Accounting and Finance

Accounting and Finance
a firm foundation

Third Edition

ALAN PIZZEY
Principal Lecturer in Accounting, Nottingham Polytechnic

CASSELL

Cassell Publishers Ltd
Villiers House
41/47 Strand
London WC2N 5JE

First edition 1980 (published by Holt, Rinehart & Winston Ltd)

Third edition 1990

British Library Cataloguing in Publication Data
Pizzey, Alan
   Accounting and finance—3rd. ed.
   1. Accounting
   I. Title
   657

   ISBN 0-304-31906-6

Typeset by Area Graphics Ltd, Arden Press Way, Letchworth, Hertfordshire

Printed and bound in Great Britain at the Alden Press, Oxford

Contents

PREFACE TO THIRD EDITION   vii

PREFACE TO FIRST EDITION   ix

PART ONE   BASIC PRINCIPLES AND TECHNIQUES   1

  1   Accounting: The Provision of Financial Information and Its Use   3
  2   The Theoretical Framework of Accounting   13
  3   The Position Statement or Balance Sheet   26
  4   The Income Statement   38
  5   Double Entry   51
  6   Depreciation   67
  7   The Accounting Treatment of Current Assets   88
  8   The Production of Accounts from a Trial Balance   106

PART TWO   THE WORK OF THE FINANCIAL ACCOUNTANT   133

  9   Miscellaneous Practical Matters   135
 10   Partnership   169
 11   The Financial Accountant as an Auditor, and Designer of
          Accounting Systems   195
 12   An Introduction to Taxation   217
 13   Disclosure: The Accounting Requirements of the Companies Act 1985 230

**PART THREE   SOME ASPECTS OF ACCOUNTING THEORY AND
          THEIR APPLICATION TO PRACTICE**   265

 14   The Recognition of Revenue   267
 15   A Critical Appraisal of Accounting Principles and Statements   273
 16   Standard Accounting Practices and the Standard Setters   288
 17   Economic Ideas and Accounting Practices   295
 18   Accounting in a Period of Rising Prices   303

**PART FOUR   BUSINESS UNITS: THEIR FINANCE AND
          VALUATION**   321

 19   Types of Business Organization   323

20 Capital Structure and Gearing 330
21 Major Sources of Finance for Business 341
22 Working Capital 355
23 The Valuation of a Business 372

PART FIVE   INTERPRETATION OF FINANCIAL STATEMENTS 395

24 The Interpretation of Accounts 397
25 Funds Flow Analysis 420

SOLUTIONS 451

INDEX 509

Preface to Third Edition

The purpose of this book has not altered since the second edition appeared six years ago, but I hope that the changes which I have incorporated within the third edition will improve the work, and help to achieve its purpose. There have been considerable developments in accounting since 1984, which I have introduced into this edition. There are five major alterations to the text.

1. In the preface to the first edition I commented that an introductory textbook was not the proper medium for a detailed explanation of Standard Accounting Practices. I still hold this view but nevertheless I have increased the coverage of SSAPs where they are relevant to the text. In some cases a standard expresses the basic principle governing the accounting treatment of an item, and it is right that students should understand such principles from an early stage in their education. The operation of the Accounting Standards Committee (ASC) has been the cause of much recent debate, and I have added a chapter on standard setting to incorporate the criticisms levelled at the ASC, and some of the suggestions made to remedy the situation.

2. I have deepened the section on accounting theory. My intention here is to meet the requirement of introductory courses for an explanation of basic ideas, and their relationship to practical accounting techniques. Since the publication of the second edition, methods suggested to guide accountants in a period of changing prices, and in the treatment of goodwill, have suffered sharp criticism, which is reflected in the text.

3. The section on finance has been strengthened. In my view some introductory courses concentrate on accounting techniques at the expense of discussion covering the management of the finance used to fund a large proportion of the assets which figure in the accounting statements.

4. The technique for drafting funds flow statements has changed in recent years to follow the format specified in SSAP 10. I have converted most of the examples in the textbook to reflect this form, although it is true to say that, in practice, a variety of forms can be found by comparing the published accounts of companies. This standard practice has suffered criticism, both academic and practical, which is covered in the text.

5. At the time of writing a Companies Bill is before Parliament, which in the course of time will emerge as yet another Companies Act. Whilst it is unlikely that this Act will usher in basic changes of such significance that they may affect an introductory course, I have included points from the Bill which are relevant to chapters in the book.

As before, the text includes tutorial questions at the end of each chapter, and, where relevant, seminar exercises with solutions in an appendix at the end of the book. There are also review questions at the end of many chapters. The solutions to these problems are contained in a Teachers' Manual which I trust colleagues will find helpful.

I would like to thank Diana Russell and Justin Vaughan for their assistance and encouragement in the preparation of this third edition.

ALAN PIZZEY

Preface to First Edition

The purpose of this book is to help students who are commencing their studies in accounting, by ensuring that the basic techniques are mastered and principal ideas understood at an early stage. Once a firm foundation is laid the young accountant can proceed to more complex matters without the disadvantage of misconceptions which might hamper his or her progress.

The book sets out to introduce the techniques of financial accounting, to discover why one method is preferred to others, and to demonstrate how to use the accounting statements which are produced. A discussion of the elements of finance follows naturally from chapters which consider the work of the financial accountant, and also acts as a prelude to the interpretation of accounting statements. In a practical subject such as accounting, the techniques are important for the student, but they must not be allowed to dominate a course or a book to the exclusion of other matters. Concepts are important to underpin the choice of technique, and to provide a basis of comprehension on which the interpretation and use of accounting statements can rest. In this book I have attempted to blend theory with practice by mixing methodology with explanation, in the hope that students will not only learn how to account, but also develop an ability to discuss their work. To this end the text includes comment of a theoretical nature alongside explanation of accounting methods. Most chapters have suggestions for discussion topics, as well as accounting exercises (with solutions) which will provide practice in applying techniques. A workbook is to be published to accompany this volume which will provide the student with further opportunities to practise the techniques discussed here.

This book has developed from the first year undergraduate course taught at Trent Polytechnic [now Nottingham Polytechnic], and represents the lecture notes, seminar problems and tutorial discussion topics built up by a team of accounting teachers over the last seven years.

I am indebted to my colleagues for their helpful suggestions, and to past students whose requirements have encouraged me in the preparation of this work. In my view tutorial discussion is an important element in an accounting course, enabling students to marshal their ideas, present them in logical form in discussion, develop the ability to make constructive criticism and use judgement to decide the relative strengths of conflicting views. Resources are scarce, however, and it is not always possible to teach in small groups where a meaningful discussion can take place. However, teachers can still inject an element of critical appraisal into a course by including some discussions in the accounting exercises. For this reason many of the exercises in the book contain discussion questions. Solutions are provided to enable students to check the mechanics of their answers, but in general suggested answers to discussion questions have not been provided, in order to encourage students to think out their own solutions.

At the present time accounting must be seen against a background of unstable economic conditions, which have promoted much discussion and not a few changes to the subject. This atmosphere of argument and development, although stimulating to the academic, is bewildering to students just starting their accounting career. I have therefore tried to explain some of the current discussions in as simple a way as possible in the hope that students will begin to appreciate the efforts made by our profession to solve the problems with which it is faced. For this reason Accounting Standards are mentioned where they fit into the text, but this is considered too early a stage for a detailed study of the standards. Ideally we need to train young people to enter the accounting profession with open minds, a capacity for independent thought and the ability to test doctrinaire views before accepting them.

One difficulty encountered in the production of an introductory textbook on accounting is that the student has little or no practical experience of the subject, and therefore terms have to be explained as they are introduced. I have tried in this book to set the subject in context with other disciplines such as law and economics, and on the practical side to introduce the systems which are necessary to provide the basic data which the accountant uses. No doubt some introductory accounting courses will include matters which I have omitted, while some teachers may not consider all the items I have covered as appropriate for their courses. Although auditing and taxation are separate subjects, in my view they need to be introduced at this early stage to familiarize students with them and to demonstrate how they stem from the more general work of the financial accountant.

The textbook *Financial Accounting Techniques* (1982) by Alan Pizzey and Alan Jennings which accompanies this text is designed to reinforce and extend the coverage of accounting techniques for students who need the practice, and for those whose course is aimed at a syllabus which contains a greater proportion of practical work.

I would like to thank B. D. Coleman, D. Hewitt and Ian A. Wright, whose comments were very useful. Also sincere thanks to Tom Perlmutter, whose encouragement and advice have proved most helpful.

ALAN PIZZEY

To Barbara, Jonathan and Joscelin

WITHOUT WHOSE FORBEARANCE AND ENCOURAGEMENT
THIS BOOK WOULD NEVER HAVE BEEN COMPLETED

'*Complacency is the enemy of study.*'

MAO TSE TUNG.

'*They should have . . . a supercilious knowledge of accounts.*'

MRS MALAPROP.

'*Receive before thou wryte, and wryte before thou paye;*
Thus wilst thou well assured be, thy counte will never decay.'

FROM THE TOMB OF AN OLD BURGHER IN CHESTER
CATHEDRAL.

Basic Principles and Techniques

1 | Accounting: The Provision of Financial Information and Its Use

THE WORK OF THE ACCOUNTANT

The work of the accountant is diverse in its nature, but basically it deals with the recording, planning and control of financial transactions, whether income or expenditure. In every organization money will be spent on administration, and thus there will be a need for an accountant. Broadly speaking, accountants can be divided into two classes: those in professional practice and executive accountants who work for organizations.

Accountants in practice have a number of clients for whom they provide a service. This service takes the form of auditing, accounting, taxation work, acting as liquidator and giving general financial advice. Auditing involves checking that the accounts of a business, which have been prepared by accountants within the business, show a true and fair view. Although the term 'true and fair' has been enshrined in company law since 1948, it has never been defined. The Companies Act 1985 states that the need to provide a true and fair view in accounts is of paramount importance, and if the strict application of rules in the Act inhibits the production of a true and fair view, such rules may be 'overridden'. The auditor must ensure:

a. that the accounts have been properly drawn up according to best accounting practice, as expressed in Statements of Standard Accounting Practice (SSAPs) approved by the professional accounting bodies;
b. that legal requirements concerning limited companies have been complied with;
c. that no fraud has taken place;
d. that the system of accounting operated by the business is such that fraud is discouraged.

A second task often undertaken by the accountant in practice is to prepare a taxation computation to translate the accounting profit into a taxable profit by applying the rules embodied in the tax laws. Some companies are large enough to employ a permanent tax specialist, but in most cases the practising accountant with special taxation expertise will undertake this work. The practitioner may find himself involved with tax planning, advising his clients, both companies and individuals, on how best to reduce the burden of taxation. He might also act as a liquidator when a company ceases trading and is wound up. Incomplete records work is important in practice, since it involves producing accounts for small firms where proper books of account have not been maintained and the basic records may be difficult to assemble. Many small businesses receive advice as to how to finance their operations from the practitioner who undertakes their accounting, auditing and tax work. This accountant may draft a statement of future cash flows for the business, and then negotiate overdraft or loan facilities with his client's bank.

Some practising accountants have joined together to form large worldwide practices. It is now a common feature of such practices to operate a financial consultancy division as a limited company (see Table 1).

Table 1. Statistics for Large Accountancy Practices
This table demonstrates the size to which some large international accountancy practices can grow, and the relative importance for each firm of the four major activities: Accounting and Auditing (A/A), Tax work, Management Consultancy (M/C) and Insurance (INS).

	UK fee income £m	Growth %	% Practice devoted to discipline				Partners	£ per partner earnings ratio
			A/A	Tax	M/C	INS		
Peat Marwick McLintock	315.6	20.2	63	18	15	4	514	614 007
Coopers and Lybrand	225.0	30.8	45	17	29	9	391	575 447
Price Waterhouse	222.0	24.4	45	24	26	4	363	611 570
Deloitte Haskins & Sells	188.8	25.0	51	26	18	5	246	767 480
Ernst and Whinney	148.4	22.7	56	22	16	6	226	656 637
Arthur Anderson	144.1	27.0	30	24	42	4	153	941 830
Touche Ross	141.8	21.6	50	20	23	7	237	598 312
Arthur Young	135.5	25.5	46	30	13	7	215	630 232
BDO Binder Hamlyn	89.0	21.6	56	31	5	3	238	373 949
Grant Thornton	86.0	14.7	47	28	5	12	253	339 921
Spicer and Oppenheim	83.2	22.2	49	25	18	8	174	478 161

(Source—*Accountancy Age*)

The current trend is for mergers among the larger firms. Prospective partners are: Price Waterhouse/Andersons; Deloitte and Touche; Ernst and Young. This would change the order at the top of the table. Price Waterhouse/Andersons could have a worldwide annual revenue of nearly £5 billion.

The type of work done by executive accountants who work for a company or some other organization, e.g. local authority, hospital board or a charity, can be further subdivided. First, there are financial accountants, whose main job is to record transactions. They are responsible for maintaining accurate records of what their company owns (its assets), and what it owes (its liabilities). They are concerned with the system of book-keeping used to record sales and purchases, the payment and receipt of cash, and keeping an accurate account of stocks, debts, and fixed or long-term assets of the company. Financial accountants act as stewards, showing the financial effect of the actions of the managers to the owners of the business. One way this effect is revealed is through accounting statements such as the balance sheet and the profit and loss account. The financial accountant drafts the published accounts which are later checked by the auditor. Such accounts provided for shareholders and available to the public are produced within the strict disclosure rules of the Companies Acts, and SSAPs. Other duties of a financial accountant may be company secretarial work dealing with insurance, pension funds, share transfers and statutory meetings, or the general management of office procedures, business systems and computerized methods of recording transactions. Some companies have an internal audit section which liaises with the external auditors, checks systems and protects the assets of the business.

The second type of executive accountant is the management accountant, whose job it is to use his expertise in any way he can to help the management of the company in the administration of the organization and the formulation of decisions. Management accountants prepare financial reports and statements which give information about the subject of a decision or show up what has happened in the recent past. In this way managers are better able to plan the future operations of the business and allocate scarce resources between alternatives, and are made more aware of the financial effect of transactions which have taken place so that they can act quickly to control a situation where, for example, losses are being incurred. Cost analysis and budgetary control are important tools for the management accountant.

THE HISTORICAL DEVELOPMENT OF ACCOUNTING

Merchants and others have kept records of their transactions from very early times. However, it was not until an Italian monk, Luca Pacioli, wrote an appendix to his mathematics book in 1494 that the system of accounting which had evolved among the merchants of Italy was formulated. Pacioli's description of the 'Italian method' is a simple one, and probably more sophisticated systems than that outlined by Pacioli existed in larger firms of merchants and manufacturers of the time. The rudiments of double-entry book-keeping had developed, as had the practice of showing a position statement for the business rather than for the individuals who owned it and the practice of accounting at regular intervals so that the profits could be computed and divided among the owners of the business. The idea of accounting once a year had not yet been adopted, since in those days businessmen tended to account for each venture as an entity, irrespective of how long it took to complete.

After Pacioli came a steady development of accounting, with the emergence of a need to account in a common monetary unit and for a set period of time, and to enable the creditworthiness of a firm to be established. Estate owners, merchant bankers and manufacturers began to operate standardized systems to reduce fraud within their large enterprises. In 1605 a Dutchman, Simon Stevin, advocated that the profit and loss account should be produced at yearly intervals, and by 1655 Jaques Savary was suggesting that the balance sheet should be drawn up at certain stated intervals. In 1673 the Code of Commerce produced in France recommended that all businesses produce a balance sheet at least every two years.

The industrial revolution increased the scale of businesses and the complexity of their transactions. The organization of finance on a large scale, the separation of loan and venture capital, the principle of limited liability, and the emergence of joint stock banks created a demand for more sophisticated methods of accounting.

The emergence of a profession of accountants with a code of ethics and standards of performance was followed by the formation of professional accounting bodies. In 1854 a Royal Charter was granted to a society of accountants in Scotland, in 1880 the Institute of Chartered Accountants in England and Wales was formed and in 1887 the Association of Public Accountants was launched in the USA.

Even at this time, however, the accounts kept by many businesses consisted of little more than the recording of cash movements in and out. Dividends were often paid before the existence of a profit had been established, and fixed assets were bought and used without providing for depreciation. As the scale of industrialization increased, however, there was a gradual divorce of management and ownership, and it became obvious that management needed accounting information of a different type from that required by shareholders and lenders. The accounting profession therefore enlarged its scope to cater for this need, and over the last forty years the provision of information to management has become the most important function of the accountant, who has in fact become a member of the management team, managing the finances of the business and providing other managers with information to help with their tasks of planning, control, and decision-making.

THE PROFESSIONAL ACCOUNTING BODIES IN GREAT BRITAIN AND IRELAND

At present there are in the UK and Ireland six separate major organizations for accountants. Each of the professional bodies possesses a charter from which its authority is derived and each gives a professional qualification with its own designatory letters. The first three are the Institutes of Chartered Accountants in England and Wales, Scotland and Ireland. These are quite separate from one another, each one having its own membership, rules, governing council, examination syllabus, and student members. The one rule which unites them is that all student members must serve a fixed period under a training contract with a member of the Institute, so that they gain the appropriate experience before they qualify. Chartered accountants dominate the practising side of accounting, although many who have qualified and have gained experience with a practising accountant then leave the practice to work in industry and commerce.

The fourth body of accountants is the Chartered Association of Certified Accountants, whose members are found mainly in industry and commerce, although there are a significant number in practice. Members of the Association, as well as members of the Institutes, are recognized by the Department of Trade and Industry and can act as auditors to public companies. The students of the Association must undergo a period of training to gain experience before they qualify, but this period may be spent either as a clerk to a practising accountant or in an accounting office in industry, commerce, nationalized industry or local authority.

The fifth body of accountants is the Chartered Institute of Management Accountants. As the name implies, the members of this body work mainly in industry or commerce, and students of this Institute must gain their experience, prior to qualifying, by training as a management accountant.

The sixth and last body of accountants is the Chartered Institute of Public Finance Accountants. Members of this body work for local authorities and Government agencies, and it is in this type of organization that the student members of this Institute gain their experience.

From time to time attempts are made to unite all or parts of our fragmented profession but so far little has been achieved. The Consultative Committee of Accountancy Bodies (CCAB) has been established by the six major bodies to encourage consultation and, where possible, the formulation and promulgation of a united view for the profession, e.g. to the Government on taxation matters.

One manifestation of co-operation between the Accountancy Bodies is the creation of the Association of Accounting Technicians. This body was organized to represent and train technician accountants, starting with Ordinary Level rather than Advanced Level school qualifications. The Assocation is now quite autonomous and the growth experienced in the last ten years is evidence of the demand for its members and students on the employment market.

Table 2. The Major Professional Accountancy Bodies

	Members	Students
Institute of Chartered Accountants in England and Wales	90 671	17 000
Chartered Association of Certified Accountants	32 329	78 000*
Chartered Institute of Management Accountants	28 959	48 000*
Chartered Institute of Public Finance Accountants	10 496	2 700
Institute of Chartered Accountants in Scotland	1 200	1 700
Association of Accounting Technicians	14 000	45 000*

*Indicates UK and Overseas

THE PURPOSE OF ACCOUNTING

The first section in this chapter demonstrates that accountants undertake a very wide range of activities in business and other organizations. A definition of accounting which is capable of satisfying all accountants has not yet been drafted. A recent attempt in the USA suggested that accounting consists of identifying, measuring and communicating business information to facilitate judgements and decision-making. This definition placed its emphasis firmly on the provision of data to users, and played down the more traditional roles of the accountant in recording, classifying and summarizing financial data. It is necessary to record and summarize transactions before financial information can be measured and used by decision-makers. Of great importance to accountants, however, is the need to communicate the information derived from their records, and if necessary to interpret that information to improve its comprehension by the users, who may have borne the cost of the information system.

Accounting has four main purposes.

1. An accountant is needed to identify, measure and record transactions. These records show the relationship of the organization with other bodies, e.g. what is owed to and by the business. Such information summarizes for managers the transactions they have initiated and gives an element of control.
2. Accounting acts as a language for business, since the commercial world communicates in accounting terms, e.g. what should be paid to a supplier or by a customer, the price for a product or a service, or the value of an asset or investment.
3. The accountant acts as a steward, using records to report to the owners of the company, i.e. the shareholders, on transactions made during a period and the effect these transactions have had on their investment. For this purpose the

balance sheet, which analyses the financial position of the business, and the profit and loss account, which measures the success or failure of its operations, are both important statements.
4. The accountant helps management to operate the business. Figures are important in planning future operations via the budget, in making decisions between alternatives, in allocating scarce resources, and in controlling the business by reporting on events soon after they have taken place and comparing them with the budget or plan.

We can now see that the task of the accountant is to look back at the past, to record, analyse and report as a steward, and also to look into the future and assist management with decision-making and control. Both aspects of this task require figures to be assembled in statements that are easily assimilated, interpreted and used in the evaluation of performance by both accountants and non-accountants.

The situation is far from static. The current trend is to emphasize the significance of accounting statements for users other than shareholders and managers, to develop the role of the accountant within society, and to refine financial reporting as a source of information for investors in the financial market place.

Accountants must now work in a situation where managerial colleagues, and some other users of accounting information, will expect the application of sophisticated quantitative techniques to its production and interpretation. The scale of some operations, and the development of computing hardware, have forced accountants to improve the old book-keeping methods into a computerized information system, perhaps using a common database established for the business as a whole. These revolutionary changes have taken place in a climate of increasing regulation as the number of standard accounting practices has steadily grown, and successive Companies Acts have increased the disclosure and technical rules with which the accountant must comply. As a background to these changes there is an increasing awareness that accounting is a social science, with the recognition that groups other than shareholders and managers are rightfully interested in financial information, and that accountants have a responsibility to provide meaningful information for such groups.

THE MAIN FINANCIAL STATEMENTS

A significant part of the task of an accountant is to explain and interpret the figures which have been produced to those who are going to use them. There are four main financial statements commonly used by accountants to produce an extract from the figures in the books so that others may use this information for their own purposes.

The more important two are the balance sheet and the profit and loss account. The balance sheet shows the financial position of the business at a particular moment in time and sets the assets of the business against the liabilities or sources from which funds have been raised to finance those assets. The profit and loss account is a summary of transactions for a stated period, e.g. a year. This sets the costs of the period against the revenue earned during the period, thus showing the profit or loss made for that period. These two statements are linked because any profit not paid out as a dividend belongs to the shareholders and is thus added to capital on the balance sheet, which records the amount invested in the business by the shareholders. Two others which are widely used are:

1. The funds flow statement, which attempts to analyse the sources from which funds have been raised and the ways in which those funds have been spent during a period between two balance sheet dates. It is now considered as part of the published financial statements of a company, since under Standard Accounting Practice 10, a funds flow statement must be appended to the published balance sheet and profit and loss account of a company.
2. The budget of a business, which sets out, in detailed financial terms, a plan for the future operations of that business. All aspects of the business are covered by the budget, e.g. sales, purchases, expenses, so that it is possible to forecast what the balance sheet and the profit and loss account might be at a future stated date. The budget is a managerial statement drafted to suit the circumstances of a particular business. It is not subject to the constraints of statute or accounting standards, which prescribe the format of the other three statements.

Current thinking emphasizes the need for financial information to show the economic reality of the situation. At first view this seems an eminently sensible principle but an argument still persists. Some authorities cling to the old idea that the accounts should be based on historically recorded costs as an objectively reliable measure, but this principle suffers if a significant difference develops between the 'value' of an item and its 'cost'. Should a balance sheet record an asset such as a building at its cost when purchased three years ago (say £800 000) or at its current value on the date of the balance sheet (say £1 500 000)? Furthermore, accountants are questioning the strict interpretation of the legal situation of a transaction. A machine leased by a company does not belong to that company, so legally it cannot appear on the balance sheet as an asset. If, however, the company has a right to the exclusive use of that machine as a term of the lease, the economic reality is that the leased asset is no different from an owned asset and should therefore appear in the balance sheet.

Another new idea is that investors should be given more information to help their assessment of a company's financial position and prospects, perhaps even as much as managers. An investor must decide whether to buy, sell, or hold a share stake in a company. In a 'management buyout', managers are in a strong position to make an accurate decision because of their inside knowledge of the business. When a takeover bid is made, a profit forecast forms part of the prospectus on which the bid is based. It is difficult to see why such extra information cannot always be made available as part of the financial statements of a business. Clearly, directors would not wish to disclose information which might be of assistance to rival companies, but perhaps funds spent on glossy public relations documents might be better employed in disclosing more useful information.

THE USERS OF ACCOUNTING INFORMATION

Many different groups use accounting information, each one requiring slightly different information from the basic financial data produced by the accountant. The accountant must therefore design reports in such a way that the appropriate information is visible and understandable. The major groups of users are as follows:

1. *Management* are perhaps the most important users of accounting information. An analysis of past and expected future revenues and expenses will provide information which is useful when plans are formulated and decisions made. Once the budget for a business is complete, the accountant can produce figures for what actually happens as the budget period unfolds, so that they can be compared with the budget to measure achievement. Management will need to know, in great detail and soon after the event, the cost consequences of a particular course of action, so that steps can be taken to control the situation if things go wrong. Speed and the ability to communicate and interpret are needed here.
2. *Shareholders and potential shareholders* are another important group of users of accounting information. This group includes the investing public at large and the stockbrokers, financial analysts and commentators who advise them. The shareholders should be informed of the manner in which management has used their funds which have been invested in the business. They are interested in the profitability and safety of their investment, which helps them to appraise the efficiency of the management. This is simply a matter of reporting on past events. However, both shareholders and potential shareholders are also interested in the future performance of the business, and use past figures as a guide to the future if they have to vote on proposals or decide whether to disinvest. Financial analysts advising institutional investors such as insurance companies, pension funds, unit trusts and investment trusts are among the most sophisticated users of accounting information, and the company contemplating a takeover bid is yet another type of potential shareholder. The accountant has an obligation to all those in this category to provide information on which they can depend when making their decisions, but the fact that some members of the group are more financially sophisticated than others causes difficulties, since the volume of information required by the financial analyst may confuse the ordinary shareholder.
3. *Employees and their trade union representatives* also use accounting information to assess the potential of the business. This information is relevant to the employee, who wishes to discover whether the company can offer him safe employment and promotion through growth over a period of years, and to the trade unionist, who uses past profits and potential profits in his calculations and claims for higher wages or better conditions. The viability of different divisions of a company are of interest to this group. Employees have invested their careers and efforts in the business, and thus have a right to accounting information. Good industrial relations are fostered if there is disclosure of such information, so that employees can participate in decisions, and negotiate profit-sharing arrangements. This fact is recognized by many companies which produce an 'employee report' based on the accounts, but highlighting certain items such as training expenditure and statistics (sales per employee, profit per employee) of interest to employees.
4. *Those who have lent money to the business.* This group includes some who have financed the business over a long period, by lending money which is to be repaid at the end of a number of years, as well as short-term creditors such as a bank which allows a company to overdraw its bank account for a number of months, and suppliers of raw materials, who permit a company to buy goods from them and pay in, say, six to twelve weeks' time. Lenders are interested in the security

of their loan, so they will look at an accounting statement to ensure that the company will be able to repay on the due date or meet the interest requirements before that date. The amount of cash available and the value of assets which form a security for the debt are of importance to this group. Credit rating agencies are interested in accounts for similar reasons. Lenders are less interested than other users in the profit disclosed by the accounts, except as a guide to the likely surplus from which interest can be paid. The generation of cash flow, and the availability of 'liquid' assets which can be turned into cash to meet repayments, are of greater interest to this group.

5. *Government agencies* also use accounting information, either when collecting statistical information to reveal trends within the economy as a whole, or, in the case of the Inland Revenue, to assess the profit on which the company's tax liability is to be computed. Businesses act as collectors of Schedule E income tax or value added tax and as such must account to the appropriate authority.

6. *Customers* of a business may use accounting data to assess the viability of a company if a long-term contract is soon to be placed. Competitors will also use the accounts for purposes of comparison. Directors may object to the disclosure of some information to shareholders, on the grounds that competitors may be able to use that information to the disadvantage of the company.

CHARACTERISTICS OF A USEFUL ACCOUNTING STATEMENT

Much thought has been given to improving the statements which accountants prepare for users, and gradually a group of basic characteristics has emerged which should be present in a useful accounting statement:

1. Relevance. This is an important characteristic, which disciplines the accountant to select and show data which are of interest to the user, say a manager, and to hold back other information which may confuse or be of little use to the manager when the information has been assimilated. Relevance implies that the accountant must be ready to adapt the form of statements to the changing needs of the users.

2. Understandability. A useful statement must be understandable, and formulated in such a way as to highlight significant figures. This characteristic faces the accountant with the dilemma of the need to disclose relevant items balanced against the danger of confusing users by presenting them with a complicated mass of detail.

3. Completeness and Lack of Bias. Accounts should be complete, showing all aspects of a situation, and at the same time free of bias, giving equal treatment to all users. It is difficult to comply with both these requirements in the same statement; for example, full information about the performance of various divisions of a company may be of great interest to shareholders if published, but it may be of greater interest to competitors, who can put such information to uses which might be harmful to the company.

4. Reliability. An accounting statement must be reliable if it is to be used with confidence. Verification by an independent auditor with a high reputation for skill and care enhances that confidence, but creates an impetus to exclude from accounting statements amounts which cannot be verified by such an objective test.

5. Timeliness. This is significant for users, be they managers, shareholders or

creditors, since they benefit from up-to-date information, which reveals the current situation, and serves as a mirror to reflect what is likely to happen in the future. Managers in particular need information at an early stage to check on performance in the immediate past and to adjust their plans for future action. Investors and creditors receive little help from data which are six months old, because the situation of the business could have changed during the intervening months.

6. Comparability. This is held to be a useful characteristic in an accounting statement. It allows the accounts of one company to be compared with those of another, or with a preconceived norm or average for the industry, which acts as a yardstick for success. Standard Accounting Practice, when applied, reduces the differences in technique experienced from one accounting statement to another, and this facilitates comparison of performance across an industry, and of the same company in previous years.

7. Cost-Effectiveness. Financial information is expensive to produce; therefore, accounting statements should only be created if the benefits derived from them exceed their cost.

The accountancy profession has attempted to identify users of accounting information and the information which they require. As yet, however, insufficient consideration has been given to the problem of whether a set of accounts produced by a business to report to shareholders (the term 'corporate report' is used) does provide all the required information, and whether other supplementary statements are needed to cover any deficiency.

TUTORIAL DISCUSSION TOPICS

1.1 Define accounting, with reference to the various operations undertaken by accountants.

1.2 Classify the users of accounting information. Discuss their different requirements for financial information and the problem for the accountant in reconciling these needs.

1.3 Name the four major accounting statements and discuss the purpose of each one.

1.4 What kind of information, other than that based on past events, can accountants provide?

1.5 It is said that accounting is the language of business. Why does accounting occupy this important position and what problems limit its usefulness as the language of business?

1.6 Discuss the characteristics of a useful accounting statement with reference to any conflicts between these characteristics.

2 | The Theoretical Framework of Accounting

If asked to point out one major weakness in the knowledge of accounting students, many teachers of the subject would say that students do not understand the framework of ideas which surrounds the practice of accounting and which is basic to its proper appreciation. The principles which concern us are the rules and conventions which govern accounting. Different authorities refer to them in different ways: some use the terms 'postulate', 'concept' and 'principle', although what is a concept for one is sometimes a principle for another. Some authorities hold that postulates are assumptions on which the principles of accounting are based, that concepts are ideas basic to a proper understanding of accounting, and that principles are rules which govern existing practice and underlie the preparation of accounting statements, the valuation of assets and the measurement of income. Students should ignore these academic differences in terminology at this stage, and make sure they understand the basis of their subject. The classifications in this chapter are simply an attempt to summarize.

These rules are general and have been adopted as a guide or basis of conduct by those practising accounting. Detailed practice must of course be tailored to fit the circumstances or company concerned, but should be within these basic guidelines. It is necessary to know the basis used in order to find the precise meaning of figures in an accounting report. For example, when an accountant says that stocks of material are valued at cost, does he mean cost when they were bought, or what it would cost to replace them at the balance sheet date, or some other measure of their cost?

It is important to realize that the principles of accounting are man-made and have evolved as the best way to solve problems which arise in accounting, and have been adopted by general consent because they work. As time passes and conditions change, however, a principle which was previously accepted may be criticized because it no longer functions usefully, and may eventually be dropped. For example, fixed assets are shown in the balance sheet at historical cost, but some accountants are criticizing this practice because it seems to them that it does not work well during a period of inflation. Unfortunately there is also criticism of the alternative methods of asset valuation suggested for accounting purposes because they lose objectivity. Accounting principles rely for their authority on acceptance by accountants that they represent 'best accounting practice'.

TOWARDS A CONCEPTUAL FRAMEWORK

It is a neat but illusory idea that a complete conceptual framework exists for accounting. All accountants would not be able to agree on the constituent parts of such a framework, although there is a fair measure of agreement as to the basic ideas or assumptions which underpin accounting techniques. Perhaps the term 'conventions' could be used for these agreed ideas. Note that 'preparers' of accounts rather than 'users' have a dominant role in identifying these conventions. It is apparent that until accountants are agreed on the meaning of such items as assets, liabilities, capital, cost and profit, it will not be possible to determine the best means to measure and account for those items.

Academic accountants suggest that accounting theory should not develop from a description of current practice, but should instead seek to base practice on a theory stemming from what *should* happen. This is the 'normative' approach, which relates back to the underlying economic circumstances of transactions, e.g. what do we understand by the term 'profit', and therefore what accounting principles and rules are required to measure profit. In contrast to the normative approach to accounting theory, the 'empirical' approach was developed, by relating back to the purpose for which financial information is to be used (usually to assist in decision-making) and basing principles on tested conclusions as to how useful was the information produced. The normative school have adapted this idea by investigating the way in which decisions *should* be made, and arguing that accounting theory should stem from the information needs of decision-makers. This difference of view is not yet resolved, manifesting itself, for example, in arguments over whether assets should be shown in accounts at their original cost or their current value. A further theory suggests that accounting information is used by managers or shareholders to decide on the allocation of scarce resources. If these resources are seen as belonging to the community, it follows that they should be invested to maximize the welfare of society, and that accounting principles should work to achieve this end. An accountant's individual stance in this argument depends on whether the accounts are seen as a stewardship document, reporting on what has happened to investors' funds, or alternatively considered to be tools for investors to use in the decision-making process.

POSTULATES

Monetary Measurement

Accounting statements are expressed in monetary terms, since money acts as a common denominator to express the many different facets of an organization, e.g. costs, sales, the value of stocks, machinery, debts and investments. If all the items covered by an accounting statement are stated as an amount of money, then the relative cost or value of these items can be seen and their aggregate cost or value determined. The disadvantage of monetary measurement is, of course, that the value of money may not remain stable, especially in a period of inflation. Not only does this hinder comparison of statements computed at different times, but it also creates difficulties when the costs of assets bought at different times are added together in the same statement. Suppose a company bought a machine two years ago for £5000, and another exactly the same last week for £8000. Would it be correct to add these two amounts together to express the two machines in a position statement? Certainly £13 000 has been invested in the assets, financed by funds entrusted to the business by investors, who will expect to be repaid £13 000 if the business is terminated. Liabilities are payable, according to the law, as an agreed amount of money, so it seems correct to record them in money terms. If the purpose of a financial statement is to disclose the legal obligation of the business to repay lenders and shareholders, then monetary measurement is a useful convention, but for decision-making purposes monetary measurement must be adjusted to reflect changing price levels.

Accountants are now beginning to realize, however, that some elements of a business, such as morale of employees and strength of competition, cannot be measured in money terms, even though they must be regarded as assets since profit derives from them. A good labour relations record in a company means that there will be little disruption of production through strikes, and thus profits will increase, but it is hard to work out exactly the profit that would have been made had labour relations in the business been less harmonious, and impossible to compute an accurate value for such an 'asset' which could be disclosed in a balance sheet. Other assets which are difficult to quantify are 'know-how', the possession of a good management team, and goodwill. This last intangible asset often appears in balance sheets of companies, though its existence and valuation may not be agreed upon by all accountants. Fixed assets can be quantified in money terms, but the figure shown makes no comment about their state of repair, or their suitability for the tasks which they undertake. The fact that a competitor has developed a new rival product and is poised to take a considerable share of a company's market does not appear on the balance sheet as a liability.

Going Concern

Unless there is evidence to the contrary, it is assumed when accounting statements are compiled that the firm which is the subject of these statements is going to continue in operation for an indefinite period. Without this postulate, year-end accounts would have to be worked out on a 'winding-up' basis, that is, on what the business is likely to be worth if sold piecemeal at the accounting date. This value is often different from its value if the present owners intend to carry on the business. Fixed assets, for example, are shown at cost less depreciation to date, rather than at their current value in the second-hand market, because they are held by the firm not for immediate resale, but to be used by the business until their working life is over. This is clearly an assumption on which the balance sheet is based, but some accountants feel that it is more a matter of common sense than something which needs to be sanctified as a postulate. Professor D. Solomons has written 'we do not need a concept to tell us that depending on whether we are accounting for a continuing concern or for one which is expected to terminate in the foreseeable future, our accounting methods should be chosen appropriately'.

Before the accounts are certified as showing a true and fair view, the auditor must be satisfied that the company is a going concern and that it will continue to function successfully in the future. The criteria to be used in this appraisal will depend on the circumstances, but some general rules are as follows:

1. The market: Is there a steady demand for the company's product which has a reasonable chance of being sustained in the future?
2. Finance: Does the company possess sufficient liquid (cash) resources to meet all known liabilities in the future? A profitable business may be brought to a halt if its creditors no longer give it financial support and it is unable to pay its way.
3. Sound capital structure: Are there sufficient long-term funds in the business to give enough strength to overcome inflation, high interest rates, a credit squeeze, increases in taxation or any other hazard of the business world?
4. What is the company's competitive condition? Here one must consider the efficiency of the company compared with that of its rivals, and its ability to acquire sufficient raw materials and labour and to replace worn-out plant and equipment.

Thus the profit measurement calculation is insulated from fluctuations in the value of fixed assets, and the spread of the capital cost of an asset over the years of its useful life, by depreciation, is supported by this postulate.

Example

Jack owns a steam roundabout which he operates at fairgrounds. The machine attracts many customers, and fares collected for the rides total £10 000 per annum. Jack would not sell his roundabout if he were to be offered £50 000 for it, but if tastes change and Jack's customers prefer a newly invented ride, his takings will fall and he will not be able to sell the machine at all, since its potential has evaporated. It will no longer be a going concern and must be accounted for at the price obtainable if sold to a museum or for scrap.

This example shows that the value of an asset is dependent on its ability to earn a profit, but cost rather than value is recorded by the accountant, since the figure for cost is an objectively determined amount. Jack can show his roundabout in the accounts at cost less depreciation to date so long as he intends to continue operating it, but this amount cannot be shown if the machine is no longer to be used, since it is now judged on what it can fetch on the scrap market.

Realization

This postulate is significant in the calculation of sales revenue and profit, since it determines the point at which the accountant feels that a transaction is certain enough to be completed for the profit made on it to be calculated and taken to the profit and loss account, and if necessary distributed to the shareholders. Realization is when a sale is made to a customer, and stock at cost becomes cash or a debt measured at selling price. The basic rule is that revenue is created at the moment a sale is made, and not when the price is later paid in cash. Profit can be taken to the profit and loss account on sales made, even though the money has not been collected. The firm has acquired a debt, and provision must be made in the profit statement for debts not likely to be collected. The sale is deemed to be made when the goods are delivered, and thus profit cannot be taken to the profit and loss account on orders received and not yet filled. Goods manufactured but not yet delivered are not deemed sold, so no element of profit can enter into the value of stocks of such goods at the accounting date. There are some exceptions to this basic rule, e.g. long-term contracts, which involve payments on account before completion of the work, and these will be fully discussed in a later chapter.

Realization implies that no increase in the value of an asset can be recognized as a profit unless it is realized. Assets are recorded at the historical cost at which they were purchased (the objectively determined amount which was paid out for them) and it is often considered prudent to keep them in the books at this amount even if there is reliable information that they are worth more. It is a matter of certainty. The prudent accountant will prefer to use the lower figure until the profit is realized, in case the value increase is only temporary. An economist would not agree with this prudent approach, preferring to recognize a value increase when it takes place.

In the example of Jack the showman, the steam roundabout would not be written up in the books to £50 000 in case this apparent increase in value could not be maintained. The profit element can be shown as such only if it is realized through the sale of the machine, or considered on reliable expert advice to stem from a permanent increase in the value of the asset.

CONCEPTS

The Business Entity

This concept separates the individuals behind a business from the business itself, and records transactions in the accounting statements as they affect the business, and not its various owners. In a large company this concept emphasizes the division between owners and managers. The accountant prepares reports to the shareholders on how the managers have used the funds entrusted to them by the owners. This aspect of accounting is sometimes called reporting on stewardship, as opposed to management accounting, where reports are prepared to assist management in their job of controlling the business and deciding on future courses of action.

In a small business run by partners or a sole trader, this concept avoids confusion between business transactions and those of private life. The accountant is trying to measure the profit made by an individual in his business, and thus a loss made when the family washing machine is scrapped and money is withdrawn from the bank account to replace it is not a business transaction. A man running a sweet shop will want to know what profit he is making, and that profit will be incorrect unless goods taken from the shop for his own consumption are accounted for as sales. Goods taken for the owner's use are part of the profit withdrawn by the man from his business. There must also be a reasonable apportionment of the costs incurred partly for the family and partly for business reasons, e.g. rent and rates of a shop or office with a flat for the proprietor above it.

The law does not recognize this distinction between owner and business, since if a business cannot pay its debts the creditors can take the possessions of the owner or partners to satisfy their claims. In the case of a company, however, the shareholders are the owners, and their liability for the debts of the business is limited to the extent of their investment in the business. The business entity concept ensures that the amount invested by the owners in the business is defined (capital) and allows a return on capital employed to be computed to show whether the investment is worthwhile. Some owners may have investments in more than one business, and in any case will be interested in the results of their business activities unencumbered by the financial details of their private lives. The capital invested by a shareholder represents the original investment when the business commenced plus undistributed profits accumulated since that time. It is the amount which the business owes to the shareholders or owners. This concept is sometimes confused with a less important idea, that of the accounting unit, which seeks to define the area of business activity to be encompassed by a set of accounts. Often the entire business is accounted for within one set of books, but more often nowadays business operations are fragmented, and the accounting unit is found at the level of subsidiary companies, divisions, or factories, which have their own accounting systems.

Objectivity

This concept holds that an accounting statement should not be influenced by personal bias on the part of the accountant who compiles it. Of course, there are times when an accountant has to use judgement when drawing up a set of accounts, but he must use his own expertise to ensure a correct result. For example, a change in value of an asset should be recognized when it can be measured in objective terms. Estimates sometimes have to be made in accounting and are permissible if they are made with care and within reasonable tolerances and accuracy, e.g. provision for doubtful debts. Another example of an objective figure is the amount actually paid out by the company when it acquires an asset. This figure is real and can be proved by documentation recording the transaction. Unfortunately, such a figure for an asset purchased many years ago is not indicative of current value.

Figures built into accounting statements should rely as little as possible on estimates or subjective decisions. Historical cost represents an amount actually paid out for an asset, which can be proved by means of a voucher and verified as the market cost of the asset at its date of purchase. This amount, it is argued, is to be preferred to a subjective valuation of an asset based on estimates of its future profitability.

Fairness

This concept follows naturally from that of objectivity, and holds that in drawing up his statement the accountant must serve all groups interested in the statement fairly and equitably. The shareholders, the creditors and long-term lenders to the business must be able to rely on an accounting statement as showing the unbiased truth. The auditor certifies the accounts as showing a true and fair view, and this is thus a protection against bias in the figures. A current trend is to preserve the independence of the auditor by urging him to sell any shareholdings he possesses in client companies, and to give up any consultancy posts he holds with them. Assets purchased in a takeover bid should be recorded for group purposes at 'fair market value', the current worth in the market, rather than the book value used in the records of the acquired company.

Consistency

The methods used to treat certain items in the accounts may differ from one company to another, although remaining within the bounds of good accounting practice. When a company chooses to treat certain transactions in a particular way in the accounts, it should go on using that method year after year. If accounting procedures are consistent from period to period, a useful comparison of results over time can be made. Thus investors can see the extent of profit or loss, comparing this year with last year, and make their investment decisions accordingly. Methods should be changed only when the income or year-end position will be shown with greater fairness as a result of the change. A note of the change must be appended to the statement concerned, since the calculation of profits may be affected as a result of the change.

Example

Suppose a company calculated depreciation at 15 per cent per annum, and applied this rate to all new plant for the year in which it was purchased. An annual investment of £60 000 in new plant would mean a charge of £9000 to the profit and loss account. Suppose also that the investment is made in the last quarter of the year, and the company decides to change its system and to calculate depreciation at 15 per cent, but pro rata to time in the first year. This means that only a quarter of £9000 will be charged to the profit and loss account, so profits in that year will be improved by £6750 at a stroke.

It would be quite unfair to use the procedure which gave the best profit each year, since the accounts would then show the best possible position rather than the true and fair position, and comparison of one year with another would be impossible.

Consistency may give a comparison over time for the same company, but it cannot offer a comparison between companies unless the same basis is consistently used in each of them. Unfortunately the idea of consistency is used as a weapon to resist change, since any new method suffers from the disadvantage that it is inconsistent with what has gone before. The answer to this dilemma is to change bases as little as possible, but when a change is made, to inform users of accounts, by means of a note to the statement, of exactly what the change is, why it has been made, and the impact it has had on the profit and loss account and balance sheet.

Materiality

Accounting statements should concern themselves with matters which are significant because of their size, and should not consider trivial matters. Analysis is expensive and the presentation of too much detail can be confusing, so insignificant items in accounting statements are merged with others, and not reported separately, since they are considered to be immaterial. The difficulty lies in setting a dividing line between what is material and what is immaterial. Individual opinions differ on this point, but perhaps the cost of collecting accounting information can be used here as a decision criterion, together with the relative importance of the item in the picture revealed by the statement as a whole. What is material in a small business may prove to be immaterial in a large business. In a case concerning an international group, the collapse of a foreign subsidiary with losses in the region of £5 million to the group was not clearly shown in the consolidated accounts. There was some criticism of the accounting treatment of these losses, and the answer made by those responsible for the accounts was that in their view the amount of £5 million was not material in such a large company when the overall position of the group profit and loss account had to be considered.

Conservatism or Prudence

This concept has resulted in accountants being thought of by businessmen as pessimists. Whenever there are alternative procedures or values, the accountant selects the one which results in a lower asset value or profit and a higher liability. The concept can be summarized by the phrase 'anticipate no profit and provide for all possible losses', and stems from the accountants' fear that if they approach the compilation of accounting statements with too much optimism they may overstate profits and cause dividends to be paid out of capital. If an unrealized profit is distributed to shareholders as dividend, the danger exists that the funds will be paid out, yet the profit may never be realized, and may even melt away. In the absence of certainty it is best to be prudent. It is considered preferable to understate profit where doubt arises, since mistakes in this direction can be corrected later when the situation is clarified.

Prudence can be misused by accountants, for it is wrong to deliberately undervalue assets and understate earnings. To understate is as bad as to overstate, and accountants must not lose sight of the need for correct, reliable figures.

Jack sells tickets in advance for rides on his roundabout. He cannot take the profit on these rides immediately because of uncertainty that the roundabout may break down and he will not be able to honour the advance-booking tickets when they are presented to him. Prudence and the realization concept are combined in this rule. If Jack has a stock of coal which costs £100 when purchased, but is worth £120 at the end of the accounting year, this apparent profit of £20 is unrealized and prudence dictates that, because of the uncertainty that coal prices will remain at this level, the profit is illusory and should not be recognized in the profit and loss account. However, if the same stock of coal was valued at £80 at the year end, the unrealized loss should be provided for in the profit computation according to the prudence concept.

Disclosure

Accounting statements must be formulated in such a way as to lay out information in a useful form, so that it can be assimilated with ease. An accounting statement should not be misleading and should be furnished with adequate footnotes to explain its contents. Where there is a departure from the concept of consistency, a note to the accounts will show the impact of the change so that comparability is maintained. The accounting requirements of the Companies Acts provide examples of matters which must be disclosed in company accounts, e.g. audit fee and directors' emoluments, and the format to be used.

Allied to the convention of disclosure is the concept of periodicity. It is generally agreed that a company should report to the shareholders at regular intervals to disclose the position and progress of the business by means of a set of accounts. Conventional wisdom supported by the Companies Acts suggests the 'accounting year' as a proper period for published accounts, but the Stock Exchange requires interim accounts for shareholders at the half-year stage. In the USA, quarterly interim accounts are produced by companies quoted on the Stock Exchange. Managerial statements may be required at more frequent intervals such as monthly or weekly according to the circumstances.

PRINCIPLES

Matching

This is sometimes called the accruals principle. Its purpose is to match effort to accomplishment by setting the cost of resources used up by a certain activity against the revenue or benefits received from that activity. When a profit statement is compiled, the cost of the goods sold should be set against the revenue from the sale of these goods, even though cash has not yet been received. Expense and revenue must be matched up so that they concern the same goods and time period, if a true profit is to be computed. Costs concerning a future period must be carried forward as a prepayment of that period, and not charged in the current profit and loss account. Expenses of the current period not yet entered in the books must be estimated and inserted as accruals. There has been much argument among accountants about whether overhead expenses should be charged against the period in which they are incurred or carried forward to the period in which the goods made when these costs were incurred are eventually sold. According to SSAP 2, the need for prudence prevails over matching in cases where they conflict, e.g. it may be wiser to write off the cost of certain stock at once rather than carry it forward to match with revenue which may not be received in the future.

Jack the showman buys coal for £50, and uses it all to power his roundabout. The bill for £50 reaches Jack one month after the coal is used. When calculating his profit, Jack must take the cost of the coal used away from his receipts, because the cost has been incurred even though the bill has not been recorded. This is an accrual.

Cost

Fixed assets are shown in the accounts at the price paid to acquire them, i.e. their historical cost less depreciation written off to date. They are acquired by a company to be used, and it is argued that their historical cost should be spread as an expense to the income statement over the years of their useful life. However, inflation or obsolescence may change the value of a long-lived asset. The concepts of consistency, objectivity and conservatism are used to support the use of historical cost in accounting for such assets. The opponents of the historical cost principle use the concepts of disclosure and materiality to support their arguments that current cost amounts are more useful to readers of accounting statements.

Accountants avoid the idea of value, since a value is often a matter of personal bias and may change according to the method of valuation used. Under the going concern postulate we account for assets at their value in use, which we interpret as the original historical cost of the asset net of depreciation to date. If this amount is out of line with the true value, then the asset should be revalued by an expert.

In the example of Jack the showman and his roundabout, if Jack's grandfather had purchased the machine eighty years ago for £500, this would be its historical cost as recorded in the books, but of course there is a great difference between what £500 could buy at that time and what it can buy now. Thus historical cost does not show the real capital employed in an asset or any fluctuations in the value of the asset that have taken place since it was bought. If depreciation written off the machine during its working life amounts to £450, then the net book value would be £50, and this amount might not be at all representative of the true value of the asset, as calculated on the basis of what it can earn if it can still attract customers at fairgrounds, or what it would fetch if sold for scrap or to a museum, or to another showman. An accountant might argue that the use of historical cost is consistent and objective, since it is based on a transaction which actually took place rather than an estimate of value, and conservative, since it does not overstate the value of the asset. Jack, however, might scoff at an accounting statement which shows his roundabout at £50, since to him such a valuation would be unrealistic!

If Jack purchased coal to power his roundabout, at £60 per tonne six months ago, and has used up that coal today, what is the cost of the fuel? Is it the historical cost of £60, or perhaps the replacement cost of £90 per tonne, which must be paid for coal at today's prices?

The Dual Aspect

This principle is the basis of double-entry book-keeping, and stems from the fact that every transaction has a double effect on the position of a business as recorded in the accounts. When an asset is acquired, either another asset (cash) is reduced, or a liability (promise to pay) is acquired, at the same time. When a sale is made, stock (an asset) is reduced, while either cash or debtors (assets) are increased. If the business borrows money, a liability to the lender is created, and at the same time an asset (cash) is increased. It follows that the assets of the business are equalled by claims on the business, either by creditors or owners, for the funds they have invested in the business and which have been translated into assets for use by the business. The balance sheet which summarizes assets and claims (liabilities) must therefore balance.

When Jack's grandfather bought the roundabout he acquired an asset, by reducing his cash, another asset, and when Jack buys coal on credit terms for the machine he acquires an asset (stock of raw material) and at the same time a liability to the coal merchant. When the liability is discharged, cash, an asset, is reduced. Thus assets equal liabilities at all times. The double-entry system is explained in Chapter 5.

Substance over Form

A new concept, which is not yet completely accepted, is that in order to show a true and fair view, it is sometimes necessary to account for the economic substance of a transaction instead of its strict legal form. Such transactions can be carefully staged so that by following the legal form of the deal, a misleading position will be disclosed in the accounting statements. The accounting profession is slowly coming to the opinion that it is preferable to ignore the legal interpretation of a transaction if accounting for the economic substance, or commercial effect, will lead to the disclosure of true and fair information. An example of substance over form concerns the accounting treatment of leases.

Suppose Jack the showman does not own his own roundabout, but instead leases it from a finance company, in return for the payment of a rental each year. The roundabout belongs to the finance company and should appear as an asset on the company's balance sheet. Jack, however, has a lease contract that gives him the right to the exclusive use of the asset for its useful economic life, and the liability to pay a series of rentals over that life. The commercial effect of the lease is that Jack can use an asset which is no different from other assets which he owns, and he has a liability to pay a series of rentals which become due as the years go by. The economic substance is that the asset and the liability should appear on Jack's balance sheet to disclose a true and fair view, but if strict legal form is followed neither asset nor liability would be disclosed. Standard Practice 21 stipulates that for finance leases, the accounting policy should follow substance over form.

CONCEPTS, STANDARDS AND THE LAW

Part of the theoretical framework of accounting is considered so important that it has been included in a Standard Accounting Practice, and in the Companies Act 1985. SSAP 2 is concerned with the disclosure of accounting policies. This standard attempts to improve the comparability of financial accounting statements by ensuring that the principles applied when the statement was drafted are clearly understood by those using the statement. If different rules are applied in subsequent statements, this fact must be clearly disclosed with information as to the effect of the change of accounting policy on the financial statements. The rule is that it can be assumed that four basic concepts have been followed in drafting a published financial statement and that a note to the accounts must state clearly the fact if any of these four fundamental accounting concepts have not been used. The concepts mentioned by the standard are the going concern concept, the accruals concept, the consistency concept and the prudence concept. The Companies Act 1985 underlines the importance of these basic ideas. Schedule 4 to the Act states that amounts included in the accounts for publication must be determined in accordance with certain accounting principles, which are:

1. The company shall be presumed to be a going concern.
2. Accounting policies must be applied consistently.
3. The amount of any item shall be determined on a prudent basis—only realized profits may be included in the profit and loss account.
4. The accruals concept must be followed.

The law states that a note to the accounts must disclose particulars of any departure from these basic principles, with the reasons for the departure and the effect of the departure on the accounting statement. In this case the law and the standard practice are in accord, but they appear to be out of step with international practice as expressed in International Accounting Standard 1 (IAS 1) 'Disclosure of accounting policies'. This world standard holds that fundamental accounting assumptions are the going concern, consistency and accruals rules, and that disclosure of such assumptions is not required in a financial statement unless they have not been followed, in which case facts and reasons should be disclosed. IAS 1 goes on to state that accounting policies should be selected and applied according to the ideas of prudence, substance over form, and materiality. Thus the international accounting fraternity seem to use slightly different basic principles from accountants in the UK.

SSAP 2 states that 'accounting bases' are the methods which have been developed by accountants to apply the fundamental concepts. Business transactions are complex, so more than one basis may be applicable as the accounting treatment of a particular item. The standard further states that 'accounting policies' are the specific accounting bases selected by a business as being most appropriate for application to its own transactions. Accounting policies should be consistently followed and disclosed as a note to the accounts so that all users of the financial statements will be aware of the rules used in their drafting. Examples of accounting policies might be the depreciation method applied, the method of stock valuation used, the accounting treatment applied to goodwill, etc. For all of these items there is more than one treatment which can be used in the accounts, and it is only fair to users of the financial statements that they are told the method adopted and can thus achieve a greater understanding of the accounting figures.

THE TRUE AND FAIR VIEW

The Companies Act 1985 states that the directors of a company are responsible for the preparation of the accounts and that those accounts must comply with the requirements of Schedule 4 of the Act (see Chapter 13). Section 228 of the Act states that the balance sheet shall give a true and fair view of the state of affairs of the company as at the end of the financial year, and the profit and loss account shall give a true and fair view of the profit or loss of the company for the financial year. The need to disclose a true and fair view is therefore enshrined in company law. The true and fair view is considered to be so important that the Act permits accountants to ignore or override other rules in the Act in order to achieve a true and fair view. In circumstances where a strict conformity to a requirement of the Act might distort the impression given by the accounts, it is permissible to ignore the rule in the Act in order to achieve a true and fair view. Sometimes it is sufficient merely to disclose extra information to achieve this end. The Act requires that the directors should substantiate their actions if they use the true and fair view override to avoid the disclosure rules contained in the Act. A note to the accounts must show the reason for the departure and the effect of such a departure on the accounts.

TUTORIAL DISCUSSION TOPICS

2.1 Is the difference between a concept, a postulate, and a principle in accounting more than a matter of terminology?

2.2 Discuss the limitations of money measurement as a postulate on which to base accounting statements.

2.3 Explain how the concepts of consistency and conservatism support the principle of historical cost, while the opponents of this principle use the concepts of disclosure and materiality in their arguments.

2.4 Is the alternative to the going concern postulate a viable one?

2.5 Why should a businessman separate the transactions of his business from those of his private life? After all, in private life the transactions concerned are mainly to spend the profits made in his business life, and thus the one is an extension of the other.

2.6 Contrast the basic concepts supported by UK law and standards with international practice.

2.7 Discuss the proposition that accounting concepts hinder change in a developing business environment.

3 | The Position Statement or Balance Sheet

This accounting statement shows the status of a firm at any given moment. It is always stated 'as at' a certain date, and is a statement of the financial position of a business on that date. The balance sheet shows the items owned by the business, which are termed assets, and sets against them a list of claims on those assets by those who have provided the funds with which the assets have been purchased; these are termed liabilities, or what the business owes. Thus when shareholders put money into a business or when a lender makes funds available to a business, a claim to the return of the funds is acquired. The funds are then invested by the business in assets which it buys and uses in its chosen trade. Thus everything owned by a business must have been financed, and the finance must have been provided by those who have claims on the business, so liabilities or claims must equal assets.

Some authorities see the balance sheet as a list of the sources of funds used in the business set against a list of the ways in which the funds have been laid out by the management. The term 'balance sheet' may give an erroneous view of this statement, since it implies that it is correct if it is able to balance assets against liabilities. Basically the statement is made up as a list of balances taken from the books of the business, and the balance of asset against liability is derived from the principle of double entry, under which every transaction has a double effect on the accounts of the business. An American term which is now being used in the UK is 'position statement', since it implies that the balance sheet should correctly reflect the position of a business rather than merely summarize the balances in its books.

The balance sheet is like a photograph in that it shows the position of a business at one point in time but does not show how that position was arrived at. It also suffers from the disadvantages of the monetary measurement postulate, in that assets which cannot be measured objectively in money terms are left out of the statement, and assets included at historical cost are shown at an unrepresentative amount after inflation.

ASSETS

An item belonging to a business is considered to be an asset to the business so long as it conforms to three conditions. These are that the asset has a value, that the value can be objectively measured, and that the ownership of the asset can be proved. An auditor will consider these conditions when verifying the situation of assets included on the balance sheet. The market value of an asset is the amount which a user is prepared to pay to control and use that asset at one point in time. Value is therefore derived from expectations of what an asset can earn. Assets are usually recorded in the books at historical cost (the amount paid out when the asset was acquired). Some assets, however, are excluded from the balance sheet because it is too difficult to obtain a precise value for them, or because they could quickly lose their value. For example, the possession of a skilled workforce will enable a business to earn extra profits, so that the workforce is considered to be an asset to the business; but employees can leave, so that this asset cannot be considered as an item completely under the control of the business. A company with an established trade connection will make extra sales, and extra profits, from repeat orders when satisfied customers return for more goods, but this advantage can rapidly disappear if a company loses its reputation. The original cost and current value of these two assets are difficult to determine.

Traditionally, accountants record assets at their historical cost and not their estimated current market value, in order to conform to the principles of objectivity, realization and prudence. It is considered imprudent to rely on a valuation for an asset which cannot be tested by a cross-market transaction, and which may subsequently be reduced by market forces and thus not realized. In some cases, however, the historical cost of an asset gets out of line with the current value of the asset, and a professional valuer is asked to revalue the asset so that the balance sheet can reflect current conditions with greater accuracy. If a building accounted for at cost of £100 000 is subsequently revalued at £150 000, and disclosed on the balance sheet at this value, the surplus of £50 000 must be shown as a reserve not available for distribution. This means that it is an unrealized profit (sometimes called a holding gain) which has not passed through the profit and loss account, and is not available for distribution to shareholders under the prudence concept.

The value of some assets cannot be assessed with accuracy. For example, a patent or trademark owned by a business, or the funds invested by a business in developing a new product, will both earn extra profits for the business but the amount of those extra profits is difficult to determine. Accordingly, 'intangible' assets of this type are recognized as assets but carried in the balance sheet at cost rather than value. An economist might wish to value an asset by determining the current value of the future stream of income to be derived from the asset. Such a value is the subject of great uncertainty and for this reason the prudent accountant prefers to use the idea of cost rather than value when stating assets in the balance sheet.

Assets can be classified as fixed assets, current assets and intangible assets. The fixed assets of the business are not held for resale but are intended as investments of the company's funds in significant items which will be used over a long period, certainly exceeding the accounting year. Such items are termed long-lived assets, and it is said that capital has been 'sunk' in them. Normally a significant proportion of the assets of a manufacturing business will be held in the form of factory buildings, plant and machinery, vehicles, and perhaps office fixtures and fittings. Most of these items are concerned with making the goods which are sold for a profit. Consequently accountants take the view that profit stems from, or is earned by, the fixed assets of the business. Another type of fixed asset is the long-term investment which takes the form of a share stake in another company owned by a business for purposes of strategy or control. An item considered to be a fixed asset for one company may be a current asset for another. For example, a car is a tangible fixed asset if it is to be driven by a salesman for the next two years, but it is a current asset if it is held as stock for sale by a car sales company.

The business entity concept requires that only assets belonging to the company or partnership, or the business assets of a sole trader, are included in the balance sheet. The going concern principle assumes that the business will continue so that the historical cost of fixed assets less any depreciation charged against them to date is used to state such assets in the balance sheet rather than the lower and more conservative scrap value of a fixed asset if it were sold immediately in the second-hand market. By tradition the assets on a balance sheet are always shown in reverse order of liquidity, i.e. the least liquid, land and buildings held more or less permanently, come at the top.

The other category of fixed assets, termed intangible assets, is shown on the balance sheet above the tangible fixed assets and long-term investments. Intangible assets are items which, although they are not visible and cannot be physically touched, nevertheless make a contribution to the profits of the business. As shown above, the possession of a patent or trademark can earn extra profits for a business and if such an asset has been purchased, its costs can be objectively valued and recorded in the balance sheet as one of the items which the business owns. Another intangible asset is goodwill, which is discussed in a later chapter.

The current assets of a business are held for a short period, traditionally less than the accounting year. This means that such assets held at the balance sheet date are expected to be turned back into cash within the passage of twelve months. These assets are said to oil the wheels of the business so that the fixed assets can make a profit more easily; it is difficult to use factory buildings and plant to manufacture goods without the current asset of raw material stock to back you up, and difficult to sell your product without working capital available to provide trade credit to your customers (debtors). The current assets of a business are also listed in reverse order of liquidity, as stock (inventory), debts, short-term investments and cash. Stocks may be in the form of raw materials, work in progress (semi-finished items in the factory), or finished goods awaiting sale. These are always shown at cost or net realizable value, whichever is the lower, to adhere to the concept of conservatism. This ensures that no element of profit is taken before stocks are sold, but that any loss made because stocks are held is taken into account at once. Debts are sums owed to the business, usually by customers who have bought goods on credit terms. It is expected that these debts will be turned back into cash in the near future when the debts are paid. Short-term investments are held to provide a safe repository for idle funds, so that they can earn some return while at the same time they can be quickly liquidated if funds are required for use elsewhere in the business. The term cash covers the money in the bank account and also money held at other points in the business, such as the tills of the shops or the petty-cash box in the office safe. All current assets are expected to work their way through the business cycle, i.e. purchase of stock for cash, storage, manufacture, sale (this is the transition from stock to a debt), and payment, which turns the current asset back into cash. This cycle is expected to be accomplished within a short period, less than the accounting year. For this reason current assets are sometimes referred to as the 'circulating' capital or assets of a business.

Accounting theory is beginning to refine the definition of an asset by considering the characteristics applicable to an asset. This new theoretical approach is changing the traditional idea of an asset as something which can be touched and objectively valued. An asset can now be considered as a probable future benefit controlled by and accruing to a particular company as a result of past transactions or events. This broad definition needs to be supported by certain recognition tests which, if satisfied, ascertain that a transaction creates an asset. When plant is shown in the balance sheet, it is not perhaps the physical item which is disclosed, so much as the value of the economic benefits to be derived from that physical item by working the plant in future periods. Control over an asset implies the ability to obtain the future benefits or to restrict the access of other parties to those benefits. If economic benefit establishes the existence of an asset, control is the critical event which decides the appropriate accounting treatment of the asset.

LIABILITIES

A liability is an amount owed by a business to any person who has provided funds to finance the assets controlled by the business. Such persons may be lenders who have provided funds for the short or long term, or the shareholders themselves (the owners) who have a right to be repaid the funds they have invested, if the business is wound up. On a traditional two-sided balance sheet the liabilities are stated in reverse order of liquidity, the claims which have to be paid soonest coming at the bottom. At the top is the capital which represents the original amount invested in the business by the owner. In a company, capital takes the form of shares owned by the various shareholders. As they are the last to be repaid in the event of the business being discontinued, they are deemed to take the biggest risk. Share capital is sometimes for this reason called venture capital. Next come the reserves of the business. They also belong to the owners or shareholders, but represent profits made by the business in the past and not distributed. When a profit is made it is appropriated or divided up, some being paid to the Inland Revenue as taxation, some being paid to the shareholders in the form of a dividend (or to the proprietor as a sole trader as drawings), and the remainder being retained in the business as a source of finance. Thus reserves or profits ploughed back into the business represent a further investment by the shareholders made out of past profits. When added together, share capital and reserves total the owner's interest in the business, being the funds provided initially and out of past profits by the legal owners of the business. Sometimes this amount is termed the equity interest, since all ordinary shareholders have an equal right to participate pro rata to their holding of shares, if these funds are repaid. Some reserves are not available for distribution as dividend for legal reasons. These are known as capital reserves and they are disclosed on the balance sheet below share capital but above general reserves.

The remaining liabilities of the business are divided according to the period for which they are lent. The long-term liabilities include loans made for periods of more than one year, and often for such long periods as to be viewed as part of the long-term capital employed in the business. These loans are sometimes termed mortgages or debentures, and are often secured on the assets of the business. This means that if the company fails to pay the annual interest on a loan, or goes into liquidation before the period of the loan is ended, the lender may take possession of some assets of the business and sell them in order to recoup the funds lent to the business.

Current liabilities are amounts lent to the business for a period of less than one year. They include trade creditors who have supplied goods and services and are awaiting payment, short-term loans from the bank, usually in the form of an overdraft, the Inland Revenue awaiting payment of tax on the due date, and the shareholders themselves awaiting payment of a dividend from the previous year's profits.

Contingent liabilities are amounts which might become liabilities of the firm, depending upon circumstances which may arise after the balance sheet date, e.g. damages in a court action where judgement is pending at the balance sheet date. These items are shown as a note under the balance sheet and do not form part of the liabilities which are added to equal the total of the assets.

A theoretical definition of a liability is that it is a present obligation of a company, which entails a probable future sacrifice when the business transfers assets, or provides a service, to another business. The term 'present obligation' has a wider scope than a mere 'legal liability' which can be proved at law.

THE FORM OF THE BALANCE SHEET

In the UK the balance sheet can take two forms. A slightly outdated form shows the assets listed on the right-hand side and the capital and other liabilities of the company on the left-hand side. An illustration of this format is shown below in the balance sheet of J. Nash, a sole trader. This business is not a company and thus it does not have a share capital. The capital of the proprietor is shown analysed as to

Balance Sheet of J. Nash as at 31 December 19..

	£	£		£	£	£
Capital:			Intangible assets:			
Original investment		175 000	Goodwill			40 000
Retained earnings		125 768	Fixed assets:	Cost	Depn	
		300 768	Land and buildings	172 000	2 000	170 000
			Plant	147 000	23 000	124 000
			Vehicles	10 412	6 208	4 204
Long-term liabilities:				329 412	31 208	298 204
Long-term loan at						
10 per cent interest		160 000				338 204
Current liabilities:			Current assets:			
Trade creditors	60 060		Stock		118 640	
Bank loan	19 618		Debtors		75 325	
Tax	4 134		Investments		10 000	
		83 812	Bank		2 411	206 376
		£544 580				£544 580

This form is slightly outdated, but is often used for the accounts of a small business, or non-profit-making organization such as a sports club. The capital in this case represents the owner's or club members' investment in the undertaking. In other countries, e.g. the USA, the assets may be found on the left and the liabilities on the right, to reflect their position in double-entry book keeping.

the original investment of £175 000 and the retained earning sof £125 768 which represent profits earned in the past but not withdrawn by the proprietor. Note that the fixed assets are shown at historical cost less the cumulative depreciation provided against those assets out of profits earned since the fixed assets were purchased. The

Balance Sheet of XYZ PLC* as at 31 December 19..

	£	£	£	£
Fixed assets:				
Intangible assets: goodwill				40 000
	Cost	*Depn*	*Net*	
Tangible assets: land and buildings	8 272 000	612 000	7 660 000	
plant	4 447 000	1 723 000	2 724 000	
vehicles	120 412	66 208	54 204	
	12 839 412	2 401 208		10 438 204
Investments				660 000
				11 138 204
Current assets:				
Stock			1 658 640	
Debtors			1 435 325	
Investments			20 000	
Cash			12 411	
			3 126 376	
Less current liabilities:				
Creditors: amounts falling due				
within one year:				
Trade creditors		1 186 310		
Bank overdraft		559 618		
Taxation		24 134		
Dividend payable		100 000		
			1 870 062	
Net current assets (working capital)				1 256 314
Total assets less current liabilities				12 394 518
Long-term liabilities: amounts falling due				
after more than one year:				
Long-term loan at 10% interest				2 000 000
				£10 394 518
Financed by:				
Capital and reserves				
Share capital				5 000 000
Capital reserve—share premium account				2 000 000
General reserve				3 394 518
Equity interest				£10 394 518

*The letters 'PLC' in the title of the company indicate that it is a public limited company, and that its shares are listed for trading on a Stock Exchange.

business has a bank loan of £19 618, repayable within twelve months of the balance sheet date and thus a current liability, and also £2411 of cash in the till and/or bank. It is not uncommon for a business to have more than one bank account, perhaps with one overdrawn whilst another contains a positive balance.

A form of balance sheet which is more easily assimilated is the vertical form, now stipulated for companies in the Companies Act 1985. This statement sets out the fixed assets and then the current assets. The amount of current liabilities is deducted from current assets to disclose the working capital which, when added to fixed assets, gives the long-term funds employed in the business. The term net current assets is sometimes used instead of working capital, implying that the current liabilities are netted off against the current assets. Amounts lent to the business over a long period (long-term liabilities) are then deducted to leave the shareholders' funds or equity interest. A second part to the statement analyses the equity interest between the amounts originally invested by the shareholders or owners (share capital) and reserves which usually represent profits reinvested over the years since the business began to trade. Capital reserves, which by law or for reasons of financial prudence are not available for distribution to shareholders as a profit, are also shown in this part of the balance sheet. The Companies Act does not favour the use of the term 'current liabilities' but prefers 'creditors: amounts falling due within one year'. By the same token, the term 'creditors: amounts falling due after more than one year' is preferred to the term 'long-term liabilities'. On the balance sheet of XYZ PLC shown above, the capital reserve takes the form of a share premium account. This means that when the £1 ordinary shares of the company were issued to the public, the issue price was £1.40 per share. Thus investors were so keen to buy shares in XYZ PLC that they were willing to pay a premium for the shares. The premium means that for each share certificate with a nominal value of £1, the shareholder was willing to pay £1.40, i.e. 5 million £1 ordinary shares issued at £1.40 raised £7 million in cash as the investment by the shareholders in XYZ PLC when it began to trade. By law the share premium account must be shown as a capital reserve since it is part of the permanent capital of the business and cannot be repaid to shareholders under normal circumstances. The capital reserve thus differs from the general reserve, which represents past profits retained in the business and reinvested by the directors on behalf of the shareholders and which are still legally available to be paid out as a dividend if necessary.

THE ACCOUNTING EQUATION

One way in which the balance sheet and its relationship to the profit and loss account can sometimes be explained is in the form of an algebraic formula or model. If symbols are allotted to the components of the balance sheet a formula will emerge which can express the interrelationship of basic ideas such as equity, liabilities, assets, revenue, and expenses. The formula can be built up in steps as follows. The amounts are taken from the balance sheet of J. Nash, already shown.

1. Assets = claims, $A = C$, £544 580 = £544 580.
   This demonstrates the basic financial position of the business as shown by the balance sheet, in that the funds invested in the business equal the assets owned by the business at any one time. The funds invested have been provided by owners and lenders, and thus these persons have claims on the assets of the business.

2. Assets = ownership investment + loans, $A = OI + L$, £544 580 = £300 768 + £243 812.

   The formula now analyses the claims, to differentiate between the funds invested by the owners in the business and the funds used in the business which have been provided by others. This relationship can also be expressed as $A - L = OI$, to reveal the extent of the investment by the legal owners in the firm. The term 'capital' is often used instead of OI, and the term ownership interest instead of ownership investment. The formula $A - L = OI$ also implies that all assets remaining after the liabilities have been repaid belong to the shareholders or the owners. This corresponds to the idea of the shareholder or entrepreneur being the risk taker and standing at the end of the queue of those with a right to be repaid out of the assets of the business. Ownership interest comprises the original capital invested in the business by the shareholders or the proprietors plus the reserves, normally arising from the reinvestment of undistributed profits belonging, of course, to the owners.

3. Assets = ownership investment + long-term liabilities + current liabilities,
   $A = OI + LTL + CL$,
   £544 580 = £300 768 + £160 000 + £83 812.

   Here long-term loans are separated from short-term liabilities to demonstrate the idea that all funds lent to the business, whether short or long term or invested permanently by the owners, are represented by the assets. There are three distinct groups of capital providers.

4. Total assets = fixed assets + current assets + intangible assets,
   $A = FA + CA + IA$,
   £544 580 = £298 204 + £206 376 + £40 000.

   This analysis of the assets side of the balance sheet shows the various types of possession which a business can buy with the funds at its disposal. Since cash is a liquid asset and can flow into any other form of asset which the firm decides to buy, there is no way of identifying particular assets with certain funds used to buy them. However, it is wise to have a fund of permanent capital at least equal to the fixed assets, since if the loan capital, long or short term, needs to be repaid, there will be sufficient current assets which can be exchanged for cash to meet the repayment.

5. Assets = loans + capital + retained earnings,
   $A = L + C + RE$,
   £544 580 = £243 812 + £175 000 + £125 768

   This development of the model divides the ownership interest into its two constituent parts: the original capital contributed by the owners at the commencement of the business, and the profits belonging to the owners which have not been distributed to them in the past, but have been retained in the business since the commencement date. In a company, owners are shareholders and retained earnings are often called reserves.

6. Assets = loans + capital + retained earnings at the start of the year + (profit − tax and drawings),
   $A = L + C + RE_{t-1} + [P - (T + D)]$, where t = this year.
   In this case the formula explains the derivation of retained earnings, showing

them to be that part of the profit figure not appropriated to pay taxes or withdrawn. This is a significant development of the model, since at this point the connection between the balance sheet and the profit and loss account begins to emerge, i.e. any amount of profit not appropriated for payment of tax or drawings is added to the capital of the business, since it is part of the owners' interest in the business. Drawings in a company are dividends paid to shareholders. If profit for the year was £38 500, and tax to be paid is £4134, whilst drawings were £17 250, the numerate proof of the equation would be:

£544 580 = £243 812 + £175 000 + £108 652 + [£38 500 − (£4134 + £17 250)].

Note that tax of £4134 has not yet been paid and is thus shown as a current liability in the balance sheet.

7. The connection between the balance sheet and the profit and loss account is underlined by the next development of the formula.

   Assets = loans + capital + retained earnings at the start of the year + [(sales − costs) − tax and drawings],

   $A = L + C + RE_{t-1} + [(S - CO) - (T + D)]$, where t = this year.

   The increase in retained earnings can be expressed as a separate formula,

   $RE = RE_{t-1} + [(S - CO) - (T + D)]$.

   If sales revenue for the year is £340 612, and the costs associated with the goods sold are £302 112, a profit of £38 500 has been earned. The numerical computation of the formula is:

   £544 580 = £243 812 + £175 000 + £108 652 +
   [(£340 612 − £302 112) − (£4134 + £17 250)].

   There is one notable flaw in this argument, which is that retained earnings or reserves can be affected by certain transactions which do not go through the profit and loss account. For example, the revaluation of fixed assets results in an increase in the asset value with a corresponding increase in the reserves which make up part of the ownership interest. Reserves of this kind should not be withdrawn, and are therefore shown as capital reserves.

The full extent of the balance sheet model can be seen by combining the formula in (4) with the formula in (7):

$$FA + CA + IA = LTL + CL + C + RE_{t-1} + [(S - CO) - (T + D)]$$

TUTORIAL DISCUSSION TOPICS

3.1 Are there any assets of a business which do not appear on the balance sheet? If so, why are they excluded and how can it be said that the assets which are shown equal the claims on the business by those who have financed the assets?

3.2 The following statement is made by a shareholder: 'The equity interest on the balance sheet shows me what my shares are worth'. Discuss the balance sheet as a statement of 'net worth'.

3.3 Define an asset for balance sheet purposes. Differentiate between current assets and fixed assets.

3.4 How, if at all, would you record the following events in the books of a business?

(a) Oil is discovered under the company's car park.
(b) The sales director leaves to work for a rival company.
(c) Political changes cause the company to be expelled from a country in which it owned mineral rights.
(d) A fire destroys the accounting department's building and all the records stored in it.
(e) The company suffers its first strike in ten years.

3.5 Many companies rely on bank overdraft as a source of funds. How is this reliance compatible with the inclusion of bank overdraft among the current or short-term liabilities on the balance sheet?

SEMINAR EXERCISES 1

1. Prepare a position statement from the following information presented to you on 31 December. Your answer should be in good form.

Company A	£
Creditors	43 614
Cash in hand	1 270
Bank balance	8 186
Stock	29 941
Freehold land	60 000
Long-term loan owed by the firm	20 000
Wages payable	1 102
Nottingham Corporation bonds	8 000
Debtors	19 487
Buildings	35 000
Expenses paid in advance	904
Share capital	50 000
Vehicles	8 000
Plant at cost	25 000
Depreciation on plant	6 000
Shares of company X	7 000
Taxation owed	13 000
Depreciation on buildings	10 000

2. Show how each of the following transactions changes the balance sheet which you produced in answer to Question 1.

(a) Shareholders invest a further £20 000 in the company.
(b) The wages payable are paid.
(c) The company buys raw material for cash, £1200.
(d) The company buys raw material for credit, £4000.
(e) The company sells its property at book value.
(f) The company pays £5000 to its creditors.
(g) The Nottingham bonds are realized for cash, £8000.
(h) £10 000 is paid to the Inland Revenue.

3. Company B has been in business for a number of years. Recently there has been a fire at the head office, in which the accounting records of the business have been destroyed. The company's accountant has left and the directors have asked you to reconstruct, as far as possible, the records. You take stock, visit the bank, inform customers, and investigate the ownership of buildings, machinery and other assets. You discover the following information:

	Balance or Market Value (£)
Cash in safe	8 000
Bank balance	36 000
Stock of raw material and finished goods	74 000
Debtors	52 000
Shares of other companies	18 000
Land and buildings	156 000
Machinery and vehicles	64 000

After a check of invoices received from creditors and statements of account received, you compute that £80 000 is owed to such creditors and a further £40 000 is owed to the Inland Revenue. The land and buildings are mortgaged in the sum of £70 000. The share register is at the office of the company's solicitor, and shows that 100 000 ordinary shares of £1 each have been issued.

(a) Draw up a balance sheet for Company B
(b) How has the accounting equation helped you to find an answer?

4. On 1 January Mr See set up business as a shopkeeper. He withdrew his life savings of £5894 from a building society and used them to open a business bank account. He borrowed a further £13 000 from a friend, and used the money to buy the freehold of a shop with storage space at the rear. It cost Mr See £2714 to fit out the shop with counter, till, window displays and display cabinets, but he has paid only £2000 of this bill to the shopfitter so far. One supplier who sold stock to Mr See at a cost of £930 demanded payment in cash, but another who sold Mr See stock for £1831 is willing to wait until the end of the month for payment. Mr See uses his car, bought recently for £2150, entirely for business purposes. He has spend £285 from the bank account to purchase a freezer for Mrs See, and has lent £500 from the same account to a business acquaintance, Mr Exe. There are no other transactions during the month of January. Draw up a balance sheet for Mr See as at 31 January.

5. (a) William Durr is the proprietor of a small building contracting firm. He does not understand the term 'balance sheet' and asks you to explain to him whether the following items should be on his balance sheet. Indicate the nature of the items, e.g. current asset, long-term liability, not applicable etc.

    (i) stock of sand and cement;
    (ii) air compressor purchased for cash;
    (iii) air compresor purchased on credit terms;
    (iv) air compressor hired for three weeks;

    (v) wages paid to labourer;
   (vi) lorry used for transporting vehicles;
  (vii) diesel fuel in lorry fuel tank;
 (viii) washing machine bought for Mrs Durr;
   (ix) bank overdraft;
    (x) £250 owing from a customer for work done;
   (xi) road fund licence for lorry;
  (xii) stock of paper and envelopes, value 90 pence;
 (xiii) petty cash in hand;
 (xiv) £2500 owing to Aunt Joan, who says William need not repay her until four years have elapsed.

(b) In respect of any of the assets in (a) above which you consider to be fixed, would it be possible for the same asset to be current in another type of business? Explain.

(c) What other items would you need in order to construct a balance sheet for William Durr?

4 | The Income Statement

Income is measured by the accountant, using the matching or accruals principle. The revenue earned in a period (sales or turnover are other words used) is calculated and the accountant then charges the cost of earning that revenue against the revenue, to reveal a surplus or a deficit. Thus income is measured by matching effort to accomplishment. The difficulty is to ascertain what costs and revenues should be recognized in a particular accounting period if a true and fair profit or loss is to be disclosed. The accountant must use judgement when profit is measured, for example:

1. Will all sales revenue be received in cash, or should a provision for doubtful debts be set against profit?
2. Have the fixed assets lost value because they have been used to earn the profit—should a provision for depreciation be charged against profit?
3. Have all costs incurred been recorded or is an accrual necessary?
4. Are all recorded costs properly chargeable to this accounting period or have expenses been paid in advance?

The income statement is designed to measure the results of transactions which have taken place between two balance sheet dates. Since it shows the result of operations for a period of time it is not a statement 'as at' but a statement 'for the year ended'. It is a summary of all trading transactions which have taken place during a period, not a statement to show the position at one moment in time.

Sometimes it is called the revenue account and sometimes the income statement, but in the UK the term 'profit and loss account' is usually used. This term, however, is a misnomer, since the income statement is often divided into four parts, one of which itself is called the profit and loss account. The parts are:

1. The manufacturing account. This reveals the cost of production and in some cases a factory profit. This part is produced only for a manufacturing company and is sometimes called the work-in-progress account.
2. The trading account, in which the cost of goods sold is set against sales revenue to show a gross profit.
3. The profit and loss account, in which the general expenses of the business are set against gross profit to reduce it to net profit.
4. The appropriation account, which shows how the net profit is divided up according to the various ways in which it is used; e.g. some is set aside for

taxation, some is used to cover dividends paid to shareholders, and the remainder is retained in the business as part of its reserves.

The manufacturing and trading accounts are produced for internal management purposes, while under the Companies Acts the shareholders and investors at large are entitled to see only certain figures on the profit and loss account and the appropriation account. Companies treat the income statement as a confidential document, since a rival business might gain a significant advantage if the full details were disclosed. Examples of the various accounts are shown below.

Dr.   Manufacturing Account   Cr.
                            £   £
Materials used   14 708   Cost of completed production
Direct labour   12 653   transferred to stores   37 207
Prime cost   27 361
Factory overheads   9 846
                       £37 207   £37 207

Factory overhead is the indirect cost of running the factory and includes such items pertinent to the factory operation as rent, light, heat, power, maintenance, depreciations and managerial salaries.

Dr.   Finished Goods Stores Account   Cr.
                            £   £
Opening stock   6 425   Cost of goods sold transferred
Cost of goods transferred   to trading account   39 448
   from factory   37 207   Balance, closing stock c/f   4 184
                       £43 632   £43 632

Dr.   Trading Account   Cr.
                            £   £
Cost of goods sold   39 448   Sales   62 871
Gross profit carried to
   profits and loss account 23 423
                       £62 871   £62 871

Note: The calculation of opening stock plus purchases less closing stock to show the cost of goods sold is sometimes undertaken in the trading account. In other systems the finished goods stores stands between the manufacturing account and the trading account.

Dr.   Profit and Loss Account   Cr.
                            £   £
Administration expenses 5 786   Gross profit brought down
Selling expenses   8 612   from trading account   23 423
Distribution expenses   4 904   Miscellaneous income   1 530
Financial expenses   2 107
Net profit transferred
   to appropriation account 3 544
                       £24 953   £24 953

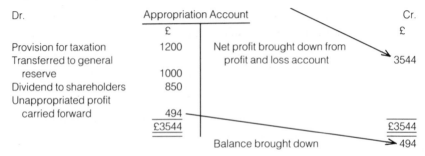

Dr.   Appropriation Account   Cr.

	£		£
Provision for taxation	1200	Net profit brought down from	
Transferred to general		profit and loss account	3544
reserve	1000		
Dividend to shareholders	850		
Unappropriated profit			
carried forward	494		
	£3544		£3544
		Balance brought down	494

This balance appears in the balance sheet as unappropriated profits, and is part of the owners' interest in the business. Transfers to reserves will be added to the amount of the reserve shown in the balance sheet. The provision for taxation is a balance sheet liability because it is waiting to be paid.

In a business which is not formed as a company, e.g. a partnership or a sole trader, the proprietor withdraws his profit instead of receiving a dividend. The term 'drawings' appears in the appropriation account instead of dividend.

Note that in the profit and loss section the expenses have been grouped under certain convenient headings. The statements could also be presented in columnar form, as will be shown in a later chapter.

A disadvantage of the balance sheet is that it shows the position at one moment in time only, but this is to some extent remedied by the income statement, which shows in part how that position has been attained. The result of the statement, the profit or loss figure, can be set against the capital employed in the business, as revealed by the balance sheet, to show as a percentage the profitability of the operation and the return earned by the management on the funds entrusted to them by the owners. This return is satisfactory only if it is sufficient to compensate for the risk taken by the owners when investing their capital in the enterprise. The return on capital employed percentage can be used to compare the performance of one company with that of another similar company, or with its own performance in previous years.

$$\frac{\text{Net profit}}{\text{Capital employed}} \times \frac{100}{1} = \frac{£50\ 000}{£250\ 000} \times \frac{100}{1} = 20\%$$

Care must be taken, however, to ensure the comparison of like with like, or a misleading conclusion may be drawn from the figures.

The choice of accounting period is important in the measurement of income. Business transactions go on from day to day, and there is never any one time at which all business transactions cease and then start again on the next day. Thus, whatever the accounting date chosen, there will always be some transactions which transcend the end of the period. The idea of an accounting period is thus an artificial one, but it would be equally false to go on recording transactions without attempting to measure their profitability. Pacioli recognized this when he wrote that frequent accounting in a partnership makes for long friendship.

The choice of accounting period depends upon the person for whom the income statement is to be prepared. Most companies publish accounts annually to show their shareholders how the business has performed during the year, and many companies also produce an interim set of accounts half-way through the year to provide investors with extra information on which to base their decisions. For management purposes accounts are usually produced monthly, and in much greater detail.

The choice of accounting period is an arbitrary one, and is determined for reasons of convenience. Some companies organize their year to run from 1 April until 31 March so that it is the same as the fiscal year of the Inland Revenue authorities. Others, however, prefer the calendar year, and their accounts are for the period 1 January to 31 December. Companies in a seasonal industry usually arrange for their year end to come after the end of the season, while others plan their year end to fall in the slack season for audit staff. Obviously, if many companies had a year-end date at 31 December there would be a heavy demand for the services of audit clerks during the months of January, February and March.

THE ACCRUALS PRINCIPLE

The accruals, or matching, principle, is the device adopted by the accountant to isolate the transactions of any one accounting period from those of the next period. If a true profit is to be computed, sales for the period must be set against the cost of goods sold during that period. This means that the cost of the products sold this year must be charged in the revenue account this year, even though those products were made last year. It also means that there is a difference between expense and expenditure, since money may be paid out for costs incurred in one accounting period, but those costs cannot be charged against sales as an expense until the next accounting period, when the goods are sold. (See figure 1.)

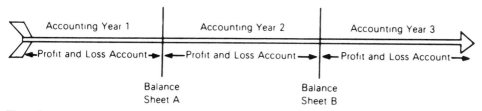

Figure 1

A cost is the amount paid out for a service or benefit received or a sacrifice made in order to achieve a stated end. The cost is entered in the books of account when it is paid for, or when a liability for such a payment is recognized, i.e. a bill is received. At this point the cost has been incurred to acquire an asset, say materials purchased and received into the stores, and this asset is charged to the profit and loss account as a cost when it is consumed or used up. At this point the asset has turned into an expense, and is no longer a balance sheet item because it must be charged to the profit and loss account as a cost for the period. The date on which the bill is paid (expenditure) is not relevant in deciding whether the cost has been incurred. The raw material purchased may be paid for in cash when the goods are received, or payment may be made weeks or months after the material has been used up if the supplier is willing to allow the purchaser a period of credit. A cost incurred in one period to make products can be carried forward at the end of the year as a balance sheet asset if the goods made have not been sold at that point in time. These costs represented by the unsold stock of finished products will be written off to the profit and loss account in the next period when they are sold, so that the revenue from the sale is correctly matched with the cost incurred to make the goods which have been sold. Cost properly chargeable to the income statement in a particular year includes the production cost of products sold that year (materials, labour and factory overhead expenses) even though the products were made in a previous year and the costs were paid for in that year. In figure 1 the stock of finished goods made in year 1 but not sold by the end of that year appears in balance sheet A as an asset at an amount equal to the costs incurred in year 1 to make the goods. This cost is not set against sales of year 1 in the profit computation but is carried forward as a balance sheet asset at the beginning of year 2 so that it can be set against revenue from the sales of these goods in the profit computation of the second year.

Four separate cases emerge:

1. A cost this year which is paid for this year: An example of such a cost is the payment of wages for labour used to make products which have been sold during the year.
2. A cost this year which was paid for last year: This means that an asset acquired last year, and shown in the balance sheet at the end of that year, becomes a cost in the profit and loss account this year. For example, raw materials purchased last year and kept in stock are charged to the income statement this year, when they are consumed in the production process.
3. The cost of a future period which is paid for this year: For example, raw materials bought during the year but not used, which appear in the closing balance sheet as an asset, stock. The calculation—opening stock plus purchases, less closing stock—computes the cost of materials used up during the period. Likewise an insurance premium paid for a year from 1 July 1990 up to 30 June 1991 in the sum of, say, £1000, should be apportioned, half of the cost being charged to the profit and loss account of 1990 for the six months covered by the premium in that year. The other half should be carried forward as a balance sheet asset in the balance sheet dated 31 December 1990, and then charged as a cost in the profit and loss account for 1991, since the premium concerns the first six months of that accounting year.
4. The cost of this year which will be paid for in a future period: For example, raw materials delivered and used up during the year for which a bill has not been received and payment has not yet been made.

Some accountants prefer to use the word 'expense' rather than cost, while others see expenses as the general administration costs of the business, e.g. rent, insurance, etc.

PREPAYMENTS AND ACCRUALS

The amounts recorded in the books of the business have to be adjusted for the four cases shown above, so that the true cost is entered in the income statement. A prepayment, or payment in advance, is such an adjustment. Suppose that rent is paid on business premises for a year in advance on 30 June. If the accounting year of the business runs from 1 January until 31 December, at the end of the year half of the rent paid on 30 June will be a cost properly chargeable for the year to 31 December, and the other half will represent the cost of the next accounting period, paid in advance. This prepayment is an asset at 31 December, since the business possesses the right to use the premises for the next six months. Technically the landlord owes the business six months' rent, or six months' use, at 31 December, and this is shown in the balance sheet as a debtor. In the next accounting period this asset will be converted to a cost and charged to the income statement. Other expenses which can be paid in advance include insurance premiums, usually paid annually, rates for a half-year, rentals on leased plant and vehicles, and the annual road fund licence for a vehicle. Two examples of case (c) for a business whose accounting year ends on 31 December are shown below.

Rent Paid in Advance

Dr.		Rent Account		Cr.
	£			£
Year 1: 30 June cash paid	1200	31 December charge to profit and loss		600
		31 December balance carried forward		600
	£1200			£1200
Year 2: 1 January balance brought down	600	31 December charge to profit and loss		1300
30 June cash paid	1400	31 December balance carried forward		700
	£2000			£2000
Year 3: 1 January balance brought down	700			

(Note that the rent has increased in the second year. It is paid annually in advance.)

Raw Materials Purchased but Not Consumed

Dr.		Materials		Cr.
	£			£
1 Jan purchased for cash	439	31 Dec charge to manufacturing account		14 387
15 May purchased on credit from J. Brown	5 617	31 Dec balance of stock carried forward		1 304
25 Sept purchased on credit from A. Smith	9 635			
	£15 691			£15 691
1 Jan balance brought down*	1 304			

*Appears in the balance sheet as a current asset.

Stock and purchases are recorded in the same account in this example. Sometimes stock is shown in a stock account which has only the opening balance on the account until that balance is transferred to the manufacturing account or trading account at the year end and replaced by the closing stock, which is the opening stock for the next year. The debit balance on both these accounts will appear as an asset on the balance sheet.

An accrued expense is a cost for the current year which has been incurred but not yet paid for or even invoiced. In this case the accountant must use his expertise to estimate what the expense is likely to be when the bill is eventually presented, and to charge this amount in the income statement so that a true profit is shown. According to the principle of duality, if a cost is entered on one side of the ledger a liability to meet the cost must be shown on the other side.

The cost of electricity provides a good example of an accrued expense. Electricity will have been used by the office and factory right up to the accounting date, but the most recent bill for electricity will show only the cost up to the date on which the meter was read, which could be a month or more before the year end. The accountant must estimate the liability for electricity for the period between the meter reading and the year end and charge it in the income statement. The balance sheet will show a liability for this amount, and when the electricity bill is presented at some date in the next year, that part of it which concerns this year will already have been charged to the profit and loss account and thus will not distort next year's costs.

Electricity Consumed but No Bill Received—an Accrual

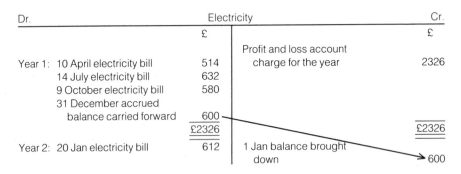

Dr.		Electricity		Cr.
		£		£
			Profit and loss account	
Year 1: 10 April electricity bill		514	charge for the year	2326
14 July electricity bill		632		
9 October electricity bill		580		
31 December accrued				
balance carried forward		600		
		£2326		£2326
Year 2: 20 Jan electricity bill		612	1 Jan balance brought	
			down	600

The accountant has estimated the missing bill for electricity consumed in the last three months of the year as £600. This has been charged to the profit and loss account of year 1 within the figure £2326. The amount of £600 is carried forward as a credit balance on the balance sheet at the end of year 1 because the accountant believes that the electricity board is owed £600 by the company at that time. This should therefore be recorded in the balance sheet as a creditor. When the bill for £612 is received on 20 January in year 2, there is a credit balance of £600 waiting in the account to offset it. Thus a year 1 expense is not allowed to interfere with profit measurement in year 2 except in so far as the accountant has incorrectly estimated the amount of the bill, by £12.

Fixed assets of a business are acquired for use in more than one accounting period. Thus the cost of a machine with a ten-year life should be charged out to the ten accounting periods covered by that life. The term used for spreading the cost of a fixed asset over several accounting periods is depreciation (see Chapter 6). A charge for depreciation is made in the income statement each year and gradually the asset is turned into an expense and written off against sales in the years in which it makes a contribution to those sales. A machine costing £5000 might be charged at £1000 per annum to the profit and loss account if it has a five-year working life.

Deferred revenue expenditure is a term applied to costs which provide a benefit in more than one accounting period and which are spread across those periods for this reason. An advertising campaign to establish a new product may give benefit by generating sales over the next two or even three years. Accordingly it may be considered fair to charge out this cost to the accounting periods which benefit from it, so that at the end of the first year the cost of advertising not yet charged out will appear in the balance sheet as an asset.

Development expenditure on a product or project yet to be marketed is sometimes carried forward as an asset until such time as there is sales revenue from that product against which the development cost can be written off (matched). An accountant, however, will defer such revenue expenditure only if he is certain that sales will follow, since it is contrary to the concept of conservatism to carry forward the cost if there is a chance that revenue will not ensue.

The accruals principle also applies to revenue from sales. Cash received is not synonymous with sales. Goods may be sold on credit, and even though the payment has not been received the sales can be counted in the income computation. Once again the concept of conservatism ensures that provision for doubtful debts is made in this case. Cash received in one year may not concern sales of that year, since it may represent payments made by debtors for sales made in a previous period. In this case one asset, a debt, has been exchanged for another, cash, with no impact on the income statement.

Some authorities hold that a true profit for the accounting period can be shown only if extraordinary or non-recurring items such as the impact of a fire or strike are separated from the main profit computation. Some entries in the income statement which correct mistakes in adjustments made in previous years will also blur the true profit for the current year. When an accountant makes adjustments such as those discussed above he must use a degree of care and professional skill, yet at the same time he must apply the concept of materiality in that where a truer estimate could be made after detailed analysis of a position, the cost of the analysis may be more than the benefit to be derived from the extra accuracy it provides.

A simple rule of thumb is: for accruals increase the recorded cost charged to the profit computation and show the accrual as a creditor in the balance sheet; for payments in advance decrease the recorded cost charged against profit and show the amount as a debtor in the balance sheet.

CAPITAL AND REVENUE EXPENDITURE

The division of expenditure between capital expenditure and revenue expenditure has a significant impact on the computation of business income, since revenue expenditure is chargeable to the income statement, while capital expenditure concerns the acquisition of an asset which is to be carried forward in the balance sheet. Any expenditure for acquiring, extending or improving assets of a permanent nature which are to be used to carry on the business or to increase the earning capacity of the business is termed capital expenditure. A revenue expenditure item is one made to carry on the normal course of the business and to maintain the capital assets in a state of efficiency, e.g. repairs and maintenance.

There are no hard and fast rules to delineate capital and revenue. The guidelines used when an accountant arrives at an opinion of how to treat a certain expenditure are as follows. Capital expenditure will improve the earning power of the business or reduce running costs. It is usually laid out to create or acquire a long-lived asset, but it need not concern a tangible asset. In cases where the labour force of the business is used in the construction of capital assets, there must be a transfer out of the costs for the year into the asset account, which will be carried forward in the balance sheet. An asset classed as a capital or fixed asset for one company may be a current asset for another company. For example, a vehicle is usually a fixed asset, since the company intends to use it over a period of years, but it could be classed as stock-in-trade if it is used for resale.

The transfer from revenue expenditure to capital expenditure will reduce cost and increase profit for the year, but depreciation provided on the new capital asset will offset part of this increase. Revenue expenditure is laid out to maintain the earning capacity of the business, and to keep the fixed assets in a fully efficient state. Since the borderline between capital and revenue expenditure is not clearly defined, individual cases are dealt with on their merits. For example, a transport business pays £15 000 for a second-hand articulated truck. Expenditure of £3000 is necessary immediately to put the vehicle into roadworthy condition, and this is considered to be capital expenditure and part of the cost paid for a roadworthy vehicle. Thus the vehicle is recorded in the books at a cost of £18 000, and this capital expenditure is spread over the economic life of the vehicle, say six years, by charging the profit and loss account of successive years a cost of £3000 for the use of the vehicle. This cost is termed depreciation. After two years perhaps the vehicle needs new tyres which might cost £2000. This expenditure is considered to be a revenue item and is charged as a cost of that year to the profit and loss account. It is not capitalized because it does not increase the operating potential of the vehicle but merely maintains that capacity. A problem arises after, say, four years, when the vehicle requires a replacement engine which may cost, say, £8000. Some accountants might consider this cost to be capital expenditure because it extends the working life of the vehicle, whilst others would consider it to be a revenue item merely maintaining the vehicle in running order. If the item can be capitalized, the profit of year 4 is increased by £8000, less depreciation of £2667, as the capitalized cost is spread over years 4, 5 and 6. Thus the capital/revenue decision has a direct effect on profit measured.

RESERVES AND PROVISIONS

A provision is an amount charged against profit for depreciation, or to provide for any known cost the exact amount of which cannot be accurately determined, such as bad debts. An accrual is a provision, since it is the charge made against profits for a cost which has been incurred but cannot be determined accurately at the accounting date. Thus provisions are charges against the profit figure before the profit is struck.

A reserve is an amount set aside for other purposes. It is an appropriation of profit and represents that part of the year's profit which is to be retained in the business for various reasons. On the balance sheet the reserves show the total of past profits retained in the business. Although these 'ploughed-back' profits represent a further investment in the business by the shareholders, the legal position is that reserves are available for distribution as dividend unless it is stated on the balance sheet that they are not available for distribution. Certain reserves cannot by law be distributed as a dividend, and are known as 'statutory reserves', e.g. share premium.

TUTORIAL DISCUSSION TOPICS

4.1 What is the difference between capital expenditure and revenue expenditure? Why is this difference important?

4.2 Differentiate between payments made in an accounting period and costs incurred in that period. Why is this difference important?

4.3 What effect will profit have on the amount of an owner's interest in the business? Are the drawings of the proprietor an expense of the business?

4.4 The terms 'revenue' and 'income' are often used interchangeably. Are they synonymous?

4.5 Differentiate between a reserve and a provision. What do the reserves represent in the balance sheet and how are they linked to the income statement?

4.6 Revenue and cost flow into and out of a business. How do accounting concepts influence the treatment of these flows?

SEMINAR EXERCISES 2

1. (a) Indicate the extent to which each of the following items is an expense of the year ended 31 December, and show the total expenses for the year.
    (i) goods received and paid for during the year, £37 712, of which items costing a total of £2430 were still in stock at the year end;
    (ii) goods received during the year but not yet paid for, £3840, of which items costing a total of £360 were still in stock at the year end;
    (iii) goods in stock at the beginning of the year, £800, and all sold during the year;
    (iv) payments during the year (additional to the above) to suppliers for goods received last year, £937;
    (v) wages paid during the year and all earned during the year, £230;

   (vi) insurance policy taken out on 30 June, one year's premium of £360, being paid in advance;

   (vii) other expenses relating to the year and all paid for in that year, £1790;

   (viii) equipment purchased in earlier years, having a value at the beginning of the year of £4000 and expected to be used for a further three years;

   (ix) you estimate electricity used but unpaid for at 31 December to be £380.

(b) Complete the following calculation of profit (or loss) for the year:

	£
Revenue for the year from sales	45 000
Less total expenses as in (a) above	
Profit (or loss) for the year	£

(c) Complete the balance sheet as it would have appeared at the beginning of the year:

	£		£
Owner's capital		Equipment	
Trade creditors		Stock	
		Debtors	2100
		Cash	450
	£		£

(d) Write up the summary of the cash book to compute the balance at the beginning of the year:

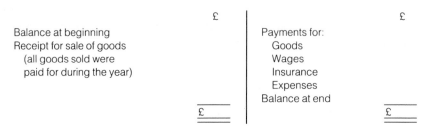

	£		£
Balance at beginning		Payments for:	
Receipt for sale of goods		Goods	
(all goods sold were		Wages	
paid for during the year)		Insurance	
		Expenses	
		Balance at end	
	£		£

(e) Draw up the balance sheet as it would appear at the end of the year:

	£		£
Owner's capital		Equipment	
Balance at 1 January		Stock	
Add profit or deduct		Debtors	
loss		Cash	
Trade creditors			
	£		£

(f) What assumptions have you made in producing these figures?

2. John Ash runs a tobacconist's shop. On 1 January his assets consisted of a stock of pipes and tobacco which had cost £10 800, a bank account containing £910, and his shop premises, which were worth £15 000. He owed suppliers £3200. On 31 December, after one year's trading, his assets were: pipes and tobacco, £7700;

debtors, £2300; cash, £1237; and his premises as above. During the year he had taken £20 per week out of the till to be used as housekeeping money. Creditors at the year end were owed £1460.

What profit has John Ash made during the year?

3. M. A. Tellow started to trade as an agent for the sale of canal cruisers on 1 January. During his first month of trading he sold boats for £53 000, comprising £10 800 for cash and the remainder on credit terms. He introduced £20 000 of his own money into the business at its inception, and an aunt lent him a further £10 000. He rented premises on 1 January and paid £500 as two months' rent in advance on that day. The costs of running his premises, including the wages of an assistant, were paid in cash on the last day of the month in the sum of £980. He was unable to pay his electricity bill as the meter had not been read, but estimated the cost for the month as £50. An insurance premium for a year's cover was paid on 1 January. It cost £1200. During the month boats were purchased for £47 000, and so far £7000 has been paid to the suppliers. Boats remaining unsold on 31 January had cost £15 000.

(a) Compute the bank balance of M. A. Tellow as at 31 January.
(b) Calculate the profit he made during January.

4. Jack Purser is a trader in leather goods who conducts his business in a London street market. He trades on both cash and credit terms. At the start of a week he had a stock which cost £1200, £400 in his bank account and debts owed to him by past customers totalling £1120. He had no assets other than his barrow (worth £800) and no liabilities. During the week he sells goods for cash at £2520 and makes credit sales of £2400. His purchases of stock amount to £2300 and he pays for them in cash. At the end of the week he still has his barrow, and a stock of goods which cost him £1360. His bank balance stands at £880, and the amount owed to him by credit customers has risen to £3040.

(a) Work out a profit figure for Jack's trading for the week and draw up his balance sheet at the end of the week.
(b) What assumptions have you made in computing the figures in (a) above?

5. The following information refers to rent, electricity and insurance account for the year to 30 June. Rent is paid quarterly in advance on the last day of March, June, September and December. Electricity is paid for half-yearly in arrears, in March and September. Insurance is an annual premium paid on 1 January.

Opening balances:
    Payment in advance   Insurance £600
    Payment in advance   Rent £400
    Accrued   Electricity £200
Payments:
    Rent   30 September £400
        31 December £400
        31 March £400
        30 June £400

Insurance	1 January £1200
Electricity	10 July £400
	30 September £500

Write up the rent, electricity and insurance account for the year.

5 | Double Entry

THE PRINCIPLES OF DOUBLE ENTRY

The principle of duality underlies the double-entry system. Every transaction has a dual effect on the business, and therefore should be recorded twice to reveal this effect. The books are divided into accounts or pages in the ledger, an account being opened not for each transaction but to summarize transactions of a similar nature on the same page, e.g. a page for repair costs, another for factory wages, another for sales revenue, and another for rent. If there are many transactions of one type, then a separate book or ledger will be opened, e.g. the cash book to record the cash part of transactions, payments or receipts, and a debtors ledger to maintain a detailed record of amounts owed to the business by customers who have bought goods on credit. In this case each debtor will have an account or page of his own in the debtors ledger. Alternatively the data can be recorded on computer tape and printed out as a statement, or shown on a visual display unit. The two-sided form may not be used but the principle of debit and credit (plus and minus) still holds true.

Each page acts as a T account, having two sides, one for debts (Dr) and one for credits (Cr). The debits are always on the left-hand side, and the credits on the right-hand side. When the two sides are added up (the old term 'cast' is sometimes used), if the entries on the debit side are greater than those on the credit side then the account is said to have a debit balance, and vice versa.

1. Each transaction is recorded twice, once on each side of separate accounts in the books, with debits traditionally on the left-hand side. Every debit must have a credit and every credit must have a debit.
2. In the ledger the assets and expenses are debit balances and the liabilities and sales revenue are credit balances. The purchase of every asset by a business is financed by funds invested in or lent to the business by owners or creditors (lenders), who then have a claim against the company for the return of their funds. Thus claims equal assets in the balance sheet. In the income statement if sales revenue (credit) exceeds costs (debit) and a profit is made, this profit is a credit and is added in the balance sheet to capital, part of the claims on the credit side to balance the increase in assets represented by the profit.
3. When an asset or cost account is to be increased the entry is on the debit side and when a liability or sales revenue account is to be increased the account is credited. When, however, an account is to be decreased, the amount is not deducted from

the side on which the balance is shown, but is instead posted to the opposite side, so that the balance is reduced in this way. For example, an asset or cost account is decreased by crediting the account and a liability or sales revenue account is decreased by debiting the account. If a loan is repaid, the appropriate entries would be debit loan account to decrease its credit balance, and credit cash or bank account (an asset) to decrease its debit balance.

4. The giving account is credited while the receiving account is debited. For example, when wages are paid, the wages account receives and is debited, while cash is given out so this account is credited, and when a debtor pays what he owes, cash receives and is debited, while the debtor gives and his account is credited (thus reducing his debit balance). This is a rather rough and ready rule which does not have a logical application in all cases.

Example

A company has £50 000 in cash in its bank account. The company buys two cars for £20 000 each and pays for them by cheque. One car is later sold for £20 000 to Mr Brown on credit terms. These transactions would be recorded in ledger account terms as follows:

Dr.	Vehicles		Cr.	Dr.	Cash		Cr.
	£		£		£		£
2 Two cars purchased for cash	40 000	**3** One car sold to Brown	20 000	**1** Balance of cash in the bank	50 000	**2** Payment for vehicles	40 000
		4 Balance c/f	20 000			**6** Balance c/f	10 000
	40 000		40 000		50 000		50 000
4 Balance b/d	20 000			**6** Balance b/d	10 000		

Dr.	Mr Brown		Cr.	Dr.	Capital		Cr.
	£		£		£		£
3 Amount owed for vehicle purchased	20 000	**5** Balance c/f	20 000			Balance invested by proprietor	50 000
	20 000		20 000				
5 Balance b/d	20 000						

These transactions can be traced by following the number code.

1 The cash account shows £50 000 on the debit side to represent an asset. The corresponding credit is in the capital account because the proprietor has invested £50 000 in the business and is therefore owed that amount by the business.

2 Some of the cash is invested in assets—vehicles; credit cash to signify that the balance of £50 000 is now reduced by £40 000, and post £40 000 to the debit side of the vehicles account to record the asset acquired. Note that £40 000 is not deducted from the debit side of the cash account but that by entering the amount on the credit side the same effect is achieved. See item **6**. The remaining balance is £10 000.

3 A vehicle is sold to Brown for £20 000, so the vehicle account balance is reduced by a credit entry of £20 000, and Brown's account is debited, thus recording how much he owes to the company and that the debt is an asset, a debit side item. If Brown were to pay what he owes, his account would be credited and cash debited, thus cancelling Brown's debit balance (a debt) and increasing the debit balance on the cash account to show how that asset had increased.

4, 5, 6 The accounts for Vehicles, Cash and Brown are balanced at the end of the accounting period. For vehicles, when the account is closed the debit side at £40 000 is found to be heavier than the credit side of £20 000, so a further credit of £20 000 must be added to balance the account. This is the balance c/f (carried forward), which is matched by a balance b/d (brought down) on the debit side below the total lines. A similar procedure will balance the other accounts.

The resultant balances can be listed thus as a trial balance:

Account	Debits £	Credits £
Vehicles	20 000	—
Cash	10 000	—
Brown	20 000	—
Capital	—	50 000
	£50 000	£50 000

If all the debit balances equal the credit balances, then the book-keeping should be correct.

RECORDING TRANSACTIONS

Before entries can be made in the ledger accounts, transactions must be recorded and evidenced on working documents from which the books themselves are written up. Some of these 'prime documents' are listed below:

(a) invoices or bills to evidence the cost, date and exact description of items purchased or expenses incurred;

(b) credit notes, which are used when an invoice is cancelled or when the amount of the bill is reduced for some reason, e.g. goods are returned;

(c) cheque book stubs to record money paid out and remittance advices to show in detail what was paid for;

(d) petty cash vouchers to show what has been bought for cash;

(e) the paying-in book to record cash received from sales, debtors etc. and which has been paid into the bank;

(f) the clock cards and wages sheets to analyse the amount paid out for labour;

(g) sales invoices to record sales made, whether for cash or credit;

(h) goods received notes to evidence the receipt of goods for which an invoice can be expected in the near future;

(i) journal vouchers for internal transactions and transfers between accounts.

There are, of course, other prime documents, but these are the major ones. These items are sometimes called 'source documents'.

BOOKS ON PRIME ENTRY

When there is a large volume of transactions the prime documents have to be summarized and analysed before they are posted into the books of account. Originally the daybook for sales or purchases was the device used for this purpose. It used to be written up daily, with a total column and sub-columns for analysis. At the end of the month the daybook would be closed, the columns cast, and the analysis column totals cross-cast to reconcile with the total of the major column. The analysis column totals were then entered into the appropriate ledger accounts and the individual items posted to the personal account of the customer or supplier. Daybooks were maintained for purchases, sales, internal transactions and transfers (the journal), and cash. Some systems had a daybook for returns inwards (goods sold sent back by the customer) and for returns outwards (purchases returned to suppliers). The cash book acted as both a book of prime entry from which items were posted to other accounts, and also as a ledger account, to record the balance of the asset cash. In the case of the purchases daybook the analysis columns would be debited to the various expense accounts to show the costs incurred, while the individual amounts in the major column would be credited to the personal accounts of suppliers in the creditors ledger. The sales daybook analysed sales to product or area (a credit entry) and allowed each sale in the major column to be debited to the customer's (debtor's) personal account.

As business became more sophisticated and the number of transactions to be accounted for increased, so the old handwritten system of keeping the books became inadequate to deal with the new volume of work. The daybook was replaced by a machine list or computer list of transactions, and analysis is now undertaken by mechanical or computer systems which sort and total entries. The ledgers produced by book-keeping machines show additions and deductions in the form of black and red entries in one total column. In some cases the account itself is little more than a set of positive and negative pulses on a computer tape which can be printed out on demand. Some systems of ledgerless book-keeping avoid the maintenance of personal ledgers by filing all invoices owed to one supplier or by one customer in the same filing pocket, adding new invoices as they arrive and extracting invoices when they are settled. Basically, however, prime documents are still summarized and analysed, and recorded both as a debit and a credit in the ledger accounts of the business no matter what form those accounts take.

THE JOURNAL

In some systems the journal for recording internal transactions and alterations is the only book still entered by hand. If by mistake the wrong account has been debited with an expense or an asset acquired, the mistake must be put right by crediting the account entered in error and debiting the correct account. A journal entry will record the appropriate account to be debited and credited with a 'narration' as to the reason for the alteration. In some systems even this book has been replaced by a file of journal vouchers which evidence the debit and credit entries made in the mechanized or computer system. Some internal transactions, however, are extremely important and must be evidenced by an extract from the minutes of the board meeting at which the decision concerning the transaction was made. The payment of dividends, transfers to reserve accounts, and changes in the share capital of the business are all examples of the type of transaction which enters the books of account through the journal.

The form of the journal is that it is ruled in four columns, with the second column wider than the others.

Date	Narration	Debit £	Credit £
1 April	Mr J. Bloggs Mr R. Goodfellow Being goods purchased by Bloggs, charged to Goodfellow in error.	500	500

The narration column names the accounts to be debited or credited, and gives a short description of the reason for the entry. In the example above Bloggs' account is debited, since he owes £500 for goods not yet paid for, and Goodfellow's account is credited to nullify the debit of £500 entered on his account in error.

THE ACCOUNTING SYSTEM

Figures 2, 3 and 4 explain the accounting system. Figure 2 shows how the recording of transactions progresses from the source documents, through the books of prime entry, and the ledgers, to the accounting statements. Figure 3 develops the analysis of the ledger accounts, and is expressed in double-entry terms. Accounts in the top line represent balance sheet items, whilst the remaining lines show how costs and sales play a part in the measurement of income. Follow the letter code to understand the debits and credits for each transaction. Figure 4 is a chart of accounts, again expressed in double-entry form, with annotations to show the prime documents from which the debits and credits are derived, e.g. materials account is debited for materials purchased evidenced by a bill or invoice, and credited for materials requisitioned from the stores into the factory to be used in the manufacturing operations.

THE TRIAL BALANCE

At the end of an accounting period, when all documents have been recorded and all amounts in the books of prime entry transferred to the ledger accounts, the total of debit entries in the ledgers should equal the total of credit entries if the double-entry

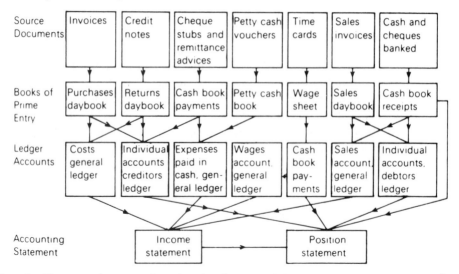

Figure 2. The accounting system, from the prime document via books of prime entry and the ledger to the accounting statement. The cash book is both a book of prime entry and a ledger account. The journal is used as a book of prime entry to transfer items between ledger accounts or to record internal transactions.

system has been properly applied. Each account must be balanced by adding up each side and finding whether a debit or a credit balance is brought down. A ledger account resembles an old-fashioned set of scales. Suppose there is more entered on the debit side than on the credit side of an account. A balancing amount must be added to the credit side to make the two sides equal. This amount is the balance carried forward to the debit side, indicating that there is a surplus of debit over credit on that account, e.g. see the accounts for rent or materials in Chapter 4 which have balances carried forward and brought down. The accounts in the ledger are then listed on a separate sheet with the balance of the account shown in a debit or a credit column. If the total of debit balances equals the total of credit balances then prima facie each transaction has been recorded as a debit and a credit. This is a valuable check on the accuracy of the book-keeping, but it does not reveal the situation where an item has been debited to the wrong account, omitted entirely, or analysed incorrectly, or where compensating errors have been made. The trial balance is a summary of the balances recorded in the ledger accounts, and can thus be used as a basis from which the income and position statements can be computed. The transactions recorded in the ledgers have to be adjusted for accruals and prepayments by extending the trial balance to include these items.

THE PETTY CASH BOOK

Small disbursements for expenses made on a day-to-day basis by local purchase are recorded in this book and analysed in a number of columns. The totals of these columns are cast and cross-cast to the main total, and the amounts are then posted as from a daybook to the appropriate account in the general ledger. These amounts are debited to various expenses, with a total credit to the petty cash account. When cash

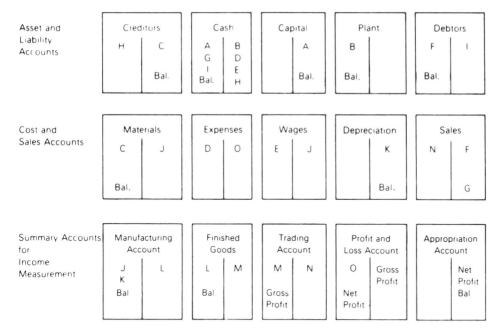

Figure 3. The accounting system, showing the debit and credit entries for transactions in the ledger accounts and the computation of the accounting statements.
The transactions are listed below, with a note about the source document and book of prime entry involved.

Transactions. Debits on the left-hand side and credits on the right-hand side. The entries for each transaction are shown by the following designatory letters.
A. Shareholders apply for shares in cash, journal entry.
B. Plant purchased for cash, invoice and cash book.
C. Materials bought on credit, invoice and purchases daybook.
D. Expenses paid in cash, bill and cash book.
E. Wages paid in cash, wage sheet.
F. Sales made on credit terms, sales invoices and daybook.
G. Sales made for cash, sales invoices and cash book.
H. Creditors paid, copy remittance advices, cheque stubs, cash book.
I. Payment received from debtors, bank paying-in book and cash book.
J. Materials used and wages charged to manufacturing account, internal transfer journal.
K. Depreciation charged to manufacturing account, internal transfer journal.
L. Cost of completed work transferred to finished goods accounts, internal transfer.
M. Cost of goods sold transferred to trading account, internal transfer.
N. Sales 'closed off' to trading account, internal transfer.
O. Expenses 'closed off' to profit and loss account.

Items marked 'Bal.' will appear in the balance sheet. The balances on the materials, manufacturing and finished goods accounts are stocks of raw materials, work in progress and finished goods. The balance on the cash book can be either a debit or a credit depending on whether the business has overdrawn its bank account.

is drawn from the bank to reimburse the petty cashier the cash book is credited and the petty cash book debited.

The imprest system is commonly used to operate a petty cash book. The system allows the petty cashier to receive a cash float (a fixed amount of money) to cover the petty cash expenses for a stated period. The expenses are totalled at the end of the month or week, and the petty cashier then draws exactly the amount that he has spent during the period from the main cash book. This amount will make up the petty cash in the till to the preordained amount of the float. Control over the system is maintained, as the cashier is required to retain vouchers for expenditure for audit

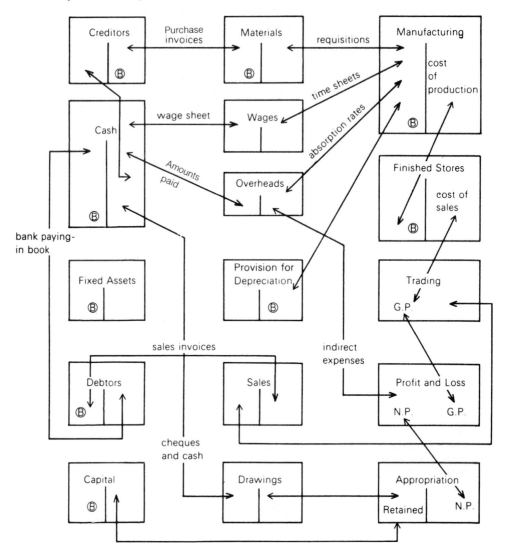

Figure 4. Simple chart of accounts for a manufacturing company. Ⓑ denotes a balance remaining at the year end after the income measurement entries have been extracted, which will appear on the balance sheet. The source documents are shown on the arrows which indicate the debit and credit entries. Note that there is an arrow at each end of each connecting line to show that every debit has a credit.

purposes. A further measure of control is that at any time the petty-cash box or till must contain cash and/or vouchers which add up to the amount of the imprest float.

BOOK-KEEPING AND THE COMPUTER

Various software packages have been developed to facilitate the application of computers, large or small, to book-keeping tasks. The principles of double entry remain the same and can easily be adapted to permit the use of a computer to process large volumes of data quickly according to a standard set of rules. The power of the computer to store, update, select, sort, calculate and print makes it a powerful tool for use in recording business data.

Daybooks and ledger accounts in T form may not exist in such a modern electronic system, but the analysis performed by the computer has the same objective as a handwritten system, and is the subject of equal if not greater disadvantages concerned with the accuracy of the data put into the system, and the accuracy with which that input is made. The device of the matrix, or grid, enables one piece of information to be recorded in two locations, one horizontal and the other vertical, to represent the debit and credit sides of the entry. The aggregate of the totals of the vertical columns must of course equal the aggregate of the totals of the horizontal rows, as with a trial balance. This format can be displayed as a spreadsheet in some systems and the program can be written to show the effect of each entry (or change) on the accounting statements.

USING A MICROCOMPUTER PACKAGE

The software associated with the microcomputer acts as a program which will undertake certain entry, sorting, analysing or listing operations at the touch of the appropriate key. The term 'menu' is sometimes applied to the list of subprograms available within the software to undertake various alternative operations. It is usual before transactions are entered into a computer that they should be batched. This means that the source documents are sorted and similar items are grouped together, e.g. a batch of purchases invoices, or a batch of sales invoices, or a batch of cheque payments. Once the source documents have been batched, it is usual to prepare a pre-list which provides a control total for all the items in a particular batch. At this stage the items are given an account code to show which accounts are to be debited and credited as a result of the transaction, and a transaction type code. Transactions can be classified as follows:

(a) cashbook receipts;
(b) cashbook payments;
(c) supplier payments;
(d) customer receipts;
(e) journal entries;
(f) purchase invoices;
(g) purchase returns;
(h) sales invoices;
(i) sales returns.

Using the data entry menu or instruction, the information on the source documents is keyed into the computer. At this point the program will check the batch total to ensure that the amount keyed in for the batch corresponds to the pre-list total already prepared. Some computer systems use a check digit in the form of a code number to ensure that the transactions classification is correct and that the data are entered correctly. Once the basic data are entered into the computer, it forms a database which can be used by various programs to provide statistics and managerial information, e.g. a batch of sales invoices entered as for a daybook can be analysed per customer, per product, per sales area or representative, or per commission classification.

The next instruction given to the computer is to activate the ledger posting menu. The items entered from the batch will be automatically posted to the correct account and if necessary to the appropriate control account or VAT account. Further checks may be built in at this stage to ensure that a transaction is posted to the proper account or rejected if it has been miscoded. In some systems the computer can be activated to produce an audit trail in the form of a printout to show the operations so far. When all batches have been entered and the 'books' are to be closed for the period, the end of period program can be activated whereby the computer will produce a trial balance, on a screen or as a printout, and either in the normal two-column form used in book-keeping, or as a spreadsheet matrix format.

A spreadsheet takes the form of a series of rows and columns. The point at which a row (horizontal line) intersects with a column (vertical line) forms a 'cell'. Cells can express titles, formulae, or values. The computer can be programmed to list the account titles in the trial balance in the same order for every trial balance requested by the operator. The formulae programmed into the software can be used to adjust the trial balance for accruals, prepayments, and provisions for depreciation, doubtful debts etc. Once all adjustments have been entered and activated according to pre-set formulae, an adjusted trial balance can be printed out with figures ready for insertion onto the manufacturing, trading, profit and loss, and appropriation accounts, or the balance sheet. Many programs have the facility for correcting errors by overtyping onto the spreadsheet, and a recalculation function to adjust totals accordingly. Some programs will print out an extended trial balance in a format similar to that shown in Chapter 8 as used by the more traditional accountants.

The computer can record all entered information on disk and when entering, posting, or adjusting operations are finished for the time being, the information to date can be stored in the memory merely by removing the disk from the machine. This simple explanation demonstrates the advantages of computerization in that accuracy is checked regularly by controls and other checks built into the program, a large volume of data can be processed, adjusted and stored, and preprogrammed analysis can be undertaken to provide almost instant information for management. The cardinal rule, however, is to check the data entered into the computer with great care because false information, once entered into the system, may not be detected and may cause error at a later stage.

THE QUADRANT AND THE SEXTANT

The quadrant is a device which helps to explain the duality of accounting transactions so far as they affect the income statement and the balance sheet. The balance sheet sets assets against liabilities, while the income statement sets costs against sales revenue. Therefore if a diagram with four boxes is drawn, showing assets and costs on the left (the debit side) and liabilities and sales revenue on the right (the credit side), the interplay of transactions on these four basic items can be demonstrated, and the rudiments of the double-entry system revealed.

Debits		Credits	
Assets	Liabilities + Capital	- - - - - - - - - -	Position Statement
Costs	Revenue	- - - - - - - - - -	Income Statement

The principle of duality states that every transaction has a double effect on the position of a business as recorded in the accounts, and thus the double-entry book-keeping system records transactions twice, once on the debit side and once on the credit side. A transaction which increases the assets or costs of the business, and thus increases the debits recorded in the books, must also either increase the liabilities or revenue on the credit side, or reduce some other asset on the debit side, so that the overall balance of debits against credits is maintained. When this device is extended to a sextant, by adding a line to analyse movements in the cash book, the impact of transactions on one single but important asset, cash, is shown.

Debits		Credits	
Assets	Liabilities + Capital	- - - - - - - - - -	Position Statement
Costs	Revenue	- - - - - - - - - -	Income Statement
Receipts	Payments	- - - - - - - - - -	Cash Book

Example

The following transactions recorded in the ledgers of a business would have the following dual impact. Consider the impact of each item on the sextant, and then relate that effect to the ledger accounts shown below. The letter code is easy to follow. The abbreviation c/f stands for 'carried forward', and b/d stands for 'brought down', and these are used to signify a balancing figure on an account transferred to the beginning of the next accounting period.

(a) Share capital subscribed, £20 000: a liability is recorded on the credit side and a receipt of cash on the debit side.

(b) Plant purchased for cash, £10 000: assets have increased on the debit side and payments in the cash book on the credit side.

(c) Material purchased on credit terms, £5000: assets have increased again but are balanced by an increased liability on the credit side.

(d) Part of the material is paid for, £4000; the payment of cash is recorded on the credit side and is balanced by a decrease of the liability by an entry on the debit side.

(e) Some of the material is used in production, £3000: an asset has decreased but it is balanced by an increase in cost, also on the debit side. If accounting statements were prepared at this moment part of the stock would be charged as a cost and the remainder carried forward as an asset in the balance sheet.

(f) Wages paid, £2000: costs have increased on the debit side and are balanced by a payment of cash on the credit side.

(g) Payment of insurance premium, £600: an increase in cost balanced by a payment of cash.

(h) Part of the insurance premium concerns the next accounting period and is thus a prepayment in the sum of £200: costs must be decreased on the debit side and balanced by an increase in assets when the provision for payment in advance is made and recorded in the balance sheet.

(i) Plant depreciated by £1000: costs have increased and are balanced by a decrease in assets. Depreciation is deducted on the balance sheet.

(j) An accrual is made for electricity costs, £100: costs have increased on the debit side and are balanced by an increased liability when the estimated amount is recorded as a creditor in the balance sheet.

(k) Goods are sold on credit terms, £12 000: the sales revenue is recorded on the credit side and is balanced by the creation of an asset, debtors, on the debit side.

(l) Some debtors pay, £6000: the decrease in the asset is balanced by the receipt of cash.

The books can now be balanced at the end of the year.

(m) Closing: in the cash book any surplus of receipts over payments will be recorded as an asset, cash, in the balance sheet. The income statement can then be completed so that the surplus of sales over costs can be added to the owner's interest on the liabilities side of the balance sheet. The other balances outstanding in the accounts in the ledger are recorded in the balance sheet, which must also balance.

(n) The board decide to pay a dividend of 10 per cent: thus £2000 is to be appropriated out of the profit and paid to the shareholders. This will increase the debit side of the costs (though a dividend is not really a cost) and, since the dividend is not yet paid, it must appear in the balance sheet as a liability. Alternatively, the provision of a dividend can be seen as a reduction in the owner's interest, since profits retained are reduced.

Share Capital Account

	£		£
		(a) Cash	20 000

Cash Account

	£		£
(a) Capital	20 000	(b) Plant	10 000
(l) Debtors	6 000	(d) Creditors	4 000
		(f) Wages	2 000
		(g) Insurance	600
		Balance c/f	9 400
	£26 000		£26 000
Balance b/d	9 400		

Plant Account

	£		£
(b) Cash	10 000		

Materials Account

	£		£
(c) Creditors	5000	(e) Income	3000
		Balance c/f	2000
	£5000		£5000
Balance	1 000		

Creditors Account

	£		£
(d) Cash	4000	(c) Materials	5000
Balance c/f	1000		
	£5000		£5000
		Balance b/d	1 000

Wages Account			
	£		£
(f) Cash	2000	(f) Income	2000

Insurance Account			
	£		£
(g) Cash	600	(h) Prepayment c/f	200
		(h) Income	400
	£600		£600
(h) Balance b/d	200		

Depreciation Account			
	£		£
		(i) Income	1000

Electricity Account			
	£		£
		(j) Accrual to income	100

Sales Account			
	£		£
(k) Income	12 000	(k) Debtors	12 000

Debtors Account			
	£		£
(k) Sales	12 000	(l) Cash	6 000
		Balance c/f	6 000
	£12 000		£12 000
Balance b/d	6 000		

Dividend Account			
	£		£
		(n) Dividend provided from income but owed to shareholders	2000

The above transactions can be entered on both sides of the ledger, and a set of accounts, such as those above, can be produced. Follow the items through the ledger accounts and onto the accounting statements below. A trial balance could be extracted after the book-keeping is complete.

Income Statement . . . Period

	£		£
Costs:		(k) Sales	12 000
(e) Materials	3 000		
(f) Wages	2 000		
(h) Insurance	400		
(i) Depreciation	1 000		
(j) Electricity	100		
(n) Dividend	2 000		
Net profit	5 500		
	£12 000		£12 000

Balance Sheet as at . . .

	£	£		£	£
			Fixed Assets:		
Capital		20 000	Plant at cost		10 000
Add net profit		3 500	Less depreciation		1 000
		23 500			9 000
Current Liabilities:			Current Assets:		
Creditors	1 000		Stock	2 000	
Dividend	2 000		Debtors	6 000	
Accruals	100		Prepayments	200	
			Cash	9 400	
		3 100			17 600
		£26 600			£26 600

Note that the provision for depreciation, a credit balance, is shown on the balance sheet as a deduction from plant on the assets side. This is because depreciation is a provision and it is normal to disclose provisions as a deduction from the amount of the asset against which they are provided, e.g. provision for doubtful debts or provision for stock losses.

TUTORIAL DISCUSSION TOPICS

5.1 How does the imprest system for the control of petty cash operate?

5.2 What is a trial balance and what are the major objects of preparing a trial balance?

5.3 Identify five documents of prime entry, and explain how each one fits into the accounting system.

SEMINAR EXERCISES 3

1. Explain how the double-entry system works and attempt to formalize the basic rules which apply in double-entry book-keeping. Illustrate your answer with a short, simple example, with specific reference to the way in which an account is balanced.

2. Brian Grange starts to trade as a wholesale dealer on 1 September at a warehouse which he owns himself and which is valued at £24 000. Grange has provided fixtures and fittings which cost £17 000, and has brought into the business his car, worth £2800, and a van valued at £900. He opens a business bank account by paying £8500 into it. He has already bought goods on credit from the following firms, and these goods comprise his opening stock: Collie and Co., £471; Lot and Mee, £360; and Edmunds, £615. Grange's capital is the amount of his investment in the business, whether injected in the form of cash or assets.

(a) Calculate Grange's capital and enter the balances shown in the appropriate books. These opening entries could be made direct to T accounts or through an opening journal entry.

(b) Record the undermentioned transactions in suitable daybooks and the cash book. Post to the ledger and prove your work by extracting a trial balance.

1 September	Bought on credit terms from Apple Ltd two typewriters at £180 each.
	Bought office stationery, £174, paid by cheque.
	Drew £250 from bank to cover petty cash expenses.
2 September	Sold goods to T. Veron for £627 and K. Jones for £460.
	Paid cheque for cartons, £61, and cleaning materials, £16.
3 September	Cash sales to date, £165, banked.
4 September	Paid wages in cash, £83.
5 September	Bought goods from J. Lewin, £190, less 10 per cent trade discount (not yet paid for).
	Paid cheques as follows: Collie and Co. £300 on account; Edmunds Ltd £600 in full settlement after deducting £15 as a cash discount.
6 September	Goods returned from T. Veron, £127.
7 September	Paid rent on premises, cheque for £181.
	Exchanged van at book value at Car Sales Ltd for a new van, costing £2800, and accepted liability for the balance.
	Returned goods costing £20 to J. Lewin.
	Sold goods on credit terms to H. Same Ltd, £430.
8 September	Withdrew goods from stock for own use, £53.
	Paid wages in cash, £76.
	Banked cash sales, £431.
	Paid office expenses in cash, £18.
9 September	Paid insurance premium by cheque, £160.
	Bought goods on credit terms from Edmunds Ltd, £280.
	Received cheque from T. Veron in settlement of his account net of 5 per cent cash discount.
10 September	Paid Lot and Mee £200 on account by cheque.
	Sold goods on credit terms to H. Same Ltd, £165.
	Drew £5 from cash to pay for Grange's lunch.
11 September	Paid carriage charge, £29, and telephone bill, £23, by cheque.
	Banked all office petty cash except a float of £50.

REVIEW QUESTIONS 1

1. This problem concerns the business of J. Nash, whose balance sheet is set out in Chapter 3. That balance sheet is the starting point of the exercise. The transactions listed below took place in the week following the balance sheet date. The opening balance sheet represents the balances of the books on the first day of that week which form a trial balance amounting to £575 788. If you open the

accounts for the balance sheet items you will have the nucleus of a set of ledger accounts. Do not forget that the balance sheet shows assets on the right-hand side whereas, in the books, asset balances are on the left-hand or debit side, and liabilities are on the right or credit side.

(a) Enter the following transactions in the appropriate ledger accounts, opening fresh accounts as required, and prove your work with a trial balance at the end.

1 January	Sold goods to Anton for cash £543 and banked the cash.
	Sold goods to Bailey Ltd on credit terms £1475.
2 January	Purchased goods from Cradshaw PLC for £2856 on credit terms.
	Three vehicles serviced for which received bill from Dixon's garage £715.
3 January	Sold investments at book value for cash £10 000.
	Sold goods to Enda Ltd for cash £4870 and banked both amounts.
	Paid half-year's interest on long-term loan.
4 January	Reduced overdraft by £2000, by paying cash into the bank.
	Received cheque in payment from Bailey less 4 per cent cash discount.
5 January	Paid wages for week £1672.
	Goods returned from Anton which had been sold to him for £60; gave cash refund from bank account.
	Received electricity bill for £243.
6 January	Bought minicomputer for workshop for £2438 on credit from Fragilistic Ltd.
	Drew £47 cash to pay office expenses.
	Mr Nash withdrew £480 to meet his personal expenses.
7 January	One of the debtors on the balance sheet paid his bill of £2463.
	The cash was banked. Payment was made to one of the creditors on the balance sheet of £2826.
	The tax was paid.

(b) At the end of the week, the remaining stock was counted and valued at £116 450. Can you compute the gross profit made during the week?

6 | Depreciation

Fixed assets have a useful economic life in excess of one year, and earn profit for a business throughout that life. Accordingly, fixed assets are gradually used up over the period of their life. Under the matching concept the original cost of the asset should be charged against the revenue earned in successive periods, to measure a true and fair profit. Thus the asset is gradually turned into an expense. The charge made each year to represent the amount of fixed asset used up during that year is depreciation. Judgement is required to calculate how much of the cost is to be charged in a particular accounting period. Under the prudence concept, a fall in value of a fixed asset should be recognized in the profit computation when it takes place, to ensure that the profit disclosed is not overstated. For this reason depreciation appears as a cost in the income statement, whilst in the balance sheet fixed assets are disclosed at cost and the cumulative depreciation to date is subtracted, revealing the unexpired portion of the original capital cost.

A traditional definition of depreciation is that it is the diminution in value of a fixed asset due to use and/or the passage of time. SSAP 12 'Accounting for Depreciation' favours the following definition: 'the measure of the wearing out, consumption or other reduction in the useful economic life of a fixed asset whether arising from use effluxion of time or obsolescence through technological or market changes'. The standard further states that depreciation should be allocated to accounting periods to charge a fair proportion of the cost or valuation of the asset to each period expected to benefit from its use. The term amortization is sometimes used to express an annual spread of the cost of a fixed asset over a predetermined life, e.g. the premium paid to purchase the lease of an office block will be spread over the remaining years of the lease.

Economists and accountants take differing views of depreciation. Economists have noted the fact that the fixed assets of a business lose their value during the course of their life, and consider that income or profit can only be correctly measured if an amount is set aside to make up for this loss in value each year. Accountants exercise caution when the term value is used because it cannot be objectively determined, and is difficult to audit. For this reason the accountant prefers to allocate the cost of a fixed asset to accounting periods during its useful economic life according to a predetermined pattern or 'profile' rather than to measure the fall in value experienced each year. Reasons for the loss in value can be analysed as follows:

1. Assets fall in price because they have been used and are second-hand. The utility

or profit-earning ability of the asset may not have changed but market forces will reduce the value of an asset for this reason, e.g. the fall in value of a new motor car on the day it is purchased and becomes technically a second-hand vehicle.

2. Assets fall in value because their earning capacity is reduced. Future earnings expected from an asset can be discounted to their present value as a means of measuring the value of the asset. A machine may be just as efficient as on the day when it was first purchased but if improved technology has produced more efficient machines to compete with it, then the future earnings of the machine are likely to be reduced, and its value will fall. An efficient machine which can make goods for which there is no longer a demand because of a change in tastes will also experience a fall in value. This phenomenon is known as 'obsolescence'.

3. Physical deterioration or wear and tear is a common reason for a fixed asset to experience a loss of value during its working life. The asset is worth less simply because its performance has deteriorated and perhaps efficiency is affected by increasing maintenance costs and a higher incidence of disruption to production caused by breakdowns.

4. For some assets the passage of time will reduce value, if the asset has a definite limit to its life. A lease or a patent right will be granted for a number of years and as those years pass so it is fair to assume that a proportion of the cost of the asset has been used up.

DEPRECIATION AS A CONCEPT

The financial accountant, true to the allocation principle, will attempt to spread the capital cost of an asset less its terminal scrap value (or residual value) over the years of the estimated useful economic life of the asset. Thus depreciation gradually translates an asset into an expense and in the balance sheet at the end of each year discloses the unexpired portion of the original capital cost. Depreciation is therefore considered to be a product of time, and not a measure of the fall in value or physical deterioration of the asset to be charged to an accounting period. Several methods can be applied by the financial accountant and it is a matter of judgement to select the appropriate depreciation policy to fit the circumstances concerned. The charge for depreciation is always made in the form of a provision because the exact amount cannot be determined, but it is considered prudent to set aside an amount out of profit to account for this cost in order not to overstate profit. A management accountant, however, might consider depreciation to be a means whereby a charge can be made against profit in a period for the use of the asset. The matching principle sets cost against revenue produced by the asset and the cost of using the asset is considered to be depreciation. In both these cases depreciation based on the historical cost of the asset does not disclose the cost of using the asset at current prices, nor does it reveal in the balance sheet the current value of that part of the asset not yet used up.

However, depreciation means that a charge is being made to the income statement to set aside out of revenue something to make up for that part of a past investment which has been used up during the accounting period. If this is not done then capital depletion will occur. A business which fails to take depreciation into account finds, at the end of the life of a particular asset, that it has used up the asset over a period of years without setting aside out of the profits of those years amounts with which to replace the capital of the company which was invested in the asset many years previously. A provision for depreciation reduces profit by an amount which might otherwise have been seen as available for distribution as a dividend. Without depreciation the fixed asset is used up, profits are overstated since no charge for the use of the asset has been made, and if those profits are all distributed in the form of a dividend, the funds invested in the business will have been run down during the life of the asset. When this asset is worthless, the store of assets representing the shareholders' funds invested in the business will have been depleted, unless the annual provision for depreciation (reinvested in the business and not distributed) maintains the general stock of assets, and thus the amount of shareholders' capital employed.

The concept of capital maintenance is crucial to the correct measurement of business income. If profit is a surplus the true profit can only be measured after making sure that the business is as well off at the end of the accounting year as it was at the beginning. The provision for depreciation which is made to avoid capital depletion ensures that the original capital invested in the business will be maintained.

Many students make a connection between depreciation and replacement, saying that the amount calculated for depreciation is set aside to provide a fund with which to replace the asset. However, this is not so. The amounts set aside for depreciation reduce the profit available for distribution and are reinvested in the business. At the end of the life of the asset these amounts are tied up in the general assets of the business and can be released by the sale of those assets to provide liquid funds (cash). These funds can be used to buy another similar asset, but need not be so used. They are available to be used in whatever way the directors of the company wish. They can be withdrawn from the business, they can be used to finance a new venture, they can be used to buy more machinery, or they can stay where they are as finance supporting the general assets of the business. It is unlikely that they will be used to buy exactly the same type of machine, since as technology is improved more sophisticated machines replace the old ones which are being retired. Depreciation is not a saving scheme to provide funds for replacement, unless of course it is linked to a 'sinking fund' whereby cash is set aside each year and invested outside the company to mature at the end of the life of the asset. The annual investment of an amount of cash, equal to the provision for depreciation, outside the business is a separate operation, and is not part of accounting for depreciation as such. Very few companies now use this sinking fund technique, since they take the view that the best use of the depreciation amount is to reinvest it in their own company and avoid an outflow of cash.

Example

Jack Spratt starts up in the demolition business and uses all his funds to buy a bulldozer for £10 000. He expects the machine to last for four years before it is worn out. Each year he receives £50 000 for work he has done and pays out £40 000 for the costs of the work. Thus his cash book will show a balance of £10 000 at the end of his first year of trading.

An accountant advises him that he has not made a profit of £10 000, and warns him that he must spread the cost of the bulldozer over the years of its useful life by charging £2500 against profit as depreciation each year. His real profit is £7500, and this is the amount he draws out of the business that year.

Opening Balance Sheet of Jack Spratt

	£		£
Capital	10 000	Cash	10 000

Balance Sheet of Jack Spratt at end of Year 1

	£		£
Capital	10 000	Bulldozer	10 000
		Less	
		depreciation	2 500
			7 500
		Cash	2 500
	£10 000		£10 000

At the end of four years his balance sheet would appear as follows:

Balance Sheet of Jack Spratt

	£		£
Capital	10 000	Bulldozer	10 000
		Less	
		depreciation	10 000
			Nil
		Cash	10 000
	£10 000		£10 000

Thus he is back in the same position as at the start of the life of the asset, with a capital of £10 000 represented by cash. The bulldozer is shown at no value, and this is a true statement of the situation. If he had failed to provide for depreciation he would have had a profit of £10 000 each year, and if he had drawn that amount his capital would have been depleted, and would have been completely consumed by the end of year 4. As it is, he now has funds in liquid form again, and it is for him to decide what he now wishes to do with them. He may buy another bulldozer, he may retire and buy a country cottage, or he may decide to invest his funds in Stock Exchange securities and live off the income from them. Unfortunately, in a period of inflation, depreciation puts back out of the profits only the money amount of the original investment used up, and this may not be sufficient to buy the same amount of goods and services as the original funds could buy. In a more sophisticated example the £10 000 of cash in the balance sheet of year 4 would instead be held in the form of general assets such as stock or debtors.

DEPRECIATION—A JUDGEMENTAL APPROACH

Depreciation is a matter of estimate and the accountant must use judgement when calculating the useful economic life of an asset, the residual value, and indeed the true cost of the asset. It may be necessary to consult specialists such as engineers who can advise on the working life of a machine, or economists who can review the market and estimate the likely effect of obsolescence on the useful economic life of the machine.

Cost

The historical cost of a fixed asset which is the basis for the depreciation calculation comprises the price for which the asset was purchased plus all other costs incurred to bring the asset to the point at which it is ready for use in the business. Such costs can include transporting a machine to the factory, or building the foundations on which the machine will be installed, or in the case of a building any legal charges and other expenses involved in the purchase. If a second-hand machine is purchased, any repairs or maintenance required to bring it up to operating capability can also be capitalized as part of the cost of the machine. If a company makes its own capital assets, using labour and raw materials within its factory, then these costs must be capitalized together with an appropriate proportion of the factory overhead costs. The cost of an improvement or an extra fitment to a machine can also be capitalized and if these costs are incurred, say, halfway through the useful economic life of the asset, then this cost should be depreciated over the remaining years of the life of the asset.

Useful Economic Life

Judgement is required to determine the period over which a fixed asset will contribute to the profitable operations of a business. Clearly physical deterioration or wear and tear is a significant factor in this estimate, which will depend upon whether the machine is used intensively, i.e. three eight-hour shifts per day, or whether it is used in an occupation where damage may shorten its life. Some companies develop an accounting policy based on past experience whereby all fixed assets are assumed to have a certain economic life, e.g. five years. Not all assets will fit into such a policy and it may be necessary to adjust the depreciation charge accordingly in certain years. A principal factor in determining this policy will be the likely expense of maintenance charges as a machine gets older.

Obsolescence is another factor which influences the economic life of an asset. Judgement concerning estimates of the speed with which new rival products will be brought to the market, or the likely introduction of improved machines, will influence the economic life of the asset. Clearly a machine which is not specific in its use and can be applied to many different tasks will have an extended working life.

Residual Value

It is difficult to estimate the eventual scrap value of a machine on the date of its purchase. The cost less the scrap value is the net amount which must be spread by means of depreciation. A business may develop a policy of renewing certain assets (company cars) after, say, two or three years, in which case the scrap value can be calculated with a little more certainty. If, however, it is intended to use a machine until it is completely worn out then the scrap value at that point will be small and thus a negligible part of the calculation.

THE METHODS USED

The methods used to account for depreciation are arbitrary and reflect the uncertainty in the estimates made by the accountant and his colleagues. It is only with the revaluation method that depreciation each year is the same as the real fall in value experienced by the asset. SSAP 12 does not recommend any one method as being better than others.

The Straight Line Method

The cost of an asset less its scrap value is divided by the years of its useful life to compute the charge per annum. Thus this method gives an equal charge per annum over the assumed life of the asset, is simple to compute, and spreads the cost in a fair way over the years of the life of the asset. The obsolescence factor can be built into the estimate of the useful life in the formula.

However, this method does not take into account use, since the same charge is made to the profit and loss account each year although the asset may not work as hard in one year as in another. Some accountants argue that even though a machine does not work it is still losing value, and that this loss is the cost of holding the asset for the year even though it is not used. Others take the view that if there is no revenue for the use of an asset during the year then the cost of holding the asset has not been matched with the revenue produced by the asset, and that it is wrong to have the same charge each year, since it is unlikely that the asset will depreciate evenly over the years of its life. They further argue that the cost of repairs for a machine is likely to be heavier in the later years of its life, while its performance will be least effective at this time, and therefore a lighter depreciation charge is needed to compensate for this situation.

In spite of this argument the straight line method remains the most widely used method of depreciation in this country. The formula for the method is:

$$\frac{\text{Cost} - \text{Scrap}}{\text{Forecast economic life}} = \text{Annual charge}$$

As a matter of policy, depreciation may be charged pro rata to time in the year when an asset is acquired, i.e. six months' use merits half the annual charge. It is usual not to charge depreciation in the year of disposal for plant sold before the end of its expected working life.

In the circumstances of the example below, a machine costing £20 000 with a scrap value of £5240 and an estimated working life of six years would be depreciated at £2460 per year.

$$\frac{£20\ 000 - £5240}{6} = £2460$$

The Reducing Balance Method

This method writes off a constant proportion of a continually reducing balance each year and has the merit of making a high charge in the early years of the asset's life and a low one later, when repair bills may be heavy. It is argued in favour of this method that this will provide a uniform expense throughout the life of the asset. Also, if the obsolescence factor of the asset is high then more is written off in the early years, so that a smaller amount is left in the later years to form a sudden loss if the asset should prove worthless before the end of its estimated life. Some accountants, however, argue that it is not right to charge a different amount of depreciation for the use of the same machine in successive years, and that the fact that repair bills are high in the later years only reflects the facts which should influence what appears in the accounting statements.

This method is nevertheless widely used, but the percentage to be written off the reducing balance each year is often decided arbitrarily. Those who wish to be more scientific in the calculation of the rate can use the formula

$$r = \left(1 - \sqrt[n]{\frac{s}{c}}\right) \times 100\%$$

where r = the rate, s = the scrap value, c = the cost, and n = the number of years.

This formula cannot be applied if there is no known scrap value, since a residual amount is required.

Example

A machine costing £20 000 is deemed to have a six-year life and a scrap value of £5240 at the end of its working life. By application of the formula a rate is found which can be applied to the reducing balance:

$$\text{Rate} = \left(1 - \sqrt[6]{\frac{5240}{20\ 000}}\right) \times 100\%$$

$$= \left(1 - \sqrt[6]{0.262}\right) \times 100\%$$

$$= (1 - 8) \times 100\%$$

$$= 20\%$$

The depreciation computation is as follows:

	£
Cost	20 000
Depreciation Year 1 (20% × £20 000)	4 000
Written-down value	16 000
Depreciation Year 2 (20% × £16 000)	3 200
Written-down value	12 800
Depreciation Year 3 (20% × £12 800)	2 560
Written-down value	10 240
Depreciation Year 4 (20% × £10 240)	2 048
Written-down value	8 192
Depreciation Year 5 (20% × £8 192)	1 638
Written-down value	6 554
Depreciation Year 6 (20% × £6 554)	1 310
Written-down value when sold	£5 244

The difference of £4 is due to rounding in the calculation.

If the machine makes 4000 articles each year, is it fair to charge for depreciation £1 to the cost of each article made by the machine in year 1, and only 33 pence to each of 4000 articles made in year 6? The difference represents no cost saving or efficiency, but is a result of the method of depreciation selected. Unless the situation is suitable to this method, the calculation may give a rate which distorts the cost and profit shown. For example, a machine costing £20 000, with a four-year life and a scrap value of £512, produces a rate of 60 per cent, which, when applied, writes off £12 000 as depreciation in the first year.

A similar method which also concentrates the bulk of the depreciation charge in the early years is the sum of the digits method. In this case the years are treated as digits and are added together. Thus the total digits for a machine with a six-year life would equal $1 + 2 + 3 + 4 + 5 + 6 = 21$. The annual depreciation charge is computed by dividing the total of the digits into the digit for a particular year to give that proportion of the total cost to be charged in that year. Thus depreciation in the first year would be $6/21$ times the cost, in the second year $5/21$ times the cost, and so on.

$$6/21 \times £14\ 760 = £4217 \text{ in year } 1$$
$$1/21 \times £14\ 760 = £703 \text{ in year } 6$$

The Revaluation Method

This method takes the view that the charge for depreciation, or the cost of holding the asset during the year, is the amount by which the asset has fallen in value during the year. Thus the asset is revalued at the end of each year and the amount of depreciation is computed. This method is advantageous where the amount of deterioration of the asset is uncertain, because objective valuation can be used to provide the amount. Items such as contractors' plant, loose tools, livestock, etc. are all examples of assets which can be depreciated in this way. However, much depends upon the efficiency of the valuer, since bias can intrude into the valuation process. If this method is to be used correctly the same valuer should be employed each year. Arguments against this method are that valuation takes time, is expensive, and is after all only an estimate. It is also difficult to separate the increase in the value of an asset caused by inflation from the decrease in the value of an asset caused by wear and tear. In certain cases special conditions could result in a negative charge for depreciation. This is the only method in which the depreciation noted by the economist equals the amount written off by the accountant.

The Production Unit Method

This method attempts to relate depreciation to the use of the asset. The cost of the asset net of the scrap value is divided by the number of units the asset is expected to produce during its useful life. Thus a rate is computed which can be applied each year to the number of units actually produced to calculate the depreciation charge. The production unit method can be operated successfully if all units produced by the asset are the same and have the same work value. It is sometimes used to depreciate the cost of excavating a mine where one can forecast the amount of ore to be produced before the mine is worked out, or of a press which should perform a certain number of operations before it is worn out. However, the depreciation charge is made only when the machine is used, so obsolescence during an idle period cannot be accounted for. Attempts are sometimes made to build an obsolescence factor into the calculation of the units in the life of the asset, but this amount is often an estimate of doubtful validity. The formula for this method is:

$$\frac{\text{Cost} - \text{Scrap}}{\text{Expected units}} = \text{Unit rate}$$

$$\text{e.g} \quad \frac{£14\ 760}{60\ 000} = £0.246 \text{ per unit}$$

If production equals 10 000 units in a year, the provision for depreciation will be £2460.

The Production Hour Method

This is a variation of the production unit method; it provides a rate per hour for depreciation rather than a rate per unit produced. To compute the rate to be used, the cost of the asset less the scrap value is divided by the working hours in the life of the asset. The advantage of this method is that it can be applied to a machine which produces different items and takes different amounts of time to produce them. A machine such as a lathe can be employed on many different operations, and since time is the common denominator depreciation can be linked directly to the product cost. Once again depreciation is related to use, and there is the disadvantage that no charge is made if the asset is not used. The formula is

$$\frac{\text{Cost} - \text{Scrap}}{\text{Hours}} = \text{Rate}$$

$$\text{e.g.} \quad \frac{£14\ 760}{120\ 000} = £0.123 \text{ per hour}$$

If the machine works for 20 000 hours in a certain year, the provision for depreciation that year will be £2460.

THE ACCOUNTING ENTRIES

The accounting entries to record depreciation have a dual purpose. They show the charge to be made in the profit and loss account for the use of the asset during the year, and in the balance sheet they show the cumulative amount of expired cost which has been provided against the original investment in the asset. In the balance sheet the tangible fixed assets are always shown at cost less total depreciation to date = net.

The method of depreciation must be disclosed as an accounting policy and the accounts must state the amount of depreciation provided that year and any additional charges for renewal. Provisions for replacement of fixed assets other than by depreciation charge, or the reason why no provision has been made, must be noted.

An interesting position arises when assets are used after they have been fully depreciated. This means that their actual life is longer than that estimated when they were first purchased, and therefore the depreciation charge in past profit and loss accounts has been too high, so profit has been understated. Similarly a machine may be revalued partway through its life.

Best accounting practice suggested by SSAP 12 is to revalue the machine, debiting the asset and crediting a capital reserve account, and then to write off the new asset value over what is considered to be the remaining life of the asset. It is of course preferable to discover that the depreciation charge is too much well before the end of the life of the asset, so that the annual charge for the remaining years can be revised. Capital expenditure on an asset during its life, e.g. the cost of an extra fitment to extend the range of a machine, should be written off over the remaining life of that machine, unless the fitment can be transferred to another machine and thus has a finite working life of its own.

Premature Retirement

Where assets are retired prematurely, i.e. their actual life is shorter than estimated, there may be a loss, since they may not be written down to their estimated realizable value at the time of their retirement. In this case past depreciation has been too small and thus past profits have been overstated. For these reasons some accountants argue that the loss on disposal should be written off at once, although they can see that is unfair to charge any of this loss to a particular product or department of the business. In this situation, however, the accountant often meets pressure from management to spread the burden of the sudden loss over more than one accounting period.

Example

Depreciation in the ledger accounts: A company acquires a machine for £2100. It decides to depreciate it over a five-year life, and assumes that its scrap value at the end of five years will be £100.

$$\frac{\text{Cost} - \text{Scrap}}{\text{Life}} = \frac{£2100 - £100}{5} = £400 \text{ p.a. as depreciation.}$$

The machine is sold at the end of four years for £300 cash.

Dr.		Machine Account		Cr.
	£			£
Year 1: Cash paid for asset	2100	Year 4: Transfer to disposal account		2100

Dr.		Cash Book		Cr.
	£			£
		Year 1: Asset bought		2100
Year 4: Asset sold	300			

Dr.		Profit and Loss Account		Cr.
	£			
Year 1: Depreciation	400			
Year 2: Depreciation	400			
Year 3: Depreciation	400			
Year 4: Depreciation	400			
Loss on sale	200			

Dr.		Depreciation Provision Account		Cr.
	£			£
		Year 1: Charge to profit and loss account		400
		Year 2: Charge to profit and loss account		400
		Year 3: Charge to profit and loss account		400
Year 4: Transfer to disposal account	1600	Year 4: Charge to profit and loss account		400
	£1600			£1 600

Dr.		Disposal Account		Cr.
	£			£
Year 4: Cost of machine	2100	Year 4: Depreciation to date		1600
		Cash		300
		Loss to profit and loss account		200
	£2100			£2100

Steps in the accounting procedure are:

1. Record the acquisition of an asset, a machine, for cash, as the reduction of another asset.

2. Record the depreciation as a cost in the income statement each year and show the year-end position, i.e. cost less depreciation to date gives the unexpired capital cost at the end of year 4 immediately before the sale.
3. Record the disposal of the asset for cash at the end of year 4 and the transfer of any profit or loss on the deal to the income statement for that year.

Note: Under the principle of duality every debit must have a credit.

Excerpt from the balance sheet as at end of year 4 but before sale of machine:

Fixed assets	Cost	Depreciation	Net
	£	£	£
Plant and machinery	2100	1600	500

In the last example the balance sheet at the end of year 4 showed as a net figure the written-down value at that time. The balances in the machinery account and the depreciation account for this asset were transferred to the disposal account, thus ensuring that they no longer appeared in the balances of those two accounts shown in the balance sheet after the sale of the machine. The term used for these entries is 'writing off' to the disposal account. The cash received from the sale of the asset was set against the written-down value of the asset in the disposal account, to reveal whether a profit or a loss had been made on the sale. A loss at this point means that depreciation to date set off against profits in previous years has not been sufficient to keep pace with the declining value of the asset, and as such shows that past profit has been overstated. The loss is transferred at once to the debit side of the profit and loss account, so that it is set off against profits in the year of its discovery. If the price received for the asset had exceeded the written-down value, then a profit on the sale would have been made. This profit would have appeared as a debit balance in the disposal account, and would have been credited to the profit and loss account.

In the case of an asset retired prematurely, the cost and depreciation to date can be written off to a retirement account, or disposal account, so that entries for the retired asset are deleted from figures which appear in the balance sheet. When an asset is retired before reaching the end of what was considered to be its useful life, there is a surplus of cost over depreciation, i.e. a debit balance on the retirement account, which is written off to the profit and loss account to charge the loss made on the scrapped asset against profits for the year. Any cash received from the sale of the asset is debited to the cash book and credited to the retirement account, thus reducing the loss on retirement.

In this way over- or under-depreciation over a period of years will distort the profit shown in each of those years and should be corrected as soon as possible. The term 'profit' or 'loss' used in this context is not strictly correct. Any surplus or deficit on disposal of an asset represents the cumulative result of error in previous years resulting from inaccurate estimate of economic life or scrap value.

Example

Taking the figures in the ledger entries example above, suppose that at the end of year 3 the machine is found to be obsolete, as the process for which it is used is no longer required. The machine is promptly written off and sold to a scrap dealer for £50.

Dr.	Machine Account		Cr.
	£		£
Year 3: Balance—original cost	2100	Year 3: Transfer to disposal account	2100

Dr.	Depreciation Provision Account		Cr.
	£		£
Year 3: Transfer to disposal account	1200	Year 3: Balance (3 × £400)	1200

Dr.	Retirement Account		Cr.
	£		£
Year 3: Transfer from asset account	2100	Year 3: Depreciation to date	1200
		Cash	50
		Loss on machine to profit and loss account	850
	£2100		£2100

Dr.	Cash Book		Cr.
	£		£
Year 3: Sale of machine for scrap	50		

In effect the loss of £850 charged against profit in year 3 is to catch up as soon as possible with the fact that profits in years 1 and 2 have been overstated, because of a mistake made when the life of the machine was originally estimated for the depreciation calculation.

SSAP 12 states that where the cost of an asset is not likely to be recouped from revenue generated by that asset, the book value of the asset must be reduced accordingly as soon as possible.

If the asset was sold for more than the written-down value (WDV) of £900, the balance on the retirement account would be on the debit side, a profit transferred to the credit of the profit and loss account. This apparent profit merely recognizes that depreciation was too high in previous years.

Extension of Useful Life

Suppose that the machine had instead worked on until the end of its calculated life, and had then been found to have several more years of useful working life left in it. The management estimate the extra life to be three years, and the value of the machine at the beginning of those three years to be £700. The eventual scrap value is still £100. The accounting entries to record these circumstances are as follows.

The balances on the machinery account and the depreciation account are closed off to a revaluation account. This means that the original cost and depreciation to date are summarized in this account as the written-down value of £100. Next the increase in the value of the asset, as disclosed by the valuer, is debited to the revaluation account and credited to a capital reserve account. The revaluation account is closed off by a credit entry of £700, which is reflected as a debit to the machinery account. Thus the new value of the machine is disclosed by this account and depreciation can go ahead normally in the forthcoming years.

Dr.		Machinery Account		Cr.
	£			£
Year 1: Purchase	2100	Year 5: Transfer to revaluation account		2100
Year 5: Revaluation of machine	700			

Dr.		Depreciation Provision Account		Cr.
	£			£
Year 5: Transfer balance to revaluation account	2000	Year 5: Accumulated depreciation		2000
		Year 6: Profit and loss account		200

Dr.		Revaluation Account		Cr.
	£			£
Year 5: Original cost	2100	Year 5: Depreciation to date		2000
Increase in value transferred to reserve	600	New value recorded in machine account		700
	£2700			£2700

Dr.		Capital Reserve Account		Cr.
	£			£
		Year 6: Revaluation of machine		600

SSAP 12 ACCOUNTING FOR DEPRECIATION—THE RULES IN THE STANDARD

This standard is in agreement with the International Accounting Standard No. 4. It is a short document, and most of its recommendations have already been mentioned.

The standard gives as the objective of depreciation the systematic allocation of the cost of an asset to accounting periods so as to charge a fair proportion to each period during the life of the asset. It seems obvious that the Accounting Standards

Committee wished to avoid a discussion of the nature of depreciation and the respective merits of the techniques used, when the standard was compiled. Unlike stock valuation in SSAP 9, no method has been outlawed, but a set of general principles are set out. The standard urges accountants to disclose in accounting statements:

(a) the depreciation method used;
(b) the lives or rates for various classes of assets;
(c) total depreciation for the period;
(d) the gross amount of depreciable assets and cumulative depreciation on them.

Users of accounting statements thus get a better view of the accounting policies which form the basis of the statements.

The standard specifies that the accountant must select the method of depreciation for use which is most appropriate to the assets to be depreciated. The argument that because the current market value of an asset is greater than its net book value, no depreciation should be charged, is not accepted. Depreciation is seen as an allocation over the life of the asset and if value increases during that life, it is appropriate to revalue the asset and allocate the new value less residual amount to the remaining years of the asset's life. The depreciation charge is to be based on the 'carrying value' of the asset. This is the amount disclosed in the balance sheet which is either the historical cost amount or the revalued amount if a revaluation has taken place. In the year when a revaluation is made a note should disclose the effect of the revaluation on the depreciation charge.

The economic life of an asset should be regularly reviewed at least once every five years. Using technical, commercial and accounting considerations the life of an asset may be revised, in which case the net book value at the date of revision should then be depreciated over the new revised life for the asset.

For example, an asset which cost £20 000 and was estimated to have a four-year life would be written down to £10 000 after two years if the straight line method is used. If at this point the useful economic life of the asset is revised and it is considered to have four more years of life from that point, the net book value of £10 000 will be allocated over the remaining life as £2500 per annum for depreciation. If there has been a permanent diminution in the value of an asset, the prudence concept must be followed and the asset should be written down immediately through the profit and loss account. The new value should be systematically depreciated over the remaining useful economic life. It is permissible to write up the asset at a later date if the reasons for making the provision against permanent diminution are considered no longer to be relevant. The standard permits a business to change from one method of depreciation to another but only if the new method will give a fairer presentation of the results and of the financial position of the business. In the year when such a change takes place a note to the accounts should disclose the reason for the change and the effect of the change on the accounts that year.

There has, however, been some argument about the section of the standard concerning the depreciation of buildings. Property companies and other owners of freehold land and buildings, such as brewers, are of the opinion that the suggestion that buildings should be depreciated is wrong. The standard clearly states that freehold land will not normally require a provision for depreciation, unless considerations such as the desirability of its location reduce its value. It also states, however, that buildings have a limited life and should be depreciated as in the case of other fixed assets. The property companies argue that:

(a) it is difficult to separate the value of a building from the value of the site on which it is built;
(b) buildings have very long lives and should therefore be accorded a special accounting treatment;
(c) buildings tend to increase in value year by year, so depreciation should not be charged.

Recent discussion among accountants tends to the view that long-lived premises, maintained in good order, should escape depreciation, even though the Companies Act 1985 states that 'any fixed asset with a useful economic life . . . shall be reduced by provisions for depreciation to write off the amount systematically over the period of the life'. The fact remains, however, that buildings wear out, so perhaps a refurbishment fund built up over twenty years, rather than an annual depreciation charge, would be more appropriate. The usual practice developing from this standard is that the value of land is separated from the value of buildings, and the buildings are depreciated over a long period—say fifty years.

A further standard, Accounting for Investment Properties (SSAP 19), has now been issued. Such properties are held as disposable investments rather than for consumption, so that changes in their current value are of greater importance than systematic depreciation. The standard practice is that such properties should be revalued annually and the valuation incorporated into the balance sheet. The names and qualifications of the valuers must be shown, as well as the basis on which the valuation was made, and whether or not they are employees of the company. Any increase or decrease in value is to be carried to an Investment Property Revaluation Reserve. If there is a large deficit in any year which exceeds this reserve, the excess must be charged to profit and loss.

TUTORIAL DISCUSSION TOPICS

6.1 'Depreciation writes down the plant to its true value'—managing director. 'Depreciation allocates the cost of plant to the years in which it is used'—accountant. Who is right?

6.2 Albert Jones is in business as a builder. He started business with equipment which cost £5800 and which he thinks will last five years before it is worn out. He has consulted an accountant, who suggests that he should depreciate his plant. What will be the result if he ignores this advice?

6.3 State the objectives of depreciating equipment by one of the decreasing charge (reducing balance) methods. Under what circumstances is this type of method particularly suitable? Are there any disadvantages in the use of this type of depreciation technique?

6.4 Advise a businessman of the major factors to be considered when deciding upon the methods and rate to be applied to depreciate a specific asset.

6.5 Albert Kerr qualified as a dentist five years ago, and borrowed £38 000 from a relation to buy the surgery equipment which he needed in order to set himself up in practice. The loan was for five years, at the end of which time the full sum was to be repaid. Mr Kerr consulted an accountant and was advised to write off one-fifth of the cost of the equipment each year. 'In that way,' said the accountant, 'you will set aside out of profits an amount equal to the proportion of your original investment which has been used up during the year.' Acting on this advice Albert drew out of the practice all the profits each year for his personal use. At the end of the five-year period his balance sheet showed that there was just enough cash in the practice bank account to repay the loan. Albert Kerr then found that his equipment was worn out and that he would have to buy new equipment. The replacement cost of similar equipment was £51 000, but there was no more cash in the bank and he faced the prospect of having to borrow even more money if he wished to continue his practice. Puzzled and not a little annoyed at the situation, he went to see his accountant. 'The business should have been able to finance the purchase of new equipment after five years' operation. You depreciated the old equipment and I withdrew only the net profits each year. Therefore the depreciation should have created a reserve for replacement,' he said. Explain the situation to A. Kerr.

SEMINAR EXERCISES 4

1. (a) The production manager of the company of which you are accountant has recently attended a one-day seminar on accounting for managers. On his return he asks you, 'Why is it necessary for accountants to depreciate the fixed assets of a business? The capital investment is sunk and gone, come what may, and even the taxation authorities allow plant to be written off in the year of acquisition, with capital allowances at 100 per cent.'
   Write a brief answer to his question.

   (b) In June, year 2, the company purchased plant for a new process at a cost of £330 000. The process was expected to operate until 31 March, year 10, when the estimated scrap value of the plant would be £10 000. The company has adopted the straight line method of depreciation. In June, year 5, further plant was purchased for £250 000, to be used specifically on this process. This plant was expected to be worn out and valueless by 31 March, year 10. In March, year 7, the process was found to be obsolete. It ceased production and the original plant bought in year 2 was sold for £146 000. A full year's depreciation is provided in the year of acquisition but none in the year of disposal.
   Record the above transactions in the ledger and show how the remaining plant would appear in the balance sheet as at 31 March, year 7.

   (c) What extra information would you require to treat the remaining plant correctly in the accounts?

2. Manor Ltd recently purchased a new machine at a basic catalogue price of £30 000. The machine is expected to have a useful life of twelve years and a scrap value of £1000 at the end of that period. Repairs and maintenance costs are

expected to be £200 in the first year and to increase thereafter by linear progression each year (that is, £200 in the first year, £400 in the second, £600 in the third etc.). Installation costs amounted to £2000. There is considerable argument within the company's accounting department about the most appropriate method of depreciation. Furthermore, the company secretary maintains that the actual method of depreciation is immaterial, and that the main advantage to be derived from the depreciation provisions accumulated over the life of the asset is that they can be used to purchase a replacement.

(a) Using the information given above to illustrate your answer, discuss the arguments for and against adopting one of the reducing balance methods of depreciation.
(b) What is the purpose of depreciation? In the light of your answer discuss the arguments put forward by the company secretary of Manor Ltd.

3. Bulford Dozers Ltd own and hire out heavy plant to the civil engineering industry. On 31 March last year the company purchased an articulated plant transporter for use in the business, at a cost of £86 000. Because equipment on building sites is usually treated roughly it is expected that the transporter will have a useful life of only five years, at the end of which its scrap value will be £1000. During its life the vehicle will travel 100 000 miles, but it is unlikely that the mileage will be the same each year, since the vehicle may stand idle for long periods.

(a) Discuss three methods of depreciation which could be applied to the transporter, recommending one of them.
(b) Show how the transporter would appear in the balance sheet of the company as at 30 September next year if depreciation was provided by the method you have chosen in (a) above.
(c) Explain the interrelationship of the provision for depreciation and the replacement of fixed assets.

REVIEW QUESTIONS 2

1. (a) The annual report of Foolhardy Ltd states: 'It is not the policy of this company to charge depreciation on fixed assets; our plant and equipment are always maintained in first-class condition, and the market value of our buildings appreciates each year.'
   Discuss critically the policy of this company towards depreciation.
   (b) The balance sheet of Deprec Ltd as at 31 December 19-8 contains the following items:

Motor vehicles	£	£
Balance at 1 January 19-8 at cost		297 000
Add purchases during 19-8 at cost		17 000
		314 000
Less sales during 19-8 (cost price)	11 000	
Depreciation provision at 31 December 19-8	71 000	82 000
		£232 000

Depreciation is charged at 20 per cent per annum on cost over five years. The depreciation charged in the year of acquisition is pro rata with time, but none is charged in the year of disposal.

During 19-9 the following motor vehicles transactions took place:

Purchases		£
31 March	Lorry	16 500
30 April	Articulated tanker	18 400
31 August	Pick-up truck	7 650
31 December	Saloon	8 200

The lorry was second-hand; it originally cost £10 000 and is expected to have a further useful life of five years.

Sales		Purchased	Cost £	Proceeds £
30 April	Fork-lift truck	31 March 19-7	3500	450
30 June	Saloon	30 June 19-5	950	75
30 September	Lorry	31 December 19-3	4000	250
30 November	Dumper	1 January 19-8	3500	800

Write up the motor vehicles account, motor vehicles depreciation provision and motor vehicles disposal account for 19-9 in the company's ledger.

Also show the relevant entries in the company's profit and loss account and balance sheet at the end of 19-9.

2. Mr Binns operates two machines in his workshop. His ideas as to book-keeping are rudimentary but he has provided the following figures which he thinks are relevant to the accounting treatment of the machines.

	£
19-4	
Machine A—cost new	3200
Machine B—second-hand cost	2000
Overhaul to machine B (this was necessary before machine B worked)	1200
Repairs to machine A	200
Annual service machine A	400
Annual service machine B	480
19-5	
Machine B—extra fitment	600
Repairs to machine B	240
Machine A—replacement bearings	400
Annual service machine A	400
Annual service machine B	480
19-6	
Machine A—repairs	800
Machine B—extra fitment	148
Machine A—repair	184
Annual service machine A	400
Annual service machine B	480

He sold machine A for £2640 and machine B for £2400 early in 19-7.
Soon after the sale he inquires whether he has made a profit on the sale of the machines and you reply that it depends on depreciation. He then remembers that

his accountant has told him that machine A is to be charged to production at 10 per cent on a straight-line basis, and machine B at 10 per cent on a reducing basis.

(a) Draft ledger accounts to record the above transactions, and explain the 'profit' situation to Mr Binns.

(b) Mr Binns meets you a few days later and is highly indignant because a replacement for machine A now costs £4000 and a similarly equipped machine to replace B is £5000. He feels his accountant has badly misled him in suggesting 10 per cent depreciation rates. Do you agree?

3. (a) You are employed as financial adviser to Finman Limited. The managing director tells you that he has heard that the main purpose of depreciation is to provide funds for the replacement of the asset. Draft a brief memorandum replying to this assertion.

(b) Finman Limited owns a large machine which at the start of 1988 was three years old. Finman's other fixed assets may be ignored for the purposes of this question. When the machine was purchased in 1985 it was estimated that it would have an operating life of 12 500 hours, and that under normal conditions the machine would be used for about 2500 hours per year. Accordingly, it was decided that its cost less anticipated scrap value should be written off in equal instalments over five years. The machine cost £22 000 and its anticipated scrap value was £2000. Therefore at 31 December 1987 the accumulated depreciation was £12 000.

State how you would deal with each of the following situations, and calculate the depreciation to be charged for this machine in 1988, *for each one*.

(i) Double shift work is to be introduced for the whole of 1988 and the machine will be operated for 5000 hours.

(ii) Owing to a change in the demand for the product, the machine was taken out of regular service on 1 January 1988. The machine was not sold but retained for use at periods of peak demand. It is expected that the machine will be used on this basis until the end of 1992, and will have a scrap value of £1000 at that time.

(iii) A spanner was left in the machine in January 1988. This necessitated major repairs costing £6000. As a result of this work the remaining life of the machine was increased by 2500 hours.

4. You are accountant to a small group of light engineering companies. The joint managing directors have recently completed secret negotiations to purchase another company to add to the group. This company has been in existence for four years, but the accounting records are incomplete. The plant register and plant account are missing, the only information being a single sheet, set out below:

Year ended	19-1	19-2	19-3	19-4
	£	£	£	£
Plant at cost	160 000	160 000	180 000	
Accumulated depreciation	32 000	57 600	73 440	
Written-down value	128 000	102 400	106 560	

You visit the factory and ask the manager what he can remember about plant bought and sold over the last four years. He informs you that only two machines have been sold.

(a) A drilling machine sold in 19-3 for £16 000 had originally cost £30 000 in 19-1, and was replaced in 19-3 by another machine, but he cannot remember what it cost.
(b) The lathe sold in 19-4 for £40 000 had originally cost £60 000 in 19-1. This machine was replaced at a cost of £100 000.

Identify the depreciation method used in this company and write up the appropriate ledger accounts to record these transactions. Show your workings.

7 | The Accounting Treatment of Current Assets

The current assets which are usually found in a balance sheet are stocks, debtors, short-term investments and cash. They are shown in reverse order of liquidity, that is, with stocks first and cash last.

INTERNATIONAL ACCOUNTING STANDARD 13: CURRENT ASSETS AND LIABILITIES

This standard, issued by the International Accounting Standards Committee, sets out two alternative views of current assets and liabilities. One view sees them as a measure of the ability of an enterprise to carry on its activities day by day, indicating its ability to pay its way from liquid resources. In this case the criterion used to identify a current asset or current liability is whether it will be liquidated (turned into cash) in the near future. The alternative view is that the classification specifies resources and obligations which are circulating in the business, and the criterion used in this case to identify current assets or liabilities is whether the items will be consumed in the production of revenue or settled during the term of a normal operating cycle. A compromise is to use a year or the operating cycle, whichever is the longer, as the realization period, to determine whether or not an item should be treated as current.

This treatment is in accordance with the view of the balance sheet as showing the financial position of an enterprise, where the segregation of current assets and current liabilities discloses the short-term financial position. Slow-moving stocks which are likely to be in store for more than a year are included as current assets, on the basis of the extended operating cycle. Trade credit or bank loans due for payment in more than a year are excluded, since current liabilities are normally understood to be obligations payable on demand or for settlement within one year. Bank balances which cannot be used because of restrictions, e.g. exchange control, should not be considered as current assets. The current portion of long-term liabilities is to be treated as a current liability unless the business intends to refinance the obligation on a long-term basis.

STOCKS

A quotation from the explanatory note to the Statement of Standard Accounting Practice 9 (SSAP 9) reads as follows: 'No area of accounting has produced wider differences in practice than the computation of the amount at which stocks and work in progress are stated as financial accounts'.

The stocks of a business may be in any of five categories:

(a) goods etc. purchased for resale, e.g. stock in a shop;
(b) consumable stores, e.g. a stock of fuel oil or stationery;
(c) raw materials and components to be used in production;
(d) finished goods awaiting sale;
(e) work in progress, or products and services at an intermediate stage of completion.

The accounting treatment accorded to stocks is significant, since it will affect both income measurement and the position statement. Opening stock plus purchases less closing stock equals the cost of goods sold, and this figure, when subtracted from sales, produces the gross profit. Thus the basis used to find the cost of stocks will affect the profit and the stock figure in the balance sheet.

The measurement of income implies that costs will be matched with related revenues, and that stocks of unused items will be carried forward to a later period when their sale produces revenue to offset their consumption. The principle of matching, however, must be subordinated to the concept of conservatism in so far as that, if there is no reasonable expectation that revenue in the future will be sufficient to cover the costs incurred and a loss is likely to be made, it is prudent to provide for that loss as soon as possible. For this reason stocks and work in progress are shown in the accounts as at the lower of cost or net realizable value. If they are worth less than their cost the loss is recognized, but if they are worth more than their cost no element of profit is taken until it is realized when a sale is made.

The standard states that the comparison of cost and net realizable value should be made for each item of stock, or at least for groups of similar items. If the total net realizable value is set against the total cost, a situation could arise where foreseeable losses are set off against unrealized profits.

The definition of 'cost' for stock purposes covers all expenditure incurred in the normal course of business to bring the product or service to its present location and condition. This includes the purchase price plus any import duties payable, as well as transport and handling costs, less trade discounts negotiated with a supplier. The cost attributable to work in progress is, however, a less straightforward matter. It is accepted that the cost of work-in-progress stocks should include the prime cost (direct labour and material) expended on them to date, but not all accountants agree with SSAP 9, which stipulates that a share of normal production overhead expenses should be added to prime cost when the value of stocks of work in progress or finished goods is computed, as forming part of the cost of converting materials to their present condition. Overhead costs such as rent, salaries, depreciation and storage are considered by some accountants to accrue over time, i.e. they are incurred on an annual basis, and as such should be matched with the revenue of the year rather than carried forward in the cost of stock to be matched with the revenue arising when the stock is eventually sold. SSAP 9 excludes abnormal conversion costs and the costs of unused production capacity from the calculation, since they should be written off against profit in the year when they are incurred. Selling and administrative overheads are not normally included in the cost of stock, but the costs of design, marketing and selling can be included if a firm sales contract has been signed. Companies which fail to follow the rules of SSAP 9 run the risk of their auditors qualifying the accounts.

Net realizable value is defined as the actual or estimated selling price of the stock net of any trade discount, from which is deducted any cost incurred to put the stock into a saleable condition, and all cost to be incurred in marketing, selling and distribution of the stock. Those who argue that it is not prudent to carry forward overhead expenses from one year to another are answered by the point that an element of prudence can best be injected into the situation through the calculation of net realizable value.

Events occurring between the balance sheet date and the date of completion of the accounts must be considered when the net realizable value is determined. If prices fall after the year end, then current stocks may not be sold at more than their cost in the future. In a famous case concerning a publishing company, the stocks of unsold magazines were carried forward at cost over a period of several years, until reporting accountants decided that a net realizable value based on their sale as scrap paper was more appropriate, and the subsequent stock write-down had a devastating impact on profits that year. Net realizable value is likely to fall below cost when selling prices fall, stocks deteriorate physically, products requiring those stocks become obsolete, a product is sold as a 'loss leader', or when mistakes in production or purchasing have been made. The length of time which stocks spend in the store before being used or sold is called the stock turnover period. A long turnover period creates an increased risk of obsolescence, deterioration or adverse price movements, and must therefore be considered when assessing the net realizable value.

The rule that stock should be valued at the lower of cost or net realizable value has been criticized by some accountants on the grounds of inconsistency. A conservative approach to profit measurement can, it is argued, lead to an understatement of profit in one year, and an overstatement in the next year. If you recognize a decrease in value which occurs before sale, but ignore an increase in value before sale, then the full amount of the increase is taken as profit in the year of realization. Academic accountants ask why, if net realizable value is better than cost when it is less than cost, it is not to be preferred for the same reasons of objectivity, certainty, verifiability etc. when it exceeds cost. No academic answer has been made to this question, but accountants continue to use the lower of cost or net realizable value rule because they consider that the advantages of conservatism outweigh the disadvantages. The same argument applies to the provision for doubtful debts.

Example

Chiltern Chairs PLC is a furniture company which imports timber from Brazil to manufacture a range of dining room chairs. For Model A there are 300 chairs in stock at the year end. Cost information discloses that 3 kilos of timber are used in each chair, which is purchased from a foreign supplier for £7 per kilo. Six thousand kilos have been purchased and used this year, incurring transport costs of £2300, port dues of £1200, and import duties of £100. Direct manufacturing costs are five hours of labour time at £4 per hour, and three hours of machine time at £3 per hour. For Model A overhead costs for the year are:

Production	£16 800
Design	£3 000
Transport	£4 000
Selling	£18 000
Administration	£9 000

Production overhead includes an abnormal cost of spoilt raw material of £1800. Model A chairs sell at £120 each, with a trade discount of 20 per cent to retailers. Packaging costs are £5 each unit.

Calculate the amount at which the stock of Model A chairs should be included in the year-end account of Chiltern Chairs PLC.

Solution:
6000 kilos of timber are purchased and used. At 3 kilos per chair this means production of 2000 Model A chairs.

Cost	£
Materials, 3 kilos at £7	21.00
Transport, port and tax charge	
[(£2300 + £1200 + £1000) ÷ 6000 kilos = £0.75 per kilo]	
3 kilos at £0.75	2.25
	23.25
Labour 5 hours × £4	20.00
Machine time 3 hours × £3	9.00
Direct cost of manufacture	52.25
Production overhead	
[(£16 800 − £1800 abnormal cost) ÷ 2000 chairs produced]	7.50
	£59.75

Net realizable value:	£
Selling price	120.00
Less discount at 20 per cent	20.00
	100.00
Less packaging costs	5.00
	95.00
Indirect overhead—design/selling/transport/admin	
(£3000 + £18 000 + £4000 + £9000) ÷ 2000 chairs	17.00
	£78.00

Cost is lower than NRV, so the amount used in the accounts would be

$$300 \times £59.75 = £17\ 925$$

Note:
(i) If market forces are likely to force a price cut on the company, the figure of £120 which starts the NRV calculation may need to be reduced, and NRV could fall below cost.
(ii) Stocks of 300 chairs on production of 2000 per annum show a ratio of stock to production of:

$$\frac{300}{2000} \times \frac{50\ \text{weeks}}{1} = 7\frac{1}{2}\ \text{weeks production}$$

This is based on a working year of 52 weeks less 2 weeks of holiday when the factory is closed down.

THE FLOW OF COSTS

The activities of a trader are to buy, store and sell, whereas a manufacturer buys raw materials, combines them with machinery and labour and converts them into manufactured goods which are then sold. Therefore costs flowing through a trading organization will follow a different pattern from the costs flowing through a manufacturing business. The flow of costs can be seen from the interrelationship of the ledger accounts used to record, accumulate and summarize the figures. Assumptions made about the flow of costs will have an impact on the profit figure eventually computed.

There is some argument as to whether factory overheads should be charged in full to the accounting period in which they are incurred, or whether part of them should be allocated to the stock of work in progress and carried forward in the cost of that stock to the next accounting period, when the work in progress is completed and perhaps sold. Some accountants see factory overheads as period costs and wish to relate them to time, since they concern such items as rent, insurance, and factory manager's salary all for the year. Other accountants prefer to match the cost of goods sold with the revenue from their sale and argue that the overhead expenses of one period must be carried forward in the cost of work in progress to set the full cost of these items against the revenue from their eventual sale, if a true profit is to be shown. They argue that this expenditure is incurred to bring the stock to its present condition and location.

This argument has never been settled and different firms adopt different practices. In a leading case some years ago the Inland Revenue authorities took the Duple Motor Body Company Ltd to the House of Lords in an attempt to define whether overhead expenses should be written off or carried forward. The answer they got was that either system is acceptable so long as it is followed consistently. Thus the cost flow assumption as to the treatment of factory overhead expenses can have an impact on the profit calculation.

STOCK VALUATION METHODS

The four main methods of valuing stocks of raw materials for inclusion in the balance sheet or operating statement are:

(a) the first in first out method (FIFO);
(b) the last in first out method (LIFO);
(c) the weighted average method (AVCO);
(d) the standard cost method.

The assumption as to the flow of raw materials through the stores will have an effect on the amounts charged from the stores into the manufacturing account for materials used, and also on the balance sheet, since it affects the cost of closing stocks. An assumption must be made as to the sequence in which stocks are used up because batches of material or components purchased at different prices cannot normally be segregated in the stores, e.g. sand bought at £10 a tonne is mixed with sand bought at £15 a tonne and the two batches cannot be easily identified when transferred to the production process. Liquids mixed in a tank cannot be segregated into different delivery batches bought at different prices.

The bases on which raw materials are valued, both for charging to the manufacturing account and for inclusion in the balance sheet, may vary. Different methods will suit firms in different industries and situations, but it must be stressed that, once a firm has chosen to use one method, then it should act consistently and not change from one method to another without very good reason. Different methods of stock valuation can, as we shall see, cause a different profit to be disclosed, and it is often tempting for a company with disappointing results to suggest a change of stock valuation method in order to show a better profit.

Some firms will assume a first in first out (FIFO) pattern, i.e. the first batches of raw materials to be bought and stored are the first to be transferred to the manufacturing processes and used up. It follows that those raw materials remaining at the end of the period under this assumption are from the most recently purchased batches. Materials used will be charged to production at cost and closing stocks will also be shown in the balance sheet at cost. If the price of raw materials fluctuates during the year so that early batches are bought at one price and later batches bought at a higher price, this assumption will ensure that the manufacturing account is charged with the lower-priced materials while the higher-priced batches are shown in the balance sheet as stocks. Thus the cost flow assumption will influence the profit figure and the balance sheet.

An alternative to FIFO is last in first out (LIFO), which assumes that the most recent batches bought and stored are the first to be used up. Thus, using LIFO, in a period of inflation the manufacturing process will be charged with materials at the later or higher price, while the balance sheet will show stocks at a lower or historical cost.

It is of course impossible to substantiate, with many raw materials, that those which have been in stock longest will be used first. If, for example, there is a large bin containing 10 000 bolts, or a pile of sand, or a vat of paint, there is no way of telling from which delivery batch the units used up in production have been drawn.

During a period of inflation the FIFO cost flow assumption shows stocks in the balance sheet at an accurate current cost, while charging raw materials to the manufacturing process at an outdated cost. Therefore it can be said that under this assumption profits are overstated, since the replacement cost of the raw materials used is not charged in measuring the profit. Conversely, the LIFO cost flow assumption will charge current cost to the manufacturing process and thus compute a truer profit, while the balance sheet figure for closing stocks will be shown at an outdated cost. If the volume of stock falls under LIFO it might seem that these old stocks are used up, and outdated costs will be set against current revenues when profit is measured. There has been some pressure from accountants in the UK to persuade the Inland Revenue to accept accounts produced on a LIFO basis, since under the FIFO system, which is approved by the Inland Revenue, profits are overstated, and it can be argued that taxation is levied on a book profit caused by inflation rather than a manufacturing profit from transactions.

The AVCO valuation method calculates a weighted average based on the price of all deliveries received during the year, and values the closing stock on the basis of this weighted average. Materials charged to production on the basis of a weighted average will measure a profit figure between the extremes of FIFO and LIFO, and the balance sheet stock figure based on AVCO will similarly produce a compromise amount. The method suffers from two disadvantages. First the weighted average must be recalculated for every fresh delivery, and second, the average produced by the calculation may not correspond with a price actually paid for materials during the year. A simple average calculated by totalling the unit price paid for all deliveries and then dividing by the number of deliveries received during the period is not used, because it fails to bring into the calculation the fact that one delivery may be for a large quantity and another delivery for only a small quantity.

While SSAP 9 does not approve of LIFO, since it states that LIFO does not bear a reasonable relationship to actual cost, it does not substantiate this view. However, International Accounting Standard 11 states that both the LIFO and base stock methods may be used, even though they are specifically rejected by SSAP 9. This international standard is otherwise in broad agreement with the UK standard, especially on the point that a proportion of production overheads used up to bring the stock to its present location and condition should be included in the cost of the stock. IAS 11 recommends the FIFO and weighted average methods, and suggests that stocks maintained for specific purposes should be segregated and accounted for at their own prices. The situation has, however, been complicated by the Companies Act 1985, which permits the use of FIFO, LIFO, AVCO, or any other similar method, and requires the directors to choose a method appropriate to the business.

The base stock method of stock valuation assumes that the same quantity and value of stock is in store or process at the end of the year as at the beginning. Thus the cost of all material movements is written off to the manufacturing account each year. This method is now rarely used, since it requires conditions in which similar volumes are in process at the beginning and the end of the year. This method is rejected by SSAP 9.

Standard costing values opening and closing stocks at a standard cost per unit computed in advance of the accounting period. Any difference between actual cost and standard is written off to the profit and loss account as a 'variance' from standard.

Example

This example demonstrates the impact on profit of the various stock valuation bases. A trading company buys the following quantity of raw materials during the first six months of the year.

	Tonnes	Price (£)	Cost (£)
3 January	40	228	9 120
15 February	60	240	14 400
21 March	50	210	10 500
19 April	80	252	20 160
15 May	30	258	7 740
25 June	20	264	5 280
Total tonnes	280	Total cost	£67 200

On 28 June the company sold 200 tonnes of material at £260 per tonne.

Under the FIFO assumption the 80 tonnes of stock remaining will comprise the most recent purchases:

		£
Purchased 25 June	20 tonnes at £264	5 280
15 May	30 tonnes at £258	7 740
19 April	30 tonnes at £252	7 560
	80	£20 580

Under the LIFO assumption the 80 tonnes of stock remaining will comprise the earliest purchases made in the period:

			£
Purchased 31 Jan	40 tonnes at £228		9 120
15 February	40 tonnes at £240		9 600
	80		£18 720

In the trading account opening stock plus purchases less closing stock determines the cost of sales, which in its turn influences the profit. Under FIFO the closing stock will be £1860 more than under LIFO, so the cost of sales will be correspondingly less and the profit correspondingly more.

Stock carried forward at the beginning of the period would have been assumed to form part of the closing stock under LIFO. In this way a batch of material can form part of the stock for several years under this system, and the balance sheet figure can become very outdated.

If the stock level eventually falls below the amount brought forward at the beginning of the year, this outdated (cheap) stock appears to have been used up in the factory, and will measure a greatly overstated profit when the products are sold at current post-inflation prices.

By the AVCO (average cost) method the 280 tonnes purchased are divided into the cost of £67 200 to give a weighted average of £240, and this figure is applied to the closing stock to calculate an amount of £19 200.

A simple average cost could be found by adding the different prices paid during the period and dividing by the number thereof, but this method would obscure the fact that far more material was bought at £252 than at £264 and therefore greater weight or significance must be given to the former price than the latter. The average calculation must be weighted for quantities purchased at different prices. In formula terms this is

$$\frac{\text{aggregate of price} \times \text{weight}}{\text{total weights (tonnes)}} = \frac{67\ 200}{280} = £240$$

The profit on the transaction is measured at different amounts according to the method used.

	FIFO	LIFO	AVCO
	£	£	£
Purchases	67 200	67 200	67 200
Less closing stock	20 580	18 720	19 200
Cost of sales	46 620	48 480	48 000
Sales	52 000	52 000	52 000
Profit	£5 380	£3 520	£4 000

Note that FIFO shows the largest profit, which is more likely to be overstated during an inflationary period when historical costs lag behind current selling prices. The AVCO result is a compromise between the other two methods, and while it is true to say in criticism that the average used, £240, was the real price paid for only one batch and is thus not a realistic figure to use in accounts, the fact remains that this method, unlike LIFO, is acceptable to the Inland Revenue in the UK.

STOCK RECORDS

Accounting for movements of stock in the stores, both receipts and issues, needs care and a measure of internal control. Many companies operate a bin card system whereby when stock is withdrawn from a bin the card is entered and a new running total calculated to show the quantity which remains in the bin. When the re-order point is reached, the buyers are automatically warned to order more stock. The re-order point is calculated with reference to the lead time. The buying department will order materials and there may be a lead time of, say, three weeks before they are delivered, during which period the factory will still be using materials. There will also be a safety margin below which, as a matter of policy, stocks are not allowed to fall. The amount of the safety margin plus the quantity which will be used during the lead time sets the re-order point. The management accountant, together with the buyers, will have computed the economic order quantity as the optimum amount to be purchased so that the advantages and disadvantages of buying and holding large quantities are finely balanced. The economic order quantity plus the amount in store at the safety margin will determine the maximum amount of storage space required for each material or component stored.

Example

A company uses 300 kilos of raw material per week, when working at normal capacity, but the usage can rise to 500 kilos in certain weeks when production is increased. The lead time between placing an order and taking delivery of the material is usually four weeks, but can be as long as six weeks. The management require a safety margin in that stock should never fall below one week's usage.

Using the most conservative figures:

Safety stock = 500 kilos	500 kg
Lead time (6 weeks × 500 kg)	3 000 kg
Re-order point (ROP)	3 500 kg
When stocks fall to 3500 kilos, a new order must be placed.	
Assume economic order quantity is 10 000 kilos	
ROP	3 500 kg
Less minimum usage in lead time*	1 200 kg
Maximum likely stock level on delivery day	2 300 kg
Delivery of EOQ	10 000 kg
Maximum stock space required	12 300 kg

* Four weeks at 300 kilos per week.

A stock record card will be maintained for each material to record receipts and issues to production. The cost at which materials are issued to the factory will depend on whether a FIFO, LIFO or AVCO system is in operation.

In many businesses the stock records are maintained on computer. This means that at the touch of a button the present stocks can be shown on a visual display unit or by a printout. The computer program is written to use the FIFO, LIFO or AVCO system and will make the same calculations as shown below in the stock record example. The computer suffers from the same difficulty as handwritten records in that mistakes can occur in recording receipts and issues of stock so that the balance shown on the stock record may not be correct. An audit check made from time to time will disclose such discrepancies.

Example

Material XD 131 has the following receipts and issues:

Date	Invoice	Receipts	Requisitions	Issues
1 January	800	1000 at 50p		
2 January			B481	500
20 January	962	800 at 60p		
25 January			B508	500
1 February			B512	500
4 February	980	700 at 80p		
20 February			B521	500

Write up a stock record card for FIFO, LIFO and AVCO for the months of January and February.

FIFO Stock Record Card, Material XD 131

Date	Receipts			Issues			Balance	
	Invoice		£	Requisition		£		£
1 January	800	1000 at 50p	500				1000 at 50p	500
2 January				B481	500 at 50p	250	500 at 50p	250
20 January	962	800 at 60p	480				500 at 50p ⎫ 800 at 60p ⎬	730
25 January				B508	500 at 50p	250	800 at 60p	480
1 February				B512	500 at 60p	300	300 at 60p	180
4 February	980	700 at 80p	560				300 at 60p ⎫ 700 at 80p ⎬	740
20 February				B521	300 at 60p	180		
					200 at 80p	160	500 at 80p	400
				Charge to production		£1140	Closing stock	

Note that lines across the issues and receipts columns help to show when each batch is used up.

LIFO Stock Record Card Material XD 131

Date	Receipts			Issues			Balance	
	Invoice		£	Requisition		£		£
1 January	800	1000 at 50p	500				1000 at 50p	500
2 January				B481	500 at 50p	250	500 at 50p	250
20 January	962	800 at 60p	480				500 at 50p ⎫ 800 at 60p ⎬	730
				B508	500 at 60p	300	500 at 50p ⎫ 300 at 60p ⎬	430
1 February				B512	300 at 60p	180		
					200 at 50p	100	300 at 50p	150
4 February	980	700 at 80p	560				300 at 50p ⎫ 700 at 80p ⎬	710
20 February				B521	500 at 80p	400	300 at 50p ⎫ 200 at 80p ⎬	310
				Charge to production		£1230	Closing stock	

Note the greater charge to production than under FIFO and that some material in stock on 1 January is assumed to be still there on 28 February.

AVCO Stock Record Card, Material XD 131

Date	Receipts			Issues			Balance	
	Invoice		£	Requisition		£		£
1 January	800	1000 at 50p	500				1000 at 50p	500
2 January				B481	500 at 50p	250	500 at 50p	250
20 January	962	800 at 60p	480				1300 at 56p	728
25 January				B508	500 at 56p	280	800 at 56p	448
1 February				B512	500 at 56p	280	300 at 56p	168
4 February	980	700 at 80p	560				1000 at 73p	730
20 February				B521	500 at 73p	365	500 at 73p	365
				Charge to		———		Closing
				production		£1175		stock

Note that a fresh weighted average is calculated after each receipt. Alternative methods of calculation may be used.

Workings

	£		£
500 at 50p	250	300 at 56p	168
800 at 60p	480	700 at 80 p	560
1300	£730	1000	£728

$$\frac{£730}{1300} = \text{say 56p} \qquad \frac{£728}{1000} = \text{say 73p}$$

LONG-TERM WORK IN PROGRESS

Some contracts in the building or engineering industry may extend over more than one accounting year. It is argued, therefore, that to take profit at the end of the job will distort the profit calculation both in that year and in the years when the job was in production. Thus at the year end the stock of work in progress on such jobs could be calculated on the basis of prime cost plus a share of overheads, plus a proportion of the profit on each job which reflects the amount of work completed and inequalities of profitability in various stages of the contract. Losses likely to be made must be provided for in full. The amount of work-in-progress stocks computed by this method should be shown net of any cash received from the customer as a progress payment. This rule, expressed in SSAP 9, does not, however, meet with wholehearted acceptance from accountants and others.

The opponents of this method argue that it is more conservative to take no profit until the job is completed, unless the management are confident that profits which appear to be made at an intermediate stage will not be diminished by losses sustained before completion. International Standard 11 expresses the view that contract work in progress can be valued by including profits on the percentage of completion method or by the completed contract method, and sets constraints on the use of the percentage method. As such it is at odds with the UK standard, SSAP 9.

Clearly it would be wrong to use the completed contract method for a large civil engineering job taking, say, three years to complete, but for a six-month contract started in one accounting year and finished in another, this method might be more appropriate.

DEBTORS

The accounting treatment of debtors ensures that all balances owed to the company are recorded, and cancelled when payment is received. Difficulties arise if payment is not made and a bad debt occurs. In this case the debt must be written off to the profit and loss account via the bad debts account. The procedure is to credit the debtor's personal account and debit the bad debts account when the debt goes bad, and to credit the bad debts account and debit the profit and loss account with the total at the end of the year. The significance of a bad debt is shown by the following example. A company sells goods to Mr A for £100. The mark-up on the goods is 25 per cent on cost, so the profit made is £20 (£80 × $^{25}/_{100}$). If Mr A fails to pay for the goods then four times the volume of goods sold to him must be sold to make a profit equal to the cost of the goods he has received. Thus it is important to ensure that goods are sold on credit terms only to customers who are likely to pay for them.

A further difficulty with bad debts concerns the matching principle. If debts go bad during the year when the goods are sold they are written off against profit in that year, but if a debt carried forward at the year end in the balance sheet is subsequently found to be bad, it will be written off against profit in the year after the sale was made. This distortion overstates profit in the first year, understates profit in the second year, and overvalues the asset in the balance sheet between those two years. At the end of an accounting year the debtor balances must be carefully reviewed to identify 'doubtful' debts which may go bad in a subsequent period, so that a provision can be made out of profits for the first year, thus matching cost with revenue and calculating profit on a conservative basis. The provision will appear in the books as a credit balance (debit profit and loss account) and in the next year bad debts can be debited against it, and thus have no impact on profit measurement in the second year. Some companies adopt a routine policy for the calculation of the provision for doubtful debts, but it must be stressed that such a provision requires the accountant to exercise judgement to recognize the loss as soon as it arises, and before it has been confirmed.

Those companies which use a formula for doubtful debt provision are not exercising judgement unless the percentage applied to debts or to credit sales is based on past experience and reviewed at frequent intervals. An accountant or credit controller should scrutinize all debtor balances, taking into account their age and what he knows about the creditworthiness of the customer, when the provision is computed.

Examples

The accounting entries are as follows:
(A) Bad Debt Written Off to the Profit and Loss Account. In this example only one

bad debt is experienced. In reality the bad debts account acts as a collecting point for bad debts before they are charged as one figure to the profit and loss account.

Kester Jon owes Jos Ltd £500, but is unable to pay. In the books of Jos Ltd:

Dr.		Kester Jon	Cr.	Dr.		Bad Debts	Cr.
	£		£		£		£
		Balance				Bad debts for	
		written				the year	
Debtor		off to bad				written off	
balance	500	debts	500			to profit and	
				Kester Jon	500	loss account	500

Dr.		Profit and Loss	Cr.
	£		£
Bad debts	500		

(B) Provision for Doubtful Debts Which Later Go Bad. Kester Jon owes Jos Ltd £500 at the year end, 31 December, and says that he is unable to pay on 30 June of the next year. Jos Ltd provides for the debt at 31 December.

Dr.		Kester Jon	Cr.	Dr.		Provision for Doubtful Debts	Cr.
	£		£		£		£
21 Dec.		31 Dec.				31 Dec.	
Debtor		Balance		31 Dec.		Charge to	
balance	500	c/f	500	Balance		profit and	
				c/f	500	loss account	500
		30 June					
1 Jan.		Bad debt		30 June		1 Jan.	
Balance		written off		Kester Jon	500	Balance b/d	500
b/d	500	to provision	500				

Note that the bad debt has not affected profit measurement in the second year, but the provision reduces profit in the first year.

(C) Bad Debt Written Off. Is Later Collected and Must Be Written Back. Suppose Kester Jon pays the £500 he owes on 31 March of the third year.

Dr.		Cash	Cr.	Dr.		Kester Jon	Cr.
	£		£		£		£
31 March				31 March			
Kester Jon	500			Bad debt		31 March	
				written		Cash	500
				back	500		

Dr.		Bad Debts	Cr.
	£		£
31 Dec.		31 March	
Other bad		Kester Jon	500
debts	2500	31 Dec.	
		Balance to	
		profit and	
		loss	2000
	2500		2500

Thus the amount written back has reduced the cost of bad debts to be written off to profit and loss in year 3.

(D) Overestimate of Provision for Doubtful Debts. Jos Ltd provided £1000 for doubtful debts last year, but only £500 of bad debts occur this year.

Dr.	Provision for Doubtful Debts		Cr.	Dr.	Bad Debts Account		Cr.
	£		£		£		£
31 Dec. Bad debts written off	500	1 Jan. Opening balance	1000	31 Dec. Bad debts of the year from personal accounts	500	31 Dec. Bad debts written off to provision	500
Balance to profit and loss account	500						
	1000		1000				

Dr.	Profit and Loss		Cr.
	£		£
		31 Dec. Doubtful debts overprovided in a previous year	500

The underutilized balance on the provision account is written back to the profit and loss account as soon as it is decided that it is not required. Profit last year was understated as the result of an excess of caution, but this is no reason why the position should not be corrected as soon as objective information is available. In practice the underutilized balance reduces the charge to the income statement for the provision next year.

Note that in these four examples every debit has a credit, and vice versa.

Debtors are shown in the balance sheet under current assets with the amount of provision for doubtful debts shown as a deduction from the total of debtor balances in the personal ledger.

INVESTMENTS

Investments made by a company can be treated as either long-term or short-term investments. The purchase of shares in another company or the loan of funds for a long period is often undertaken for strategic purposes, e.g. some commercial advantage gained by the possession of a share stake in a supplier of raw materials or chain of retail outlets. Investments of this nature are shown separately in the balance sheet, as part of the fixed assets, above the current assets. This indicates that the investment has been made for a long-term reason, and is not for resale or a short-term repository of idle funds which cannot be gainfully employed in the business in the near future. Short-term investments such as deposits with local authorities or commercial banks, as well as investments in shares intended for resale within a year, are current assets.

The basic rule for accounting for investments is to show them in the balance sheet at cost. Long-term investments can be revalued from time to time, but this is wise only if the change in value is permanent and not a short-term fluctuation. It is considered prudent to recognize a rise in the value of an investment only when it is realized. Although investments are shown at historical cost, their correct worth ought to be communicated to shareholders and others. For this reason the Companies Act 1981 requires that investments listed on a recognized stock exchange must be the subject of a note to the accounts disclosing the market value of the quoted investments.

TUTORIAL DISCUSSION TOPICS

7.1 Discuss the impact of the matching and conservatism concepts on the accounting treatment of stocks.

7.2 What is the significance of a FIFO or LIFO assumption for income measurement and the position statement?

7.3 What costs should be included when the amount of work in progress and finished goods stock for a manufacturing company is computed? What difficulties exist in measuring these costs?

7.4 Why should an enterprise provide for doubtful debts?

7.5 Discuss the accounting treatment of investments in the balance sheet.

SEMINAR EXERCISES 5

1. General Accounting Machines Ltd is a business which sells accounting machines entirely on credit terms to a wide range of customers. The following balances were extracted from its ledgers at 30 November.

	£	£
Sales		538 112
Creditors, balance at 30 November last year		36 118
Debtors, balance at 30 November last year	61 803	
Purchases of components	275 480	
Discounts allowed	4 762	
Discounts received		6 184
Cash received from debtors	519 267	
Cash paid to creditors		247 981
Returns inwards	26 916	
Carriage outwards	2 794	
Overdraft interest	8 106	
Provision for doubtful debts, balance at 30 November last year		4 300

A cheque for £1015 from J. Smith, a customer, has been returned from the bank marked 'refer to drawer'. Bad debts totalling £4328 are to be written off, and the provision for doubtful debts is to be raised to 10 per cent of the debtor balances at 30 November this year.

Produce for the period ended 30 November this year:

(a) a total figure for debtors;
(b) the bad and doubtful debts account;
(c) the balance sheet entry for debtors as at that date.

2. Trentvend Ltd are wholesalers for a packaged article in the grocery business. The data below summarize their transactions during the first three months of this year.

| Period | | Purchase | | | | Sales | |
	Units	Price £	Total £	Units	Price £	Total £
January	1000	5	5 000	—	—	—
	600	8	4 800	900	9	8 100
February	600	9	5 400	—	—	—
	400	10	4 000	1100	10	11 000
March	1200	11	13 200	600	12	7 200

(a) Compare the effect on profit for the quarter, and the closing balance sheet if stocks are valued using the FIFO, LIFO and weighted average methods.
(b) Explain the different impacts of the FIFO and LIFO systems upon the profit and loss account and balance sheet.

3. A shop near the Houses of Parliament has recently been buying from the Wedgwood Pottery Co. Ltd replicas of 'Big Ben', affectionately known as 'Wedgwood Bens', for sale to American souvenir hunters. The shop started off on 1 January with 10 'Bens' in stock, which had cost £30 each in December. From 1 January to the end of May they bought 20 'Bens' per month, but each month the cost per 'Ben' had risen by £1 on the previous month. During the same period 80 'Bens' were sold to customers.

(a) Calculate, on the basis of FIFO and LIFO, the stock valuation as at 31 May, and the impact on profit of a change from FIFO to LIFO.
(b) Discuss the impact of inflation on stocks in a business. State, with reasons, why a business may be better or worse off as a result of inflation on stocks.

REVIEW QUESTIONS 3

1. (a) Name five groups into which business stocks can be categorized. State the general rule for the accounting treatment of stock and relate that rule to the concepts or conventions on which accounting is based.
(b) Explain how best accounting practice, embodied in Statement of Standard Accounting Practice 9, follows the general rule.

(c) Purser Leather Goods operate a shop selling ladies' shoes and handbags. Until recently they had always purchased goods for resale, but have decided to make all the handbags they sell, from 1 January 19-1.

The trading account for the year to 31 December 19-1 shows the following figures for handbag sales through the shop.

	£
Opening stock at cost (500 × £6)	3 000
Received from workshop at transfer price (10 000 × £8)	80 000
	83 000
Less: Closing stock (1000 × £8)	8 000
Cost of sales	75 000
Gross profit	45 000
Sales	£120 000

Mr Purser comments that buying the bags from his own workshop at £8 each was a mistake, since he could have bought them through the trade at £7.60. However, he says the workshop did well to produce them at £7.00 each and show a profit of £1 on each one.

Show how the stock of handbags would appear in the balance sheet as at 31 December 19-1.

2. Marmalade Ltd uses ginger in a manufacturing process and presents the following information concerning its purchases, requisitions and balances for the year ending 30 October 19-2. Each unit is a small keg of ginger.

Date	Received (units)	Quantities issued to production (units)	Balance (units)	Unit price of purchases (£)
19-1				
1 November	—	—	200	150
24 November	600	—	800	156
8 December	—	160	640	—
19-2				
16 January	—	280	360	—
11 April	300	—	660	160
18 June	—	260	400	—
6 July	—	220	180	—
15 August	300	—	480	170
29 October	—	280	200	—

Calculate the cost of the closing inventory and the cost of material used under:

(a) first in, first out method;
(b) last in, first out method;
(c) weighted average method (to three decimal places).

3. Mr Spice is in business as a general import and export merchant. In December 19-7 he decided to enter the pepper market. Purchases of pepper were made by Mr Spice as follows:

	Tonnes	Price (per tonne) £
3 January 19-8	20	114
18 February 19-8	30	120
11 March 19-8	25	105
20 April 19-8	40	126
12 May 19-8	15	129
20 June 19-8	10	132

On 27 June 19-8 Mr Spice sold 100 tonnes of pepper at £130 a tonne, he received payment on 8 July 19-8.

(a) Compute the value of stock on hand on 30 June 19-8 by each of the following stock-pricing systems:

  (i) first in, first out (FIFO);
  (ii) last in, first out (LIFO);
  (iii) weighted average cost.

(b) Show the effect of each system in (a) on Mr Spice's pepper trading profits for the six months ended on 30 June 19-8.
(c) Explain briefly why stock is always accounted for at the lower of cost or net realizable value.

4. Simoco Limited sells used cars, which the company acquires through contacts in the motor trade or from customers who have part-exchanged them for newer models. The company has a service department, which often has to repair cars bought to bring them up to 'retail' condition. This department charges the sales department the cost of materials and labour plus 50 percent of cost to cover the service department's profit. The company's year end is 31 August and the stock of used vehicles at that date included the following:

Car	A	B	C	D
Cost	2750	1500	4800	3450
Service department charges				
(Cost + 50 per cent) work done	450	270	120	150
Work needed to bring car to good retail condition				
(Cost + 50 per cent)	60	—	90	120
'Black Book'* retail market values:				
When bought:	4000	1800	5500	3800
At 31 August:	3750	1650	5400	3500
Sales manager's estimated sale price if sold in September	3600	1600	5700	3850

* The 'Black Book' is a national publication available to the motor trade which estimates the retail sale value of used cars in good condition. The cars detailed above are deemed to be in good condition.

(a) Explain the major principle of stock valuation used by accountants, with reference to fundamental accounting concepts.
(b) Calculate the value at which each car should be included in the company's stock as at 31 August. Relate your answer to (a) above.
(c) By using different stock valuation methods a company can influence its annual reported profit and therefore its share price. Discuss.

8 | The Production of Accounts from a Trial Balance

The purpose of this chapter is to show how a list of balances is converted into a trial balance, to make the adjustments necessary at the year end, and to produce detailed accounts in vertical form.

The following balances have been extracted from the books of Columnar Ltd at 31 December last, by the inexperienced book-keeper who is employed by the company as an office manager. Mr Doric, the Managing Director and majority shareholder, has asked you to act as the company's accountant, and to prepare a manufacturing account, trading account, profit and loss account and appopriation account, for the year ended 31 December last, and a balance sheet as at that date. He says that the accounts should be presented in vertical form to facilitate their assimilation by the managers of the business.

Balances on the Books of Columnar Ltd at 31 December Last

	£
Advertising	920
Bad debts	711
Bank account, overdrawn	1 064
Bank charges	230
Cash in hand	409
Creditors	3 290
Debtors	11 680
Depreciation of plant at 1 January	2 000
Dividend paid	4 500
Discount received	641
Doubtful debts, provision	1 200
Factory power	4 729
Fixtures and fittings, office	2 000
General expenses	687
Insurance	1 146
Interest on loan stock	500
Investment in Ionic Industries Ltd	28 837
Light and heat	595
Loan stock, 10 per cent interest rate	10 000
Plant and machinery	18 000
Purchases of raw material	36 219
Packaging expenses	964
Profit and loss account (unappropriated profit b/d)	7 809
Repairs and renewals to plant	853
Rent	1 571

Balances on the Books of Columnar Ltd at 31 December Last (continued)

Returns outwards	58
Salaries	8 690
Sales	103 662
Share capital	45 000
Stocks, 1 January: finished goods	8 438
raw material	6 118
work in progress	2 147
Transport expenses	1 204
Wages	30 715
Warehouse expenses	2 861
	£349 448

An investigation of the ledger accounts and some conversations with Mr Doric produce the following significant factors which will necessitate the adjustment of the book figures before the accounts are prepared.

1. The following liabilities are to be provided for: factory power £625, rent £429, light and heat £125.
2. Mr Doric says that in his view 80 per cent of the expense for rent, light, heat and insurance should be allocated to the factory, the balance being an administrative cost. The general expenses are to be apportioned one-third as an administration expense and the balance to the factory.
3. The following payments have been made in advance: insurance £196, road fund licences (included in transport expenses) £210.
4. Depreciation is to be provided on the straight line basis at 10 per cent per annum on machinery (pro rata to time) and at 5 per cent per annum on furniture. Mr Doric informs you that plant costing £3000 was purchased on 30 June and has been included in the balance in the books.
5. Stock is taken on 31 December and the stock sheets reveal that closing stocks are: raw material £4683, work in progress £1274, finished goods £7926 and packing materials £217. Work-in-progress stocks contain no overhead expense allocation.
6. Mr Doric has examined the debtors ledger and decides that the provision for doubtful debts should be increased by a further £300.
7. Interest on the loan stock has been paid only up to 30 June last.
8. An analysis of the salaries account shows it to include £5000 paid to the factory manager. Analysis of the wages account shows it to include £6000 paid to the warehousemen and £2800 paid to drivers.
9. Mr Doric says he would like to know whether the factory operation has made a profit separate from the profitability of the trading operation. He has maintained a careful check on the quantity of finished goods transferred from the factory to the finished goods store and estimates its value on the wholesale market to be £80 000. Mr Doric also intends to pay his factory manager a commission of 10 per cent of the factory profit.
10. You decide to provide £2000 for tax on the profit made which is payable in the future, and a final dividend of 10 pence per share.

PROCEDURE

Step 1

To produce the set of accounts, first convert the list of balances to a trial balance in order to check that the book-keeping is accurate. If the credit balances are separated from the main list and then added together, they should total half the total of the whole list. Credit balances are liabilities, capital, accumulated depreciation, sales, and other miscellaneous income. Thus the items remaining in the debit or left-hand column are balances representing assets or costs. It should be remembered that provisions are deducted from assets on the face of the balance sheet and are thus represented in the ledger accounts by credit balances. Armed with this information it is a fairly simple task to compute a trial balance which totals £174 724 on each side.

Trial Balance at 31 December

	Debits (Assets + Expenses) £	Credits (Liabilities + Sales + Provisions + Capital) £
Advertising	920	
Bad debts	711	
Bank account, overdrawn		1 064
Bank charges	230	
Cash in hand	409	
Debtors and creditors	11 680	3 290
Depreciation on plant at 1 January		2 000
Dividend paid	4 500	
Discount received		641
Doubtful debts, provision		1 200
Factory power	4 729	
Fixtures and fittings, office	2 000	
General expenses	687	
Insurance	1 146	
Interest on loan stock	500	
Shares in Ionic Industries Ltd.	28 837	
Light and heat	595	
Loan stock (10 per cent interest rate)		10 000
Plant and machinery	18 000	
Purchases of raw material	36 219	
Packaging expenses	964	
Profit and loss (unappropriated)		7 809
Repairs and renewals	853	
Rent	1 571	
Returns outwards		58
Salaries	8 690	
Sales		103 662
Share capital		45 000
Stocks 1 January: finished goods	8 438	
raw material	6 118	
work in progress	2 147	
Transport expenses	1 204	
Wages	30 715	
Warehouse expenses	2 861	
	£174 724	£174 724

Step 2

The next step is to adjust the balances in the ledgers by the amounts in the notes, so that the amounts to be entered in the accounts will be computed. It is important to make sure that the trial balance still balances debit against credit, after each adjustment. In the examination room many students write the adjustments onto the trial balance in the question. An adjusted trial balance annotated with the adjustments in the question is shown below as step 3.

Note 1. Liabilities to be provided for are accruals. The accounts for factory power, rent, and light and heat will be debited with £625, £429 and £125 respectively, while accrued charges or creditors will be increased in the balance sheet by £1179 to complete the double entry. The costs for the year will therefore be: factory power £5354, transferred to the manufacturing account; rent £2000, apportioned £1600 to the manufacturing account and £400 to the profit and loss account; and light and heat £720 apportioned £576 to the manufacturing account and £144 to the profit and loss account. The ledger account for light and heat would appear as follows:

Dr.		Light and Heat		Cr.
	£			£
31 Dec.		31 Dec.		
Balance (costs recorded)	595	Charge to manufacturing account		576
Accrual c/f	125	Charge to profit and loss account		144
	£720			£720
	(x)	1 Jan. balance b/d	(y)	125

Thus when the bill is received in the next accounting period and debited to the account (x), the credit balance of £125 (y) will automatically reduce the impact of that bill on the costs of that period.

Note 2. This is a simple apportionment. The adjusted amounts for rent, light and heat, and insurance are divided by five, and four-fifths are allocated to the manufacturing account. The remainder will be debited to the profit and loss account. General expenses are treated similarly, but divided by three. Thus the general expenses account is credited with £687 while the manufacturing account and profit and loss account are debited with £458 and £229 respectively.

Dr.		Rent		Cr.
	£			£
Balance b/d	1571	Charge to manufacturing account		1600
Accrual c/f	429	Charge to profit and loss account		400
	£2000			£2000
		Balance b/d		429

Note 3. Payments in advance must be deducted from the recorded costs, since they concern the next accounting period. They should not be debited to the current profit and loss account. An amount of £210 will be carried forward as a debit balance on the transport expenses account (appearing in the balance sheet as a debtor or prepaid expense), while £994 will be debited to the profit and loss account.

In the insurance account, the balance of £1146 will be reduced to £950 as the cost for the year, to be apportioned £760 to the manufacturing account and £190 to the profit and loss account. The debit balance carried forward will be a cost chargeable to the next accounting period. The ledger account will appear as follows:

Dr.		Insurance	Cr.
	£		£
31 Dec.		31 Dec.	
Balance (costs recorded)	1146	Charge to manufacturing account	760
		Charge to profit and loss account	190
		Payment c/f	196
	£1146		£1146
1 Jan. Balance b/d	196		

Note 4. Depreciation on plant, to be charged to the manufacturing account as a factory expense, is to be computed at a rate of 10 per cent per annum on cost. Plant costing £3000 was purchased on 30 June, and will bear depreciation for only a half year, pro rata to time, i.e. £150, while depreciation on the other plant, which cost £15 000, will be £1500 for the year. The manufacturing account is debited and the accumulated depreciation account is credited with £1650, the balance of depreciation to date (£3650) being deducted from the cost of the asset on the face of the balance sheet.

Dr.		Depreciation on Plant	Cr.
	£		£
Balance c/f	3650	Balance b/d	2000
		Charge to profit and loss account	1650
	£3650		£3650
		Balance b/d	3650

Depreciation on fixtures and fittings will be provided in the sum of £100 (5 per cent of £2000), resulting in entries similar to those above except that the profit and loss account will be charged (debited). The fixtures may be new, since they have not been depreciated in previous years.

Dr.		Depreciation on Fixtures and Fittings	Cr.
	£		£
Balance c/f	100	Charge to profit and loss account	100
		Balance b/d	100

Note 5. The closing stock figures are derived from a physical check of the stock quantities as recorded and priced on the stock sheets. The usage of raw material, or the cost of goods sold, is computed by adding opening stock to purchases (or production) and deducting closing stock. This sum is worked out in the manufacturing and trading accounts and means that opening stocks are debited to those accounts (credit the stock account, thus closing it) while closing stocks are credited to the manufacturing account or trading account (debit the stock account, thus re-opening it and leaving a debit balance on the account to be recorded as an asset in the balance sheet). The closing stock is often credited to the manufacturing account by deducting it from the debit side. With a columnar approach it is a

deduction. This set of postings is often called a 'stock adjustment'. Such an adjustment is needed in the manufacturing account to convert the figure for factory cost incurred during the period to the cost of production completed during the period. The opening stock of work in progress (partly completed work in the factory) is added to factory cost during the period, and the closing stock figure for work in progress is deducted, so that the cost of work completed during the period is isolated, for transfer to the finished goods account or direct to the trading account on the debit side.

Note 6. The provision for bad and doubtful debts is made to charge the profit and loss account in one period with the cost of debts of that period, which might go bad in a subsequent period. It is yet another example of matching cost with revenue. The profit and loss account is debited, and the provision is credited and carried forward as a credit balance which is shown in the balance sheet as a deduction from the current asset, debtors. When in the next accounting period bad debts are incurred, they are written off to the provision account (credit the debtor and debit the provision), where the balance carried forward on the credit side is waiting to neutralize their effect on the current profit and loss account. The amount of the provision made is a matter for estimate. If the estimate is wrong, an over- or under-provision will arise which will distort the current profit figure.

Dr.		Provision for Doubtful Debts	Cr.
	£		£
31 Dec.		1 Jan.	
Bad debts written off	711	Balance b/d (old provision)	1200
		31 Dec.	
Increased provision c/f	1500	Charge to profit and loss account	1011
	£2211		£2211
		1 Jan.	
		Balance b/d	1500

The charge to the profit and loss account is this year's provision of £1500 less last year's provision no longer required, £489 (£1200 − 711) which equals £1011.

Alternatively, bad debts could be debited direct to the profit and loss account so that the increased provision of £300 could be credited to the provision account and debited to profit and loss as a separate item.

$$[£711 + £300 = £1011]$$

Note 7. The annual interest on the loan stock is £1000, but only £500 has been paid. Thus £500 of unpaid interest should be charged to the profit and loss account (a debit) and credited to the creditors or accrued charges, which will show up in the balance sheet as a current liability.

Note 8. The factory manager's salary of £5000 should be charged to the factory overhead expenses in the manufacturing account, while the balance of salaries are debited to administration expenses in the profit and loss account. Warehouse wages and driver's wages are charged to selling and distribution expenses, and the balance on the wages account is debited to the manufacturing account.

Note 9. As Mr Doric can supply a wholesale price for the finished goods transferred from the factory to the stores, it is possible to set the cost of finished production against this figure to compute a notional profit for the factory. The profit is a debit item in the manufacturing account, and is credited to the profit and loss account along with the trading profit and other miscellaneous income. The factory manager's commission has not yet been paid, and so must appear in the balance sheet among the creditors, as well as being debited to the manufacturing account. The amount of 10 per cent on the profit will equal one-ninth of the profit remaining after charging the commission.

$$£3365 \div 10 = £337$$
$$£3028 \div 9 = £337$$

Note 10. Tax is an appropriation of profit, so the amount set aside to meet future tax will be debited to the appropriation account and credited to a provision for future tax account, the balance of which appears on the balance sheet with the current liabilities until it is paid.

A dividend of 10 pence per share (£4500) must be provided—debit the appropriation account and show the credit on the balance sheet as a current liability.

Once the adjustments have been made to the figures in the ledgers, the accounts can be prepared.

Step 3

As a matter of examination technique the adjustments can be entered onto the trial balance given in the question. Check the annotated adjustments onto the trial balance shown below, checking debit against credit. Note that certain entries such as depreciation and appropriations for tax and dividend can be entered below the total but in the appropriate column to maintain the all-important balance.

Trial Balance (including adjustments in brackets annotated to the example)

	Debits £	Credits £	
Advertising	920		
Bad debts (6) W/O to P/L	711		
Bank account, overdrawn		1 064	
Bank charges	230		
Cash in hand	409		
Debtors (2) + 196 + 210	11 680		
Creditors		3 290	(1) + 1179
Depreciation on plant		2 000	(4) + 1650
Dividend paid (10) + 4500	4 500		
Discount received		641	
Doubtful debts provision		1 200	(6) + 300
(6) W/O to P/L + 300	—		
Factory power (1) + 625	4 729		
Fixtures and fittings	2 000		
General expenses	687		
(Manf. a/c 458 + P/L 229)			
Insurance (2) minus 196	1 146		
(Manf. a/c 760 and P/L 190)			

Trial Balance (including adjustments in brackets annotated to the example) (continued)

	Debits £	Credits £	
Interest (7) + 500	500		(7) + 500 B/S
Shares in Ionic Industries Ltd	28 837		
Light and heat (1) + 125	595		
(Manf. a/c 576 and P/L 144)			
Loan stock		10 000	
Plant	18 000		
Purchases of raw material	36 219		
Packaging expenses	964		
Unappropriated profit b/d		7 809	
Repairs and renewals	853		
Rent (1) + 429	1 571		
(Manf. a/c 1600 and P/L 400)			
Returns outwards		58	
Salaries	8 690		
Sales		103 662	
Share capital		45 000	
Stocks 1 January:			
Finished goods	8 438		
Raw materials	6 118		
Work in progress	2 147		
Transport expenses (2) minus 210	1 204		
Wages (8) apportion	30 715		
Warehouse expenses	2 861		
	£174 724	£174 724	
Depreciation (4):			
Manf. a/c	1 650		
P/L a/c	100	100	B/S as fixtures
Closing stock (5) B/S	14 100	4683	Manf. a/c
		1274	Manf. a/c
		7926	Trading a/c
		117	P/L
Managers' commission (9)			
P/L	337	337	B/S as current liability
Appropriation a/c (10):			
Tax	2 000	2000	B/S as current liability
Dividend	4 500	4500	B/S as current liability

Note: All adjustments have been made and the debits still equal the credits. The accounts should now balance if figures from the trial balance are entered into the statement correctly and in the right place.

An alternative method is to enter the adjustments in the appropriate column of an 'extended trial balance' and draft the income statement and balance sheet therefrom. This alternative self-balancing method is often used by the practising accountant, but is not suitable as an examination technique.

Trial Balance as at 31 December

	1 Debit	2 Credit	3 Prepaid	4 Accruals
	Balances		Provisions	
Advertising	920			
Bad debts	711			
Commission owed	—	—		
Doubtful debts, provision		1 200		
Bank account, overdrawn		1 064		
Bank charges	230			
Cash in hand	409			
Debtors	11 680			
Creditors		3 290		
Depreciation, plant		2 000		
Dividend paid	4 500			
Discount received		641		
Factory power	4 729			625
Fixtures and fittings, office	2 000			
Fixtures and fittings, office, depreciation	—	—		
General expenses	687			
Insurance	1 146		196	
Interest on loan stock	500			
Shares in Ionic Industries Ltd	28 837			
Light and heat	595			125
Loan stock		10 000		
Plant	18 000			
Purchases of raw material	36 219			
Packaging expenses	964			
Profit and loss (unappropriated)		7 809		
Repairs and renewals	853			
Rent	1 571			429
Returns outwards		58		
Taxation outwards	—	—		
Salaries	8 690			
Sales		103 662		
Share capital		45 000		
Stocks. 1 January: finished goods	8 438			
raw material	6 118			
work in progress	2 147			
Transport expenses	1 204		210	
Wages	30 715			
Warehouse expenses	2 861			
	£174 724	£174 724	406	1179

5 Expense	6 Income	7 Asset	8 Liability
Income Statement		*Balance Sheet*	
Expense	Income	Asset	Liability
920			
711			
337			337
300			1 500
			1 064
230			
		409	
		11 680	
			3 290
1 650			3 650
9 000			4 500
	641		
5 354			
		2 000	
100			100
687			
950			
1 000			500
		28 837	
720			
			10 000
		18 000	
36 219			
747		217	
			7 809
853			
2 000			
	58		
2 000			2 000
8 690			
	103 662		
			45 000
8 438	7 926	7 926	
6 118	4 683	4 683	
2 147	1 274	1 274	
994			
30 715			
2 861			
123 741	118 244	75 026	79 750

Note 1. Entries in columns 3–8 cross-cast on each line to equal the entries in columns 1 and 2.

Note 2. The income statement columns carry all the entries for manufacturing, trading, profit and loss and appropriation accounts.

Note 3. The difference between the income and expense is profit retained, in this case a negative figure, since capital is depleted. Drawings exceed profit for the year.

Note 4. Closing stocks are credited to the income statement and debited to the balance sheet.

Note 5. Provisions for commission, taxation and interest are entered in the balance sheet liability columns, to balance the income statement entry.

Note 6. Expenses, assets and prepayments are equal to income, liabilities and accruals. This proves that the adjustments have been correctly made and that debits still equal credits, so the financial statements can now be written out.

£
123 741
75 026
406
£199 173
118 244
79 750
1 179
£199 173

Step 4

Enter the figures from the trial balance onto the accounting statements.

*Columnar Ltd. Manufacturing, Trading and Profit and Loss Accounts
for the Year ended 31 December*

		£	£
Manufacturing	Raw material opening stock	6 118	
Account	Add purchases less returns	36 161	
		42 279	
	Less closing stock	4 683	
	Cost of material used	37 596	
	Labour	21 915	
	Prime cost		59 511
	Add opening stock of work in progress	2 147	
	Less closing stock of work in progress	1 274	873
	Prime cost of completed production		60 384
	Factory overhead expenses:		
	Power	5 354	
	Rent	1 600	
	Insurance	760	
	Light and heat	576	
	Plant repairs	853	
	Plant depreciation	1 650	
	General expenses	458	
	Factory manager's salary	5 000	
	Factory manager's commission	337	16 588
	Cost of production		76 972
	Factory profit carried to profit and loss account		3 028
	Value of completed production on wholesale market		£80 000
Trading	Sales		103 662
Account	Opening stock of finished goods	8 438	
	Add completed production transferred to stores	80 000	
		88 438	
	Less closing stock of finished goods	7 926	
	Cost of goods sold		80 512
	Gross profit		£23 150

Note: Usually the cost of goods produced is transferred to the finished goods stock account, and from there to the trading account as the cost of goods sold. In this example the market value of completed production has been introduced to enable a factory profit to be computed.

		£	£	£
Profit and	Gross profit			23 150
Loss	Factory profit			3 028
Account	Discount received			641
	Total revenue			26 819
	Less administration expenses:			
	Salaries	3 690		
	Rent	400		
	Light and heat	144		
	Insurance	190		
	General expenses	229		
	Depreciation on fixtures	100	4 753	
	Less selling and distribution expenses:			
	Advertising	920		
	Packing net of closing stock	747		
	Transport expenses	3 794		
	Warehouse expenses	8 861	14 322	
	Less financial expenses:			
	Bank charges	230		
	Bad and doubtful debts	1 011		
	Loan interest	1 000	2 241	21 316
	Net profit			5 503
Appropriation	Undistributed profits b/d			7 809
Account	(from previous year)			
				13 312
	Provision for taxation		2 000	
	Dividend interim paid		4 500	
	Final provided		4 500	11 000
	Unappropriated profit c/f			£2 312

Columnar Ltd Balance Sheet as at 31 December

	£	£	£
Capital:			
45 000 ordinary shares of £1 each, authorized, issued and fully paid			45 000
Unappropriated profit			2 312
Equity interest			£47 312

	Cost	Accumulated depreciation to date	Net
Fixed assets:			
Plant and machinery	18 000	3 650	14 350
Fixtures and fittings	2 000	100	1 900
	20 000	3 750	16 250
Investment in Ionic Industries Ltd			28 837
			£45 087

Columnar Ltd Balance Sheet as at 31 December (continued)

	£	£	£
Current assets:			
Stock (see note 5 below)		14 100	
Debtors	11 680		
Less provision	1 500	10 180	
Prepayments		406	
Cash in hand		409	
		25 095	
Less current liabilities:			
Creditors	3 290		
Interest outstanding	500		
Commission owed	337		
Accrued expenses	1 179		
Taxation due	2 000		
Dividend	4 500		
Bank overdraft	1 064	12 870	
Working capital			12 225
			57 312
Less long-term liabilities:			
10 per cent loan stock			10 000
Net assets			£47 312

A careful survey of the accounts of Columnar Ltd will bring to light some interesting points.

1. A dividend has been paid on the ordinary shares at a rate of 20 per cent, or 20 pence per share, while profit for the year after tax is insufficient to cover this dividend, and consequently the equity interest in the business has been depleted. If a loss is made in any one year it is still legal to pay a dividend out of the general reserves as they represent past profits reinvested in the business.
2. There is a large investment in another company, Ionic Industries Ltd, but there appears to be no income from this investment during the year. It follows that the market value of an apparently unprofitable investment may have fallen below its book value, so the balance sheet may give a false impression of this asset.
3. Although there are transport expenses, including drivers' wages and road fund licences, in the profit and loss account, there are no vehicles shown as assets in the balance sheet. Perhaps it will be discovered on further investigation that the vehicles are hired, and thus have no place as assets in the balance sheet.
4. The ratio of gross profit to sales is £23 150 ÷ £103 662 × 100/1, which is calculated at 22 per cent. This ratio reflects the profit margin on sales, and if it is different from the mark-up used to compute prices, it points to an error in the accounts such as a wrong stock figure or some sales made but not recorded. The significance of this ratio will be developed in a later chapter. For example, a 25 per cent mark-up added to cost as a profit margin will show up as a 20 per cent gross profit on sales.
5. Finished goods are transferred from the factory after a factory profit has been added to them. If the closing stock of finished goods is shown at a figure which includes this profit element, a provision must be made. No profit can be taken until it is earned.

SEMINAR EXERCISES 6

1. The trial balance of John Doe, a baker, at 31 December was:

	£	£
Drawings	7 650	
Sales		140 500
Investment and loan interest		2 380
Purchases of raw materials	34 630	
Manufacturing wages	39 720	
Repairs and renewals	1 580	
Rent	2 600	
Heat and light	3 574	
Power	8 600	
Office expenses	2 140	
Telephone	662	
Supervisory wages	8 656	
Office salaries	5 460	
Selling and distribution expenses	10 400	
Land, at cost	8 500	
Factory etc. buildings, at cost	25 000	
Depreciation on buildings		8 000
Plant and machinery, at cost	54 000	
Depreciation on plant and machinery		22 000
Investments at cost	8 000	
Opening stocks 1 January:		
Raw materials	7 800	
Finished goods	21 600	29 400
Debtors	19 600	
Loans	5 000	
Creditors		27 970
Capital account		68 400
Provision for doubtful debts		750
Insurance	1 460	
Bank overdraft		6 632
	£276 632	£276 632

Notes

(a) Closing stocks (at cost) were:

	£
Raw materials	8 240
Finished goods	23 420

(b) Rent for the ½ year to 31 March next year had been paid, £2040. The rented building is used 80 per cent for manufacturing and 20 per cent for administration.

(c) The following accruals were estimated:

	£
Heat and light	140
Power	430
Telephone	31

(d) Insurance had been paid:

2 Jan. whole year	340
24 June whole year	642

(e) Office repairs were analysed at £83.
(f) The factory occupies four-fifths of the buildings, and this fraction is applied to insurances, as well as to heat and light to apportion these costs.
(g) Bad debt provision is to be adjusted to 5 per cent of debtors.
(h) Depreciation on cost is 5 per cent on buildings and 10 per cent on plant and machinery, using the straight line method.

Prepare a manufacturing, trading and profit and loss account for the year ended and balance sheet as at 31 December.

2. Paul Over carries on business in the knitting industry. Being a firm believer in the delegation of authority, he has organized his business into two parts, manufacturing and selling. Each part is under the authority of a manager, who receives a bonus of 12½ per cent of the profits after charging the bonus of his department. Finished goods are transferred from the factory, run by Mr Smith, to the sales department, run by Mr Jones, at cost (exclusive of manager's bonus) plus 20 per cent. The trial balance of the firm as at 30 April is as follows:

	£	£
Capital account, Paul Over		95 000
Freehold factory at cost (including land £27 000)	75 000	
Plant and machinery at cost	18 600	
Salesmen's cars	9 900	
Provision for depreciation b/d, factory		7 820
Provision for depreciation b/d, plant		6 900
Provision for depreciation b/d, cars		5 650
Stocks as at 1 May last year		
Raw material at cost	24 200	
Finished goods at transfer price	7 800	
Finished goods stock provision		1 300
Trade debtors and creditors	14 200	15 600
Provision for doubtful debts		1 120
Raw materials purchased	125 600	
Cash discount received		600
Wages and salaries	71 200	
Insurance	4 210	
Postage and stationery	1 120	
Factory power	1 808	
Sundry expenses	7 320	
Maintenance of machinery	615	
Motor expenses	1 206	
Sales		255 000
Bank	26 211	
	£388 990	£388 990

The following information is relevant:

(a) Stocks at 30 April were: raw material at cost, £28 000; finished goods at transfer value, £8400.
(b) Analysis of the wages and salaries account shows that salaries paid to Smith and Jones were £4500 and £4200 respectively, that Paul's drawing of £6600 had been debited to the account and that sales department wages and salaries were £7100.

(c) Depreciation is computed on the factory building, plant and cars at 2 per cent, 10 per cent and 25 per cent on cost, respectively.

(d) Expenses common to the factory and the sales department are to be apportioned in the ratio 4 : 1, e.g. insurance, postage and sundries.

(e) An invoice for £490 for fuel oil delivered to the factory has not been entered in the books, and insurance paid in advance is £600.

(f) Bad debts totalling £298 are to be written off. These debts concern a previous accounting period and provision has already been made for them. The provision for doubtful debts is to stand at 0.5 per cent of sales.

Required:

(i) Prepare a revenue account for Paul Over for the year ended 30 April showing prime and factory cost, and the profit made by each department.

(ii) Prepare a balance sheet as at that date.

(iii) State one serious flaw in the system for paying bonus to the factory manager.

Note: Calculations to the nearest £1.

3. Andy Pinder is in business manufacturing and selling light fittings, and operates from a small factory on the outskirts of a large town. A trial balance extracted from his books on 31 May was as follows:

	£	£
Capital account, Andy Pinder		57 112
Drawings account, Andy Pinder	4 220	
Cash at bank and in hand	4 384	
Sundry trade debtors and creditors	17 732	5 866
Land and buildings at cost	25 000	
Plant and machinery at cost	20 000	
Plant and machinery depreciation		10 000
Motor vehicles at cost	2 604	
Motor vehicles at depreciation		1 500
Fixtures and fittings at cost	3 438	
Fixtures and fittings depreciation		1 470
Stock 1 June last year: raw materials	17 456	
work in progress	15 900	
finished goods	18 700	
Provision for doubtful debts		
Bad debts	181	356
Insurance	1 432	
Wages	17 020	
Factory power	4 511	
Light and heat	4 120	
Maintenance	3 114	
Salaries	15 200	
Returns inwards and outwards	263	518
Advertising	1 400	
Transport expenses	1 670	
Bank charges	415	
Sundry expenses	800	
Purchases, sales	52 880	123 788
10 per cent loan account, Lite Finance Ltd		30 000
Discounts received		1 830
	£232 440	£232 440

The following notes are relevant:

(a) Provision for doubtful debts is to be adjusted to a figure equal to 10 per cent of debtors (to nearest £1).

(b) Depreciation is to be provided, using the reducing balance method and applying rates of 15 per cent on plant, 25 per cent on vehicles and 10 per cent on fixtures and fittings.

(c) At 31 May:

Electricity accrued was £52

Insurance prepaid was £107

Stocks were valued at:

raw material	£18 760
work in progress	£14 900
finished goods	£19 100

(d) Light and heat, insurance, and sundry expenses were to be apportioned in the ratio 3 : 1 between the factory and administrative overheads. An amount of £2200 posted to the salaries account concerns the factory manager.

(e) Included in the sales are goods which cost £338 and which have been charged out with a profit margin of £78 added. It has been agreed that these goods will be accepted back from the customer without charge.

(f) Loan interest has not yet been paid this year.

Prepare, in good vertical form, manufacturing, trading and profit and loss accounts for the year ended 31 May, and a balance sheet as at that date.

4. Sally and Denise (Hair Styles) Ltd runs a small chain of hairdressing salons. Their books of account show the following balances at 30 April 19-8 (in £000).

	Debit £	Credit £
Cash in bank	435	
Cash in hand	25	
Cleaning expenses	160	
Creditors		590
Debtors	250	
Directors' salaries	40	
Equipment and machines, cost	1500	
Equipment and machines, provision for depreciation		300
Freehold premises, cost	860	
Freehold premises, provision for depreciation		80
Hairdressing materials, shampoos etc.	400	
Heat, light and power	480	
Receipts		4510
Rent	490	
Reserves		540
Salon expenses	920	
Salon furnishings, cost	1460	
Salon furnishings, provision for depreciation		430
Share capital, ordinary shares of £1		2000
Stock of materials, 1 May 19-7	140	
Telephone and office expenses	210	
Wages	1080	
	£8450	£8450

The following information is also relevant:

(a) Depreciation is charged on fixed assets on a straight line basis at the following rates: buildings (but not land), 2 per cent p.a.; equipment and machines, 20 per cent p.a.; salon furnishings, 10 per cent p.a. Freehold premises is considered to be made up of land £360 000, and buildings, £500 000.

(b) Included in rent are half a year's rent for the main salon for the period April–September 19-8, £84 000, and a quarter's rent for some other rented properties for April–June 19-8, £60 000.

(c) Closing stock at cost is £160 000.

(d) Wages outstanding amounted to £40 000.

(e) Some of the customers who owe the company money are proving difficult to trace, and the company wishes to provide for doubtful debts of £12 000.

(f) Some of the closing stock has deteriorated in store, and £8000 write-down is required.

(g) Corporation tax of £90 000 is to be provided, and a dividend of 6p per ordinary share is proposed.

Prepare a profit and loss account for the company for the year ended 30 April 19-8, and a balance sheet as at that date. Comment on the company's proposed dividend policy.

5. Karl August PLC are garment manufacturers, and their trial balance at 31 December 19-8 was as follows (in £000).

	Debit £	Credit £
Share capital		3 000
Share premium		1 715
Profit and loss account, balance at 1 January 19-8		980
Long term loan—8 per cent debenture, redeemable 19-9–20-3		2 000
Stocks at 1 January 19-8: raw materials	1 810	
work in progress	935	
finished goods	1 280	
Purchases of raw materials	6 035	
Creditors		1 805
Land, at cost	600	
Factory and office building, at cost	1 750	
Factory, provision for depreciation, 1 January 19-8		175
Plant and machinery, at cost	1 260	
Plant, provision for depreciation, 1 January 19-8		400
Motor vehicles, at cost	420	
Motor vehicles, provision for depreciation, 1 January 19-8		180
Sales, less returns		11 275
Debtors	2 420	
Factory wages, direct labour	1 190	
Factory wages, other	480	
Factory heat, light and power	555	
Factory overhead expenses	892	
Repairs and renewals	410	
Distribution expenses	635	
Selling expenses	275	
Administration expenses	292	
Interest	80	
Bank balance	196	
Cash in hand	15	
	£21 530	£21 530

The following items are relevant:

(a) Stocks at 31 December were valued at:

raw materials	£1 720 000
work in progress	£995 000
finished goods	£1 465 000

All stocks are at cost.

(b) Depreciation is calculated as follows: on factory and office buildings at 2 per cent per annum on cost; on plant and machinery at 10 per cent per annum on cost; on motor vehicles at 25 per cent per annum on reducing balance. Factory and office buildings are regarded as six-sevenths factory; motor vehicles as 75 per cent for distribution and 25 per cent sales.

(c) Although no provision for bad or doubtful debts had been made previously, it is considered necessary now to write off a debt of £20 000 and to make a provision of 1 per cent of the balance for doubtful debts.

(d) No entries have yet been made in the books of the company in respect of the following items to accrue at the year end: electricity account (December) £32 000, repairs to machines £8000, salesmen's travelling expenses (December) £6000, haulage contractor (for delivery of finished goods) £7000, director's remuneration £25 000.

(e) In addition, a consignment of raw materials was received between Christmas and New Year, and due to the factory being closed, was stored in the gatekeeper's garage. The invoice for £17 000 for the consignment has not hitherto been recorded, and the goods were not counted on the stocktake at year end.

(f) Rates of £96 000 have been paid in respect of the half-year from 1 October 19-8. In the accounts these have been divided between factory overheads and administration expenses in the proportion 5 : 1.

(g) Annual insurance premiums of £90 000 were paid for the year commencing 1 May 19-8. These were apportioned between factory overhead distribution expenses and administration expenses in the ratio 4 : 1 : 1.

(h) A commission on profit is payable to certain key management staff of the company. A provision of 10 per cent of the company's profit *after* charging this commission is to be made, and this will be shared in agreed proportions between certain senior managers.

(i) As a result of the profit for the year, the tax charge, payable on 1 October 19-9, is provisionally estimated at £50 000.

(j) The directors propose a dividend of 2p for each ordinary share of 50p payable a month after the annual general meeting, if approved by the shareholders.

Prepare the manufacturing, trading and profit and loss account for Karl August PLC for the year ended 31 December 19-8, and the balance sheet of the company as at that date.

REVIEW QUESTIONS 4

1. The following final balance was extracted from the books of Yeats, a trader, at 31 December 19-9.

	£	£
Carriage inwards	631	
Capital account at 1 January 19-9		50 000
Motor vans	20 000	
Stock at 1 January 19-9	16 400	
Balance at bank	11 686	
Purchases	159 369	
Sales		222 400
Trade debtors	29 000	
Trade creditors		15 760
Rent	5 608	
Salaries	35 040	
General expenses	4 472	
Motor expenses	2 560	
Discounts allowed	4 040	
Discounts received		3 760
Insurance	1 760	
Bad debts	3 040	
Provision for doubtful debts 1 January 19-9		800
Provision for depreciation on vans		6 000
Drawings	5 000	
Profit on sale of van		600
Returns inwards	714	
	£299 320	£299 320

The following matters are to be taken into account:

(a) After examination of the sales ledger, it was decided to:

    (i) write off a bad debt of £200;

    (ii) make a specific provision in the accounts for the following doubtful debts
    £500 from Wordsworth
    £300 from Coleridge;

    (iii) make a general provision of 5 per cent on the other debtors.

(b) Goods unsold at 31 December 19-9 had cost £20 160 but Yeats expected to sell them at £23 247.

(c) Salaries accrued at 31 December 19-9 amounted to £3200.

(d) The rent for the premises is £4000 a year payable quarterly in arrears but the instalment due on 31 December 19-9 was not paid until 15 January in the next year.

(e) Insurance paid in advance at 31 December 19-9 amounted to £200.

(f) Depreciation is to be provided for on the new motor vans at the rate of 20 per cent per annum straight line on cost.

(g) General expenses include £306 relating to the telephone account which is made up of
    Rent—three months in advance from 30 November 19-9 at £42
    Calls—three months ended 30 November 19-9 at £264

(h) It has been agreed with the Inland Revenue that 25 per cent of the motor expenses relate to private use.

Prepare a trading and profit and loss account for the year to 31 December 19-9, and a balance sheet as at that date.

2. Mr Rusty trades as a retailer of hardware products. Most goods in which he trades are purchased from various suppliers in a finished form, but, in addition, a separate department of the firm manufactures several types of brushes from bought-in raw materials and, when finished, the brushes are transferred for resale to the shop, at agreed transfer prices. No brushes are sold other than through the shop. Some sales made by Mr Rusty are on credit terms.

The book-keeper draws up the following trial balance at 30 June 19-2.

Mr Rusty—Trial Balance as at 30 June 19-2

	£	£
Capital		70 800
Drawings	26 000	
Long-term loan (15 per cent interest)		24 000
Fixtures and fittings:		
Cost	80 000	
Accumulated depreciation to 30 June 19-2		40 000
Motor vehicles:		
Cost	20 800	
Accumulated depreciation to 30 June 19-2		6 000
Stock at 1 July 19-1 (at cost):		
Raw materials for brushmaking	4 000	
Finished brushes held in shop	2 000	
Other goods	34 000	
Sales ledger balance (debtors)	12 000	
Purchase ledger balances (creditors)		9 700
Bank balance	10 000	
Sales		400 000
Purchases: raw materials for brushmaking	86 000	
other goods	230 000	
Wages	31 400	
Rent	4 400	
Heat and light	2 100	
Motor expenses	1 080	
Repairs and renewals	1 400	
Interest on loan	3 600	
Bank charges	200	
Accountancy charges	100	
Sundry expenses	1 420	
	£550 500	£550 500

Notes:

(i) At 30 June 19-1 the firm owned only one motor van (A) which was sold during the year for £1200 and replaced by a new vehicle (B) costing £12 000. Both transactions have been posted to the motor vehicles (cost account).

(ii) Depreciation is provided using the straight line method over the following periods: motor vehicles—five years fixtures and fittings—ten years.
A full year's depreciation is charged in the year of acquisition and none in the year of disposal.

(iii) A trade debt of £2000 is not expected to be realized and a provision is required.

(iv) The agreed transfer price for brushes produced was £4 per brush. The number of brushes transferred to the shop was 25 000.

(v) Wages include those of the only brushmaking employee, who is paid £100 per week plus a bonus of £200 paid in May. In addition, he is entitled to commission of 10 per cent on the annual profit of his department after charging such commission.

(vi) On the basis of floor space, the apportionment of rent and heat and light to the brushmaking department is 25 per cent.

(vii) Rent includes a prepayment of £400.

(viii) Accruals at 30 June 19-2 were:

	£
Electricity and gas bills	300
Accountancy charges	200

(ix) Stocks at 30 June 19-2 were:

	£
Brushmaking raw materials (cost)	8 000
Finished goods (at transfer price)	3 000
Other goods (cost)	43 000

(a) Prepare a manufacturing account for the brush department, a trading account for the shop, and a profit and loss account, all for the year ended 30 June 19-2.

(b) Prepare a balance sheet as at 30 June 19-2.

Your workings should be shown.

3. The following trial balance has been extracted from the books of Grumbleweed Ltd:

Trial Balance as at 31 December 19-2

	Debit £	Credit £
Ordinary shares		200 000
Preference shares		100 000
Profit and loss account, 1 January 19-2		21 000
Plant and machinery: cost	300 000	
Office equipment: cost	205 000	
Motor vehicles: cost	100 000	
Accumulated depreciation at 1 January 19-2		
Plant and machinery		80 000
Office equipment		44 500
Motor vehicles		40 000
Debtors/creditors	250 000	178 000
General provision for bad debts at 1 January 19-2		500
Manufacturing wages	250 000	
Stocks at 1 January 19-2: raw materials	35 000	
work in progress	63 000	
finished goods	125 000	
Purchase of raw materials	260 000	
Sales		1 300 000
Bank balance		30 000

127

Trial Balance as at 31 December 19-2 (continued)

	Debit £	Credit £
Carriage outwards	25 000	
Directors' salaries	80 000	
Rent	60 000	
Advertising	95 000	
Insurance	5 900	
Office salaries	83 000	
Light and heat	8 000	
Factory power	10 000	
Bank interest	3 500	
Interim dividend on preference shares	5 000	
General administration expenses	30 600	
	£1 994 000	£1 994 000

(a) Depreciation is to be provided on the fixed assets as follows:

Plant and machinery	15 per cent on cost
Office equipment	10 per cent on cost
Motor vehicles	25 per cent written-down value

(b) Prepayment of rent £6000.
Prepayment of insurance £500.
(c) Amount owing for light and heat £1000.
(d) Rent, light and heat and insurance to be apportioned ⅚ to the factor and ⅙ to office expenses.
(e) The bad debt provision is to be 1 per cent of the debtors.
(f) The share capital (all authorized and fully paid) is:

400 000 ordinary shares of 50p
100 000 10 per cent preference shares of £1

A dividend of 10p per share is to be provided on the ordinary shares, together with the second half-year preference dividend. Ignore ACT.
(g) A staff bonus is to be provided at 10 per cent of the net profit (before tax) after having charged the bonus. Directors' salaries include the production director at £15 000.
(h) Corporation tax of £100 000 is to be provided.
(i) The trade price of manufactured goods transferred to the trading account is £700 000. Provision is to be made in these accounts for any profit on finished goods remaining unsold at the year end.
(j) Stocks at cost at 31 December 19-2 were as follows:

	£
Raw materials	28 000 at cost
Work in progress	47 000 at cost
Finished goods	100 000 at transfer price

Prepare from the above trial balance, for the directors of the company only, a manufacturing, trading and profit and loss account and profit and loss appropriation account for the year ended 31 December 19-2 and a balance sheet as at that date, having first adjusted for points (a) to (j) above.

4. John Stokes trades as a manufacturer of electrical time switches from a small factory. He is proud of his status as a sole trader and of the success and financial stability of his business.

Trial Balance of John Stokes and Co., as at 31 December 19-6

	Debit £	Credit £
Drawings	22 650	
Sales		417 900
Investment income and loan interest		6 480
Purchase of raw materials	103 560	
Manufacturing wages	119 790	
Repairs and renewals	5 550	
Rent	7 500	
Heat and light	11 250	
Power	25 500	
Office expenses	6 600	
Telephone	1 950	
Supervisory wages	26 100	
Office salaries	16 050	
Selling and distribution expenses	31 800	
Land at cost	24 000	
Factory etc., buildings at cost	72 000	
Depreciation on buildings		24 000
Plant at cost	168 000	
Depreciation on plant		72 000
Investments at cost	30 000	
Loans	17 470	
Stocks, 1 January 19-6:		
raw materials	23 700	
finished goods	65 400	89 100
Debtors	59 280	
Creditors		86 370
Capital account		211 200
Provision for doubtful debts		2 550
Insurances	3 660	
Bank overdraft		21 810
Overdraft interest	500	
	£842 310	£842 310

Notes:
(a) Closing stocks (at cost) were:

	£
Raw materials	25 260
Finished goods	69 720

(b) Rent for the year to 31 March 19-7 had been paid £6120.
(c) The following accruals were estimated:

	£
Accountancy fee	1000
Heat and light	405
Power	1230
Telephone	75

(d) Insurance had been paid—annual premiums on

1 January 19-6	£960
30 June 19-6	£1872

(e) Office repairs were analysed at £225.

(f) The factory occupies four-fifths of the buildings, and this fraction also applies to insurances, as well as to rent and to heat and light.
(g) Bad debt provision is to be adjusted to 5 per cent of debtors.
(h) Depreciation on cost is 5 per cent on buildings and 10 per cent on plant and machinery, using the straight line method.
(i) The loans are repayable to John Stokes in ten years' time. The investments are a 10 per cent shareholding in a supplier.

Prepare manufacturing, trading and profit and loss accounts for the year ended and balance sheet as at 31 December 19-6.

5. Automatic Amplifiers PLC operate from a medium-sized factory near London. The following trial balance has been extracted from the books of the company.

Trial Balance as at 31 December 19-3

	Debit £	Credit £
Ordinary share		400 000
Preference shares		200 000
Profit and loss account, 1 January 19-3		42 475
Office block (freehold land £40 000)	170 000	
Plant and machinery: cost	730 000	
Office equipment: cost	110 000	
Motor vehicles: cost	200 000	
Accumulated depreciation at 1 January 19-3:		
Plant and machinery		224 500
Office equipment		24 500
Motor vehicles		80 000
Debtors/creditors	500 000	356 226
General provision for bad debts		1 000
Manufacturing wages	503 400	
Stocks at 1 January 19-3, at cost:		
Raw materials	60 000	
Work in progress	126 000	
Finished goods	260 000	
Transport expenses	85 013	
Returns inwards	15 106	
Purchases of raw materials	528 600	
Sales		2 610 147
Bank balance		60 020
Directors' salaries	60 114	
Maintenance of plant and buildings	28 102	
Rent	90 234	
Advertising	192 048	
Insurance	20 116	
Office salaries	166 013	
Light and heat	46 027	
Factory power	30 014	
Bank interest	5 070	
Interim dividend on preference shares	10 000	
General administration expenses	63 011	
	£3 998 868	£3 998 868

Further information is as follows:

(a) Depreciation is to be provided on the fixed assets as follows:

Plant and machinery	15 per cent on cost
Office equipment	10 per cent on cost
Motor vehicles	25 per cent on written-down value

New office block built during the year—2 per cent straight line.

(b) Prepayment of rent at 31 December 19-3 was £819.

(c) An insurance premium for public liability cover in the sum of £3360 was paid for the year to 31 March 19-4.

The amount owing for light and heat is £1214 at 31 December 19-3.

(d) Rent, light and heat and insurance to be apportioned ⅚ to the factory and ⅙ to office expenses.

(e) The bad debt provision to be 1 per cent of the debtors.

(f) The share capital (all authorized and fully paid) is:

> 800 000 ordinary shares of 50p each
> 200 000 10 per cent preference shares of £1 each

A dividend of 22.5p per share is to be provided on the ordinary shares, together with the second half-year preference dividend. Ignore ACT.

(g) The production director acts as factory manager, his salary being £20 000. Office salaries include amounts paid to sales representatives £64 237.

(h) Corporation tax of £100 000 is to be provided.

(i) The trade price of completed amplifiers transferred to the stores during the year was 1500 amplifiers at £1000 each.

(j) Stocks at cost or trade price at 31 December 19-3 were as follows:

	£
Raw materials at cost	56 200
Work in progress at cost	47 190
Finished goods at trade price	100 000 (100 amplifiers)

Note that this year by a change of accounting policy the closing stock of finished goods is shown at trade price.

Prepare for the information of the directors of the company a manufacturing, trading and profit and loss account, and a profit and loss appropriation account for the year ending 31 December 19-3 and a balance sheet as at that date.

6. Kohlslau Kitchens Ltd owns a couple of healthfood restaurants and a shop catering for similar tastes. At 31 December 19-7 the company's trial balance was as follows (in £000):

	Debit £	Credit £
Cash at bank	9.8	
Cash in hand	0.9	
Consumable supplies	26.5	
Creditors		45.0
Debtors	26.2	
Directors' salaries	24.0	
Fixtures and fittings, cost	102.0	
Provision for depreciation, 1.1.19-7		18.4
Freehold land and buildings, cost	340.0	
Provision for depreciation, 1.1.19-7		10.0
Heat, light and power	24.0	
Interest on loan	8.0	
Loan—8 per cent debenture 20-1		200.0

	Debit £	Credit £
Motor expenses	13.8	
Motor vehicles, cost	48.0	
Provision for depreciation, 1.1.19-7		12.0
Office expenses	4.2	
Purchase of food etc.	369.0	
Rent	7.2	
Retained profits		37.5
Share capital, 50p ordinary shares, fully paid		100.0
Share premium		20.0
Shop expenses	15.5	
Sales		832.5
Stock, 1.1.19-7	46.0	
Telephone	2.3	
Wages	208.0	
	£1275.4	£1275.4

The following information may be relevant to the preparation of year end accounts:

(a) The company provides for depreciation on fixed assets as follows:

Freehold buildings	2 per cent on cost
Fixtures and fittings	10 per cent on cost
Motor vehicles	25 per cent on written-down value

(b) The cost of the freehold land part of freehold land and buildings is deemed to be £90 000.

(c) The closing stock at 31.12.19-7 is £68 000.

(d) No allowance has yet been made for bonuses of £1200 to be paid to employees at the end of February in respect of this year's sales.

(e) Late invoices, not yet entered in the books, are as follows:

| Purchases of food | £600 | Electricity bill | £1200 |
| Motor repairs | £200 | Consumable supplies | £300 |

(f) The rent for the year to 31 March 19-8, which amounts to £6000, has been paid in full.

(g) Included in shop expenses is insurance, for which premiums are paid annually in advance, on 1.7.19-7, amounting to £800.

(h) Motor expenses includes the annual road fund tax on six vehicles at £100 each, all expiring on 31 August 19-8.

(i) Normally, credit is only allowed to highly regarded customers, but recently the directors have become concerned about the future of one of their restaurant credit customers, Smarthouse Ltd, who have incurred bills of £2220 and are now widely felt to be experiencing trading difficulties. The directors wish to provide 50 per cent in respect of this doubtful debt.

(j) A provision for corporation tax payable of £25 000 should be made.

(k) The directors wish to provide a dividend of 10p for each ordinary share of 50p, to be approved by the shareholders at the annual general meeting.

Prepare the trading and profit and loss account for Kohlslau Kitchens Ltd for the year ended 31 December 19-7, and the balance sheet as at that date.

PART TWO

The Work of the Financial Accountant

9 | Miscellaneous Practical Matters

ACCOUNTS FROM INCOMPLETE RECORDS

It is not every business that maintains a complete double-entry accounting system; indeed, in many firms the records fall short of a complete system. In some cases the reason for this shortfall is neglect, the absence of good systems analysis when the accounting system was first designed, or the piecemeal growth of the accounting system over a number of years without the direction of a firm organizing hand. In other cases the lack of a complete set of records, or indeed of any records at all, is caused by their loss, for example in a fire or a burglary.

Some systems will be more complete than others, and the procedure adopted by an accountant to produce sensible statements will depend on the records and documents he discovers when he begins the job. Sometimes there will be what is called a single-entry system where one side of each transaction has been recorded in the cash book, for example, so that all that is needed to complete the system is to post the single entries to the appropriate accounts in order to produce a set of double-entry records. The bank statement is a very useful document in this respect, since all movements in and out of the bank account of the firm will be shown here, even though some of the items on the bank statement are not shown in the cash book. In more primitive systems the accountant will have to build up the figures by drawing conclusions from the answers to enquiries he makes, and by deduction from other scraps of information which he can glean from the business.

The starting point for the production of accounts from incomplete records is the computation of an opening statement of affairs. This is a list of assets and a list of liabilities, so that when liabilities are deducted from assets the capital invested in the business at the beginning of the period will be found.

It is often difficult to set a value on the assets of the business as they stood at the beginning of the accounting period, and some accountants prefer to use for such assets the figure of original cost less an amount to represent accumulated depreciation up to the opening date of the accounting period. The figures for stock, debts and liabilities have to be estimated, but the bank balance can be determined with some accuracy from the bank statement. If an account is opened for each of the fixed and current assets and the liabilities and capital amount, then the foundation of the double-entry system has been laid.

The next step is usually to analyse the bank statement, on which will be found the receipts and payments of cash during the period. Receipts are generated by cash takings paid into the bank and money received from debtors. Other receipts include miscellaneous income, amounts of fresh capital introduced into the business, and liquid funds generated by the sale of assets. The payments shown on the bank statement can be analysed into separate columns for expenses paid in cash, amounts paid to creditors, wages paid, petty cash expenses paid, cash drawn out by the proprietor or expenses paid for the proprietor through the business bank account, and assets purchased. The bank statement may not show a complete picture of all monies received, since some amounts received from cash takings may not have been paid into the bank because they were used to pay the running expenses of the business, or because they were used by the proprietor for personal expenditure. Enquiries must be instigated to determine such amounts so that sales and costs or drawings can be increased by the appropriate amount. Further enquiries should determine the amounts of stock drawn from the business for the personal use of the proprietor or his family. The appropriate entry in this case is to debit drawings and reduce the cost of goods sold. The opening cash float should be included in the statement of affairs, and this float will have an impact on the cash takings figure.

Once this analysis has been made, the totals of the analysis columns can be posted to the relevant accounts, and a set of double-entry accounts emerges. Journal entries will be needed to introduce into the system the amounts of takings used to pay cash expenses or withdrawn by the proprietors. Estimates must be made in the normal way of amounts prepaid and accrued expenses.

From records produced so far it is now possible to compute the sales and purchases figures by deduction. Purchases can be computed from the creditors figures by taking the amount paid to creditors during the year, subtracting the amount owed to creditors at the beginning of the year, and adding on the amount owed to creditors at the end of the year. One disadvantage of this technique is that it produces a figure for credit purchases only, so the amount of cash purchases must be added on if the correct total is to be obtained. In the same way the figure for sales can be computed from the debtors figures by taking the amount paid by debtors during the period, subtracting from it the amount owed by debtors at the start of the period, and adding on the amount owed by debtors at the end of the period. Once again this formula provides a figure for credit sales only and any cash sales must be added to this amount if the correct total is to be found. Cash sales are not always the same as cash takings banked, since this amount must be increased to cover those cash takings which have been spent in cash to pay the running expenses of the business.

Sometimes the use of the mark-up or gross profit percentage is helpful as a check on the accuracy of figures. The application of the mark-up to the cost of goods sold will show a figure for sales, and likewise if the gross profit percentage is applied to sales an amount for costs can be worked out. For example, if the cost of goods sold is £1000 and the mark-up on cost is 20 per cent, then the figure for sales must equal £1200. Likewise sales minus a gross profit margin of 20 per cent on cost will show the cost figure, so £1200 minus one-sixth of £1200 equals £1000, the cost of goods sold.

Note: A mark-up of one-fifth on cost means that one-sixth must be subtracted from the sales figure to get back to the cost figure. Five-fifths plus one-fifth equals six-fifths, and this figure must be divided by six to get back to one-fifth of cost.

Example

The incomplete records technique is similar to using a child's building bricks to compute the figure needed from the evidence available.

	£
Cash paid to creditors during period	5000
Less opening creditors	2000
	3000
Plus closing creditors	1000
Purchases on credit terms	£4000

Add cash purchases, if any, to find total purchases. Ensure that all cash paid to creditors is for revenue rather than capital items. By a simple rearrangement you can deduce the missing cash figure if the purchases and opening and closing creditors are known.

	£
Opening creditors	2000
Plus purchases	4000
	6000
Less closing creditors	1000
Cash paid	£5000

The same logic can be applied to the credit sales figure by using cash received and the opening and closing debtors. The computation of the overall sales figure does, however, require more information.

	£
Cheques received from debtors	14 000
Less opening debtors	4 000
	10 000
Plus closing debtors	5 000
Credit sales	15 000
Plus cash takings banked	8 000
Plus cash takings spent on expenses	3 000
Plus increase in cash float	500
Plus cash drawn from till by proprietor	1 000
Total sales	£27 500

If any debts have been written off during the year they must be added back in the computation to show the true sales figure.

The gross profit percentage or mark-up can often be used to compute the sales figure. If the cost of goods sold can be found, then by applying the gross profit percentage, the figure can be 'grossed up' to sales. The sales figure can also be used to work back to cost of sales.

Sales of £440 000 at a mark-up on cost of 10 per cent means a deduction of 1/11 from sales to get back to cost, £400 000. Once the cost of sales is determined, by using the opening and closing stocks, the purchases figure can be worked out. Then, if the opening and closing creditors are known, the cash paid to creditors can be found, or, if cash paid and opening creditors are known, the closing creditors' figure can be computed.

Example

Peter Bean commenced business on 1 January as a wholesaler of frozen vegetables. The accounting system used in the business is rudimentary, and you have been asked to produce accounts for the year ended 31 December.

The following is a summary of the bank statements for the year:

Receipts. Cash introduced as capital on 1 January, £22 000; banked from cash received from customers, £50 800.

Payments. Motor van £4000; freezer equipment £10 000; office furniture £1500; factory rent £1500; wages £7088; commission to sales manager £4800; goods purchased for resale £39 600; electricity £800; repairs £250; insurance £220; van expenses £746.

Note: The following cash payments were made before banking the balance of the takings: motor expenses £516; wages £593; sundry expenses £100; drawings by Peter Bean £54 per week.

The following information is also relevant:

1. Discounts allowed to customers during the year were £490, while discounts received totalled £220. Goods sold to Rooster during the year amounted to £800, but he has now disappeared without paying for them. Peter Bean has taken goods for his own use which could have been sold for £500.
2. On 31 December £3000 was owed to suppliers and £6200 was owed by customers. The prepayment of insurance was £120. Stock at cost amounted to £4820. The factory had been occupied since 1 January at an annual rent of £2000.
3. Peter Bean tells you that in his view the van will have a useful life of four years, and the office and freezer equipment will last ten years.
4. On 31 December there was £10 in the petty cash box.

Do not forget that depreciation should be provided on the van at 25 per cent of cost, and on the freezer and office equipment at 10 per cent of cost. In the absence of a scrap value it is best to act conservatively and assume that the assets will be worthless when worn out.

The first step is to write up the petty cash account to determine as the balancing figure the amount of sales receipts raised to pay expenses. Do not forget the £10 closing balance, especially in the balance sheet.

Dr.		Petty Cash Account		Cr.
	£			£
Sales receipts	4026	Motor expenses		516
(balancing figure)		Wages		592
		Sundries		100
		Drawings		2808
		Balance c/f		10
	£4026			£4026
Balance b/d	10			

The next step is to write up the cash book to find the closing bank balance. If, instead, the bank balance is found from the bank statement the figure for cash received from customers can be computed as the balancing figure on the account, e.g. if £2296 is known then £50 800 can be found by deduction.

Dr.		Cash Book	Cr.
	£		£
Capital	22 000	Motor van	4 000
Received from		Freezer equipment	10 000
customers	50 800	Office furniture	1 500
		Rent	1 500
		Wages	7 088
		Sales commission	4 800
		Purchases paid for	39 600
		Electricity	800
		Repairs	250
		Insurance	220
		Van expenses	746
		Balance c/f	2 296
	£72 800		£72 800
Balance b/d	2 296		

In practice it would be possible to start a set of double-entry accounts by recording the other side of these cash transactions. Do not forget, however, that there is a difference between cash recorded and the profit and loss account amount. Some cash items will need to be capitalized.

The next step is to write up accounts for creditors and debtors, to find the amounts needed for the trading account, purchases and sales. There are no opening balances because the business only commenced on 1 January.

Dr.		Creditors Account	Cr.
	£		£
Bank, payments	39 600	Trading account—purchases	42 820
Discounts received	200	(balancing figure)	
Creditors on 31			
December c/f	3 000		
	£42 820		£42 820
		Balance of creditors b/d	3 000

Dr.		Debtors Account	Cr.
	£		£
Trading account—sales	62 816	Petty cash	4 026
(balancing figure)		Bank	50 800
		Drawings in kind	500
		Discounts allowed	490
		Bad debts, Rooster	800
		Debtors on 31	
		December c/f	6 200
	£62 816		£62 816
Balance of debtors			
b/d	6 200		

The trading and profit and loss accounts can now be prepared, together with a balance sheet.

Trading and Profit and Loss Account for the Year Ended 31 December

	£	£
Sales		62 816
Purchases	42 820	
Less closing stock	4 820	38 000
Gross profit		24 816
Add discounts received		220
		25 036
Expenses:		
Wages, £(592 + 7088)	7 680	
Rent, £(1500 cash + 500 accrued)	2 000	
Electricity	800	
Insurance, £(220 cash − 120 prepaid)	100	
Sales commission	4 800	
Motor expenses, £(516 + 746)	1 262	
Bad debt, Rooster	800	
Discounts allowed	490	
Repairs	250	
Sundries	100	
Depreciation:		
Van	1 000	
Freezer equipment	1 000	
Office furniture	150	20 432
Net profit		£4 604

Peter Bean, Balance Sheet as at 31 December

	£ Cost	£ Depreciation	£
Fixed assets:			
Freezer equipment	10 000	1 000	9 000
Office equipment	1 500	150	1 350
Vehicle	4 000	1 000	3 000
	15 500	2 150	13 350
Current assets:			
Stock		4 820	
Debtors (including prepayments of £120)		6 320	
Bank		2 296	
Cash		10	
		13 446	
Less current liabilities:			
Trade creditors	3 000		
Accruals—rent	500	3 500	
Working capital			9 946
Net assets			£23 296
Financed by:			
Peter Bean capital			22 000
Add net profit		4 604	
Less drawings, £(500 + 2808)		3 308	1 296
Net capital employed			£23 296

RECEIPTS AND PAYMENTS ACCOUNTS, AND INCOME AND EXPENDITURE ACCOUNTS

When the transactions of a club or a non-trading organization are recorded the double-entry system is not often used, so the production of accounting statements for such organizations presents the accountant with a single-entry or incomplete records problem.

Bills are received and paid through the bank account operated by the organization or from its cash resources, and monies are received by the organization for various reasons. The majority of transactions are therefore on a cash basis and thus it is easy to prepare from the vouchers of the organization a receipts and payments account. This account, as its name implies, shows on one side the monies received and on the other side the payments made by the organization. It is a summary of the cash book and combines movements through the bank account with cash transactions. The account is operated on debit and credit lines, beginning with a balance which represents the cash and bank account resources of the organization on the first day of the accounting period. It is debited with funds received and credited with payments made so that its closing balance represents the cash and bank account resources of the organization on the last day of the accounting period. It must be stressed that the receipts and payments account is merely a cash account; there is no attempt to distinguish capital transactions from revenue ones, or to bring into the account accruals or prepayments, so any balance shown cannot be described as a surplus or profit revealed by the account.

The income and expenditure account represents the profit and loss account of a club or non-trading organization. In this account the expenses of a period are set against the revenue of that period so that a profit, or excess of revenue over expense, can be revealed for the period and added to the accumulated fund, which is the term used for the capital account in the balance sheet of clubs and societies etc.

Thus the major differences between these two accounts are that the receipts and payments account deals only with cash transactions, includes capital items as well as revenue ones, and shows as its balance the total of funds held in cash or in the bank account of the organization, while the income and expenditure account includes expenses and revenues which have not been the subject of movement of cash, i.e. accruals and prepayments, excludes capital transactions and shows as its balance the surplus or deficit (profit or loss) made by the organization during the period.

It is often the lot of an accountant to prepare an income and expenditure account from a receipts and payments account, since as a member of the society he has been persuaded by the committee to do so. His first step is to analyse the receipts and payments account so that the costs of various activities are grouped together, and receipts from such activities are separated, and then to post the items to the income and expenditure account. This account will be credited with such items as subscriptions, fees, grants received and other items of miscellaneous income, all of which have appeared on the debit side of the receipts and payments account. The costs of the organization shown on the credit or payments side of the receipts and payments account are debited to the income and expenditure account.

The next step is to adjust the receipts and payments for any accruals and prepayments which are revealed by enquiries made about them. Once expenditure has been adjusted to show expense the account can be tidied up, and in this respect it is important to show separately the effect on income of the separate ventures undertaken by the organization. Transactions of a capital nature shown in the receipts and payments account should be posted to accounts in the general ledger and thus appear in the balance sheet. Any surplus of assets over liabilities at the beginning of the accounting period will be balanced in the general ledger by the amount in the accumulated fund account, to which any surplus or profit made during the period is added.

The production of accounts for a non-trading organization is not always straightforward, since certain problems can arise. In some cases the accumulated fund is not the only capital account of the organization; there may also be an account for life members' subscriptions or for a building fund. Some clubs and societies may hold part of their accumulated capital in such separate funds since they have been raised separately from the main capital of the society for a distinct purpose.

The treatment in the accounts of the subscriptions of life members is sometimes a source of confusion. A life member makes a large single payment instead of paying a subscription each year and for this he is allowed to be a member of a club or society until his death. Thus a life fund can be built up from these subscriptions which is represented, as is the accumulated fund, by the general assets of the club. As new life subscriptions are made they should not be taken to the credit of the income and expenditure account, but should be added to the balance on the life members fund, and when a life member dies that part of the life fund represented by his payment should be transferred to the credit of the accumulated fund.

A similar difficulty concerns entrance fees to a club where these are separate from the annual subscription. There is some confusion about whether these are of an income or of a capital nature. Opinion is divided on this point, the only principle to guide the accountant being that their treatment should be consistent from year to year. A major argument in this debate is that if entrance fees are written off to the income and expenditure account the profit of the club or society could be distorted in a year when many new members join.

Another problem encountered in this type of accounting concerns the position of subscriptions in arrears. Such subscriptions are technically debtors of the club, but in many cases they are likely never to be received. Thus a decision has to be made as to whether this asset should be ignored or revealed, the criterion for the decision being an objective and realistic review of the probability that subscriptions in arrears will eventually be paid. Such subscriptions can also have an impact on the income and expenditure account, since, although it is wrong to credit that account with subscriptions which are not likely to be received, if such subscriptions are not taken into account in one period they could distort the profit of a subsequent period if many arrears are paid in that year and counted as income of that period.

Example

This example combines the incomplete records technique with the production of the accounts of a non-trading organization.

The following balances were taken from the books of Paddington Green Golf Club, as at 1 January.

	£	£
Course at cost		80 000
Clubhouse at cost		20 000
Building fund, represented by investments		
£20 000 4 per cent consolidated stock	7 400	
Deposit with East Acton Building Society	12 000	19 400
Subscriptions in advance (this year to 31 Dec.)		400
Creditors for bar supplies		350
Life membership fund		5 000
Subscriptions in arrears		600
Bar stock		4 850
Clubhouse equipment at cost		3 400
Cash in hand	100	
Cash in bank	950	1 050

An analysis of the bank account operated by the club showed the following summary of receipts and payments during the year ended 31 December.

		£
Receipts	Subscriptions	26 000
	Life members	2 000
	Sale of instruction manuals	800
	Green fees	200
	Sale of old carpet from clubhouse	22
	Bar takings	28 600
	Consolidated stock interest	800
Payments	Upkeep of course	17 150
	General clubhouse expenses (including bar	
	wages of £4200)	12 150
	Petty cash, expenses paid to treasurer	1 550
	Bar supplies	23 150
	Purchase of instruction manuals	350
	Piano	700
	Deposited with East Acton Building Society	800
	Replacement carpet for clubhouse	1 250

The following information is relevant to the preparation of club accounts.

1. The club maintains a building fund separate from the capital fund and life membership fund. The building fund is invested in consolidated stock and a building society, while the capital fund and life membership fund are represented by the general assets of the club.
2. The East Acton Building Society has been instructed to credit the interest on the club's account direct to the account at each half year. The Society computes interest half-yearly on 30 June and 31 December. This year the interest amounted to £840. Interest paid on the consolidated stock is also added to the building fund by paying it into the building society account.
3. There were five life members at the beginning of the year, one of whom has since died. Two other life members have joined the club.
4. Renewals of clubhouse furnishings are to be treated as revenue expenditure.
5. Outstanding at 31 December were:

	£
Creditors for bar supplies	1600
Subscriptions in advance (next year)	900
Subscriptions in arrears (this year)	300
Bar chits not yet settled	65

143

6. Bar stocks at 31 December were valued at £4350.
7. It is a rule of the club that a cash float of £100 should be maintained in the treasurer's hands. To this end an imprest petty cash account is operated.
8. An insurance premium of £480 has been paid by cheque during this year for the year to 31 March next year.

Produce an income and expenditure account for the year ended 31 December, and a balance sheet as that date, ignoring taxation.

The best method of approaching this problem is to compute as 'workings' some significant figures, using the process of deduction already described, and then build them into the accounting statement.

1. *The Opening Accumulated Fund.* This is the recorded amount of the net assets of the club at the start of the accounting period.

	£	£
Course and clubhouse at cost		100 000
Subscriptions in arrears		600
Bar stock		4 850
Equipment		3 400
Cash (at bank and in hand)		1 050
		109 900
Less Creditors	350	
Subscriptions in advance	400	
Life fund	5000	5 750
		£104 150

2. *Subscriptions.* During the year.

	£	£
Amounts paid in cash		26 000
Plus Opening subscriptions in advance	400	
Closing subscriptions in arrears	300	
		700
		26 700
Less Opening subscriptions in arrears	600	
Closing subscriptions in advance	900	
		1 500
		£25 200

3. *Renewals.*

	£
Cost of a new carpet	1260
Less scrap value of old	22
	£1238

4. *Bar Trading Account.*

	£		£
Paid to creditors	23 150	Opening stock	4 850
Less owed at start	350	Plus purchases	24 400
	22 800		29 250
Plus owed at end	1 600	Less closing stock	4 350
Purchases	£24 400	Cost of sales	24 900
		Wages	4 200
Takings Banked	28 600		29 100
Chits	65	Bar takings	28 665
Total takings	£28 665	Loss	£435

5. *General Expenses.*

	£
Payments less bar wages	7950
Petty cash	1550
Less prepayment (3/12 × 480)	(120)
	£9380

6. *Instruction Manuals.* Sales £800 − Costs £350 = Profit £450. Note: No closing stocks.

7. *Life Fund.* Opening balance, £5000, minus one deceased plus two new members, £6000. (Life membership £1000.)

8. *Building Fund.*

	£
Opening balance	19 400
Add interest on stock (£20 000 × 4 per cent)	800
Building society interest	840
Closing balance	£21 040

Note: £1640 of interest is added to building society deposit.

9. *Bank Account.*

	£
Opening balance	950
Add total of receipts	58 422
Less total of payments	(57 110)
Closing balance	£2 262

Note: A petty cash float of £100 appears on the balance sheet.
Once these 'workings' are completed, the accounts can be produced as follows.

Paddington Green Golf Club

Dr.	Income and Expenditure Account Year Ended 31 December				Cr.
	£	£		£	£
Course upkeep		17 150	Subscriptions		25 200
General expenses		9 380	Green fees		200
Renewals (net)		1 238	Profit on manuals		450
Bar loss:			Deficit for year		2 353
Cost of sales	24 900				
Wages	4 200				
	29 100				
Takings	28 665				
		435			
		£28 203			£28 203

Paddington Green Golf Club Balance Sheet as at 31 December

	£	£	£
Capital fund as at 1 January			104 150
Transfer from life membership fund			1 000
			105 150
Less deficit for the year			2 353
			102 797
Building fund as at 1 January		19 400	
Add interest consolidated stock		800	
East Acton Building Society		840	21 040
Life members' fund as at 1 January		5 000	
Less transfer to capital fund		(1 000)	
Add new life members		2 000	6 000
Funds employed			£129 837
Represented by:			
Fixed assets			
Course at cost			80 000
Clubhouse at cost			20 000
Clubhouse equipment at cost		3 400	
Additions: piano		700	
			4 100
Investments, building fund			
20 000 4 per cent consolidated stock at cost		7 400	
Deposit with East Acton Building Society		13 640	21 040
Current assets			
Bar stocks			
Subscriptions in arrears		4 350	
Prepayments		300	
Debtors		120	
Bank		65	
Cash in hand		2 262	
		100	
		7 197	
Less current liabilities	900		
Subscriptions in advance	1 600		
Creditors for bar supplies			
		2 500	
			4 697
Net assets			£129 837

ADJUSTMENTS TO ACCOUNTS

Mistakes often occur in the accounting system, and when they are discovered the books and accounts have to be adjusted. Some adjustments will have an effect on the profit figure, some on items in the balance sheet, and some on both the position and income statements. In some cases a compensating error will be found, the adjustment of which shows no change in a figure on an accounting statement; for example, if money received from debtor A is posted to debtor B's account, when this is adjusted the overall debtor figure on the balance sheet will not have changed. Such adjustments can be used as a test to prove the ability of an accountant to understand the impact and extent of mistakes and to see what is needed to correct them. For this reason this has been a fertile source of examination questions.

The major types of adjustment are as follows.

The Capital/Revenue Allocation. It often happens that items which should be capitalized are written off to the income statement as revenue expenses, so they have to be adjusted by increasing the asset in the balance sheet and reducing the charge in the income statement, thus increasing the profit for the period. If the fixed assets are increased, the depreciation charge for the period which has been set against profit must be updated to include the newly capitalized amount, so an extra depreciation charge will have to be made, with a consequent reduction of the profit figure. A common example of this type of adjustment occurs where a company uses its own labour to install a new machine. In this case the wages account must be credited and the asset account debited with the cost of labour so used.

Drawings of the Proprietor Charged in the Salaries Account. It must be recognized that an amount drawn out by a proprietor is an appropriation of profit and not a charge to be borne before that profit is computed. In this case salaries must be reduced and thus profits increased, but at the same time drawings increased so that the amount of ploughed-back profit remains the same.

Prepayments or Accruals Omitted When the Accounting Statements Were Made Up. An expense large enough to be considered material may be discovered after the income statement has been completed. Such an expense must be debited to the profit and loss account, thus reducing the profit figure, and shown in the balance sheet as an accrual or creditor among the current liabilities. If the accountant has forgotten to apportion a payment such as rent or insurance premium, which concerns a time period other than the accounting period, the appropriate part of the expense to be carried forward must be calculated, credited to the profit and loss account, thus increasing the profit, and shown in the balance sheet as a prepayment or debtor among the current assets.

Credit Sales Understated. If sales made to some customers on credit terms have been omitted, the amount of such sales must be credited to the trading account, thus directly increasing the profit while debtors are similarly increased in the balance sheet. Note that the profit is increased by the full amount of this transaction, since the cost of goods sold has already been debited to the trading account as the closing stock was taken after the goods had been sold.

Depreciation at the Wrong Rate, or on the Wrong Basis. If depreciation was charged on the written-down value instead of on the cost of the asset, the adjustment required would need a computation of the correct amount so that the difference could be added to or subtracted from the costs, with a consequent effect on profit, and also shown as an adjustment to accumulated depreciation in the balance sheet.

Goods on Sale or Return Counted As Sold. Such goods are placed with an agent in the hope that they will be sold, but until the agent sells them they are still the property of the business and should be counted in the closing stock shown in the balance sheet. The adjustment required in this case is to reverse the entries made, so that sales are reduced, stock is increased, and the profit figure is reduced by the profit margin on this transaction.

A Stock Write-down. If stock is old or has lost its value for some other reason a realistic value must be placed upon it, which may be less than the figure shown in the balance sheet. In this case stock in the balance sheet is reduced and the amount of the reduction is written off against profit in the income statement.

Errors in the Cash Book. There are many errors which can be made when a cash book is written up, for example, an amount of £86 posted as £68, in which case the appropriate increase must be made, or a payment posted on the receipts side, in which case the adjustment is to post double the amount to the payments side.

Loan Interest Outstanding. If this expense has been omitted it must be debited to the profit and loss account, thus reducing profit, and shown among the creditors on the balance sheet. Sometimes interest is paid half-yearly so that the first instalment may appear in the trial balance, but an accrual is needed for the remainder. The loan and interest rate must be checked to find out how much has been paid.

A Vehicle Sold without Any Record of the Transaction Entered in the Books. The asset account for vehicles must be reduced and the accumulated depreciation on the vehicle sold must be written out of the depreciation account. Both these items are transferred to a vehicle disposal account so that the written-down value can be set against the price received for the vehicle which has been posted from the cash book to the credit of the vehicle disposal account. This adjustment will affect the profit figure and the balance sheet.

A Debtor Balance Which Goes Bad after the Accounting Date. An extra provision must be raised to reduce the profit and to appear as a deduction from debtors among the current assets of the balance sheet.

Cost or Appropriation Omitted When the Profit Figure Is Struck. Sometimes an amount for taxation due to be paid, or salary, or manager's commission computed after the profit figure has been struck, is forgotten. The provision is debited to the profit and loss account (appropriation section for taxation), thus reducing profit, and the amount thus provided appears on the balance sheet among the creditors, since payment has not yet been made.

Debit Balances Listed as Credits, or Debits Posted as Credits. The adjustment in this case is to reverse the wrong posting, remembering to double the amount involved.

Casting Errors. Pages in the ledger may be under- or over-cast, in which case the difference between the wrong figure and the right figure must be calculated, and this amount added to or subtracted from cost (and profit), or the appropriate asset account as the case may be.

The list of likely adjustments shown above is not exhaustive, since the practical application of double-entry book-keeping produces many types of error. Suffice it to say that a cool head is needed to work out the impact of mistakes and see what is required to correct them.

JOURNAL ENTRIES

The means by which adjustments are made in the books is the journal entry. The journal is written up in a two-column ledger so that the dual aspect of each adjustment can be seen. It is customary to explain the reason for each adjustment by means of a 'narration' or 'narrative'. In a well-organized system only authorized persons are allowed to make journal entries, and a file of journal vouchers is maintained as a form of internal control.

A typical journal ruling is.

Date	Narration	£	£
1.4.19..	Plant and machinery Direct labour Being cost of own labour used to install plant, capitalized	1423	1423

SUSPENSE ACCOUNT

Where a trial balance will not balance it is sometimes the practice to open a suspense account, entering therein the difference. As errors are found they can be posted to the suspense account and the difference will gradually be eliminated.

CONTROL ACCOUNTS

In most businesses a number of suppliers provide materials on credit terms and a number of customers purchase goods on credit. Thus the asset debtors and the liability trade creditors which appear in the balance sheet are the total figures for a number of debtor balances and a number of creditor balances. To record this situation properly a subsidiary ledger is maintained for debtors and creditors. The individual account of each debtor is kept in the debtors ledger while the total figure for amounts owed by all the debtors is shown in the general ledger.

When there is a large number of accounts for debtors or creditors, book-keeping mistakes are bound to be made, so the device of the control or total account is used in an attempt to reveal them. Suppose there are 5000 customers of a business all buying goods on credit terms, so that 5000 individual debtor accounts must be maintained. Goods purchased will be debited to each individual's personal account and the sales account will be credited. Cash paid by customers, discount allowed to them and goods returned by them will be credited to the personal account of each customer and debited to cash discounts and returns.

If the amounts for the goods bought, goods returned, cash paid and discount allowed for all debtors are totalled and the total figures entered into a control account, the balance of this account must equal the total of the balances of the individual accounts. If it does not, then a book-keeping mistake has been made which must be sought and rectified. Total figures from the daybooks and cash book can be used for this purpose, since they summarize the transactions entered from those books to the individual debtor or creditor accounts.

A total account can be used to control the situation wherever a large number of postings are made to individual accounts in a subsidiary ledger, for example the cost ledger control, or the handwritten control used to check the accuracy of amounts entered into a mechanized or computerized book-keeping system. The balance on the control account will appear in the trial balance taken out from the general ledger, while the total of balances in the subsidiary ledger must be reconciled to this figure. Thus the trial balance can be extended and accounts produced without delay while petty mistakes on the personal ledgers are located.

Other advantages of the control account are that errors are localized within one section of the books so that the area of search for a mistake can be reduced to only those accounts covered by the control, and that fraud may be disclosed, unless the senior clerk who operates the control account is involved.

Typical Entries in a Creditors Ledger Control Account

Dr.		Creditors Ledger Control Account		Cr.
	£			£
Cash paid		Opening balance b/d		
Discounts received		Purchases		
Returns outwards				
Closing balance c/f				

The totals for the month are entered into the account from the following sources: purchases from the daybook, returns from the returns daybook (written up from credit notes received), cash and discounts from the cash book.

Typical Entries in a Debtors Ledger Control Account

Dr.		Debtors Ledger Control Account		Cr.
	£			£
Opening balance b/d		Cash received		
Credit sales		Discounts allowed		
Dishonoured cheques		Returns inwards		
(written back)		Bad debts written off		
		Closing balance c/f		

The amounts entered in the account are totals for the month (hence the name total account) and are posted from the following books: cash received and discounts allowed from the cash book, returns inwards from the sales daybook or a separate book for credit notes if one is maintained, bad debts written off from the journal, sales from the daybook, cheques written back from the cash book. The procedure when a customer's cheque 'bounces' is to reverse the entry made when it was first received, credit the cash book and debit the customer's account in the debtors ledger. If the control account is to reflect the total of accounts in the personal ledger, then it too must be debited. At first glance this seems to be two debits for one credit, but the debtors ledger is now treated as a subsidiary ledger for memorandum purposes only, to give a detailed analysis of the total debtors figure shown in the control account. It is this total figure which appears in the trial balance and which is used in the computation of accounting statements.

Example

Shaw and Steadfast Ltd keep a debtors control account in their general ledger, and maintain individual accounts for each customer in a subsidiary debtors ledger. There are 150 accounts in the debtors ledger. The first eight are as follows:

	Balance at 1 January
	£
T. R. Andrews & Co.	126
Arnold & Palmer	264
Ankler Ltd	20
Bageholt & Drew	—
Bell Garages Ltd	300
T. C. Belling	60
Bright and Co.	136
Broadbent & Neames	240

The total of the balances outstanding at 1 January (including the above) is £19 284.
    Transactions during January affecting these accounts were:

	Sales	Returns	Bad Debts	Cash Received	Cash Discounts
	£	£	£	£	£
T. R. Andrews & Co.	280	—	—	126	—
Arnold & Palmer	—	—	—	200	—
Ankler Ltd	164	28	—	154	2
Bageholt & Drew	70	—	—	48	2
Bell Garages Ltd	—	—	—	294	6
T. C. Belling	—	—	60	—	—
Bright and Co.	128	—	—	136	—
Broadbent & Neames	70	6	—	236	4
All other accounts	13 560	174	84	14 862	206
	14 272	208	144	16 056	220

Head up accounts for the debtors control and for the first eight accounts in the debtors ledger. Add a further account to represent all the other customers' accounts.

Enter the above transactions. Balance all the accounts and check that the total of the balances in the debtors ledger agrees with the control account balance at 31 January.

Dr.	T. R. Andrews & Co.		Cr.
Balance b/d	126	Cash	126
Sales	280	Balance c/f	280
	£406		£406
Balance b/d	280		

Dr.	Arnold & Palmer		Cr.
Balance b/d	264	Cash	200
		Balance c/f	64
	£264		£264
Balance b/d	64		

Dr.	Ankler Ltd		Cr.
Balance b/d	20	Returns	28
Sales	164	Cash	154
		Discount	2
	£184		£184

Dr.	Bageholt and Drew		Cr.
Sales	70	Cash	48
		Discount	2
		Balance c/f	20
	£70		£70
Balance b/d	20		

Dr.	Bell Garages Ltd		Cr.
Balance b/d	300	Cash	294
		Discount	6
	£300		£300

Dr.	T. C. Belling		Cr.
Balance b/d	£60	Bad debts	£60

Dr.	Bright & Co.		Cr.
Balance b/d	136	Cash	136
Sales	128	Balance c/f	128
	£264		£264
Balance b/d	128		

Dr.	Broadbent & Neames		Cr.
Balance b/d	240	Returns	6
Sales	70	Cash	236
		Discount	4
		Balance c/f	64
	£310		£310
Balance b/d	64		

Dr.	All Other Accounts		Cr.
Balance b/d	18 138	Returns	174
Sales	13 560	Bad debts	84
		Cash	14 862
		Discount	206
		Balance c/f	16 372
	£31 698		£31 698
Balance b/d	16 372		

Dr.		Debtors Ledger Control	Cr.
Balance b/d	19 284	Returns	208
Sales	14 272	Bad debts	144
		Cash	16 056
		Discount	220
		Balance c/f	16 928
	£33 556		£33 556
Balance b/d	16 928		

List of Balances	£
T. R. Andrews & Co.	280
Arnold & Palmer	64
Bageholt & Drew	20
Bright and Co.	128
Broadbent & Neames	64
Others	16 372
Total debtors per personal accounts	£16 928

BANK RECONCILIATIONS

At the end of an accounting period a statement will be received from the bank showing all amounts paid into or drawn out of the business bank account. The balance on this statement represents the funds of the business held at the bank or the amount overdrawn. It is rare for the balance on the statement to agree with the balance in the cash book maintained at the office of the business. It may seem strange that two records made up from the same basic documents should disagree as to the bank balance at a particular time, but this is because certain items which appear on the bank statement are not in the cash book, and vice versa.

One such item concerns cheques drawn by a company in favour of its creditors and entered in its cash book, but not yet presented at its bank for payment by those creditors. A cheque is drawn, entered on the payments side of the cash book, and then put into an envelope and sent off to the creditor. There is a time lag while the cheque is in the post, while it is at the creditor's office, and while it is filtering through the banking system from the creditor's bank, where it has been paid in, to the debtor company's bank, where it is presented for payment. Thus cheques not yet presented are payments made by a business but which have not yet been paid out of its bank account.

Another difference concerns cheques received from debtors and entered into the cash book on the receipts side, but not yet entered on the bank statement because of the time lag while they are entered on a paying-in slip, taken to the bank and deposited, and then entered by the bank on to the appropriate bank statement page.

The third difference between cash book and bank statement is caused by receipts or payments made by banker's order, standing order or direct debit. These are payments made not by cheque but by an instruction to a bank to make the payment.

Thus the transaction is completed within the banking system by the transfer of funds from one bank account to another. If no prime document is produced to inform the recipient that the payment has arrived, he discovers this only when he receives his bank statement. In this case the bank statement itself acts as the document of prime entry which evidences the transaction and initiates its entry into the cash book.

Occasionally, miscellaneous income of a business is collected by its bank and will therefore appear on the bank statement rather than in the cash book. Dividends from an associate company, or the interest on a loan, can be paid by a warrant sent directly to the bank of the recipient, so that if no separate notice is sent to the office of the recipient no entry will be made in the cash book until the item is picked up from the bank statement. Many companies make routine payments by standing order, and these are posted on the credit side of the cash book from the bank statement, and from there debited to the appropriate expense account. Other items which are first notified to the company through its bank statement concern the costs of running the bank account itself, i.e. bank charges and interest charged on overdrawn balances. Once again these amounts must be identified on the bank statement and entered from there into the cash book.

When a cheque received from a debtor and banked is dishonoured, this too will appear on the bank statement but not in the first instance in the cash book. The company receives the cheque, enters it in its cash book, and posts it from there to the credit of the debtor's account. The cheque is then banked and presented by the creditor company's bank to the debtor's bank for payment. If the debtor does not have sufficient funds in his account to meet that cheque his bank will return the cheque to the creditor company's bank marked 'refer to drawer'. This means that the cheque has 'bounced', i.e. that it has been returned from the debtor's bank. The creditor company's bank will therefore write it back out of their client's account, so that it appears on the payments side of the bank statement to contra its earlier appearance on the receipts side. The bank will notify its client of its action, but often such dishonoured cheques are found to be a source of difference between the bank statement and the cash book.

Thus the differences between the cash book and the bank statement have two main causes. These are items not yet processed completely through the banking system, and items not yet notified by the bank to the business so that they are not in the cash book. At the end of each month, when the cash book is closed, cross-cast, and posted to the accounts in the general ledger, a bank reconciliation must take place. This means that all the items causing a difference between the cash book and the bank statement must be identified, those not yet entered in the cash book must be entered, and the remaining difference must be set out in the form of a reconciliation statement so that no items are 'lost' between the bank and the business, and the cash book total as entered in the accounts shows the correct amount for cash belonging to the business. Such a reconciliation will also eliminate errors in the cash book.

The procedure is a simple one. First the items in the cash book and in the bank statement are checked off against one another to find the transactions which are not shown on both statements. A list of cheques sent out to creditors entered in the cash book but not yet presented by their recipients can be computed and deducted from the bank statement balance or added to the overdraft. The amounts paid in before the end of the period but not yet shown on the bank statement must be added to the bank statement total, which should then agree with the cash book. It is important to list these outstanding amounts so that at the end of the next month it can be easily ascertained that they have gone through the system correctly and are not still outstanding for some other reason. At this time extraordinary items, such as cheques on the bank statement which do not correspond with the cheque number sequence used by the company, or standing orders not authorized by the company, can come to light.

Example

A book-keeper has written up the cash book of Nolling Ltd for the month of June but the balance shown by his work does not agree with the corresponding amount on the bank statement. Check the cash book for errors, reconcile it to the bank statement, and comment briefly on any matters you discover which might merit further investigation.

Dr.   Cash Book of Nolling Ltd   Cr.

	Receipts				*Payments*		
June	*Account*	*£*	*June*	*Cheque*	*Accounts*	*Ref.*	*£*
6	Dawson & Co.	47.50	2		Opening balance		2761.75
7	James	29.29			b/d		
15	Shaw	10.00	6	473	T. Maint	M13	32.00
24	Dingle Ltd	70.00	6	474	L. Brock	B7	25.00
24	Weather Ltd	36.32	8	475	IKI Ltd	I2	18.20
28	Mitchells	41.29	9	476	Clumber Ltd	C4	59.14
28	Ronalds	88.00	13	477	Crackle Ltd	C7	40.00
	Total lodgements	322.40	16	478	Lamp & Co.	L17	39.98
30	Balance c/f	2496.59	19	479	Print & Co.	P42	100.25
			20	480	Bandelle Ltd	M3	22.67
			25	481	Petty Cash	PC14	50.00
			27	482	Crumble	C4	35.00
			27	483	Anderton	A7	30.00
			29	484	Nimble Ltd	N21	105.00
		£3318.99					£3318.99
			July				
			1		Opening balance		2469.59
					b/d		

Eastmid Bank Ltd, Statement of Account with Nolling Ltd

	Particulars	*Debit* £	*Credit* £	*Date* *June*	*Balance* £
Balance forward				2	2761.75 (o/d)
Lodged			47.50	9	2714.25
	476	59.14		10	2773.39
	473	32.00			
S.O.		16.32		12	2821.71
	477	40.00			
	475	18.20		13	2879.91
Lodged			29.29	20	2850.62
	478	39.98		22	2890.60
S.O.		36.00		23	2926.60
Lodged			70.00	24	2856.60
C.T.			23.34	25	2833.26
	481	50.00			
	9437	21.50		26	2904.76
	482	35.00		29	2939.76
C.T.			46.32	30	2893.44

S.O. = Standing Order
C.T. = Credit Transfer

Note that the cash book shows payments in excess of receipts, which means an overdrawn account at the bank. The cash book balance has been computed in error. There has been a transposition of figures when the balance was carried down and a casting error in the balance calculation. The correct balance carried forward should be £2996.59.

	£	£
Correct balance per cash book (overdrawn)		2996.59
Deducted lodgements not entered in cash book (credit transfers)	23.34	
	46.32	69.66
		2926.93
Add payments not entered in cash book	16.32	
	36.00	
	21.50	73.82
		3000.75
Real balance per cash book (overdrawn)		
Less cheques not yet presented	105.00	
	30.00	
	25.00	
	22.67	
	100.25	282.92
		2717.83
Add lodgements not yet credited	36.32	
	10.00	
	41.29	
	88.00	175.61
Balance per bank statement		£2893.44

The following points should be noted.

1. Cheque 9437 is out of sequence on bank statement. Enquire of bank whether this is the correct account.
2. Reference C4 is used twice on the payments side of the cash book. Is there a misposting? The accounts of Clumber Ltd and Crumble are not likely to be on the same page in the creditors ledger.
3. £29.29 was received from James on 7 June according to the cash book but was not banked until 20 June according to the bank statement. Why was there a delay in banking funds when the account is overdrawn?
4. Check authority for standing orders.
5. Bandelle Ltd is given posting folio M3 in the cash book. Is this correct? Should it not be a 'B' posting?

SEMINAR EXERCISES 7

1. Mr Feckless holds the view that a system of stock record cards is an expensive luxury for a business such as his. He says, 'When quarterly accounts are compiled, all that is needed for accuracy is a physical stock-take and the extension of the physical totals at cost to provide the figure for closing stock.' Stock was taken on 30 November, but Mr Feckless has lost his briefcase containing the stock sheets.

    The quarterly accounts are needed urgently. It is now 15 December, so stocktaking carried out now would not necessarily reflect the position at 30 November, and in any case would take time and effort to undertake.

Your enquiries uncover the following facts:

(a) Sales invoiced to customers during the months September, October and November amounted to £85 627, but this figure includes £7346 which relates to goods despatched in August.

(b) Goods despatched in November but not yet invoiced total £7912 at selling price.

(c) Stocks at 31 August were £53 278.

(d) An examination of the stock sheets for 31 August reveals the following errors. The total of page three was £24 690, but it had been carried forward on to page four as £26 490. Four hundred items which had cost £17 each had been extended at £1.70 each. Page five had been overcast by £81.

(e) The mark-up on stock sold is 33⅓ per cent.

(f) Items in stock at £725 on 31 August had been scrapped in October.

(g) Purchase invoices entered in the bought daybook during September, October and November totalled £64 539, but included goods received in August totalling £2643. Goods received in November but not yet entered in the daybook totalled £3129.

(h) Sales returns during the quarter recorded in the sales daybook were £796 and purchase returns in the bought daybook were £958.

Compute the stock figure as at 30 November for inclusion in the accounts and make a brief comment on stock levels in the firm.

2. A summary of the cash book of Reconcile Ltd for the year to 30 September is as follows:

Dr.		Cash Book	Cr.
	£		£
Opening balance c/d	912	Payments	175 638
Receipts	176 614	Closing balance c/f	1 888
	177 526		177 526

After investigation of the cash book and vouchers you discover that:

(a) Standing orders appearing on the bank statement have not yet been entered in the cash book.
  (i) Interest for the half year to 31 March on a loan of £30 000 at 8 per cent per annum.
  (ii) Hire purchase repayments on the managing director's car. 12 months at £61 per month.
  (iii) Dividend received on a trade investment, £1248.

(b) The company owes £789 to the Electricity Board.

(c) A cheque for £112 has been debited to the company's account in error by the bank.

(d) Cheques paid to suppliers totalling £830 have not yet been presented at the bank, and payments into the bank of £780 on 31 May have not yet been credited to the company's account.

(e) An error of transposition has occurred in that the opening balance of the cash book should have been brought down at £921.

(f) A cheque received from a customer of £167 has been returned by the bank marked 'refer to drawer', but it has not yet been written back in the cash book.

(g) A cheque drawn for £69 has been entered in the cash book as £96, and another drawn for £341 has been entered as a receipt.

(h) Bank charges of £213 shown on the bank statement have not yet been entered in the cash book.

(i) A page of the receipts side of the cash book has been undercast by £400.

(j) The bank statement shows a balance of £516.

Produce well-presented statements to adjust the cash book in the light of the above discoveries, and reconcile the adjusted cash book to the bank statement.

3. The books of account of Naunton Knitwear are handwritten with great care by a small team of book-keepers under the eagle eye of the office manager. However, the manager has recently taken extended leave to visit relations abroad, with unfortunate results, since the month end trial balance will not balance, credits exceeding debits by £1227.

   You are asked to help and after inspection of the ledgers discover the following errors:

(a) A balance of £57 on a debtors account had been omitted from the schedule of debtors, the total of which was entered as debtors in the trial balance.

(b) A small piece of machinery purchased for £1138 had been written off to repairs.

(c) The receipts side of the cash book had been undercast by £400.

(d) The total of one page of the sales daybook had been carried forward as £3209, but the correct amount was £3292.

(e) A credit note for £271 received from a supplier had been posted to the wrong side of his account.

(f) An electricity bill for the sum of £78, not yet accrued for, was discovered in a filing basket.

(g) Mr Exe, whose past debts to the company had been the subject of a provision, at last paid £311 to clear his account. His personal account has been credited but the cheque has not yet passed through the cash book.

Write up the suspense account and make the entries to clear the balance thereon. State the effect of each error on the accounts.

4. The balance sheet of Harold Darby as at 30 June is as follows:

	£	£	*Fixed Assets*	£ Cost	£ Accumulated Depreciation	£ Net
Capital		48 500				
Profit	12 500		Buildings	40 000	—	40 000
Less drawings	9 500	3 000	Plant	22 000	11 000	11 000
		51 500	Vehicles	9 000	6 000	3 000
				£71 000	£17 000	54 000
Loan at 12 per cent p.a.		20 000				
Current liabilities			*Current assets*			
Creditors	27 500		Stock	23 000		
Tax payable	6 000	33 500	Debtors	19 000		
			Cash	9 000		51 000
		£105 000				£105 000

Scrutiny of the accounts revealed the following information:

(a) The company's own workmen were employed to construct the foundation for a new machine. No adjustment has been made in the books for the labour cost of £2930.

(b) Interest on the loan for the half year to 30 June is outstanding, and has not yet been recorded in the books.

(c) Goods costing £2400 have been sent to an agent on a 'sale or return' basis. These goods have been invoiced at a mark-up of 25 per cent on cost and are included in sales for the year. The goods also appear in stock.

(d) Repairs in the sum of £179 made to a flat occupied by Mr Darby have been charged to maintenance expenses.

(e) A vehicle, four years old, has been sold at its written-down value, but no entry has been made in the books to record this transaction. The original cost of the vehicle was £1600. Depreciation on vehicles is at 25 per cent on reducing balance.

(f) A debtor of the firm who owes £800 has gone bankrupt. Reliable evidence confirms that his estate is likely to pay 50p in the pound.

Draft the journal entries required to adjust the books in the light of the above information, and produce a statement to reconcile the present profit figure to the true profit for the year.

5. Dear Mrs Jones,   31 December 19..

I am very pleased that you have agreed to help me to sort out the accounts of my second-hand business, which as you know commenced on 1 January last. Such records as I have kept are, unfortunately, to be found on tattered scraps of paper kept in an old cardboard box. I expect you will want to examine these records for yourself, but I thought it might help you if I were to summarize my business dealings up to 31 December 19.. as I recall them.

I was lucky enough to win £10 000 on the football pools, and with this and £2000 lent to me by an aunt (I agreed, incidentally, to pay her 10 per cent per year interest) I started my business. I put £11 000 into the bank immediately, in a separate business account. I needed a lorry to enable me to collect and deliver the second-hand goods, and I'm pleased to say I made a profit of £920 here; a dealer was asking £2600 for a second-hand lorry, but I beat him down to £1680. I've paid by cheque only £400 of this so far, but as I will finish paying the full £1680 in three years, it will be mine before it falls to pieces in another five years from now.

I rent an old shed with a yard, and I pay only £700 a year. I've paid by cheque this year's rent and also £100 in respect of next year.

My first deal was to buy a job lot of 4000 dresses for £12 000. I've paid a cheque for £8000 so far and my supplier is pressing me for the rest. To date I've sold 3000 dresses and received £11 600, which I promptly banked as it was all in cheques. I reckon I'm still owed £1000, most of which I should be able to collect.

I bought 2000 ties for £2400 out of my bank account. I've sold 1500 of these for cash (£3000 in all) but as the remainder have been damaged I'd be lucky if I got £100 for them.

I managed to get some cigarette lighters cheaply—100 of them cost me only £800. I'm rather pleased I haven't paid for them yet, as I think there is something wrong with them. My supplier has indicated that he will in fact accept £400 for them, and I intend to take up his offer, as I reckon I can repair them for £2 each and then sell them at £16 a time—a good profit.

I haven't paid my cash into the bank at all, as the cash I got for the T-shirts and my initial float enabled me to pay for my diesel, £800, and odd expenses, £500. Also it enabled me to draw £40 per week for myself. As I've done so well I also took my wife on holiday. It made a bit of a hole in the bank account but it was worth all £1200 of it.

Perhaps from what I've told you you can work out what profit I've made—only keep it as small as possible as I don't want to pay too much tax.

Yours sincerely,
Don Lerr

(a) From the data provided by Mr Lerr prepare a business trading, and profit and loss account for the period ended 31 December and a balance sheet as at that date. Show clearly all your workings and assumptions as notes to the accounts.
(b) Write a short report to Mr Lerr highlighting what you consider to be the most important features revealed by the accounts you have prepared.

6. Your friend John Grey is in business as a sole trader, and you act as his accountant. His book-keeper draws up the accounts each year and you check them for mistakes. The balance sheet as at 31 May is as follows:

John Grey, Balance Sheet as at 31 May 19..

	£ Cost	£ Accumulated depreciation	£
Fixed assets:			
Buildings	100 000	—	100 000
Plant	111 346	44 554	66 792
Vehicles	24 838	11 212	13 626
	£236 184	£55 766	£180 418
Current assets:			
Stock		49 080	
Debtors	73 102		
Less provision	8 000	65 102	
Cash in safe		1 446	115 628
			£296 046
Financed by:			
Capital account			174 000
Add profit for the year			52 944
			226 944
Less drawings			(18 614)
			208 330
Long-term loan			
Mr Green			
(interest			
11 per cent)			60 000
Current liabilities:			
Trade creditors		21 254	
Overdraft		6 462	27 716
			£296 046

When the accounts are checked the following facts emerge:

(a) Part of the stock is considered to have a net realizable value of less than its cost, necessitating a stock write-down of £8000.

(b) A debt of £12 000 owed by Mr Black is considered to be bad. The provision for doubtful debts is to be maintained at 10 per cent of debtors after this bad debt is written off.

(c) Machinery costing £10 000 was bought on credit from Mr Black during January but no entry has yet been made in the books.

(d) John Grey has taken goods costing £1032 for his own use during the year.

(e) Loan interest for the half year to 31 May is outstanding.

(f) Bank charges and interest of £1260 are shown on the bank statement but have not yet been entered in the cash book.

(g) A vehicle was sold on 31 May at book value £400. Its original cost was £2400. No entry has yet been made in the books for this transaction.

Raise journal entries in good form for the above adjustments and prepare a balance sheet in vertical form, after the adjustments have been made.

7. Albert Green carries on a retail business and asks you to draw up his accounts for the year to 30 June 19-8. Proper records have not been kept.
You ascertain the following information:

(a) At 1 July 19-7 Green's assets were:

	£
Shop	20 000
Fixtures	6 000
Stocks	16 000
Rent in advance	2 000
Debtors	3 000
Cash in hand	100
Cash at bank	1 500

He owed £10 500 to suppliers.

(b) A summary of his bank account is as follows:

	£		£
Balance as at		Bonus to assistant in	
1 July 19-7	1 500	shop	1 000
Bankings	144 700	Drawings	10 000
		Lighting and heating	
		for the year	2 500
		Rent	8 800
		Bought ledger payments	120 000
		Balance as at 30 June	
		19-8	3 900
	146 200		146 200

(c) Green pays some expenses from takings before banking them. During the year he paid:

	£
Wages	24 160
Repairs	480
Drawings	8 800
Printing and sundries	3 760
Cash to bought ledger	12 780

He received £16 300 from sales ledger debtors.

Unfortunately the cash takings book has been lost but Green is confident that he has given you sufficient information to calculate them with substantial accuracy.

(d) Green has bought goods valued at £1680 from Jones, who was also a debtor on the sales ledger. It was decided to clear these balances by contra between the bought and sales ledgers.

Green allowed £456 in discount to debtors in the year.

(e) Depreciation of the shop has been agreed at 2 per cent and of the fixtures at 25 per cent of the written-down values.

(f) Rent paid during the year was as follows:

	£
Paid 30 October 19-7 in advance to 31 March 19-8	4000
Paid 15 April 19-8 in advance to 30 September 19-8	4800
	8800

(g) At the close of business 30 June 19-8 debtors owed £6084 and £12 160 was due to creditors. Stocks amounted to £19 440 and cash in hand £200.

Write up accounts for cash, debtors, creditors and rent, and draw up a trading and profit and loss account for the year ended 30 June 19-8 and a balance sheet as at that date.

REVIEW QUESTIONS 5

1. John Napier is a wholesaler in the motor accessories trade. He has other business interests, so he employs a full-time manager to operate the warehouse business. Accounting records are maintained by the office manager, who informs John Napier that in her opinion the general manager has been misappropriating money from the business. You are asked to investigate and extract the following information from the books and records:

	£
Stock taken 31 December 19-1	154 800
Stock taken 31 December 19-2	151 090
Debtor balances 31 December 19-1	133 670
Debtor balances 31 December 19-2	94 510
Creditors owed for goods purchased for resale	
31 December 19-1	155 080
Creditors owed for goods purchased for resale	
31 December 19-2	138 260

A mark-up of 33⅓ per cent on cost is used to set selling prices.

The bank statement revealed that takings in the sum of £1 590 740 had been banked and the cash book showed that suppliers of goods for resale had been paid by cheque £1 384 150. Before banking the takings the general manager had made the following payments:

> John Napier drawings £25 000
> General manager salary £18 000
> Goods for resale bought for cash £186 040; Wages £2200 per week
> Salaries £480 per week, petty cash expenditure £14 237
> Rent £750 per calendar month

You also discover that depreciation for the year was £173 820 and that at the year end bills for electricity were unpaid in the sum of £2180, and that bank interest of £790 had been deducted by the bank on the bank statement. Compute the amount of the general manager's defalcation. Beware of information in the question which is not relevant to the solution.

2. Jack Daw, who has recently completed his first year of study as an undergraduate, received a payment from a matured insurance policy, and set off for a summer holiday in the USA. He found that jeans were cheap to buy there and bought 360 pairs for the sterling equivalent of £1260 (all his remaining funds) before he returned to the UK. It cost him a further £47 to bring them home.

When the college term began he spent £8 on stationery and produced handbills 'Jeans £7 per pair' for distribution amongst the students. Business was brisk and Jack sold 180 pairs in a fortnight. A friend approached him with a deal offering T-shirts for sale at £1 each. Jack's grant cheque of £490 had recently arrived so he spent it all on T-shirts, and began offering them for sale at £1.50 each.

Jack found that he had a transport and storage problem so he purchased an old van for £370. The van broke down one week later and cost a further £240 to repair. Road tax on the van cost Jack £85 and insurance a further £211. As winter approached, Jack heard of a camping shop that was closing down, and bought up 200 sleeping bags for £9 each. He offered these for sale at £20 each but by March he had sold only 130 bags. By this time his bank manager was beginning to complain at the size of Jack's overdraft. In the last week of the spring term the van failed its MOT test and was sold for scrap at £30. A replacement van cost Jack £1200, much to the distress of the bank manager.

Hoping to recoup his fortunes, Jack bought 50 films from a man he met in a pub. The films cost only £2 each, but after selling ten of them at £4 each, Jack discovered they were all faulty and had to refund the money to his customers.

Jack Daw asks you to sort out his muddled financial affairs. He tells you that he still has 15 pairs of jeans, 80 T-shirts and 40 sleeping bags in the van, but 12 T-shirts are unsaleable because of faulty stitching. The bank statement shows that £5580 has been banked from the sale of goods. Jack tells you that he has spent some of the sales cash on personal expenditure (£600) and £25 on stationery before banking the remainder. Bank interest is £50. Cheque book stubs reveal further expenditure by Jack Daw as:

	£
Hall fees	750
Motor expenses (petrol and repairs)	560
Drum kit	693
Miscellaneous personal expenditure	470

Jack considers that half of the van expenses relate to his personal use. A student owes him for one sleeping bag and he has £5 of cash from sales which he has not yet banked.

(a) Prepare accounting statements to show the effect of the above transactions on:

    (i) Jack Daw's income;
    (ii) Jack Daw's bank account;
    (iii) Jack Daw's present position.

(b) Advise Jack Daw.

3. Ruddington Sports Club provided facilities for archery, soccer, cricket, tennis and bowls. Each sport was managed by a separate section, and each section was required to make an annual contribution to the parent sports club which provided, managed and maintained the clubhouse and grounds. The club's financial records were a cash and bank account, backed by such documentary evidence as members remembered to hand to the treasurer. A club member (an accountant) was asked to draw up a set of accounts for the year ended 31 December 19-7.

The accountant first sought the assistance of the treasurer, who was able to supply summaries of the bank and cash accounts for 19-7, as follows:

Bank Account for the Period 1 January 19-7 to 31 December 19-7

Receipts	£	Payments	£
Cash banked	45 000	Electricity	2 900
Contributions from sections:		Water rates	1 000
19-6/7	4 000	Maintenance of clubhouse	4 200
19-7/8	9 000	Maintenance of machinery	850
Sundry income	800	Improvements to bar	9 500
Bank interest	600	Rent of ground	1 800
		Loan repayment and interest	2 500
		Petrol	1 250
		Bar purchases	31 600

Dr.		Cash Account	Cr.
Receipts	£	Payments	£
Bar sales	59 500	Bar purchases	9 700
Donations	100	Wages of cleaner	1 400
		Sundry light fittings	300
		Lodgements at bank	45 000
		Miscellaneous expenses	400

It was evident from the records and bank statement that the balance in the bank current account had been £11 000 on 1 January 19-7, and that the cash in hand at that date had been £2000. The bank interest proved attributable to a bank deposit account of £4900 which had remained constant at that level during the period. The bar sales were listed daily in a 'bar book' and the bar maintained a strict control on prices in order to ensure a gross margin on sales of 33⅓ per cent. The bar chairman explained that although he had not taken stock during 19-7 he had done so on 1 January 19-7 when the bar stock, at cost, had been valued at £5300. All bar sales were for cash, although at the end of the period there were 'IOUs' in the till which amounted to £500. Until 1 January 19-7 all bar purchases had been for cash, but with growing sales volume credit facilities had been granted, and at 31 December 19-7 bar creditors were owed £2400.

The club secretary was also able to provide some information based on the club minutes. The clubhouse, he explained, had been built in 19-1, for a cost of £100 000 and, given the type of construction, it was considered to be suitable for use for 25 years. The building had been made possible, in part, by a loan from a National Sports Association of £20 000 which was repayable at £2000 per year. Interest for the year to 31 December 19-7 was £500. The club had acquired some new mowing machinery at a cost of £6000 which, with luck and careful use, would last six years, i.e. until 31 December 19-9.

The contributions or levy from the sections were based on a financial year which ran from April to March, to align with the playing seasons. The levy for 19-6/7 (which had been completely paid) was £12 000 and that for 19-7/8 was £14 000. The sections were required to complete their levies by the end of March each year, but had no fixed time for paying any instalments during the year.

The accountant sought copies of all invoices from the treasurer, and, from those that were available, concluded that at 31 December 19-7 the club owed a further £300 for electricity and the annual charge for the rent of the ground which was £2400. Both these accounts were paid up to date at 1 January 19-7. Armed, therefore, with information from the secretary, treasurer and bar chairman together with his own findings, he prepared the accounts for the year ended 31 December 19-7.

(a) Prepare the income and expenditure account at the Ruddington Sports Club for the year ended 31 December 19-7 and a balance sheet as at that date. Show clearly all your workings, and state as a footnote to the accounts any assumptions you have made.
(b) The secretary, having received the accounts, comments that he finds it difficult to understand how the club's bank balance has risen by only a few hundred pounds while there is a healthy surplus on the income and expenditure account. Explain to him why this has occurred.

4. The sales ledger supervisor of Fisheries Ltd has been taken ill and the inexperienced ledger clerk is having problems balancing the ledgers for the month of February. He presents you with the following information and asks for your help.
The balances on the individual accounts at 28 February are:

	£
R. Herring & Son	1 100
S. Newt Ltd	11 600
C. Lion & Co. Ltd	28 350
Fish Food Ltd	4 900
The Eating Plaice	1 950
Fred's Restaurant	2 350
H. Addock	1 800
Trout Farms	7 300
	£59 350

The balance brought forward on the control account for 1 February is £68 300. The clerk says he has entered the following items on the customers' account cards to get the above balances:

	Sales £	Cash received £	Discount allowed £	Goods returned £
R. Herring & Son	2 500	1 900		
S. Newt Ltd	4 900	9 600	400	
C. Lion & Co. Ltd	3 650	7 450	150	1250
Fish Food Ltd	450	850		300
The Eating Plaice	—	250		
Fred's Restaurant	700	500		
H. Addock	2 300	300		
Trout Farms	5 100	2 900	300	
Total	£19 600	£23 750	£850	£1550

When he enters the above totals in the sales ledger control account it does not balance to the total of the customers' accounts.

On investigation you find that:

(i) The sales to S. Newt Ltd have been mistakenly entered on S. Newt's account in the creditors ledger.

(ii) A contra has been entered on the account of Fred's Restaurant for £650 against his account on the creditors ledger. This has not been recorded on the control account.

(iii) An invoice for £2100 in respect of C. Lion & Co. Ltd has been omitted from the list of sales and is not included in the individual account balances on 28 February.

(iv) The account for Mr C. Horse showing a balance of £1650 has been removed from the sales ledger as the debt has been proved to be bad.

(v) The cheque from R. Herring & Son has been returned by the bank marked 'refer to drawer'.

(vi) A credit note for £4500 has been posted to the account of Trout Farms but not to the control account.

(vii) The cash received from C. Lion & Co. Ltd had not been entered on the customer account card.

(viii) The chief accountant has been looking at the account of Codds Ltd. You have reason to believe the customer account card showing a credit balance of £1850 is locked in his filing cabinet.

(a) Complete the sales ledger control account.

(b) Reconcile the list of individual debtors account balances to the control account balance.

5. The first draft of the final accounts of Wysall Weavers Ltd disclosed a net profit of £52 617 and a capital employed of £441 500 before providing for the manager's efficiency bonus, but including £8778 (credit balance) for errors held in suspense. Mr Smith, the manager, receives a basic salary plus an annual bonus of £400 for every complete percentage point by which the net profit to capital employed percentage exceeds 10 per cent. In this context, net profit is calculated before

charging the manager's bonus, and capital employed is defined as fixed assets plus working capital. The bonus calculation is not carried out until the figures have been audited. During the course of the audit, it was discovered that:

(a) Discounts allowed £611 had been credited to discounts received.
(b) The sale for cash of some disused fixtures and fittings which had been completely written off in a previous year had been credited to fixtures and fittings £650.
(c) An amount of £265 owed by M & Co. for goods supplied had been settled in contra against an amount of £850 owing to M & Co. but the ledger entries had not yet been made.
(d) A glass carboy containing chemicals, which was kept in the warehouse, had sprung a leak. The resultant seepage had caused irreparable damage to stock, valued at £1000, but no account has yet been taken of this fact.
(e) Due to an oversight, credit sales for the last three days of the accounting year, amounting to £1693, have been completely omitted from the sales daybook.
(f) In the purchases daybook, a subtotal of £36 411 had been carried forward as £46 411—creditors, however, have been correctly posted.
(g) A credit sale invoice of £845 had been entered in the sales daybook as £548.
(h) A credit note from a supplier for £51 in respect of faulty goods had not been posted.

  (i) Recalculate the net profit and capital employed figures after the above errors have been corrected.
 (ii) Calculate the manager's bonus.
(iii) Open the suspense account and post the eliminating entries.

6. Henry Dids (an old-established marine store dealer), in view of advancing years and failing health, reluctantly agreed to merge his business with a similar establishment run as a partnership between William Coy and his sons Fred and Alec. The new firm started trading on 1 May 19-8 under the name Didicoy and Co.

From 1 May 19-8 the Didicoy book-keeper made all cash-book and sales-journal entries in Coy and Sons books. Both businesses used similar loose-leaf binders for their sales ledgers. Alec Coy (who completed part of a Polytechnic accountancy foundation course in 19-6 before entering the family business) merged the two sales ledgers on 7 May 19-8, without realizing that Dids' books were balanced only up to 31 March 19-8 (Coy and Sons' books were balanced up to 30 April 19-8). Alec went on to produce the May 19-8 sales ledger control account for Didicoy and Co. as follows:

Dr.				Cr.
		£		£
Balances 1 May 19-8:			Returns and allowances	715
Coy and Sons		1 738	Cash	11 021
H. Dids (B)		714	Balances 31 May 19-8 (A)	4 099
Sales		12 715		
Discounts allowed		256		
Sales debt satisfied by transfer				
to purchases ledger		412		
		£15 835		£15 835

The schedule of balances at 31 May 19-8 (extracted by the book-keeper) showed a net debit balance of £4099 which Alec entered (at A above) and to complete the control account Alec assumed that £714 (the balancing figure) must be Dids' net debit balances at 1 May 19-8 (entered at B above). H. Dids stated that his trade debtors were at least £1500 higher than the figure of £714, and that Alec's calculations were 'a load of old rubbish'.

At this stage, William Coy decides to seek professional help, and you have been sent (from your firm of accountants) to resolve the problems. You find Dids' books (except the sales ledger) and correctly complete all entries up to 30 April 19-8; the following information for April 19-8 refers to the sales ledger (the pages of which have now been incorporated into Didicoy and Co.'s sales ledger):

	£
Opening balances (1 April 19-8)	2241
Sales	5851
Returns, allowances and discounts	519
Bad debts written off	53
Cash received	4870
Customer's cheque dishonoured	140
Contra account with purchases ledger	307

It had also been agreed that the following balances would not be transferred to the new firm (any value/liability to concern H. Dids personally):

Special bad debts	£280
Very old credit balances	£28

You further discover the following from the sales ledger and the May 19-8 accounts:

(a) The merger adjustments (above) have not been made.
(b) The book-keeper had omitted from the list of balances the following:

	Dr.	Cr.
	£	£
Arkwright stores	403	
Byron Ltd	190	
Chaucers the ironmongers		15

(c) Dryden and Co. had been credited with £72 for goods returned but no entry had been made in the returns and allowances journal.
(d) A May 19-8 payment of £117 by Maudslay had been correctly entered in the control account but had been posted to the sales ledger as June 19-8.
(e) The sales journal had been undercast by £100.

(i) Prepare the sales ledger control account for H. Dids for April 19-8.
(ii) Correct the sales ledger control account for Didicoy and Co. for May 19-8 and prepare the adjusted schedule of balances at 31 May 19-8.

10 | Partnership

Partnership has been defined as 'the relationship which exists between persons carrying on a business in common with a view to profit'. Case law abounds with instances where an attempt has been made to prove a partnership, and it is clear that three essentials must exist before partnership can be established. These three essentials are (a) carrying on a business, (b) in common, and (c) with a view to profit. It is sometimes important to know whether a partnership exists, since if such a business ceases trading because of lack of funds, there is no limited liability to protect the private assets of the partners. If creditors can establish that somebody is a member of a partnership they can use the private assets of that person to make good the debts of the partnership. Alternatively, if a person can establish a claim to partnership, that person can also claim a share of the profits and a share of the assets of the business when it ceases trading.

Partnership, of course, means that there is a mutual agency in existence between the partners. Each partner can act as an agent for the other, and also as a principal for the business. Thus a partner, when acting on behalf of the business, can bind the other partners in law. A partnership in the UK is governed by the Partnership Act of 1890 and by the Limited Partnership Act of 1907. The Act of 1890 lays down that partnerships shall be limited to a maximum of twenty partners, unless the partnership is a banking partnership, in which case the limit is ten partners. Partnerships in banking can apply to the Department of Trade and Industry to extend the partnership to twenty. Under the Companies Act of 1967, now 1985, firms of solicitors or accountants qualified to audit public companies, or members of stock exchanges, may have any number of partners.

Because the action of a partner, whether careless, inefficient or dishonest, can affect the future of others in the partnership, the relationship between partners is one 'uberrimae fidei'. This means that the utmost good faith must exist between partners, and that one partner can rely on information given by other partners when entering the partnership and during the term of the partnership. If such information is found to be false, a claim for damages can be sustained in the courts. Partnerships can be established for a limited period by agreeement, or 'at will', which means they can be wound up by the partners at any point in time, subject to reasonable notice being given.

A partnership is a relationship which exists between the partners, and it may be expected, therefore, that some agreement between the partners will be used as an instrument to govern this relationship. The Partnership Act lays down the rules to be applied in a partnership in the absence of an agreement, but wherever there is a partnership agreement, the rules in the Act are subordinated to the terms of the agreement.

THE PARTNERSHIP AGREEMENT

Partnership agreements vary according to the partnership concerned, but in general they cover the following matters.

Capital. Is capital per partner to be a fixed amount settled at the beginning of the partnership or is it to vary from year to year?

The Division of Profits. The profit-sharing ratio which exists between the partners states what proportion of the business profit each partner is to receive.

Current Accounts. These are maintained to record the remuneration of partners by means of salary, interest and share of profits, and to set against this remuneration the amount of drawings made by each partner. It is usual in a partnership agreement to decide that capitals will be of a fixed amount, and that the shares of profit etc. and drawings shall be passed through a current account.

Interest on Capital or Drawings. The agreement should specify whether partners are to be entitled to interest on their capital, and the rate at which such interest is to be computed. Where partners have contributed widely different amounts of capital, interest is seen as a method of compensating the partner who has contributed most. Alternatively, it may be agreed among the partners that they should pay interest on their drawings, so that any partner who draws out part of his profit share before it is earned and is thus overdrawn will still contribute to the partnership.

Interest on Current Accounts. If partners leave their share of profits in the business and do not draw them out entirely, this is equivalent to the profits ploughed back into the reserves of a limited company. If one partner contributes more to the partnership than his fellows, it would seem right that he should be paid interest on his current account balance, which is an extension of his fixed capital amount.

A Limit to Drawings. The partners may wish to stop any one of their number from drawing out of his current account more than there is in it, or alternatively they may put a limit on the amount by which partners can overdraw.

The Remuneration of Partners. Some partners may work harder for the business than others, and thus the profits are more attributable to their efforts than to those of their fellows. The senior partner has probably contributed more in capital to the partnership, but the junior partner with a much smaller capital may work harder. Accordingly if interest is paid on capital it is only right that salaries should be paid to those partners who contribute most in terms of effort. It must be stated, however, that such partnership salaries are an appropriation of profit, and not a charge thereto, but that both interest on capital, and partners' salaries, must be deducted from profit before the figure to be divided in the profit-sharing ratio is computed.

The Preparation of Accounts. The agreement will often contain a clause about the preparation of accounts, usually stipulating that they should be produced once per annum. This part of the partnership agreement also stipulates that the accounts shall be binding on the partners once they are agreed inter se.

Goodwill. Goodwill arises from time to time in partnerships when a new partner joins the original team or when one of the original partners leaves. In order to ensure that a new partner pays a fair price for a share of the partnership assets, or that a retiring partner takes with him the appropriate amount, goodwill is valued on these occasions. There are many different ways of making such a valuation, and the method to be used for each particular partnership should be contained in the agreement.

Retirement. The agreement should state how the amount to be paid to a partner on retirement shall be determined, and what steps shall be taken to pay this amount. If a retiring partner does not withdraw capital, the amount is transferred to a loan account.

THE PARTNERSHIP ACT

At all times in partnership the terms of the Act of 1890 are subordinated to those in the partnership agreement, but where there is no agreement or where the agreement is silent on any point, then the terms of the Act apply. Section 24 of the Act lays out the terms which are to apply in partnership accounts.

1. Partners are deemed to have an equal share of capital on cessation of business and to share equally any profits or losses made during periods of trading.
2. The partnership firm undertakes to indemnify a partner for payments made on behalf of the partnership business. This means that if a partner pays a partnership expense out of a private bank account, he has a right to draw that money from the partnership bank account, although usually such an adjustment is made through the current account. This indemnity extends to payments or contracts made by partners on behalf of the firm in the ordinary course of business or in order to preserve the business. Thus if a partner buys raw material for the business the other partners cannot refuse in the name of the partnership to accept what has been purchased in the normal course of business. Payments made to preserve the business are more difficult to define, but if a partner sees vacant shop premises near those already occupied by the partnership business and decides to lease them on behalf of the partnership, this action could be construed as an act to preserve the business, since the partner could claim that this action denied the premises to a rival and allowed the partnership business to expand. Although there was no consultation with other partners prior to this action they would have to ratify what has been done.

3. Interest to be paid on loans made to the business by partners at a rate of 5 per cent. A loan in this context is defined as an advance beyond the amount of a partner's agreed capital.
4. Interest on capital is not payable.
5. All partners are allowed to play an equal part in managing the business.
6. Partners are not to be paid salaries.
7. Before a new partner can be admitted to the business all existing partners must consent to the change. One dissenting voice will be sufficient to keep out the joining partner.
8. In all decisions of the partnership the majority is seen to rule. However, in any decision which changes the nature of the business all partners must agree before that change can take place.
9. The books of account of the partnership must be maintained at the partnership office, and all partners must be able to view them on request.

THE APPROPRIATION ACCOUNT

The appropriation account is used in partnerships to make adjustments for the rights of partners *inter se*, so that the accounting profit is reduced by any interest payable on the capital of the partners, by any salaries payable to the partners, and by other similar adjustments before the profit to be divided among the partners in their profit-sharing ratio is revealed. Once the accounting profit has been appropriated, the amounts debited to the appropriation account are credited to the current account, drawings are set against them, and the balance of undrawn profits is carried forward and shown on the balance sheet. If there are several partners a current account in columnar form will be easy to assimilate, and can also be used to show up adjustments between the partners, such as where partner A guarantees partner B a certain minimum income. In such a case, if partner B's income does not reach the guaranteed minimum, he will be credited with the appropriate amount and partner A will be debited.

Example

There are three partners, Frank, Fearless and Bold, who agree to share profits in the ratio 3 : 2 : 1. Their partnership agreement stipulates that partners will receive interest on their capital at 10 per cent per annum, that Bold is entitled to a salary of £1000, and that 10 per cent interest is to be charged on drawings. Frank has guaranteed Fearless a minimum income of £4000 per annum. The last agreed capitals of the partners were: Frank, £50 000; Fearless, £10 000; and Bold, £15 000. The opening balances on their current accounts stood at £1300 for Frank, £200 for Bold and £600 overdrawn for Fearless. The net profit as disclosed by the accounts was £14 500 for the year. Partners' drawings during the year to date were Frank £5000, Fearless £3000 and Bold £3000. The accounts to record these circumstances would appear as follows.

Calculation of income of Fearless:

	£
Profit share	2367
Interest on capital	1000
	3367
Less interest on drawings	300
	3067
From Frank	933
	4000

Frank, Fearless and Bold, Appropriation Account

		Year Ending
	£	£
Net profit per accounts		14 500
Add interest on drawings:		
Frank	500	
Fearless	300	
Bold	300	1 100
		15 600
Deduct salary, Bold		1 000
		14 600
Deduct interest on capital:		
Frank	5000	
Fearless	1000	
Bold	1500	7 500
		7 100
Deduct share of profits:		
Frank (3/6)	3550	
Fearless (2/6)	2367	
Bold (1/6)	1183	
		7 100

Frank, Fearless and Bold, Current Accounts

	Frank £	Fearless £	Bold £		Frank £	Fearless £	Bold £
Opening balance b/d	—	600	—	Opening balance b/d	1300	—	200
Transfer to Fearless per agreement	933			Salary			1000
				Interest on capital	5000	1000	1500
Drawings	5000	3000	3000	Share of profit	3550	2367	1183
Interest on drawings	500	300	300	Transfer from Frank per agreement		933	
Balance c/f	3417	400	583				
	£9850	£4300	£3883		£9850	£4300	£3883
				Balance b/d	3417	400	583

CHANGE OF PARTNERS

Accounting for a partnership becomes slightly more complicated when there is a change in the personnel involved in the partnership, either by the addition of one or more extra partners or by the retirement or death of an existing partner. Often the retirement of one partner is accompanied by the addition of a new partner. Before such an addition can take place, however, all the existing partners must agree about the person involved and the terms on which the new partner joins the group. The legal position is that the partnership ends when an existing partner retires or dies and a new partnership is started by those remaining, with or without a new partner to replace the one who has retired.

The incoming partner usually introduces capital into the firm, often in the form of cash or assets such as cars or plant, but occasionally in the form of goodwill. The accounting entry here is to debit the appropriate asset account and credit the capital account of the new partner with the agreed value of the items introduced. It is important to revalue assets whenever there is a change of partner, since if the real value of the assets is more or less than their book value, the true value must be used in transactions between the partners at this point. An incoming partner will be entitled to a share of the assets and, if there is a surplus of real value over book value, the new partner will receive a share of this surplus without paying for it, unless the surplus is recognized when he joins the firm.

A retiring partner will wish to ensure that the assets are properly valued on the date of retirement, so that the share of partnership capital due to him is accurately computed and adequate compensation is paid by those who are going to continue the business after the retirement for the items which are left behind. Goodwill is a significant item in such a valuation. Sometimes a business is worth more as a whole than the aggregate value of all its individual assets less liabilities. This surplus is called goodwill, and arises from a number of factors, which will be discussed in a later chapter. Goodwill is generated because a business is a going concern with established customers, or because its owners have knowhow and experience, or because it makes more profit than is expected from the assets involved.

There are several methods by which the revaluation of assets and the creation of goodwill can be treated in the accounts of a partnership. The most common method is to recognize the true value of the assets and the existence of goodwill, and to apportion the surplus or capital profit to the existing partners in their profit-sharing ratio before a new partner joins the firm. This involves the creation of a revaluation account to which the debit balances of the asset accounts are written off, while the newly agreed values of the assets are credited to the revaluation account and debited in turn to the asset accounts. A credit balance on the revaluation account means that there is a surplus on revaluation which is divided among the partners in their profit-sharing ratio and credited to their capital accounts.

An alternative method is to compute the share of goodwill or revalued assets attributable to an incoming partner and make that partner pay for this share when joining the business by debiting the new partner's capital account and crediting the capital accounts of the other partners from whom he is buying this part of the surplus. If the partners do not wish a revaluation or goodwill account to be raised in their books, the matter can be settled by a payment from the incoming partner in cash direct to the existing partners, or by dividing the amount of goodwill in the old profit-sharing ratio and crediting it to partners' capital accounts, and then debiting it to partners' capital accounts in the new profit-sharing ratio, as in Review Question 6.2.

The third way of dealing with this situation allows the new partner to earn a share of the goodwill over a period of years without paying for it. In this case a goodwill account is raised and written off against the old partner's capital accounts over a period of years, in the profit-sharing ratio which existed before the arrival of the new partner. Thus, when goodwill is valued at a later date, it can be apportioned between all the partners in their new profit-sharing ratio.

Example

Albert and Brian are in partnership sharing profits in the ratio 2 : 1. Albert has capital of £17 000 invested in the business, while Brian's capital is £7000. This means that the net assets of the business have a book value of £24 000. The partners agree that Charles shall join them as a partner, and that in return for introducing capital of £3000 in cash and £2000 in the form of machinery, he is to receive a fifth share of future profits. The net assets are revalued at £27 000 at this point, and a goodwill account of £6000 is also to be created.

A balance sheet before revaluation of the assets would show:

	£	£
Capital:		
Albert	17 000	
Brian	7 000	£24 000
Represented by		
net assets		£24 000

Goodwill is computed as three years' purchase of the superprofits, which are defined as the excess of past weighted average profits over the profits that should be earned by a business when the risk involved is considered. Albert and Brian reckon a 15 per cent return is needed to compensate for the risk they are taking, so on capital employed of £24 000 they should earn £3600. The profits of the last three years are as follows:

	£			£
This year	6000 × weighting	3	=	18 000
Last year	5500 × weighting	2	=	11 000
Year before last	4600 × weighting	1	=	4 600
	Total	6		33 600 ÷ weights (6) = £5600

Past weighted average profit of £5600 less required profit of £3600 = superprofit of £2000. Three years' purchase of superprofit gives goodwill a value of 3 × £2000 = £6000.

The greatest weighting or significance in the calculation was given to the most recent year because that is most likely to reflect the current situation and the amount of profit which will probably be made in the immediate future.

The journal entries to record the transactions are as follows.

Journal Entries

	Dr. £	Cr. £
Asset accounts	3000	
Revaluation account		3000
Being surplus on revaluation as assets		
Revaluation account	3000	
Capital account:		
Albert		2000
Brian		1000
Being apportionment of surplus on revaluation to partners' capital accounts in the ratio 2 : 1		
Goodwill	6000	
Capital account:		
Albert		4000
Brian		2000
Being creation of a goodwill account and its apportionment between the partners in their profit-sharing ratio 2 : 1		
Cash	3000	
Assets	2000	
Capital account: Charles		5000
Being capital introduced by Charles		

A balance sheet at this point would show:

	£	£
Capital:		
Albert	23 000	
Brian	10 000	
Charles	5 000	£38 000
Represented by:		
Goodwill		6 000
Net assets		29 000
Cash		3 000
		£38 000

The new profit-sharing ratio is computed as follows. At present A and B share 2 : 1 and C is in future to get one-fifth. Thus four-fifths will be left for A and B to share in ratio 2 : 1 ($3 \times 5 = 15$). In future A gets $8/15$, B gets $4/15$ and C gets $3/15$.

With the alternative method of accounting for goodwill on the admission of a new partner, no goodwill account is raised but part of the cash introduced by the new partner is deemed to be to pay for his share of goodwill. The entries are to debit cash and credit the old partners' capital accounts in their original profit-sharing ratio.

If the partners do not want any entry in the books concerning goodwill the amount can be paid direct to Albert and Brian by Charles.

If the goodwill is valued at £6000, Charles will be entitled to a fifth share as a partner, and must therefore pay £1200 to Albert and Brian, in the ratio 2 : 1, from the £3000 of cash which he introduced into the business.

Appropriate journal entries are:

	Dr. £	Cr. £
Cash	1200	
Capital account:		
Albert		800
Brian		400
Being payment from Charles for a fifth share of		
goodwill apportioned between Albert and Brian in		
their profit-sharing ratio.		
Cash	1800	
Assets	2000	
Capital account: Charles		3800
Being capital introduced by Charles		

A balance sheet would now show:

	£	£
Capital:		
Albert	19 800	
Brian	8 400	
Charles	3 800	£32 000
Represented by:		
Net assets		29 000
Cash		3 000
		£32 000

If the goodwill is now valued at £6000, it will be shared by the partners in the ratio 8 : 4 : 3, and Charles will get what he has paid for. The balance sheet will then show:

		£	£
Capital:			
Albert	(19 800 + 3200)	23 000	
Brian	(8400 + 1600)	10 000	
Charles	(3800 + 1200)	5 000	£38 000
Represented by:			
Goodwill			6 000
Net assets			29 000
Cash			3 000
			£38 000

When a partner dies or retires the assets, including goodwill, are revalued to compute accurately his share of the business. It is usual to pay out the retiring partner in cash, for which the entries are credit cash and debit the capital accounts of the remaining partners in their capital ratio. Alternatively, the balance on the capital account of the retiring partner will be transferred to a loan account.

Example

Suppose, in the partnership above, Brian decides to retire and goodwill is valued at £7500 at this point. His share will amount to $4/15$ of the extra value placed on the goodwill, £7500 − £6000 = £1500, which is £400. If the partners do not wish to change the goodwill at this stage the entries would be:

	Dr. £	Cr. £
Either (a)		
Goodwill	400	
Capital account: Brian		400
Being Brian's share of increase in value of goodwill		
Or (b)		
Capital accounts:		
Albert	291	
Charles	109	
Brian		400
Being Brian's share of increase in value of goodwill paid for by his partners in the ratio 8 : 3		

With either alternative Brian would receive £10 400 on his retirement. Until he is paid, the balance sheet would show, for alternative (a):

	£	£
Capital:		
Albert	23 000	
Charles	5 000	£28 000
Represented by:		
Goodwill		6 400
Net assets		29 000
Cash		3 000
		38 000
Less loan account: Brian		10 400
		£28 000

Perhaps under these circumstances it is better to revalue goodwill at £7500 and distribute the extra £1500 to the partners in the ratio 8 : 4 : 3.

In law a retired partner is liable for the debts of the partnership as at the date of retirement. This liability may be offset by persuading the remaining partners to indemnify the retiring partner against such claims, or by the use of a contract of novation whereby the creditors of the firm agree to look to a new partner, as a substitute for the retiring partner, to meet their claims. In certain circumstances a retired partner could be liable for debts of the business incurred after retirement, for example if a creditor did not know of the retirement and lent money to the partnership because the creditor still believed him to be a partner. In the example quoted above, Brian should give specific notice of his retirement to all present creditors of the firm and past creditors who may advance credit again in the future, so that he is not 'held out' as a partner and 'estopped' from denying liability if existing partners cannot repay.

DISSOLUTION OF A PARTNERSHIP

A partnership is dissolved whenever there is a change of partners, but often the business carries on and a new partnership comes into existence. If there is bankruptcy or all partners retire, the business will cease when the partnership is dissolved. The assets are sold for cash (and/or shares if they are sold to a company), the debts are collected, the liabilities are paid and any funds remaining are repaid to the partners. Profit or loss on the sale of the assets is apportioned in the profit-sharing ratio and posted to the credit of the capital accounts.

Section 44 of the Partnership Act 1890 lays down rules for the disbursement of partnership funds on a dissolution. The assets of the firm are to be applied first to repay the debts and liabilities of the firm to persons who are not partners, second to repay partners' loans to the firm, third to repay partners' capital balances, and last to pay out any surplus on dissolution to the partners in their profit-sharing ratio. If the assets are insufficient to meet the liabilities of the firm the deficiency shall be met out of profits and, if they are insufficient, out of capital, and if that is still not enough then the partners must contribute to the remaining deficiency in their profit-sharing ratio. If at this stage one partner is bankrupt and is unable to contribute a share of the deficiency, under the rule in *Garner* v. *Murray*, a case decided in 1904, the solvent partners must make up the share of the deficiency of an insolvent partner, in the ratio of their *capital* accounts before the dissolution commenced.

Example

Alan, Ben and Chris share profits equally. Their balance sheet is as follows:

Balance Sheet of Alan, Ben and Chris as at 31 December

	£	£
Capital:		
Alan	5000	
Ben	2000	
Chris	500	7500
Current accounts:		
Alan	1000	
Ben	1000	
Chris	(1600)	400
Loan account: Alan		2000
		£9900
Represented by:		
Assets:		
Cash		7800
Losses on realization		2100
		£9900

Chris is found to be bankrupt and cannot contribute his share of the loss. The cash would be apportioned among the partners as follows: first Alan would be repaid his loan of £2000, leaving cash available of £5800.

Capital and Current Accounts

	Alan £	Ben £	Chris £
Opening balances	6000	3000	(1100)
Share of loss	(700)	(700)	(700)
	5300	2300	(1800)
Chris deficit, apportioned in opening capital ratio 5 : 2	(1286)	(514)	1800
Cash paid out	£4014	£1786	Nil

These amounts equal the cash of £5800.

SALE OF PARTNERSHIP TO A LIMITED COMPANY

When a partnership is sold to a company and the partners either retire or carry on in business as directors of the company, a realization account is used to sort out the transactions. First the fixed asset accounts are closed off to the realization account, i.e. credit fixed assets and debit the realization account. Care must be taken to ignore any assets which are not being sold. Sometimes retiring partners may take certain assets in lieu of cash, and if they agree to take such assets at a price in excess of their book value, this constitutes a sale at a profit. The appropriate entries are: credit the asset with the agreed price, debit the partner's capital account, and transfer the balance on the asset account to the realization account (as a credit if it is a profit and a debit if it is a loss).

The next step is to compute the price or consideration to be paid. This may be in cash or in the form of shares, or a mixture of cash and shares. The amount should be debited to the purchaser's account and credited to the realization account. When the price is paid, the purchaser should be credited and either shares or cash should be debited.

The debtors and any investments should next be realized for cash. A profit on the sale of investments should be posted from the debit side of the investment account to the credit side of the realization account. If debtors do not realize the book amount (some bad debts are encountered or discounts allowed for early payment) then the difference is debited to the realization account. When creditors are paid (credit cash and debit creditors) any discount received will go to the credit side of the realization account. The costs of realization will be credited to cash and debited to the realization account. A credit balance on the realization account means that the consideration is greater than the book value of assets sold, and a profit on realization has been made. The profit is apportioned in the profit-sharing ratio and posted to the credit of the partners' capital accounts. The balance on the capital account is then settled in cash or shares, or both, and at this point all accounts will be closed.

Example

William and Samuel were in business as partners sharing profits in the rato 3 : 1. A summarized balance sheet for their business as at 31 December is as follows:

	£	£
Capital accounts:		
William	30 000	
Samuel	10 000	
		£40 000
Represented by:		
Fixed assets (net)		18 400
Investments		4 800
Current assets:		
Stock	9 000	
Debtors	16 800	
Cash	2 520	
	28 320	
Less trade creditors	11 520	
		16 800
		£40 000

Included in the fixed assets were two motor cars at book values of £1800 and £1340 respectively, i.e. a total of £3140.

The partners have decided to cease trading as a partnership and have sold their stock and fixed assets to Stockholders Ltd for a price of £44 000, to be satisfied by a payment in cash of £16 000 and the issue to the partners of 28 000 ordinary shares of £1 each in Stockholders Ltd. The two vehicles mentioned above were excluded from the sale, since William had agreed to take over the first car at a valuation of £2200, and Samuel had agreed to take over the other car at £1280.

On final realization £16 600 was received from the debtors, the investments were sold for £5200, and creditors settled for £11 400. The costs of dissolving the firm were paid in cash for £240.

The partners agreed that the ordinary shares were to be allocated in proportion to the capitals shown in the balance sheet above, with any final balance to be settled by cash.

Record the above transactions to close the books of the partnership.

Dr.			Realization Account			Cr.
	£	£		£	£	
Fixed assets			Stockholders Ltd			
£(18 400 − 3140)		15 260	Purchase consideration:			
Stock		9 000	Shares	28 000		
Dissolution costs		240	Cash	16 000	44 000	
Debtors and bad debts		200	Profit on sale of			
Loss on Samuel's vehicle		60	investments		400	
Profit on realization:			Profit on William's vehicle		400	
William (3/4)	15 120		Creditors'			
Samuel (1/4)	5 040		discount received		120	
		20 160				
		£44 920			£44 920	

Dr.		Fixed Asset Account		Cr.
	£		£	
Balance	18 400	Vehicle A—Disposal account	1 800	
		Vehicle B—Disposal account	1 340	
		Realization account	15 260	
	£18 400		£18 400	

Dr.		Vehicle A Disposal Account		Cr.
	£		£	
Fixed assets—Book value	1800	William's capital account	2200	
Profit on disposal to realization	400			
	£2200		£2200	

Dr.		Vehicle B Disposal Account		Cr.
	£		£	
Fixed assets—Book value	1340	Samuel's capital account	1280	
		Loss on disposal to realization	60	
	£1340		£1340	

Note: The profit on William's vehicle arises since he has agreed to take it over at a valuation in excess of its book value. Samuel takes over his car at a value which is less than its book value, so a loss is made. The investments were sold for more than their book value. The accounting entries are:

Dr.		Investment Account		Cr.
	£			£
Balance	4800	Cash		5200
Profit to realization				
account	400			
	£5200			£5200

Dr.		Cash Book		Cr.
	£			£
Balance b/d	2 520	Creditors		11 400
Stockholders Ltd	16 000	Dissolution costs		240
Sale of investments	5 200	William's capital account		21 920
Debtors	16 600	Samuel's capital account		6 760
	£40 320			£40 320

Dr.		Stockholders Ltd		Cr.
	£			£
Purchase consideration	44 000	Cash		16 000
		Shares in Stockholders		28 000
	£44 000			£44 000

Dr.		Shares in Stockholders Ltd		Cr.
	£			£
Stockholders Ltd	28 000	William's capital account		21 000
		Samuel's capital account		7 000
	£28 000			£28 000

The shares are apportioned between the partners according to their capital ratio, i.e. 30 : 10.

Partners' Capital Accounts

	William	Samuel		William	Samuel
	£	£		£	£
Motor cars	2 200	1 280	Balances b/d	30 000	10 000
Shares	21 000	7 000	Profit on		
			realization	15 120	5 040
Cash	21 920	6 760			
	£45 120	£15 040		£45 120	£15 040

The capital account tells a simple story: how much each partner had before realization, what his share of profit was on realization, and how he withdrew his capital—shares, cash and goods.

The partnership assets will now be recorded in the books of Stockholders Ltd. If the consideration paid for them exceeds their book value, the amount of the excess will appear as an extra asset, goodwill.

CONVERSION OF A PARTNERSHIP TO A LIMITED COMPANY

Sometimes partners may decide to change the form of their business to a limited company. The accounting entries for this manoeuvre are similar to those for the sale of a partnership to the company. The fixed and current assets and current liabilities are transferred to the company, and shares are issued to the partners in place of their capital accounts. Often the partnership books are used for the company's accounts and in some cases the conversion entries are not made until after the event. If the conversion takes place during an accounting year it is necessary to apportion the profit for the year to a partnership period, when it will be divided into profit-sharing ratio, and a company period, when it will be divided pro rata to share holdings. If a partner retires on the conversion date he will not be a shareholder and cannot receive a share of post-conversion profits, but if his capital was not repaid to him on the conversion date it will appear as a loan in the company's accounts and interest thereon would normally be provided.

Partnership assets are usually revalued at the conversion date. The consideration for net assets in the partnership is the amount of shares issued to the partners. It seems logical to allocate the shares on the basis of partners' capital accounts, but if this is done profits in the company will be shared on a different basis from that ruling in the partnership. Agreement can be reached if partners become directors and draw salaries or fees which will compensate for any loss of income.

Example

Frank, Victor and Jon are in partnership sharing profits and losses equally. Their balance sheet as at 30 October is as follows:

Frank, Victor and Jon, Balance Sheet as at 30 October

	£		£	£
Capitals:		Fixed assets (net of		
Frank	240 000	depreciation):		
Victor	120 000	Buildings		120 000
Jon	14 000	Fixtures and fittings		34 000
	374 000			154 000
Current liabilities:		Current assets:		
Creditors	26 000	Stock	125 000	
		Debtors	115 000	
		Cash	6 000	246 000
	£400 000			£400 000

The partners decide to convert their business to a limited company, Factors Ltd, as from 1 November, but Jon decides to retire on that date, leaving his capital in the business as a loan at 10 per cent interest per annum. The buildings were revalued at £28 000, and £1 ordinary shares in Factors Ltd were issued to Frank and Victor in settlement of their capital accounts.

A profit of £108 000 (£228 000 − £120 000) is disclosed on revaluation and divided equally among the partners. Frank and Victor now have capitals of £276 000 and £156 000 respectively, so shares issued by Factors Ltd equal £432 000.

Factors Ltd Balance Sheet as at 1 November

	£		£	£
Share capital:		Fixed assets net of depreciation:		
66 000 ordinary shares		Buildings		228 000
of £1 each	432 000	Fixtures and fittings		34 000
				262 000
Long-term loan:		Current assets:		
Owed to Jon at 10 per cent		Stock	125 000	
interest (14 000 + 26 000)	50 000	Debtors	115 000	
Current liabilities:		Cash	6 000	
Creditors	26 000			246 000
	£508 000			£508 000

The business uses the same set of books until the year end of 31 August in the following year, when a trading and profit and loss account is prepared:

	£	£
Sales		442 000
Less cost of sales		322 200
Gross profit		79 800
Expenses:		
Selling expenses	12 202	
Carriage outwards	1 460	
Management salaries	18 400	
Office expenses	1 248	
Directors' fees	4 500	
Preliminary expenses	1 200	39 010
		£40 790

Depreciation on buildings is at 5 per cent on book value and on fixtures 10 per cent on book value.

The next problem is to compute a true profit and apportion it between the partnership which existed until 31 October and the company. Your enquiries reveal that the goods sold in the year are of one kind and have been priced at the same level throughout the year. The average monthly sales for the first two months (September and October) were half those of the average monthly sales for the remaining months in the accounting year. This means that the gross profit can be apportioned as follows:

$$\text{September and October: two months at half each} = 1 = \frac{1}{11}$$

$$\text{November to August: ten months at 1 each} = 10 = \frac{10}{11}$$

$$\text{Ratio 1:10} \qquad\qquad \frac{}{11}$$

Further information available is that £16 000 paid to partners as salaries is included in management salaries.

Remember to provide loan interest (£58 000 × 10 per cent × $^{10}/_{12}$ = £4166) and depreciation: buildings (£228 000 × 5 per cent × $^{10}/_{12}$ = £9500); and fixtures (£34 000 × 10 per cent × $^{10}/_{12}$ = £2833). The buildings and fixtures were taken over at a valuation, so no depreciation can be charged against the partnership profit. Any depreciation so charged would merely increase the profit on revaluation.

Factors Ltd. Statement Showing Apportionment of Profit for Year Ended 31 August

	£	£	Basis of Apportionment		Partnership		Company	
Gross profit		79 800	Turnover	1 : 10		7255		72 545
Selling expenses	12 202		Turnover	1 : 10	1109		11 093	
Carriage outwards	1 460		Turnover	1 : 10	133		1 327	
Salaries:								
Partners	1 600		Actual		1600		—	
Others	16 800		Time	2 : 10	2800		14 000	
Office expenses	1 248		Time	2 : 10	208		1 040	
Directors' fees	4 500		Company		—		4 500	
Preliminary expenses	1 200		Company		—		1 200	
Depreciation:								
Building	9 500		Company		—		9 540	
Fixtures	2 833		Company		—		2 833	
Loan interest	4 166	55 509	Company		—	4250	4 166	49 659
Net profit		£24 291				£3005		£22 886

The partnership period shows a profit which would be divided equally among Frank, Victor and Jon as £1001.66 each.

JOINT VENTURES

A trading agreement where two or more parties already in business in their own right agree to act together for a specific transaction is known as a joint venture. The transactions concerned are usually of a trading nature, where one venturer, perhaps a sole trader, consigns goods to the other, who sells them. Joint ventures are not, however, confined to small operations, since this form of trading can be adopted when companies co-operate to undertake a large project, perhaps with one partner providing expertise and the other providing local production facilities.

The difficulty of accounting for such transactions concerns the recognition of expenses of the venture borne by the venturers, and the computation of the profit made. Sometimes a separate set of books is kept for the joint venture, but the more usual method employed is for each venturer to record his own transactions in a joint venture account in his books and then these accounts are brought together in a memorandum joint venture account which will disclose the profit made. Each venturer's share of the profit is posted back to the joint venture account in his own books, and the balance on that account will disclose the cash to be received from, or paid to, the other venturer.

Example

Charles and Roger agreed upon a joint venture to buy up a bankrupt's stock, with a view to selling it later at a profit. The stock was valued by the receiver at £8000, and Charles agreed to contribute £3000 towards its cost, leaving Roger to find the balance. Other expenses were paid by Charles and Roger as they occurred. The venturers agreed to share profits equally, but decided to credit a 10 per cent commission to each party on the sales he made. A separate set of books was not opened for the venture.

The following transactions took place:

May 1	Stock purchased.	
2	Charles bought a van to transport the stock, £1500.	
3	Advertisements were placed: by Charles, £70; by Roger, £90.	
5	Sales were made: Charles, £2500; Roger, £2600.	
9	The van broke down and Roger paid a repair bill, £100.	
12	Sales were made: Charles, £1300; Roger, £800.	
16	Sales were made: Charles, £2800; Roger, £3000.	
18	Petrol bills were settled by Charles, £80.	
20	The venture being over, Roger agreed to take the van at a price of £1100.	
25	Settlement was effected between the partners, after the agreement that petty cash expenses paid out for travelling should be £30 each, and for general expenses, Charles, £70 and Roger, £120.	

These transactions would be recorded as follows:

Charles's books:

Dr.   Joint Venture Account with Roger   Cr.

	£		£
Stock	3000	Sales	2500
Van	1500	Sales	1300
Advertising	70	Sales	2800
Petrol	80		6600
Travelling	30	Balance—cash from Roger	165
General expenses	70		
Commission	660		
Share of profit	1355		
	£6765		£6765

Roger's books:

Dr.   Joint Venture Account with Charles   Cr.

	£		£
Stock	5000	Sales	2600
Advertising	90	Sales	800
Van repairs	100	Sales	3000
Travelling	30		6400
General expenses	120	Van taken over	1100
Commission	640		
Share of profit	1355		
Cash to Charles	165		
	£7500		£7500

Dr.		Memorandum Joint Venture Account		Cr.
May	£	May		£
1 Stock purchased	8 000	5 Sales		5 100
2 Van purchased	1 500	12 Sales		2 100
3 Advertising	160	16 Sales		5 800
9 Van repairs	100	20 Sale of van		1 100
18 Petrol	80			
25 Travelling	60			
25 General expenses	190			
25 Commission				
Charles 10 per cent of £6600	660			
Roger 10 per cent of £6400	640			
	11 390			
Net profit: £				
Charles (½) 1355				
Roger (½) 1355				
	2 710			
	£14 100			£14 100

SEMINAR EXERCISES 8

1. (a) The books of Check and Mate, who are equal partners, are balanced annually on 31 December. Before profits are ascertained and divided, 5 per cent interest is allowed upon partners' capital. Depreciation (based on cost) is written off plant at the rate of 5 per cent per annum and off motor vehicles at the rate of 25 per cent per annum. A provision of 5 per cent on debtors is to be made for bad and doubtful debts. One year's interest at the rate of 6 per cent is due on the loan, and has not yet been passed through the books. The stock in hand as on 31 December was valued at £3225. The following are the final balances as on 31 December:

	£		£
Purchases	16 450	Carriage inwards	400
Manufacturing wages	2 150	Motor vehicles (at cost £3200)	2 400
Sales	24 800	Sundry creditors	15 345
Check's capital	5 000	Loan on mortgage	5 000
Check's current account			
(overdrawn)	550	Freehold land and buildings	8 000
Mate's capital	2 000	Plant (at cost £6000)	4 000
Mate's current account		Provision for bad and doubtful	
(overdrawn)	350	debts (1 January)	600
Stock (1 January)	3 000	Sundry debtors	13 100
Salaries	820	Cash at bank	1 200
Rent	325		

Check is to receive a salary of £575 but guarantee Mate a profit share of £1300. Prepare a trading, profit and loss and appropriation account for the year ended 31 December, and a balance sheet as at that date. Show current accounts as workings.

(b) Distinguish between appropriations of profit and charges made against profit. Use examples from (a) above to illustrate your answer.

2. Hope and Crosby are in partnership and have been trading as The Utopia Road Nurseries for several years. Neither partner is skilled at accounting. They have presented you with such books and vouchers as they have kept and have asked you to prepare the annual accounts. You discover the following:

(a) Bank Account.

	£		£
Balance 1 April last year	1 200	Purchases	81 035
Bankings	101 349	Drawings	
		Hope	6 000
		Crosby	5 500
		Van hire	2 400
		Cash	3 000
		Electricity	1 660
		Balance this year	2 954
	£102 549		£102 549

(b) Bankings. Cash takings have been paid into the bank twice a week. Payments made from takings were:

	£
Wages	16 080
Repairs	670
Insurance	835
Sundries	2 982
Electricity	1 300
Purchases	2 900
Tractor expenses	877

Cash in hand at 1 April last year was £92 and at 31 March this year £110.

(c) Partners. Crosby is to be credited with a salary of £2500 and the partners will be credited with 10 per cent interest on their capital as at 1 April last year. Hope owns the freehold land and a notional rent of £1500 is to be charged in the accounts. The partners took, at retail prices, some goods for their own consumption. They amounted to £350 for Hope and £520 for Crosby. Profits are shared in the ratio Hope 60 per cent and Crosby 40 per cent. At 1 April last year the capital amounts were Hope £10 000 and Crosby £5000.

(d) Assets and Liabilities. Debtors and creditors are:

	This Year £	Last Year £
Purchases: creditor	3250	2820
Electricity: creditor	300	180
Sales account: debtor	352	773
Stocks of goods and plants for resale	9080	7935

Fixed assets at 1 April last year were:

	Cost	Accumulated Depreciation	Depreciation Rate
Tractor	1 800	600	25 per cent on cost
Greenhouses	12 000	5200	10 per cent on cost

Present the trading and profit and loss account for the year ended 31 March and a balance sheet as at that date.

3. Leek and Bean were in partnership as lawnmower manufacturers. Leek being responsible for the factory and Bean for the warehouse. Completed lawnmowers were transferred from the factory to the warehouse at agreed prices. Profits are to be shared as follows:

	Factory	Warehouse
Leek	75%	25%
Bean	25%	75%

The following trial balance was extracted from the books on 30 June this year.

	£	£
Capital accounts:		
Leek		48 000
Bean		49 000
Drawings:		
Leek	6 000	
Bean	5 000	
Freehold factory at cost	42 150	
Factory plant at cost	25 750	
Provision for depreciation to 30 June last year		6 050
Delivery vans at cost	8 050	
Provision for depreciation to 30 June last year		3 450
Stocks at 30 June last year:		
Raw materials	4 028	
Work in progress	3 400	
Lawnmowers completed (1200 @ £40 each)	48 000	
Sales (1820 lawnmowers)		111 020
Purchase of raw materials	28 650	
Factory wages	15 020	
Warehouse wages	6 030	
Expenses:		
Factory	12 070	
Warehouse	10 020	
Provision for doubtful debts		1 600
Trade debtors and creditors	18 000	6 000
Bank overdraft		7 048
	£232 168	£232 168

During the year 1520 lawnmowers at £45 each were transferred to the warehouse; lawnmowers in stock at the end of the year were to be valued at £45 each. Closing stock of raw materials was £3180 and work in progress was valued at £5050.

Accrued expenses outstanding on 30 June this year were:

	Factory	Warehouse
Expenses	£2090	£1080
Factory wages	£ 280	—

The general provision for bad debts was to be maintained at 10 per cent of the trade debtors.

During the year Leek bought a new car for £4000 out of his own money and brought it into the partnership business, but this has not yet been entered in the books. It is to be charged against the warehouse.

Provision for depreciation is to be made as follows: factory plant 10 per cent per annum on cost; motor vehicles 20 per cent per annum on cost.

Interest is to be charged on drawings at 10 per cent and paid on opening capital at 5 per cent, and satisfied by a contra entry between the partners' profit shares.

Prepare manufacturing, trading, profit and loss and appropriation accounts for the year ended 30 June this year and a balance sheet as at that date.

4. The following is a trial balance of a partnership at 31 December last year.

	£	£
Capital accounts as at 1 January last year:		
Henrietta		10 000
Maud		8 000
Nellie		2 000
Freehold property	20 000	
Fixtures and fittings	4 000	
Stock	5 000	
Debtors	1 000	
Cash at bank	2 500	
Creditors		2 500
Net profit for the year		
to 31 December		10 000
	£32 500	£32 500

The net profit for the year is to be divided as follows: Henrietta ½, Maud ¼, Nellie ¼, after allowing for interest at the rate of 10 per cent per annum on the capital account balances at 1 January and after allowing a salary of £1000 per annum to Maud.

On 31 December Henrietta retired from the partnership. On this date the assets were revalued as follows:

	£
Freehold property	25 000
Fixtures and fittings	2 000
Stock	3 000

Goodwill was valued at £6000. On this date and after adjusting for the foregoing, Henrietta received payment of the amount due to her.

On 1 January this year Emma was admitted to the partnership, sharing profits equally with the two remaining partners. It was agreed that she should introduce capital of £5000 in cash and that goodwill should not appear in the balance sheet of the new partnership. Emma also brought a car worth £2000 into the business.

Draw up the balance sheet of the new partnership on 1 January this year after the admission of Emma.

5. (a) Red, Green and Blue are in partnership sharing profits and losses equally. At close of business on 31 May, Green decided to retire, and Red and Blue

agreed to continue in partnership sharing profits and losses in the ratio of
2 : 1. The balance sheet at 31 May before the retirement of Green was:

	£	£		£	£
Capital accounts:			Freehold property		1 500
Red	13 000		Plant and machinery		4 000
Green	5 000				5 500
Blue	7 000				
		25 000			
			Stock	9100	
			Debtors	6900	
Sundry creditors		5 000	Bank	8500	24 500
		£30 000			£30 000

The partners also agreed the following:
  (i) In computing the amount due to Green, goodwill is to be valued at £9000
      but no goodwill account is to be opened in the books.
 (ii) Revaluation of assets is to take place, which results in revised amounts as
      follows: freehold property £2500, plant and machinery £3000, stock
      £7300.
(iii) Green is to be paid £4000 in cash and it is agreed that the balance due to
      him is to be retained in the form of a loan.
Prepare the partners' capital accounts recording the above and also the
balance sheet of Red and Blue after Green has retired.
  (b) In drawing up a partnership agreement provision is often made for the
      partners to be entitled to salaries and interest on the capital invested in the
      firm, as well as the balance of profits to be shared in an agreed ratio. Why is
      this so?

REVIEW QUESTIONS 6

1. Alan, Bill and Chris are in partnership and have traded together successfully for
   many years making and selling identification equipment for the export packaging
   trade. Early in 19-2 Bill perceived a new business opportunity which he intended
   to develop on his own and advised his partners that he would leave the
   partnership on 31 December 19-2. Alan and Chris considered the situation and
   agreed to convert the business to a limited company on that date. The new
   company was to be incorporated as Alchris Ltd.
   The balance sheet of the partnership as at 31 December 19-2 is as follows:

	£	£		£	£
Partners' capital:			Fixed assets:		
Alan	300 000		Freehold property	600 000	
Bill	300 000		Plant	255 272	
Chris	150 000		Vehicles	42 613	
		750 000			
			Fixtures and		
			fittings	32 505	

	£	£		£	£
Current accounts:					930 390
Alan	41 118		Current assets:		
Bill	94 260				
Chris	36 209		Stock	328 422	
		171 587	Debtors	181 875	
			Cash	15 624	
					525 921
Loan account:					
Alan		210 000			
Current liabilities:					
Trade creditors	.	324 724			
		£1 456 311			£1 456 311

During December 19-2 the partners met to agree the terms of the changes outlined above. They agreed that:

(a) Part of the premises was not required by the new company and was to be sold for £112 500. Bill was to be allowed to retain his car at a valuation of £6000, and he would also take out of the business some stock valued for balance sheet purposes at £30 000.

(b) The remaining assets and current liabilities of the partnership, except cash, were to be purchased by Alchris Ltd for a consideration of £1 050 000. Legal and valuation expenses related to these changes were £751 and were to be borne by the partnership, and paid immediately.

(c) The consideration was to be paid partly by the issue of 14 per cent debentures to Alan in lieu of his loan account, and to Bill to cover his remaining investment in the partnership after he has been paid all the cash in the partnership bank account. The balance of the consideration would be settled by the issue of ordinary shares of £1 each to Alan and Chris.

Draft the closing entries for the partnership books.

2. Eric, Fred and Geoff are in partnership sharing profits and losses in the ratio 3 : 2 : 1. The balance sheet for the partnership as at 30 June 19-2 is as follows:

	£	£		£	£
Capital:			Fixed assets:		
Eric	92 500		Premises	88 000	
Fred	67 500		Plant	39 000	
Geoff	25 000		Vehicles	14 000	
	185 000		Fixtures	3 000	
				144 000	
Current account:			Current assets:		
Eric	4714		Stock	63 479	
Fred	(2009)		Debtors	33 880	
Geoff	4178	6 883	Cash	560	97 919
Loan Geoff		27 000			
Current liabilities:					
Creditors		20 036			
Bank overdraft		3 000			
		241 919			241 919

Geoff decides to retire from the business on 30 June 19-2 and Hal is admitted as a partner on that date. The following matters are agreed:

(i) Certain assets were revalued:

	£
Premises	118 000
Plant	37 000
Stock	54 279

(ii) Provision is to be made for doubtful debts in the sum of £2000.

(iii) Goodwill is to be recorded in the books on the date Geoff retires in the sum of £21 000. The partners in the new firm do not wish to maintain a goodwill account so that amount is to be written back against the new partners' capital accounts.

(iv) Eric and Fred are to share profits in the same ratio as before, and Hal is to have the same share of profits as Fred.

(v) Geoff is to take his car at its book value of £2900 in part payment, and the balance of all he is owed by the firm in cash, except £30 000, which he is willing to leave as a loan account.

(vi) Hal is to contribute £79 000 in cash as his capital. Eric is to transfer £10 000 from current account to capital account.

(a) Account for the above transactions, including goodwill and retiring partners' accounts.

(b) Draft a balance sheet for the partnership of Eric, Fred and Hal as at 30 June 19-2.

3. Garner, Murray and Wilkins are trading in partnership together, sharing profits and losses equally. The balance sheet of the business as at 31 December 19-3 is as shown below.

	£	£
Capital:		
Garner		140 000
Murray		70 000
Wilkins		42 000
		252 000
Current accounts:		
Garner	10 000	
Murray	16 000	
Wilkins	(6 000)	20 000
Loan account:		
Ms Wilkins		200 000
Net capital employed		472 000
Represented by:		
Fixed assets, at book value:		
Land and buildings		901 640
Plant		154 230
Vehicles		36 130
		1 092 000

	£	£
Current assets:		
Stock	74 000	
Debtors	102 000	
	176 000	
Less current liabilities:		
Trade creditors	(182 800)	
Hire purchase on car	(6 000)	
Overdraft	(607 200)	
		(620 000)
		£472 000

The partnership business has made losses in recent years and the bank and trade creditors are pressing for repayment of funds advanced to the business. Garner and Murray consider the suggestion that they should inject more capital into the business, but decide against this plan. Wilkins is now bankrupt and so cannot advance more funds. The partners decide to sell the business as at 31 December 19-3 to Scott PLC, a company in the same trade:

The terms of the sale are as follows:

(a) Scott PLC agree to purchase the land and buildings, plant, two of the vehicles and the stock, all for £1 002 000.

(b) The third vehicle, a car, which has a book value of £12 000, is to be taken by Murray as part of his capital repayment. The price agreed for the car is £8000 but Murray also agrees to settle personally the hire purchase debt owing on the car.

(c) The partners collect the debts of their business but, because of their haste, £8000 of bad debts are incurred and £4000 of cash discounts are allowed.

(d) The consideration is to be partly settled by Scott PLC by the payment of £737 200 in cash and the assumption of the trade creditors (all except a personal contact of Garner, who is owed £20 000 and is paid separately by the partnership). The balance of the consideration is to be settled by the issue of £1 ordinary shares in Scott PLC at par to the partners.

Draft ledger accounts to close the books of the partnership.

11 | The Financial Accountant as an Auditor, and Designer of Accounting Systems

A well-proven definition of an audit is 'the examination by an auditor of the evidence from which the income statement and balance sheet have been prepared, to ascertain that they represent a true and fair view of the transactions under review, and of the financial state of the organization at the closing date of the period'. An auditor is one who asks questions, listens to answers, checks facts, eventually forms an opinion about the correctness of the financial statements, and then reports his views to the shareholders of the company. The auditor's opinion is contained in the audit certificate which is appended to the published accounts. The evidence on which this opinion is founded is derived from the accounting records, and especially the vouchers which provide the basic data from which the accounting records are prepared, e.g. invoices, goods received notes, orders, sales invoices, wage sheets and bank statements. All provide evidence to confirm that the books properly represent the transactions which have taken place and that the accounts are based firmly on those book entries. Apart from this paper evidence the auditor must examine the actual assets themselves, where possible, to ascertain that they really exist and are correctly shown in the books and the accounts. Justification is important to ascertain that the transactions which have been recorded have received the correct accounting treatment according to best accounting practice as expressed in accounting standards and the Companies Acts.

Part of the object of an audit is to reveal errors in the accounts, and to discover any fraud which has taken place, but another objective of equal importance is to prevent error and fraud from taking place. It is the professional duty of an auditor to report, to those who employ him, on the accounting systems in operation in the business. The system must be tested to ensure that it is good enough to account adequately for the transactions which take place and that it is being operated properly. If the system is weak, or the operation of a good system is less than thorough, what is called a 'letter of weakness' is sent to the client. When working for a company the auditor is employed by the shareholders to comment to them on the accounts prepared for them by the management, but the letter of weakness is sent to the management of the company so that they can act to put matters right.

In a leading case, *Fomento (Sterling Area) Ltd* v. *Selsdon Fountain Pen Co. Ltd* (1958) WLR 45, Lord Denning, then Master of the Rolls, had this to say:

'An Auditor is not confined to the mechanics of checking vouchers and making arithmetical computations. He is not to be written off as a professional adder upper and subtractor. His vital task is to take care to see that errors are not made, be they errors of computation or errors of omission or commission or downright untruths. To perform this task properly he must come to it with an enquiring mind—not suspicious of dishonesty, but suspecting that someone may have made a mistake somewhere, and that a check must be made to ensure there has been none.'

The audit forms an important part of the corporate reporting system. When the auditor certifies that the accounts are 'true and fair' he is supporting them with the weight of his own reputation, creating confidence in the statements and increasing their credibility in the eyes of all parties who may use and rely on these statements. The auditor must be satisfied that the accounts have been drawn up according to best accounting practice as expressed in the Statements of Standard Accounting Practice, and the statutory rules embodied in the Companies Act 1985. The relevance of accounting policies used, and the adequacy of notes to accounts in disclosing significant information, must be considered by the accountant before the audit certificate is completed.

TYPES OF AUDIT

It is customary to classify audits according to their type, i.e. private, statutory and internal. The private audit takes place when an accountant acts as auditor to a sole trader or partnership. In this case there may be an agreed limit of work, the task to be undertaken being the subject of an agreement between auditor and client, who is the sole trader or the partners. It is wise to formalize the nature and scope of the work to be undertaken in a written agreement in order to protect the auditor from difficulties which can arise at a later date. In a private audit the auditor works directly for the manager, who may also be the owner of the business, and therefore the extent of the work can be limited to what the client requires. Often this requirement is to certify the accounts, so that they can be used as reliable evidence for tax purposes or for the valuation of a business if it is to be sold. The client may ask the auditor to verify the accounts, but stipulate that a full stock audit is not required. If the stock figures are later proved to be wrong, then the client cannot seek redress from the auditor for damage he suffered from this mistake.

The second type of audit is the statutory audit, so called because it is carried out under the provision of the Companies Act 1985. Such an audit is undertaken for a public limited company, i.e. one whose shares are traded on the Stock Exchange. In this type of audit the auditor is working for the shareholders and commenting to them on the accounts produced by their management for their company. The general public as investors may also rely on the audited accounts to guide their investment policy. For this reason the auditor must do whatever he considers necessary for a satisfactory audit, and there can be no restriction on what is checked and the amount of work done. There can be no agreement between the auditor and the management to limit the scope of the investigation or the area of search. Because the auditor accepts no restrictions he alone is responsible for determining how much work needs to be done for a proper audit.

The third classification is the internal audit. In this case the auditor is an employee of the company and reports to its managers. The task is to review the systems set up in the business, to ensure that they are efficient, to comment on the safety and security of the assets, and to discover and prevent fraud where possible. The work of the internal auditor is very detailed, involving much checking and vouching of prime documents, and is often closely connected to the systems design and organization and methods departments. The relationship of the internal auditor and the external auditor is one of friendly co-operation. The external auditor can decide to ignore the work undertaken by the internal audit department. Usually, however, having tested the abilities and standards of the internal auditor, the external auditor is able to avoid the duplication of much detailed checking by relying on some of the work already completed by the internal auditor. The programmes of work undertaken by the internal audit department are usually designed after consultation with the external auditor. Vouching is a term used to describe the substantiation of a transaction by the inspection of a voucher which provides evidence to support the entry made in the books.

AUDITING METHODS

There are several different methods of undertaking an audit. The traditional method is that of the final audit, where the auditor, with a team of clerks, attends the business premises after the accounts have been produced and checks and vouches them thoroughly at one sitting. This may take several weeks or, in a large company, even several months. With a small business the practising accountant may find that he has to produce accounts from incomplete records and then audit them as a separate task.

The final audit has been shown to be impractical for large businesses, since it concentrates the work into one period, and the fact that it may take many weeks to complete the checking required can delay the publication of the company's accounts. Also, concentration into one period, for example in February after a year-end date of 31 December, creates a peak demand for auditors' services and may cause difficulties in an accounting practice. For these reasons the interim audit has been developed. This method entails the attendance of the auditors on two or three occasions in the year. They work through the books, checking and vouching according to their audit programme, until they have checked the transactions of, for example, the first six months of the accounting year, and then they stop, carefully noting the point at which their checking ceases, and return later in the year. Thus the device of the interim audit accelerates the production of audited accounts at the year end and enables companies to produce audited accounts at the half-way stage, on the basis of which the board can decide to pay an interim dividend to the shareholders.

In some very large organizations, however, even the interim audit has proved inadequate from a timing point of view, and has been replaced by the continuous audit. This method necessitates the attendance of auditors throughout the year at various parts of the organization. The small permanent team of auditors will constantly check the transactions which have taken place so that when the year end approaches most of the checking has been completed. The auditor of a large group of companies, perhaps with subsidiaries in many different countries, may find that a continuous audit is the only way in which the many thousands of transactions which have taken place can be checked in time to meet the deadline of the annual general meeting for which the published accounts are produced.

The audit of a large volume of transactions requires the application of special techniques. The auditor cannot check everything, since this would be too time-consuming. To save time, auditors have adopted two techniques, sampling and depth checking. Sampling, to the auditor, is the selection of a statistical sample of the transactions which have taken place and their careful checking and vouching by the auditor. The auditor knows that he can rely on this sample, if it is large enough, as being representative of the whole, so that if the transactions in the sample are found to be correct it is probable that the remainder, which have not been checked, are also correct. The success of sampling is largely dependent on the selection of the sample, and it should be ensured that the sample is large enough to be a significant guide to the whole 'population'. The auditor must use judgement to select a 'confidence level' appropriate to each item to be tested, which will in turn influence the size of the sample.

Depth checking is a term used to describe the audit method whereby a single transaction is selected and checked in depth, which means that the auditor follows the transaction from beginning to end in great detail. For example, the auditor may select the purchase of a certain delivery of raw materials, and will check every prime document and every entry in the books needed to record that transaction from the moment that the purchase is requisitioned right through until the point at which the supplier is paid by cheque. This will show whether the system is operating correctly. If a large enough sample of transactions is selected to give confidence in the reliability of the remainder, depth checking removes the need to check every transaction.

It must be emphasized that the extent to which the auditor can rely on his work depends upon the selection and size of the sample.

It is customary for an auditor to draw up a programme of the checks needed to complete the task. Thus if the work is interrupted, the audit programme ensures that nothing is missed, and if another auditor comes to finish the job, he will know exactly what has been done to date. Auditing is a systematic and painstaking business, e.g. careful notes are maintained in an audit file of questions asked and answers received, so that a comprehensive record is built up on which the auditor's opinion can be based. The file contains the Internal Control Questionnaires (ICQs) completed at the beginning of the audit. The auditor will review the system of internal control in operation in the business and interview those responsible for its operation, gradually completing an ICQ which in time will form the basis of a letter of weakness.

APPOINTMENT OF AN AUDITOR

It is considered a matter of professional ethics that when a new auditor takes up his appointment to audit the accounts of a company he should ascertain from the retiring auditor whether there is any reason why he should not act. The new auditor should not accept nomination for the post without having had written communication with the retiring auditor to ensure that all is well. This simple stratagem ensures that a new auditor is given full information by the previous auditor of any disagreements with the management over the production of the accounts, or of any pressure which the board may have tried to put on the auditor to accept certain accounting policies which are considered to be undesirable. This will inhibit the ability of a board to change its auditors in order to gain acceptance of questionable accounting policies. The shareholders have a right to change their auditor, and it is their votes at the annual general meeting which will be needed to make the change, but they will often accept the advice of the board of directors when a change of auditors is proposed by the board.

The auditor has a right to act independently, since he is employed by the shareholders to comment on what the management have done so far as the accounting statements are concerned. This implies that the auditor must be able to form and express an opinion openly. This principle is supported in the appointment, rights and duties of auditors which are laid down in the various sections of the Companies Act 1985.

Section 384 of the Companies Act 1985 deals with the appointment of auditors. It lays down that the auditor of a public company shall be appointed by the shareholders at each annual general meeting, and shall be entitled to hold the appointment from the end of that meeting until the end of the next annual general meeting. This ensures that an auditor will have the right to attend the AGM and speak if necessary, especially if another auditor has been appointed at that meeting.

If no auditor is appointed at the annual general meeting, the Secretary of State for Trade and Industry has the right to appoint an auditor to serve until the next annual general meeting and the company must notify him that this power has become exercisable within one week of the event. In the case of the first auditor of a company, the directors are empowered to appoint an auditor to serve until the end of the first annual general meeting of the shareholders.

The directors are also empowered to fill a casual vacancy caused by the death or retirement of an auditor during the accounting year. The auditor's fee is fixed by the shareholders at the annual general meeting, unless the Secretary of State or the directors have made the appointment. The fee is, however, usually agreed with the board before the AGM. It is also stated in the Act (s.389) that only professional accountants who are members of accounting bodies recognized by the Department of Trade and Industry can act as auditors of a public company. The Institutes of Chartered Accountants and the Chartered Association of Certified Accountants are the only bodies recognized for this task in the UK, although a few individuals who are not members of these bodies are authorized by the Board of Trade to act as auditors. The Companies Act 1989 makes some changes to the situation of the auditor. Private limited companies will be allowed to opt out of the obligation to appoint an auditor annually so that there will be an automatic reappointment of the auditor until the company or the auditor decide otherwise.

There is a new regime for the regulation of auditors in the UK in line with the EEC 8th Directive. Only 'registered auditors' will be eligible for appointment as auditors of a company. A registered auditor can be either an individual or a firm but must be supervised by a Recognized Supervisory Body (RSB). Individual auditors must hold appropriate qualifications and an auditing firm must be controlled by qualified persons. Members of the existing recognized bodies under section 389 of the 1985 Act will be deemed to hold an appropriate qualification but from the commencement of the scheme in January 1991 Recognized Qualifying Bodies (RQBs) will be appointed by the Secretary of State to award appropriate qualifications. Clearly the bodies recognized under section 389 of the 1985 Act will apply for recognition but will need to comply with detailed requirements on education and training. In future it may be necessary for the qualified accountant to undertake two years of post-qualification experience and at least three years of practical audit training before becoming a qualified auditor. The RSBs are intended to be regulators of the auditing profession with established rules covering professional integrity, the achievement of technical standards, monitoring and enforcement of procedures for maintaining competence, and the investigation of complaints. If an auditor is sued for negligence the RSB which has licensed that auditor will, however, be immune from litigation. Although in future an auditing firm will be controlled by qualified persons, under the new rules non-auditors will be allowed as partners in audit firms. A question which is very much open at this time is the possibility that firms of accountants and auditors might be able to transfer from partnership status and incorporate a business as a limited liability company, thus reducing the impact of claims for negligence against the partners. Such a development will only take place, however, if there are adequate rules for insurance against such claims for negligence.

Some persons are forbidden by law to act as auditors to public companies. Section 389 also states that an officer or servant of the company cannot act as its auditor. The term 'officer of the company' applies to directors and the company secretary, while a 'servant of the company' is somebody in its employ. It is also stated that the partner or employee of an officer or servant of the company cannot act as auditor to that company. These measures are written into the law to ensure the independence of the auditor and to prohibit the appointment as auditor of any person who owes a debt of loyalty to those running the company and who are the subject of the auditor's investigation. Neither can a body corporate (another company) act as an auditor. The separation in practice of auditing duties from consultancy work undertaken for a client is an important feature of this independence. A practice should ensure that it does not have as an audit client a company in which a partner is the beneficial holder of shares. A shareholder employed by a practice should not work on the audit of the company concerned.

RIGHTS AND DUTIES

The auditor has certain rights which are embodied in the Companies Act 1985. In the case of the audit of a private company the rights of an auditor depend on the agreement or contract with the person who is employing the auditor, i.e. the principal shareholder. An auditor has a lien on the books of the company for any unpaid audit fees. This means that in the event of non-payment of the fee for services, the auditor can withhold the books and papers of the company in his possession until the fee is paid.

The auditor has a right at all times to have access to the books, accounts and vouchers of the business which is under audit, and he is expected to use all available information. If necessary a previous opinion should be reviewed in the light of fresh information which becomes available. The auditor has a right to such explanations as he shall require from the officers and employees of the company, and must be invited to all meetings of the company, i.e. the AGM and any special meetings held for the shareholders. Any officer of a company who knowingly or recklessly makes a misleading statement to an auditor is guilty of an offence.

The rights of the auditor are especially significant when it is suggested that he should be removed from office or replaced by another auditor. To protect the auditor from pressure from management, the auditor has the right to receive special notice of a resolution to appoint as auditor a person other than the retiring auditor, or to remove the auditor before the expiry of the term of office, and on receipt of such a notice the auditor can make representations of a reasonable length to the company, and these must be sent out to all shareholders at the company's expense. Even after removal, an auditor has the right to attend the AGM at which the term of office would have expired, or a meeting held to fill a casual vacancy, and to be heard at such meetings.

An auditor may resign the office by written notice deposited at the company's registered office. Such notice must contain a statement to the effect that there are no circumstances connected with the resignation which should be brought to the attention of shareholders or creditors, or an appropriate statement. This statement must be circulated to all shareholders and the resigning auditor can convene an extraordinary general meeting to consider it.

Whenever rights are granted to a person in law it is usual for that person to be charged with certain duties which must be undertaken, and standards which must be maintained. The main duties of an auditor are to make a proper investigation of the books and vouchers of the company, and to form an opinion as to whether proper books have been maintained and whether the accounts are in agreement with those books. To quote Lindley L. J. in the London and General Bank Case of 1895, 'He must be honest, that is, he must not certify what he does not believe to be true, and he must take reasonable care and skill before he believes that what he certifies is true'. Having formed an opinion, the auditor has a duty to report to the shareholders at the AGM that the accounts have been properly prepared in accordance with the law, and that they show a true and fair view. A typical auditor's report might read as follows:

'I have obtained all the information and explanations which, to the best of my knowledge and belief, were necessary for the purpose of my audit. In my opinion proper books of account have been kept by the company so far as appears from my examination of those books. I have examined the above balance sheet and profit and loss account, which are in agreement with the books of account. In my opinion and to the best of my knowledge the profit and loss account and balance sheet give information required by the Companies Act 1985 in the manner so required, and the balance sheet gives a true and fair view of the state of the company's affairs as at . . . and the profit and loss account gives a true and fair view of the profit for the year ended on that date.'

An auditor's report phrased in a similar manner will be found appended to the published balance sheets of all public companies.

QUALIFICATION OF AN AUDITOR'S REPORT

The most powerful weapon in the armoury of the auditor is the threat to qualify the audit report. This means that a public comment will be made in the audit report on matters which are considered to be improper, unless the directors and management of the firm take advice and act to set matters right. When an auditor is not satisfied with an accounting policy, or a system, or certain transactions, it is a matter of duty to say so in the report, so that the shareholders and potential shareholders are made aware of factors which may adversely affect their interest.

An auditor will qualify the report if the accounts are not drawn up in conformity with recognized accounting principles. If in any respect the standard accounting practices agreed by the major accounting bodies in the UK acting through the Accounting Standards Committee have been ignored, this must also be mentioned. Not all companies agree with the recommended treatment of some accounting transactions laid down in the standards, and their boards of directors sometimes set the standards aside when drawing up their accounts. The auditor must draw the attention of the shareholders to this fact, but some large and influential companies who cannot be rightfully accused of accounting malpractice have chosen to account in ways not approved by the accounting standards. When their accounts are qualified by an auditor for this reason this tends to increase the number of qualifications made to accounts during a calendar year, and reduces the impact of a more serious qualification made by the auditors of another company. In the past a qualification by the auditor was considered a very serious matter, but nowadays, as qualifications increase and are often the subject of a disagreement with the terms of a technical accounting standard, the significance of a qualification has been reduced.

If the accounts have been drawn up to follow a policy or method which is inconsistent with past accounting statements of the company, the auditor must mention this in the report, unless an adequate explanation by way of a note to the accounts has been made. Such an explanation should, of course, reveal the extent of the impact on profits or balance sheet items of a change to a different accounting policy. If the auditor does not agree with the amount stated in the balance sheet for an asset, or with an item shown in the profit and loss account, he must say so. Qualifications of this nature often concern the directors' valuation of investments in subsidiary companies or fixed assets such as buildings. Another reason for qualification is where the accounts fail to disclose some information which the auditor feels is significant if a true and fair view of the position is to be read from the accounts.

Thus the auditor has a duty to ensure that all pertinent information is revealed and that the accounts are free from bias. Indeed, the auditor has a duty to qualify the accounts by revealing any inconsistencies where, for example, a note to the accounts changes the view given by the accounting statements themselves. Such qualifications should be concise, clear and specific, and should express the auditor's opinion in such a way that the comments cannot be misinterpreted.

LIABILITY OF THE AUDITOR

Because the auditor holds himself out as a professional expert, great care must be taken to ensure that the work done is absolutely correct. Shareholders and potential investors will rely to some extent on the auditor's certificate to confirm to them that the accounting statements show a true and fair view. If it can be proved that an auditor did not bring to the work the normal skill expected of a professional person, and as a result of this negligence some other person suffered, then the auditor may be held liable under both civil and criminal law to make good any loss so suffered. Auditing firms insure against this liability by taking out a professional indemnity insurance policy. Some accountants believe that companies and their auditors should be free to agree limitations on the auditor's liability for negligence. This move has arisen because potential claims for liability may run into millions of pounds, and accordingly the premium for such insurance has become expensive. It is, however, difficult to see how an agreement between the auditor and the company can in any way limit the liability of the auditor to users of the accounts other than the company itself.

Under common law the auditor is considered as an agent of the company, and as a professional person he must bring to his work a high standard of care, skill and diligence. If it can be proved that he has been negligent in discharging this duty, he will be liable to the clients for any losses they may suffer as a result.

In one leading case, *Re London and General Bank* [1895] CH 673, the auditor informed the directors that loans had been made on poor security, but they did not act on his advice. The auditor qualified the report by saying that the value of the assets was dependent on the realization of these loans. It was held, however, that such a qualification was not in sufficiently strong terms and acted only as a hint. In the *Kingston Cotton Mill* case [1896] CH 279, the stocks were overvalued and profits thus inflated. In the course of his judgement, Lord Justice Lopes remarked that an auditor must use reasonable care and skill in the execution of his duties, but was not a detective, next making his now famous remark that the auditor is a watchdog but not a bloodhound. The relevance of his remark in this case was that the auditor was justified in believing the trusted servants of the company in whom confidence is placed by the company, and is entitled to assume that they are honest. In later cases, however, it has been held that the auditor must, to the best of his ability, use all available information when forming an opinion, and should make an attempt to check the accuracy of information given by employees of the company. It is difficult in practice for an auditor to decide how far to go with an investigation when suspicions are aroused which may later prove to be unfounded.

If an auditor is negligent a liability may be established to third parties if they have relied on his statements and suffered damage by so doing. The leading case here is that of *Hedley Byrne* v. *Heller and Partners* (1963), which does not directly concern an auditor. In this case a banker gave a negligent reference about a client, and the plaintiff suffered loss by relying on this reference and sued the bankers. From the result of this case it appears that an auditor is not now immune from a liability to make good the losses of third parties caused by his negligence. However, such cases rarely come to court as they are settled between the parties as part of a claim on the professional liability indemnity insurance carried by practising accountants. Under the City Code on Mergers and Takeover Bids, the auditor or reporting accountant is required to report on the accounting bases used and calculations made in any statement which forecasts the income of a company, and he must use the care and skill reasonably expected of a professional expert in this work.

Two recent cases have suggested a change in the law on auditors' liability. In the case of *Caparo and Touche Ross* it was held that an auditor owes a duty of care to the company which is the subject of the audit and to that company's individual shareholders, which limits the classes to which an auditor owes a duty of care. In the case of *Clark Pixley*, yet to be tried before the House of Lords, it was held that the auditor was not liable to banks that had lent money to a company which went into liquidation after receiving a clean audit report. In this case a duty of care was not established because the auditors were not obliged to send accounts to the banks and were not aware that the banks would receive those accounts. In this case the auditor appears to have relied solely on assurances from the directors of the company that the accounting records were complete but subsequently the main asset of the company was found to be valueless. The banks who had lent money to the company secured on this asset subsequently found that their security was worthless. Clearly the question of whether an auditor is liable to a third party for the standard of care used when preparing an audit report has yet to be determined.

DIVISIBLE PROFITS

One important consideration of the auditor when he seeks to determine a true and fair view is that profit shall not be overstated, because if it is the directors of the company will get a false impression of the efficiency of their organization, and of the amount which they can distribute in the form of dividend. In an extreme case the directors may distribute in dividend more than the true profit earned, thus paying part of the dividend out of capital rather than profit. Such action is imprudent financially since it reduces the capital employed, and does not have regard to the long-term survival of the business. It is also illegal, since it prejudices the rights of the creditors of the business if capital is repaid to shareholders by way of dividend before the claims of creditors have been met. As we have seen, the amount of a true profit is often the subject of estimate and argument, but the amount of profit available for dividend is subject to the requirements of statute, case law, and prudent accounting policy. Prudence dictates that the profit available for dividend shall be a surplus left after adequate provision has been made for items such as depreciation and doubtful debts, and after sufficient funds have been set aside in the reserves to finance expansion or ensure the long-term survival of the business. The Companies Act 1985, section 263, states that a distribution can only be made out of profits available for that purpose, and such profits are defined as accumulated realized profit not previously distributed or capitalized or written off in a reduction of capital, less accumulated realized losses. The term 'distribution' means any distribution of a company's assets in cash or otherwise, except bonus shares, the redemption of shares out of capital, a reduction of capital by reducing shareholders' liability on uncalled capital, or on a 'winding up'. Section 264 of the Companies Act 1985 states that a distribution can only be made in a public limited company if the net assets of the company are greater than the aggregate of called-up share capital and undistributable reserves. (Defined as share premium; capital redemption reserves and the surplus of accumulated unrealized profits over accumulated unrealized losses.) Any development costs capitalized and shown as an asset in the balance sheet are to be treated as a realized loss. A provision other than for a diminution in value of a fixed asset is to be treated as a realized loss, but depreciation written off a revaluation surplus is considered to be a realized profit.

Under section 271 of the Companies Act 1985 a distribution can only be made if accounts have been properly prepared and audited as true and fair. Any qualification of the audit report may mean that a distribution would be in contravention of section 264 (above), and the auditor must state in writing that the matter concerned in the qualification does not have this effect before a distribution can be made. From the requirements of the statute and of good business practice, a body of case law has developed some general rules to be followed.

A problem which has been the subject of some activity within the courts is to establish the position of capital profits such as the revaluation of property and to determine whether they are available for dividend. Some early cases at the turn of the century established that capital profits could be distributed in the form of dividend if they were realized, that is turned into cash rather than a paper profit; if they remained after all other assets had been realistically valued; and if the articles permitted such a distribution. It is interesting, however, to note that two more recent cases have had a significant effect on this position. In 1960 the *Westburn Sugar Refineries* case supported the traditional view that a capital profit could not be distributed until it was realized. This position has, however, been eroded by the decision in the case of the *Dimbula Tea Company* v. *Laurie*, which sought to determine the correct treatment for unrealized reserves. When assets are revalued the corresponding credit is placed in a reserve not available for distribution, but such a reserve can be used to pay up unissued shares so that they can be distributed to the shareholders as a 'bonus' or 'scrip' issue. Thus, although it still has not been established that a capital profit can be distributed in specie unless it has been realized, it is now possible to distribute it in the form of extra shares on which dividend can later be paid.

Example

To calculate the profits available for distribution in a business it is necessary to identify profits and losses, realized and unrealized. The accounts of Giant PLC at 31 December 19.. contain the following balances:

	£000's
Share premium account	500
General reserve	1600
Profit and loss account—balance unappropriated	700
Fixed asset revaluation reserve	980
Capital reserve (arising from profits on sale of fixed assets)	300
Cost of developing new products which has been capitalized as an asset	200
Adjustments have not yet been made for the following items:	
Provision for uninsured fire loss	150
Loss on translation of assets held abroad into sterling	60

	Realized		Unrealized	
	Profit	Loss	Profit	Loss
General reserve	1600			
Profit and loss account	700			
Fixed asset revaluation reserve			980	
Capital reserve	300			
Capitalized development cost		200		
Provision for uninsured fire loss		150		
Loss on currency translation				60
	2600	350	980	60
Less realized losses	350			
Profit available for distribution	2250			

205

Note:

1. If unrealized losses had exceeded unrealized profits, this excess would be deducted from profits available.
2. Share premium account does not enter the calculation because it is a statutory capital reserve and thus not available for distribution.

THE CLASSIFICATION AND LOCATION OF ERRORS

Once a trial balance is extracted from the books a check on the accuracy of the book-keeping is available, since if every debit has a credit, then the two columns of the trial balance should add up to the same figure. If they do not, an error has occurred and a search must be organized to locate the error and correct it. Errors which occur in book-keeping can be classified according to their type.

First, there are errors of omission, which concern the complete omission of a transaction from the books. Such an error will not affect the balance of the books, since both the debit and credit elements have been omitted. If, for example, an invoice for goods sold has been overlooked and is discovered after completion of the accounting statements, the books will not record the sale or the existence of the debt as an asset. An efficient system to record transactions, especially sales, will reduce the incidence of such errors. If, in the example above, the sales invoices had each been given a serial number, the fact that one of the series was missing would have been recognized and a search initiated.

Next there are errors of commission, which occur when transactions are wrongly recorded in the books. Such errors may or may not affect the trial balance, according to the circumstances. A sale amounting to £5000 may be recorded as £500 in both the sales account and the debtors account without disrupting the balance of the books, but if it is correctly recorded as a sale, but is shown as £500 in the debtors account, then the trial balance debits will not agree with the credits. Other errors of commission concern mistakes in casting when columns are added up, posting errors when items are posted to the wrong account or to the wrong side of the right account, and errors of transposition when figures are changed before they are entered or carried from one page to another as the wrong amount, e.g. £8950 carried forward or entered as £8590.

A third class is errors of principle, which, although they do not affect the balance of the books, will certainly influence the validity of accounting statements computed from the books. Such errors concern the incorrect treatment of a transaction in the books of account; for example, where a revenue expense is capitalized by being posted to a fixed asset account, the profit will be understated and the balance sheet will also be wrong.

Compensating errors are mistakes which take place when, by coincidence, two mistakes of similar amounts are made on opposite sides of the books. Such errors are not discovered immediately, since they cancel each other out, and the trial balance appears to be correct; e.g. a total of £910 carried forward as £900 on the credit side will compensate for £10 undercast on the debit side. Mistakes which nearly compensate can also cause problems, since if an error of £5000 on the debit side is accompanied by an error of £4800 on the credit side, the book-keepers will be searching for an amount of £200, which they will not find. It is important to understand that some mistakes can occur which will not be shown up by the trial balance.

The location of errors is a science in its own right. A common practice is to open a suspense account and post the amount of the difference to it. Then, as successive errors are discovered, they too can be posted to the suspense account so that the outstanding amount is readily available to the team who are searching for the error. A useful step is to try to trace the difference to a control account, to isolate and reduce the area of the search. If a control account total is proved to be correct, the accounts can be produced using that figure, while a search is continuing to find the mistake in a subsidiary ledger and adjust it to the control account total. An early step to locate an error is to check all balances from the ledger to the trial balance, and to check the accuracy of the opening balances in the books. If the amount of the difference is divided by two, a figure is provided which, if posted to the wrong side in the books, could account for the error. A check should be made for transposition of figures; e.g. £15 posted as £1.50 gives a difference of £13.50. All totals carried forward from one page to another should be checked, and if the error is still not located then columns and crossfooters should be recast in case an error of addition or subtraction has taken place. If the error still cannot be found, it is necessary to check the postings from the daybooks to the ledger, checking for badly formed figures which may give rise to a mistake.

In a well-organized business the system will be designed to minimize the occurrence of error.

INTERNAL CONTROL AND INTERNAL CHECK

The term 'internal control' is given to the whole system of controls existing in an organization, which have been set up to ensure that the accounting records are accurate and reliable, and that the assets of the organization are adequately protected. Such controls may not be entirely financial, but will arrange the systems of working within the business to achieve the aforementioned goals. A system of stock control or credit control and the existence of internal checks built into the system will, together with an internal audit department, lead to the appropriate level of control, whereby management are sure that all revenue to which they are entitled is received and recorded, and that no expenditure is made without proper authorization. If the assets of the business are adequately accounted for they cannot be lost, stolen or misused, and if liabilities are systematically recorded it will be difficult to ignore such claims or to fail to provide for known losses when the accounting statements are produced.

Internal check comprises the routine checks on the day-to-day transactions which operate as part of the system. A major feature of internal check is to ensure that the work of one person is proved independently or is complementary to the work of another, so that errors are found and prevented, or at least detected, at an early stage. It is virtually impossible to prevent all fraud, but a well-planned system can reduce temptation, increase the difficulties encountered by the fraudulent employee and improve the chances of his being detected. Internal check seeks to define the responsibility of individuals with a view to arranging matters so that no one person can undertake all the activities involved in any one transaction. A single clerk who can order goods, check their receipt, pass the invoice for payment, and then draw a cheque, is in a position of great temptation, since it would be comparatively easy to pass fictitious entries through the books and make payments to friends and accomplices. If more than one clerk is involved in the system, however, collusion must take place before fraud can be effected, and if employees are frequently rotated within the system then any collusion will not last long.

There is more to internal check than the prevention of collusion between employees. Test checks can be built into the system so that one record provides an independent confirmation of another, e.g. comparison of order with invoice. A well-organized accounting system will ensure that costs are classified and coded so that they are entered in the correct accounts, and that control accounts are maintained for sections of the books (especially the personal ledgers) so that mistakes or differences can be isolated. If the debtors ledger control account is written up by a senior clerk, this acts as a check on the accuracy of the junior clerk who maintains the debtors ledger, and collusion must take place between the two before fraud can be accomplished. The simple tactic of putting serial numbers on invoice pads will highlight any missing documents, and colour coding will serve to show where a copy of an accounting record, say an order, has strayed to the wrong department.

Authorization is an important feature of internal check, since it limits the ability of employees to act irresponsibly with the company's assets. If all orders, discounts, cheques, bad debts written off, etc. must be authorized by the signature of a trusted employee, judgement will be exercised before the company is committed in any way. The safe custody of order pads, cheque books, and receipt books is part of the system. A close check is particularly important at the points where transactions enter the accounting system. There must be a prime document to support each entry, and it must be authorized before an accounting record is made. The existence of the internal audit department will ensure that the system is reviewed from time to time to test its efficiency, and, most important, to test that an efficient system, once established, is operated properly by all concerned.

SOME SYSTEMS EXPLAINED

The Payment of Wages

This is a function which is to be found in most enterprises. The basic records are as follows:

(a) the employee's record card, which shows personal details of the employee, including rate of pay;

(b) the clock card, which the employee punches through a time clock when starting and stopping work to provide a record of working hours;

(c) the wage sheet, which is written up from the clock cards, to show for each employee the wage earned and deductions such as tax, national insurance, holiday savings scheme, pension deductions etc.; totals from the wage sheet give the amount to be drawn from the bank for wages, and the amounts for Schedule E tax deduction etc.;

(d) if the wage sheet is produced using a carbon copy system, the tear-off slip for each worker's pay packet is produced, and the individual's tax deduction card is written up at the same time.

The system could operate as follows:

1. Alterations to rates of pay should be initialled on the personal record card by a senior manager.
2. Time clocks should be installed to record hours worked on clock cards. Precautions should be taken to ensure that one employee does not clock in for another as well as himself. The supervisor or gate security staff can carry out this check.
3. Overtime should be separately recorded and authorized by a senior manager.
4. Wage sheets should be ruled in columns to record any pay details and deductions, e.g. national insurance and tax. Each employee should have a line on the wage sheet. The wage sheet should be written up from the time cards and then extended. This work should be undertaken by two clerks, one to check the work of the other. Thus collusion will have to take place if fraud is to remain undetected.
5. A separate cheque for the total wages should be drawn, and the amounts put into the wage packets with the individual pay slips. All cash should be accounted for in this operation.
6. Payment of wages should be made by a person who has no part in making them up, and to whom all employees are known, e.g. the departmental supervisor. All unclaimed packets should be recorded and returned to the wages office. In this way 'dead men' or non-existent employees injected into the system will be discovered.
7. The system should be strictly adhered to, and supervised by those responsible for the business. The management should review the wage sheet frequently and attend the payment of wages from time to time.
8. In many companies the wage payment routine is computerized, and payment is made direct to a named bank account by cheque. Accounting information for tax, payments, and labour costs must still be produced but the computer will avoid the drudgery of repetitive calculations and accuracy checks. However, with a computerized system it is even more important to maintain vigilance as to the details for individual employees that are entered into the system. If details of non-existent employees, or of enhanced wage rates, are fraudulently entered into the system, the speed of the computerized system may allow false payments to be made for some time before the fraud or error is discovered.

The Purchase of and Payment for Raw Materials

As a matter of internal control all purchases must be made through the buying office, which should be the only department allowed to place orders. When goods are required by the stores or by another department, a requisition signed by a responsible official must be submitted to the buying office. The requisition will contain details of quantity, quality, delivery date and address, as well as a full description of the goods. The buyers negotiate a price with the supplier and place an official order, which contains the information on the requisition and any variations.

All orders must be countersigned by the chief buyer. A copy of the order is sent to the requisitioning department, the gatehouse or goods receiving bay, and the invoice department, for information. A copy is filed for reference in the buying office.

When the goods arrive they are checked against the order for type, quantity and quality before being stored, and a goods received note is raised by the checker, to accompany the goods to the store. Copy GRNs are sent to the buying office and to the invoice department, and a copy is filed for reference in the receiving bay. Next the invoice arrives and is checked by the invoice department against the order and the GRN, and only when this check proves satisfactory is the invoice passed and entered in the creditors ledger. This check is to ensure that the quantity, quality and price on the invoice are as agreed, and that only those so authorized can pledge the firm's credit. It is important that in the system so far the buyer, checker, stores clerk and invoice clerk are separate, so that collusion must take place before fraud can occur.

The next step in the system occurs when a statement of account is received from the supplier. This is compared with the ledger and if they agree, and if the period of credit has expired or the appropriate discount has been taken, the account can be passed for payment and a cheque drawn. If possible the clerk in charge of the creditors ledger should be separated from the cashier who draws the cheque. The cheque sent to the supplier will be accompanied by a remittance advice which explains the various items covered by the cheque. The cheque should be signed by a trusted official of the firm who is appointed as a signatory. This system can be expressed as a flow chart (figure 5).

Cash Sales

The system to account for the handling of cash must be designed with care, since it is at this point that the company's assets are often most vulnerable to mis-appropriation. The selling points at which cash is received may be remote from the central administration or accounts department, so control is difficult to achieve. The operation should be divided into spheres of responsibility, with a particular employee responsible for each area and reporting to a trusted manager.

For a branch shop with, for example, five counters, each counter selling a different product, the system might be designed as follows. All goods should be invoiced to the shop at selling prices, with a record of goods despatched maintained at head office. Therefore stock at the shop plus cash sales banked must equal the amount sent to the shop. An internal auditor should visit to make spot checks on the stock at random intervals, when each counter should have cash collected and banked, or goods, equal to the amount issued to it by the manager. The shop as a whole should also pass this test.

Sales should be evidenced by a bill given to the customer and a copy retained by the assistant. Cash received should be put into the till immediately, and tills emptied every day, when the amount removed, net of float, must equal the total shown on the till roll and the total of the copy bills. The assistant should initial the till roll amount and date, and this should be countersigned by another assistant, in order to prevent collusion between the manager and the assistant. The amount from each till should be entered daily by the manager in a cash book, amounting to a total to be banked per the paying-in slip. A copy paying-in slip should be sent to the main

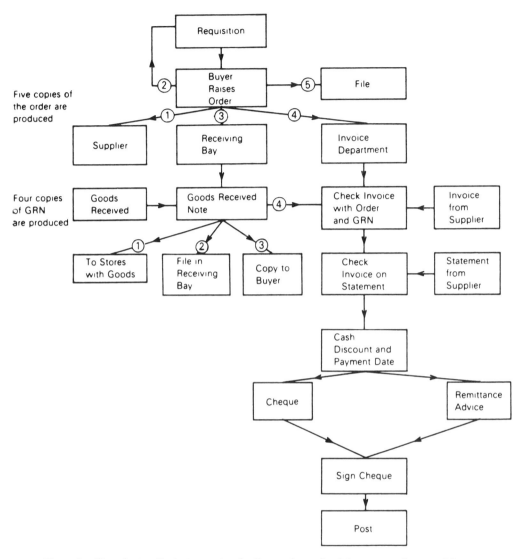

Figure 5. Flow chart to illustrate a system for the purchase of and the payment for materials.

office, for entry in the main cash book. Pads of bills should be printed with serial numbers and issued to assistants by the manager only. The internal auditor should check that all the numbered pads are accounted for. No cash refunds should be made unless authorized by the manager.

The total of the copy bills should be entered each day in a sales journal analysed for each counter, and a summary sent to the main office each week for entry in the sales account. A trusted clerk at the head office should check cash banked against the bank statement and against sales. All cash takings should be banked, and local expenses and wages dealt with by a separate imprest system. Head office should check the date on which bankings appear on the bank statement against the date on the copy paying-in book, so that cash received on one day cannot remain in the possession of the branch manager for several days before being banked. Thus the manager cannot use this cash for his own purposes and make it up from takings at a later date (teaming and lading) without detection.

Sales on Credit Terms

A system to account for this type of transaction must contain steps to check the creditworthiness of the prospective customer and to check whether the goods required are in stock. Multipart stationery can be used to distribute copies of documents such as the sales invoice, to ensure that important information is received by all persons working in the system. Follow the system through on the flow chart (figure 6).

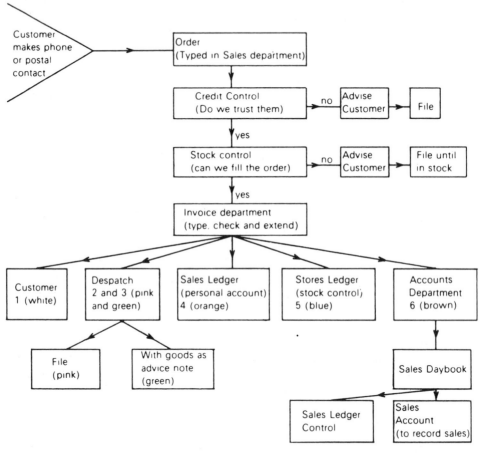

Figure 6. Flow chart of a sales accounting system. The sales ledger records what is owed by each customer and should check with the total of the sales daybook as entered in the sales ledger control account. Note that the invoice department could type the invoices on a six-part stationery set, colour coded to ensure proper distribution.

SYSTEMS AND THE COMPUTER

The term 'computer' covers a wide range of hardware, of varying sizes. Clearly the documentation system to be applied will depend upon the capabilities of the computer which is to be used to process the transactions, e.g. how fast can it process documents, how much information can it store, and how easy is it to retrieve data from the store for further processing? A large or 'mainframe' computer can be operated from a central processing unit, or computing department, and can serve many different needs in an organization, with on-line terminals in various offices giving access to the system. Data entered into the system form the 'database', which the computer can be programmed to analyse in a number of different ways, e.g. customers' names and addresses held in a customer file can be used to prepare invoices, to despatch sales promotional information, or for regional sales customer analysis. The mainframe requires special operating conditions and a team of programmers and operators to make the best use of its sophisticated information processing capabilities. A minicomputer is medium-sized and can be operated by a smaller team for a localized part of the organization. Its capacity and speed of operation cannot match those of the mainframe, but it is cheaper to purchase and operate and can be more flexible in providing a service to a specific segment of the business. Microcomputers are smaller still, providing computer support for operations at a very local level, from word-processing to record-keeping and analysis. The memory storage to retain and file information on such small computers is comparatively limited when compared with the minicomputer or mainframe.

The operations undertaken by a computer can be classified as follows:

(a) recording and storage of basic data such as customer information, or employee information, which might otherwise be retained on file in the personnel department;
(b) recording transactions once the prime documents have been batched and entered into the computer system, e.g. orders received from customers or cheque payments to be made to suppliers;
(c) processing transactions according to a pre-set program of instructions whereby newly entered transactions data are combined with basic data stored in the memory of the computer, e.g. orders are processed with customer information, or wages are calculated from clock cards and information in the personnel file;
(d) printing new documents as a result of the processing undertaken, e.g. sales invoices or wage payment slips, and updating old information filed in the computer memory to a current information file;
(e) retrieving information on request either for display on a visual display unit (VDU) or by means of a printout, e.g. the current spare parts situation or product availability level required to see if an order can be serviced;
(f) analysis of the database to provide reports, financial and otherwise, which will assist management, e.g. sales analysis.

Data can be stored in a computer system in 'files' held on disks or tapes. The data can be updated by creating a new file from the old file and the batch of new data; for example, customer balances less a batch of cheques received gives a file of new balances. Other files can store basic data such as customer name and address lists, and the programs themselves can also be held on tape or disk and used to instruct the computer as to the operations it is to perform, e.g. searching, updating or reporting.

Example

As an extension of the credit sales system explained in figure 6, the computer could be applied to this system as follows. When an order is received two basic questions must be answered:

1. Is the item in stock?
2. Can we sell to this customer on credit terms without exceeding the credit limit?

The computer system can be organized to accept such enquiries and provide answers quickly, either by showing the current stock situation on a VDU, or perhaps by producing a printout of the current balance and credit limit of customers. The reliability of this information will depend on the accuracy with which data are input to the computer system, and also on the frequency with which the computer files are updated. The company must make a policy decision to trade off the cost of frequent updates against the benefit of supplying efficient operational data from the system.

If the answer to the first two questions is in the affirmative, the order can be passed for processing and an official form can be raised, batched with other orders, and entered into the computer system. The computer will be programmed to produce an invoice, perhaps with a printout of six copies as shown in figure 6. The computer information held on file will also be updated as part of the same operation but all operations may not necessarily be carried out at the same time. A likely sequence of operations is as follows:

1. Print the customer's copy of the invoice (white) and two copies for the despatch department. This program should be run as frequently as possible, say daily, to reduce delays in delivering goods to customers. It may not be necessary to print and retain a copy of the invoice in the despatch department if a weekly printout of all despatches is available from the computer, or if queries can be answered by retrieval of individual items, say on a VDU or by printout.
2. Update the sales ledger whose individual customer accounts may be held on a customer file, so that the information discloses the current balance owed by each customer. If there is instant access (by VDU) to this information, the orange copy (4) in figure 6 may not need to be printed and stored. Conversely, frequent processing on the computer is expensive so a balance up to one week old may be adequate for the purposes of credit control. If customers know of this time lag they may be able to exploit the system to exceed their credit limits.
3. Update the stores ledger file to record items despatched to customers, thus reducing stock levels. A priority should exist for this file to be updated frequently if accurate, dependable stock records are to be available as part of the system. The blue copy (5) shown in figure 6 will no longer be needed to trigger an entry on the stock record card if the computer can update the file automatically so that current information is ready for retrieval when enquiries are made. Again, the cost of frequent updating must be set off against the needs of efficiency and operating convenience.
4. The transactions must be notified to the accounts department for 'daybook'-type analysis and entry into the sales account and sales ledger control account. The transactions file can be used for this updating, perhaps as infrequently as once a month, and the same data can then be analysed for sales department statistics.
5. The updated customer file can be used to print monthly statements for the purposes of the accounts department and to provide management information in the form of an ageing debtors list. A flowchart of the computerized system might be as shown in figure 7. Updating usually concerns the creation of a new tape file, from the old tape and fresh transactions data—the 'father and son' technique. The old tape is then 'dumped' as a back-up file, stored separately, which does not interfere with the operation of the main system. The files are available if for any reason records need to be re-created, and as part of the 'audit trail' allowing the

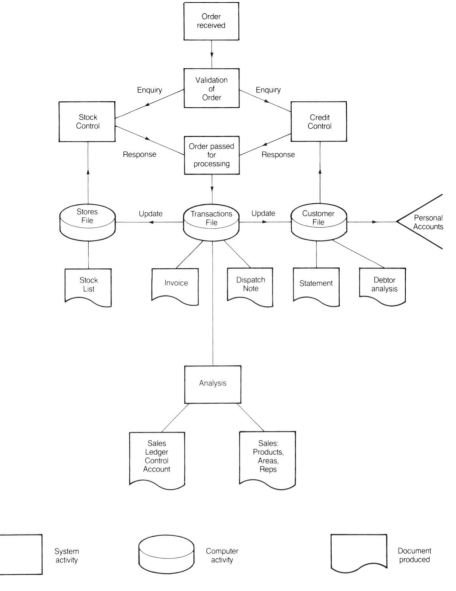

Figure 7. Flow chart of a computerized sales system.

auditor to follow through transactions as part of a depth check on the operation of the system.

TUTORIAL DISCUSSION TOPICS

11.1 'The prime reason for employing an auditor is to discover and prevent fraud.' 'The purpose of an audit is to test the lines of communication.' Discuss these two views.

11.2 What action should an accountant take before accepting the audit of a limited company? What information would he require on commencing the audit if he were subsequently appointed?

11.3 What are the main statutory duties of an auditor of a limited company, and what powers does he have to enable him to carry out these duties?

11.4 Discuss the ability of an auditor to withstand pressure put upon him by management with special reference to the weapons he can use in his defence.

11.5 How far can an external auditor rely upon the work of an internal auditor and what relationship should exist between these two parties?

11.6 Describe, with examples, each of the major types of error which affect the accuracy of accounting statements.

11.7 Trace the steps you would follow to locate an error when the two sides of a trial balance do not agree.

11.8 What do you understand by the term 'internal check' and how is it related to internal control?

11.9 Discuss the aims of the system of internal check with reference to the ways in which those aims are achieved.

SEMINAR EXERCISE 9

Draw a diagram or flow chart to illustrate an accounting system with which you are familiar. Annotate your charts to show the original records from which basic data are gathered, and the points at which internal check applies.

12 | An Introduction to Taxation

Taxation is levied by the Government to meet the expenses of governing, administering and protecting the country. The Government uses its revenue to provide education, the health service, social security, defence and roads, and to pay for the administration of Government schemes. A secondary use of taxation is an instrument of economic policy, to encourage saving instead of consumption, to inhibit inflation, to increase economic activity to avert a recession, and to give aid to newly established and growing industries or declining industries so that employment opportunities are safeguarded. Tariffs can be used to reduce the competitiveness of imports and thus influence the balance of payments. Taxation can also be used to redistribute wealth for political and social reasons.

A taxation policy must be based on the need to structure taxes in such a way that their effects are beneficial to the economy. An understanding of the incidence of taxation, by recognizing the class on which the weight of a tax falls, is important to this end; for example, if the business rate paid to meet local government expenditure is increased on shop premises, the shop-keepers will pay the tax, but may pass it on to the consumer in the form of increased prices. Their ability to pass on the tax is influenced by supply and demand, and the availability of substitutes to which customers can transfer their trade when prices are increased. It is also important to realize the limits to which taxation can be successfully levied. If business profits are taxed too heavily the net of tax return for risk taking will not compensate for the risk, and this will affect enterprise and the provision of venture capital to finance business undertakings. The Government itself participates in the provision of goods and services within the economy, through its control of the remaining nationalized industries and other agencies. Taxation may be used to influence events in the public sector as well as the private sector of the economy. The Government can use its ability to levy taxation or undertake public expenditure to bring about desired economic consequences. Capital grants or tax concessions may persuade companies to site new factories in areas of high unemployment, and may attract investing companies from abroad.

A direct tax, e.g. income tax, is levied directly on the individual, but an indirect tax, e.g. value added tax (VAT), is levied on goods or services and is paid when the item is consumed. For example, an individual pays VAT when he buys a television set or pays for a haircut. The indirect tax is collected by the seller of the goods on behalf of the Government and paid over at a later date. An indirect tax can usually be passed on to the ultimate consumer in the form of a price increase by the collecting agency. Indirect tax can be avoided by forgoing the consumption of the items on which it is levied. Direct taxes may be passed on to the consumer by manufacturers who raise their prices to maintain their net profits after tax, when corporation tax rises. The ability to transfer the incidence of tax depends on the elasticity of demand for the product.

PROGRESSIVE AND REGRESSIVE TAXES

The effect of taxation is not felt to the same extent by all taxpayers. Those with higher incomes can probably afford to pay more than those who earn less. The annual road fund licence of £100 paid by the owner of a Rolls-Royce means little to him, whereas the same sum paid by the owner of a Mini may be equal to a half or more of his weekly income. For reasons of fairness it is suggested that taxation should be progressive, and that each should pay according to his means and ability to pay. Income tax is progressive, because incomes up to a certain level are exempt and then the rates of taxation get higher as income increases. As a matter of administration it is not worth the cost of collecting small amounts of tax from the lower income brackets, but as a matter of political policy progressive taxes can be used to transfer income from one class, the richer members of society, to another, the poor.

In the case of the road fund licence, however, a poll tax (so much per head) is levied on all road users. The person who drives 50 000 kilometres a year pays the same as another who drives only 10 000 kilometres, and the owner of a large car pays the same as the owner of a small car. This tax is regressive, since the higher the income the lower the proportion of it which is used to put a car on the road.

It has been suggested that there should be a negative income tax whereby those who receive low incomes should receive a subsidy to bring their standard of living up to a set minimum level, but if progressive taxation is carried too far it can have unfortunate effects on the economy. The impact of high marginal tax rates will inhibit the willingness of wage earners to forgo leisure in order to work overtime, will reduce the desire for promotion among managers if they do not consider the extra salary net of tax to be worth the burden of increased responsibility, and may decrease the supply of venture capital if the net of tax return is considered inadequate to compensate for the risks taken.

Indirect taxes, such as VAT, may be considered to be slightly regressive, since the tax per article is the same irrespective of the purchaser's ability to pay and if it is true that the rich spend a smaller proportion of their income than the poor. For this reason it is suggested that higher rates of VAT should be levied on luxury items to add a progressive element to VAT.

FORMS OF TAX

Income is an obvious base on which to compute an individual's liability for taxation. Some members of society, however, may not receive their income in monetary form, e.g. a farmer providing his own food, so it may be difficult to measure. This dilemma can be solved by placing an arbitrary value on business drawings in kind.

Other problems associated with income tax are that it ignores the existing wealth of the individual and the effort he has made to earn his income. In the UK unearned income (mainly from invested wealth) is taxed as rigorously as earned income, and assets held for capital gain are also subject to taxation when gains are realized (capital gains tax). The income tax system has also tried to take into account the various needs of individuals by developing a system of allowances which consider the circumstances of each case. Other allowances concern expenses 'wholly and exclusively' paid out in order to earn the income. The income of a company is subject to corporation tax, but a number of allowances embodied in tax law will be applied to convert net profit to taxable profit.

A wealth tax has been considered, as a supplement to income tax rather than as an alternative, but the suggestion has encountered the difficulty of measuring wealth at frequent intervals. At present, wealth is taxed, by means of inheritance tax, when it is transferred, either on the death of its owner or when he gives it away during his lifetime.

Figure 8 shows the various taxes levied in the UK. The percentages shown in figure 8 are the proportions of total Government income raised from each tax.

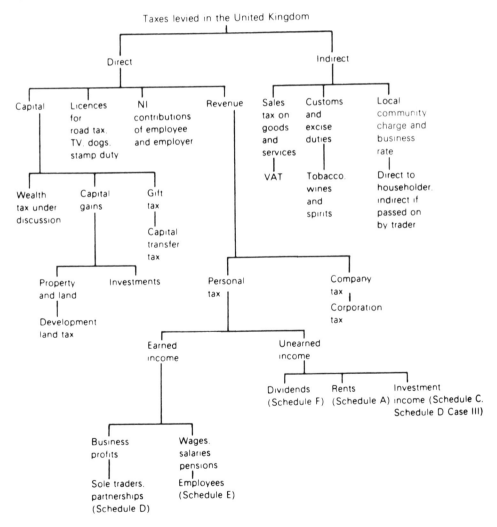

Figure 8. Taxes levied in the UK.

The taxes levied by the Government are a matter of political policy according to the Government of the day. For example, in the UK there is no longer a development land tax and local rates have now been replaced by the community charge, but such taxes could return if there is a change of political influence at the next election. In the days before the electricity industry is privatized, it is a nationalized industry. The Government can influence the price charged for electricity, so that when the electricity industry makes a profit, this profit goes into the Government coffers. This is a very indirect tax in that higher electricity costs are passed on by manufacturers to consumers of a wide range of products in the prices charged.

THE SCHEDULES

An individual may have income under more than one schedule.

Schedule A. This covers income from rent received (less statutory repairs) from land and buildings. This schedule used to cover a notional rent for owner/occupiers.

Schedule B. There is now no Schedule B, which used to cover income from the occupation of land, e.g. woodlands.

Schedule C. This covers income from investment in Government securities. This is taxed at source and the net amount paid to the recipients.

Schedule D. Cases I and II concern income from trades, professions and vocations. Case III concerns income from interest, annuities and other annual payments. Cases IV and V concern income from abroad. Sometimes UK taxation can be levied only on that part of the income that comes to the UK, and sometimes under a double taxation agreement with a foreign government such income is treated as franked investment income, and is not taxed again since it has already been taxed in its country of origin. Case VI concerns miscellaneous income.

Schedule E. This covers wages, salaries and pensions.

Schedule F. This covers dividends received from companies, advance corporation tax.

TAXABLE PROFIT

Business income is subject to corporation tax, if it is earned by a company, and income tax Schedule D Case I if it is earned by a sole trader or partnership. The definition of taxable profit is not the same as that of accounting profit, since certain expenses are not allowable against the taxation liability. Therefore the taxation computation of a company will start with net profit, and will then list the adjustments needed to convert it to the profit to which the corporation tax rate or income tax rate is applied to compute the tax payable. The major adjustments are as follows.

Depreciation

This cost is added back to net profit and an amount for capital allowances is deducted. Thus the rate at which depreciation is applied to compute accounting profit cannot be influenced by taxation. All businesses are treated the same so far as long-lived assets are concerned. Taxation policy allows 25 per cent of the cost of plant to be set off against profit each year on a reducing balance, to encourage industrial concerns to install modern plant and equipment. When a capital asset is sold, a balancing charge may be set off against capital allowances on new purchases that year. If the original cost less allowances received to date is less than the scrap value, the difference is the balancing charge.

Domestic Expenditure

Any disbursements or expenses of maintenance of the partners, their families or establishments, or any sums expended for domestic or private purposes distinct from the purposes of the trade, are not allowed to be set against taxable profit. Thus, for a partnership or sole trader, domestic expenditure must be identified in the accounts and added back to profit. However, some expenditure may lie in a grey area between business and domestic purposes, and this must be negotiated between the tax inspector and the accountant representing the tax payer. If a car is used partly for business purposes, part of its running costs will be an allowable expense. The same logic can be applied to private telephones used for business purposes and premises used for domestic as well as business purposes, e.g. a flat over a shop or office.

Entertaining

This can be expensive, but for some years now it has not been a tax allowable expense. It can be argued that entertaining a customer is a legitimate tactic of the salesman who is seeking an order, but the system can easily be abused and the Inland Revenue made to contribute to items of consumption rather than allowing the expense of a justifiable business activity.

Miscellaneous Items of Expenditure

These may be disallowed if it cannot be proved that they are 'wholly and exclusively' for the purpose of the business. Fines for parking etc. incurred by salesmen but paid by their employers are a case in point. Some companies will pay their employees' subscriptions to golf clubs etc. to encourage them to meet potential customers, but these expenses are disallowed, although subscriptions to trade associations are allowable. An accountant's subscription to his professional body is a tax deductible expense. Gifts to charities and donations to political parties are not tax deductible. Charitable donations made over a period of three years under a deed of covenant are deemed to be net in the hands of a registered charity which can then claim a refund of the tax. Gifts to charities may be allowed if incurred wholly and inclusively for the trade.

Debtors

A general provision for doubtful debts based on a percentage of debtors is not allowed as a deductible expense for tax purposes, relief in this direction being limited to provisions against specific debts which are considered doubtful. If a bad debt which has been written off is later paid, then it would be treated as business income in that year.

Stocks

The amount at which stocks are included in the accounts can have a significant effect on the profit figures. Although there is no strict legal definition of how stocks are to be valued for tax purposes, a business must be consistent in its use of one method or another. Case law has developed over the years, and the general rule is that stocks are to be valued at the lower of cost or market value, and that FIFO is favoured as a method of deriving cost whereas LIFO is not acceptable.

Example

The firm of Terry's Taxis has been in existence for a number of years. The proprietor lives on the premises. The income statement for the twelve months to 31 March this year was:

	£	£
Gross profit (after charging petrol, oil, drivers' wages)		19 630
Add		
Profit on sale of old taxis	300	
Football pool winnings	2350	
Advertising fees received	60	
Rent for sub-letting part of premises	400	
		3 110
		22 740
Less		
Office:		
Salaries (part-time staff)	1800	
Rent (25 per cent private)	800	
Lighting and heating (30 per cent private)	250	
Postage and stationery	130	
Advertising	340	
Telephones (20 per cent private)	600	
Repairs:		
Premises (5 per cent private)	120	
Vehicles	910	
Loss on sale of office equipment	10	
Audit fee	150	
Depreciation	2100	
General expenses	970	
		8 180
Net profit		£14 560

Notes:
1. Capital allowances of £1600 have been agreed with the Inland Revenue.
2. General expenses include.

	£
Taxi Proprietors Association subscription	20
Golf club subscription	25
Fines for speeding and illegal parking	130
Entertaining	60
Employees' Christmas gifts	45
Donation to RSPCA	10

Prepare a statement showing the profits adjusted for Schedule D Case I purposes.

Terry's Taxis, Schedule D Case I Taxation Computation

	£	£
Net profit		14 560
Add back disallowed items		
Office:		
Rent (25 per cent of £800)	200	
Lighting and heating (30 per cent of £250)	75	
Telephones (20 per cent of £600)	120	
Repairs to premises (5 per cent of £120)	6	
Loss on sale of office equipment	10	
Depreciation	2100	
General expenses:		
Golf club subscription	25	
Fines	130	
Entertaining	60	
Christmas gifts	45	
Donation to RSPCA	10	
		2 781
		17 341
Deduct receipts not taxable, already taxed, or taxable under another case or schedule		
Profit on sale of old taxis	300	
Football pool winnings	2350	
Rent for sub-letting	400	
		3 050
Taxable profit		14 291
Less capital allowances		1 600
Schedule D Case I assessment		£12 691

The donation to the RSPCA may be allowed if it is incurred wholly and exclusively for the purpose of the trade concerned. If a business makes a gift to charity as part of its advertising or sales budget then such a donation may be tax allowable.

THE IMPUTATION SYSTEM

The treatment of taxation in company accounts is closely connected to the imputation system whereby advance corporation tax (ACT) is levied on dividends paid by companies. SSAP 8 has been issued to lay down the agreed procedure.

Company income, whether distributed or not, is subject to corporation tax. If no dividend is paid, the whole amount of this tax is payable, depending on the circumstances, as a single sum nine months after the end of the accounting period to which it relates.

If a company pays a dividend, the 'qualifying distribution', as it is called, necessitates an amount of advance corporation tax (ACT), equal to tax at standard income tax rate on the notional gross dividend, to be paid to the Inland Revenue within thirteen weeks of the dividend payment date.

The company must deduct income tax at the standard rate from imputed gross dividend paid to its shareholders. The dividend paid out in cash, the 'qualifying distribution', is deemed to be a net amount and must be grossed up, by adding to it the amount of income tax which would have been deducted at the standard rate from a notional gross amount. The amount added is paid over and this is ACT.

The standard rate applied is that in force at the date of the dividend payment (which of course may be different from that obtaining at the date of the dividend declaration when the provision for ACT would be raised). ACT can be recovered at a later date.

Example

Share capital 100 000 £1 ordinary shares. A dividend of 20 pence per share is proposed, which calls for an entry in the appropriation account and a payout of £20 000. This is deemed to be net of tax, so to find the amount of tax due on the dividend it must be 'grossed up' to tax. If the standard income tax rate is 25p in the pound, then the ACT payable on the dividend would be $25/75 \times £20\ 000 = £6667$, so this is the amount of tax at the standard income tax rate that shareholders would have paid on this dividend if they had received the gross amount. The amount is proved by the fact that 25 per cent of £26 667 = £6667, so this is the amount of tax at the standard income tax rate that shareholders would have paid on this dividend if they had received the gross amount.

The amount is deemed to have been collected from them by the company when the dividend was paid, and must therefore be paid over to the Inland Revenue by the company within two weeks of the end of the quarter in which the dividend is paid. Thus at the year end the company will show, as current liabilities, £6667 ACT payable and £20 000 dividend payable. However, the company has the right to set off ACT paid against corporation tax payable in a future period, so the £6667 should also appear in the balance sheet as a deferred asset. In practice ACT recoverable is usually included in the balance sheet as a deduction from a long-term liability, the deferred tax account. If the standard rate of income tax is 29 per cent the appropriate fraction becomes 29/71, or for 20 per cent the fraction is 20/80.

When the ACT recoverable is set off against corporation tax, the net amount payable is termed mainstream corporation tax (MCT). ACT can be recouped in the first instance from corporation tax payable on the taxable income of the year in which the dividend is paid. Thus if a company makes a profit in year 1, and pays a dividend and ACT on that profit during year 2, the ACT can be recovered from corporation tax on the profit of year 2 when that tax is paid, which may be in year 3. ACT on an interim dividend paid during year 1 can be recouped from corporation tax paid on the profit of year 1. Until the ACT is recovered it should appear in the balance sheet as a deduction from other deferred tax liabilities. If ACT cannot be recouped because corporation tax on future years' profits is insufficient, it can be carried back for six years or carried forward indefinitely, unless recoverability is uncertain, when it should be written off to the profit and loss account as a separate item.

In the balance sheet ACT recoverable in the forthcoming year is netted off against the corporation tax charge on the profit for the period, and the net liability (MCT) is shown as a current liability. Where dividends have been proposed but not paid at the date of the balance sheet, the related ACT is provided and shown as a current liability, and as a deferred asset.

If a company receives a dividend from which tax has been deducted by the paying company, SSAP 8 requires that the amount must be grossed up to tax and this amount is termed 'franked investment income'. The gross amount must appear as income in the profit and loss account and the tax suffered must be disclosed as part of the tax charged in the profit and loss account. A similar rule applies to interest or a royalty received by a business and paid to it net of tax. The paying company is deemed to be the collector of income tax on such payments, and must therefore account to the revenue authorities for the tax deducted. Thus royalties or interest are paid net of income tax and received net of tax. The book-keeping entries are disclosed in the example below.

A company receives a dividend of £21 000, a royalty of £15 000 and pays interest on £240 000 of 10 per cent debentures. The ledger accounts would show:

Dividends Received Account

	£		£
Investment		Cash	*21 000
income	£28 000	Tax	
to P/L		to P/L	7 000
	£28 000		£28 000

Royalty Received Account

	£		£
P/L income	**20 000	Cash	15 000
		Income	
		tax suffered	5 000
	£20 000		£20 000

N.B. * The cash received has been grossed up using the standard rate of income tax, 25 per cent.

$^{25}/_{75} \times £21\ 000 = £7000$

** The true royalty was £20 000 but the payer deducted income tax before making the payment.

Interest Paid Account

	£		£
Cash	18 000	Interest	24 000
Income tax		to P/L	
deducted	6 000		
	£24 000		£24 000

Income Tax Account

	£		£
Suffered on		Deducted	
royalty	5000	from	
Balance		interest	6000
owed	1000		
	£6000		£6000
		Balance b/d	1000

PAYMENT OF MAINSTREAM CORPORATION TAX

In 1965 the taxation system was changed, and companies which previously had paid income tax were subject to corporation tax from then onwards. Corporation tax, like income tax on business profits, is payable after the end of the accounting year in which the profit arose. An accounting year can be timed to end on any date; many companies use 31 December. The tax year runs from 6 April to 5 April.

The rate of corporation tax can be changed by the Government by a clause in the annual Finance Act. The rate has been held at 35 per cent for some years, but it is now expected to fall. The amount of corporation tax to be paid is often a matter of negotiation with the Inland Revenue, so an amount is provided in the accounts, but subsequently a different sum may be paid over. Negotiations usually concern whether or not certain expenses are to be allowed as deductions in the computation of taxable profit.

There are two rules for the payment of MCT:

1. Corporation tax will be paid nine months after the accounting year end.
2. For companies in protracted negotiation with the revenue, corporation tax is payable one month after an assessment is agreed and issued.

Example

For the accounting year ending 31 December 19-2, a company would pay corporation tax on those profits by 1 October 19-3. A Schedule D income tax payer who has been in business for some years would pay his tax in a similar year but in two equal instalments on 1 January 19-4 and 1 July 19-4.

Tax payable within twelve months of the balance sheet date should be treated as a current liability, but tax payable more than twelve months into the future should be shown separately as 'future taxation payable on . . .' with the appropriate date.

This is a creditor payable more than twelve months from the balance sheet date and does not form part of the shareholders' interest in the company.

DEFERRED TAXATION

The reserve under the name 'deferred taxation' contains the total of tax liabilities arising from various transactions which may or may not have to be paid at some future date. Profits computed for taxation purposes include items of income and expenditure in periods different from those in which they are included in the financial accounts, i.e. timing differences occur. The objective of such a reserve is to eliminate fluctuations in net profit after tax which are caused by tax regulations rather than economic activity. A true profit will lead to a prudent dividend policy, a correct statement of tax liabilities in the balance sheet and a reliable price/earnings ratio. These tax liabilities arise in a number of ways.

First, capital allowances at rates of 25 per cent on reducing balance may exceed the provision for depreciation made by a company in a single year. This difference is called a 'timing difference' because after a number of years the depreciation charged each year will have caught up with the capital allowances. The original timing difference will be reversed. If, however, the asset is sold before the original timing differences have reversed, a balancing charge will be made in the tax computation, so that the liability to tax in that year will increase. This extra tax payable has got nothing to do with the profit made in that year so that the figure for net profit after tax will be distorted merely because of timing differences. Accounting for deferred taxation attempts to isolate the tax attributable to a timing difference and hold it in a deferred taxation reserve until the difference no longer exists. If the asset concerned is sold for more than its tax written-down value, the balancing charge in that year can be compensated by an amount transferred from the provision for deferred taxation. Capital allowances are now normally at 25 per cent per annum on the reducing balance, so this reason for a deferred taxation reserve is no longer so important as in the past, when it was possible to write off an asset at 100 per cent against taxation in the year during which it was purchased.

Second, certain items may be dealt with in different time periods for the accounts than for the tax computation, and are held in the deferred tax account. For example, a provision for bad debts may not be tax deductible, until the debts go bad in a subsequent period, or a provision for interest receivable may not count as taxable income until the period in which the interest is actually received—short-term timing differences.

A third reason for the creation of a deferred taxation reserve arises from the revaluation of buildings and other fixed assets. If the assets were sold at their enhanced value, a capital gains tax liability might arise, and a provision must be made against this eventuality. Some businessmen do not agree with this provision, since the accounts are drawn up on a going concern basis, and this implies that fixed assets such as buildings are not likely to be sold in the future. Capital gains are taxed in the hands of a company at corporation tax rates.

A fourth reason for creating a deferred tax account concerns fixed assets which are sold for a capital gain. Usually this gain would attract capital gains tax, but if the funds produced by the sale are used immediately to replace the assets sold, there is a dispensation termed 'roll-over relief', which delays the payment of capital gains tax until the funds so employed are no longer invested in replacement assets. Clearly the case here for a provision against this deferred taxation liability is weak, because the date on which the liability crystallizes is remote.

The impact of timing differences and the creation of a deferred taxation reserve have met with much opposition in industry, and SSAP 11, which dealt with these matters, has been replaced by SSAP 15 (which is itself under review). It is argued that some of the reasons for creating the account are not likely to occur, but it is suspected that at the root of the opposition lies the depressing effect of a provision to the deferred tax account, which reduces profits after tax and thus affects the price/earnings ratio, which is used as a Stock Exchange indicator.

Example

A company purchases plant for £100 000 during the year 19-1. This plant is depreciated by the straight line method over a ten-year life but it attracts capital allowances of 25 per cent based on the cost for that year. A computation of the net profit after tax of the business, assuming a net trading profit of £100 000, is as follows:

	£	£
Net trading profit 19-1		100 000
Less depreciation		10 000
Profit disclosed to shareholders		90 000
Tax computation—business profit	90 000	
Add back depreciation	10 000	
	100 000	

	£	£
Less capital allowances		
£100 000 × 0.25	25000	
Taxable profit	£75 000	
Corporation tax on £75 000 at 35 per cent		26 250
Net profit after tax		63 750
Transfer to reserve for deferred taxation		
(£25 000 − 10 000 × 0.35)		5 250
Disclosed net profit after tax	£58 500	

In the financial accounts net profit after tax would be £63 750, all of which would appear in the earnings per share calculation, and all of which could be paid out as a dividend if necessary. The timing difference is the amount of the capital allowance (£25 000) less the depreciation (£10 000), a net figure of £15 000. This means that there is a difference of £15 000 between the accounting profit and the profit on which the tax is calculated. SSAP 15 'Accounting for Deferred Taxation' suggests that tax at 35 per cent on the timing difference, i.e. £5250, should be charged against profits in 19-1 and credited to a reserve for deferred taxation. This would reduce the disclosed profit to £58 500.

If the company makes a net trading profit of £100 000 in the year 19-2 and sells the plant for its written-down value of £80 000 at the end of that year, this sale would have no effect on the accounting profit. However, after two years of capital allowances at £25 000 and £18 750 respectively, the tax written-down value of the plant would be £56 250. If the plant is sold for £80 000 a balancing charge of £23 750 will then affect the tax charge for 19-2. As shown in the computation, the taxable profit for that year would be £105 000, which at 35 per cent corporation tax would give tax paid of £36 750. Thus in 19-1 and 19-2, although the same net trading profit has been made, a very different figure for net profit after tax would appear in the accounts. If, however, in 19-2 the amount in the reserve for deferred taxation is transferred as a credit to the tax charge for the year, the net profit after tax will be £58 500, the same as for 19-1.

	£	£
Net trading profit 19-2		100 000
Less depreciation		10 000
Trading profit disclosed to shareholders		90 000
Tax computation—business profit	90 000	
Add back depreciation	10 000	
	100 000	
Less capital allowance		
(25 per cent of £75 000)	(18 750)	
Balancing charge		
(£80 000 − £56 250)	23 750	
Taxable profit	£105 000	
Corporation tax on £105 000 at 35 per cent		36 750
Net profit after tax		53250
Add transfer from deferred taxation		5 250
Disclosed net profit after tax		£58 500

Under SSAP 15 the tax effect of the timing difference should be set aside out of profit in one year and released in later years to iron out fluctuations to the disclosed profit figure caused by the tax system. If the plant was not sold until the end of its life, then part of the reserve would be released to the profit and loss account each year. SSAP 15 requires that all short-term timing differences shall be the subject of a deferred tax reserve. Other originating timing differences should be reserved unless the directors can demonstrate a reasonable probability that they will continue into the foreseeable future, which for this purpose is a period of three years. Capital allowances, reduced from 100 to 25 per cent on the reducing balance, have made tax deferral less important than in previous years. The third and fourth reasons shown above for creating a deferred taxation reserve are also less important because they are not likely to attract tax within a three-year period and can thus be excluded from the rule in the standard.

TUTORIAL DISCUSSION TOPICS

12.1 Explain how taxation can be used as an instrument of economic policy.

12.2 What is the difference between progressive and regressive taxes? Give examples of each type.

12.3 What is the imputation system and how does it affect the balance sheet of a company?

12.4 State the rules which govern the payment of corporation tax and Schedule D income tax in the UK.

13 | Disclosure: The Accounting Requirements of the Companies Act 1985

Financial information disclosed to shareholders and the general public gives much less detail than is provided for managers.

The Companies Acts of 1948, 1967, 1980 and 1981 set out rules as to the information which companies must disclose in their annual accounts. These Acts have now been consolidated into the Companies Act 1985. The requirements of the Act represent the legal minimum for disclosure but many companies show more than is required by law in their annual accounts. The 1985 Act lays down special formats in which company accounts are to be prepared. The company must select the form of balance sheet and income statement which it wishes to use, and use it consistently.

The information specified in the Act can be shown either on the face of the profit and loss account or balance sheet, or in the form of notes appended thereto. It is fairly common for companies to show their profit and loss account and balance sheet in published form as an austere statement with as few figures and as little information as possible. The bulk of the information is provided in the form of notes appended to the accounting statements. One item of information which is always shown in published accounts is data concerning the previous year's statement, so that a comparison can be made.

Accounts are prepared for use within the firm as in Chapter 8, and then these detailed statements are edited into a form which discloses only what is required by statute.

A requirement is written into the 1985 Act (section 228) that every balance sheet and profit and loss account shall give a true and fair view, and shall be based on certain accounting principles, i.e.

1. The company is presumed to be a going concern.
2. Accounting policies shall be applied consistently.
3. Items shall be determined on a prudent basis, e.g. only profits realized at the accounting date shall be included, whereas account shall be taken of liabilities and losses which are likely to arise in respect of the financial year. Information only becoming apparent after the end of the year but before the accounts are signed must be included.
4. Income and charges for the financial year shall be taken into account without regard to the date of receipt or payment (matching).

A note covering departure from these principles with reasons must be shown in the accounts. This section of the Act brings the accounting principles required by SSAP 2 into the legal requirements for company accounts. A further note will disclose the accounting policies adopted when the accounts were drafted.

The true and fair view requirement overrides other legal rules in so far as extra information not required by statute must be disclosed if it is significant for a true and fair view, and that where compliance with statute would inhibit a true and fair view, a statutory requirement can be ignored. The 'true and fair view override' only operates in special circumstances which must be noted in the accounts.

The 1985 Act specifies two alternative forms of balance sheet and four alternative formats for the profit and loss account. Companies must adopt their chosen format in subsequent years unless there are special reasons for changes, which must be noted in the accounts.

Three items are mentioned which shall not be treated as items in the balance sheet. They are:

(a) preliminary expenses;
(b) expenses or commission on issue of shares or debentures;
(c) costs of research.

This means that such costs must be charged against profit and not carried forward as assets. The profit or loss on ordinary activities before tax must be shown, together with amounts added to, or withdrawn from, reserves, and aggregate dividends paid and proposed. A heading or subheading may be excluded from the format if there is no amount for that item in the year or preceding year. Amounts to which an arabic numeral is assigned in the format can be combined at the discretion of the directors if the amounts are not material, or if the combination facilitates an assessment of the true state of affairs. Corresponding amounts for the previous year must be shown. The formats specified are as follows, but are freely adapted by accountants, whose task is to draft sensible statements. Figures are not given in the 1985 Act but have been included here to add meaning to the examples.

Balance sheet—format 1

Comparative figures for the previous year are usually inserted to the left of the description.

The figures below represent thousands.

	£	£	£
A. Called-up share capital not paid			5
B. Fixed assets			
I Intangible assets			
1. Development costs	200		
2. Concessions, patents, licences, trademarks and			
similar rights and assets	500		
3. Goodwill	400		
4. Payments on account	10	1110	
II Tangible assets			
1. Land and buildings	2000		
2. Plant and machinery	1200		
3. Fixtures, fittings, tools and equipment	700		
4. Payments on account and assets in course of			
construction	50	3550	

	£	£	£
III Investments			
1. Shares in group companies	800		
2. Loans to group companies	75		
3. Shares in related companies	100		
4. Loans to related companies	25		
5. Other investments other than loans	47		
6. Other loans	20		
7. Own shares	25	1092	
			5752
C. Current assets			5757
I Stocks			
1. Raw materials and consumables	630		
2. Work in progress	940		
3. Finished goods and goods for resale	560		
4. Payments on account	15	2145	
II Debtors			
1. Trade debtors	870		
2. Amounts owed by group companies	36		
3. Amounts owed by related companies	27		
4. Other debtors	12		
5. Called-up share capital not paid	8		
6. Prepayments and accrued income	11	964	
III Investments			
1. Shares in group companies	4		
2. Own shares	7		
3. Other investments	29	40	
IV Cash at bank and in hand		59	
		3208	
D. Prepayments and accrued income		—	
		3208	
E. Creditors: amounts falling due within one year			
1. Debenture loans	10		
2. Bank loans and overdrafts	150		
3. Payments received on account	21		
4. Trade creditors	463		
5. Bills of exchange payable	56		
6. Amounts owed to group companies	18		
7. Amounts owed to related companies	4		
8. Other creditors including taxation and social security	175		
9. Accruals and deferred income	26	923	
F. Net current assets/liabilities			2285
G. Total assets less current liabilities			8042
H. Creditors: amounts falling due after more than one year			
1. Debenture loans	1000		
2. Bank loans and overdrafts	10		
3. Payments received on account	20		
4. Trade creditors	6		
5. Bills of exchange payable	8		
6. Amounts owed to group companies	40		
7. Amounts owed to related companies	25		
8. Other creditors including taxation and social security	115		
9. Accruals and deferred income	5	1229	

		£	£	£
I.	Provisions for liabilities and charges			
	1. Pensions and similar obligations	68		
	2. Taxation, including deferred taxation	1420		
	3. Other provisions	86	1574	(2803)
J.	Accruals and deferred income			
				£5239
K.	Capital and reserves			
	I Called-up share capital			4000
	II Share premium account			100
	III Revaluation reserve			400
	IV Other reserves			
	1. Capital redemption reserve fund		350	
	2. Reserve for own shares		25	
	3. Reserves provided for by the articles of association		80	
	4. Other reserves		50	505
	V Profit and loss account			234
				£5239

Format 1 for balance sheet and income statement is most popular in practice.

Balance sheet—format 2

This format is the same as for format 1 except that there are two sections, namely, assets and liabilities, which balance at equal amounts. The assets section is not reproduced here since it is the same as sections A to D in format 1, but it will show a total (£5757 + £3208) of £8965 for all the assets. The liabilities section which balances to £8965 is shown below. The items here are essentially the same as for sections E, H, I, J and K of format 1, except that long-term and short-term creditors (E and H) have been amalgamated into one section.

As in the old-style format, the comparative figures for the previous year are usually inserted to the left of the description.

The figures below represent thousands.

		£	£	£
LIABILITIES				
A.	Capital and reserves			
	I Called-up share capital		4000	
	II Share premium account		100	
	III Revaluation reserve		400	
	IV Other reserves			
	1. Capital redemption reserve fund	350		
	2. Reserve for own shares	25		
	3. Reserves provided for by the articles of association	80		
	4. Other reserves	50	505	
	V Profit and loss account		234	5239
B.	Provisions for liabilities and charges			
	1. Pensions and similar obligations		68	
	2. Taxation including deferred taxation		1420	
	3. Other provisions		86	1574

		£	£	£
C.	Creditors			
	1. Debenture loans		1010	
	2. Bank loans and overdrafts		160	
	3. Payments received on account		41	
	4. Trade creditors		469	
	5. Bills of exchange payable		64	
	6. Amounts owed to group companies		58	
	7. Amounts owed to related companies		29	
	8. Other creditors including taxation and social security		290	
	9. Accruals and deferred income		31	2152
D.	Accruals and deferred income			
				£8965

Note 1. Prepayments and accrued income (C II 6 and D in format 1). This item may be shown in either of the two positions given.

Note 2. Accruals and deferred income (E 9, H 9 and J). Long-term or short-term accruals have an alternative position at J in format 1 and can be shown at either C 9 or D in the liabilities section of format 2.

Profit and loss account—format 1

As in the old-style format, the comparative figures for the previous year are usually inserted to the left of the description.

The figures below represent thousands.

	£	£
1. Turnover		10 414
2. Cost of sales		8 213
3. Gross profit or loss		2 201
4. Distribution costs		(209)
5. Administrative expenses		(941)
6. Other operating income		64
7. Income from shares in group companies		112
8. Income from shares in related companies		26
9. Income from other fixed asset investments		37
10. Other interest receivable and similar income		21
11. Amounts written off investments		(15)
12. Interest payable and similar charges		(470)
13. Tax on profit or loss on ordinary activities		(314)
14. Profit or loss on ordinary activities after taxation		512
15. Extraordinary income	71	
16. Extraordinary charges	(30)	
17. Extraordinary profit or loss		41
18. Tax on extraordinary profit or loss		(15)
19. Other taxes not shown under the above items		(5)
20. Profit or loss for the financial year		£533

Profit and loss account—format 2

	£
1. Turnover	10 414
2. Change in stocks of finished goods and in work in progress (increase—see note)	51

	£	£
3. Own work capitalized		100
4. Other operating income:		64
5. (a) Raw materials and consumables	(2416)	
(b) Other external charges	(1795)	(4 211)
6. Staff costs:		
(a) Wages and salaries	(3831)	
(b) Social security costs	(546)	
(c) Other pension costs	(203)	(4 580)
7. (a) Depreciation and other amounts written off tangible and		
intangible fixed assets	(667)	
(b) Exceptional amounts written off current assets	(16)	(683)
8. Other operating charges		(40)
9. Income from shares in group companies		112
10. Income from shares in related companies		26
11. Income from other fixed asset investments		37
12. Other interest receivable and similar income		21
13. Amounts written off investments		(15)
14. Interest payable and similar charges		(470)
15. Tax on profit or loss on ordinary activities		(314)
16. Profit or loss on ordinary activities after taxation		512
17. Extraordinary income	71	
18. Extraordinary charges	(30)	
19. Extraordinary profit or loss		41
20. Tax on extraordinary profit or loss		(15)
21. Other taxes not shown under the above items		(5)
22. Profit or loss for the financial year		£533

Note. Change in stocks (format 2). A stock increase reduces the amount of costs for the year to be charged against sales. Therefore a stock increase is added to turnover, since in this format it is not deducted from the costs. See format 4 B 2.

Profit and loss account—format 3

As in the old-style format, the comparative figures for the previous year are usually inserted to the left of the description.
   The figures below represent thousands.

	£
A. Charges	
1. Cost of sales	8 213
2. Distribution costs	209
3. Administrative expenses	941
4. Amounts written off investments	15
5. Interest payable and similar charges	470
6. Tax on profit or loss on ordinary activities	314
7. Profit or loss on ordinary activities after taxation	—
8. Extraordinary charges	30
9. Tax on extraordinary profit or loss	15
10. Other taxes not shown under the above items	5
11. Profit for the financial year	533
	£10 745

	£
B. Income	
1. Turnover	10 414
2. Other operating income	64
3. Income from shares in group companies	112
4. Income from shares in related companies	26
5. Income from other fixed asset investments	37
6. Other interest receivable and similar income	21
*7. Profit or loss on ordinary activities after taxation	—
8. Extraordinary income	71
9. Loss for the financial year	—
	£10 745

* *Note.* Profit or loss on ordinary activities after taxation—this item appears in both charges and income sections of this format. This would seem to be a drafting error since clearly a profit cannot be a charge and a loss cannot be income. It is also difficult to understand how this item fits into a statement where the total of A equals the total of B, when the item iself is calculated as showing the difference between income items 1 to 6 and charges 1 to 6. This criticism also applies to format 4. Perhaps these formats in Schedule 1 of the Act were not designed to balance A against B but to show in detail the items which the published profit and loss account must reveal.

Profit and loss account—format 4

As in the old-style format, the comparative figures for the previous year are usually inserted to the left of the description.
The figures below represent thousands.

	£	£
A. Charges		
1. Reduction in stocks of finished goods and in work in progress		—
2. (a) Raw materials and consumables	2416	
(b) Other external charges	1795	4211
3. Staff costs:		
(a) Wages and salaries	3831	
(b) Social security costs	546	
(c) Other pension costs	203	4 580
4. (a) Depreciation and other amounts written off tangible and intangible fixed assets	667	
(b) Exceptional amounts written off current assets	16	683
5. Other operating charges		40
6. Amounts written off investments		15
7. Interest payable and similar charges		470
8. Tax on profit or loss on ordinary activities		314
9. Profit or loss on ordinary activities after taxation		—
10. Extraordinary charges		30
11. Tax on extraordinary profit or loss		15
12. Other taxes not shown under the above items		5
13. Profit or loss for the financial year		533
		£10 896

	£	£
B. Income		
1. Turnover		10 414
2. Increase in stocks of finished goods and in work in progress		51
3. Own work capitalized		100
4. Other operating income		64
5. Income from shares in group companies		112
6. Income from shares in related companies		26
7. Income from other fixed asset investments		37
8. Other interest receivable and similar income		21
9. Profit or loss on ordinary activities after taxation		—
10. Extraordinary income		71
11. Profit or loss for the financial year		—
		£10 896

THE PUBLISHED PROFIT AND LOSS ACCOUNT

Certain information, specified by statute, must be disclosed in the income statement or by notes thereto.

1. Turnover—the amount of turnover (total sales or other income) and the basis on which it is computed must be disclosed, i.e. turnover of ordinary activities should be stated after deduction of trade discounts and VAT. Turnover and profit must be analysed for substantially different classes of business, and turnover for substantially different geographic markets, unless the directors consider that such disclosure would prejudice the interests of the company, in which case they must say so in a note to the accounts. Turnover from banking operations, whether all or part of the business, need not be disclosed, but its omission must be noted.
2. Employees—the average number of employees during the year must be noted, and analysed in categories of persons. The aggregate amounts of wages and salaries, social security costs and pension costs must be disclosed. This analysis of turnover, profits and employees is part of a process referred to as 'disaggregation' or segmental analysis whereby more detail is disclosed in public accounts.
3. Directors' emoluments—these must be divided between fees received as directors, amounts received for other services, e.g. salaries, and the cost of directors' pensions. The aggregate of all emoluments must be disclosed, including directors' and past directors' pensions, and compensation paid for loss of office. Where aggregate directors' emoluments exceed £60 000, a note should reveal the number of directors who have waived rights to emoluments during the year and the amount waived, the emoluments net of pension contributions of the chairman, highest paid director, and the number of UK directors whose emoluments net of pension contributions fall into brackets of £5000.
Note: These starting amounts can be increased by order in council so the figures quoted above may become outdated.

4. Depreciation—the amount provided for tangible or intangible fixed assets must be shown, together with additional provisions for temporary or permanent diminution, or amounts written back because no longer necessary. Assets which have been revalued but which are still depreciated on the basis of historical cost must be noted, with the difference between the charge and the amount based on the new value. This requirement is usually covered by a note to the accounts concerning fixed assets and depreciation.

5. Auditor's remuneration, including expenses. It is important that the shareholders should be informed as to the amount paid to the auditors because, in theory at least, the auditors are employed by and report to the shareholders.

6. Charges for the hire of plant or machinery.

7. Revenue from rents if material, net of outgoings.

8. Interest paid analysed between:
   (a) loans and overdrafts repayable by instalments within five years;
   (b) loans and overdrafts repayable other than by instalments within five years;
   (c) other loans.

9. Income from investments listed on a stock exchange. This will be part of 'other operating income' in the profit and loss account, so a note should provide the detail required.

10. Amounts provided for the redemption of share capital and loans.

11. The profit or loss on ordinary activities before taxation.

12. Taxation on ordinary activities—the amount of:
    (a) UK income tax;
    (b) UK corporation tax;
    (c) tax imposed outside the UK.
    A note should cover any special circumstances affecting taxation, and the basis on which UK tax has been computed.

13. The aggregate amount of dividend paid and proposed. This is usually analysed by note to the various classes of capital.

14. Reserves—amounts set aside or withdrawn from reserves.

15. Extraordinary items—information must be disclosed to show:
    (a) details of extraordinary items, and the tax thereon, per SSAP 6;
    (b) the effect of amounts charged or credited that relate to preceding financial years;
    (c) any items which although they are part of the ordinary activities of the company are exceptional because of their size or incidence.

THE BALANCE SHEET

The following information must be shown either on the face of the balance sheet or by way of note.

Share Capital

The amount for authorized and issued capital must be summarized. The authorized capital is the amount which the company is authorized to raise, under its Memorandum and Articles of Association, and the issued capital is the proportion of authorized capital which has been issued to subscribers. Where redeemable shares have been issued, the details of redemption dates, whether the redemption is optional, and any redemption premium which may be payable must be shown. Obviously such details cannot be shown on the face of the balance sheet, and are usually revealed in the form of a note. Analysis must show the number and aggregate nominal value of each class of shares allotted. Where shares are allotted during the year a note must explain the reason for the issue, the numbers issued, their aggregate nominal value and the consideration received. A further note is required to give details of the aggregate amount recommended for dividend and any arrears of fixed cumulative dividend together with the arrears period. Further information concerning share capital, which does not often appear in the accounts, covers particulars of share capital on which interest has been paid out of capital, together with the rate and details of any loans made by the company for the purchase of its shares, with particulars of options outstanding to any person to subscribe for the company's shares.

Reserves and Provisions

Amounts transferred to or from reserves or provisions must be disclosed by note or as part of the appropriation section in the profit and loss account. The sources from which increases in reserves and provisions have been made must be shown, as must the ways in which any reduction of a reserve has been applied. If there is a share premium account this should be shown separately. Such an account arises in circumstances where a company issues shares at more than their face value. If there is a strong demand for its shares, a company will be able to offer a new issue of fresh shares to the general public at a premium, i.e. the public would be willing to subscribe, say, £1.50 for every £1 ordinary share they take up. If 100 000 shares are the subject of such an issue, then the capital will increase by £100 000, the share premium account will increase by £50 000 and, on the other side of the balance sheet, cash will go up by £150 000. It must be remembered that a share premium account is a statutory reserve, not available for distribution, and the uses to which such an account can be put are severely limited.

Transfers from a provision for a purpose other than that for which the provision was created must be explained.

Loans

Creditors must be analysed between amounts falling due within one year and after one year. Loans repayable more than one year from the balance sheet date must be separated from other loans, amounts repayable in more than five years, by instalment and otherwise must have the repayment terms and rate of interest shown. A note should reveal any debentures of the company which have been redeemed and which the company has power to re-issue, together with details of any debentures of the company held by a nominee for the company. For debentures issued during the year, the reasons, class, amount and consideration should be disclosed. Any loans or other liabilities which are secured on the assets of the company must be the subject of a note detailing the assets concerned in such a security. In cases where there is a charge on the assets of the company to secure the liabilities of another person, this too must be stated.

Current Liabilities

The Acts say little about how current liabilities should be shown except that amounts owed for tax and social security must be separated from other creditors, as must proposed dividends. Since the introduction of advance corporation tax under the imputation system there has been a significant change in the way in which proposed dividends are shown. Dividends proposed, but not yet paid, are the same as creditors of the company. The amount to be paid to the shareholders is thus shown as a current liability. Under the imputation system advance corporation tax on dividends is liable to be paid to the Inland Revenue within thirteen weeks of the payment of that dividend, but it can be reclaimed later by being set off against mainstream corporation tax. Thus advance corporation tax liable as a result of a dividend must be shown as a current liability on the balance sheet, and also as a deferred asset, since it can be reclaimed later. It does not, however, always appear on the balance sheet as an asset, since it may be deducted from the deferred taxation reserve.

Contingent Liabilities

These must be noted. They are not part of the balance sheet computation, since they are not owed at the balance sheet date, but they relate to transactions which took place before the balance sheet date and which may or may not become liabilities after the balance sheet date, contingent upon some further circumstances which cannot be accurately forecast. Figures must be shown for capital expenditure authorized by the board and not yet contracted for, separate from authorized capital expenditure for which contracts have been placed.

Material contingent losses (SSAP 18) must be provided for where a future event may confirm the loss. A note must disclose the nature of the contingency, the uncertainties, and a prudent estimate of the financial effect of the contingent event if it is practicable to make such an estimate.

Intangible Assets

Any amount not yet written off for goodwill, patents and trademarks, and share and debenture issue expenses and commissions, must be stated.

Pension Commitments

A note is required to show particulars of provisions made and items for which no provision has been made.

Loans to Directors and Officers

As a general rule a company may not make a loan to a director or act as guarantor or security for a loan to a director. This prohibition extends to 'quasi loans', whereby the company agrees to reimburse a person who has lent money to a director, unless the quasi loan is for less than £5000 and repayable within two months. Small loans up to £5000 in aggregate, minor business transactions up to £5000, and advances up to £10 000 to meet directors' business expenditure are excepted from the general rule, as are loans from 'money-lending companies' up to £100 000 (other than from banks). Particulars of such loans, if considered as material by the board, must be disclosed. Amounts, with names, at the beginning and end of the year, and any unpaid interest or provision for a doubtful debt must be stated.

Loans, guarantees, quasi loans and credit transactions in favour of officers of the company must also be noted if in excess of £2500 each. The aggregate figure at the beginning and end of the year must be shown together with the number of officers involved.

The amounts shown are as in the Companies Act 1989.

Tangible Fixed Assets

The accounts must show the cost or valuation of fixed assets net of depreciation to date, analysed to disclose movements during the year: opening cost, plus or minus revaluations, plus acquisitions, less disposals, to give cost at the end of the year.

Cumulative depreciation is similarly analysed to show provision at the beginning of the year, plus provision for the year, less depreciation transferred to disposals account, leaving cumulative provision at the end of the year. Usually one figure for net book value is given in the accounts, with an extensive note to provide the required analysis. Any significant difference between book value and real value must be mentioned in the directors' report.

For fixed assets carried in the accounts at a valuation rather than historical cost, details must be disclosed of the value and year of valuation. In the year of valuation the names and qualifications of the valuer and the basis of the valuation must be shown. Thus investors can assess the validity of any new value set upon the fixed assets of the business, and can see when they were last valued.

Land and buildings must be analysed between freehold, long leaseholds (fifty or more years to run) and short leaseholds. A note concerning depreciation methods will appear with the other accounting policies.

Intangible Fixed Assets

Notes must disclose:

1. Capitalized development costs—the reason for capitalizing such costs and the period over which they are to be amortized.
2. Purchased goodwill—the amortization period chosen by the directors, which may not exceed the economic life of the goodwill, and reasons for their choice. This is a similar analysis as that for tangible fixed assets.

Investments

Whether fixed or current assets, investments are normally shown at cost, with notes to explain further details.

1. The amount of listed investments with a note as to their current stock exchange value or market value if that is different, e.g. in the case of a large shareholding.
2. The nominal value of its own shares held by a company must be shown.
3. Investments carried at directors' valuation must be accompanied by an explanation of the valuation method.
4. If the company holds more than 10 per cent of any class of another company's shares it must show the name, and country of origin of the company and proportion held.
5. Holdings of more than 20 per cent of the capital of another company (a related company) should be accounted for under the equity method (SSAP 1). This method adds the appropriate proportion of undistributed income of the associate company to the cost of shares in the associate company. An item 'net profit retained in associate' is added to undistributed profit on the other side of the balance sheet. Clearly the possession of a 20 per cent or more share stake in another company brings an element of control with it, and to account only for dividends received rather than a proportion of all profit made would be misleading. This is part of the consolidation of group accounts, which is beyond the scope of this book.

Stocks

Stocks are to be shown at the lower of net realizable value or purchase price or production cost. A note about the basis of the valuation will appear with other accounting policies.

The 1985 Act refers to 'fungible assets', meaning those short-term assets which are interchangeable in function or value and for this reason cannot be distinguished from one another, i.e. debtors and investments. The purchase price or production cost of stocks or fungible assets can be determined by an appropriate method chosen by the directors from those mentioned in the Act, i.e. FIFO, LIFO, weighted average and any similar method. At this point the Act is in direct contravention of SSAP 9, which does not allow the use of the LIFO method. If the amount shown differs materially from the replacement cost of the asset this difference must be noted. The Act also allows stocks to be included at a fixed quantity and value where this is not subject to material variation. This could be construed to permit the use of the base stock method banned by SSAP 9.

Debtors

Amounts recoverable after more than one year must be disclosed separately from other debtors.

Example

Grande PLC has an authorized share capital of £3 750 000, consisting of ordinary shares of £1 each. The company prepares its accounts as on 31 March in each year and the trial balance, before final adjustments, extracted on 31 March 19-6 showed:

	£	£
Goodwill	20 000	
Ordinary share capital, issued and fully paid		3 600 000
General reserve		18 000
Retained profit as on 1 April, 19-5		18 000
Debenture stock 6 per cent		120 000
Unsecured loan stock 6 per cent		30 000
Freehold office premises:	3 000 000	
accumulated depreciation		12 000
Leasehold factory: cost at beginning of year	600 000	
accumulated depreciation		228 000
Plant and machinery: cost at beginning of year	260 000	
accumulated depreciation		105 000
additions in year	30 000	
Interest on debenture stock	7 200	
Interest on loan stock	1 800	
Directors' emoluments	108 000	
Auditors' remuneration	7 500	518 000
Creditors and accrued expenses		
Stock as on 31 March 19-6	480 000	
Debtors and prepayments	582 000	
Balance at bank	204 000	3 240 000
Sales: invoiced value less allowances		
Cost of sales	2 100 000	
Distribution costs	250 500	
Administration expenses	400 000	
	£8 051 000	£8 051 000

You ascertain that:

1. The unsecured loan stock is repayable at par on 31 December 19-6. The debentures are secured on the leasehold factory and are repayable in ten years' time.

2. The lease of the factory is for 50 years, with 20 years expired. Freehold premises are split—£600 000 for the buildings and £2 400 000 for the land.
3. Directors' remuneration comprises (a) salaries of chairman £30 000, managing director £33 000, sales director £33 000, (b) fee of non-executive director £5500, and (c) pension contributions £6500.
4. The managing director is entitled to a commission of 5 per cent per annum on the net profit, after deducting all charges except taxation and the commission. The company secretary has been paid a salary of £31 000.
5. Annual depreciation is calculated as to:
   Leasehold factory and freehold building—2 per cent on cost
   Plant and machinery—20 per cent on written-down value 1 April 19-5, plus additions in year. Plant costing £20 000 was sold for its WDV of £5000 cash on 31 March, but no entry has yet been made in the books for this transaction.
6. Stock has been valued consistently at the lower of cost and net realizable value.
7. A dividend of 3.33 pence per share net of income tax is proposed.
8. Corporation tax on the profit of the year has been computed at £120 000 and is payable on 1 January 19-7.
9. The directors have placed contracts for new plant costing £75 000 and have authorized further expenditure on new plant costing £60 000.
10. Sales are at invoiced value less allowances.
11. The directors have decided to amortize goodwill to the profit and loss account over a five-year period starting this year.

You are required to prepare in a form suitable for publication and in conformity with the provisions of the Companies Acts:

(a) a balance sheet as on 31 March 19-6;
(b) a profit and loss account for the year ended 31 March 19-6; and
(c) notes to the accounts.

The first step is to calculate depreciation, and then compute the trading profit, since it is not shown in the trial balance. Note that freehold land is not depreciated.

	Freehold buildings 2 per cent	Leasehold 2 per cent	Plant 20 per cent WDV	Goodwill 20 per cent
	£	£	£	£
Cost	600 000	600 000	270 000	20 000
Less cumulative depreciation			90 000	
			180 000	
Depreciation	12 000	12 000	36 000	4 000

The plant figure is after deducting cost and depreciation for disposals. Cost of £20 000 – WDV £5000 = Cumulative depreciation of £15 000.

	£	£
Sales		3 240 000
Less:		
Cost of sales	2 100 000	
Distribution costs	250 500	
Administration expenses	400 000	
Interest: debentures	7 200	
loan stock	1 800	
Audit fee: administration	7 500	
Depreciation: factory (COS)	12 000	
office (administration)	12 000	
plant (COS)	36 000	
goodwill (administration)	4 000	
Directors (£33 000 distribution)		
(Remainder—administration)	108 000	2 939 000
		301 000
Managing director's commission (administration) ($\frac{1}{11}$)		15 050
Net profit		£285 950

1. Do not forget that the commission is a current liability.
2. Costs are allocated to cost of sales (COS), distribution costs or administration expenses so that they can be slotted into the appropriate heading in the published profit and loss account format, e.g. administration expenses are £400 000 + £7500 + £12 000 + £4000 + £75 000 + £15 050 = £513 550. Interest is disclosed separately. The accounts would disclose the following information using format 1.

Grande PLC Profit and Loss Account for Year Ending 31 March 19-6

	£	£
Sales		3 240 000
Less cost of sales		2 148 000
		1 092 000
Less distribution costs:	283 500	
Administration expenses	513 550	
Interest on loans repayable within one year	1 800	
Interest on loans repayable otherwise than by instalments		
in more than five years time	7 200	
		806 050
Net profit before taxation		285 950
UK corporation tax based on profit for the year		120 000
*Net profit after taxation		165 950
Less: proposed dividend at 3.33 pence per share	119 880	
transfer to general reserve	30 000	
		149 880
Unappropriated profit for the year		16 070
Balance of unappropriated profit b/d		18 000
Balance of unappropriated profit c/f		£34 070
Earnings per share		
*[£165 950 ÷ 3 600 000 shares] 4.6 pence per share		

Note:
Earnings per share is calculated by dividing the net profit, *after* tax but *before* extraordinary items, by the number of shares at issue.

Grande PLC Balance Sheet as at 31 March 19-6

	£	£	£
Fixed assets:			
Intangible assets: goodwill		16 000	
Tangible assets: land and buildings		3 336 000	
plant and machinery		144 000	
			3 496 000
Deferred assets: ACT recoverable			51 377
Current assets: stocks		480 000	
debtors		582 000	
bank		209 000	
		1 271 000	
Creditors—amounts falling due within one year:			
Unsecured loan stock 6 per cent	30 000		
Trade creditors	533 050		
Corporation tax	120 000		
ACT payable	51 377		
Proposed dividend	119 880		
		854 307	
Net current assets			416 693
Total assets less current liabilities			3 964 070
Creditors falling due after more than one year			
6 per cent debentures			120 000
			£3 844 070
Capital and reserves:			
Called-up share capital			3 600 000
General reserve			210 000
Unappropriated profits			34 070
			£3 844 070

Note:
ACT payable and recoverable is calculated as $3/7$ × the dividend payable (119 880) = £51 377. ACT recoverable is shown as a deferred asset because in this company there is no reserve for deferred taxation against which it can be offset.

Notes to the accounts:

1. Accounting policies:
   stock is accounted for at the lower of cost or net realizable value.
   Depreciation: freehold building 2 per cent on cost on a straight line basis
   leasehold building 2 per cent on cost on a straight line basis
   plant—20 per cent on net book value
   Goodwill: the directors have decided to amortize it over a five-year economic life starting this year.

2. Fixed assets:

	Freehold land and buildings	Leasehold buildings	Plant	Goodwill	Total
	£	£	£	£	£
At cost 1 April 19-5	3 000 00	600 000	260 000	20 000	3 880 000
Acquisitions	—	—	30 000	—	30 000
Disposal	—	—	(20 000)	—	(20 000)
Cost 31 March 19-6	3 000 000	600 000	270 000	20 000	3 890 000
Depreciation				—	345 000
Balance 1 April 19-5	12 000	228 000	105 000	4 000	64 000
Provision	12 000	12 000	36 000	—	(15 000)
Disposals	—	—	(15 000)		
Balance 31 March 19-6	24 000	240 000	126 000	4 000	394 000
WDV	2 976 000	360 000	144 000	16 000	3 496 000

Freehold buildings cost £600 000.
The lease is a short lease.

3. The 6 per cent debentures are repayable in ten years' time and are secured on the leasehold property.
4. Directors' emoluments:

	£
Salaries	110 050
Fees	5 500
Pension contributions	6 500
	122 050

Chairman—£30 000
Highest-paid director—£48 050
   salary band £30 001—£35 000 = one;
   salary band £5 001—£10 000 = one.

5. Capital expenditure: contracts placed—£75 000
                   contracts authorized—£60 000.

THE DIRECTORS' REPORT

This is a formal statement that is appended to the published accounts. The auditor must certify that it is consistent with the financial statements. In the report the directors must set out a fair review of the development of the company during the year and its position at the end of the year.

Once again, a minimum of information is required by the Act, but many companies exceed these limits in the cause of good public relations. The manner in which the required information is presented often reflects the character of the board.

Many companies now produce a chairman's statement as a public relations item, accompanying the published accounts. The report is separate from the directors' report, the contents of which are specified in the Companies Act 1985. The report should cover the following matters:

1. A fair review of the development of the business of the company and its subsidiaries during the year, and their position at the end of the year.
2. The principal activities of the company and its subsidiaries during the accounting period, with details of any significant changes to those activities. For example, if a construction company acquires a bank as a subsidiary company during the year, this fact must be mentioned in the directors' report.
3. Details concerning the directors:
    (a) The names of all persons who acted as directors at any part of the accounting period.
    (b) The interests of directors in shares or debentures of the company showing amounts at the beginning and end of the year. This information is to be given for each person who was a director of the business at the end of the financial year. As an alternative the directors' interests in shares or debentures may be given as a note to the accounts rather than being set out in the directors' report.
4. The amount of dividends proposed and paid during the year and the amount proposed to be transferred to or from the reserves.
5. A comment concerning future developments. This comment should give users of the accounts an idea of the board's future policy, but it is more often honoured in the breach than in the act, in that a bland but meaningless comment is made which fulfils the strict requirement but not the spirit of the law.
6. Details of any post-balance-sheet events which have taken place since the end of the accounting year but before the accounts are signed as approved by the directors.
7. If a company purchases or otherwise acquires its own shares during the course of the year, the directors must disclose the number of shares purchased, their nominal value, the aggregate consideration paid, and an explanation of the reasons for the purchase. If less shares are held at the end of the year than were held during the year, the maximum number and nominal value must be shown. The number and nominal value of shares disposed of or cancelled during the year, and any charge on the shares if they have been used as security, must be disclosed.
8. If the average number of employees in the business exceeds 250, the directors' report must state the company's policy as to the employment of disabled persons and the training, career development and promotion of disabled persons.
9. If the company employs more than 250 people in the UK, the directors' report must disclose policy and actions to provide employees with information on matters of significance to them, to consult with employees or their representatives and to operate an employee share scheme.
10. The total figure for political and charitable contributions made by the company during the year must be disclosed unless the combined total is less than £200. The amount given and the name of any political party, or person paid, for each contribution for political purposes in excess of £200 must be shown.

THE SIGNIFICANCE FOR DISCLOSURE OF STATEMENTS OF STANDARD ACCOUNTING PRACTICE

Statements of Standard Accounting Practice (SSAPs) specify methods of accounting practice approved by the councils of the major professional accounting bodies in the UK, for application to all financial accounts intended to give a true and fair view of the financial position, or profit and loss. Professional accountants, whether acting in the capacity of director, executive, or auditor, must observe the requirements of these standards and explain departures from them. Failure to do this may lead to the qualification by an auditor of his certificate on a set of published accounts.

SSAPs reflect best accounting practice, and often stipulate disclosures beyond what is required by statute. The requirements of some SSAPs have been incorporated into subsequent Companies Acts, and in one case at least an SSAP is in conflict with the law. The major disclosure rules are as follows.

SSAP 2, as mentioned in Chapter 2, deals with the disclosure of accounting policies. In the absence of an explanatory statement of facts to the contrary, the four fundamental concepts, i.e. going concern, accruals, consistency and conservatism, are presumed to have been observed in the preparation of the accounts. The accounting policies (i.e. the specific accounting basis used) followed for dealing with items judged to be material in determining profit or loss for the year and in stating the financial position, should be disclosed by way of a note to the accounts. Disclosure of policy adopted would be required for such matters as depreciation of fixed assets, treatment and amortization of intangible assets, research and development expenditure, stocks and work in progress, long-term contracts, deferred taxation, hire purchase and instalment transactions, and repairs and renewals.

SSAP 3 stipulates that earnings per share (EPS) should be shown on the face of the profit and loss account of companies listed on the Stock Exchange. The calculation is usually made by dividing net profit after tax, but before extraordinary items, by the number of ordinary shares at issue. The basis of the calculation, which in certain circumstances can be complicated, must be noted in the accounts.

SSAP 6 deals with extraordinary items and prior-year adjustments. In this standard extraordinary items are those material items which derive from events or transactions outside the ordinary activities of the business. They do not include prior-year adjustments or those items which, although exceptional as to their size and incidence, arise from the ordinary activities of the business and which should be reflected in the net profit (before tax) for the year and disclosed separately if necessary. The profit and loss account should show the net profit (after tax) before extraordinary items, then the extraordinary items themselves, with their nature and amounts specified, less any tax liability attributable to such items. The statement can conclude with the net profit after tax and after extraordinary items. Prior-year adjustments in this context are limited to the effects of changes in accounting policies and the correction of fundamental errors. They do not include corrections and adjustments to previous periods' estimates. In the cases of correction of fundamental errors and change in accounting policy, such as a change in the basis of depreciation of fixed assets, or in the basis of stock valuation, the cumulative adjustments relating to prior years should not be included when calculating a current year's profit. Such cumulative amounts should be adjusted in the opening balance of retained profits with an adequate note to disclose the nature of the adjustment and separate amounts where necessary (see Chapter 14).

SSAP 8 (Chapter 12) deals with the treatment of taxation in accounts. The imputation system requires the payment of ACT, and it appears as an asset and as a liability in the balance sheet. Dividends paid are shown net of taxes, but franked investment income is grossed up in the profit and loss account, and the associated tax credit is shown as part of the tax charge for the year.

SSAP 9—Stocks and Work in Progress. This requires that stocks should be classified in the accounts or notes, in a manner appropriate to the business. This standard also stipulates rules and methods for the calculation of stocks, but methods forbidden by the standard appear to be permissible under the Companies Act 1985 (see above and Chapter 7).

SSAP 10 requires that any business with a turnover in excess of £25 000 per annum must publish a statement of sources and application of funds as an appendix to the accounts. The methods whereby such statements are drafted are explained in Chapter 24.

SSAP 12—Depreciation. This stipulates that details of the methods, economic lives and depreciation rates must be disclosed with other accounting policies. The opening and closing provision, together with amounts added to or taken from that provision during the year, must be shown.

SSAP 13—Research and Development. This standard requires that expenditure on pure and applied research must be written off to the profit and loss account in the year it is incurred, and that development costs should receive a similar treatment unless there is likely to be sufficient profit derived from the development to cover the cost. Details to be shown are the opening and closing balance of deferred development expenditure carried forward and any addition or reduction of the amount during the year. The accounting policy must be clearly explained.

SSAP 15—Deferred Taxation. All movement to or from the deferred taxation reserve must be disclosed, with a note as to the reason for the movement.

SSAP 17—Post-Balance-Sheet Events. The 1985 Act requires the directors' report to give details of important events affecting the company which may have occurred since the end of the accounting year, but this standard goes further. Events between the balance sheet date, and the date on which the accounts are approved by the board, are analysed into two classes: one which requires adjustment to the figures in the accounts and another of 'non-adjustable events', which must be the subject of a note to the accounts. The note should cover the nature of the event and an estimate of its financial effect on the business.

SSAP 18—Contingencies. Under the 1985 Act a note must show contingent liabilities not provided for in the accounts, disclosing the amount, legal nature and any security given. The standard requires that material contingent losses must be provided for in the accounts if they can be estimated with reasonable accuracy and certainty, and that otherwise a note must disclose the contingency, giving details of its nature, and uncertainties affecting it, and the likely financial effect it may have.

Exemptions for Small and Medium-Sized Companies

These exemptions are granted to non-public companies to which two or more of the qualifying conditions apply:

1. Small companies:

(a) Turnover not exeeding £2 million net or £2.4 million gross;

(b) Balance sheet total £1 million net or £1.2 million gross;

(c) Average number of employees less than 50.

2. Medium-sized companies:

(a) Turnover not exceeding £8 million net or 9.6 million gross;

(b) Balance sheet total £3 million net or £4.7 million gross;

(c) Average number of employees less than 250.

The amounts for turnover and balance sheet total were increased in the 1989 Companies Act and also net and gross figures were included. The net figure is calculated after adjustments are made in the consolidated accounts to eliminate inter-company balances.

Full information must still be produced and audited; the exemptions apply only to what needs to be filed with the registrar of companies.

The exemptions from the disclosure rules mean that the company concerned may deliver copies of modified accounts to the Registrar of Companies. A small company need not submit a profit and loss account or a directors' report, but must submit a modified balance sheet with notes to cover accounting policies, share capital, share allotments, debts, foreign currency translation and comparative figures. A medium-sized company can submit a modified profit and loss account without particulars of turnover, but must submit a full balance sheet. Information concerning the salaries of directors and higher-paid employees is not required for small companies.

Analysis of turnover and profit by class of business, and turnover by geographic area, is not required from either medium-sized or small businesses. The directors must state that they are claiming these exemptions, and the auditor must report that the requirements for exemption are satisfied.

Alternative Accounting Rules

The disadvantages of historical cost accounting and the need for some alternative system of accounting were recognized when the European Fourth Directive was drafted, and when the Companies Act 1985 was passed. The Act states the need for company accounts to show a true and fair view, but recognizes the fact that there is not a single method which can lead exclusively to a true and fair view. Accordingly, permissive sections of the Act set out alternative accounting rules which companies can apply or ignore as they wish.

These rules are as follows:

1. Intangible fixed assets other than goodwill may be stated at their current cost. Tangible fixed assets may be stated at either market value on their last valuation date, or at current cost.

2. Fixed asset investments may be shown at market value when last valued or on a basis thought appropriate by the directors. Details of the methods and reasons for its adoption must be stated.
3. Current asset investments and stock may be stated at current cost.

Thus accounts can be drafted according to the historical cost convention or using current cost rules, or mixing the two systems by revaluing certain items. There is no certainty as to how current cost is to be determined, as the Act does not require companies to comply with the rules of SSAP 16, which has now been withdrawn. Any differences between an alternative rule value and the historical cost value for an asset must be credited or if necessary debited to a revaluation reserve, after taking account of any provision for depreciation. For the purpose of depreciation the value of an asset determined according to the latest application of current cost valuation rules is significant, because although historical cost-based depreciation can still be used, if the charge is not based on current cost, the difference must be disclosed.

Certain historical cost information must be given if the alternative rules are used. Notes must state which assets have been revalued, the basis of the revaluation, and either the historical cost amounts for the asset or the difference between the historical cost and the value according to the alternative rules.

Summarized Accounts

The Companies Act 1989 contains rules which allow companies to send abbreviated accounts to shareholders. A large company may have many shareholders, e.g. the Trustee Savings Bank has 1.8 million shareholders, and it is very expensive to send out a full set of accounts to each of these members, when it is probable that the detailed notes contained therein will not be appreciated by a large proportion of the shareholders. Two-thirds of the shareholders of the TSB indicated in a recent survey that they would rather see a simpler technical report than the full set of accounts they currently receive. This problem has beset accountants and companies for some time because the published accounts distributed to shareholders must be meaningful to a population with a widely differing financial awareness. A full set of accounts with accompanying notes will be of great interest to a qualified accountant but may be just a meaningless jumble of figures to a financially unsophisticated shareholder who owns, say, 100 shares. It is argued by some companies that they should send to their members an easily understood summary instead of full accounts. Not all accountants agree with this position, arguing that it is wrong to cater to shareholders' lack of knowledge about accounts by telling them less. Already much significant information is hidden in the notes to the accounts, and to allow a summary to be distributed to shareholders could lead to the publication of misleading information. It is not enough, argue the accountants, that the Companies Act 1989 should stipulate that the summarized accounts are audited before being sent to shareholders. The real cure is for accounting statements themselves to be presented in a more understandable form. The new rule is that shareholders will have to request a full set of accounts if they require more information than that given by the summary statement. So far detailed proposals for items to be included in the summary have not been very informative and there may be a considerable risk that important information could be missed from summarized accounts.

Segmental Reporting

In a complex business group it is to be expected that operations will be undertaken in different countries and perhaps in different industries. A financial statement which merely aggregates together the results of these very different operations into one set of financial statements will not be very helpful to readers of the accounts. It is necessary to explain the variety within the group and to analyse the results of the various segments of the business. A company such as Cadbury-Schweppes has three clear areas of activity, i.e. confectionery, beverages, and foods, and conducts its business in four main areas, i.e. the UK, Europe, North America and Australasia. It would be misleading to combine the results of this diverse activity, and therefore financial information concerning the segments of the business must be provided in the published accounts. Thus users may judge the profitability and growth of separate parts of the business, and poor performance from some parts of the business cannot be hidden amongst the figures for other business segments. Investors will be able to make a more trustworthy estimate of future earnings, and employees will be able to see the effect of their part of the business on the whole. Governments are interested in segmental information because with multinational companies they are able to interpret the corporate strategy of the company and to see in which geographic areas the company is investing and making profits.

Clearly not all accountants are convinced by these arguments. Some hold the view that segmental information just produces further confusing detail for unsophisticated users of financial statements, and that shareholders have invested in a business as a whole and are more interested in the overall result than in an analysis. So far there are no standard rules to determine just how much segmental information should be shown in published accounts, and perhaps more significantly just how that segmental information should be calculated. It is left to directors to decide how to divide up the business into segments for this purpose, and how to calculate the figures disclosed. An international accounting standard argues that accounts should disclose for each segment of the business:

(a) a description of the activities undertaken;
(b) sales or other operating revenues;
(c) the profit made by the segment;
(d) the assets employed in the segment.

Clearly such information would be of the greatest assistance to users of financial statements.

STATISTICAL SUPPLEMENTS TO PUBLISHED ACCOUNTS

Many companies present a statistical supplement to their published accounts. The purpose of such extra data is to highlight the salient features of the accounts, to put current events in the company into perspective, and to provide background information to help shareholders and potential shareholders to interpret the accounting statements. Advantage is often taken of such statements to undertake a public relations exercise and, in the process of simplification and explanation, to ensure that the company's activities and performance are shown in the best possible light. This type of appendix to the published accounts can help to maintain the price of the shares by showing the company to be a good investment.

Statistics of this type should be easy to assimilate. Companies often work to the nearest £1000 and use percentages and ratios so that comparisons can be made easily, trends revealed, and key figures accentuated. A good statistical supplement avoids presenting a mass of figures by using forms of visual presentation other than tables of figures. Such devices as graphs, bar charts and pie charts are very useful in this respect. For example, an international company may show a map of the world with a dot or company emblem in every area in which the group has an interest.

A pie chart is a useful device for showing the proportion of parts to a whole. An example of the use of such a chart is in demonstrating how the profit figure is appropriated. A large slice of the pie would go in taxation, another large slice would be ploughed back into the company, and a comparatively small slice would be dividend to the shareholders. Such a pie diagram might be useful in undermining the arguments of trade union officials for higher wages based on the large return achieved by the shareholders.

A value added statement is an alternative method of disclosing the income of a business, which can be usefully combined with statistical or graphic presentation which is often shown as a supplement to the published accounts.

SEMINAR EXERCISES 10

Solutions to these questions have been prepared by calculating ACT on the basis of 30 pence in the pound as the standard rate of income tax.

1. Assembly PLC, a company which manufactures electronic equipment, has an issued share capital of 1 000 000 6 per cent cumulative preference shares of £1 each, and 2 000 000 ordinary shares of 50p each, both fully paid.

    The company's accounts are made up to 31 December in each year, and the balances in the books on 31 December 19-6 included the following:

	£
Office fixtures and fittings, at cost	75 000
Plant, at cost	724 650
Stock of raw materials, at cost, 31 December 19-5	164 290
Stock of finished goods, at cost, 31 December 19-5	83 460
Work in progress, at cost, 31 December 19-5	23 460
Advertising	13 560
Bank commission	1 430
Carriage inwards	34 670
Delivery expenses	14 950
Directors' fees (chairman £25 000, two other non-executive directors £10 000 each)	45 000
Insurances	2 420
Loan interest paid	30 000
Office salaries (including the executive director's salary £43 100, and company secretary £35 000)	204 000
Office lighting and heating	1 400
Repairs to plant	15 150

	£
Postage, stationery and telephone	4 190
Factory power and lighting	24 620
Profit and loss account, undistributed balance, 31 December 19-5	86 520
Purchases	1 396 730
Rent: factory	10 400
office	5 200
Sales	2 996 800
Sales department salaries	49 500
Factory wages	367 200
Trade debtors	506 000
Provision for doubtful debts, 31 December 19-5	5 500

You are also given the following relevant information:

(i) Depreciation is to be provided for the year on plant at a rate of 20 per cent on cost, and on office fixtures at 15 per cent on cost.

(ii) Provision for doubtful debts is to be adjusted to 2 per cent of outstanding trade debtors on 31 December 19-6.

(iii) On 31 December 19-6, stocks and work in progress, valued at cost, amounted to:

	£
Raw materials	130 470
Finished goods	75 430
Work in progress	25 490

(iv) Provision is to be made for audit fee £6000, also for an amount due for factory power and lighting £2460.

(v) The liability for corporation tax for the year ended 31 December 19-6, is £250 000, based on a rate of 35 per cent.

(vi) The directors wish to transfer £200 000 to a plant replacement reserve, and to recommend payment of the preference dividend and a dividend of 12½ per cent on the ordinary shares, both for the year.

(a) Prepare manufacturing, trading and profit and loss accounts for the year ended 31 December 19-6, for presentation to the directors; and

(b) Prepare a profit and loss account for the year ended 31 December 19-6, suitable for presentation to the members and in accordance with the provisions of the Companies Act.

Corresponding figures are not required, and the information given may be taken as all that is necessary to satisfy the requirements of the Companies Acts.

2. Sandal Ltd, a retail company which sells footwear, makes up its accounts to 31 December in each year. The company has an authorized share capital of £300 000 divided into 150 000 7½ per cent preference shares of £1 each and 300 000 ordinary shares of 50p each. On average there are six employees apart from the directors.

The following draft accounts for the year ended 31 December were presented to the auditors for consideration.

Dr.   Profit and Loss Account   Cr.

	£		£
Cost of sales	1 333 871	Sales	1 638 740
Motor expenses	78 482	Discounts received	685
Depreciation on: buildings	2 000	Income from investments	—
motor vehicles	6 509	Trade	800
Overhead expenses	38 240	Quoted	1 170
Wages and salaries	91 179		
General expenses	6 564		
Audit fee	1 050		
Depreciation on fixtures and			
fittings	540		
Pension to a former director's			
widow	950		
Superannuation scheme	8 250		
Corporation tax	13 104		
Debenture interest	800		
Preference dividend	7 500		
Net profit for year	52 356		
	£1 641 395		£1 641 395

Dr.   Balance Sheet   Cr.

	£		£
8 per cent debentures			
1990/2001	10 000	Cash in hand	1 763
Ordinary share			
capital	100 000	Balance at bank	59 149
Preference share		Stock in hand,	
capital	100 000	at cost	105 246
Creditors	73 105	Motor vehicles	12 800
Provision for		Fixtures and	
doubtful debts	7 500	fittings	5 560
Profit and loss			
account	84 691	Debtors	170 022
		Freehold land and	
Corporation tax	29 244	buildings	85 000
General reserve	30 000	Investments at cost	15 000
Share premium	20 000		
	£454 540		£454 540

You are given the following additional information:

(a) The issued share capital is all fully paid.
(b) The charge for wages and salaries includes the salaries of the managing director, £26 500, and sales director, £16 000. The superannuation scheme also includes £2858 on their behalf. Provision is to be made for directors' fees of £16 500, being £5500 for each director, including the chairman, who does not receive a salary. The charge for wages and salaries includes administration salaries of £20 000.
(c) The charge for corporation tax in the profit and loss account is the amount estimated to be payable on the profits for the year, and due on 1 January in the year after next.
(d) There have been no additions to, or sales of, motor vehicles or fixtures and fittings, but freehold land and buildings includes an amount of £20 000 spent

on a new extension built during the year. The cost of fixed assets was: freehold land and buildings, £90 000; motor vehicles, £25 600; and fixtures and fittings, £10 400.

(e) The quoted investments, which cost £10 000, had a market value on 31 December of £17 582.

(f) The directors recommend payment of an ordinary dividend of 10 per cent.

Prepare the company's profit and loss account for the year ended 31 December, and a balance sheet as on that date in a form suitable for publication.

Corresponding figures are not required, and the information given may be taken as if it included all that is necessary to satisfy the requirements of the Companies Act.

3. The following list of balances was extracted from the books of Candlestickmakers PLC on 31 December 19-2. The company is involved in the manufacture and sale of lighting equipment.

	£
Sales (net of VAT)	2 884 782
Cost of sales	1 886 666
Administration expenses	330 623
Distribution costs	213 211
Directors' emoluments	143 241
Debenture interest	25 000
Land and buildings	820 000
Vehicles	62 462
Plant	479 000
Fittings	57 850
Depreciation at 1 January 19-2: land and buildings	20 000
vehicles	26 462
plant	63 000
fittings	19 500
Stock	292 452
Debtors	70 450
Creditors	66 409
Overdraft	8 322
Cash	675
Share capital	750 000
Unappropriated profit	25 955
Reserves	75 000
10 per cent debentures	500 000
Pension contributions	60 000
Provision for doubtful debts	2 200

The following adjustments are to be made:

(i) Directors' remuneration is split amongst the four directors as follows:

Salaries:	£
Production director	36 000
Chairman	14 000
Marketing director	40 000
Finance director	33 241
Pension contributions	20 000
	£143 241

(ii) Depreciation is to be provided in the accounts for the year as follows:

Office buildings	2 per cent on cost
Plant	20 per cent on cost
Motor vehicles	25 per cent on written-down value
Fixtures and fittings	10 per cent on cost

(iii) Messrs Checkit and See, Chartered Accountants, rendered an account in early March 19-3 as follows:

Assistance in preparation of the accounts for the year ended 31 December 19-1	500
Audit of those accounts	1000
	£1500

(iv) The debtors include a balance of £4000 owed by Custard Catering Suppliers Ltd. This is to be written off as it has proved irrecoverable. The provision for bad debts is to be adjusted to 10 per cent of debtors.

(v) Corporation tax based upon the profits of the year at the rate of 35 per cent amounting to £40 000 is to be provided.

(vi) A dividend of 4 pence per share is to be provided on the ordinary share capital. The authorized ordinary share capital is £1 000 000 divided into £1 shares. All issued shares are fully paid.

(vii) £8000 is to be transferred to general reserve.

(viii) Assume the basic rate of income tax to be 30 per cent.

(ix) Plant costing £61 000 and fittings costing £14 000 were purchased during the year. Plant which has cost £28 000 was sold for its written-down value of £8000 during the year. The buildings owned cost £120 000 when they were purchased two years ago.

(x) The debentures are secured on the freehold property. They are repayable in ten years' time. Interest is payable half-yearly on 30 June and 31 December.

Within the limits of the information given, prepare a profit and loss account and balance sheet for submission to the members of the company in accordance with the requirements of the Companies Act.

REVIEW QUESTIONS 7

1. Replant PLC are major suppliers of replacement parts for the agricultural engineering industry. Their accountant has produced the following financial statements for the year ended 31 December 19-9.

   Prepare in a form suitable for publication based on the requirements of the Companies Act, a profit and loss account and a balance sheet for the year ended 31 December 19-9.

   Corresponding figures for the previous year are not required and the additional information set out below should be regarded as sufficient for this exercise.

Profit and Loss Account

	£000	£000
Income:		
Sales		105 000
Discount received		20
Investment income		150
Scrap		5
Total income		105 175
Less expenditure:		
Cost of goods sold	75 000	
Selling expenses	2 830	
Administration	1 760	
Debenture interest	360	
Directors' salaries	120	
Audit fee	25	
Total expenses		80 095
Net profit for the year added to general reserve		£25 080

Balance Sheet

	£000	£000
Fixed assets		53 500
Investments		1 000
Current assets:		
Stock	24 540	
Debtors	11 345	
Bank	205	
Cash in hand	8	36 098
		90 598
Current liabilities:		
Trade creditors	9 540	
Corporation tax	8 500	
Accrued charges	115	(18 155)
		£72 443

	£000	£000
Financed by:		
Ordinary shares		8 000
8 per cent preference shares		4 000
Debentures		4 000
Share premium		5 000
Capital reserve		5 500
General reserve		45 943
		£72 443

The following items have not yet been accounted for by Replant PLC and/or may be required for the statements.

(a) Directors' fees of £4000 each are to be provided.
The salaries are split as follows:

Chairman	£30 000
Managing director	£47 000
Sales director	£28 000
Finance director	£15 000

(b) Depreciation based on cost for the year to 31 December 19-9 is to be charged as follows:

	Cost	
	£000	
Freehold property	15 000	2 per cent p.a.
Plant	64 200	10 per cent p.a.
Motor vehicles	680	25 per cent p.a.

Accumulated depreciation at the beginning of the year was:

	£000
Freehold property	3 000
Plant	33 160
Motor vehicles	220

Land at cost amounted to £10 million.

(c) Corporation tax at 35 per cent has been computed to be £11 500 000. The previous year's corporation tax has been agreed and is payable on January 19-0.

(d) All shares are of £1 each fully paid. 10 000 000 ordinary shares and 5 000 000 preference shares have been authorized but have not yet all been issued. The preference dividend is due but has not yet been paid. An ordinary dividend of 15p per share is proposed. Income tax is currently at a rate of 30p in the pound. All undistributed profits are to be added to general reserve.

(e) The investment is in Plantex PLC and is to secure trade links. The market value of the shares is £850 000 above their book value as at the year end.

(f) The debenture interest rate is 9 per cent. Repayment of the loan is due in the year 2010. The debentures are secured on the freehold property.

(g) Capital expenditure of £4 million pounds has been proposed. The board have not yet met to consider the project.

Note: All figures should be rounded to the nearest £1000.

2. Digger PLC is a manufacturer of gardening tools. Set out below is a trial balance extracted from the books of the company as at 31 December 19-3.

	Debit	Credit
	£	£
Sales		3 425 900 ⏤7000
Cost of sales	1 985 789	
Distribution costs	140 000	
Administrative expenses	699 269	
Debtors/creditors	489 531	201 122
Provision for doubtful debts		23 610
Directors' remuneration	201 500	
Audit fee	4 000	
Debenture interest paid	7 500	
Half-year preference dividend paid on 30 June 19-3	2 100	
ACT paid on 14 July 19-3	900	
Premises at cost	700 000	
Plant and machinery at cost	185 000	
Provision for depreciation on plant and machinery at 1 January 19-3		65 000
Motor vehicles at cost (salesmen's cars)	64 000	
Provision for depreciation on motor vehicles at 1 January 19-3		34 000

	Debit £	Credit £
Stock in trade and work in progress at 31 December 19-3	291 628	
Trade investment at cost	75 000	
Bank overdraft		275 382
Profit and loss account balance at 1 January 19-3		71 203
General reserve		240 000
Ordinary share capital		300 000
7 per cent preference share capital		60 000
10 per cent debentures (19-9) secured on premises		150 000
	£4 846 217	£4 846 217

The following information is also related to the accounts for the year to 31 December 19-3.

(a) The bad debt provision is to be increased to an amount which is equal to 1 per cent of the turnover for the year.
(b) The directors' remuneration is divided amongst the four directors of the company as follows:

Salaries:	£
Chairman	24 000
Managing director	60 000
Finance director	49 500
Sales director	48 000
	181 500

There are also directors' pension contributions of	£20 000

In addition provision must be made for directors' fees of £4000 to each of the above directors.

(c) Depreciation is to be provided for the year as follows:

Buildings	2 per cent on cost
Plant and machinery	10 per cent on cost
Motor vehicles	25 per cent on written-down value

The only changes in fixed assets during the year were an addition to plant and machinery in early January 19-3 costing £40 000, and the purchase of premises for £700 000 comprising £150 000 for buildings and £550 000 for land.

(d) A provision of £160 000 is to be made for corporation tax at 35 per cent based upon the profits for the year. This will be payable on 30 September 19-4.
(e) The half-year preference dividend to 31 December 19-3 and a final dividend of 6.5p a share on the ordinary share capital are to be provided in the accounts.
(f) The sum of £75 000 is to be transferred to general reserve.
(g) The authorized preference share capital is £60 000 in £1 shares.
(h) The authorized ordinary share capital is £600 000 in 50p shares. All shares in issue are fully paid.
(i) Assume the standard rate of income tax to be 30 per cent.

(j) Administrative expenses include £4134 interest on the overdraft.
(k) The value of the trade investment at current Stock Exchange price is £35 000. The investment consists of 10 000 20p ordinary shares in Fork PLC, a company with an issued share capital of 200 000 ordinary shares. Investment income this year was £7000 and has been credited to sales in error.

Within the limits of the above information, prepare the final accounts of Digger PLC for the year ended 31 December 19-3 in a form suitable for presentation to the members and which complies with the requirements of the Companies Act.

The required information should be shown as part of the accounting statements or by way of note, whichever is considered more appropriate.

3. Golf PLC is a manufacturer of sports equipment. The following is the trial balance as at 31 December 19-6.

	Debit £	Credit £
Sales		1 975 300
Cost of sales	1 395 299	
Distribution costs	140 000	
Administrative expenses	116 432	
Debtors/creditors	256 444	159 531
Provision for bad debts		7 500
Directors' remuneration	90 500	
Audit fee	1 000	
Debenture interest	2 500	
Half-year preference dividend paid on 20 July 19-6	4 800	
ACT paid on 30 July 39-6 (re above)	2 057	
Freehold land at cost	650 000	
Freehold office buildings at cost	150 000	
Plant and machinery at cost	45 000	
Provision for depreciation on plant and machinery at 1 January 19-6		20 000
Motor vehicles at cost	18 000	
Provisions for depreciation on motor vehicles at 1 January 19-6		8 000
Stock in trade and work in progress at 31 December 19-6	194 176	
Trade investments at cost in Swing PLC	24 000	
Bank overdraft		18 176
Profit and loss account balance, 1 January 19-6		21 701
General reserve		10 000
Ordinary share capital		700 000
Preference share capital		120 000
10 per cent debentures (2005/2008)		50 000
	£3 090 208	£3 090 208

The following information is also related to the accounts for the year to 31 December 19-6.

(a) The bad debts provision is to be increased to an amount which is equal to 0.5 per cent of the turnover for the year.
(b) The directors' remuneration is divided amongst the four directors of the company as follows:

Salaries:	£
Mr Andrews—Chairman	8 000
Mr Turnberry—Production director	30 000
Mr Wentworth—Finance director	26 500
Mr Stoylake—Sales director	26 000
	£90 500

In addition provision must be made for directors' fees of £4000 to each of the above directors.

(c) Depreciation is to be provided for the year as follows:

Buildings	2 per cent on cost
Plant and machinery	10 per cent on cost
Motor vehicles	25 per cent on written-down value

The only change in fixed assets during the year was an addition to plant and machinery in early January 19-6 costing £10 000.

(d) A provision of £60 000 is to be made for corporation tax at 35 per cent based upon the profits for the year. This will be payable on 30 September 19-7.

(e) The half-year preference dividend to 31 December 19-6 and a dividend of 6p per share on the ordinary share capital are to be provided in the accounts.

(f) The sum of £25 000 is to be transferred to general reserve.

(g) The authorized preference share capital is £120 000 in £1 shares.

(h) The authorized ordinary share capital is £800 000 in 50p shares. All shares in issue are fully paid.

(i) Assume the standard rate of income tax to be 30 per cent.

(j) Administrative expenses include £1748 interest on the overdraft.

(k) The market value of the investment in Swing PLC is £5000. No dividend has been paid by Swing PLC this year.

(l) The 10 per cent debentures are secured on the land and buildings.

Within the limits of the given information, prepare the accounts of Golf PLC in a form suitable for presentation to the members and which comply with the Companies Act, for year ended 31 December 19-6.

PART
THREE

Some Aspects of Accounting Theory and Their Application to Practice

14 | The Recognition of Revenue

Our discussion of the measurement of income covered the accruals principle, by which the costs of a product are matched against the revenue from its sale. A development of the accruals principle is that revenue for one accounting year brought into the income statement is not necessarily the total of the cash received in that year, since some cash received may have been received from customers for goods sold in a previous year, while other payments may concern goods not yet delivered. Care must be taken, therefore, to differentiate between cash received during a period and that part of the cash which can be counted as revenue. A further step in the measurement of income is to define the point in a transaction at which profit can be considered as earned and taken to the profit and loss account. A good accountant is conservative and will not wish to show a profit in the income statement for a period unless certain that that profit has been made, and that circumstances which may transpire in a later period will not reduce that profit. If a dividend is paid out of a profit which is later found to be illusory, the capital of the business will be depleted. For this reason there is a well-defined rule governing when profit can be recognized in the income statement and, like most general rules, it has a number of exceptions.

The earning of profit is a gradual process, sometimes termed a cycle. A manufacturer will change raw materials into finished goods during the production process, then transport, store and sell them. At the point of sale an asset, stock, is exchanged for another asset, debt, the difference between the values of the two being the profit. The debt is eventually collected and thus the asset, stock, is translated into cash. The recognition of revenue concerns the definition of the point in the cycle at which profit will be recognized and considered, for accounting purposes, to have been made. If profit can be regarded as the reward for enterprise or risk taking, it follows that a profit can only be distributed in the form of a dividend when it is safe to assume that the profit has been made, and that it is permanent because there is certainty that all costs concerning the transactions have been taken into account. Some accountants hold that the point in the cycle when the most critical decision has been made or the most difficult task completed is the point at which profit can be recognized, and this is usually taken to be the time of sale. At this point profit has been earned, since the revenue-earning activity is complete, and the profit can be measured objectively since it has undergone the test of the market. Even though the price may not yet have been collected from the customer the basic transaction is complete, and any doubt about the eventual payment of the price can be dealt with in the accounts by a provision for doubtful debts.

This is the certainty theory which holds that revenue can be recognized at the point beyond which there is no further uncertainty about the completion of the transaction. Three rules can be applied by the accountant to determine whether certainty exists.

1. The revenue has been earned by a change in value.
2. The revenue-earning activity has been accomplished, i.e. the manufactured goods are successfully delivered, or a service has been appropriately provided to the customer. It does not seem proper to recognize revenue once goods are made but before they have been sold because the revenue-earning activity is not yet complete. Similarly, if a payment is made in advance for a service to be given by the business, the profit on the transaction cannot be taken until the service has been satisfactorily provided.
3. The transaction must be capable of objective measurement. This means that an external comparator must be used to verify the amounts concerned in a transaction, e.g. a sale made across the market.

The certainty theory supports the application by accountants of the completed contract method where, if a transaction is undertaken over a period of time, it is not considered prudent to take any profit until the entire transaction is complete. An alternative method is the percentage of completion method where if the performance of a contract requires the execution of more than one act, revenue can be recognized proportionately to the amount of total performance which has been completed. This method can be applied to service contracts which provide for a number of service visits to maintain a machine over a specific period of time, or allow an indeterminate number of visits as required during the service period, e.g. if a service contract runs from 1 July until the following 30 June, it will be 50 per cent complete on 31 December and therefore 50 per cent of the profit of the contract can be taken into the profit and loss account up to that date. A new idea, that of the critical event concept, holds that for every transaction there is a critical event in the cycle which acts as a decision point for the recognition of revenue from the transaction.

For most transactions the three conditions certainly can be said to exist at the point when the sale is made, and this is the general rule which accountants follow when recognizing revenue. In England the law is quite precise about the moment at which the property in the goods passes from seller to buyer and a sale can be said to be made. It is a matter between the buyer and the seller when they intend the property to pass. For specific goods, i.e. the goods identified by the buyer and the seller as those concerned in the transaction, the buyer is bound to take delivery when the seller sends the goods to his place of business. Thus delivery is not the critical event, but rather the agreement between the buyer and the seller for the transaction to take place. However, with 'unascertained' goods (goods not identified when the contract was made) property passes when the goods of that description are unconditionally appropriated to the contract by the seller with the assent of the buyer. Delivery instructions from the buyer are construed as assent to such an appropriation. Thus, when a warehouseman separates a specified lot from the bulk in his warehouse and instructs the carrier to load, on receipt of delivery instructions, the critical event has taken place, since the goods will not be returned unless they are not of merchantable quality. It is, however, normal commercial practice to confirm receipt of an order in writing.

A further factor in identifying the critical event is the point in the transaction at which the risks and rewards of holding the asset are transferred from the seller to the buyer.

EXCEPTIONS TO THE GENERAL RULE

The first exception to the general rule concerns long-term contracts. In the building and civil engineering industries it could take five years or more to complete a job for a client. It is wrong to take all the profit on a five-year job at the end of the five-year period, since if in any one accounting year no jobs are completed then no profit will be shown that year, but in another year, when more than one job is completed, profits will be high. Thus fluctuations in profit will occur unless the profit is spread over the years of the contract. The price for the work is usually determined in advance, so once part of the contract is completed it is possible to take profit on that part. The quantity surveyors in the building industry will decide with the architects how much of the contract is completed, and the management will be given technical advice about what could go wrong on the contract before it is finalized, so that an estimate of profit to date can be made. Sometimes it is possible to take a percentage of the final expected profit based on the percentage of the job completed to date. Such methods are uncertain, so conservatism is important when profit is measured in this way. However, the value is added, the revenue is objectively measured, and if acceptance by the architect is considered to be the critical event, then the profit on work to date covered by an architect's certificate can be recognized.

SSAP 9, referring to work-in-progress stocks on long-term contracts, lays down that the profit recognized, if any, should reflect the proportion of the work carried out at the accounting date and any known inequalities of profitability of various stages of the contract. If the outcome cannot be reasonably assessed before the work is completed then no profit should be taken. Conservatism should be exercised at all times and future estimated costs compared with future estimated revenues in case losses may accrue. The profit computation would include costs to date plus future estimated costs to completion, including estimates of future rectification costs and work under any guarantee scheme, and amounts to provide for any penalties which might arise out of the contract. Once the total cost has been estimated, having taken into consideration likely increases in wages, materials and overheads, the amount can be set against the sales value of the contract to show what profit is likely to be made, and an appropriate proportion of this figure, less any profit already taken in previous years, can be taken to the credit of the profit and loss account.

A second exception to the general rule concerns accretion, where the value of work in progress increases gradually through natural growth or an ageing process. Examples of this are timber, which gradually increases in value as it grows year by year, animals, for the same reason, and commodities such as brandy or whisky, which mature over a long period. It is possible to value the stocks of such items at the beginning and end of an accounting period and to gauge the increase in value achieved during the year. This increase is an income even though it has not arisen from transactions, and has yet to be realized. Such an income cannot be made available for distribution, but this does not mean that it cannot be recognized, if realization and the realization price can be estimated with certainty and provision can be made for costs yet to be incurred. A prudent accountant might show such a profit as a note to his accounts rather than credit it to the income statement. If the stocks are shown at their current value in the balance sheet, the increase in the value of this asset during the accounting period could be balanced by the creation of a reserve not available for distribution as part of the equity interest.

A third exception to the general rule concerns sales made on instalment or hire purchase terms. The sale is made at one point in time and the customer is obligated to pay for the goods over a period. Revenue could be recognized at the time of sale, but since customers are sometimes poor credit risks it is more conservative to spread the profit over the period of the instalments. In practice this is usually accomplished by the use of percentages, i.e. when 70 per cent of the total price has been paid, then 70 per cent of the profit to be made from the transaction can be credited to the profit and loss account. Goods on hire purchase should not be confused with goods on a 'sale or return' basis. In this case the goods might be consigned by a wholesaler to a retailer but revenue cannot be recognized at this point since, if the retailer is unable to sell the goods, he will return them to the wholesaler and owe nothing. Transactions of this nature are merely the movement of the wholesaler's stock from his warehouse to another place. The stock still belongs to him and property in it passes only when the retailer makes a sale to a customer.

A fourth exception to the general rule is that in some cases revenue is recognized only when cash is received from a sale. This is an extension of the third exception, but occurs in slightly different conditions. If the customer has a poor credit rating, or if circumstances outside the control of the parties to the transaction can interfere with the payment of the price, the critical event for the transaction must be considered to be collection of the price. In this case it is conservative not to recognize the revenue until the price is paid.

A fifth exception to this rule concerns interest on a loan. If a loan contract is arranged between borrower and lender, it could be argued that the interest payable on the loan is earned once the contract is signed, and the full amount could be taken to the credit of the profit and loss account at once. It is, however, a much more prudent practice to spread the interest over the period of the loan. A similar argument is expressed for the treatment of profit on a leasing transaction, but once again income is spread, by one means or another, over the period of the lease.

In some transactions payment is made before delivery of the goods, but this is no case for the recognition of revenue, since a successful delivery, and in some cases production of the goods, must take place before the transaction is completed. In this case it is not payment, but delivery, which is critical. An example of this case is subscriptions to a monthly magazine. Such subscriptions are usually purchased a year in advance and then the magazine is printed and delivered monthly throughout the period of the subscription. If production costs are certain then there is a temptation to recognize revenue at the time of sale rather than at the time of delivery, but this is not conservative practice. Some accountants try to make out a special case for the recognition of revenue at the completion of the production process. They argue that at this point the costs are no longer uncertain, since they have been incurred, and if the product is covered by a contract for its sale, or is to be sold in a market where the price is fixed, then uncertainty is removed and revenue can be recognized before the point of sale. This exception to the general rule concerns only products which conform to the above conditions, and examples of these are difficult to find. American textbooks give as an example the production and refining of gold, where the market is certain and the price is fixed by the Government but this is no longer the case in practice.

Extraordinary Items and Prior Year Adjustments

An extraordinary item is derived from events or transactions which fall outside the ordinary activities of a company. There are two schools of thought as to the best accounting practice when dealing with such items.

1. The all-inclusive school believe that the profit and loss account should show the outcome of *all* transactions which have affected the income of the business during the year. If extraordinary items are excluded from the profit computation the resulting figure may mislead shareholders as to the overall performance of the business. If the profit and loss account is to be considered a significant financial statement, then all items of revenue and cost should be passed through that account.
2. Alternatively, the current operating profit school believe that the revenue statement should disclose the result of normal operations of the business each year in order to effect a comparison of the performance of a company over a number of years.

SSAP 6 combines the beliefs of these two schools in a neat compromise, since it requires that the normal operating profit of the business should be disclosed, and that extraordinary items should be disclosed separately 'below the line', thus showing a profit before and after extraordinary items.

The earnings per share figure is calculated on the basis of normal activities. Extraordinary items are not expected to recur frequently or regularly. They do not include items which, though exceptional because of their size and incidence, derive from the ordinary activities of the business, e.g. redundancy costs relating to an ongoing business are considered to be exceptional whereas redundancy costs for a discontinued part of the business are considered as extraordinary.

An exceptional item is one which, although derived from normal business activities, is considered significant because of its size or incidence. Such items must be disclosed by way of a note to the financial statements so that readers of a statement will be able to appreciate the influence of such significant exceptional items. SSAP 6 lists a number of circumstances which are considered to be extraordinary, or exceptional, in an attempt to assist the accountant using judgement to determine the appropriate accounting treatment for a particular item.

SSAP 6 defines a prior-year adjustment as a material adjustment applicable to prior years arising from changes in accounting policies, or the correction of fundamental errors. It is clearly recognized that from time to time a company may change its accounting policies and will accordingly need to adjust balance sheet items to bring them into line with the new accounting policy, e.g. a change in the method of depreciation used may necessitate a recalculation of the depreciation to be charged on the plant in the business. Such a recalculation may disclose that in past years insufficient depreciation has been provided. Clearly it would not be fair to charge this 'back depreciation' against the current year's profits, so it is treated as a prior-year adjustment. A further example concerns the situation when fundamental errors made in previous years are discovered. Again it would not be fair to charge the adjustments to correct such errors against the profit of the current year. The standard therefore requires that such adjustments of items affecting prior years should be set against the opening balance of retained profits brought forward from prior years in the profit and loss account.

TUTORIAL DISCUSSION TOPICS

14.1 Discuss the basic conditions for the recognition of revenue.

14.2 Explain the differences between the certainty theory, the completion of transaction theory and the critical event concept.

14.3 What is an 'arm's length' transaction? Give examples of transactions which are, and are not, in this category.

14.4 What are the exceptions to the general rule for the recognition of revenue?

14.5 How would you determine the amount of profit to be taken in any one year on a five-year civil engineering contract?

15 | A Critical Appraisal of Accounting Principles and Statements

CONCEPTS IN THE REAL WORLD

There is still much mystery attached to accounting, almost to the extent that its practitioners behave somewhat as though it were a medieval guild from which intruders must be excluded.

In accounting, despite recognition of the fact that accounting statements should be easily assimilated and understood by those for whom they are prepared, there remains a great deal which is not properly explained, and a tendency for the accountant to use special terminology and professional jargon to confuse those who are attempting to argue or advance a contrary opinion.

The misuse of the accounting or tax terminology in this way, and the application of the prudence concept, have done much to create a reputation for accountants in some parts of industry as being obstructive, over-cautious and entirely involved in their own subject. Gradually, however, this view of the accountant is being dispelled as accountants do their best to translate their subject for those who use it, and merge themselves more with the management team in industrial concerns.

Accounting concepts are criticized as being merely matters of convention, relying for their authority on their acceptance by practitioners, and as such cannot support a coherent theory of accounting. The historical cost principle is the one which is most criticized today. The balance sheet may show the original cost paid for an asset less amounts charged to previous accounting periods, but the layperson, seeing the figures in the balance sheet, attributes value to them and concludes that the unexpired portion of the capital cost is in fact the current worth of the asset shown. It is hard to convince him that the balance sheet is not a statement of value and that if it were, a certain degree of bias and uncertainty would be inevitable because of the methods by which such figures would be produced. The impact of inflation on accounting statements has undermined the cost principle. The unreality of using historical figures which mean different amounts in real terms at current prices is now apparent to accountants and to users of accounting statements, but inflation-adjusted accounts, once a supplement to the historical cost statements, are now rarely disclosed because the methods proposed so far have not received wholehearted acceptance.

The *realization postulate*, under which an increase in value is not recognized until realized, can cause distortion in accounting statements. Thus only when stock is sold can the difference between the price and the cost be taken as profit. If a fixed asset shows a permanent increase in value over and above its cost it would seem short-sighted to continue to show the owners of the business what it cost when new, rather than what it is now worth. For this reason a company will have its property revalued from time to time by an expert. If the increase is deemed to be permanent and the estimate is a conservative one, then the asset can be written up to current value. Because the surplus has not been realized, it cannot be shown in the profit and loss account, or distributed as a dividend. The increase in value must, however, be recognized, and is usually shown on both sides of the balance sheet. This is achieved by increasing the amounts of the fixed assets, and on the liability side by creating a reserve, not available for distribution, which is part of the equity interest in the business.

The *going concern postulate* has been criticized as being more a matter of common sense than a postulate, in that if fixed assets are held for future production and not for resale it seems obvious that they should be accounted for as though the company is going to continue using them, rather than at their current second-hand market price. This means, however, that the charge for using the asset during the year is a proportion of the historical cost and not the fall in value or loss to the company experienced as a result of holding that asset during the year. The significance of the going concern principle is felt in circumstances where the company is not a going concern, and the auditor must qualify the accounts drawn up on normally accepted principles to warn users of the accounts of these circumstances. Under statute it can now be assumed that the going concern convention has been followed, since a statement must be appended to the accounts if this is not so. One question which still has to be answered is how to decide whether a company is a going concern. Opinion may differ on this point. If it can be established that the market for the firm's product is steady, that there is sufficient working capital to prevent liquidity problems, that the company is able to compete with its rivals, to attract sufficient labour, and to replace equipment when necessary, then it is true and fair to assume that it is a going concern which will survive through the next accounting period.

The *matching* or *accruals principle* is often misunderstood by non-accountants who seek to equate net cash income with profit. Expense is not always matched with revenue when, for example, development costs or advertising expenditure are written off before the benefits derived from them are received in full, or when the fall in value over a period of time of a fixed asset differs from the amount written off the asset in the form of depreciation. Prudence and caution are often mistaken for pessimism or a lack of dynamism in these circumstances.

Accountants themselves cannot agree about the principles to be followed. There is no complete set of accounting principles to cover every eventuality, and there is no international agreement about the areas which should be covered by accounting principles and what those principles should be. In the UK, the Accounting Standards Committee has produced exposure documents which have become standards, but the Committee is often defied by companies which do not wish to follow these standards in the accounts that they prepare for their shareholders.

The multiplicity of practice among accountants in the EEC and the contrasts between American and European practice are evidence of the wide differences that still confront accountants. Even within the UK there are often different applications of accounting principles, perhaps because true alternative treatments exist, but still generating the criticism that there is too much flexibility of method in accounting so that a profit may be neither true nor comparable. The assumptions behind the valuation of stock, the fact that SSAP 9 on stocks discredits practices which are permissible under the Companies Act 1985, the treatment of research and development expenses, the inclusion or exclusion of goodwill in the balance sheet and the period over which it should be amortized, and the various methods of depreciation, are all matters about which accountants may not agree. Many of these differences are matters of opinion or judgement of each situation, but they can still lead to considerable differences in the figures entered in the accounting statements. The opinion of one accountant about the amount to be provided for bad and doubtful debts will not necessarily be the same as that of another accountant reviewing the same debtor balances.

Probably the concept which causes more differences of opinion than any other is the concept of *materiality*. For example, one accountant may consider that an alteration required by another (perhaps the auditor) is not material to the overall view shown by the accounting statements and should therefore be ignored. Recently an accountant commenting on a loss of £5 million made by a subsidiary of a group excused the fact that the loss had not been shown separately in the accounts by saying that it was not material to the overall view of the position of the business. Obviously size is important for materiality, but often this is used as an excuse for not presenting the facts explicitly in an accounting statement.

The scope of business is wide, and its operations are complex, so no single set of rules could cover all the situations to be found in business, and the accountant often has to treat each circumstance on its merits. The rule of consistency prevents such diversity from becoming chaos, but it is also often used as an excuse to continue to use outdated methods and to avoid change that is perhaps overdue. The historical cost principle has proved inadequate in the current period of inflation. While the reports, exposure drafts and standards of accounting practice reflect a careful search for an alternative, the amount of argument and discussion suggests a rearguard action in defence of the historical cost principle by those who are opposed to change, as well as a lack of agreement as to suitable methods to replace historical cost accounting.

A major limitation of accounting principles is that they cannot show a complete and accurate picture of the complexities of business within the accounting statements. Reporting in monetary terms is necessary, but the statement cannot show the impact of matters which cannot be quantified in monetary terms. Estimates of the future have to be built into the statements, but since they are subject to human error it is sometimes deemed more accurate to exclude them. Accountants are aware of these limitations, but non-accountants may not realize their impact. To overcome this problem accountants produce, along with accounting statements, a number of notes explaining the accounting policies followed when the accounts were computed. Also published with the accounting statements is a directors' report which is required by statute and must be audited, and a chairman's statement which deals with items not quantified in the accounts. Naturally a chairman reporting to his shareholders will try to use his statement to show the business in the best possible light, and while the Companies Act gives strict legal control over what the directors' report should cover, the two documents together are often used to promote good public relations.

Even when accounting statements have been certified by an auditor as showing a true and fair view, they still have their limitations. They do not always show the reader what is required, but rather provide information which can be used to draw conclusions if the reader is skilled enough to interpret them. Investors require information about the future, but accountants steadfastly refuse to forecast, and report only what has happened. In any case an accounting statement must be read with caution, and it is important for the reader to realize its shortcomings.

THE BALANCE SHEET

The balance sheet has been criticized for many reasons, not least the fact that it shows up the position of the company at one point in time, and this can be very different from the position of the same company only a few days earlier or later than the balance sheet date. Some accountants see the balance sheet as a type of photograph catching the image of the business for a fleeting moment only, and are aware that some photographs are not at all representative of their subject matter. The term 'window dressing' is used to describe the action taken by a company to temporarily improve its balance sheet position at or near to the year end, with a view to showing a healthy balance sheet in the published accounts, although of course there are limits to what can be done to make a poor position appear a much better one. SSAP 17 on post-balance-sheet events requires that adequate notes should explain significant events which have taken place soon after the balance sheet date, but which affect a proper understanding of the accounts, or reverse significant transactions undertaken during the year.

The balance sheet gives no information about the past or the future, it does not tell the reader how the business reached its present position, and it provides little information from which a trend can be deduced unless comparison is made with figures from previous years. The fixed assets of the business are recorded at historical cost less depreciation, leaving the unexpired portion of the capital cost. This historical record is not a statement of current worth of the assets, but many investors confuse the book value of the assets with their real or market value. The balance sheet may be consistent and drawn up along conservative lines, but it is not a realistic guide to the value of the business or of individual assets. Some companies revalue their assets from time to time so that their balance sheets are updated to meet the changes in the value of assets owned by the business, but such valuations are expensive and liable to personal bias on the part of the valuer, so they are rarely carried out annually and the asset values shown in the balance sheet soon become outdated again. A recent takeover bid valued a public company at £130 million. The company was engaged in property management and building but shareholders were unable to assess the true value of their assets since if the property portfolio had been revalued since the company was first listed on the Stock Exchange, ten years before the date of the bid, no details of such revaluation had appeared in the published accounts. Even though the terms 'owner's equity' and sometimes 'net worth' are used when a balance sheet is drawn up, it is misleading to think of the balance sheet as a means of valuation, because the value of shares in a business depends upon the financial climate in the market where they are likely to change hands, and the potential which a likely buyer sees in the business. The figure for owner's equity or shareholders' funds is an amalgam of accretions over the years when profits have been ploughed back at varying price levels.

Not all the 'assets' of a business are shown in the balance sheet; those which cannot be quantified, such as good labour relations, know-how, or a team of hard-working executives, are ignored. Some liabilities are also excluded; for example, the rentals due in future years on a contract made by the business will be excluded since they are not outstanding at the balance sheet date, but if the business were to cease the other party to the rental contract would no doubt seek assurance that arrangements would be made for the amounts due under the contract to be paid at the proper times. In a recent case of a large group of companies in financial trouble, the liquidator who was turning the enterprise into cash to pay the creditors was presented with a demand for £30 million from a leasing company for future rentals under contract. These items were omitted from the balance sheet because they were not immediately payable, and yet that balance sheet was claimed to show a true and fair view of the current position. SSAP 21, on the financial accounting treatment of leases, proposes a cure for this situation.

Accountants often disagree about matters of accounting policy or the treatment of items in the balance sheet. They may have opposing views about the treatment of intangible assets, the valuation of freehold property, the rate for plant depreciation, the method by which stocks of raw materials or finished goods are to be valued, the valuation of unquoted investments owned by a business, or the provision for doubtful debts. When such differences occur (usually between the auditor and the firm's accountant) they undermine the general public's confidence in the veracity of the position statement.

Some of the terms used in a balance sheet can limit the value of the statement; the term 'net worth' has been dealt with above. A simple term such as capital employed has four basic definitions. It is sometimes used to describe the aggregate of share capital and reserves, being the capital employed in the business by its legal owners and separate from capital used which has been borrowed from others. A second definition is that of net capital employed, where the capital contributed by the owners is combined with the long-term loans. This definition excludes the current liabilities as part of the capital employed and therefore leaves out bank overdrafts, taxation owed and trade credit, all of which are important sources of funds. A third definition of capital employed considers the book value of all the assets under the control of management as being the capital employed by them in the business. This is known as the 'gross assets' definition of capital employed. It is, however, unreal because some of the assets may be included in the balance sheet at historical cost, so their true current value is not revealed. A fourth definition of capital employed attempts to arrive at the full value of the funds used by the management in the business by taking the gross assets and valuing them at current replacement cost.

Example

Calculation of capital employed:

Makers PLC Balance Sheet as at 31.12.19..

	£		£
Share capital	4 000 000	Fixed assets:	
Share premium	500 000	Premises	5 400 000
General reserve	780 000	Plant	2 330 000
Unappropriated		Vehicles	117 619
profit	53 417	Fittings	230 412
	£5 333 417		£8 078 031
Long-term liabilities		Current assets:	
16 per cent debentures	3 000 000	Stock	1 861 473
	8 333 417	Debtors	1 539 248
		Cash	479 603
			3 880 324

		£		£
Current liabilities:				
Trade creditors	1 161 288			
Overdraft	1 850 000			
Tax	213 650			
Dividend	400 000			
		3 624 938		
		£11 958 355		£11 958 355

First definition—Shareholders' funds £5 333 417 represents the owners' capital invested in the business.

Second definition—Net capital employed £8 333 417 represents the long-term funds invested in the business.

Third definition—Gross assets £11 958 355 represents all the funds invested in the business, and all the assets at the disposal of the management with which to earn a profit.

Fourth definition—Current value of gross assets £? represents the aggregate of today's value of the individual assets employed.

THE INCOME STATEMENT

The income statement is also often the subject of critical comment. Some authorities take the view that, while this statement shows the profit or loss that has been made, it makes no mention of the risks taken to make that profit or the potential of the business in terms of what profit could or should have been made during the period under review. The income statement summarizes the past year's trading but makes no comment about the maximization or optimization of profit. Nor does it give any forecast for the future to assist those who have to decide on future policies. The idea of the accounting year could also be considered as a limitation of the income statement, since a year is hardly a long enough period over which to make a worthwhile comment about a capital project with a life of perhaps ten or fifteen years.

The task of the income statement is one of profit measurement, not profit determination. The profit calculation is, however, affected by the accounting policies adopted and by the estimates made in its computation, so accountants using different bases could produce different profit figures for the same period for the same business. Once again the rate and method of depreciation, the basis of stock valuation, the method of absorption of overheads (whether they should be carried forward or written off during the period) and the treatment of advertising or research and development expenditure are all matters where the judgement, outlook, or view developed by the accountant can have an impact on the profit figure. In the face of such criticism of accounting methods the alternative method of computing profit advanced by the economists, that of viewing the business at two points in time and considering any increase in value over a period as the profit made, seems attractive, until the practicalities of its operation are considered.

The major weaknesses of the profit figure shown by the income statement derive from the multiplicity of measurement practices in use, an over-reliance on the stability of the monetary unit, and a failure to incorporate contemporary values into the statement. Conservatism acted in the past to prevent optimistic claims of solvency in position statements laid before creditors, but in recent times this concept, together with those of realization and objectivity, has acted to obscure the true profit. What the accountant shows as a profit in the income statement is not the full gain attributable to the period, but only that part of the gain which has been realized, and to this he adds gains from previous periods realized this year, and deducts unrealized losses which he estimates may be experienced in the future. It is difficult to support such a heterogeneous collection of items as the product of a coherent theory of income measurement, yet it is accepted by practitioners as the most useful measure of income.

In recent years a dynamic view of accounting has moved the published profit and loss account into a more central position of attention than that of the published balance sheet. There are many reasons for this change of emphasis, not least of which are the shortcomings of the balance sheet, where fixed assets, long-term liabilities and share capital are shown at historical monetary values, stocks and work in progress may be valued on a number of bases, and the reserves are a combination of accretions over a number of years at varying price levels. The concept of conservatism only accentuates these shortcomings, while in the current economic climate of inflation investors will pay more attention to the profit and loss account, since this shows performance from which a price/earnings ratio (the ratio of current share price to earnings per share) can be computed. Also, profit is of course the motivating force of business, and therefore the profit and loss account can be expected to assume major importance for those who have risked their funds and are seeking a return. While the balance sheet is a 'snapshot' of the financial position at one point in time, the profit and loss account summarizes the figures for a whole period and is a better vehicle for the extrapolation of trends. If losses are made by a business they will be shown in the profit and loss account, but will not be visible on the balance sheet, since they are covered by reserves; it may even be possible to pay a dividend out of general reserves if profits are low without a marked impact on the balance sheet. The profit and loss account owes its greater significance partly to the fact that the appropriation section reveals the policy of management so far as the payment of dividend and the retention of profits in the business is concerned.

These two accounting statements should really be considered as a pair rather than separately, but even when they are combined their limitations are such that companies need to show a movement of funds statement in their published accounts to further interpret what has happened in the business during the accounting year. The market value and book value of a company are very different, so what is shown in the balance sheet is of secondary importance to investors, but if the value of a business is computed as the present value of future profits, then a statement which reveals current profits will be of some interest.

THE POSITION STATEMENT VERSUS THE INCOME STATEMENT: AN ACADEMIC VIEW

There has recently been some academic argument about whether the position statement or the income statement is the embodiment of the most fundamental elements of accounting theory. To those who use accounting statements, the income statement is probably the more important, but the argument here is not one of practicality but rather to determine which of these two statements is nearer to the theoretic base of accounting.

Some accountants see the balance sheet as merely a sheet of balances which are left in the books after the measurement of income has taken place, and for them accounting theory stems from the income statement, with the accruals or matching principle as the most important part of the entire system. They reject the economist's view of income as the increase in wealth or the owner's interest during a period, preferring to match cost against revenue in the profit and loss account to show a profit on a transactions basis. These accountants seek to divide the flow of costs by channelling some of them into a pool to be deferred and used up in a future period, while the balance of the flow is channelled into the income statement. According to this theory the balance sheet is created as a byproduct of the matching process, and the assets shown therein are merely items which are not yet required as costs in the income statement. The opponents of the *sheet-of-balances* view hold that income is best measured as a change in value during a period, and that the accruals principle leads to nothing more than a set of estimates made in an attempt to match costs with revenue. Such estimates, they say, are value judgements, depending on individual preference and bias, and cannot be part of a consistent theory. The supporters of the accruals principle, however, reply that estimates are made only where uncertainty exists, and that the accountant's response to uncertainty is conservatism, consistency, disclosure and objectivity, and this, they argue, is a sound theoretic base for the principle. Matching seems to emerge from this argument not as a principle but as a system which is adopted because it works. Its success depends upon the ability of the accountants who operate it, so rules such as conservatism have had to be made as parameters within which the accountant is able to exercise his judgement.

A second view of the balance sheet is as a *statement of static funds*, showing the sources from which capital has been obtained and the ways in which that capital is used in the business to finance assets. Here the balance sheet is seen as a statement of what is owed and what is owned by the business. This view corresponds closely to the 'commander' theory, whereby the balance sheet is seen as being prepared for the chief executive of the business, showing the sources from which capital has been recruited and the ways in which that capital is employed. The accountant preparing a balance sheet as a statement of static funds is acting as a steward, explaining the current position of the business to the owners or managers. The opponents of the static funds view of the balance sheet point out that some of the items included cannot be conveniently classified as either sources or uses of funds. Some liabilities arise as a result of transactions which have nothing to do with the raising of funds; for example, when a dividend is declared but not yet paid, a liability is created, but this can hardly be viewed as a source of funds to the business. The treatment of taxation due in the balance sheet as a current liability is also used as an argument against the static funds view, since it is argued that because tax due has not yet been paid this is not a source from which there has been an inflow of funds. However, this is a difficult argument to maintain, since credit taken from taxation authorities is an important liability in most companies, and it can be argued that funds set aside to meet future taxation which are ploughed into the business up to the point when payment is made are a source of finance just as much as trade credit is. The opponents of the static funds view also turn their attention to the assets of the business and argue that when fixed assets are revalued and a reserve is created on the liabilities side of the business this cannot be said to be a source of capital. They further state that a movement of funds statement will show up the flow of funds in and out of the business during a period in a far more vivid manner than can a balance sheet as at one point in time.

A third view of the balance sheet is as a *statement of financial position*, showing the assets and liabilities of the business. An asset can be defined as something owned by the business from which future economic benefits or rights will be derived, while liabilities are described as obligations to convey assets or perform services at a future time. Liabilities, it is said, arise from past transactions which have to be settled at some future date. This idea of assets and liabilities goes much further than the concept of them as merely balances remaining in the books. The net assets of the business can be equated to the owner's equity, and when during a period the net assets increase, the consequent change in owner's equity is seen as the income of the business. Thus the measurement of income, it is argued, is dependent upon the measurement of the value of assets and liabilities. Transactions therefore should be analysed in terms of their effect on the assets, the liabilities and the owner's equity of the business, so the revenue account is needed only as an analysis of the sources from which income is received.

Another argument in favour of the financial position view of the balance sheet is that the items therein can be so arranged as to give information and ratios which help to interpret the financial position, for example the working capital and acid test ratios. In the balance sheet of Makers PLC shown above, the working capital ratio of current assets to current liabilities is calculated as £3 880 324 ÷ £3 624 938, giving a ratio of 1.07 : 1. The balance sheet as a vehicle for the interpretation of the financial position is far more important than a mere dumping ground for surplus balances remaining in the books at the year end. The critics of this view, however, argue that the financial position and static funds views of the balance sheet are very similar, and that the financial position is of more interest to creditors than managers or past investors. The counterpoint to this argument is of course that anything which has a bearing on the view taken by the creditors of a business is important for the owners and the managers, since both these groups rely heavily upon trade credit to finance the operations of the firm.

To summarize these arguments, one view is that the revenue account is a summary of one class of transactions only, that the measurement of income depends upon the measurement of assets, and that it thus follows that the concept of income is dependent upon the concept of assets and liabilities as shown in the position statement. The counter-argument is that the balance sheet is sometimes seen as a summary of stocks or residual items left after the measurement of income has taken place. This argument is supported by the belief that the value of an asset depends on the future income it can provide and that current earnings are the best guide to this future income. Thus it is argued that the concept of assets is dependent upon income, and the position statement is therefore of secondary importance to the income statement.

There are of course some very original views held by academics. One such view is that the balance sheet should be seen as a statement of resources and future commitments of the business, resources being seen as items likely to produce a future cash inflow and commitments as items likely to produce a future cash outflow. Those who hold this view of the balance sheet say that it need not balance, since at any one time the resources available to a business may be more than the future commitments made on its behalf, or indeed less than those commitments, since the term commitment implies a future use of resources and there is thus time to increase resources to meet commitments at a future date or to commit surplus resources.

THE CORPORATE REPORT

In 1975 the Accounting Standards Committee issued this consultative document in an attempt to initiate a debate on the objectives and form of published financial statements. New ideas for appendices to company accounts were suggested, including, among others, the value added statement. Although it was published some time ago, *The Corporate Report* is still very relevant to company accounts.

The report first attempts to analyse the users of accounting statements and investigate the special needs of each group of users. The fundamental objective of accounting statements is to communicate economic measurements of, and information about, the resources and performance of an enterprise, in a form that is useful and understandable to those who need this information. To fulfil this aim statements should contain certain basic characteristics.

1. Relevance. The information provided should be what the users need, not what the accountant thinks they should have. Users of statements may develop different requirements for information as time goes by, and accountants must be ready to provide for changing requirements.
2. Understandability. Complex business affairs cannot be simplified, but accountants must balance the need to disclose against the danger of confusion arising from a detailed presentation. Perhaps what is required is a simple presentation for the less sophisticated and a more detailed statement for those who need more detailed information. To some extent statements fulfil this need by including notes to explain in depth some of the figures in the statement.
3. Reliability. The fact that an accounting statement has been verified by an independent auditor will increase the user's confidence in that statement. Audited information should be clearly segregated from unaudited information. High standards on the part of auditors will help accountants to achieve reliability. The reputation of the accounting profession is important if users are to rely on the statements accountants produce.
4. Completeness. Accounting statements should show all aspects of the enterprise.
5. Lack of bias. This means that accountants should not bias their statements towards the need of one category of user. Accounting standards are helpful in this respect.
6. Timeliness. Accounting statements should be published as soon as possible after the end of the accounting period to which they relate, to provide users with up-to-date information. This is especially important for accountants providing information for managers.
7. Comparability. Information is more meaningful if comparisons are made, so that the significance of a particular piece of information can be measured. Accountants should therefore prepare statements in a form which facilitates comparison with other enterprises and, if possible, also provide figures for comparison, e.g. those of a previous period.

The profit and loss account and the balance sheet are criticized because, although the information they provide is of great use to shareholders and creditors, it is of much less use to other users of accounting information. The profit figure is given great prominence, but it is a short-term measure of the result of one slice of the life of the business, and as such may mask the significance of the long-term view. If too much emphasis is placed on making a profit in the short run, this may obscure the long-term aim of management, which is to ensure the survival of the enterprise and maximize the value of the business in the future.

The auditors who certify that the accounting statements show the true and fair view give the impression that this is the only view, whereas, as we have already seen, the use of different bases of accounting and estimates can show a very different profit figure. The chairman of one public company was irritated when the accounts of his company were qualified by the auditors since they did not comply with SSAP 9 but adopted a more conservative view of stock valuation. He sought counsel's opinion and received the advice that it was possible to have more than one true and fair view, and that the one he had adopted was as good as the view proposed by the auditor. Therefore, although accounting standards can help to reduce the multiplicity of practices used in the production of accounting statements, if they are applied too rigidly this can lead to public argument, which reduces the users' confidence in the figures produced by accountants.

The Corporate Report suggests that the disadvantages of accounting statements might be reduced if additional statements were produced to give a more comprehensive picture of the economic activities of the enterprise. The fact that under SSAP 10 a funds flow statement is to be appended to the published accounts of a company is an improvement, but other additional statements recommended are as follows:

Value Added Statement

The profit of an enterprise is seen as the product of the combination of capital, labour and management. Value added is the wealth created by the efforts of managers, employees and shareholders, and it provides a fund from which shareholders, employees, the state and the company, through reinvestment, receive a share. This form of presentation underlines the interdependence of the elements in the enterprise which have combined to make it successful.

Example

All that is required to produce a statement of value added is to rearrange the data already available in the financial statements.

Note the use of percentages to bring out the significance of the figures as parts of a whole and for comparison between years.

Tinpot Manufacturing Co. Ltd, Statement of Value Added

	Year to 31 December £(000s)	%	Last Year £(000s)	%
Turnover	217.5	100	186.8	100
Less materials and services bought outside the organization	146.9	68	131.4	70
Value added	£70.6	32	£55.4	30

Applied as follows:		Year to 31 December £(000s)	%	Last Year £(000s)	%
To pay employees:					
(wages, pensions, fringe benefits)		49.8	70.5	38.7	69.8
To pay providers of capital:					
Interest on loans	1.9			1.2	
Dividends to shareholders	2.1			1.7	
		4.0	5.7	2.9	5.2
To pay the Government:					
Corporation tax		8.3	11.8	6.5	11.7
To provide for maintenance and expansion of assets:					
Depreciation	3.9			3.2	
Retained profits	4.6			4.1	
		8.5	12.0	7.3	13.3
		£70.6	100%	£55.4	100%

Arguments in Favour of Value Added Statements

Value added can be used as an alternative measure of performance of a business, instead of the profit figure. The statement emphasizes the interdependence of shareholders, lenders, management and employees in the operation of an efficient business. If value added is considered as the wealth created by the business, then the statement shows how this amount is divided up amongst the members of the team who created that wealth, thus fostering an atmosphere of co-operation within the business. Value added can be used to indicate the productivity of the workforce and to act as the basis for a bonus scheme. Some companies produce a value added statement as a supplement to the published accounts or as part of the statistics that are sent to shareholders with the accounts. It can also be argued in favour of value added that as a concept it does not conflict with the basic conventions on which accounting statements rely, that it can be used as a useful comparitor of one company with another or of one company over time, and that in a wider context it discloses the contribution made by a business to the national income. It is a useful and interesting statement, no doubt, but only a few firms have adopted this statement for inclusion in their corporate report. Some accountants argue that the concept of value added falsely assumes that a company is a team of co-operative groups, working together to produce the wealth of the business. Lenders and the Inland Revenue may not be considered as members of such a team by the labour force and its management, and in some companies there is unfortunately little team work existing between labour and management in any case. A value added statement can be criticized as one further accounting statement for users to assimilate when they read the published accounts of the business. It is argued that the financial statements are complicated enough already without adding a further statement which is costly to produce and may not be worth that cost in terms of information supplied to users of the financial statements. Any statement which reduces the significance of the profit figure may militate against the efficiency with which the business is organized. There is of course no standard practice to specify how the figures in value added statements should be calculated so that figures may be distorted to disclose a required picture rather than a true one.

Employment Report

The workforce in an enterprise is its human asset, but accountants do not show that asset on the balance sheet because it is difficult to value the asset and prove ownership rights to it. This does not prevent the provision of information about the workforce in the published accounts. An employment report would include statistics about the number of employees, labour turnover, age and sex distribution, and geographic location of the workforce. Details of hours worked, rates of pay, pension contributions by the company, and training and safety costs should all be included in such a report.

This report is to inform users of the financial statements about employment as one particular factor contributing to the progress and performance of the business. An employee report differs from an employment report because it is designed to report to employees, a single factor, about the overall performance of the business. An employee report draws together all information from the published accounts which might be of interest to employees with a view to improving labour relations and teamwork within the business. A value added statement in the form of a diagram might form part of an employee report. Clearly information other than that provided by the published accounts will be included in an employee report such as a message from the Chairman designed to have a public relations effect. The corporate report supported the use of employee reports to satisfy the employees' right to know about the company for which they work, to improve industrial relations and demonstrate to investors that a good record of labour relations exists, and as part of social responsibility accounting whereby the company provides information to a group who 'ought' to receive it.

Statement of Money Exchanges with the Government

Such a statement can reveal the contribution made by a company to the activities of the state, and the help given to the Government by the company in its role as a collector of taxes. Income tax deductions collected from employees and VAT collected from customers should be shown, as well as corporation tax and local rates paid by the company. Figures for capital grants and employment subsidies received should also be shown on this statement.

Other Statements

Other statements which the corporate report suggests are:

(a) a statement of transactions made in foreign currencies to show the impact of the enterprise on the balance of payments;
(b) a statement of future prospects;
(c) a statement of corporate objectives.

The last two of these three might be of interest to investors but from the accounting point of view they would be difficult to compute objectively and to audit. If a statement of future prospects were to be made a compulsory appendix to published accounts, managers would lower their sights and try to achieve less so that they could be certain of meeting their profit forecasts. As for objectives, many firms would object to being asked to reveal their goals to rival organizations.

TUTORIAL DISCUSSION TOPICS

15.1 What criticisms have been made of the balance sheet as a useful accounting statement? Does such criticism make out a valid case?

15.2 Some accountants see the balance sheet as simply a sheet of balances, and therefore of secondary importance to the profit and loss account. The opponents of this view seek to demolish the accruals principle to gain victory in the debate. How and why do they do this?

15.3 'A balance sheet is mainly a historical document which does not purport to show the realizable value of the assets' (ICA N18). Comment on this statement.

15.4 What criteria are used to establish the fact that a business is a going concern?

15.5 Discuss the basic characteristics which you consider to be desirable in an accounting statement.

SEMINAR EXERCISES 11

1. The following balances are extracted from the ledgers of Value PLC. You are required to draft a value added statement for Value PLC.

	£(000s)
Turnover	24 926
Cost of raw materials consumed	6 431
Factory wages	7 903
Work subcontracted	1 211
Factory salaries	1 064
Factory overhead expenses	3 461
Depreciation of plant	874
Administration salaries	1 085
Office electricity charge	312
Postage, stationery and telephone	479

	£(000s)
Depreciation of office equipment	83
Depreciation of company cars	98
Directors' fees	100
Insurance cost	57
Employer's contribution to state pension scheme	106
Employer's contribution to company pension scheme	309
Cost of fringe benefits	181
Interest on loan	400
Corporation tax	358
Dividends	220
Retained profit for the year	194

16 | Standard Accounting Practices and the Standard Setters

THE NEED TO STANDARDIZE

The Accounting Standards Steering Committee (now Accounting Standards Committee—ASC) was established in 1969 to 'narrow the areas of difference and variety in accounting practices by publishing authoritative statements', and this it has tried to do. Accounting principles, unlike the laws of natural science, are man-made, and they rely on the fact that accountants accept each principle because they consider it to be correct and a matter of good practice. The publication of Statements of Standard Accounting Practice (SSAPs) seeks to codify some existing methods and prohibit other methods which are considered to be of doubtful validity. The reason for developing accounting standards was to publicize and gain acceptance for new ideas, thus improving accounting practice, to give guidance in sensitive areas, and above all to promote the comparability of accounting statements produced by companies across the economy. If a set of agreed rules could be developed, then it was argued that this would facilitate the comparison of the performance of one company with another and thus strengthen the utility of published accounts for investors and other users. A cynical view is that the publication of standards was motivated by a need to improve the image and reputation of the profession after several well-publicized cases in which the accounts of companies had been questioned and shown to present neither a true nor a fair view; and was also an attempt to head off moves by Government authorities to impose some sort of control over the profession. A more charitable view, however, might be that the standards are an attempt to produce basic rules for accountants to follow in sensitive areas of practice where doubt and confusion are present. There is a need to standardize if those who use published accounts are to understand them properly, and to be able to compare the accounting statements of one company with those of another, and if those who produce accounting statements are to be encouraged to improve their performance. The standards also give accountants and auditors some means of protection from those who may try to pressurize them into accepting methods of which they do not approve. After twenty years of work by the ASC, 24 standards have been produced, and 48 exposure drafts issued for comment.

A number of criticisms are now being made, suggesting that accounting standards are not achieving their objectives. Critics point to the range of topics covered by the standards, some of which are in very contentious areas of accounting. Acceptability has always been the keynote of accounting principles, and to impose standards which are not accepted by some, and to ban methods which are seen as perfectly proper by others, would seem to have departed from this basic idea. Detailed procedures in some standard practices have been included in subsequent legislation, but in one or two cases an outdated standard appears to be at variance with the law. Some standards have been so unsuccessful that they have been withdrawn.

HAS STANDARD SETTING ACHIEVED ITS OBJECTIVE?

In order for the accounts to be prepared and checked in accordance with the standards, the workload of accountants and auditors has increased, but it is questionable whether the informativeness and accuracy of the final product have improved enough to warrant the extra cost involved. If one accepts standardization as an answer to the need to convey essential financial information to a wide range of consumers, the point remains that perhaps the attempt to impose uniformity of practice on disparate operations has gone too far. Accountants offer their expertise to many different industries, and it seems foolish to suppose that what is good practice in one situation will be acceptable in another. Accounting methods should fit the circumstances of the industry or company, and when ideas which work well elsewhere are imposed by standard in places where they do not quite fit, a difficult situation is bound to develop. The difficulties produced by SSAP 9 are a good example. Perhaps consistency and a statement of accounting policies, as proposed by SSAP 2, would be a preferable course of action when there is a strong objection by a company to a practice laid down by a standard. The ASC is now considering the issue of standards for particular industries with individual idiosyncracies in their accounting practices.

A further criticism of the standards is that they are applied with too little flexibility by those in the auditing profession. In the past, when a set of accounts was qualified it meant that something was seriously wrong, but the impact of qualification has been eroded by its use as a sanction against companies whose accounts do not conform to standards. It has not improved the reputation of the accounting profession for auditors to be seen to be in public contention with their clients, invariably companies of high repute, over what must seem to the onlooker to be a too rigid application of an inappropriate rule. An explanatory foreword written when the ASC was being set up said 'Accounting practitioners involved in the preparation of financial statements must ensure that, if the standards are not observed, significant departures are disclosed and explained in the accounts and their effect, if material, is disclosed', and a later statement contained the words 'all significant departures from accounting standards should be referred to in the audit report'. There is, however, no firm definition of the word 'significant', and in some cases rather trivial infringements have been the subject of an auditor's qualification, and hence its devaluation in the eyes of investors and others. Perhaps we should try to return to the position laid out in the Statement of Intent of 1969, which proposed that 'only departures from definitive standards, which are not disclosed in the accounts should be mentioned in the auditor's report'. In spite of the standards, there are still too many unfortunate occurrences where published accounts fall short of excellence, and it is suggested by some critics that these lapses are more the result of poor auditing than poor accounting.

STANDARD SETTING—THE PROCEDURES

The ASC is sponsored by the Consultative Committee for Accountancy Bodies (CCAB), which represents the six major accountancy bodies in the UK and Ireland. The CCAB bodies propose individual accountants to be members of the ASC according to a pre-agreed formula and contribute to the costs of the ASC on the basis of that formula. The idea is that individual members should represent themselves but in effect they tend to represent the views of the body which has proposed them for membership. This gives a dominance on the ASC to the Institutes of Chartered Accountants in England and Wales and Scotland, i.e. the practitioners with a strong connection to the auditing side of the profession. The total of 23 members is completed by the addition of members representing the users of accounting statements such as the Stock Exchange. The budget of the ASC pays for a small full-time secretariat but the committee members and those who work on subcommittees and working parties receive only expenses for the large amount of time and effort which they expend on standard setting.

The programme of work for the ASC is generated by discussion within the committee and the secretariat. Issues are targeted, problems emerge, and a subcommittee or working party is selected to begin preliminary discussions. The working party will often produce a consultative document or discussion paper which is published by the ASC for distribution to interested parties. The discussion paper usually sets out the problem or issue which is under review, together with the alternative practices which are currently in operation, and then discusses the difficulties and poses specific questions, to which interested parties are asked to respond. After an interval for debate amongst accountants, the subcommittee reviews the responses it has received, weighing the evidence and formalizing proposals in an 'exposure draft'. This document is a formal proposition for what is likely to become a standard practice. The draft is exposed for a six-month period and after the closing date further comments and objections are analysed by the subcommittee. A formal standard practice (SSAP) is then drafted to include any adjustments to the exposure draft which the committee feels to be necessary. The standard practice must then be approved by the council of each of the six sponsoring bodies, and it is possible even at this stage for one of those councils to delay approval and consequent promulgation of the standard if further adjustment is required. These procedures are designed to generate discussion over a fairly lengthy period, and to persuade accountants to accept a recommendation for what is termed 'best accounting practice' in the self-regulating accountancy profession.

The ASC has also issued statements of recommended practice (SORPs) as a further effort to define best accounting practice. Although the procedure to draft a SORP is similar to that for the development of a SSAP, the SORP does not have the same mandatory status given to a SSAP. Accountants should comply with SSAPs when drafting financial statements, and a departure from a standard must be justified by a note to the accounts and may necessitate an adverse comment by the auditor in the audit report appended to those accounts. In the case of a SORP, however, non-compliance need not be disclosed. SORPs are issued to cover matters of limited application, or matters which have widespread application but which are not of fundamental importance, e.g. Pension scheme accounts—SORP 1. The ASC uses the device of a SORP to give guidance to accountants on problems which are specific to a certain industry or which are of less central importance to the development of accounting practice. Recently the ASC has issued 'franked' SORPs which have been developed by a specific industry (e.g. oil and gas) and receive the approval of the ASC. SORPs can be issued by the ASC itself without the approval of the CCAB bodies. For this reason they are not mandatory upon accountants but derive their authority from the ASC itself.

STATEMENTS OF STANDARD ACCOUNTING PRACTICE ISSUED

1. Accounting for the results of associated companies 1971, revised 1974 and 1986.
2. Disclosure of accounting policies 1971.
3. Earnings per share 1972, revised 1974.
4. The accounting treatment of government grants 1974, revised 1988.
5. Accounting for value added tax, 1974.
6. Extraordinary items and prior-year adjustments, 1974, revised 1975 and 1985.
7. Accounting for changes in the purchasing powers of money 1974 (provisional, withdrawn 1978).
8. The treatment of taxation under the imputation system in the accounts of companies 1974, revised 1977.
9. Stocks and work in progress 1975, revised 1986.
10. Statements of source and application of funds 1975.
11. Accounting for deferred taxation 1975, withdrawn 1978.
12. Accounting for depreciation 1977, amended 1978, revised 1985.
13. Accounting for research and development 1977, revised 1988.
14. Group accounts, September 1978.
15. Accounting for deferred taxation, October 1978.
16. Accounting for price level changes—current cost accounting 1981, non-mandatory 1986, withdrawn 1988.
17. Accounting for post-balance-sheet events 1981.
18. Accounting for contingencies 1981.
19. Accounting for investment properties 1982.
20. Accounting for foreign currency translation 1982.
21. Accounting for leases and hire purchase contracts 1984.
22. Accounting for goodwill 1985.
23. Accounting for acquisitions and mergers 1985.
24. Accounting for pensions 1989.

RECENT CRITICISMS OF THE ASC

Apart from criticisms levelled at individual standards, there has been much adverse comment in recent years concerning the activities and operation of the ASC. These criticisms fall into five separate groups.

The Programme

Critics argue that the programme of work undertaken by the ASC is not developed from a careful review of the needs of users of financial statements but rather as a response to current problems as they develop. This approach is termed 'putting out brush fires' and lacks the consistent logical approach to the development of standards based on the needs of users and within the scope of accounting theory.

Preparers Dominate

It is argued that accountants and auditors who prepare accounting statements hold the majority of places on the ASC and undertake much of the work of its subcommittees and working parties. Accordingly, the opinions and requirements of users of financial statements may not be given appropriate weight when standards are devised. The CCAB bodies act to approve standards in the last resort. Clearly, accountants with technical expertise must be involved in the setting of individual standards, but at present there seems to be only a small minority of ASC members who are responsible for putting forward the views of users. Published accounts are extremely complex documents which might be simplified if the views of users were given greater weight.

Compliance

The ASC does not have power to enforce the standards which it promulgates. Whilst the CCAB bodies may be able to influence accountants who are their members, the profession can have little influence over directors who are not qualified accountants. At law the Board is responsible for the accounts of the company, but non-compliance with a standard brings no legal penalty and little more than the qualification by the auditor of the audit report.

Resources

The ASC relies on funds provided by the CCAB and is criticized for being underfunded. There is only a small professional secretariat working full-time for the ASC and the bulk of the work is undertaken by panels and working parties of experts who give their services free. It is argued that a larger professional secretariat is required to give both professional expertise and continuity to the work of the ASC.

Harmonization

Standards set by the ASC are relevant for accountants within the UK and Ireland, and as such should also be harmonized with the directives of the European Economic Community and International Accounting Standards put forward by the International Accounting Standards Committee (IASC). Although the IASC is based in London and adopts an Anglo-Saxon approach to accounting, there are some significant points at which differences remain between the ASC and the IASC. It is argued that such differences should be speedily resolved in the interests of international comparability and the harmonization of accounting standards and methods across the world.

THE DEARING REPORT

Criticism of the operations of the ASC reached a critical level and in 1988 the CCAB bodies commissioned the Dearing Report to suggest ways in which the ASC could be reformed. Major points in the Dearing Report are as follows:

1. The Government and the law should have increased influence over the standard-setting and -enforcing process. It was suggested that the ASC should be abolished and replaced by a new standard-setting authority empowered to issue standards without reference to the CCAB. It is proposed that users will have greater representation in a more comprehensive membership. This proposal will perhaps reduce the dominance of preparers and increase the weight given to the opinions of users when standards are set.

2. A four-tiered system. If the ASC is abolished, the report suggests that it should be replaced by four separate entities.

   (a) There should be a *Financial Reporting Council* (FRC) to act as a policy-making body to guide on the development of the work programme, on matters of public concern and to promote good practice and issue an annual report. The FRC is envisaged as controlling the budgets of the other tiers. This senior body should meet three or four times per annum with a suggested membership of twenty. Half of this membership is to be appointed by the CCAB, representing practice, industry, commerce, and the public sector. The remaining members are to be drawn from the Stock Exchange, institutional investors, users, employees, and Government observers. The Chairman of the FRC is to be appointed by the Department of Trade and Industry after consultation with the Bank of England and the CCAB.

   (b) The *Accounting Standards Board* (ASB) is envisaged as the second tier in this arrangement. It is proposed that the ASB should have a Chairman and Technical Director as full-time executives and should comprise nine members acting on a part-time basis but paid for their services, working with a paid secretariat. This body will be much stronger than the ASC which it replaces, being independent and able to promulgate standards, being streamlined to reduce time lags when standards are set, and with provision for a two-thirds majority in the event of disagreement to avoid compromise and the issue of standard practices which appear to favour more than one alternative method.

(c) The FRC and ASB are to be supported by a *Review Panel*, chaired by a QC. Membership of this Panel will be drawn from a pool of members appointed by the FRC. It is the purpose of the Panel to consider cases of non-compliance with standards by large companies. The Review Panel will be able to initiate its own enquiries or receive cases referred to it by auditors and other interested parties. This panel would expect co-operation of directors and accountants and would be able to force companies to revise their financial statements or make extra disclosures if appropriate.

(d) The fourth tier is a *Task Force*, whose objective is to deal with emerging issues arising on a day-to-day or month-to-month basis. This force would advise on brush fire problems and on the interpretation of standards and is included in the report to remove short-term problems from the major standard-setting activity.

3. Standards and the law. The Dearing Report emphasizes that the objective of enforcing compliance with standards is to improve financial reporting, and not to punish or penalize offenders. Company directors are responsible in law for the accounts of a company and at present defective accounts can lead to a criminal offence and a fine. The report urges the courts to suggest accounting standards as the expression of good accounting practice but suggests that statute should put the onus on the company to demonstrate a true and fair view when standards are breached. This proposal does not give SSAPs statutory force, but establishes a rebuttable presumption that compliance gives a true and fair view. The report suggests that a new civil offence should be established whereby the Review Panel can apply to the court for an order requiring a company to amplify or modify its accounts and that such extra information should be audited and circulated to users. This suggestion is seen as a reserve power to be used only when companies will not co-operate with the Review Panel.

4. Setting Standards. It is suggested that the ASB should set standards on its own authority and that each standard should include an explanatory statement setting out the principles behind the standards and the reasons for rejecting alternative methods. New standards should be accompanied by a statement setting out how far the standard should apply to the accounts of small businesses.

5. Resources. The report suggests that a paid secretariat of at least twenty professional and support staff are required and that this would increase the funding required to at least three times the current budget of £440 000. The CCAB bodies are expected to contribute as at present, but it is suggested that the remainder of the finance required could be funded by a Stock Exchange levy on published accounts or an addition to the filing fee for accounts at the Companies Registry.

TUTORIAL DISCUSSION TOPICS

16.1 What are the objectives to be achieved by establishing Standard Accounting Practices?

16.2 Discuss recent criticisms of the operations of the ASC.

16.3 How far have the proposals in the Dearing Report met recent criticisms of the ASC?

17 | Economic Ideas and Accounting Practices

THE ACCOUNTANT AND THE ECONOMIST

The accountant and the economist both study the workings of a business and use such terms as income, expenditure, profit, capital and value. However, from a common starting point they face in opposite directions, and from the same basic data they produce very different end products. The economist uses information produced by the accountant to attempt to answer problems raised within economics, but usually sees the information in a different perspective. For example, an accountant will attempt to measure a profit to give shareholders and managers an objective report summarizing transactions up to a certain point in time in terms of funds actually paid out or received, but to the economist profit is the motive force in the market system which guides the allocation of resources between competing purposes. Profit to an economist does not necessarily have the same definition as profit computed by an accountant.

The accountant and the economist are closest together when the firm is discussed, but here again there are different perspectives. The accountant sees each firm as an entity, to be accounted for as such, while the economist usually views the firm as a small part of the whole which comprises the market, and constructs theories which will improve our understanding of the workings of the economy, and the forces which motivate its constituent parts. A major difference is in their views of the position statement, where the economist would prefer to see all assets of the business included and those assets shown at their current value, while the accountant records only items which are quantifiable, and records them at cost. In financial statements the accountant shows what has happened in the past and what is the current position, while the economist is more interested in what might have occurred and how the optimum position for the business can be identified and achieved in the future. The businessman is sometimes caught between these two opposing views, when the economist talks about the future potential and an optimum, but is unable to measure them with any accuracy, while the accountant is accurate in his measurement of past events but hesitant when asked to predict the future.

The accountant shows in the income statement and balance sheet what has actually happened. The economist, however, deals in variables, always seeking to define an outcome under differing conditions so that potential and an optimum position will emerge. Perhaps it can be said of profit that the accountant seeks to measure what the economist seeks to improve, but this is a little unjust since as management accountants have moved more into the area of business decision-making, they have become concerned with the evaluation of future cash flows and the selection of the best alternative. In doing so the accountant in his role as financial manager accepts economic ideas, such as discounted present value, and puts them to work in the real world. The economist often assumes perfection either in the market or in knowledge of future events, so that it is conceivable to him that at one point in time the best alternative can be chosen. The accountant, however, is far more concerned with the real world and has to produce accounting statements for firms which are working under conditions of oligopoly, imperfect competition, etc. The motives of the entrepreneur interest the economist, i.e. whether a firm is seeking to maximize its profits or whether it is a 'satisficer' (content with less than a maximum profit). The accountant, however, is content to measure what the firm has actually achieved in real-life situations. Unlike the economist, the accountant cannot assume perfection and carry analysis to its logical conclusion. The accountant is reluctant to comment on subjective measurement in terms of potential and optimum, but will compare the actual result with a budget or a pre-set plan and show variances which have occurred.

Incremental analysis for decision-making, where only costs which change as a result of a decision are considered significant for that decision, is another point at which accountant and economist converge. The accountant, however, will want to measure the marginal or incremental cost to see the impact on total cost of a particular decision, whereas the economist sees the margin as a small increment which brings into balance a delicate economic mechanism, e.g. the price mechanism. Moreover, the economist sees cost from several different points of view according to the purpose for which the cost is to be used. The management accountant is learning to fit these ideas into decision-making techniques, e.g. opportunity cost, where the identification of costs which are relevant to a decision is significant for successful analysis.

Accountants and economists also differ in their attitudes towards inflation. The economist will investigate the reasons which have caused inflation to develop and the ways in which inflationary pressure can be controlled within the economy as a whole. The accountant, on the other hand, is interested in inflation only in so far as it affects the individual business for which he is accounting, and seeks to determine the impact which inflation will have upon accounting statements and on the capital structure and future of the individual business, with a view to achieving a true and fair view.

CAPITAL, INCOME AND VALUE

The accountant and the economist certainly have different ideas about capital and income and, so far as value is concerned, the economist has many ideas and suggestions, but the accountant is unwilling to be involved with the subjective theories put forward.

Capital

To an investor capital is important as the amount of his wealth committed to a certain economic project and from which an income is expected to flow. The investor has given up control over the use of funds and sees profit as the return for risk and use forgone. The capital has probably been created in the first place by saving, which represents consumption of income forgone in order to accumulate wealth. This is the stock and flow concept, with capital as the stock and income flowing from it. The accountant sees capital as the amount invested in an enterprise by its legal owners (share capital plus reserves saved out of profits), or lent to the firm over a long period (debentures). The shareholders' interest in the firm is of a residual nature, since they are entitled to whatever is left after all liabilities have been met. The accountant's concept of capital is derived from the assets owned by shareholders to whom he reports. These assets, from which it is hoped that an income will be earned, are recorded on the basis of the transaction undertaken to own them, i.e. historical cost or book value. Capital then, is the book value net of liabilities of those debit balances left on the books after the income measurement exercise has taken place. It represents payments not yet matched as expenses against revenue, but left over after the profit figure is struck. All assets will eventually become expenses when they are used up by the business.

In economics, capital is considered to be the present value of future earnings derived from an asset or enterprise as a whole, so capital and income are again linked together. An economist might prefer a broader definition of capital employed, and might suggest that some assets, such as human resources, are omitted by accountants because they cannot be quantified and recorded in the books. The accountant measures capital with reference to tangible assets whose existence, ownership and cost can be verified. To the economist capital is an expression of the potential future earning power of the enterprise, and is measured in order to derive income from the change in capital between two points in time. If the capital value of the business has increased during the year this is an income, and should be included when profit is determined.

Accountants are, however, drawing closer to the position of economists so far as assets are concerned. Exposure Draft 42 suggests that it is more important to account for the substance of a transaction than for its legal form, and that an improved definition of what is an asset or a liability will generate clear thinking on the commercial reality of a transaction. It is suggested than an asset is a probable future benefit controlled by and accruing to a particular company as a result of past transactions or events. This idea is a significant departure from traditional accounting beliefs because it assumes that when plant is shown in the balance sheet, as an asset, it is not the physical item which underpins its presence there, but rather the fact that economic benefits are expected to be derived from the physical item and it is this present value of future expected income flows which supports the plant as an asset of the business.

Income

Thus the concept of income is a significant point of difference between the accountant and the economist. Accountants measure income and try to ensure that their measurements are as accurate and near to the truth as possible, but economists take the view that income is used for several purposes, and that perhaps a different method of measuring income should be applied according to the purpose for which the income measurement is required. Income is seen as a determinant of company dividend policy, since the rights of creditors would be prejudiced if a dividend was paid when losses had been made. Accounting income is a surplus derived from business activity and is measured by the use of the matching principle, when cost is set against revenue for a given time period. This is an 'ex post' measurement, since it is made from objectively recorded amounts after the event has taken place.

Economists and accountants see profits as a guide to future investment in a business, using the past to assess future prospects. The best investment, of course, is the one which leads to the greatest future benefits, and these can be discounted and measured at their present value. Thus capital investment is oriented towards the improvement of the present value of future receipts from the investments made by the company. From this premise it is only a short step for the economist to regard income as growth in the present value of future receipts, or the capital value of the business. An economist, Sir John Hicks, defined income as the maximum amount an individual could consume during a period while remaining as well off at the end of the period as at the beginning. The success of this idea depends upon the definition of the term 'well off', which can mean possession of capital, or wealth. It follows, therefore, that income is the amount by which capital or net worth has increased during a period plus what has been withdrawn for consumption, less new capital that has been introduced into the business. For the economist, then, the net worth of the business is the capital value of expected future receipts, and any increase in the value of those future receipts will be a profit. This valuation-based idea is very different from the accountant's view of net assets, which is the unexpired portion of the capital cost, stemming from recorded transactions.

An economist would hold that the accountant's definition of income is of little use as a measure of business success because it ignores value changes, other than to write off depreciation and adjust stock values downward if required. Unrealized profits are ignored by accountants unless there is a certainty of their permanence, since it would not be conservative to distribute them. The accountant, however, might ask the economist how to compute a profit figure from the concept of present value, how far into the future receipts are to be forecast, and how accurate such a forecast should be. The accountant would also wish to know the criterion for the selection of the discount factor on which the present value calculation is based. The Hicksian concept of income can be linked to the idea of maintaining the capital invested in the enterprise, if income is defined as the maximum amount that can be consumed in a period without a reduction in the expected level of consumption in the next period. Thus depreciation is a common factor in the definition of income by both accountant and economist.

The two views can be reconciled by formulae. If Y_e is economic income, C is consumption, and S is savings

$$Y_e = C + S$$

This formula can be expressed as

$$Y_e = C + (K_N - K_{N-1})$$

K is the notation for capital, and N stands for time, i.e. now. K_{N-1} will therefore represent capital a year ago. Income is what has been consumed plus the increase in wealth during the year. Accounting income can be expressed in the same way:

$$Y_a = D + (R_N - R_{N-1})$$

In this expression D stands for dividend paid and R stands for reserves. Thus income equals the dividend paid out and the increase in reserves (profit ploughed back) during the year. The influence of the Hicksian concept is that the true growth in reserves can only be measured after an amount has been set aside out of profit to maintain the capital of the business. Thus the principle of capital maintenance (as well off at the end of the year as at the beginning) acts in part to reconcile the views of accountants and economists on income measurement. Depreciation is one method which accountants use to maintain the capital of the business.

Value

When a value is attributed to an asset or a whole enterprise, the asset or enterprise is appraised and ranked in order of preference against other items which have greater or lesser values. These preferences are expressed in money terms, so value allows us to measure an asset against others in terms of the amount of purchasing power we must sacrifice to possess the valued item. Money shows what must be paid to exercise economic choice and to show a preference for one item over another, since money spent cannot be used to purchase alternatives which are competing for scarce resources in the market.

The accountant records as objective the value laid out to purchase an asset, i.e. historical cost, but will use current market value if it is lower than historical cost for reasons of conservatism (the lower of cost or market-value rule for stocks) or if a permanent increase in value above historical cost is established (a building revalued and written up in the books). Many accountants do not trust value, since it implies a subjective judgement or estimate which may be influenced by bias on the part of the valuer and may not be permanent, although it should be remembered that accountants themselves make subjective judgements when providing for doubtful debts or accrued expenses, and when fixing a rate of depreciation. Many users of balance sheets mistakenly believe that they are reading a statement which discloses the value of the business, and the use of the term 'net worth' to describe net capital employed only serves to strengthen this belief.

As we have seen, the economic or capital value of an asset is the present value of the future income stream expected to be derived from the asset. The price of the asset is the value set on it in the market place by the interaction of supply and demand. This is an exchange value for the asset whereby its worth is expressed in money, so that when that price is compared with the price of other assets its worth can be measured. The economic value computed for an asset simply reflects the expectations of the company or individual and sets the maximum price they would be willing to pay for it on the market. Therefore individuals with different expectations of the potential of an asset to produce income would value it at different amounts.

An asset may have different values according to the purpose for which the valuation is made. For example, the following are different ways of valuing an ocean-going liner.

1. Scrap value, i.e. what it is worth at break-up value. This reflects the intrinsic value of its parts less the cost of dismantling them.

2. Going concern value, i.e. what it is worth to the shipping company that owns it. They intend to operate it together with other ships in their fleet and other assets which they possess (docks, know-how etc.). This value approaches economic value, as it is the present value of the expected income stream.
3. Historical cost. This is an input value—what was spent when the asset was acquired. This value is soon outdated and does not represent earning potential.
4. Book value, i.e. the asset as recorded in the books. Usually this is historical cost less depreciation to date, the unexpired portion of the capital cost. The depreciation profile adopted by the enterprise may not reflect the real fall in value from use and/or the passing of time.
5. Net realizable value or market value. This is an exit value, since it represents what another ship-owner would be willing to pay for the liner for use as part of a fleet. It is impractical, however, to put assets up for sale simply to value them. The market price of specialized assets with a narrow market will not be easy to establish. The difference between this value and (2) above is the difference in the expectation of future income between its present owner and the potential buyer, and the cost of the transaction. Supply and demand will affect this value.
6. Replacement value, i.e. the cost of another liner to do the same job. It will be difficult to establish a price for an exactly similar asset, and also to appraise the amount to be deducted for years of expired service since the liner is not new.
7. Opportunity cost. This is a value based on the returns expected from the asset in its next best alternative use, for example as a cruise ship rather than in passenger service. This could be the same as net realizable value, but would be very difficult to calculate. An exit value shows the amount forgone by a business because it prefers to hold and use the asset rather than realize it on the market. The replacement value, an entry value, shows the amount which a business is willing to invest to control and use an asset. Net realizable value represents the view taken by the market as a whole, but replacement value concerns only the view of an asset by an individual business.

Faced with so many different bases on which a valuation can be made, accountants hesitate to incorporate valuation in their statements, preferring to use the objective basis of recorded historical cost adjusted for conservatism. SSAP 16 on current cost accounting introduced 'value to the business' (deprival value) as a basis for recording assets. This method combines market value, replacement value, and historical cost, updated by appropriate indices.

Deprival Value

This concept equates to value to the business as expressed in SSAP 16, and has developed to enable entry values (replacement values), exit values (NRV), and economic values to be combined in selecting an appropriate amount at which to express assets in a financial statement. Theoretically, in a perfect economy values based on each of these methods should be the same for a certain asset, but in the real world this is not so. The cost of replacing an asset may not be the same as the amount of cash released by the sale of such an asset and neither of these amounts will necessarily equal the present value of the earnings stream expected from the asset.

Deprival value builds a model which enables the accountant to select which of these alternatives best suits the individual asset concerned, based on the idea of the loss which would be suffered by the business if it were deprived of the use of an asset.

If a business is deprived of the use of an asset the loss will be either:

(a) the cost of replacing that asset; or
(b) the funds which could have been realized by selling the asset; or
(c) the income stream derived from the future employment of the asset expressed in present value terms.

Clearly an asset would only be replaced if its future earnings were expected to be greater than the replacement cost and only then if replacement cost is less than the net realization value. No business would buy an asset for more than it expects to earn from it, or for more than the net realizable value of the asset. Thus, the first rule of deprival value is that it is the lower of replacement cost or the value to the business of the future services of the asset. If replacement cost exceeds the value of future services it will not be worth replacing, and a different logic is then applied. To calculate the value to the business of the future services of the asset it is necessary to compare the net realizable value (what is it worth if sold at once) with the economic value (what can the asset earn if it is not sold). The value to the business of the future services of an asset is therefore the greater of the net realizable value and the economic value. Thus deprival value can be expressed in the form of the following diagram:

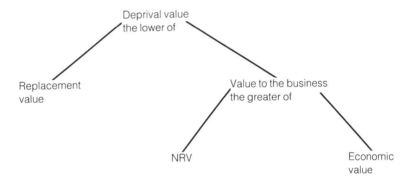

The logic behind deprival value argues:

1. If future services are worth more than replacement cost, the asset would be replaced so replacement cost is the best guide to value.
2. If future services are worth less than replacement cost, the asset would not be replaced so the next decision must be made, i.e. whether to keep the asset for operation or sell it for its net realizable value. Thus deprival value is selective and acts as a logic to guide choice in varying circumstances.

TUTORIAL DISCUSSION TOPICS

17.1 What are the different meanings of the term 'capital'?

17.2   Discuss the relationship of income to capital from the point of view of both an economist and an accountant.

17.3   How does the Hicksian concept of income differ from the profit computed by an accountant? How far do the rules concerning depreciation and the payment of dividends only out of profit help to bridge this gap?

17.4   Accountants are loath to use the 'value' of assets in a balance sheet. Why is this so?

17.5   How many different values can you define for the same asset, for example a large item of industrial machinery?

17.6   Calculate the deprival value of the following assets:

Asset	Replacement cost	Net realisable value	Economic value
A	£20 000	£8 000	£40 000
B	£20 000	£8 000	£16 000
C	£16 000	£8 000	£4 000

Justify your choice.

18 | Accounting in a Period of Rising Prices

THE IMPACT OF INFLATION ON ACCOUNTING STATEMENTS

During a period of inflation prices rise, so a fixed amount of money buys less in terms of goods and services after inflation than it could before. Thus the 'real' value of money is said to fall in an inflationary period. However, accountants still record transactions in the money terms applying at the date of the transaction, even long after the date of that transaction. This is called historical cost accounting. The historical cost convention claims to use values which have been derived from actual events, so this system has the advantage of objectivity. It is suggested that if assets and costs are given estimated current values rather than actual recorded values when accounting statements are compiled, the results derived from such statements could become matters of opinion, where uncertainty and bias influence the figures. It is argued that conservatism in accounting supports the historical cost convention, since it is prudent to ignore increases in value caused by inflation, but if such actions cause an accountant to set historical costs against sales at current prices, profit will be overstated, and will certainly not have been computed on a conservative basis. Accountants in the UK would not add together assets or costs expressed in dollars, yen, marks and francs, but would take care to convert them to pounds, yet they are willing to mix pounds of 1975 with pounds of 1989, although the difference in the amounts of goods and services commanded by them is as great as the difference in the amounts of goods and services currently commanded by the pound and the dollar. There are four major points at which inflation can influence the accounting statements.

Fixed Assets and Depreciation

First, as the value of money falls, fixed assets recorded at historical cost will not reflect the purchasing power of capital invested in them at current prices, and depreciation based on historical cost will fail to set aside a large enough amount out of profit to replace the investment that has been used up at current prices. Thus depreciation based on historical cost will overstate profit and can lead to the depletion of capital in the business if such profit is distributed. For example, if an asset purchased ten years ago for £1000 is depreciated at £100 per year, although at the end of its ten-year life the original £1000 invested in it will have been set aside out of profits, after ten years of inflation £1000 can command less in terms of goods and services than could the original amount. So although the capital of the business has been protected in money terms, this amount means less in real terms. Assets stated in the balance sheet at historical cost fail to show the shareholders the current value of what the company owns, and cause the capital-employed figure to be understated.

Example

A. Mann is in the haulage industry on his own account and owns his own lorry. He started business with £5000 in cash, which he invested in the vehicle. His opening balance sheet would be:

Dr.		A. Mann	Cr.
	£		£
Capital	5 000	Vehicle	5 000

During his first year of trading revenue is £20 000 but he charges £10 000 for his services and pays £8000 as expenses. The vehicle has a life of five years, and no scrap value, so depreciation of £1000 per annum is provided, and a net profit of £1000 is computed. A balance sheet at the end of the first year would show:

Dr.		A. Mann	Cr.
	£		£
Capital	5 000	Vehicle	5 000
Undistributed		Less accumulated	
profit	1 000	depreciation	1 000
			4 000
		Cash	2 000
	£6 000		£6 000

At the end of five years, if no profit is distributed, the balance sheet might show:

Dr.		A. Mann	Cr.
	£		£
Capital	5 000	Vehicle	5 000
Undistributed		Less accumulated	
profit	5 000	depreciation	5 000
			Nil
		Cash	10 000
	£10 000		£10 000

The statement shows the vehicle as being fully depreciated and the funds set aside by depreciation held in the form of other assets, cash. But what if A. Mann tries to replace his fixed asset and finds that a similar vehicle now costs £8000? His balance sheet, after replacement, will be:

Dr.		A. Mann	Cr.
	£		£
Capital	5 000	Vehicle	8 000
Undistributed profit	5 000	Cash	2 000
	£10 000		£10 000

He is now in exactly the same position as when he started in business five years ago (the owner of one vehicle) except that he has £2000 of cash. He might question the validity of the measurement technique which shows him to have made a profit of £5000 in that period when he is £2000 better off as a result of his efforts. Depreciation based on historical cost has replaced the original investment in money terms but not in real terms. If A. Mann had withdrawn his profits year by year he would not now be able to continue in business without recruiting fresh capital to help pay for the replacement vehicle. Capital depletion would have taken place, and the operating capability of the business would have been reduced. Depreciation is needed to maintain the capital in the business, but depreciation based on historical cost fails to maintain the operating capability of the business, measured in terms of assets.

The Cost of Sales

The second point at which the impact of inflation is felt on accounting statements concerns the measurement of profit when costs incurred in one period are set against revenue received in a later period. The revenue will be counted at higher (post-inflation) prices, while the costs, for example raw materials, will be charged at low (pre-inflation) prices, and an enlarged profit will thus be disclosed. If, however, the raw material used up in the transaction is charged in the profit computation at replacement cost rather than historical cost, then both the revenue and cost side of the sum will be expressed in current price terms and the true profit will emerge. Some accountants argue that the next in first out (NIFO) assumption should be used to compute profit in an inflationary period.

Example

John Green is a trader. He buys 500 shirts at £1 each and sells them one month later for £2 each. His expenses are £200, so a profit is calculated at £300. He returns to his supplier for another batch of 500 shirts, but this time they cost £1.50 each. John Green asks himself how much better off he is now than he was a month ago. Then he had 500 shirts and no cash, and now he has 500 shirts and £50 in cash. The profit of £300 has been overstated, since it sets historical cost of sales against current selling price. A calculation using replacement cost of sales shows a truer profit during an inflation.

Historical Cost	£	£	Current Cost	£	£
Sales		1000	Sales		1 000
Cost of sales	500		Cost of sales	750	
Expenses	200		Expenses	200	
		700			950
Net profit		£300	Net profit		£50

Perhaps the current cost profit is also distorted if sales during the year are set against a cost of sales calculated at an end-of-year price. The cost of sales might be more suitable if computed at the average cost ruling during the year, weighted for quantities involved. The fact remains that more capital is needed to finance the same quantity of stock at post-inflation prices (500 shirts at an extra 50 pence each) and unless sufficient is set aside for this purpose operating capability will be reduced.

Monetary Items

Third, certain items in the balance sheet, termed monetary items, such as creditors, debtors and cash, are shown in the accounting statements in current terms so that they appear to be correctly stated at a time of inflation. However, if a firm holds its assets in a monetary form, i.e. cash and debtors, during a period of inflation, when it eventually turns its monetary assets into tangible assets such as machinery or stock, prices will have risen, so it will get less for its money than if it had spent the money earlier. Thus to hold a monetary asset is to make a loss during a period of inflation. By the same token a company which obtains its funds from borrowing will gain during an inflationary period, since when it repays its creditors, overdraft, or long-term loans, the amount paid out will equal the amount borrowed, but since inflation has taken place during the period of the loan the amount paid out will mean less in terms of goods and services than it meant when the loan was made.

Example

The sole asset possessed by an investment company is an investment of £100 000 lent to a client at 10 per cent interest and repayable after one year. At the end of the year the client repays £100 000 of principal plus £10 000 interest. The investment company's balance sheet now appears as follows:

Dr.		Investment Company		Cr.
	£			£
Capital	100 000	Cash		110 000
Undistributed profit	10 000			
	£110 000			£110 000

If, for the sake of argument, inflation at 10 per cent has been experienced during the year, the cash of £110 000 can now buy exactly the same quantity of goods and services as the original capital of £100 000 could have bought a year ago. It is difficult to see how a profit has been made in these circumstances, since the company is no better off in real terms than it was at the beginning of the year. The client, however, is in a favourable position, since he has repaid (including interest) the same amount in real terms as he borrowed, and the use of the money for a year has cost him nothing. Thus inflation brings an element of profit to a company with creditors in the balance sheet, but a loss if debtors are held as an asset. There is also the need to invest more in working capital (debtors less creditors) since the same volume is expressed in larger money amounts post-inflation.

Capital and Growth

The fourth point at which inflation affects the accounting statements concerns the way in which conventional accounting protects the money capital of the business but fails to show how that money capital is being eroded in terms of purchasing power during a period of inflation. The original investment by the shareholders in a business is shown by the amount of the share capital, and the amount of their investment since the inception of the business is represented by ploughed-back profits or reserves in the balance sheet. If 100 000 £1 shares were raised by a company in 1960 it seems wrong to show that amount as £100 000 in a current balance sheet, since the quantity of goods and services which can be commanded by that amount has fallen since the capital was first raised. At the same time profits have been ploughed back into the reserves year after year since the company began. The accountant records this by adding to the reserves each year, but this adds an amount of profit computed at the price level of each year, so the figure for reserves is an amalgam of many different price levels shown as one figure, below the share capital, which is stated in a single but outdated price level. In this way the true growth of the owners' equity in the business is not shown, and the amount required to equal at current prices the shareholders' original investment is obscured.

Clearly, part of the reserves should be shown as an addition to share capital to represent the amount which must be set aside out of profit to maintain the purchasing power of the shareholders' original investment. The remainder of the reserves would then represent a true growth figure. Throughout this discussion the terms 'better off' and 'well off' have been used and this relates back to the Hicksian concept of income measured as the surplus after making sure that the business is as well off at the end of the year as it was at the beginning of that year. This calculation of the wealth of the business should be undertaken in terms of current prices rather than historical cost, but there is still argument as to how best to measure the wealth of a business. One body of opinion argues that the wealth of a business, or the capital to be maintained, should be measured in terms of purchasing power, i.e. what the money could buy if it were distributed to the shareholders. This school believes that the solution to the inflation accounting problem is to maintain the purchasing power of the shareholders' original investment and favours the current purchasing power method of accounting. The rival school believes that the wealth of a business should best be measured in terms of what that business can produce, i.e. assets representing productive capability rather than pounds invested by shareholders. This school argues that enough must be set aside out of profits to maintain the operating capability of the business before a profit can be determined and thus supports the current cost accounting method.

SHOULD HISTORICAL COST ACCOUNTS BE ADJUSTED?

The points made above show that there is a case for adjusting accounting statements to show the impact of inflation, and the case is strengthened as follows. Historical cost is a true view of the cost of an asset only at the time when the asset is purchased. If the historical costs of a number of assets purchased at different dates are added together, the total cannot be said to express the cost in terms of one monetary unit. Historical cost accounting will cause profits to be overstated, while the capital employed, as shown by the balance sheet, will be understated, so the use of the ratio of net profit to capital employed as a measure of managerial efficiency is impaired.

Example

A company purchases a plot of land for £5000. Three years later an adjacent plot of the same size comes up for sale and the company buys it for £10 000. Two years after this a third similar plot is purchased for £15 000. The balance sheet would show the historical cost of these assets as £30 000, yet at the time of purchasing the third plot the market value of the three plots would be £45 000 (3 × £15 000). If a net profit of £4500 is made in year 6, and the land is the only asset possessed by the company, the return on the capital employed recorded at historical cost would be

$$\frac{£4500}{£30\ 000} \times \frac{100}{1} = 15 \text{ per cent}$$

but the return on the current value of the assets used would be only

$$\frac{£4500}{£45\ 000} \times \frac{100}{1} = 10 \text{ per cent}$$

If a company pays out a high proportion of its profit in dividends, and if the profit is overstated because historical costs have been set against revenue computed at current prices, then there is a danger that a dividend could be paid out of capital if the dividend exceeds the amount of the real profit made. If insufficient profit is retained in the business to maintain the purchasing power of the original capital investment, capital depletion in real terms will have taken place. It is necessary, therefore, in a time of inflation, to identify that proportion of the reserves of the business which is needed to maintain the purchasing power of the original investment, and that proportion of the reserves which represents real growth. When profits are overstated this gives a false picture to investors and employees alike, and thus the former are encouraged to expect high dividends and the latter to submit high wage demands. If the accounting statements are computed in terms of current rather than historical costs they become more realistic, and when inter-firm comparison takes place it will be possible to judge the capital structure best suited to inflationary conditions.

Thus the true position of long-term loans repaid in post-inflation pounds becomes apparent. The case against adjusting accounting statements for the effect of inflation is no longer considered to be strong. Its arguments centre around the fear that such adjustments could have a depressing effect on profits, and that if investors could see the real return their funds were earning, the supply of risk capital might be inhibited. The refusal of the Inland Revenue authorities to accept for taxation purposes accounts which have been computed in other than historical terms has also long delayed implementation of this much needed reform. The inadequacy of the remedies proposed so far as a basis for taxation or investment decisions has aggravated the situation. The main argument remaining between accountants and others on this subject concerns the methods by which the accounting statements are to be adjusted for the impact of inflation. Most suggest that assets and costs should be updated at the accounting date so that they are expressed in current terms, but they cannot agree how it should be done.

The current purchasing power method and the current cost accounting method are still favoured by certain factions of accountants. The current cost accounting method seemed to have been accepted but has been so severely criticized that the majority of the accounting profession have now rejected it, and accordingly SSAP 16 has been withdrawn. In the absence of complete support for one of the two rival methods by accountants in general, no method for the adjustment of accounts in a period of changing prices is currently the subject of a standard and the outdated and sometimes misleading historical cost accounting system continues to be used.

THE RIVAL REMEDIES PROPOSED

The current purchasing power (CPP) system (as proposed in SSAP 7, withdrawn in 1978) suggests that a supplementary statement should be added to the historical cost accounts to reveal the impact of inflation on the figures. This statement should be produced by converting the historical figures to current purchasing-power terms by applying an appropriate price index. A general index, the retail price index (RPI), is suggested as appropriate, since it reflects the general movement in prices of goods and services. The critics of this system argue that the impact of inflation is not general in its nature, and that it depends on what assets and costs are involved. For example, if a business consumes a material whose price has not changed then it has not suffered inflation, but if the raw material it uses has increased in price at twice the rate of the RPI, then this index is of little use as a measure of the effect of inflation on that particular company. The supporters of CPP, however, claim that when the shareholders come to spend the profits, they would be able to buy less after inflation, and thus profit should be stated in CPP terms. Their opponents also criticize the RPI, saying that it is based on the budget of a typical family and has little to do with the assets or consumption of large industrial enterprises. What is required, they say, is the updating of historical cost to current terms by the application of price indices which are specific to the assets or expenses which are under review—the current cost accounting (CCA) system.

The production of two sets of accounting statements is complicated for users, and those who support CCA at first suggested that the system should replace historical cost accounting, with one set of accounts expressed in terms of current costs. The CCA system proposes the use of specific indices and other devices for measuring current value, so that the inflation adjustment would be more closely related to the assets or costs concerned. For example, some assets may fall in value during an inflationary period, or may inflate faster than the movement of general purchasing power. The values used in accounting for the assets held by a company under CCA could be based on entry prices (replacement cost), or exit values (realizable market value), or economic value (capital value of future earnings). There are, of course, difficulties in computing these values and combining them. For example, some machines do not have a current replacement model with which to compare them, and how would one account for expired service in the replacement cost of an old machine? The capital value of future earnings depends on a number of estimates and assumptions, and can hardly be said to be an objective measure. A convincing system of detailed specific indices has yet to be provided. The suggestion that for convenience the same index can be used for stocks, debtors and creditors reduces the impact of the principle of specific indices in CCA.

The argument as to which is the preferred system has continued for many years and has been complicated by a rearguard action fought on behalf of the supporters of the historical cost accounting system. The CPP system was first proposed in SSAP 7, introduced in 1974 but finally withdrawn in 1978 as a result of fierce criticism from the Sandilands report which supported the CCA system. Exposure Draft 18 was advanced in 1976 advocating the CCA system to replace the historical cost accounting system, but this exposure draft was rejected by the accounting profession. After such a rebuff the supporters of CCA issued the Hyde guidelines, which suggested the voluntary use by companies of the less controversial CCA provisions of ED 18. ED 24 was then drafted and after much discussion and argument became SSAP 16 'Accounting for Price Level Changes—Current Cost Accounting' in 1981. Gradually users and accountants became disillusioned with this standard and despite the issue of ED 35 in 1985, which suggested adjustments to the system, the exposure draft was rejected, and SSAP 16 was made non-mandatory in 1986 and finally withdrawn in 1988. The latest developments concern proposals in a discussion document to combine CCA with CPP accounting in a more meaningful set of accounts. As yet, however, it appears most unlikely that the historical cost accounting system will be replaced by a system of accounting for price level changes; it seems more likely that this difficult problem will be resolved by the addition of extra inflation-adjusted accounting statements to the normal published accounts.

MONETARY ITEMS

One of the major differences between CPP and CCA is in the treatment of monetary items. The CCA system at first denied the gains and losses attributable to monetary liabilities and assets. This was unfortunate, since it obscured the fact that differences of capital structure could influence profit during an inflationary period. As a compromise a monetary adjustment was included in the Hyde guidelines, but this was only a short-term solution to the problem and in any case did not meet with universal acceptance.

It is difficult to find an index which is specific to monetary items, unless the RPI is used. A useful suggestion is that the gains or losses on monetary items should be separated from the operating profit, if only to make sure that they do not attract the attention of the Inland Revenue.

The fact remains, however, that debts and cash in a balance sheet will cause an element of loss during inflation, since when they are eventually spent on goods or services they will command less than if they had been spent at an earlier date. Companies with long- or short-term liabilities gain during an inflation, since they repay a fixed amount of money, which means less in terms of purchasing power after inflation. This is an important matter for banks with deposits and loans, and for highly geared companies with a large proportion of loan capital in their capital structure.

SSAP 16

This standard is the fourth attempt by the ASC to produce a workable system of accounting in an inflationary period, and has now been withdrawn. It favoured current cost accounting, but limited the mandatory application of the system to enterprises with an annual turnover of £5 million or more, with the further exception of property companies, insurance companies and investment and unit trusts. The recommended practice was for a company to produce historical cost accounts accompanied by a current cost profit and loss account and a current cost balance sheet and explanatory notes, which must all be covered by the auditor's certficate.

Three major adjustments are made to the historical cost profit to arrive at a current cost operating profit, and a fourth adjustment is then made.

1. Depreciation adjustment, to allow for the impact of price changes when determining the charge against revenue for that part of the fixed assets consumed in the period. The amount will be the difference between the value to the business of fixed assets used up and historical cost depreciation for the year, and will be deducted from the historical cost profit.
2. Cost of sales adjustment, to allow for the impact of price changes when computing the cost of stock used up in the period. The difference between the value to the business of stock consumed and the historical cost charge therefore will be deducted from the historical cost profit.
3. Monetary working capital adjustment, to recognize the need to maintain the real value of the monetary assets in the business. Sales made on credit terms cause the business to finance any inflationary price changes which take place in the credit period before the goods are paid for. Conversely, any purchases on credit terms reduce the working capital belonging to the firm which is tied up in stocks and debtors, so that the real value of this proportion of funds invested in current assets does not need to be maintained by the business. It is suggested that cash or overdrafts should be excluded from the monetary working capital adjustment unless the exclusion will give a misleading result.

Example

A company achieves sales of £120 000 p.a. with three months' credit allowed to customers, so that £30 000 ($\frac{3}{12} \times$ £120 000) is invested as working capital in debtors at any moment.

The company makes purchases of £96 000 p.a. on terms of two months' credit from its suppliers. Thus £16 000 ($\frac{2}{12} \times$ £96 000) of the finance tied up in debtors will be provided by trade creditors, and the company itself will need to finance only £14 000 as working capital.

Suppose that in the following year the volume of trade remains the same but that the prices of sales and purchases increase by ten per cent. How much extra will be required as working capital for the same volume of business?

			£	
Sales: £120 000 + £12 000 = £132 000	3/12 × £132 000		33 000	—Debtors
Purchases: £96 000 + £9600 = £105 600	2/12 × £105 600		17 600	—Creditors

New working capital	15 400
Old working capital	14 000
Extra working capital	£1 400

4. Gearing adjustment. The total funds employed in the business, other than trade credit, are derived from the equity interest (S = share capital plus reserves) plus loans (L), both long-term and short-term. These funds finance the assets of the business, and the three previous adjustments have ensured that enough is set aside out of profits to maintain that investment at current prices. However, the borrowed proportion of these funds $(\frac{L}{L+S})$ will be repaid at historical cost amounts, so that any funds set aside to maintain that proportion of the assets will not be repaid, but will remain in the business and rightly belong to the shareholders. Accordingly the gearing proportion $(\frac{L}{L+S})$ of these previous adjustments is added back to the computation of current cost profit, after subtracting from it the amount of interest paid during the year.

Current Cost Profit and Loss Account

	£	£
Historical cost profit before interest and tax		XXXX
Less:		
Depreciation adjustment	XX	
Cost of sales adjustment	XX	
Monetary working capital adjustment	XX	
		XX
Current cost operating profit		XXX
Add gearing adjustment	XX	
Less interest	X	
		XX
Current cost profit before tax		XXX
Less taxation		XX
Current cost profit attributable to shareholders		XX
Dividend		XX
Retained for the year		£ XX

The current cost balance sheet will contain:

(a) fixed assets and stock at their value to the business:

(b) investments in associated companies—the company's proportion of the current cost net assets of the subsidiary company:

(c) other investments at directors' valuation:

(d) intangible assets and goodwill at current replacement cost, but if this is impracticable the historical cost basis:

(e) current assets other than stocks at historical cost;

(f) all liabilities at historical cost;

(g) current cost reserve or capital maintenance reserve which will reflect revaluation surpluses on fixed assets and stocks, and the working capital and gearing adjustments.

Examples of the four adjustments suggested to mitigate the impact of inflation on financial statements are as follows.

EXAMPLE OF CURRENT COST ACCOUNTING

Cost of Sales Adjustment

The purpose of the adjustment is to revise the opening and closing stock figures to the average current cost for the year. An index, specific to the raw material in stock, is used in the adjustment. Suppose the index stood at 100 on 30 November 19-2, and at 120 on 30 November 19-3, that the average index over the year is 110, and that raw material purchases are spread evenly over the year. The company year end is 31 December but since stocks are assumed to have a holding period of two months then the index at the end of November typifies stock bought before and after that date.

	Historical Cost Data	*Index*	*Current Cost Data*
	£		£
Opening stock	700	$\times \dfrac{110}{100}$	770
Add purchases	4 600		4 600
	5 300		5 370
Less closing stock	1 080	$\times \dfrac{110}{120}$	990
Cost of materials used	£4 220		£4 380

This adjustment would reduce profit by £160. It is an attempt to isolate the inflationary effect of setting costs at historical prices against sales at current prices.

The adjustment can be computed in a more complicated manner using the formula:

$$\left(\text{Historical cost closing stock} \times \frac{\text{Average index number}}{\text{Closing index number}}\right) -$$

$$\left(\text{Historical cost opening stock} \times \frac{\text{Average index number}}{\text{Opening index number}}\right)$$

$$\left(\frac{1080}{1} \times \frac{110}{120}\right) - \left(\frac{700}{1} \times \frac{110}{100}\right) = 990 - 770 = £220$$

Stocks have increased by £220 when opening and closing stocks are calculated at mid-year prices. This increase can be attributed to a greater volume of stock. The amount is deducted from the historical cost stock increase for the period, £380 − £220 = £160 as the adjustment.

The total increase, £380, less the volume increase, £220, is the amount required to finance stocks at higher post-inflation prices, which must be set aside out of profits to maintain operating capability so far as stocks are concerned.

Depreciation Adjustment

The value to the business of a fixed asset is its net current replacement cost. This amount can be computed by applying relevant indices to the original historical cost of the asset and deducting therefrom a proportion for the expired life of the asset. First it is necessary to find an appropriate index, which is specific either to the industry concerned or to the assets involved, then to apply it to historical cost and then subtract the expired service proportion from the figure calculated. The adjustment is the difference between the depreciation on the revised cost and the historical depreciation for the year.

A machine was bought a year ago for £10 000 and it has a ten-year life. The appropriate index has moved from 100 to 120 during the year.

	Historical Cost Data	Index	Current Cost Data
	£		£
Cost	10 000	$\dfrac{120}{100}$	12 000
Depreciation	1 000	$\dfrac{120}{100}$	1 200
Net book value	£9 000	$\dfrac{120}{100}$	£10 800

This adjustment would reduce profit by £200. The increase of £2000 in the cost of the asset as stated in the current cost balance sheet would be balanced by £2000 transferred to the capital maintenance reserve (sometimes called current cost reserve), part of the equity interest on that balance sheet.

Monetary Working Capital Adjustment

This adjustment represents that part of the change in working capital which has resulted from a change in prices and not from a change in volume. Stocks are excluded since they are adjusted under cost of sales, and amounts owed to the Inland Revenue are excluded since they form part of the gearing adjustment.

Debtors (£1000) less creditors (£500) at start = £500 MWC.

Debtors (£1400) less creditors (£600) at end = £800 MWC.

This represents an increase of £300 on the year in historical cost terms. The formula is:

$$\left[\text{Closing MWC} \times \frac{\text{Average index}}{\text{Closing index}} \right] - \left[\text{Opening MWC} \times \frac{\text{Average index}}{\text{Opening index}} \right]$$

$$= \left[\frac{800}{1} \times \frac{100}{120} \right] - \left[\frac{500}{1} \times \frac{110}{100} \right]$$

$$= 733 - 550 = 183$$

This amount is deducted from the increase for the year. £300 − £183 = £117 as the adjustment.

The total increase (£300) less the volume increase (£183) equals the increase in MWC caused by price changes.

The Gearing Adjustment

Net borrowings are the total of long-term liabilities, deferred taxation, hire purchase creditors and bank overdraft less any cash balances. The gearing proportion is derived from the formula ($\frac{L}{L \times S}$) computed as an average figure for the year.

$$\frac{\text{Opening Net Borrowings} + \text{Closing Net Borrowings} + 2}{(\text{Opening} + \text{Closing Net Borrowings}) + (\text{Opening} + \text{Closing Equity Interest from Current Cost Balance Sheet}) + 2} \times \frac{100}{1}$$

This proportion is applied to the amount of the first three adjustments, and the current cost profit is increased by the figure produced. The effect of this adjustment is to add back to profit the proportion of the other adjustments which has been financed by interests other than those of the shareholders.

Example

$$\frac{[8550 + 9650] \div 2}{[(8550 + 9650) + (24\,230 + 25\,310)] \div 2} \times \frac{100}{1}$$

$$= \frac{9100}{33\,870} \times \frac{100}{1} = 27 \text{ per cent}$$

	£
Cost of sales adjustment	160
Depreciation adjustment	200
Monetary working capital adjustment	117
Total adjustments	477

Gearing adjustment adds back 27 per cent of
477   129
[Less whatever interest has been paid on the loans.]

HOLDING GAINS

If a company holds an asset which rises in price during the`holding period, the company is said to have made a holding gain, since costs have been saved because stocks were purchased at pre-inflation prices instead of at prices current when the stock was sold or used. This element of profit has not come from operations but from stockholding. Historical cost accounting combines the holding gain and the operating profit in one profit figure, but current cost accounting separates these important items.

Example

A company buys 100 components for £5000 on 1 June 19-1. At the year end, 31 December 19-1, the components are still in stock, but it would cost £5500 to replace them. In current cost terms an unrealized holding gain (UHG) of £500 has been made in 19-1, and although it is not yet realized and available for distribution as a dividend, perhaps shareholders should be told of this gain. The historical cost system would not disclose such a gain because stocks are accounted for at the lower of cost or net realizable value.

Suppose the components are sold (or used) on 31 March 19-2 for £6000, when it would cost the company £5800 to replace them. In current cost terms the UHG of £500 from 19-1 is now realized, and a further realized holding gain (RHG) of £300 is made. The operating profit is the difference between the selling price and the replacement cost on the date of the sale, which is £200.

	Historical Cost £	Current Cost £	
Cost on 1 June 19-1	5000	5000	
Replacement cost on 31 December 19-1		5500	
Unrealized holding gain 19-1			500
(realized in 19-2)			
Replacement cost 31 March 19-2		5800	
Realized holding gain 19-2			300
Selling price	6000	6000	
Operating profit 19-2			200
Historical cost profit 19-2	£1000		

The historical cost profit of £1000 fails to distinguish between the operating profit and the holding gains, unrealized and realized. This is important not only because users should be informed, but also because the holding gain should not be distributed as a dividend. One hundred components which cost £5000 (£50 each) will now cost £5800 (£58 each) to replace, and an extra £800 (the holding gain) is required to finance the working capital invested in component stocks. In Hicksian terms, an extra £800 must be retained out of profit to maintain the capital of the business, expressed as operating capacity. If the £800 of holding gain is distributed as a dividend, the company would not be able to buy for £5000 the 100 components it requires to maintain its operating capability; it would only have 86 (£5000 ÷ £58) components in stock. Accordingly only the operating profit is available for distribution, and historical cost accounting, by confusing holding gains with the true profit, may encourage a company to pay out in dividend funds which are needed to maintain capacity post-inflation.

The CPP system relates the cost of materials to the current value of money and shows as a profit any surplus of sales revenue over the current purchasing power equivalent of the original cost. Thus under CPP, holding gains calculated according to a general index (the RPI) are separated from operating profit, but real holding gains are ignored.

Example

Fictional Ltd sells goods for £150 000 during the year. The historical cost of goods sold was £100 000, but to replace the goods it has sold Fictional must pay £130 000. The RPI has risen by 10 per cent during the year. An income statement for Fictional Ltd could be produced on the following bases.

	Historical £	CPP £	CCA £
Sales	150 000	150 000	150 000
Cost of sales	100 000		
Adjustments for RPI		110 000	
At current cost			130 000
Profit	£50 000	£40 000	20 000
Holding gain (replacement cost minus historical cost)			30 000
			£50 000

In terms of the Hicksian concept of income, which seeks to maintain the 'well-offness' of the company before showing a profit, the CPP system is trying to maintain capital in terms of what money can buy in general, but the CCA system is trying to maintain the real value of those assets owned by the company. This distinction is sometimes expressed as the difference between real capital (what money can buy) and physical capital (the assets of a firm irrespective of their original cost). This example can be shown on a graph (figure 9).

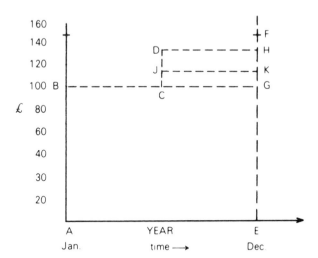

Figure 9.
Historical cost = AB
Inflationary increase in value of materials = CD
Sale price = EF
Holding gain = GH
CCA operating profit = HF
Historical cost profit = GF

Fall in purchasing power of money as shown by:
  RPI = CJ
CPP profit = KF

THE WAY FORWARD

Since the withdrawal of SSAP 16 in 1987, most companies have discontinued the practice of publishing current cost accounts as an appendix to the published accounts prepared on a historical cost basis. However, the problem of inflation remains, and accountants should prepare for the need to adjust financial statements when the inflation rate increases. The ASC has offered advice in the form of a handbook, supporting the idea of current cost accounting, though it is now termed the 'Operating Capital Maintenance Concept'.

CCA maintains operating capability, because the effects of inflation are calculated as they affect the capital employed in a business expressed in terms of assets (plant, stock and monetary working capital), rather than the shareholders' funds invested. The new relaxed view suggests that there is no need for a current cost balance sheet, and that the monetary working capital and gearing adjustments can also be omitted, if the company considers that they are not helpful. Comparability appears to have been forsaken.

The ASC also accepts the alternative view that capital can be measured in financial terms as a fund attributable to shareholders. If profit is the difference between the opening and closing fund, any measurement of such a fund must take into account the erosion of the fund by the reduction in the purchasing power of money during a period of inflation. Thus the financial capital maintenance concept seeks to ensure that the current cost adjustments are sufficient to maintain the financial capital (shareholders' funds) in real terms. This means that the shareholders' funds must be able to buy as much in terms of goods and services at the end of the financial year as at the beginning.

The amount of shareholders' funds at the start of the year is adjusted by the RPI for the year, to show the amount they should have grown to, to keep pace with general inflation. This amount is compared with the shareholders' funds based on the current cost asset values at the end of the year. If the difference is negative then the real financial capital has not been maintained, and more must be set aside out of profit for this purpose. Thus an amended version of the former CPP method is now used in conjunction with the CCA method, and the rivals are used together to improve the quality of financial information—the real-terms system.

TUTORIAL DISCUSSION TOPICS

18.1 Why should accountants adjust historical cost accounts for the effects of inflation?

18.2 How does a cost of sales adjustment reduce the effect of inflation on profit?

18.3 Why should accounts be adjusted for the effect of inflation on monetary items?

18.4 What is a holding gain? Should accountants include it with the profit they measure?

18.5 What is the difference between a general index and a specific index? How does the use of either affect the profit adjusted for inflation?

SEMINAR EXERCISE 12

For several years Mr Grant has been employed as branch manager of a butcher's shop owned by a retail chain store. Last year he received an inheritance, and this provided him with sufficient funds to buy a shop in the main street of the town for £30 000.

At the end of his first full year of business he thought he had done moderately well, and he was therefore somewhat annoyed when his accountant sent him figures which indicated he had operated at a loss.

His accountant requested him to submit the accounts for inspection. Schedule I shows the figures which Mr Grant prepared.

Schedule I. James Grant, Statement of Profit for First Year's Trading

	£	£
Sales		53 000
Cost of goods sold		41 000
Gross profit:		12 000
Salaries and wages	4 800	
Advertising	800	
Stationery and postage	500	
Insurance on and improvements to shop (£700)	900	
Heat, light and power	300	
Depreciation of equipment	250	
Sundry expenses	800	
Income tax	1 550	
Repairs to flat above shop	112	10 012
		£1 988

The accountant asked for more information concerning salaries and the rent value of the building. Mr Grant answered as follows:

'I own my own business so there is no point in my charging a salary. I drew £3000 from the business last year and paid my wife £20 per week from the till. My salary as a manager was £3200 per annum, although I don't see what relevance this figure has.

I thought I made it clear to you that I own my own shop. It would cost me £2400 a year to rent a similar building, and you can see I save a lot of money by not being forced to rent, as well as living on the premises rent free, since flats in this area cost £400 a year.'

On the basis of this information the accountant revised Mr Grant's figures and sent him the revised statement shown in Schedule II.

Schedule II. James Grant, Statement of Loss for Year

	£	£
Sales		53 000
Cost of goods sold		41 000
Gross profit:		12 000
Salaries and wages	8 000	
Advertising	800	
Stationery and postage	500	
Rent	2 000	
Insurance	200	
Heat, light and power	300	
Depreciation	320	
Sundry expenses	800	12 920
Net loss		(920)
Add drawings in excess of salary charged		(840)
Capital depletion		(£1 760)

(a) How much profit did Mr Grant's shop earn in the year? How do you explain the difference between the profit of Schedule I and the loss of Schedule II?
(b) What, if any, accounting principles are violated in either statement?
(c) Does either statement show an 'economic' profit?
(d) Should Mr Grant continue to operate his own shop? Has he been successful?

PART FOUR

Business Units: Their Finance and Valuation

19 | Types of Business Organization

There are many ways in which a business enterprise can be organized, the main difference between the forms being the number and types of owners who join together in a business.

THE SOLE TRADER

In the case of a sole trader there is one proprietor who both owns and operates the business. The proprietor acts as manager and is the only person responsible for the success or failure of the business. Although free from the control of others, the business success of a sole trader is limited to what can be achieved by the ability of the operator, and the finance of the business is limited to the amount which the proprietor can raise. This form of business organization is very flexible in that business decisions can be made quickly and with the minimum of delay. Bearing responsibility for the success or failure of the business motivates a sole trader to work very hard. The success of the business depends upon the efforts and ability of the proprietor, who has a legal right to all the profits after tax but must also bear all the losses which are made. Certain types of business where there is a high degree of skill or professional content, e.g. an accountant or a dentist, are perhaps best organized in the form of a proprietor or sole trader.

THE PARTNERSHIP

The success of the business of a sole trader may be limited by the ability of the proprietor and by the amount of capital a single person can invest, but these limitations are to some extent overcome by the amalgamation of two or more sole traders into a partnership. The business can expand if more principals join it and bring capital with them, while each partner will bring a measure of expertise to the running of the business. Decisions in a partnership are no longer the responsibility of an individual, but are usually the outcome of discussion among the partners. It is necessary for partners to have absolute trust in one another, and therefore it is important to select one's partners with care. This is very important, because one partner can bind the whole of the partnership by his actions and, as in the case of a sole trader, the debts of the business can be recovered by the creditors from the private resources of the partners. The Limited Partnership Act 1907 allowed a certain class of partners, who provided capital but took no part in the management of the business, to have their liability for its debts limited to their investment.

THE COMPANY

The company is a 'body corporate' comprising persons who have united together to form a separate legal entity. A company is considered to be a legal person, separate in law from the people who own and manage it. As such it can sue or be sued in its own right. A creditor or any other person seeking to establish a legal right against a sole trader or a partnership must sue the trader or the partners as individuals. (The legal liability of a partnership is 'joint and several', which means that it is possible to sue individual partners or the group as a whole.) A person with a debt or legal right to establish against a company must sue the company, and cannot sue its members, the shareholders. It follows from this idea of legal personality that the law gives a company perpetual succession. The company itself will continue even though the composition of the group of people who own it is changed. This is a distinct advantage over partnership as a form of business organization, since a partnership is deemed to be discontinued when one or more partners join or leave the group. A shareholder in a company can sell shares in the business, die or go bankrupt, but the company itself still continues. Since the company is a separate legal person it has a seal to signify its will. There is a divorce of management from ownership, with a board of directors elected by the members or owners to control on their behalf the day-to-day operations of the business. For certain types of contract the board will agree to bind the company, and the company secretary will affix the seal of the company to the contract, thus expressing this decision.

As a form of business organization, the company allows a large number of people to be organized to own and finance the business, while a small committee, the board, manages it on their behalf. The shareholders, or owners, have the privilege of limited liability, which means that if the company's ventures are unsuccessful the liability of the shareholder for the debts of the company is limited to the amount of the original investment plus any amount unpaid on the shares.

It has long been a cardinal principle of English law that no corporation or company can be formed without the permission of the Crown. In historical times companies which were formed required a royal charter to establish their existence. Such companies as the Hudson's Bay Company and the East India Company are examples of this type of company formation. In the nineteenth century, with the establishment of the principle of limited liability, the company form of business organization became more common, and companies began to be incorporated by Act of Parliament. Many of the early railway companies and water and electricity authorities were established by private Act of Parliament in this way. The most common form for the incorporation of companies, however, is by registration under the terms of the Companies Act. A memorandum and articles of incorporation are prepared and submitted to the Registrar. Once he has approved these documents he will issue a certificate of incorporation which proves the existence of the company. The memorandum includes an objects clause which sets out what the company proposes to do. Any transaction undertaken by the company which is not within the scope of its objects will be considered as 'ultra vires', which means that it is beyond the powers of the company to undertake it. The articles of the company contain the rules under which the company is to operate, and will cover such matters as the regulations for the issue of shares, the rules concerning directors and managing directors, the proceedings and powers of the board, the rights of the members inter se (between themselves) and the extent of the company's borrowing powers.

There are three main types of company. First, there is the most common type, which is the company limited by shares. In this type, as explained above, the liability of the members for the debts of the company is limited to their investment in the company. The creditors can levy no further contribution from the shareholders to meet their claims against the business. The second type of company is that limited by guarantee. This form of organization calls for the members of the company to undertake to contribute a specified sum to the liabilities of the company if it ceases to trade and has insufficient funds to meet its creditors. They are not so much shareholders as members who have promised to pay a stated amount towards the debts of the company if required. This arrangement provides the business with a measure of security which it can offer to normal trade creditors. Guarantee companies are not a normal form of business undertaking; this type is usually restricted to non-profit-making organizations such as charities. The third type of company is the unlimited company. In this form the members or shareholders have the same liabilities as partners and cannot claim the protection of limited liability if the creditors wish to pursue their debts to the full extent of the shareholders' private fortunes. However, this form of business undertaking does give the advantages of a body corporate, of transferability of shares, and of perpetual succession.

In companies limited by shares there is yet another division. Such companies can be either public (PLC), or private (Ltd). A public company is a company limited by shares or by guarantee with a memorandum that states that it is a public company. It must have at least two members (shareholders) and be registered as such. All other companies are private companies. It is an offence for a private company to offer shares or debentures to the public for subscription. The registrar will not issue a certificate to a public company unless the nominal value of its allotted share capital exceeds the 'authorized minimum', which is normally £50 000. If the company is deemed to be a private company it has certain privileges. These privileges can be summarized as follows:

1. A private company can have only one director, whereas a public company must have two.
2. A private company need not issue a prospectus, and can commence business immediately on incorporation, whereas a public company has to obtain a trading certificate from the Registrar of Companies after fulfilling conditions laid down in the Companies Act.
3. A director of a private company is not forced to retire when he reaches seventy years of age, whereas in a public company such directors must retire and be re-elected each year.
4. The directors of a private company can be appointed as a board by a single resolution, whereas in a public company directors must be appointed individually by separate resolutions.

5. A public company must have a statutory meeting and a statutory report, but these are not required by law for a private company.
6. In a private company proxy holders may speak at meetings. A proxy holder is somebody who attends the meetings of a company to represent one of its shareholders and to vote on his behalf. In a public company the proxy holder cannot speak, although he can vote.
7. A private company can restrict the right to transfer shares, thus maintaining control in the hands of family shareholders. This may be a disadvantage to a shareholder who wishes to sell shares.

The major differences between the company form of business organization and the partnership may be summarized as follows:

1. A company is a legal person in its own right, whereas a partnership is not a separate legal entity from its members. This gives to the member of a company the right to transfer a share in the company without the termination of the business, as would happen with a partnership. This is known as perpetual succession.
2. Shareholders in a company are protected by limited liability, whereas in a partnership each partner may be made liable for the debts of the firm to the full extent of his private fortune.
3. A limit of twenty is usually put upon the number of partners who can engage in a partnership business, but in a public company the only limit to the number of shareholders is the number of shares authorized. This means that a public company can recruit capital from a much wider market than can a partnership or a private limited company.
4. In a partnership all partners have a right to join in the management of the business and have access to the books and vouchers, but in the company form of business organization management is delegated by the shareholders to the board, and once that delegation has taken place the shareholders have only a statutory right to the information specified in the Companies Act 1985.
5. Since a company is incorporated by registering under the Companies Act, it must file certain information about its accounts etc. with the Registrar. A partnership, however, does not have to disclose information about itself to the public.
6. The Partnership Act 1890 lays down the rules within which a partnership is administered, unless there is an agreement among the partners which can override the Act. The Companies Act 1985 lays down rules by which companies must abide, even though in some cases they might wish to vary those rules.
7. The capital of a company is authorized by the terms and conditions laid down in its memorandum. It is an administrative matter to increase the capital, but to reduce capital is a matter for the court. In a partnership, however, capital is fixed only by agreement and can be changed if the partners so wish.
8. Under the Companies Act, a company must appoint an auditor and must maintain certain books. There is no such requirement for the audit of a partnership and nowhere in the Partnership Act is a list of statutory books laid down.
9. The profit of a partnership business is divided among the partners according to their agreed profit-sharing ratio, and can be withdrawn by them if they so wish. The profit of a company is distributed as a dividend pro rata to shareholding at a rate determined by the company in a general meeting. The board decides how much of the profit is to be paid out in dividend and recommends its decision to be adopted by the shareholders.

CO-OPERATIVE SOCIETIES

This form of enterprise occurs when groups of consumers or producers band together to form an organization to represent them in the market. A co-operative of farmers may develop in order to purchase seeds and fertilizers for the group as a whole or to market a specific product, say a local type of cheese. In the retail field a co-operative society is set up to sell goods to customers, who may or may not be members, and to pay back some part of the profit made by the co-operative to its members in the form of a dividend based on the amount of goods purchased by the member in the period. A consumers' co-operative attempts to cut out the middleman and provide supplies at a cheap rate.

A co-operative is a business enterprise, and as such will need the services of competent managers. Whereas in a company the board is elected by the shareholders, in a co-op the members elect a governing body to which managers will report, and which is responsible for overall policy decisions. Under the Industrial and Provident Societies Act 1965 each society is constituted as a corporate body with limited liability, with a maximum shareholding for each member of £1000.

BUILDING SOCIETIES

This form of enterprise brings together the saver and the borrower in the domestic property market. The object of the society is to take deposits, or subscriptions to share accounts, from those members who wish to use the society as a means of saving, and then to lend out the funds accumulated to other members, on the security of freehold or leasehold property.

The Building Societies Act 1962 governs the operation of this form of enterprise. Depositors and shareholders are paid a rate of interest on their funds invested in the society and can withdraw their investment at short notice, e.g. on demand, or else they can receive a slightly higher rate of interest if they agree to give three months' notice of withdrawal. Building societies are seen as a safe form of investment for the small saver, who has little fear of loss, since deposits will be repaid at par and the rate of interest to be received is indicated in advance, and maintained without fluctuation, where possible. The rate may fluctuate from time to time on the initiative of the society. The interest received by the investor is deemed to be net of tax at the standard rate.

At first sight it appears a doubtful commercial practice to borrow on short-term repayment terms and lend to a householder for a twenty-year period. The societies do, however, note carefully the amount of funds flowing in to them each month from deposits and repayments from borrowers and, if withdrawals increase, they can increase the rate of interest they offer to tempt more deposits and discourage withdrawals. When this occurs the increase in the rate is passed on to the house buyers who have outstanding mortgage loans with the societies.

Recently the building societies have extended the range of services provided to their members. The business of lending to prospective buyers has suffered competition from banks eager to enter this lending market, and in retaliation the building societies have offered cheque accounts, and deposit withdrawal card services, so that they have become more like banks. One of the largest building societies has now changed its form to that of a public limited company and has offered shares in this new company to former depositors and borrowers as well as to the public.

UNIT TRUSTS

This is another form of savings institution, established under a trust deed. Investors buy units in the trust, and the board of management invest the funds in a portfolio of securities, which are usually specified in the trust deed. A trust may invest only in certain shares, e.g. of banks and insurance companies, or the deed may specify companies in a specific area, e.g. Yorkshire, or 'Japan small business situations', or with a particular emphasis, e.g. growth or income. The idea is that the small investor can obtain a stake in a large and prosperous business, can spread the risk across the portfolio of the trust, and can receive the benefit of the expertise of the trust managers. The 'managers' are usually a company associated with a number of trusts, to which they make a management charge for their services. This charge is passed on to the unit holders by a loading charge, applied when they buy their units, and an annual service charge. The actions of the trust managers are overseen by the trustee, usually a large corporation whose task it is to hold the investments of the trust. Some unit trusts are quoted on the Stock Exchange, but in others the buying and selling prices of the units are specified from time to time by the managers.

Unit trusts must not be confused with investment trusts. An investment trust is invariably not a trust but is instead a company whose funds are invested by the board in a number of other investment opportunities.

NATIONALIZED INDUSTRIES

A number of enterprises may be under the control of the Government. Such undertakings usually provide important public services such as transport, electricity or water, or operate in a strategically important area of the economy, e.g. the production of steel, oil and coal. The Government controls the operation of these undertakings, through the responsibility of management to a minister of state and through him to Parliament. Each nationalized industry produces an annual report which can be debated by MPs, but it is unusual for a minister of state to face questions on the day-to-day running of a nationalized industry. A nationalized industry is expected to operate as efficiently as possible, but often there is a claim for it to be run in the national interest, which usually implies the provision of a service at less than its cost, the subsequent loss being recouped by a grant out of revenue raised from taxation. The profit of a nationalized industry makes a contribution to the Treasury, just like a tax. Industries under Government control should be free of political pressure in order to make sensible commercial decisions, e.g. British Coal may prefer to buy American equipment rather than machinery built in the UK. However, in practice the effect of political manoeuvre is often obscured when their accounts are drawn up and their efficiency discussed. The Government can control a nationalized venture by setting up an authority or corporation under statute or by holding shares in a company. The present political trend is for the Government to disinvest from nationalized industries and to 'privatize' them by transforming them into public companies and offering shares in those companies for sale to the public via the Stock Exchange.

TUTORIAL DISCUSSION TOPICS

19.1 What advantages accrue to the sole trader form of business organization and what further advantages can be achieved if a sole trader joins with a partner?

19.2 Discuss the different types of company that can be found in the UK.

19.3 What are the major differences between a company and a partnership?

19.4 Discuss the function of a building society.

20 | Capital Structure and Gearing

CAPITAL STRUCTURE

The funds used to finance the assets of a company can be recruited from several sources. In most companies a combination of share capital, long-term loan capital, and short-term facilities is used. It is important that a significant proportion of the finance is provided by ordinary shareholders, who are the legal owners of the business. The existence of a sizeable fund of permanent capital invested in the business will increase the confidence of other lenders, whereas overdependence on finance provided by sources other than the legal owners is seen as a sign of weakness. The authorized capital of the business is the number of shares stated in its memorandum of association which it has authority to issue to investors. The proportion of that capital which has been taken up by the public and subscribed for is termed the issued capital, and is usually in the form of ordinary or preference shares.

Ordinary Shares

An ordinary share is a fixed unit of the common fund of the company, and it gives its holder a right to a proportionate interest in the company as to a share of the profit or loss, and as to the return of capital in the event of a winding up. When business ceases, the assets are realized and the funds used to repay claims on the business. Thus the term 'equity shares' means that ordinary shareholders have a right to share pro rata to their holdings, the profits made by the business, and any surplus available on a winding up after all other liabilities have been paid. Most ordinary shares carry with them the right to attend and vote at all meetings of the company. Thus the shareholders elect the board and the auditors, and approve or disapprove the level of dividend which is proposed by the board. They can also vote to accept or reject a takeover offer made by another company. There are, however, some ordinary shares, sometimes known as 'A' shares, which do not possess voting rights. Some companies have ordinary shares and 'A' ordinary shares in issue at the same time and it is interesting to note the low value set on the vote by the investors, which is shown by the small difference in price between the shares. Yet another class of

330

shares is sometimes called 'founders' shares. These are issued to members of the family which built up the business before it changed from a private to a public company, or others who founded the company. Such shares usually carry enhanced voting rights such as ten votes per share, and are used as a means whereby a small group of people can maintain control over an old family business after it has expanded. Needless to say, the Stock Exchange disapproves of these various classes of shares with different voting rights, and encourages the issue of shares on a one vote per share basis.

In the final analysis the ordinary shareholders with their votes can approve or disapprove the board's policy and vote to remove the directors from office. Anyone who possesses over 50 per cent of the voting shares is said to have a controlling interest in a company, while the other shareholders in this instance comprise the minority interest. It is, of course, possible to maintain control of a company by owning a share stake with less than 50 per cent of the votes if the other shares are disposed over a large number of small holdings whose owners find it difficult to join together to formulate a policy of concerted action.

The ordinary shareholder has a right to sell his shares on the market, and the company has a duty to record this transfer in its share register and issue the appropriate share certificate. The marketability of shares in a private limited company is restricted, since such shares cannot be traded on the Stock Exchange. Financial managers see the issue of ordinary shares as advantageous, since there is no liability to repay the investment on the part of the company, and the rate of dividend can fluctuate with profits. If losses are made, the dividend on ordinary shares can be 'passed'. Investors see other advantages in holding ordinary shares, such as the possession of the right to participate in all surpluses remaining after prior right capital (preference shares) has been satisfied, and the potential capital growth from profits retained in the business to buy assets, which provides a hedge against inflation. Of course any increase in the value of ordinary shares is subject to capital gains tax when the shares are realized, but an investor with a large income would prefer to pay this rather than high marginal rates of income tax on distributed profits. The main disadvantages of issuing ordinary shares are that the creation of extra votes may change control in a company and give more investors the chance to join in the distribution of profits.

When an issue of ordinary shares is floated on the market it is first advertised in what is called a prospectus. The terms of this document must be absolutely correct and within the rules laid down by the Council of the Stock Exchange and the Companies Act so that the potential investor is not misled in any way. The investor will apply for shares which are to be issued, sending in his application money as he does so. The terms of the issue of a £1 share may be 25p on application and 25p on allotment, with one call thereafter. This means that when a potential shareholder applies for shares in the issue, he must send application money of 25p per share for all the shares he wants. The board of the company will review the applications for their issue, and if it is oversubscribed (more applications for the shares than there are shares available) they will scale down applications by lottery or selection, selecting only those potential shareholders whom they wish to be members of the company. An investor who is not allotted shares has his application money returned with a letter of regret, while the successful subscriber is sent a letter of allotment whereupon he must pay a further 25p on allotment of the shares. Often application and allotment money is paid when the application is made. Once share certificates have been issued to the new shareholders the company may, at its discretion, 'call up' the remainder of the capital. A letter is sent to the new shareholders asking them for a further 50p per share, so that they have all contributed £1 for every share issued to them. If a shareholder is unable to make payment of a call or instalment on a share, the company may forfeit that member's shares. This means that according to authority in the articles of association of a company, the shares are taken away from the member by a resolution of the board of directors. The company then has the power to sell or re-allot the forfeited shares to other shareholders. Sometimes if a share is popular with the investing public it is possible to issue it at a premium, i.e. a £1 share can be issued for £1.50. If 10 000 such shares are issued the ordinary share capital of the company is increased by £10 000 and a share premium of £5000 is also created. This is a statutory reserve not available for distribution, since it is the same as the ordinarily subscribed capital. There is little which can be done with this type of reserve, except to use it to pay up new shares to be issued as a bonus or scrip issue, or to write off against it the expense of an issue or the premium on repayment of a debenture.

Bonus Shares

Bonus shares are extra shares issued to ordinary shareholders pro rata to their holdings. They do not need to be paid for since they represent reserves which are already part of the equity interest of the business. A bonus issue is a means by which the share capital of a company can be brought more into line with the value of assets owned by the company, since reserves not available for distribution can be used to 'pay up' the issue.

Example

Dr.	Balance Sheet of Bonus Ltd (before bonus issue)		Cr.
	£		£
Capital		Fixed assets	120 000
100 000 £1 ordinary shares	100 000	Current assets	80 000
Capital redemption reserve fund	20 000		
Share premium account	5 000		
Reserve arising on revaluation			
of fixed assets	5 000		
General reserve	50 000		
	180 000		
Current liabilities	20 000		
	£200 000		£200 000

A bonus issue of three new shares for every ten now held is made. The new shares are to be paid up out of reserves not available for distribution.

Dr.		Balance Sheet of Bonus Ltd (after bonus issue)	Cr.
	£		£
Capital		Fixed assets	120 000
130 000 £1 ordinary shares	130 000	Current assets	80 000
General reserve	50 000		
	180 000		
Current liabilities	20 000		
	£200 000		£200 000

The shareholders have been given nothing except what was already theirs. They will, however, benefit if the existing rate of dividend is maintained on the newly increased capital.

Preference Shares

Another class of shares, separate from ordinary shares, is preference shares. These shares are so termed since they have a preferential right to receive their dividend if profits exist, and repayment of capital before other shareholders. The exact rights of preference shareholders will be found in the articles of association of the company. The dividend on such shares is, however, limited to a fixed percentage of the face value (nominal or par value) which is stated on the share certificate. We can thus speak of 8 per cent preference shares, being shares whose owner has a right to a dividend of 8 per cent each year, but no more. If a company has issued 10 000 8 per cent £1 preference shares, and has made a profit of only £800, then the preference shareholders will have a right to receive their dividend before any payment is made to the ordinary shareholders, who in this case will receive nothing. The same rule normally applies in the event of a winding up, so that the preference shareholders are repaid the face value of their shares before any money is paid to ordinary shareholders. Thus preference shares give investors a steady return with a high degree of safety. However, the ordinary shareholders have a right to all the profits that are made after the preference dividend has been paid, and a right to divide equally among themselves the entire value of the business on a winding up after the preference shareholders have received the face value of their shares. Thus the ordinary shareholders take the greater risk, since they are the last group to receive their share of profit or their money back on a winding up, although they do have a right to all the surplus that is earned. This is why ordinary shares are often referred to as risk or venture capital. Preference shares also suffer by restriction of their voting rights. Normally the articles specify that they carry no right to vote at a general meeting of the company, but if an extraordinary meeting is called to discuss matters which prejudice their preferential rights, e.g. a capital reorganization scheme, then it is usual for preference shareholders to be allowed to vote.

Some companies will issue cumulative preference shares to avoid the difficulty which occurs in a year when profits are too small to pay either the preference or ordinary share dividends. In this case a normal preference shareholder will receive nothing, and will have to wait until next year for a normal fixed percentage dividend. The holder of a cumulative preference share will, in a subsequent year, receive arrears of dividend which have accumulated in the past, before any dividend is paid on the ordinary shares. Yet another variation of the preference share is the participating preference share. A holder of such a share has a right to a fixed preference dividend, and then has a further right to participate in exceptionally high profits when they are made and divided. The terms of issue of such a share usually state that when the ordinary shares have received a dividend of, for example, 30 per cent, the participating preference shareholders will receive an extra x per cent for every further y per cent paid to the ordinary shareholders. Thus the preference shareholder is in a safer position than the ordinary shareholder because of these preferential rights. Less risk means a lower return. The entire surplus of the business, after the preference shareholders and creditors have had their due, belongs to the ordinary shareholders. For this reason the equity interest in the business comprises the ordinary share capital and the reserves which belong to the ordinary shareholders.

Some classes of share are redeemable. This means that the capital sum can be repaid by the company to the shareholders. The normal rules for such a redemption state that it can be made out of profits or reserves available for distribution, or it can be financed by a fresh issue of shares. If the redemption is made out of reserves, then a capital redemption reserve must be established. In effect this means that part of the reserves available for dividend are transferred to a capital redemption reserve, which is a reserve not available for dividend. Thus if a company repays part of its share capital without raising fresh capital it must establish a reserve not available for distribution to replace the share capital repaid, so that the rights of the creditors to be repaid before shareholders are not prejudiced in any way. Like the share premium account, the use of the capital redemption reserve is restricted. It can be used only to pay up new shares which can be issued as a bonus or scrip issue, or to offset the effect of writing off preliminary expenses or the premium paid on the redemption of a debenture, or to write off discounts on issue of shares or debentures.

Debentures

A debenture is the written acknowledgement of a debt. When this acknowledgement is made by a company it is a contract made under seal of the company, providing for a fixed rate of interest to be paid on the sum loaned to the company and specifying terms for the repayment of the principal at the end of the period. The debenture, therefore, is a long-term loan. There is, however, some confusion about terminology. In the legal sense the term debenture is used to describe any long-term loan, evidenced by a deed or contract, whether it is secured or not, but in the financial press the term debenture is usually restricted to cover only long-term loans which are secured, while unsecured long-term loans are called loan stock. A debenture deed has a trustee whose task it is to protect the interests of the debenture holders or lenders. In normal circumstances the trustee has little to do, since the interest will be paid on the due date regularly each quarter or half-year as specified in the agreement. However, if the interest is not paid, then the trustee can act to demand its payment or, in the event of the collapse of the borrowing business, he can demand the repayment of the debenture holders' principal. If the debenture is secured, then the trustee can take charge of the assets which comprise the security and sell them to provide funds from which the debenture holders will be paid. Often the security will be fixed on a specific asset of the company, e.g. the buildings, and it is these which will be taken over by the trustee and sold to meet the repayment. Sometimes, however, the security is of a floating nature, which means that the trustee can take control of any of the assets of the business when the need arises. The term used in this case is that the floating security 'crystallizes' on a certain asset. A floating security is useful in cases where the assets of the business are unsuitable for a fixed charge, or where the assets of the business fluctuate on a day-to-day basis. This means that if a company has little in the way of fixed assets such as property or plant but carries a large volume of stock, this asset which is turned over every day can be taken as security for a debenture. Clearly the value of the stock will fluctuate and may be uncertain at the time when the debenture is issued. A floating charge is subject to the further disadvantage that a seller of goods may 'reserve title' until payment is made, or a fixed security may already exist as a prior charge on certain assets; in both of these cases the floating charge will not attach to the assets concerned. The holder of a floating security can only move against the assets of a business when interest remains unpaid or on a winding up, but an individual trade creditor can prove a debt before the court and levy execution of that debt on the assets of a business before winding-up proceedings are commenced. A naked debenture is one which has no security at all. The holder of a naked debenture will rank *pari passu* with the ordinary creditors of the business at the time of a winding up.

A debenture holder is not a member of a company, but a creditor thereof with a claim against the business. As such the fixed interest is paid on this debt whether or not a profit has been made and this interest is considered a charge against, not an appropriation of, profit. This means that such interest is held by the Inland Revenue to be an expense of the business allowable as a deduction against profits for corporation tax purposes. In effect the burden of debenture interest will be borne partly by the state, since for every pound of interest paid taxable profit will be reduced and corporation tax at, say, 35 per cent in the pound will be saved. Thus it is cheaper to finance the business by means of debentures, whose holders are not members of the company, than by the issue of fixed return preference shares which do not have this tax advantage, until the corporation tax rate falls. The real rate of interest on a 15 per cent debenture is $0.65 \times 15\% = 9.75\%$, after tax is taken into account.

From the viewpoint of the investor a debenture with its priority right and certainty of interest and repayment is much less risky than preference or ordinary shares. A debenture holder can sell a holding on the market, but the price offered for a fixed return security will fluctuate with the general rate of interest. Debentures with a coupon rate of 10 per cent will be worth 10/8 of their face value when the market rate of interest stands at 8 per cent. But if the market rate rises to 16 per cent, the 10 per cent debentures will only be worth 10/16 of their face value. Debenture holders do not possess voting rights, so there will be no dilution of control with the issue of debentures. The need to repay the debt eventually, and the cost of interest up to that time, may prove a burden if profits fall, and will act to reduce cash flow.

Sometimes a debenture carries with it the right to convert to an ordinary share at the option of the holder. Conversion rights state a date or dates by which the option must be exercised, and the number of ordinary shares to be acquired for each £100 worth of debentures. Usually fewer shares are offered as succeeding dates are passed. The debenture holder gains the advantage that, if he thinks the company has good growth prospects, he can switch his investment to equity, or, if he is doubtful about future results, he can stay safe with loan capital. In return for this advantage he usually receives a slightly lower rate of interest.

CAPITAL GEARING

Gearing, or leverage, as the American textbooks call it, is the relationship between the fixed return capital and equity capital used to finance the operations of a business. It is sometimes expressed as a ratio whereby one sets fixed return capital against equity, or alternatively against the aggregate of fixed return and equity capital. As one would expect, there is some debate among accountants as to the precise definition of the parts of this ratio. The capital structure of the business is built up by recruiting capital from ordinary shares, preference shares and long-term loans, and gearing is the relationship between the fixed return and equity proportions of this structure. Fixed return capital is generally taken to mean preference shares, debentures and loan stock, all of which are serviced by a fixed rate of dividend or interest. Some authorities, however, argue that bank loans and overdrafts receive a fixed rate of return and should be included in the definition. There is some degree of acceptance for this idea, but much less for the suggestion that loans from trade creditors should be included, since they are of a fluctuating nature and bear no interest charge at all. Equity capital is sometimes included as the par value of ordinary shares only, but in most cases the reserves are added to this amount to change it to the equity interest in the business.

Gearing is said to be high when there is a large proportion of fixed return capital in the capital structure of a company, and low when the equity interest comprises a large proportion of the capital. The following example shows the effect on the return to equity of profit fluctuation in a highly geared situation.

Example

Company A has a share capital of 400 000 £1 ordinary shares, 40 000 £1 14 per cent preference shares, and £60 000 of 16 per cent debentures. Company B has a share capital of 200 000 £1 ordinary shares, 40 000 £1 14 per cent preference shares, and £260 000 of 16 per cent debentures.

	A £	B £
Ordinary shares	400 000	200 000
14 per cent preference shares	40 000	40 000
16 per cent debentures	60 000	260 000
Net capital employed	£500 000	£500 000

$$\text{Gearing} \quad \frac{\text{Fixed return capital}}{\text{Total capital}} \times \frac{100}{1}$$

	A	B
	$\dfrac{100}{500} \times \dfrac{100}{1}$	$\dfrac{300}{500} \times \dfrac{100}{1}$
	20%	60%
	Low	High

Assume that in year 1 each company makes a profit before interest but after tax of £125 000, and that in year 2 there is a 20 per cent increase in this profit figure to £150 000. The return on capital employed for both companies is 125/500 × 100/1 = 25% in year 1. In year 1 the profit would be allocated as follows:

	A £	B £
Net profit before interest but after tax	125 000	125 000
Interest and dividend to fixed return capital:		
Debentures	(9 600)	(41 600)
Preference shares	(5 600)	(5 600)
Profit available for ordinary shareholders	£109 800	£77 800
Earnings per share [EPS]	27.45 pence	38.9 pence

Clearly shareholders in B receive a better return on their investment than those in A. Remember B is a highly geared company, and has recruited a large proportion of its funds at 16 per cent, which have been invested to earn a ROCE of 25 per cent. This surplus belongs to the shareholders and boosts their earnings. The situation changes in year 2, when as profit increases the benefits of high gearing are felt by the shareholders of company B.

	A £	B £
Net profit before interest but after tax	150 000	150 000
Interest and dividend to fixed return capital (as before)	15 200	47 200
Profit available for ordinary shareholders	£134 800	£102 800
Earnings per share	33.7 pence	51.4 pence
Increase in EPS over year 1	6.25 pence	12.5 pence
Increase in EPS as a percentage of year 1	22%	32%

All the increased profit belongs to ordinary shareholders, since the rights of prior right capital are already covered, but in B there are fewer shareholders to divide up the increase.

Now assume that in year 3 the profit of both companies falls by 33 per cent from £150 000 to £100 000.

	A £	B £
Net profit before interest but after tax	100 000	100 000
Interest and dividend to fixed return capital	15 200	47 200
Profit available for ordinary shareholders	£ 84 800	£ 52 800
Earnings per share	21.2 pence	26.4 pence
Percentage fall in EPS	34%	48.6%

In B, a fall in profit of one-third causes a near 50 per cent reduction in shareholders' earnings. High gearing seems to be advantageous when profit is increasing, but shareholders may be penalized if profit falls. Remember that in B, if in year 4 profit falls below £47 200, the ordinary shareholders will have earned nothing, but shareholders in A would still have an EPS of eight pence per share (£47 200 − £15 200 ÷ 400 000 shares).

This example shows that a disproportionate increase in the profit available to one class of capital providers is the consequence of the highly geared capital structure whereby profit is made from the fixed return funds invested in the business, and any surplus of that profit over the interest required to service the fixed return capital can be used to increase the return on the ordinary shares. Another benefit is that debenture interest is a tax deductible expense, and the cost net of tax is much less than the coupon rate.

Thus we are led to the conclusion that if the management of a company are able to raise the gearing of the company by recruiting fresh fixed return capital, and make more in profit from the use of that capital than is needed to service it, then the surplus will increase the return available to ordinary shareholders. The equity interest is thus claimed to benefit from a highly geared situation. However, this is not always true. What if profits fluctuate in a downward direction? The fixed return would still need to be serviced, and if, as in year 4 of the above example, there were no surplus after interest had been paid, then the dividend would be passed. Real problems would follow if profit in one year was not sufficient to cover the fixed return, as interest must be paid whether or not a profit exists. It seems, therefore, that although the ordinary shareholder who bears the risk in the company receives all the super profits when they are made, he will also be the first to suffer if profits fall away.

A final point with regard to raising the gearing in a company concerns the repayment of capital and the risk borne by the ordinary shareholders. When the gearing is raised by increasing fixed return capital, perhaps using the fixed assets as security, this new group from whom finance has been raised now has a prior right to interest or dividend out of profit and repayment of principal before the claims of ordinary shareholders are met. Because this group has been interposed in front of the ordinary shareholders, the risk borne by the ordinary shareholders may be said to have increased and thus the return they would expect for taking a greater risk would also need to increase.

Example

The true cost of funds raised to finance a business by debentures should be calculated after tax because interest is a tax allowable expense, e.g. a 16 per cent debenture after allowing for corporation tax at 35 per cent costs 16% × 0.65 = 10.4%.

The significance of gearing on profit available for reinvestment in the business is shown by the following computation, assuming facts as for companies A and B above, and a profit of £150 000 and a dividend of 15 pence per share.

	A	B
	£	£
Net operating profit	150 000	150 000
Less debenture interest (16 per cent)	9 600	41 600
Taxable profit	140 400	108 400
Corporation tax at 35 per cent	49 140	37 940
	91 260	37 940
Dividend on preference shares	5 600	5 600
	85 660	64 860
Ordinary dividend at 10p per share	60 000	30 000
Profit available for retention	£25 660	£34 860

B, the highly geared company, has more profit available as a source of finance to fund future expansion. However, A has greater flexibility within its capital structure, because a smaller proportion of its assets are tied up as security for the debentures. Thus the low-geared company is able to finance expansion by raising long-term loans secured against this uncharged property, but if it raises its gearing in this way, the risk to shareholders will increase.

A highly geared company must always ensure that sufficient profit is earned to cover interest payments and take full advantage of corporation tax relief. Common sense suggests that gearing should be raised to give shareholders an advantage, but not too high in case profits cannot be maintained. A norm of 30 per cent is suggested, but an appropriate figure depends upon the circumstances of each individual company, e.g. the fixed assets available as security and likely fluctuations of profit.

TUTORIAL DISCUSSION TOPICS

20.1

Balance Sheet of X Ltd			
	£		£
£1 ordinary shares	40 000	Fixed assets	70 000
7 per cent £1 preference shares	16 000	Current assets	20 000
Reserves	24 000		
Liabilities	10 000		
	£90 000		£90 000

(a) Distinguish between the ordinary and the preference shares as regards dividend, return of capital on winding up, and voting rights.
(b) What does the expression 'cumulative' mean in connection with preference shares? Are the above preference shares cumulative?

20.2

Balance Sheet of Y Ltd			
	£		£
Ordinary shares, par value	60 000	Fixed assets	100 000
7 per cent £1 preference shares	20 000	Current assets	60 000
6 per cent debentures	24 000		
Reserves	36 000		
Liabilities	20 000		
	£160 000		£160 000

(a) Distinguish between the preference shares and the debentures as regards security of holders' investments, return on investments (certainty and treatment in accounts), and status of holders.

(b) Why is the rate of interest on the debentures lower than the dividend on the preference shares?

20.3 Ordinary share capital is sometimes referred to as the equity of a company. Why?

20.4

Balance Sheet of Z Ltd			
	£		£
Ordinary shares, par value	60 000	Fixed assets	140 000
Share premium			
account	20 000	Current assets	60 000
Revenue reserves	100 000		
Creditors	20 000		
	£200 000		£200 000

(a) How will the share premium account have arisen, and for what purposes can it be used?

(b) If the company was to declare a dividend of 33⅓ pence per share of £1 ordinary shares, how could you reply to the criticism that shareholders were getting their money back in three years?

(c) What are the arguments for capitalizing part of the reserves?

20.5 The promoters of a new company estimate that it will initially need £100 000 in long-term funds to finance its activities. The following capital structures have been suggested:

	(1)	(2)
	£	£
Ordinary shares	80 000	30 000
8 per cent cumulative		
preference shares	10 000	20 000
7 per cent debentures	5 000	50 000
6 per cent convertible loan		
stock (repayable 1980)	5 000	—
	£100 000	£100 000

(a) Discuss the advantages and disadvantages of the above alternatives.

(b) What additional information would you require in order to advise the promoters on the two alternatives suggested?

21 | Major Sources of Finance for Business

Business finance is concerned with the provision of funds for investment in business enterprise. Whatever is invested in this way must be provided by an investor, and this means that the investor must forgo consumption and save to provide the funds. Savers and the users of their funds come together in the market for finance, where the normal rules of supply and demand apply unless there is Government interference with interest rates. The price of money is the rate of return paid for its use. If the demand for investment funds is greater than the funds offered for investment by savers, then the rate of interest will rise until people in the economy are induced to forgo consumption and make their savings available for investment. The money market is worldwide, and is limited only by communication difficulties and problems of transferring funds from one economy to another. Within each country the money market tends to be concentrated in one place, where the important institutions of the market have their offices, e.g. in the City of London there is the Stock Exchange, the banks, and pension and life assurance companies. However, finance is also local, e.g. the banks have established a network of branches nationwide.

The mechanics of the market for finance are not as simple as, for example, a local country market for eggs or butter, where buyers and sellers meet. The market for finance involves the use of many intermediary institutions such as banks, stockbrokers, unit trusts, pension funds and life assurance companies, which are geared to accepting the savings of many individuals and channelling them to the businesses which need the funds for investment. Savers can invest their funds in a wide range of different industries and companies, and at different levels of risk. They can also choose from many types of investment, e.g. an ordinary share in or a loan to a company, or a deposit in a bank, which is lent in turn by the bank to a company in the form of an overdraft or loan. In this way the saver may not be directly connected to the business which uses his money. An important influence in the financial market is the Government, which borrows in advance of tax revenue, and sometimes in excess of tax revenue, in order to pay for its current expenditure.

A small business may be limited to the amount of money that the proprietor can invest in it. If it is to expand extra funds must be recruited from elsewhere, and the return for the use of these funds must be met out of profits. The proprietor may offer a share of the business and its profits to tempt a saver to entrust funds to the firm, but on the other hand the saver may prefer to lend money to a firm on the understanding that the interest is to be paid whether a profit is made or not, and that the funds can be disinvested and returned on a certain date. This depends perhaps on the investor's need to use the funds at a future time, or perhaps on his psychological make-up, i.e. whether he is a risk seeker or a risk averter.

The risks encountered in business can be caused by natural hazards such as drought, flood, or the death of a key employee, or calamities such as war or revolution. Other risks encountered are of an economic nature, for example a fall in demand for a product because of a change in taste or fashion, or losses as the consequence of inefficient management, bad product design, or strikes caused by poor industrial relations. The causes of some types of risk are thus outside the control of the business, while others are a direct consequence of circumstances within the business. If an investor is to take a risk there must be the chance of high reward as well as the chance of failure.

The funds needed to finance a business can be divided between fixed capital and working capital. The fixed element of the capital employed is sunk into fixed assets such as machinery and buildings, while the working capital is turned over in the short term, in a cycle from cash to stock, work in progress, finished goods, debtors and back to cash again. Some funds will be provided to finance current assets from bank overdrafts and trade creditors for goods supplied, thus reducing the amount of funds from the firm's own resources needed to finance stocks, debtors etc. The level of stocks and debtors in the business may fluctuate over time, but usually an amount below which they will not fall can be established. It is necessary, therefore, when reviewing the capital structure of a business, to compute the amount of funds which will be needed permanently in the business and thus discover the amount of funds needed during peak periods of activity only.

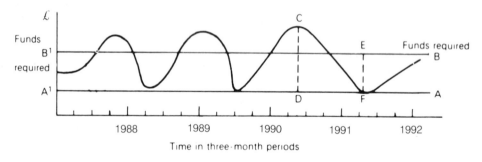

Figure 10. The fluctuations of funds required are caused by varying levels of stocks, debtors and work in progress, in what appears to be a seasonal trade. If the company grows over the period the lines A^1A and B^1B will slope upwards from left to right.

The business must determine whether to raise long-term funds up to level A^1A or B^1B (figure 10). If finance is raised up to level A^1A then the amount DC will be needed as short-term funds at peak periods of activity. In the situation where short-term borrowing is more costly than long-term finance, this could be expensive. However, if long-term funds are borrowed up to level B^1B, while the expensive short-term requirement is reduced, some of the long-term finance may lie idle during periods when business activity slumps (FE). Even though they are not utilized to earn a profit, such funds will still need to be serviced by way of interest. The decision as to the form of the company's financial structure is one in which the flexibility of expensive short-term finance must be set off against the cost of servicing long-term funds during periods when they are not fully employed. Another factor which influences this decision is the ability to raise short-term funds at the precise time when they are needed, and the availability of assets to act as security for long-term loans. Gearing and its effect on the riskiness of the business as perceived by potential shareholders is also significant for this decision.

The cost of long-term finance will vary according to when it is raised. If it is raised at a time when interest rates are high the company, once it is committed, will have to pay these rates for many years. It may therefore be preferable to borrow short term and delay a long-term commitment until rates improve.

PROFIT RETENTION AS A SOURCE OF FUNDS

A large and well-established business will have access to the market of the Stock Exchange as a means of raising funds, since, as a public company, it can offer its shares to investors in general. Despite the presence of this wide market for funds, the fact remains that the most significant source of capital for British industry is ploughed-back profits, or profits retained in the business. The appropriation of profit is in three main directions: a proportion is paid to the Inland Revenue as corporation tax; a proportion is paid out to the shareholders as dividends; and the remainder is reinvested in the business. Profits retained in the business are shown in the balance sheet as reserves, and the funds they represent are invested in the general assets of the business. The board of directors decides how much of the profit available for dividend is to be paid out. This decision is important, since it involves a fine calculation of the amount needed to satisfy the shareholders and thus maintain the price of the shares, while ensuring that sufficient funds are reinvested in the business to maintain its financial health. If too little profit is retained the business may find itself starved of funds and be unable to expand or modernize, while if a large proportion of profit is retained the dividend payment to shareholders will be small, and the shareholders may express their dissatisfaction through comment at the annual general meeting or by selling their shares and reinvesting in another company. If this happens the price of the shares on the Stock Exchange will fall and, although the company is financially healthy, it may be the subject of a takeover bid, since the share price undervalues the assets involved. The profit-retention decision is thus a difficult one, since the need to modernize or to support the present level of activity during an inflationary period must be balanced against the need to maintain the confidence of the shareholders.

THE LONG-TERM CAPITAL MARKET

A public company can raise fresh capital from the market by an issue of shares, debentures or loan stock. Sometimes loan stock is issued with a conversion right which allows the owner to convert his stock to ordinary shares at a future date. The decision about whether to issue shares or fixed-return securities such as debentures will be determined by the ability to provide security for the debentures, the need to retain control so that the issue of voting shares is avoided, and the impact of a new issue on the gearing of the business.

There are several methods by which a public company can issue shares:

1. The best known one is a *public issue by prospectus*. In this activity the company is helped by an issuing house, usually a subsidiary or department of a merchant bank, which organizes the issue. A prospectus is compiled which gives full details of the shares to be offered, the company and its prospects, and what it intends to do with the funds once they are raised. The prospectus is accompanied by an advertisement, strictly governed by the rules of the Stock Exchange, and special bank accounts are opened for the application and allotment monies. The advertisement ends with an invitation to the public to apply for the shares, loan stock or debentures. The issuing house has given advice about the timing of the issue and the price at which the shares or fixed-return stock are to be issued. If the shares of a company are popular it will be possible to issue them at a premium, but if the market is dull or there is some doubt about the success of the issue, then debentures or loan stock (but not shares unless sanctioned by the High Court) may be issued at a discount, e.g. £97 for a £100 stock certificate. Such an issue is usually underwritten by a firm of professional underwriters who contract to take up any shares or debentures not subscribed for by the public. In this way the company is guaranteed a successful issue so far as raising its funds is concerned. However, the underwriters will try to unload the blocks of shares or stock they have taken up from an unsuccessful issue, so the price of these securities could be depressed for some months. A public issue by prospectus is an expensive method to use, since underwriting, bank commission, advertising, legal and accounting fees, capital duty and issuing house expenses must be paid, and it has been estimated that as much as 6 or 7 per cent of the money raised by the issue goes to meet these costs. Accordingly, this method is only used to raise large amounts, say £1 million at least. Sometimes the technique of a *rights issue* is used. In this case the shareholders of the business are circularized and told of the offer, which is made to them at what appears to be an advantageous price. They are then able to take up the offer and subscribe for the shares or sell their rights to the offer to another investor.

2. An *offer for sale* has now to some extent superseded the prospectus method. In this case the company issues shares directly to an issuing house, which then offers them for sale to the public at a fixed price. This is also an expensive method, and is best used when the size of the issue is too small to merit a public issue by prospectus, or when a significant shareholder in the business decides to retire or sell his interest. In cases where the company requiring the finance is not well known to potential investors it will rely on the reputation of the issuing house to attract funds. The issuing houses are very particular about the shares they offer to the public, since an unsuccessful issue could harm their reputation from which their ability to act is derived.

3. The technique of a *'placing'* is one which can be used in both private and public companies. The shares to be issued are placed with a number of investors by an intermediary. In the case of a large placing, a merchant bank or issuing house will be used, and it will communicate via an offer document with other institutions such as pension funds and insurance companies in order to place the shares with them without the expense of a public issue. A placing on a smaller scale can be undertaken by a solicitor or broker who has contacts with companies or

individuals who will take up a share stake in the business if it is offered at the right price. A placing avoids the expense of going to the market and allows a smaller amount of funds to be raised than is economic for a public issue, but it can still be underwritten. The Stock Exchange authorities keep a close watch on placings by public companies, since these avoid the mechanism of the market. The institutions are more likely to invest if they trust the intermediary to prepare and present appropriate material, and to enquire diligently into the performance and position of the company.

4. An *offer by tender* is sometimes used as an alternative to a public issue by prospectus. In this event shares or loan stock are offered to the public with a prospectus attached, but the offer is not made at a fixed price. The investors are left to tender or offer the price at which they are willing to invest in the shares or debentures. The company states a minimum price below which shares will not be offered, but the shares are issued at what is termed the striking price, which is the lowest price offered by those tendering for the shares at which the shares on issue are all taken up. This means that if an investor offers to take up shares at a price above the striking price he will receive those shares at the striking price, but if an investor offers below the striking price he will be unsuccessful.

5. *An introduction.* The mechanism of the finance market so far as the flotation of share issues is concerned is really open only to larger companies, because the costs of an issue are too great to make it economic for small issues. When the small company expands it can do so by recruiting finance from short-term sources, but a point is reached when it can expand no further from these sources, and requires an injection of long-term funds. If such a company has not grown to a size which makes it economic to come to the market, it will find it difficult to obtain finance for further expansion. Many large private companies seek to change to public status by a Stock Exchange introduction, which is effected by an offer for sale or a public placing, after the strict regulations of the Exchange have been met.

   If the shares of a public limited company are to be 'listed' or traded on the Stock Exchange, it is necessary to ensure that sufficient shares are available to 'make a market' and that those shares are not concentrated in the hands of relatively few shareholders who may not wish to buy or sell on a regular basis. Marketability of those shares is important to a company seeking an introduction. The company need not prepare a prospectus as with a public issue, but will need to supply the information required by the Stock Exchange, whose regulations are to be found in 'The Yellow Book' issued by the Stock Exchange. The issuer must disclose all material facts in these listing documents and compensation may be payable to investors for false or misleading statements. To be successful in an application for listing, the company should have at least £700 000 of equity shares, but in fact companies applying for listing usually have a market capitalization of at least £5 000 000. A further rule is that at least 25 per cent of any class of ordinary shares in a company must be in the hands of the public to ensure that there is a fair market in the shares. A good trading record over at least a five-year period preceding the application, and the possession of significant assets, are other requirements for a successful introduction. Many growing companies prefer to achieve quotation on the unlisted securities market and then, having grown some more, transfer their listing to the main Stock Exchange. A common procedure is to combine an introduction onto the Stock Exchange with either a public issue or an offer for sale.

A company may expand by using short-term finance, which it later replaces by a funding operation. Long-term funds are raised and used to repay the short-term finance, which is then available for use in the next stage of expansion.

THE INSTITUTIONAL INVESTORS

There seems to be a size beyond which companies cannot grow without an injection of long-term funds, but sometimes there is a gap between the size to which they can grow by the use of their own resources and the size which they need to be before they are big enough to make a public issue. To help small companies to expand across this gap or step (the MacMillan gap), other financial institutions have been developed. First there is Finance for Industry, which has taken over the Industrial and Commercial Finance Corporation. This was a body set up under the auspices of the Bank of England which made available to small companies money provided by the major banks. A subsidiary of ICFC was Technical Development Capital Ltd, which still uses funds provided by the major banks to encourage technical innovations and improvements. A similar institution is the Estate Duties Investment Trust, which uses its funds, provided by insurance companies and investment trusts, to help private companies over the awkward period when the payment of inheritance tax consequent upon the death of a major shareholder causes problems of cash shortage within the family who run the business. 'Edith', as this institution is known, acts as an investment trust to buy a share stake in such businesses to encourage them to grow, and then to sell its share stake when eventually the business is large enough to go public.

A number of other institutions have also developed to assist the small company to grow until it becomes large enough to go public. Foremost among these are the merchant banks, which are large banks in private ownership (their shares can be bought and sold on the Stock Exchange) which, as their name implies, used to be involved in the finance of foreign trade by means of bills of exchange. Over the last twenty years, however, they have changed the market in which they operate and, although the bill market is still important, they are now more involved in the provision of finance to growing businesses. Most merchant banks have an issuing house department, and some provide an underwriting service. They also provide advice and financial assistance in takeover battles on the sides of both the attacker and the defender. A merchant bank likes to make contact with a small growing company early in its existence and help it to expand by providing loan capital or by taking a stake in its shares. Sometimes a merchant bank will appoint a director to the board of the company to watch over its interests and to provide helpful financial advice. When the company has grown large enough to cross the gap and apply to the Stock Exchange for a public quotation of its shares with a view to making a public issue, the issuing house department of its merchant bank will organize the issue. Later in the life of the company, when amalgamations or takeover negotiations take place, the merchant bank gives help and advice.

A similar institution in the finance market is the investment trust, which is not a trust in the normal sense of the word, but is really a public company whose shares can be traded on the Stock Exchange. An investment trust is a company which holds the shares of other companies. Its task is to invest its funds in a portfolio of other companies, both large and small, so that it spreads its risk and makes a profit from the investment expertise of its directors.

There is often no clear line of demarcation between merchant banks and investment trusts, since both will operate what are called 'city nurseries', where a number of small but profitable private businesses are encouraged to expand and then are helped to go public.

Unit trusts are institutions within the finance market whose task it is to channel savings from their many unit holders to be invested in companies. The unit trusts, the life assurance companies, and the pension funds collect the savings of many people and convert them to investment by buying shares and debentures both privately and on the market. These institutions spread their risk and do not want to dominate any company in which they invest, but during a takeover bid the institutions, with their large block holdings of shares, are the ones whose votes are most significant in deciding whether or not the bid is successful. When a merchant bank has a block of shares to place, it contacts unit trusts, assurance companies and pension funds, and is usually able to place the shares with them without much difficulty.

THE UNLISTED SECURITIES MARKET (USM)

This market was opened in 1980 to give medium-sized but growing businesses some access to a wider financial market for their shares. A successful launch in this market followed by a sound record of profit and dividend makes it easier for a company to gain a full listing on the Stock Exchange. A three-year record of successful operations and a market capitalization in excess of £1 million are required. The costs of entry to the USM are considerably less than for a quotation on the main Stock Exchange and a company need only offer 10 per cent of its equity to the public to make a market on this exchange.

Other advantages of a quotation on the USM include the ability to raise capital from a wider spectrum of investors, and, to directors who have founded a private limited company, the ability to realize part of their initial investment without losing control of their business. The fact that the company now has a quote increases its reputation amongst financial institutions, who may now be more willing to lend money to the business. If shares are quoted on the market it is possible to motivate management by setting up a share incentive scheme. If a company wishes to expand by acquisition, the fact that its shares are quoted enables it to bid for another company in terms of shares as well as cash. Considerable public relations advantages accrue to a business which is listed in this way.

The advantage of listing brings also the liability to disclose more information to the public and puts managerial performance under the spotlight of scrutiny from investors and financial commentators. If a growing business has a share quote, it may find that another quoted 'predator' company may be tempted to make a takeover bid for what it sees as a profitable investment. In general the USM has been successful in its objective to provide finance for small but growing companies, helping such companies to achieve a full listing. In 1987 a 'third market' began trading in the shares of eight companies. This market is available to help companies which have not yet progressed to a situation where they can join the USM. Only one set of statutory accounts need be produced but there are no requirements to announce half-year profit figures or any minimum proportion of the share capital which must be in the public hands.

VENTURE CAPITAL

Capital of this type is provided by an institution or individual to a small but growing firm and can take the form of a share stake in the business, or a loan. Such growth situations are inevitably risky and the venture capitalist seeks a good return in a relatively short period by selling the investment after the company has made significant progress. Venture capital can take the form of 'start-up' funds for a new business, assistance for young companies after they have traded successfully, and development capital for specific situations in established companies. The venture capitalist may also assist in a management buy-out. An entrepreneur running a profitable private limited company may be unable to finance the growth required from the retention of profits and may find that the more traditional providers of finance are too cautious to invest in a high-growth/high-margin situation. In this situation the proprietor/manager may be forced to consider offering a minority share stake to a venture capitalist in return for the funds which are desperately needed by the business.

To be successful in raising funds from a venture capitalist, a small firm must be able to demonstrate that it has certain qualities:

(a) a competent and skilled management team which is motivated to work hard and achieve high growth;
(b) a product capable of making progress in the market;
(c) ability to keep up with technological change and to compete adequately with other companies in the same business;
(d) the absence of dependence on suppliers or other financial institutions.

A feasible venture investment will also be equipped with an exit route, whereby the venture capitalist can recoup the investment either when the company goes public by a listing on the USM, or perhaps if it is likely to be acquired by a larger company in a takeover bid. A significant factor in a venture capital proposal is that the company should have developed a sound business plan providing the information which the venture capitalist requires about its products, management, operations, marketing methods, and financial situations.

MANAGEMENT BUY-OUTS (MBOs)

This is a specialist form of transaction, whereby a group of managers combine to make an offer for a part, or the whole, of a business. Finance to pay for the purchase is partly provided from the managers' own resources, but most of the funds are derived from long-term loans furnished by financial institutions. Accordingly the resulting company is owned by its former managers but is encumbered by a significant measure of debt. Such a capital structure is highly geared, and, for this reason, MBOs are often referred to as 'leveraged bids'.

An MBO will take place when a large company reviews the significance of a segment of the business for the overall group strategy with the intention of concentrating on core activities. When a receiver sells a failed business as a going concern, or when major shareholders in a private company wish to retire and sell their controlling interest in the business, a further opportunity may occur for managers to buy a share stake in a business. In these circumstances the existing managers are well placed to gauge the likely success of the business they are buying, and to make a bid.

The vendor company may wish to divest itself of a division of the business which does not fit well into the core activity of the group, and to release funds to finance the development of the core. A group of companies will regularly review the portfolio of its investments, or may wish to sell part of a business which it has recently purchased. For example, a firm of publishers taken over by a large newspaper company might have an academic publishing division, which is not in line with the core activity of the new group. Such a division will be hived off and sold.

Participation in an MBO is a risky activity for the managers concerned, since they stand to lose a significant part of their private fortune if the new company fails. However, the bid is based on their confidence in their own ability to run the business successfully. The financier will be satisfied with an investment at favourable rates, probably secured on the assets of the business, and perhaps with a part of the equity of the business included. A management 'buy-in' is where an enterprising manager sees an investment opportunity in another company, and organizes the finance to buy a share of that company for himself or herself.

THE COST OF CAPITAL

If it is the main objective of a business to maximize the wealth of shareholders in the long run, the management should only invest in projects which give a return in excess of the cost of investment funds used to finance such projects. If the capital employed in the business has been recruited from a range of sources, it may be difficult to determine the cost of funds applied to individual projects.

The measurement of a true business profit is dependent on adequate capital maintenance included in the calculation, but the measurement of the likely return from an investment before funds are committed is dependent upon an estimate of cash flows throughout the life of the investment. Clearly it is only profitable to invest in a project if cash flowing in from the project exceeds cash flowing out. Since flows in are experienced over a period of years they must be discounted to show their present value, in order to be accurately compared with cash flowing out at the commencement of the project. The discount factor which is usually applied in this calculation of present value is the cost of capital to the firm. If a project results in a cash inflow pattern which exceeds the outflows and the cost of capital tied up in the project, then a profit is assured. The cost of capital is difficult to define because a business will recruit funds from various sources, so a weighted average cost of capital is calculated based on the capital structure of the firm. Risk, which is influenced by gearing, will in turn influence the cost of capital of the various types of finance in the capital structure. Tax must of course be taken into account where it is relevant.

Equity

Shareholders will expect a dividend on their investment but they also require growth. The cost of equity is therefore the dividend yield necessary to satisfy investors in the market, plus a factor to account for growth expectations. Expressed as a formula this amount can be calculated as

$$\text{Cost of equity} = \frac{\text{Dividend}}{\text{Current share price}} + \text{Growth}$$

For example, assume that a company has issued £1 ordinary shares on which it is currently paying a dividend of 10.2 pence per share, and that these shares are currently priced in the market at 150 pence each with an expected growth factor of 10 per cent. When the formula is applied to these figures the calculation is

$$10.2/150 \text{ expressed as a percentage} + 10\% = 16.8\%$$

Retained earnings, the reserves in the business, generated from past profits, have the same cost of capital as ordinary shares, because if a company expects shareholders to leave profits in a business then a similar return to that earned on the shares must be made on these shareholders' funds.

Debt

The cost of debt is the rate of interest adjusted for the fact that interest is an allowable expense for corporation tax purposes. Assuming debentures with an interest rate of 16 per cent, and applying a corporation tax rate of 35 per cent, the formula is

$$\text{Cost} = \text{Interest}\,(1 - \text{tax rate}) = 16 \times (1 - 0.35) = 16 \times 0.65 = 10.4\%$$

The same logic can be applied to overdraft or other short-term bank loans. Assuming a short-term bank loan at 18 per cent, the formula gives the cost of capital of 11.7 per cent for this part of the company's capital structure. The next step is to apply these rates to the capital structure of the company weighted for the various types of capital. Assume that the company has issued 8 million ordinary shares of £1 each, that it has retained earnings of £5 million, 16 per cent debentures of £4 million and a short-term bank loan of £3 million at a rate of 18 per cent. The following computation will calculate the weighted average cost of capital for this business.

	Capital structure	Weighting	×	Cost	=	Weighted Cost
£8 000 000	£1 ordinary shares 8/20	40%		16.8%		6.720
£5 000 000	Retained earnings 5/20	25%		16.8%		4.200
£4 000 000	16 per cent debentures 4/20	20%		10.4%		2.080
£3 000 000	Bank loan on 18 per cent 3/20	15%		11.7%		1.755
£20 000 000		100%				14.755%

As an approximation a cost of capital of 15 per cent could be used.

OTHER METHODS OF FINANCE

There are other ways in which a company can finance the purchase of an asset which it needs without raising capital. A company may undertake a sale and lease-back operation, which is a financial technique to set free some funds that are tied up in fixed assets so that they can be used elsewhere in the business. For example, suppose a company owns a large office block as its headquarters, and wishes to invest £500 000 in new plant for its factory. The company may contact a city institution or property company with a view to selling its headquarters office block to the institution, a term of the contract of sale being that the company can lease back the premises for the payment of a rent. In this way the manufacturing company can continue to use the building, while at the same time it now has the funds it needs to purchase the machinery. The property company or city institution has a good investment, since it now possesses a prime piece of property let to a reputable company at a fair rental, and it also gains any increase in value achieved by the property because of inflation or other reasons. This technique thus has advantages for both parties. If the company had mortgaged its office block it could have borrowed the required funds and retained ownership of the building, but the payment of interest and repayment of the loan may have created cash flow problems. Sale and lease back releases the full market value of the asset, whereas a mortgage only raises funds equal to a proportion of this value. The mortgage alternative does, however, mean that the company retains the ownership of the property, so any increase in value falls to the company rather than the financier.

The practice of leasing is another way in which a company can gain the use of an asset without investing a capital sum. Instead of borrowing money to buy an asset it can lease or rent the asset from a leasing company. In the UK it is possible to lease a wide range of assets, from typewriters for a period of months, through vehicles for several years, to large pieces of plant for longer periods. There is usually a distinction between an operating lease for a short period and a capital or finance lease for a large item over a long period. The leasing company (lessor) which is usually a subsidiary of one of the larger banks or insurance companies, buys the asset and is the legal owner, but the lessee company uses the asset in its business in return for paying a rental or hire charge to the lessor. The accounting procedure involved in leasing means that, since the asset does not belong to the user company, it does not appear in the balance sheet. Nor does the liability to pay future rentals under the lease agreement, although this is certainly a liability which exists at law. Thus the balance sheet fails to show the asset and the liability. It is now suggested that in the case of finance leases the accounts of the lessee company should reflect the true situation. SSAP 21 separates long-term finance leases from short-term operating leases and stipulates that assets acquired under a finance lease should appear on the balance sheet, even though they do not belong to the lessee company; that such assets should be depreciated in the normal way, and that the future rental liability should also be disclosed as a balance sheet item.

It is also possible for a company to enter into a hire purchase agreement with a finance company, whereby it can pay for assets which it uses, not before it possesses them but out of the profits created while it is using them. With hire purchase the asset eventually becomes the property of the user company, whereas with leasing, the asset remains the property of the lessor, unless there is a clause in the lease whereby the lessee can purchase the asset at some time. The significance of the difference is that under the Inland Revenue rules capital allowances can be claimed by the owner of the plant, which in leasing is the lessor company, and under a hire purchase agreement is the user company.

It is Government policy to encourage the modernization of industrial plant, to promote industrial activity in areas of high unemployment and to nurture the growth of small businesses. To promote these ends a whole series of schemes have been established whereby Government grants and other financial incentives are available, and these schemes should always be considered as potential sources of capital when an investment in plant or premises is under review.

SHORT-TERM FINANCIAL REQUIREMENTS

There are several sources of short-term capital available to companies.

1. *Overdraft*. The commercial banks provide short-term funds to finance working capital items, either by loans repayable at short notice or by overdraft facilities. An overdraft is usually considered to be preferable to a loan, since interest is payable only on the overdrawn amount, whereas with a loan, interest is payable on the whole amount, whether or not it is used in its entirety in the business. The rate of interest payable on such short-term facilities offered by the banks depends on the creditworthiness of the borrower, and is also linked to the minimum lending rate of the Bank of England. In some cases commercial banks require security for such a short-term loan, and with a small business it may be that the security needed is a guarantee on the part of the proprietor to repay the loan if the business fails to do so. In this way the banks can avoid the difficulties they would encounter if, once they had lent money to a company, the owner of the company claimed protection as a shareholder under the limited liability rule. The large commercial banks have been criticized for not supporting industry by advancing funds for the long and medium term. They have, however, introduced medium-term and variable interest rate loans, as well as taking a significant share of the hire purchase and leasing markets through the operation of subsidiary companies.

2. *Trade Credit* advanced by suppliers. This is usually governed by the terms of trade in a particular industry and by the contract between the purchaser and supplier of its goods. The amount of credit advanced to a company by its suppliers depends on their view of the company's creditworthiness, and whether the company is an important customer. Trade credit is often viewed as being a source of interest-free funds, since apparently there is no rate of interest attached to it. This is not always true, since if a cash discount is offered by the supplier, the fact that the customer does not pay early net of the discount shows the amount he is prepared to forgo in order to extend the payment period. Although a business should try to maximize the amount of trade credit it takes from its suppliers, there is a limit at which its reputation as a good payer begins to suffer, and at which the creditors begin to emerge as a significant pressure group in the running of the business. Both bank finance and trade credit are important sources of finance for the small firm, but they can also be the reason for its sudden demise if they withdraw their financial support at a crucial moment. The Inland Revenue is also a provider of short-term funds in that the tax on business profits is not payable until some months after the end of the accounting year, and during the

intervening period funds needed eventually to pay tax can be used to finance business operations.

3. *Invoice Discounting or Factoring.* If a company makes sales to a number of customers on credit terms it will have to wait for two or even three months before its debtors pay what they owe. This means that the debtors must be financed by the company, and the idea of factoring is to pass over the finance of debtors from the selling company to a special factoring or finance company. The factoring company, after reviewing the amount of the debts and the creditworthiness of the debtors, will pay the selling company, at the end of the month in which the sales were made, the amount it can expect to receive from the debtors (less a percentage). In this way the selling company receives its money one or two months earlier than would normally be the case. The factoring company will then collect the debts from the selling company's customers when they fall due. A company with sales of, for example, £20 000 a month can release up to £40 000 of working capital for use elsewhere in the business if it sells its debts to a factoring company. However, debt factoring has some disadvantages, such as the expense of the discount charged by the factoring company, and the procedures whereby the factor collects the debts from debtors who are not his customers. The factor may not be too courteous in the way it collects the money and therefore an element of goodwill on the part of the selling company may be lost. Factoring companies are very particular about what debts they are willing to buy, and will often accept only balances owed by the larger and more reputable customers, so the selling company may be unable to factor all its debtor balances, and will also have to bear the cost of all bad debts involved. Some companies like to hide the fact that they factor their debts in case this harms their financial standing, while others factor their debts with a company which not only undertakes collection later, but also takes on the task of recording sales and book-keeping.

Thus there is a range of facilities open to a company to raise funds in both the long and short term, and it is up to the business itself to select the source of funds which is cheapest and most convenient for it. Often, however, a decision cannot be made on this basis, since once the cheapest and most suitable source has been utilized the business still needs finance, and less suitable and more expensive methods must be used.

TUTORIAL DISCUSSION TOPICS

21.1 Why is the decision about how much profit to retain in the business an important one?

21.2 Outline the institutions which operate in the long-term capital market.

21.3 What methods are open to a company which intends to raise long-term funds on the capital market?

21.4 What facilities are available in the market to meet the short-term financial requirements of a business?

21.5 What role is played by merchant banks in the progress of a company from its early days to financial maturity?

21.6. A business acquaintance owns and operates a small construction company. You meet him for lunch, and he tells you that he has interviewed his bank manager that morning, with a view to increasing the overdraft facilities extended to his business. The bank manager said 'Your business is overtrading and the gearing ratio is too high; you must control the situation before the overdraft limit can be raised', but your friend does not understand financial jargon.

Explain the bank manager's comment, and advise your friend of the action he must take to improve the financial position of his business.

22 | Working Capital

The working capital of a business is computed by deducting the current liabilities from the current assets at any point in time. It is sometimes expressed as a ratio of current assets to current liabilities. The current assets of a business, as shown on the balance sheet, consist of stock, valued at the lower of cost or net realizable value, debtors, less a provision for doubtful debts, short-term investments, prepayments and amounts of cash and bank deposits. The current liabilities show the sources from which short-term funds have been recruited by the business, and are trade creditors, accrued charges, short-term loans, amounts owed to the Inland Revenue, bank overdraft and any dividends which are payable in the near future. The amount owed to the Inland Revenue may consist of corporation tax to be paid within twelve months, or amounts of value added tax, or income tax deductions made from wages paid to employees, which are collected by the company and later paid over to the revenue authorities. Thus the working capital of a business shows the amount of the firm's own funds which have been used to finance the current assets after short-term borrowings have been deducted. From the viewpoint of a creditor, the existence of working capital denotes a safety margin of current assets over current liabilities, which is seen as a pool from which a short-term loan to the business can be repaid. In the past the current or working capital ratio shown above has been thought to be satisfactory if a relationship of two to one existed. This idea has fallen into disrepute and now it is considered that the extent of a satisfactory margin of current assets over current liabilities depends upon the company concerned, the trade, and the season of the year, as well as other factors.

Working capital is often viewed by accountants as that portion of the finances of the firm which is used to 'oil the wheels of business'. The funds employed as fixed assets are directly concerned with the production of the goods which the business sells, but it is the function of working capital to facilitate that production and selling activity. For example, working capital invested in stock eases production problems, since production without stock would be difficult, and working capital invested in debtors allows the sales force of the company to support their activities by offering trade credit. Where negative working capital exists, this means that current liabilities exceed current assets, and that short-term funds are used not only to finance short-term assets, but also to finance some long-term assets. Such a situation is financially imprudent, since it will be difficult to disinvest from fixed assets if repayment is required.

The importance of adequate working capital for a business is demonstrated by the disadvantages suffered by firms which operate with insufficient working capital. Such firms are in a financial straitjacket, as their operations are hindered and their growth stunted by a lack of funds to finance extra stock and debtors. The weakness of such firms is also demonstrated by their dependence on short-term sources of funds to finance their operations, since at times of great dependence the providers of funds may begin to dictate the policy of the business and, in extreme cases, may bring profitable operations to a halt by calling a creditors' meeting and appointing a liquidator. A business must always have adequate funds to finance the continuity of its operations. If it can be proved that the directors or managers authorized the company to borrow money at a time when they knew it was already insolvent, they can be charged with fraud.

DISADVANTAGES OF INSUFFICIENT WORKING CAPITAL

The disadvantages suffered by a company with insufficient working capital are as follows:

1. The company is unable to take advantage of new opportunities or adapt to changes. Since it does not have sufficient financial elbow-room, it is unable to finance the development of new products or the alteration to production techniques needed when new opportunities occur. A company which has used up all its overdraft facility is unable to take advantage of a cheap line of raw material when a supplier offers it.
2. Trade discounts are lost. A company with ample working capital is able to finance large stocks and can therefore place large orders. The bigger the order the more generous the trade discount offered by the supplier, who uses it as a method of reducing the price so that the company is induced to place an order. If a company is unable to place large orders it will find that the prices it has to pay for raw materials and components are higher than those paid by its rivals, so it is at a competitive disadvantage in the market. Large stocks also act as a cushion against the disruption of production consequent upon a 'stock out', if there are supply problems.
3. Cash discounts are lost. Some companies will try to persuade their debtors to pay early by offering them a cash discount off the price owed. Discounts of 2½ per cent for cash in one month (instead of taking two or three months' credit) or even 4 per cent for cash within seven days are not uncommon. A discount of 2½ per cent for payment one month early is equivalent to an annual rate of interest on the money of about 30 per cent,

   i.e. $\dfrac{2\frac{1}{2}}{97\frac{1}{2}} \times 12 = 30.67$ per cent
4. The advantages of being able to offer a credit line to customers are forgone. If the sales force can back up their efforts by making credit available to the customer this will give them an advantage over rival organizations whose credit facilities are less extensive. In the case of contracts for large items of heavy engineering plant where the goods offered for sale are of equal efficiency, the credit line may be the deciding factor.
5. Financial reputation is lost. A company with ample working capital is able to pay its bills to suppliers and other creditors in good time. Thus is achieves a

reputation as being a good payer, and this will enhance the goodwill of the business. A company with a good reputation can expect co-operation from trade creditors at times of financial difficulty; for example, it would be possible for a firm that is well known in the trade to negotiate with suppliers as much as two or three months' extra credit at a time when funds are short because a large item of capital equipment has been purchased. Suppliers will value their connection with a company with a good reputation and may be willing to offer advantageous prices to maintain the connection. Conversely, a company with a bad reputation can expect credit controllers in the trade to be on their guard if it attempts to exceed the credit limits they have set. At such times a credit controller may cut off supplies of raw materials to a factory, thus seriously disrupting production.

6. There may be concerted action by creditors. If the working capital of a business is grossly inadequate it will be forced to finance its operations more and more by short-term borrowings such as overdraft and trade credit. Eventually the point will be reached beyond which the short-term lenders are not willing to extend credit, and it is at this point that the policy, and indeed the continuation of the business, is dependent not on the wishes of the owners, shareholders or directors, but on the actions of the creditors. Even though the business is a profitable one, at this weak stage in its development a creditors' meeting can decide that, in the absence of repayment, the creditors will apply to the court to appoint a liquidator or force the company to commence a voluntary winding-up.

Over-trading is often the reason for the development of such adverse credit conditions in a business. In simple terms, to over-trade means to attempt to finance a certain volume of production and sales with inadequate working capital. If the company does not have enough funds of its own to finance stock and debtors it is forced, if it wishes to expand, to borrow from creditors and from the bank on overdraft. Sooner or later such expansion, financed completely by the funds of others, will lead to a chronic imbalance in the working capital ratio. At this point the creditors and the bank may withdraw their support and a creditors' meeting will take place. A careful scrutiny of the working capital and acid test ratios of a business may enable the accountant to predict the onset of financial distress. A business which changes its suppliers to raise extra credit, whose payments to creditors, including the Inland Revenue, are rarely made on the due date, and whose overdraft facilities are fully committed, is a business in which the slightest breath of change on the part of current liabilities can blow down the fragile credit structure which supports its operations.

CONSERVING THE RESOURCES OF CAPITAL EMPLOYED IN A BUSINESS

A much used measure of the profitability of a business is to set net profit against the capital employed and show it as a percentage thereof. This is known as the return on capital employed. A good accountant or financial manager will attempt to manage the resources of the business in such a way that the capital employed is used efficiently and not wasted. If the capital employed can be reduced and profit maintained, then an improved return on capital employed will be achieved. Conversely, if the capital employed in current operations is reduced, funds are released for use in other activities, and the profit on capital employed is increased. The financial manager should review the asset structure of the business to seek out idle, under-utilized and non-profitable assets, so that they can be turned back into cash which can then be re-employed in the business, or elsewhere, at a much greater return. Fixed assets are as important in this operation as are current assets, since when they are squeezed, liquidity, or funds for use elsewhere in the business, is the result. Some fixed assets, especially plant of a specific nature, may not be easy to sell unless at a price well below book value, and there will also be redundancy payments if staff are involved.

The land and buildings belonging to and used by the company should be investigated. The accountant must attempt to find out whether they are fully utilized, and to discover idle or underused space or space being used for wasteful or unprofitable purposes. Discussions with the technical experts in the business will indicate ways to rearrange the factory area, to re-route goods and stocks of work in progress which travel round the factory so that some space is released. Such space can then be sold, rented out, or used to house a new operation; any of these courses of action should improve the cash flow of the business.

A review of machinery used in the business should be made to discover the level of idle time experienced each week or day by individual machines. This survey will reveal whether the plant and machinery is working at full capacity, whether the same volume of work could be produced from a smaller number of machines, and how much extra work could be undertaken using the existing plant and machinery. Once again, the level of spare capacity, if it exists, will be shown, so that it can be put to work or sold. Care must be taken in such economy reviews that back-up capacity is not seen as an idle resource, but as a form of insurance against breakdown.

Vehicles should also be brought under scrutiny. Investigation, with the transport manager, into routes and mileages driven per week or per month, would pinpoint those vehicles which do not earn their keep, and perhaps produce ideas so that fewer vehicles can be used to undertake the work of the company.

Investments made by the business also tie up capital, and therefore they too should be analysed. The return received from an investment should be set against its current value to determine whether it is worthwhile. In cases of low return, perhaps the investment is held for strategic reasons, e.g. a share stake in a supplier or customer company. It is difficult to quantify such strategic benefits, but an attempt should be made to find out whether the benefit is considered to be worth tying up the amount of capital in the investment. Perhaps the same strategic benefit could be gained by holding a smaller share stake, thus releasing some funds for use elsewhere in the business.

CONSERVING FUNDS INVESTED IN CURRENT ASSETS: STOCKS

So far the accountant's activities to husband the capital employed have been directed towards achieving the same volume of turnover and activity from a reduced quantity of fixed assets. A review of the current assets of the business should also be made to ascertain whether levels of stocks and debtors could be the subject of economy measures.

The stocks of a manufacturing business are usually of three types. They consist of stocks of raw material waiting in the store to be used in the productive process, stocks of work in progress or semi-finished goods being worked on in the factory, and stocks of finished goods waiting to be sold. The computation of ratios is a useful device to determine the stock-holding period.

In the case of raw material, the stock should be set against the usage of each material. If the amount of stock is divided by the average weekly issue, a figure for the number of weeks' usage held in stock will emerge, and this can be compared with the lead time between placing an order and receiving delivery in order to find out whether the stock held is excessive. For example, if one can buy raw material at a fortnight's notice, it seems wrong to finance two months' usage of that raw material in stock. The executive responsible for this is the buyer and, if the raw material stock-holding period is increasing, he must be called to account for the change. It may be that the rate of production has slowed down while he has continued to buy material at the same rate, or that he is buying more than is required for production quantities. On the other hand, the buyer may be attempting to build up stocks in anticipation of a forthcoming seasonal demand or as a hedge against inflation.

Example

One hundred tonnes of material A are held in stock and normal usage of this material is 10 tonnes per week:

$$\frac{\text{Stock}}{\text{Weekly usage}} \times \frac{100}{10} = 10$$

Therefore, sufficient stock for ten weeks is held in the stores. If this material can be replaced two weeks after ordering, there should be good strategic or cost reasons to justify this overstocking situation. A system currently coming into use is 'just in time' stock control, whereby deliveries and usage are planned together.

The ratio of stocks of work in progress to the cost of production when computed as a number of days or weeks will show how long it takes for semi-finished articles to progress through the factory. This time period must be compared with the normally expected production cycle and discrepancies analysed. If, for example, there are fifty working weeks in the year and it takes a week to complete the production process, but work-in-progress stocks are $^4\!/_{50}$ of the production cost for a year, then there is too much work-in-progress stock in the factory, and the bottlenecks which are disrupting production must be discovered and eliminated.

The ratio of finished goods to the cost of goods sold will, when expressed as a time period, show how long the finished goods wait in the stores before they are sold. In this way one can discover whether production is co-ordinated properly to sales, or whether the factory goes on producing at its normal rate while sales are falling away. For example,

$$\frac{\text{Stock}}{\text{Cost of sales}} \times \frac{52}{1} = \text{The number of weeks}$$

These ratios are discussed, with examples, in Chapter 23.

The establishment of a correct stock level is a decision affected by many different factors. The management team must trade off the advantages of holding large stocks against the disadvantages. The advantages of holding large stocks can be summarized as follows: that large orders can be placed with suppliers so that trade discounts are secured, that there is a reduction of buying costs if orders are placed less often, and the advantage of a smooth flow of production, since a large buffer stock of raw materials will reduce the possibility of a 'stock out'. The disadvantages of holding a large stock of raw materials stem from the costs of financing and maintaining the stock. Interest paid on overdraft used to finance the stock, the cost of running the stores, i.e. rent, rates, light, heat, insurance, the costs of spoilage, spillage and pilferage, the losses inherent in the operation of breaking bulk, and the fear of obsolescence followed by a stock write-down must be set against the advantages shown above.

The accountant must ensure that stocks are examined to discover slow-moving and obsolescent items so that the quantities involved can be reduced to realistic levels and funds released. Any action taken to improve the flow of products through the factory will reduce the time lag involved in the conversion of raw material to a sold product.

The working capital cycle can be expressed in terms of the number of days it takes to convert raw materials to finished goods, and then after they are sold to collect the price from the company's debtors. Such a computation will reveal the time period in which the company must finance the working capital cycle, and from this period it is possible to deduct the amount of credit received from suppliers. For example, if the raw material waits thirty days in the stores before being used, is then transferred to the factory for a ten-day production cycle, then waits for fifteen days in the finished goods store before being sold, and the person to whom the goods are sold delays a further sixty days before he pays his bill, it will take 115 days to change the funds invested in raw materials back into cash or liquid resources. This means that the company will have to finance this period, but if it in its turn takes ninety days of credit from the supplier of raw materials, the period to be financed is reduced to 25 days. Thus the amount of working capital tied up in raw materials for this transaction will be the cost of 25 times an average day's usage of raw materials.

Example

	Days
Storage	30
Production	10
Finished goods store	15
Payment delay	60
	115
Less credit from suppliers	90
Days to finance	25

This simple sum emphasizes the importance in the working capital cycle of the management of debtors and creditors, since if debtors can be induced to pay sooner and creditors can be persuaded to wait for their money, the amount of the company's own funds tied up in the transaction will be reduced. Any other factor which can shorten the time period, such as a shorter production cycle or a reduced lead time between the delivery and use of raw material stocks, will also reduce the amount of working capital required. Thus planning and the reduction of production bottlenecks can help to turn over stocks faster and allow the same amount of money to finance more transactions, and earn more profit margins from each transaction, in an accounting period.

DEBTORS AND CREDITORS

The accountant must approach debtors with some caution to conserve the working capital of the company. There is less control over debtors than, for example, over stock, since the period of credit which the company must give depends to some extent on the activity of the other party to the transaction, i.e. the customer. The volume of funds required to finance debtors may grow without an increase in the volume of transactions, merely because in a period of inflation prices rise and more capital is needed to finance the same number of transactions.

Many companies employ a credit controller in an attempt to economize on their working capital tied up in the form of debtors. The credit controller has four main tasks:

1. To vet new customers and set a credit limit (an amount beyond which goods will not be sold to the customer without the payment of previous bills).
2. To review the credit position of old customers and set new credit limits for them.
3. To ensure that credit limits are not exceeded.
4. To hasten the slow payers by means of carefully worded letters encouraging them to pay.

The credit controller is in a delicate position, since money must be collected from the firm's customers, but without rudeness while collecting the money, since this may discourage them from buying from the company in the future. Thus the credit controller is the rope in a tug of war between the accounting department, who wish to collect debts and reduce working capital wastefully tied up in debtors, and the sales department, who wish to extend the credit line and maintain customer goodwill. A useful device in the control of trade credit is the ageing debtors list. This is merely an analysis of all debtor balances to show how long they have been outstanding. Thus the poor payers are revealed and the credit controller can try to make them pay. The danger with debtor balances which are four or five months or more overdue is that they may, unless the credit controller is careful, become bad debts.

Another aspect of the management of working capital which a financial accountant must monitor with care is the amount of trade credit which he can take on behalf of his company from the suppliers of raw materials. The general rule is to take as much as possible, since it is free, but not too much, since slow payment of bills harms the reputation of the company and its goodwill, and may affect future prices charged to the company for raw materials. Long-delayed payment may result in a stop on the delivery of vital raw materials to the factory. Some companies adopt the policy of always paying promptly where they are offered a cash discount, while others, through careful programming with their suppliers, organize the deliveries to co-ordinate with the needs of the factory and thus reduce the stock-holding period.

Cash balances, or funds lying in the bank, are viewed by many companies as idle assets, since they are earning nothing. They are, however, a useful safety margin to ensure that urgent bills can always be paid. Forward planning in the form of a cash budget can show up the impact of future transactions on the cash balance, so that when an overdraft is required it can be requested well in advance.

WORKING CAPITAL TRADE-OFF STRATEGIES

Working capital management comprises a trade-off or constant effort to balance the advantage achieved by a certain strategy against the costs of securing that advantage.

Assume that a sales organization allows two months (sixty days) credit to its customers. The company decides to offer a 4 per cent discount for cash within ten days of sale, i.e. payment fifty days sooner than at present. Then

$$\frac{4}{96} \times \frac{365}{50} = 30.4 \text{ per cent}$$

is the annual rate of interest which this strategy costs the company, and this cost must be balanced against the overdraft interest avoided because the money is collected sooner, or the profit which can be earned if that money is put to work in the business for fifty days. From the customers' point of view it would be profitable to borrow on overdraft at 18 per cent, in order to pay bills fifty days early, and earn a discount giving an annual rate of 30 per cent.

An alternative strategy might be to allow improved credit terms to customers in an attempt to increase sales. The profit from the extra sales must be set off against the cost of providing finance for the extra period to new and existing customers. An extension of the period before payment may also increase the number of bad debts experienced by the business.

Example

A company has annual sales of £6 million, earning a gross profit of 20 per cent. The sales director suggests that all customers should be allowed to extend their credit period from one month to two months, and estimates that sales will increase by 30 per cent as a result of this strategy. Clearly this will earn extra revenue of £1 800 000, and an increase in profit of £360 000, providing that there is no increase in administrative costs. Extra credit must be financed, and will be expensive at an overdraft rate of, say, 17 per cent.

$$\text{Existing sales £6 million} \div 12 = £500\ 000 \text{ per month}$$

Therefore extra funds of £500 000 would be required throughout the year to finance this extra credit each month. Interest at 17 per cent on this sum would cost £85 000 per annum.

The extra sales would also need to be financed for two months, but the money tied up in these sales represents only the cost of the items sold, i.e.

$$
\begin{aligned}
£1\ 800\ 000 \times 0.8 &= £1\ 440\ 000 \\
\text{Cost of finance} &= £1\ 440\ 000 \div 6 = £240\ 000 \\
\text{Borrowed at 17\%} &= £40\ 800 \text{ in extra interest}
\end{aligned}
$$

The credit controller expects bad debts to increase from the present 1 per cent of sales to 2½ per cent of sales despite more stringent credit control achieved by expanding the credit control department at a cost of £30 000 per annum.

Bad debts 1½ per cent on existing sales of £6 million	=	£90 000
2½ per cent on new sales of £1 800 000	=	£45 000
		£165 000

The overall trade-off is:

	£	£
Revenue from extra sales		360 000
Increased costs		
Interest on extra working capital:		
Existing sales	85 000	
New sales	40 800	
Bad debts	165 000	
Administration cost of credit control	30 000	320 800
Surplus		£39 200

Affirmative—the strategy is worth adopting. This surplus would have been even greater if the post-tax cost of borrowed funds had been used in the calculation.

CASH BUDGETS

A matter of such importance as the amount of liquid funds available to the company cannot be left to chance. Cash planning or budgeting implies that as part of the general budgeting procedure an accountant will forecast the flows of cash into and out of the company's bank account, so that any excess of payments over receipts will show up well in advance, and action can be taken to provide for a shortfall of liquid funds. This can be done on a quarterly, monthly, or even weekly basis, according to the needs of management and the situation of the company. It is especially important if the firm has an overdraft and wishes to ensure that the limit placed by its bank is not exceeded. Also, it is a useful tactic to be able to approach a bank for overdraft facilities well in advance of the date on which the funds will be needed, since such evidence of financial planning and control will improve the credit-worthiness of the company in the eyes of the bank. Finance cannot be raised at short notice without extra expense. It is preferable to make arrangements in good time so that funds are available when required.

The technique of cash budgeting is a simple one. The accountant needs to discover the receipts and payments of cash which are likely to take place in the future, and the dates on which they will happen, so that a forecast of the balance at the end of the month or week can be computed. The accountant must find out the length of lead time between incurring an expense and paying for it, and the time lag between making a sale and collecting the price from debtors. The art of cash budgeting is to work out accurately the timing of receipts and expenditure. If, for example, a firm takes two months' credit on its purchases, materials delivered in January will need to be paid for in March, and so on. The same applies to cash collected from credit sales. If a firm gives three months' credit to its customers, then cash from January credit sales will be received by the end of April. Care must be taken in this forecast to take into account the likely percentage of bad debts which will reduce the cash received, and to separate cash sales from credit sales, since these will be banked at once. Cash discounts may also affect this figure.

With labour costs the timing is a little more predictable, but computation may be difficult, since some companies pay a week in arrears. This means that in a monthly cash budget each quarter, divided into thirteen weeks, must be analysed for the number of weeks in each month. If January and February each contain four pay days then March will cover five weeks of wage payments. If the firm pays one week in arrears the cash paid out in February will equal one week of January's wages (¼) and three weeks of February's wages (¾), whereas in March the wages paid out will be a quarter of February's labour cost and four-fifths of March's labour cost. It must be remembered that in cash budgeting the actual wage sheets are not available and figures must be assessed from estimates of monthly costs.

Expenses are usually easier to forecast, since they are often paid one month in arrears, e.g. salaries. Certain expenses are paid quarterly, e.g. rent, or half-yearly, e.g. loan interest, or annually, e.g. insurance premiums or annual bonus. Some expenses, such as depreciation, do not cause an outflow of cash and therefore should be ignored for cash budgeting purposes. Care must be taken when budgeting for miscellaneous items, both receipts and payments. Dividends received from an investment should be allotted to the correct month, together with projected receipts from the sale of fixed assets, while the amount and date of capital expenditure and payments of tax and dividend should be entered on the statement. It then remains only to set off the receipts against the payments each month to compute the surplus or deficit, and to show the impact of this cash flow on the bank balance or overdraft. A columnar approach facilitates the compilation of a cash budget.

Example

Alpha PLC has a balance of £150 000 in its bank account on 1 January. The company has negotiated overdraft facilities of £100 000 with its bankers. Materials, all purchased on credit, usually cost £500 000 per month, but a reduction of £100 000 is planned during December. Suppliers allow two months' credit terms to the company. Labour costs for December, January, February and March are expected to be £250 000, £280 000, £320 000, and £400 000 respectively. Wages are paid one week in arrears, and December and March are considered to be five-week months. Expenses paid monthly in arrears amount to £80 000 each month, the rent of £60 000 is paid on each quarter day, and industrial rates of £12 000 per annum are paid half-yearly on 31 December and 30 June. An annual insurance premium of £45 000 falls due on 30 January and corporation tax of £205 000 must be paid in January. Capital expenditure to purchase new machinery for £400 000 is planned, and a progress payment of 25 per cent is to be made in March.

A dividend from an associated company is expected to be received in February, and should amount to £200 000. The company expects to raise a long-term loan of £250 000 by a mortgage on its property during March.

Expected sales are as follows: October, £800 000; November, £750 000; December, £1 090 000; January, £650 000; February, £800 000; and March, £900 000. Ten per cent of sales are for cash, and the remainder are on terms of three months' credit. Bad debts are expected at the rate of 5 per cent on credit sales.

Compute a cash budget for January, February and March.

Note: A simple way of remembering the quarter days is as follows:

25 March (five letters in March)
24 June (four letters in June)

29 September (nine letters in September)
25 December (Christmas)

This is an old-fashioned set of dates, but sometimes still occurs in questions. The modern convention is to work to the last day of March, June, September and December.

Alpha PLC Cash Budget (£000s)

	January	February	March
Receipts:			
Cash sales	65	80.00	90.00
Debtors	684 (95% × 720)	641.25 (95% × 675)	931.95 (95% × 981)
Loan			250.00
Investment income	—	200.00	—
Total receipts	749	921.25	1271.95
Payments:			
Materials	500 (Nov.)	400.00 (Dec.)	500.00 (Jan.)
Labour	50 (1/5)	70.00 (1/4)	80.00 (1/4)
	210 (3/4)	240.00 (3/4)	320.00 (4/5)
Expenses	80	80.00	80.00
Rent and insurance	45	—	60
Taxation	205	—	—
Capital expenditure	—	—	100.00
Total payments	1090	790.00	1140.00
Surplus/deficit	(341)	131.25	131.95
Opening balance	150	(191.00)	(59.75)
Closing balance	(191)	(59.75)	72.20

The closing balance of January is of course the opening balance for February. This cash budget shows that the overdraft limit will be exceeded during January, but the situation will be under control by the end of February, and the facility will not be required by the end of March. Managers must decide now how best to employ the surplus at the end of March.

Note that the quarter day for rent is 25 March and that rates are ignored since they are not paid during this period. This computation shows month-end balances, based on the assumption that receipts and payments flow in and out evenly during each month. A substantial payment early in a month could upset this computation.

In conclusion, the differences between a cash budget and a profit and loss account must be discussed, since the two are often confused. A cash budget does not contain the non-cash expenses found in the profit and loss account, such as the provision for depreciation. The provision for doubtful debts cannot be included in the cash budget, but actual bad debts will reduce the cash received from sales. Conversely, income and expenditure of a capital nature will appear in the cash budget but not in the profit and loss account. Appropriations of profit for tax and dividend will cause an outflow of cash, but cannot influence the profit figure before it is struck.

TUTORIAL DISCUSSION TOPICS

22.1 What is working capital and why does a creditor see it as a significant figure on the balance sheet?

22.2 Why is it so important for a business to have an adequate fund of working capital?

22.3 What is the working capital cycle and how can an accountant use an understanding of this cycle to benefit the firm?

22.4 Discuss the task of a credit controller, with specific reference to the pressure to which he is subjected.

22.5 Outline the advantages of a cash budget.

SEMINAR EXERCISES 13

1. From the two balance sheets of Ginger Ltd shown below calculate the change in working capital over the year and show how this change has arisen:

Ginger Ltd Balance Sheets as at

	£ 1 Jan.	£ 31 Dec.		£ 1 Jan.	£ 31 Dec.
Share capital	60 000	65 000	Freehold land and buildings	22 000	25 000
General reserve	4 000	5 000			
			Plant and machinery	38 000	40 000
Profit and loss balance	9 000	11 000			
Long-term loan	—	50 000			
				60 000	65 000
Current liabilities:			Current assets:		
Trade creditors	12 000	14 000	Stocks	17 000	70 000
Tax	11 000	12 000	Debtors	7 000	10 000
Proposed final dividend	6 000	8 000	Cash	18 000	20 000
	£102 000	£165 000		£102 000	£165 000

2. Mr Smith is considering commencing a small business on 1 January 19–9, with a capital sum of £5000. He has made estimates covering the first six months of trading, as follows:

(a) Sales. January, £6000; February, £8000; March, £10 000; April to July inclusive, £12 000 per month. Debtors are expected to settle their accounts at the end of the month following that of the sale; e.g. goods sold in February are paid for in March. The gross profit on sales is 25 per cent throughout.

(b) Purchases. A stock is retained to cover the succeeding months' sales. All suppliers are paid at the end of the month following that of purchase.

(c) Wages and salaries. These are estimated to be: January, £350; February, £450; thereafter £500 per month.

(d) Expenses. General expenses of £350 per month are paid in the month in which they are incurred. Rent of £2000 per annum is payable quarterly in advance, the first payment being on 1 January. Insurance of £160 is to be paid on 1 April 19-9.

(e) Fittings and plant to be purchased in January, £3000; motor van to be purchased in February, £1500.

Prepare a cash budget showing the estimated cash position at the end of each of the six months to June 19-9.

3. The managers of Alpha PLC plan to commence business as a wholesaler on 1 July by issuing 50 000 £1 ordinary shares for cash which will be paid into a business bank account. The company forecasts sales for July of £40 000 and expects sales to increase at the rate of £20 000 per month until October when they will be £120 000. The reason for this increase in sales is that a promotion campaign is planned for the months of September and October. Advertisements costing £40 000 will be paid for in September. In the months of November and December sales are forecast at £100 000 for each month. It is intended that the gross profit percentage earned in each month will be 40 per cent of sales, with the exception of October when it will be 30 per cent due to a reduction in prices during the promotion drive. To service this sales pattern the company plans to hold stock costing £10 000 at the end of July and to increase the stock level by £5000 per month throughout the first six months of trading activity. All sales are on credit terms and the average period of credit allowed to debtors will be two months (except for sales to Hard Up Ltd referred to below).

Creditors for the goods purchased for resale have indicated that they will allow one month's credit only to Alpha PLC. A sales manager has been employed by the company to be paid a commission of 2 per cent on the sales value. This commission will be paid in the months after which the sales are effected.

The business plans to lease premises at a rental of £12 000 per annum, payable quarterly, the first payment falling due on 1 July. Wages and salaries are estimated to cost £5000 per month and other overheads will cost £3000 per month for the first three months, and £4000 per month of the next three months. These expenses will be paid in the month to which they relate. On 1 September, Alpha PLC have contracted to purchase warehouse equipment for £6000 which will be paid for on 30 November. On 1 October it is planned to purchase and pay for vehicles costing £24 000.

Included in the sales figure for July is an amount of £4000 to Hard Up Ltd. It is intended to grant Hard Up Ltd extended credit and it is confidently predicted that Hard Up Ltd will settle its debt in March of the next year.

Depreciation is to be provided pro rata to time at the rate of 10 per cent per annum on the cost of warehouse equipment, and 25 per cent per annum on the cost of the vehicles.

(a) Prepare a cash budget for each of the first six months of trading showing the anticipated bank balance at the end of each month.

(b) Prepare a forecast trading and profit and loss account for the six months ending 31 December.

(c) Discuss the differences between a cash budget and a profit and loss account.

4. During the Christmas holiday you went on a skiing holiday in the north of Scotland, and stayed with a relative who has developed a farm on ranching principles. One day he confided in you that he was rather worried that he might be in temporary financial difficulty during the early part of the year, and you agreed to put your business knowledge at his disposal in order that he might negotiate an overdraft with his bank in Fort William.

Prepare a cash budget for the months of January to April (inclusive) from the information given below:

(a) Balance at bank was expected to be £2000 on 1 January.

(b) Incomings: sales of cattle. There is a contract with an exporter for the supply of forty head of cattle each month for which forward prices have been negotiated and agreed: September to February inclusive, £115 per head; March to August inclusive, £100 per head. The money is paid over in the second month after the date of sale.

Surplus cattle, together with any suitable steers, are sent to the auctions, at which prices are expected to be: steers, £50 per head; beef cattle, £125 per head. The money for these is received immediately. The numbers of these expected to be available for auction are:

	Jan.	Feb.	Mar.	Apr.
Steers	12	20	20	26
Beef cattle	8	16	16	20

(c) Other income:

(i) There is a variation clause in the contract with the cattle exporters by which additional lump sum payments are made when weighted-average export prices exceed a certain figure. Taking price trends into account, the amounts likely to be received are: interim distribution, February, £700; final distribution, April, £2100.

(ii) He is due to receive a subsidy of £1000 from the Highlands Agricultural Development Board in March.

(d) Outgoings: labour. The salaries of the ranch manager and foreman together amount to £800 per month plus a bonus of 5 per cent of the combined sales value of the steers and beef cattle auctioned that month.

In addition to the nine permanently employed 'hands' hired at £150 per month each, a certain amount of part-time casual labour is employed at an average wage of £100 per month each. Numbers of casual hands expected to be hired are: January, fifteen; February, twelve; March, twelve; April, nine.

(e) Other costs:

(i) Fodder etc. During the spring and summer the cattle can obtain sufficient food by free ranging. This is gradually supplemented in early autumn and superseded in winter by bought-in fodder.

The cost of this and of vitamin concentrates, veterinary vaccines etc. is likely to be: December, £900; January, £900; February, £900; March, £500; and April, £300. These sums are paid to the suppliers one month after the items have been acquired.

 (ii) The cost of grazing rights (£300) is paid to local landowners in advance in the month of February.
(iii) Payments for the use of rights of way are made to neighbouring landowners half-yearly in advance at the rate of £200 per annum. The first payment is made in January.
(iv) All other costs (paid currently) for vehicle running expenses, repairs, electricity etc. are expected to amount to £400 per month.

 (f) Capital expenditure. It is proposed to acquire another truck in March at a cost of £6000 on hire purchase. The terms are 20 per cent deposit in March and 32 equal monthly instalments from April onwards.

In February the final instalment of £6000 is due for the supply and erection of some outbuildings.
 (g) Personal drawings. To meet living expenses etc. he intends to withdraw £1000 per month.
 (h) Taxation. An instalment of £5000 tax on business profits is to be paid in January.

REVIEW QUESTIONS 8

1. The management of Shortfall PLC require £60 000 in early December to purchase additional plant and equipment. They are hoping to obtain the funds from internal sources:

The cash balance at 31 May was £10 540 (debit) and they have an overdraft limit of £30 000.

Estimates of items which will affect the cash flow are given below:
 (i) The cost of goods sold for April and May was £100 000 and £103 200 respectively.

Management estimates the cost of goods sold for the next six months will be as follows:

June	July	August	September	October	November
108 000	114 000	118 000	112 000	100 000	90 000

 (ii) The stock level at the end of May was considered too high at £35 600. Attempts will be made to reduce it by £1500 each month for the next four months, to a level which will be more acceptable.
(iii) The company operates on a 25 per cent mark-up. All sales are on credit terms and cash is normally received at the beginning of the second month following the month of sale.

(iv) Purchases are paid for in the month they are received in order to take advantage of a 5 per cent settlement discount.

(v) Wages of £12 000 are paid each month. A 10 per cent pay increase has just been negotiated and this will be paid to all staff in July, and backdated to 1 March.

(vi) Administration expenses are £5000 per month payable in the month they arise.

(vii) Interest charges currently amount to £2000 every month and the company has £50 000 of 12 per cent debentures which must be redeemed on 31 October.

(a) Prepare a cash budget for the next six months commencing 1 June.

(b) Advise the management of Shortfall whether the funds are available within the business and, if not, suggest possible other sources.

2. Messrs Cash and Short have decided to form a partnership to sell in this country a new Japanese photocopier. They have carried out a survey of the potential market for the new product and have investigated the technical requirements and financial implications of embarking on this new business venture. The following is a summary of the forecasts and conclusions they have made:

(i) Sales are expected to commence in February, 19-1. The projected figures for monthly sales from February to June inclusive are £1000, £2000, £5000, £8000 and £10 000. Thereafter sales of £10 000 are expected each month.

(ii) The cost of the product to them will be 50 per cent of its selling price. Cash and Short will require an initial stock of £1500 (at cost) to be purchased in January, but thereafter stock on hand at the end of each month should be sufficient to meet the expected demand of the following two months.

(iii) One month's credit will be received from the manufacturer, whereas it is expected that two months' credit will have to be allowed to customers.

(iv) Wages, salaries and general expenses are expected to be £3000 per month. These costs would be payable from 1 January 19-1.

(v) Variable selling expenses would be 3 per cent of sales and would be payable one month in arrear of sales.

(vi) In the first three months of 19-1, £500 per month would be spent on promotional activity. This would be reduced to £200 per month thereafter.

(vii) Motor vehicles and other equipment necessary for the business are estimated to cost £6000 and will have to be purchased and paid for in January 19-1. Depreciation of £900 is to be provided for the first nine-month period.

Messrs Cash and Short have available £10 000 each for investment in the business. They are anxious to know if this will be sufficient to meet the financial requirements of the partnership, and if not, what additional finance would be required. They also want to know what profit the partnership should make in the first nine months (to the end of September 19-1).

(a) Prepare a detailed cash budget for the partnership for the nine months to 30 September 19-1, on a month-by-month basis, stating the maximum bank overdraft (or minimum cash balance) reached each month.

(b) State the maximum bank overdraft expected to be reached during the nine-month period and the month this is reached.
(c) Prepare a projected profit and loss account and balance sheet for the nine months to 30 September 19-1; you may assume that profits and losses are shared equally and that the partners will make no drawings during the period.

23 | The Valuation of a Business

A business is valued when it is sold, when there is a change of partners, or when the proprietor dies and the value is computed to be added to his estate for the purposes of inheritance tax. In the case of a limited company there may be a need to value the company in order to put a price on individual shares when a takeover or merger is proposed. Several methods are employed to find the value of shares in a business. A share in a public company will have a market value, since it is quoted on a stock exchange, but if a steady demand is experienced as an investor who intends to make a takeover bid seeks to build up a significant share stake in the business, the price will rise. The extent to which the investor will continue to buy as prices rise will be determined by the valuation he puts on the company. In the case of a private limited company there will be no such market value, and an offer will be made direct to an existing shareholder or his agent. The terms of such an offer will be in line with the valuation put on the business.

Accountants use several methods to value a business, but it must be emphasized that the value reached by their computation may bear little relation to the final price arrived at through bargaining, since various factors will influence the negotiations. Such factors are concerned with business strategy and include the re-employment of assets, the establishment of a monopoly or a foothold in a market, diversification, and integration. These factors may cause the business to be worth more than the accountant's valuation of it to a particular buyer who wants it very much.

From the accountant's viewpoint when shares are purchased the buyer gains two things. Each shareholder has (1) a right to share in the assets of the business if and when the business is wound up, and (2) a right to a share of the profits. Thus shares can be valued on the basis of the underlying assets which they represent, or on the basis of the income which they provide. When a small holding of shares is to be valued (this is termed a minority interest, since it does not give voting control of the company) recognition must be made of the fact that the buyer cannot dictate decisions at a general meeting of the company, and has little influence over board policy. Therefore such a holding is best valued on the basis of the income it yields. Such a valuation is made by comparing the yield on the share with the yield which can be earned on similar shares bearing an equivalent risk. Dividend is declared as a percentage of the face value of a share, e.g. a 20 per cent dividend on a £1 share provides a dividend of 20p for every share held; but yield is expressed by computing the percentage of the dividend paid over the current market price of the share, e.g. if a £1 share has been purchased for £2, a dividend thereon of 20 pence per share will yield 10 per cent. This method of valuation can be expressed in formula terms as the yield over the expected yield times the face value.

$$\frac{\text{Yield}}{\text{Expected yield}} \times \text{Face value} = \frac{20\%}{10\%} \times £1 = £2, \text{ or } \frac{8\%}{10\%} \times £1 = 80p$$

Preference shares and securities, such as debentures or loan stock, which have a fixed rate of return can also be valued by means of this formula. The fixed return is set against the expected return or market rate of interest, as the case may be, and then applied to the face value. The value thus produced is what a prudent investor would expect to pay for the income involved at current market rates.

$$\frac{\text{Debenture coupon rate}}{\text{Market rate of interest}} \times \text{Face value} = \text{Price},$$

$$\frac{10\%}{15\%} \times £100 = £66 \ (15\% \text{ of } £66 = £10)$$

The £10 interest gives the investor the market rate of 15 per cent if he pays £66 for the right to receive that interest.

RISK

The most significant factor in the above formula is the expected yield from the shares. This figure can be derived from the expectations of investors revealed by the Stock Exchange, but these expectations themselves are an amalgam of a number of factors which determine whether or not an investment is a risky one.

The nature of the business itself will help to determine the risk, since in general the luxury trades are considered more risky than trades providing necessities, and the home market is considered less risky than the export market. Any factor which promotes the likelihood of fluctuation in the market, or of obsolescence, will increase the risk of an investment. The past record of a business, its earnings, and the dividends it has paid out will show the pay-out or plough-back policy of the directors. This financial policy can be compared with that of similar firms, and the result of this comparison will have an effect on risk. The trend of profits in a business will show whether there is growth or recession, and whether future earnings are likely to be sufficient to maintain the required rate of dividend. The ratio of net profit to capital employed can also be used in this context to show the return earned by a business on its capital to compensate for the risk taken in investing the capital in that way. Another factor influencing risk is gearing. A highly geared position is considered more risky than a low-geared position, since a large volume of prior right capital must be serviced before the highly geared ordinary shares can receive a return.

The nature of the assets in a firm also contributes to the riskiness of an investment. A large proportion of fixed, as opposed to current, assets means that the capital has been sunk into the business and it may be difficult to disinvest it. Current assets are relatively easy to turn back into cash. The degree of specificity of the fixed assets of a business will help to determine their marketability and also their ability to act as security for loan capital. Risk is also affected by the amount of goodwill existing in a business. It is necessary to investigate the factors which support the existence of the goodwill to determine whether they are easily transferable to a new management, whether they have been calculated properly, and whether the amount of goodwill is excessive when compared with the tangible assets and current earnings. The demand for the product, the share of the market, the level of competition, and the supply of raw materials and labour are other factors which can affect the risk of the business, and accordingly the return required from it. When a bid is made by one company for the shares of another, a number of factors concerning the economic logic of the merger and the advantages of the economies of large scale (vertical or horizontal integration) will influence the price that the buyer is willing to pay. Risk is also determined by 'cover'. This word is used to express the safety margin of the investor in two distinct ways. First, the excess of net assets less long-term liabilities over the ordinary share capital of the business will show up the extent of the reserves and the asset base on which the value of the shares rests. Second, the relationship of profits available to the amount of the expected dividend will show whether profits are sufficient to meet the required level of dividend and comment on the risk of non-payment of a dividend.

A CONTROLLING INTEREST

The valuation of a controlling interest in a company is undertaken by a somewhat different method. The controlling shareholder will be able to outvote others at general meetings of the company, and is thus in a position to determine its policy. When such an investor buys a controlling interest, he will buy the assets and what they earn, and accordingly the value of his shares could be computed on the basis of the underlying assets, and on their capacity to earn profit. The assets, however, must be realistically revalued so that their true current worth is known. The term used in this case is net tangible assets, being the value of all the physical assets which the company possesses less the liabilities which it owes. Once this amount has been computed it can be divided by the number of shares in issue, so that the asset value per share is found. To this amount must be added the value of the goodwill, which is expressed as the value placed by an investor on the extra profits which the business is likely to make. Goodwill is sometimes defined as the capital value of future superprofits based on past superprofits. It is the amount which a prudent investor would pay for the fact that the business can earn more in profit than would be expected from that class of business taking that type of risk with its capital employed.

First, the amount of capital employed is computed, and the appropriate risk factor is applied to that amount to show what profits should be made by this business if a fair return to compensate for the risk taken is to be achieved. This is termed the expected profit.

Second, the past adjusted weighted average profit is computed. Profits for a number of past years are included, so that no single or abnormal year can affect the value of the goodwill, and these profits are adjusted to remove influences which will not apply after the business has changed hands. If an owner/manager is paid £25 000 a year for doing a job which a hired manager would do for £20 000 a year, then £5000 must be added back to profits to show the level they are likely to achieve under new management. Past profits for a number of years are used to give a fair spread of the normal ups and downs of business, but these profits must be weighted to give greater significance to the profits of the most recent years, since they are more likely to reflect future conditions and should therefore have a greater significance when the average profits are calculated. Profits from periods too far into the past will not reflect current conditions. Depending on the circumstances of the industry, a three-year spread is often considered suitable for a weighted average calculation. During a period of inflation, past profits may not reflect future earnings, and for this reason there is now a tendency to adjust them. It must, however, be recognized that the basis for such an adjustment will be an estimate, and difficult to substantiate. An alternative method is to use future expected profits derived from budgets, again giving the greatest weight to the most recent year. This method is risky since it relies on estimates of future profit rather than audited figures for past performance.

Next the expected profit is subtracted from the past adjusted weighted average profit to determine whether excess or superprofits have been earned. The capital value of superprofits to be earned in the future is computed by multiplying superprofits by an agreed number of years' purchase thereof or by finding their capital value at an agreed rate. This is goodwill.

Example

The ABC Company Ltd has a balance sheet as follows:

	£	£
Share capital 1 000 000 ordinary shares of £1 each		1 000 000
Reserves		750 000
Equity interest		1 750 000
Debentures (10 per cent)		600 000
Net capital employed		£2 350 000
Represented by:		
Fixed assets (net of depreciation):		
Buildings		1 200 000
Plant		400 000
Vehicles		150 000
		1 750 000
Current assets:		
Stock	400 000	
Debtors	200 000	
Cash	100 000	
	700 000	
Curent liabilities: creditors	100 000	600 000
Net worth		£2 350 000

Book value of assets as disclosed by the balance sheet is unlikely to reflect the correct market value of the assets.

Suppose the buildings are revalued at £1 500 000, stock is written down to £300 000, and vehicles are considered to be worth only £50 000. The net capital employed figure would then be £2 450 000 less £600 000 for debentures, equalling £1 850 000 as net tangible assets. This figure is divided by 1 000 000 ordinary shares to give an asset value of £1.85 per share, showing what the shares are worth in terms of assets, and representing a floor below which negotiations to purchase the shares will not allow the price to fall.

	£
Buildings	+ 300 000
Stock	− 100 000
Vehicles	− 100 000
Net	+ 100 000
Equity interest	+ 1 750 000
Net tangible assets	1 850 000

Another significant factor of an asset valuation based on adjusted balance sheet figures is that the balance sheet itself may be out of date by anything up to a year, and profits or losses made in the intervening period will have increased or decreased the net assets of the business.

But what of the profits of the business? Suppose they have been: this year, £500 000; last year, £450 000; and the year before last, £400 000. The shareholders who act as directors are paid salaries totalling £150 000 p.a. but could be replaced by managers for a salary of £70 000. Thus profits for all years will have to be adjusted by adding £80 000. If it is discovered that an extraordinary transaction last year which brought in a profit of £30 000 is not likely to be repeated in the future, a further adjustment is needed so that past profits reflect future conditions.

The past adjusted weighted profits will be: this year, £580 000; last year, £500 000; and the year before last, £480 000. These profit figures need to be weighted for averaging purposes to allow the results of the most recent years to have a major influence on the past average profit figure.

	£	Weights	Product
This year	580 000	3	1 740 000
Last year	500 000	2	1 000 000
Year before last	480 000	1	480 000
		6	3 220 000

£3 220 000 ÷ 6 = £536 666 = PAWAP (past adjusted weighted average profits).

If a return of 20 per cent is considered sufficient to compensate for the risk involved, then a profit of 20 per cent on net tangible assets of £1 850 000 will be required, i.e. £370 000, so superprofits of £166 666 in excess of this figure can be expected in the future. The amount of the goodwill is the value to an investor of these superprofits. It can be computed as so many years' purchase of the superprofits, say three, so that goodwill is worth £499 998 and the company is then worth net tangible assets plus goodwill, an amount of £1 850 000 + £499 998 = £2 349 998, say £2 350 000.

	£
Profit required, 20 per cent of £1 850 000	370 000
Past adjusted weighted average profits	536 660
Superprofits	£166 666

	£
Goodwill at three years' purchase of superprofits	499 998
Net tangible assets	1 850 000
Value of business (£2.35 per share)	£2 349 998

The goodwill multiplier is either agreed by the buyer and the seller or is a rate normally used in the particular trade or industry.

Alternatively, the superprofits can be capitalized at an appropriate rate. Since they represent a non-tangible and thus risky asset, this rate can be expected to be above the normal expected return. Suppose 30 per cent is considered appropriate. The superprofits would then be worth £166 666 $\times \dfrac{100}{30}$, i.e. £555 553, and this amount of goodwill could be added to the net tangible assets to compute the valuation of the business at £2 405 553.

Capital Value of Superprofits

	£
£166 666 $\times \dfrac{100}{30}$	555 553
Net tangible assets	1 850 000
Value of business (£2.40 per share)	£2 405 553

Three years' purchase of superprofits is equal to a capitalization rate of 33 per cent. Appropriate multipliers must be carefully selected since these subjective factors inserted into the calculation have a significant effect on the value derived therefrom.

Yet another method can be used to value the shares by capitalizing the profits on the basis of the required yield. With past adjusted weighted profits of £536 666 and a required rate of return of 20 per cent, this would value the entire business at £536 666 $\times \dfrac{100}{20}$, say £2 700 000. If the value of net tangible assets at £1 850 000 is subtracted from this figure, the difference of £850 000 would be goodwill.

Capital Value of Expected Profits

	£	
£53 666 $\times \dfrac{100}{20}$	2 700 000	(£2.70 per share)
Net tangible assets	1 850 000	
Goodwill	£850 000	

Thus we have seen three methods for the valuation of shares which have computed three different values for goodwill. This example illustrates the idea that share valuation methods are far from precise, and also shows the significance of the calculation of such estimates as the required rate of return etc.

The price/earnings ratio is another multiplier which can be used as a share valuation tool. This ratio sets earnings net of tax per share (EPS) against the current market price of the share, and is expressed as a number. It can be seen as the number of years which the investor must wait to recoup his invested sum out of earnings, whether they are distributed as a dividend or not. In a public company a net profit of £500 000 this year would give earnings of £325 000 after corporation tax at 35 per cent. Thus, with 1 000 000 ordinary shares, EPS would be 32.5 pence per share. If the market price of the shares was £2, the price/earnings ratio would be 6.15. This ratio reflects the market price of the share, which is the product of investors' expectations. Where growth and a capital profit are expected, investors will bid up the share price and thus increase the price/earnings multiple. Companies of a similar size and prospects within the same industry can be expected to have a similar price/earnings ratio, so this figure can be used as a basis for valuing a private company of the same type. The appropriate price/earnings number, decreased slightly to take into account the extra risk concerned with the lack of marketability of a private company, is multiplied by the net profit after tax but before extraordinary items, and a value is found. For example, suppose a price/earnings ratio of twelve is normal for companies like ABC Ltd that are quoted on the Stock Exchange, then deduct, say, two, since ABC Ltd is a private company, and calculate a multiplier of 10. A net profit of £500 000 after tax at 35 per cent gives £325 000. If the multiplier of 10 is applied to this figure, a value for the business of £3 250 000 is found. The rule in SSAP 6 concerning the calculation of net profit after tax ensures that extraordinary items in the profit and loss account are not allowed to affect this sensitive Stock Exchange comparator. If the rate of corporation tax falls, then EPS will increase. Thus changes in base rates can influence share values.

Note that the term 'net worth' on the balance sheet has little to do with the value of the share as computed by any of the methods shown above.

GOODWILL

This phenomenon is an important factor in the valuation of a business, but there has been considerable discussion about the precise meaning of the term and reasons for the existence of goodwill. The legal profession and accountants see goodwill in somewhat different terms, as the following two quotations from past judgements will show. First, Judge Warrington in *Hill* v. *Fearis* [1905] 1 CH 466 defined goodwill as 'the advantage, whatever it may be, which a person gets by continuing to carry on, and being entitled to represent to the outside world that he is carrying on, a business which has been carried on for some time previously'. This legal definition seems to suggest that the goodwill of the business is derived from the fact that it is a going concern with an established clientele and reputation. In another case, that of *CIR* v. *Muller* [1901] AC 217, Lord MacNaughton remarked that goodwill was 'a thing very easy to describe, very difficult to define. The benefit and advantage of a good name, reputation and connection of a business. The attractive force that brings in custom. The one thing which distinguishes an old established business from a new business at its first start. Goodwill is composed of a variety of elements. It differs in its composition in different trades, and in different businesses in the same trade. One element may preponderate here and another there.'

This definition attempts to explain some of the reasons why goodwill exists, and the elements in a business which improve its profitability, such as reputation and trade connection, which attract custom and increase turnover. The accountant also sees goodwill as a force which attracts custom. Thus there is a need to value goodwill, since as turnover is improved so profit will increase. To an accountant, goodwill is that element arising from the connection and reputation which enables a business to earn larger profits than would otherwise be expected, and it is at this point that the idea of superprofits and their connection with goodwill emerges. The ability of a business to be more than normally profitable can be determined by a number of factors:

1. The business's reputation for the quality of its products, the service that it gives, and the fair trading of its managers or proprietors. While a good reputation will attract customers, the possession of a well-known trade name built up through advertising campaigns will persuade customers to ask for a specific product by name, and thus increase turnover and profit.
2. Location. If a company possesses business premises in a favourable place, e.g. a shop in a prime high street site or a factory well positioned for communication, then it can expect to derive advantages from its location. These advantages can be turned into superprofits, and thus contribute towards the goodwill of the business.
3. 'Knowhow' and experience. A company which has carried on business in a certain trade for a number of years builds up a body of knowledge of the best methods to employ in its chosen trade, so that it knows how best to tackle awkward projects and overcome difficult problems. This type of experience avoids mistakes, which can increase costs and reduce profits. The very fact that a company is a going concern means that it has an established body of customers who are used to trading with it, and who may return with repeat orders. A new entrant to a certain trade must not only build up its clientele but also learn by its own mistakes while it is establishing itself in the trade.
4. The possession of favourable contracts. A lease on good premises brings its own advantages of site, but a long-term contract to supply to a reputable customer, or a licence to manufacture or a dealership from a well-known company, will reduce the riskiness of the business and profits will thus be assured.
5. A team of keen and experienced executives and a body of contented and efficient employees will also contribute towards superprofits. Good relations with union representatives can reduce the disruption of business through strikes, and improve profitability.

Some of the above factors which contribute to the existence of goodwill are derived from the circumstances of the firm, while others are the product of the character of the managers or proprietors. Some of these elements of goodwill can be transferred easily and quickly to a new proprietor or management at the time of takeover, so the continued existence of goodwill will depend on them rather than on the actions of the proprietor who built up the business. If goodwill is derived from short-term factors this will be taken into account when the number of years' purchase of the superprofits is negotiated.

Example

Jon is the proprietor of an established business which has a good reputation for service and good labour relations. Raw materials for the business are bought from a trade supplier owned by Jon's father-in-law. Jon wishes to sell his business and emigrate with his capital to Canada. He has prepared a forecast of profits he expects the business to achieve over the next five years from the net tangible assets of £150 000.

	19-5	19-6	19-7	19-8	19-9
Net profit	£31 000	£32 000	£36 000	£40 000	£45 000
Return on capital	20%	21%	24%	26%	30%

Jon is a shrewd businessman, and has recently employed a specialist to revalue his assets, which are well maintained and in a good condition. The figure of £150 000 quoted above is a good indication of their net realizable value.

Jos has just graduated from a business school and wishes to start up a business of her own. She has no business connections, but intends to combine youthful enthusiasm with an inheritance of £150 000. Her projections of profit for the next five years are as follows:

	19-5	19-6	19-7	19-8	19-9
Net profit	£9 000	£15 000	£22 500	£30 000	£45 000
Return on capital	6%	10%	15%	20%	30%

Jon meets Jos and the conversation rapidly turns to the valuation of businesses. Jon points out that he will expect more than the net tangible asset value of £150 000 for his business.

As adviser to Jos what value would you put on Jon's business, and what arguments would you suggest that Jos uses to reduce the price which Jon might ask?

The answer to this problem can be in only the vaguest of terms, since much necessary information has been omitted. Briefly, however, Jon's position is that he is in an established business with a trade connection already built up, that his reputation is good, and this enhances his business connection, that his business has good labour relations and no disruptions through strikes, that there is experience and knowhow in the business, and that he benefits from certain family connections when buying his raw materials. All these factors contribute to Jon's profit, but it is difficult to quantify that contribution with any accuracy. It is equally certain that without these advantages the business would not be as successful as it is at present. Since the plant is well maintained and recently valued, an amount of £150 000 can be assumed for the net tangible assets of the business.

The profit forecasts of Jon and Jos are not really comparable, since the figures of Jos reflect the fact that she must learn the business in the early years. Jos has a faster rate of growth than Jon. Can she nearly catch up after five years of trading? Is the 50 per cent increase in profit for 19-9 a feasible forecast?

The net asset value of £150 000 provides a good starting point for the valuation of Jon's business. Jon will want to value goodwill by computing the worth of his superprofits. If we assume a 20 per cent return on net tangible assets, the required profits from Jon's business are 20 per cent of £150 000, or £30 000. Thus superprofits to be made by Jon in years 19-5 to 19-9 are £1000, £2000, £6000, £10 000 and £15 000 respectively. The factors which underpin the goodwill are largely connected with the personality of the proprietor, and do not seem to be permanent. Therefore it could be argued that goodwill should be valued as three years' purchase of the weighted average superprofits computed from the forecast figures for the next three years. Note that when weights are allocated to years the greatest weight is given to the most recent year.

	£	Weights	Multiple
19-5	1000	3	3 000
19-6	2000	2	4 000
19-7	6000	1	6 000
		6	13 000

13 000 ÷ 6 = £2167 superprofits
Three years of purchase = £6501 goodwill
Value of business = £156 501

The arguments which Jos can use to reduce the value which Jon sets on his business will revolve around the valuation of goodwill, which in this business appears to be closely linked to the personality of the retiring proprietor. Jos will argue that many of the advantages from which Jon derives his superprofits may not be transferred when the business is sold. For example, Jon's personal reputation and his purchasing advantages with a relation will certainly not enhance the business when it is owned by Jos. What is more, Jos will have to work very hard to maintain some of the other advantages, such as the trade connection and good labour relations. The experience and knowhow on which future superprofits depend may also leave with Jon; unless key employees of the business have agreed to remain under Jos's management and continue to contribute their experience and knowhow in the future. Jos may argue that much of the superprofitability depends on her ability to continue to operate the business as well as Jon, and that it is unfair to ask her to pay Jon for profits she has to earn by her own efforts. Jon, of course, will answer that he has built up the firm, that the potential is there, and that he cannot be expected to give this away for nothing.

Jos may challenge Jon's figures in an attempt to reduce the value of the goodwill. If it is a risky business a return of 25 or even 30 per cent on capital employed might be expected to compensate for the risk, with a corresponding reduction of the amount of superprofits. Jos might also argue that three years' purchase of the superprofits is too long a period for the calculation, since the goodwill transfers much sooner to the new manager and must be maintained by her. An alternative computation of the value of the firm, computed on the basis of the 30 per cent expected return, would show no superprofits, or goodwill computed at 1½ years' purchase of the superprofits would further reduce the value of the goodwill. Jon may counter this argument by pointing out that a 30 per cent return is too much to expect, since Jos's own profit forecast does not reach 25 per cent even after a five-year period of experience.

As an accountant giving advice to Jos, you might comment that this is the wrong business for her to buy, and that she should try to find another. She cannot afford to pay more than £150 000 for a business without recourse to borrowing, and the cost of the interest on borrowed funds would reduce the profitability of the business. The profit forecasts of Jon and Jos are very different, and suggest that Jos is willing to accept a low return in the early years while she builds up experience, while Jon, on the other hand, is trying to sell an established business at as high a price as possible. Jos must decide whether she wishes to leapfrog the next few years of low profits, whether she can afford to buy her way into this profitable business, and whether she should take the risk of borrowing and investing in an established business which she may not be able to operate successfully. It would be wise to point out to Jos that if she fails the goodwill of the business for which she has paid will rapidly evaporate, but she will still have to meet her creditors' demands for interest and repayment of principal, and that her own funds will be fully committed.

Example

W. Rambler and Co. Ltd (founded in 1920) is engaged in fellmongery and hide and skin merchanting. It is based in Bermondsey (south-east London) and operates in hide and skin markets in Devon and Cornwall.

The summarized profit and loss accounts and balance sheet are set out below. No accounts have been drawn up in respect of any period subsequent to 30 September 19-8, and no dividends paid.

Profit and Loss Accounts, Years Ended 30 September

	19-6	19-7	19-8
	£	£	£
Sales	982 373	989 660	865 550
Cost of sales	(894 933)	(920 798)	(763 464)
	87 440	68 862	102 086
Investment income (note 1)	20 483	14 832	23 800
Profit before taxation	107 923	83 694	125 886
Taxation	(40 338)	(43 573)	66 754)
Profit attributable to shareholders	67 585	40 121	59 132
Dividends	12 120	12 120	20 200
Retained profit	£55 465	£28 001	£38 932

Balance Sheet at 30 September 19-8

	£	£	£
Fixed assets:	*Cost*	*Depreciation*	
Land and buildings, freehold	98 265	—	98 265
(Note 2), long leasehold	13 365	2 258	11 107
Plant, equipment and vehicles	68 512	52 898	15 614
	180 142	55 156	124 986
Investments (note 1)			279 611
Current assets:			
Stock and work in progress	43 300		
Debtors	62 613		
Bank and cash	69 602		
		175 515	
Less current liabilities:			
Creditors	20 915		
Taxation	93 069		
Proposed dividends	20 200		
		134 184	
Net current assets			41 331
			£445 928
Representing:			
Share capital: ordinary shares of £1		10 100	
Reserves		435 828	£445 928

Notes:

1. Investments:

   (a) At 30 September 19-8 investments comprised:

	£
Quoted investments (market value £71 001)	82 750
Corporation loans	190 000
Loans to employees	6 861
	£279 611

   (b) The market value of the quoted investments as at 1 June 19-9 was £89 750.
   (c) The investment income includes the related tax credit.

2. Land and buildings. The land and buildings have been valued on a going concern basis at 31 May 19-9 by Messrs Hope, Eternal and Co., Chartered Surveyors, as follows:

	£	
Freehold	90 000	
Long leasehold	28 500	£118 500

Amalgamated Leather Holdings Ltd has liquid funds available for investment and is contemplating purchasing for cash as at 1 June 19-9 all the shares in Ramblers from Mr W. Rambler, who is retiring because of old age and poor health. The executive directors of Ramblers (the managing director and the fellmongery director) will continue to be associated with the business in their present capacities. The acquisition of Ramblers will increase the supply of raw materials to Amalgamated's tanneries.

(a) Assuming that the normal return on capital is 20 per cent (before tax) for the leather industry, and using weighted average profits, calculate the price you would expect Amalgamated to pay as at 1 June 19-9 for all the shares in Ramblers:

   (i) on an asset basis, valuing goodwill as two years' purchase of superprofits;
   (ii) on an earnings basis (for the trading profit/assets) plus investments.

(b) List six items (other than the information used in (a)) which might be taken into account in determining the actual price Amalgamated would be willing to pay for Ramblers. (The effect of capital gains tax can be ignored.)

The first step toward a solution is to calculate the weighted average trading profits. Investment income can be ignored here, since the investments will be valued separately according to the information in note (1).

$$\frac{£87\ 440 + 2(£68\ 862) + 3(£102\ 086)}{6} = £88\ 570$$

Note that the greatest weighting has been accorded to the profits of the most recent years. No adjustment has been made to the figures so they must be considered to adequately reflect future trading conditions.

Next the trading assets should be valued according to their current, rather than their book value.

	£	£
Trading assets:		
Land and buildings	118 500	
Plant etc.	15 614	
Net current assets	41 331	175 445
Investments at market value		
(£89 750 + £190 000 + £6861)		286 611
(Check: £445 928 + £7000 investment surplus + £9128		
property surplus)		462 056
Post-balance-sheet profit		
8 months net profit (1 October 19-8 to 1 June 19-9)		

$$\frac{8}{12} \times \frac{£67\ 585 + 2\ (£40\ 121) + 3\ (£59\ 132)}{6} = \frac{8}{12} \times £54\ 204 =$$

		36 136
Total assets (excluding goodwill)		498 192

The balance sheet is the basis of this valuation, but the assets shown therein will have increased by the valuation date by the amount of profit made net of tax since 30 September 19-8.

	£	£
Total assets excluding goodwill		498 192
Superprofit calculation:		
Assets £175 445 × 20 per cent	35 089	
Actual profit (WA)	88 570	
Superprofit	£53 481	
Goodwill:		
2 × £53 481		106 962
Value on assets basis plus goodwill		£605 154

Part (ii) of (a) is calculated as follows:

$$\text{Profit: } £88\,570 \times \frac{100}{20}$$

	£
	442 850 = Capital value of trading assets
Investments as above	286 611
Value on earnings basis	£729 461

Other items which might be considered when the company is valued would include matters which affected the future return of the business, and adjustments which might affect the present position. The valuation above is based on past profits, but estimates of future profits, perhaps even weighted in favour of the most recent year, might be used. If Mr Rambler has drawn a salary in excess of the market rate for the work he has performed, the amount of this excess must be added back to past profits so that they are adjusted to reflect the future after Mr Rambler has retired. The general economic prospects for the industry as a whole will affect the confidence of the purchasers, while the particular situation of Rambler Ltd (e.g. whether it is a forced sale, or whether a rival bidder is likely to make a counter offer) will also influence the price. If Rambler Ltd fits neatly into the operations of Amalgamated Leather Holdings (e.g. if Amalgamated Leather Holdings do not have a subsidiary in Devon or Cornwall and wish to expand in that area) this will improve the value of Rambler Ltd in the view of the management of Amalgamated.

The valuation above has been made on the basis of the book value of the plant, although a current value would be more helpful. The profits for the eight months since the last accounting date have been estimated, although actual figures may be available for use instead. If the goodwill is likely to evaporate when Mr Rambler leaves the business, because it is caused by factors related to his management, then the two-year purchase period for superprofits in the goodwill computation might be reduced.

The Accounting Treatment of Goodwill

Accountants differentiate between purchased goodwill and inherent goodwill as discussed above. Purchased goodwill arises on consolidation, and is calculated as that part of the price paid for the assets of a business which is in excess of their fair market value. Purchased goodwill does not rely on a doubtful computation for its identification, but is the product of an open market transaction. When a business is purchased for a price in excess of the fair market value of the net tangible assets, this is tacit recognition of the fact that, when combined, the assets concerned possess the capacity to earn superprofits.

There is no difference between inherent goodwill and purchased goodwill, since they represent the same idea, except that the inherent goodwill in a business is capable of accurate valuation as purchased goodwill when the business changes hands at a market price.

An examination of the characteristics of this intangible asset provides further evidence of the difficulties encountered in the search for best accounting practice concerning goodwill:

1. It is difficult to identify and value the factors from which inherent goodwill is derived in a business. It follows from this that goodwill is unique to every business, and cannot fairly be compared with goodwill in other businesses, and that goodwill is attached to the business as a whole and cannot easily be sold separately from the business.
2. Any value attaching to goodwill belongs to the shareholders as owners of the business, and should be disclosed to them in any accounting statement which purports to reveal the position of the business, but that value can fluctuate from year to year according to the influence of factors which are either internal or external to the business.
3. The value of goodwill may be influenced by the subjective assessments or bias of individual valuers, and often bears no relation to the costs incurred in its creation.
4. The value or cost is not used up when profits are earned from the asset, although certain expenditures may have to be made each year to maintain the factors from which inherent goodwill is derived.

A further question concerns 'badwill' (negative goodwill) which may exist in companies which are not profitable enough to compensate the shareholders for the risk they take and, if so, how should the accountant treat this item in accounting statements?

Opinion among accountants as to the proper treatment for goodwill is divided. One group holds that goodwill is not like the other fixed assets, especially as it cannot be realized separately from the business. Expenditure on purchased goodwill is a once-only payment for an intangible asset whose value and life cannot be accurately determined. To disclose such an asset is of little help to users reading a balance sheet, so it is best to write off purchased goodwill to reserves when it is acquired, and to ignore inherent goodwill altogether. It is argued that this accounting treatment gives comparability between the treatment accorded to inherent and purchased goodwill. However, to ignore one item and to write off the other can hardly be considered a matter of comparability.

The opposing group believes that purchased goodwill is not substantially different from other assets employed in the business, that it has a finite useful life, and that it should be charged to the profit computation over that life. They argue that the purchase of goodwill is a payment for extra profit in the future, and the amount paid should be written off against that profit as it is earned. However, the rules which have been suggested so far to give guidance in the determination of the useful economic life of goodwill are not very precise.

Accounting practice varies widely in the treatment of goodwill. In the USA and Canada an accounting standard states that goodwill should be written off over its useful economic life, giving forty years as the maximum period. The maximum has become the norm as directors have tried to minimize the impact of the write-off on profits. The International Accounting Standards Committee holds the view that goodwill should be written off over its life, since it is a payment for future anticipated income. The EEC Fourth Directive followed the usual practice in European countries, which is to write off goodwill over a maximum period of five years. In the UK the Companies Act 1985 mentions goodwill, considering it to be an intangible fixed asset disclosed in the balance sheet separate from patents, trademarks etc. The accounting treatment specified in the Act is that goodwill should be written off systematically but that the directors must choose the period of the write-off, which must not exceed the useful economic life of the goodwill. A note to the accounts must disclose the period chosen and the reasons behind that choice (Sch. 4, Part II, Para. 21). The statute, however, refers specifically to purchased goodwill, which includes goodwill arising on consolidation, but does not include inherent goodwill. Under the Companies Act any provision should be treated as a realizable loss when distributable profits are computed, and this applies to goodwill whether it is written off at once or gradually over its economic life.

The Accounting Standards Committee (ASC) in seeking to guide accountants through this difficult situation has issued SSAP 22 with four main proposals.

1. No amount should be attributed to non-purchased goodwill in accounting statements—inherent goodwill is to be ignored.
2. Purchased goodwill should be calculated as the difference between the fair value of the consideration given (shares, loan stock or cash) and the fair value of assets acquired. In a contested takeover bid this difference could be of considerable size.
3. Purchased goodwill should not include any value for separable intangibles such as patents, trademarks etc.
4. Purchased goodwill should not be carried in the balance sheet as a permanent item, but must be eliminated from the accounts by the consistent use of one of the two alternative policies. Either:

   (a) write off immediately to general reserves; or
   (b) amortize to profit and loss over the economic life.

Alternative (a) is preferred but (b) is permitted.

Alternative (a) appears at first glance to be at variance with the requirements of the Companies Act 1985, but may be within statutory requirements if the directors choose a very short economic life, and if the provision forms part of the calculation of distributable profits under the Act. Most directors would prefer to spread the effect of amortization over as long a period as possible, to minimize its effects on profit, so policy (b) may prove to be most popular. However, the point must be made that any proposal which allows such divergent methods as (a) and (b) above, can hardly be classed as a 'standard' seeking to improve comparability of accounting statements.

Accountants who favour amortization argue that goodwill is a long-term asset acquired with capital recruited to finance the business and must be treated in the same way as other fixed assets, and that the cost of the asset should be matched against the extra earnings derived from it. Their opponents hold that comparability between companies is reduced if non-purchased goodwill is ignored while purchased goodwill is capitalized and amortized, and that comparability between years is reduced if goodwill is amortized in one year but not in another. The case against amortization also covers the difficulty of determining the economic life of purchased goodwill, and the fact that it may not fall in value, or that it may disappear rapidly. A uniform accounting treatment will not work well in conditions where uniformity does not exist. SSAP 22 defines useful economic life as the period over which benefits may reasonably be expected to accrue from goodwill in existence at the date of acquisition, expressed as 'the directors' best estimate of the life, at that date.' This figure will be difficult to audit! The key to the problem lies in the assertion that purchased goodwill diminishes after its acquisition, and is replaced by non-purchased (inherent) goodwill created from the activities of the business designed to preserve this important asset. The standard suggests the following rules to help towards a solution of these problems.

1. Useful economic life should not include any allowance for the effect of subsequent expenditure to create non-purchased goodwill.
2. Purchased goodwill should not be revalued, but any permanent diminution of its value should be written off at once to the profit and loss account.
3. Estimated useful life of goodwill may be shortened but not increased, and should not exceed twenty years.

Presumably amortization will affect the earnings per share calculation, which in turn will change the price/earnings ratio which is so important to investors.

Accountants who favour an immediate write-off to reserves on acquisition argue that goodwill is not a normal fixed asset, that it cannot be realized independently of the business and that it can disappear without warning because of factors outside the control of the business. In this situation it is imprudent to carry goodwill as an asset. It is a premium paid on acquisition, and must be treated as part of the acquisition. Their opponents hold that it is excessively prudent to write off this asset immediately, and that such a write-off will reduce the distributable profits of the company. If reserves are reduced, the equity interest in the company will fall and this will increase the gearing ratio. The company appears more risky than a similar company using the amortization method, but since the profit is not reduced by amortization, but the capital employed is decreased because of the write-off, the ratio of net profit to capital employed will give the impression of a better performance when comparing companies using the write-off method with companies using the amortization method. Companies whose borrowing powers are limited to a certain proportion of share capital and reserves may find that their ability to raise long-term loan finance is inhibited if goodwill is written off against reserves. In some companies goodwill forms a large proportion of the fixed assets, e.g. retailers or service companies, and a write-off in these circumstances might be positively misleading.

TUTORIAL DISCUSSION TOPICS

23.1 What factors influence the risk attached to an investment in a company?

23.2 Why should a controlling interest in a public company be valued differently from a minority interest in a private company?

23.3 Why is it necessary to adjust past profits when using them to compute a value for a business?

23.4 Reconcile the legal view of goodwill with that of the accountant.

23.5 Outline the factors which support the existence of goodwill in a company, and show how they can be related to the number of years' purchase of goodwill when a business is valued.

23.6 You are examining the published accounts of a public company to establish whether to subcontract part of a job to that company. The term 'intangible assets' appears on the balance sheet, and on further investigation you learn that this asset is goodwill. Explain the term 'goodwill', and discuss the difficulties encountered in accounting for this intangible asset.

SEMINAR EXERCISES 14

1. As you are leaving the AGM of the Institution of Civil Engineers, you meet an old friend who is managing director and principal shareholder in a medium-sized construction company. Recently you have inherited £50 000 from an aunt, and your friend offers to sell you a 10 per cent stake in his business for just that sum. He explains that he has a set of audited accounts, for publication under the Companies Act 1985, which will prove to you that he is offering a sound investment.

   (a) Discuss briefly the limitations of published accounts in a situation such as that outlined above.
   (b) Explain *three* items which you consider would need deeper investigation in such an investment decision.

2. (a) 'Surely the balance sheet provides all the information required to value a business. After all, it usually shows an item labelled "shareholders' funds".' Comment.
   (b) The following is the balance sheet of Boozles, a wholesale wine merchanting business, at 31 March, year 5.

	£	£
Liabilities:		
Owners' capital		60 000
Creditors		10 000
		70 000
Assets (at written-down value):		
Land and buildings		20 000
Fixtures and fittings		10 000
		30 000
Current assets:		
Stock	30 000	
Debtors	7 000	
Cash	3 000	40 000
		70 000

You ascertain the following information:

(i) The land and buildings are currently valued at £50 000.
(ii) Included in the debtors is a balance of £1000 which may prove irrecoverable.
(iii) Businesses of this type usually provide a return of 25 per cent on the gross assets employed.
(iv) The profits over the past five years (before charging any remuneration for the owner) were as follows:

Year ended 31 March	Year 1	Year 2	Year 3	Year 4	Year 5
	£	£	£	£	£
Profits	25 000	30 000	35 000	40 000	40 000

It is anticipated that growth of profit in the future is extremely unlikely.

Suggest three alternative methods of valuation for the business, stating clearly any assumptions you make.

3. Ever since Mr Carrott died, his wife has retained the family business, which has been run completely by Mr Parsnip. Mr Parsnip is now due to retire. Mrs Carrott is therefore considering selling the business. For every £1000 that she receives from the sale of the business she can buy a pension of £218 per annum, ceasing on her death.

The following figures include the relevant extracts from the profit and loss account for the year to 31 December.

	£
Wages of department heads:	
Mr Parsnip	7 000
Mr Turnip	7 000
Mr Swede	7 000
Wages of other staff	49 000
Directors' emoluments:	
Mr Parsnip	5 000
Mrs Carrott	7 500
Transport	16 000
Interest	4 000
Heat and light	7 000
Bad debts	3 120
Loss on sale of car	2 500
Net profit	30 000

Balance sheet for the last three years:

	Year Before Last	Last Year	This Year
	£	£	£
Share capital	20 000	20 000	40 000
Reserves	50 000	65 000	70 000
Loans	—	—	20 000
Current liabilities	32 000	40 000	30 000
	£102 000	£125 000	£160 000

	Year Before Last	Last Year	This Year
Fixed assets cost	60 000	60 000	120 000
Less depreciation	30 000	40 000	60 000
	30 000	20 000	60 000
Current assets:			
Stock	40 000	40 000	40 000
Debtors	20 000	30 000	25 000
Cash	12 000	35 000	35 000
	£102 000	£125 000	£160 000

Mr Ward is interested in buying the business and holds the following assets:

	Capital £	Income per annum £
Building society	10 000	900
Quoted shares	10 000	400
Shares in private company	10 000	300

(a) Calculate the superprofit for the current year, indicating any assumptions you would wish to confirm.

(b) What is the purchase price of the business? (The basis of calculation of goodwill is to be the next two years' projected superprofits with the last three years assumed to indicate a constant trend in profit. This year's depreciation is to be reduced from 20 per cent to 15 per cent (there were no disposals).)

4. There has been a recent decline in the market for decorative watergarden plants, and Mr C. Weed is considering the sale of his business, Waterweeds Ltd, in which he owns all the shares, to Underwater Plants Ltd.

The most recent balance sheet and profits for the last five years are as follows.

Balance Sheet at Waterweeds Ltd as at 31 December 15

	£		£	£
Share capital and reserves:		Fixed assets:		
Ordinary share capital		Freehold land and		
of £1 each	30 000	buildings		20 000
General reserve	10 000	Plant and		
	40 000	equipment		10 000
Less deficit on profit and loss				
account	(20 000)			
	20 000			
Current liabilities:		Current assets:		
Creditors	30 000	Stock	30 000	
Bank overdraft	30 000	Debtors	20 000	50 000
	£80 000			£80 000

The stock is revalued at £20 000 and the land and buildings are considered to be undervalued by £10 000. All other assets represent market value.

Profits for the last five years are: year 11, £10 000 loss; year 12, £5000 loss; year 13, £5000 profit; year 14, £10 000 profit; year 15, £15 000 profit.

Profit and loss accounts have been prepared on a uniform basis and Mr Weed has charged only a nominal management fee for his services, taking out profits by way of dividends. A fair return for this kind of business is 20 per cent. Losses made in the past are not likely to recur.

(a) Compute a value for each ordinary share in Waterweeds Ltd.

(b) Discuss briefly those factors which cause goodwill to arise in a business.

5. Almond Ltd is an old family company in the south-west of England. The company, which manufactures gliders, has an enviable reputation for good workmanship, prompt delivery and low prices. Purchases of raw materials are made from another business, also owned by Mr Almond, which is not for sale. Mr Almond offers all of the issued share capital in the glider manufacturing business to Mr Cherry at the net asset value on 31 December plus the adjusted profits of the last three accounting years.

Any adjustments to profit are to be ignored for the purpose of calculating the net asset value.

For the purpose of the selling negotiations Almond produces the following information:

Balance Sheet Extract as at 31 December

	£	£	£
Issued share capital:			20 000
20 000 ordinary shares of £1 each			
Reserves:			
General reserve		10 000	
Profit and loss account:			
Profit for year	100 000		
Less losses brought forward	60 000		
		40 000	
			50 000
Long-term loan			60 000
			130 000
Current liabilities:			
Trade creditors	10 000		
Director's salary	60 000		
			70 000
			£200 000

A Statement of Past Profitability for the Three Years Ended 31 December

Year Before Last	Last Year	This Year
£60 000	£90 000	£100 000

The following information is also relevant:

(a) A reasonable management remuneration is estimated to be £40 000 per annum, not £60 000 per annum as deducted by Almond.
(b) Depreciation has been understated in each year by: £10 000 the year before last; £15 000 last year; and £20 000 this year.

Calculate the office price and advise Mr Cherry.

REVIEW QUESTIONS 9

1. (a) The balance sheet of Value Ltd as at 31 December 19-2 was as follows:

	£	£		£	£
Ordinary share capital:			Fixed assets:		
100 000 £1 shares	100 000		Premises at cost	80 000	
			Plant and machinery		
Revenue reserves	20 000	120 000	at cost, less		
			depreciation	20 000	100 000
Current liabilities:			Current assets:		
Creditors	70 000		Stocks at cost	51 500	
Bank overdraft	21 500	91 500	Debtors	60 000	111 500
		£211 500			£211 500

The following additional information is available:

(i) A fair after-tax return on net assets for the type of business involved is 10 per cent.

(ii) Premises are to be revalued at £125 000.

(iii) Plant and machinery is overvalued by £5000.

(iv) Trade debts of £5000 are regarded as irrecoverable.

(v) Stocks are considered to have a net realizable value of £45 000.

(vi) Goodwill in this type of business is normally valued as threè years' superprofits, or by capitalization of annual superprofits at 25 per cent.

(vii) Taxed profits for the five years up to 31 December 19-2 were as follows: [£18 000, £20 250, £22 000, £21 500, £24 000.]

Calculate the value of the equity of Value Ltd using three different bases. State any assumptions you make, and show all your workings.

(b) What do you understand by the term 'goodwill'?

Under what circumstances would you expect to see goodwill in the accounts of:

(i) a partnership?

(ii) a limited company?

2. A client who owns 10 000 shares in Leen Valley Trading Limited has received an offer by Buyit Ltd for his holding. The price suggested is £1.70.

You are asked to produce a report detailing your calculations of the various alternative prices along with your recommendation of whether the offer should be accepted. Supporting arguments for your view are required. (Note: working papers should be submitted as necessary.)

The information detailed below has been made available to you.

Leen Valley Trading Limited Balance Sheet as at 31 December 19-1

	£	£
Capital and reserves:		
2 000 000 Ordinary shares of £1 each fully paid		2 000 000
General reserves		700 000
Total shareholder interest		£2 700 000
Represented by:		
Fixed assets:		£
(At cost less depreciation)		
Freehold property		1 400 000
Plant and machinery		600 000
		2 000 000

	£	£
Current assets:		
Stock at cost	560 000	
Debtors	600 000	
Cash	40 000	
	1 200 000	
Less current liabilities:		
Trade creditors	450 000	
Accrued charges	50 000	
	500 000	
Working capital		700 000
Total net assets		£2 700 000

Notes:

(a) Profits over the past five years have been approximately £300 000 per annum. The dividend has averaged 10 per cent of the nominal value of the shares.

(b) The freehold property was recently valued by a professional surveyor at £2 000 000, plant and machinery being worth around £400 000. Stock is estimated to be realizable for £500 000 and it is thought that bad debts (not previously provided for) would amount to £20 000.

(c) Liquidation cost if the company was wound up would be £120 000.

(d) The earnings yield of similar firms sold recently is currently in the region of 15 per cent and the dividends paid represent a return on the market value of the shares of 6 per cent.

(e) Goodwill is said to be computed as two years' purchase of net profits in this trade.

Interpretation of Financial Statements

24 | The Interpretation of Accounts

The means by which an accountant is able to understand a set of accounts and reveal their meaning to a non-accountant are among the most advanced techniques he can use. A blend of skill and experience is required to explain the relative importance of the figures and the relationship between one figure and another. A good accountant can translate what the statements show to be happening to a company, and can comment on the significance of the figures for the efficient operation of the business. This is not always a matter of hindsight, since comment on future planned positions is also helpful.

The accountant must bear in mind the recipient of his interpretation when drawing out the meaning of a set of accounts, as what is significant to one user may be less so to another. He may be commenting to management on the performance of various divisions in a group of companies, or, as an extension of the annual accounts, providing helpful statistics for the shareholders, or demonstrating the optimal use of the capacity available to the management. The accountant may also be called on to comment on the business to potential investors, such as a city institution or the client of a stockbroker, or to his own managers when they are considering a takeover bid. The profit record, dividend cover and growth potential will be important to an investor, whereas the asset base and price/earnings ratio will usually be of greater interest in a takeover bid. When interpreting a set of accounts for a creditor or potential creditor, the accountant will accentuate the company's ability to repay a loan on the due date, to meet the interest required, or to provide security to cover the loan.

THE BASIC QUESTIONS

There is a set of basic questions to which the interpreter will seek answers. The answer to each question will lead to further questions, so that gradually a picture of what is happening in the company will emerge.

1. The first question usually concerns profitability. It is not enough to discover whether a profit or a loss is being made, since a measure of the adequacy of profit is needed. The return on capital employed should show whether profits are

sufficient to warrant the amount of funds invested in a business, the risk taken by investing those funds, and whether a better return for the same class of risk could be earned by an alternative employment of the funds. This approach leads on to questions to determine whether the assets are employed in the right way or in the best combination, and whether the company is on the threshold of a profit breakthrough after some lean years when reorganization has taken place.

2. The second question investigates solvency, or the ability of the firm to pay its way. Some argue that this should be the first question asked, as sometimes a profitable business is brought to a halt through insufficient liquid funds. The interpretation of the solvency position revolves around the availability of cash to repay creditors and the adequacy of working capital resources to finance the level of activity required by management. The liquidity of the current assets, the rate of expansion of stocks and debtors to an 'overtrading' position, and the ability of the business to borrow are all significant in this part of the pattern.

3. The third major question concerns ownership of the business. One individual or group may control a firm through significant shareholdings, and thus may be in a position to influence management policy. The voting rights of various classes of capital are important in this case. Rights to dividend and repayment of capital if the business is wound up are important matters to a potential shareholder. Often the ownership of shares is obscured through the use of nominee holdings. Ownership, however, has a deeper significance, since it can be used to comment on the relative importance of the various groups who have supplied the funds utilized to finance the business. In this sense all those who have provided funds for use in the business, shareholders, long-term lenders and current liabilities, are seen as owners of the assets which their finance has helped to buy, especially since, if the firm ceased trading, they would expect to be repaid out of the proceeds of those assets. If, for example, the trade creditors become a significant provider of finance, they may begin to have more power over the destiny of the firm than its legal owners, the shareholders. When assets are charged as security for loans the actions of the management may be inhibited, since they cannot dispose of certain assets without permission of the lender.

4. The fourth major question deals with financial strength. A weak company is one which has used up all its credit facilities and thus can borrow no more or one which is overdependent on sources of finance outside the business. If a company has unused overdraft facilities or uncharged assets which can act as security it can use this extra finance to extricate itself from financial difficulties or mount an expansion scheme. A different view of financial strength measures the amount of assets which the company controls year by year, so that growth in the assets, financed by increasing reserves from profits retained in the business, is seen as a healthy sign.

5. A fifth avenue of approach is to investigate trends. If the accounting statements for several years are expressed in columnar form and placed side by side, changes in the relative importance of certain items can be identified. For example, when all costs are expressed as a percentage of sales, the fact that one cost is becoming a larger proportion of the total as year succeeds year can be seen; or when all sources of finance are expressed as a percentage of total capital employed, the changing relative importance of the various classes of capital providers can be noted. When variations from a settled pattern are observed an attempt should be made to discover the cause. If, for example, the proportion of debtors or stocks to total assets has increased, further investigation to establish the reason for such a

change should be initiated. It is also possible to extrapolate the figures to forecast what is likely to happen if the present rate of change is maintained.

6. The last basic question concerns cover, to reveal the adequacy of the margin of profits over a required rate of dividend, or the value of a secured asset over the principal of the loan. Further questions concerning gearing are raised from this point to find the effect of a fluctuation in profit on the ability of the company to pay a dividend or to meet its liability for loan interest.

Once the answers to these six basic questions and their associated queries have been found, the accountant knows a great deal about the position of a business. Three techniques are used to answer these questions and to help form an opinion of a set of accounts. They are ratio analysis, funds flow statements, and balance sheet criticism. These techniques are not used in isolation, but together, each providing evidence to support the conclusions drawn from another.

RATIO ANALYSIS

A ratio shows the relationship of one figure to another and can be used in accounting to demonstrate the interplay between balance sheet items, or between features of the profit and loss account and the balance sheet. Ratios are useful in that they summarize a position and simplify an explanation of a complicated statement by its expression in one figure. However, a major disadvantage of their use is that they sometimes over-simplify a situation, and thus without a proper understanding of the definition of the constituent parts false conclusions may be drawn; e.g. the definition of net profit (before or after tax), or of capital employed, can seriously affect the return on capital employed. Accountants often use ratios to focus attention on important items in accounting statements or to illustrate points made in reports, but these techniques must be treated with caution. Ratios should be used as a guide, not as a basis for definitive conclusions. Too much reliance should not be placed on the impression gained from one ratio alone. The findings should be checked against other ratios, and perhaps against a movement of funds statement, until gradually a clearer picture emerges. Sometimes compensating changes in the constituent parts of a ratio can obscure the extent of the change that has taken place; e.g. although profit and capital employed may double, this important change does not show up in the ratio of net profit to capital employed. A change in both constituent parts at the same time will alter the ratios, but can cause confusion when the reason for the change is investigated.

Another use for ratios is as comparators. Absolute figures in an accounting statement are made more meaningful when they are put into perspective by comparison. Although the profit made by a company is always interesting, its significance is properly demonstrated only when it is measured against the capital employed in making that profit. An increase in profit may be considered as a good result until the extent of the extra capital employed to earn it is shown. The comparison of ratios of one company with those of another, or with the average ratios of a group of similar companies, is helpful, and comparison of the ratios of the same company at different time periods will reveal important changes from the established pattern for the company, which should prompt an investigation. Some companies treat ratios as guidelines or targets to be reached during the planning and budgeting operation. Because ratios reflect a relationship they can transcend national barriers. The ROCE, compiled from figures expressed in pounds, dollars or yen, enables international comparison to take place.

Ratios can be expressed as percentages, e.g. the rate of gross profit to sales, say 25 per cent; or as a relationship, e.g. current assets to current liabilities, say 1.7 : 1; or as one figure times another, e.g. the turnover of capital employed is, say, 2.4 times in a year; or in terms of time, e.g. debtors to credit sales may reveal an average credit period of sixty days.

RETURN ON CAPITAL EMPLOYED (ROCE)

One approach to ratio analysis is to compute the ratios in figure 11 and use their interaction to interpret the position of the company.

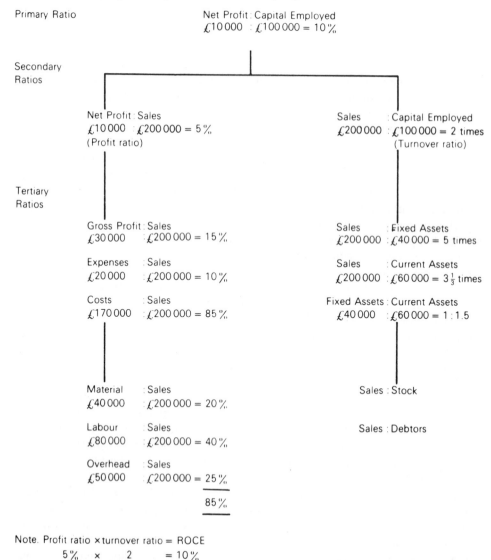

Primary Ratio

Net Profit : Capital Employed
£10 000 : £100 000 = 10 %

Secondary Ratios

Net Profit : Sales
£10 000 : £200 000 = 5 %
(Profit ratio)

Sales : Capital Employed
£200 000 : £100 000 = 2 times
(Turnover ratio)

Tertiary Ratios

Gross Profit : Sales
£30 000 : £200 000 = 15 %

Sales : Fixed Assets
£200 000 : £40 000 = 5 times

Expenses : Sales
£20 000 : £200 000 = 10 %

Sales : Current Assets
£200 000 : £60 000 = 3⅓ times

Costs : Sales
£170 000 : £200 000 = 85 %

Fixed Assets : Current Assets
£40 000 : £60 000 = 1 : 1.5

Material : Sales
£40 000 : £200 000 = 20 %

Sales : Stock

Labour : Sales
£80 000 : £200 000 = 40 %

Sales : Debtors

Overhead : Sales
£50 000 : £200 000 = 25 %

85 %

Note. Profit ratio × turnover ratio = ROCE
5 % × 2 = 10 %

Figure 11. Ratio diagram.

The first ratio is the ratio of net profit to capital employed. It is known as the primary ratio, since it reveals the return on capital employed and comments on the efficiency of management in employing the funds placed at their disposal by shareholders and lenders. This ratio is often expressed as a percentage and can be used to compare performance with other companies in the same industry, or other industries, or other economies, or at other time periods. The return on capital employed is seen by the investor as the return received for placing funds at risk, and is compared with the return available for alternative investments in the same risk category.

The definition of capital employed remains the subject of discussion among accountants. The ratio of net profit to shareholders' funds (share capital and reserves) expresses the return on the capital contributed by the legal owners of the business. This figure is a valuable guide to the profitability of the shareholders' investment, but, since it uses a limited definition of capital employed, cannot comment well on managerial efficiency. The net capital employed, defined as fixed assets plus working capital, is often used for ROCE in published accounts. It provides an acceptable figure, but of course does not set profit against all the capital employed, since current liabilities, an important source of capital employed, are ignored. It is argued that current liabilities provide finance for only a few weeks or months and should therefore be ignored, but when one current liability is repaid, usually another takes its place, so the total funds employed do not fluctuate very much. It seems wrong to calculate the ROCE after excluding bank overdraft and taxation awaiting payment.

Some authorities prefer to set net profit against gross capital employed (fixed and current assets) to show what the management have really produced from all the assets at their disposal. This definition is incomplete if it uses historical figures derived from a balance sheet. Perhaps a fairer view of managerial efficiency is found by setting net profit against the current value of all the assets, but this of course presupposes that the current value can be determined easily. Where net profit is set against the net capital employed, which includes long-term liabilities, there is a case for adding back loan interest to the net profit figure so that a true return on the capital employed is shown. If this argument is carried to its logical conclusion, overdraft interest should be added back to profit if the gross capital definition is favoured. Whichever definition is chosen it must be used consistently if true comparability is to be achieved. Some accountants prefer to use opening capital employed as opposed to closing capital employed, whilst other use an average of these two figures.

There is some difference of opinion among accountants about whether net profit before or after tax should be used for this ratio. Some argue that managerial efficiency should be measured before tax is deducted, while others hold the view that a good management should minimize the tax burden, and that profit after tax shows what is available for dividend or reinvestment in the company.

Analysis of ROCE Using Accounting Ratios

A good or bad ROCE can be explained by two basic reasons. Either (1) the profit on the activity is not large enough, or (2) the capital employed is not worked hard enough. Further investigation of these reasons can be achieved by the use of secondary ratios. Net profit to sales shows the profitability of sales made, and can be expressed as a percentage or as so many pence of profit for every pound of sales. This ratio can be further analysed by the tertiary ratios. If net profit to sales is not satisfactory the cause may be either in the pricing policy of the firm, if the mark-up is insufficient, or in the cost structure, if expenses and costs are too high. The difference between the percentage of net profit and gross profit to sales is the percentage of expenses to sales. When the gross profit margin is adequate, the reason for an unsatisfactory profit to sales ratio should lie in the cost structure, which can be further analysed by computing the percentage of various costs to sales, and revealing the changing position of the various cost headings.

Alternatively, if net profit to sales shows an adequate return, the reason for low profitability could be that not enough sales are being made. In other words, the productive capacity or assets of the firm are not working hard enough. The ratio of sales to capital employed (the turnover ratio) shows how many pounds of sales are earned by each pound of capital employed, or how many times the capital is turned over, the idea being that every time a firm turns over its capital it makes the profit margin. When the ratio of net profit to sales is multiplied by the turnover ratio, the result is equal to the primary ratio. If the turnover ratio is inadequate further analysis to pinpoint that part of the asset structure where underutilized capacity exists will investigate the ratios of sales to fixed assets, and sales to current assets (or sales to working capital if the net capital employed definition is used in the primary ratio). The ratio of fixed assets to current assets will show whether the business has the right combination in its asset structure or whether there is a preponderance of current or fixed assets. Sales can then be set against the individual assets to reveal over-investment in any one classification. The ratio of stock to sales in this context shows how many pounds of sales are earned for each pound of stock held. In other circumstances stocks would not be set against sales since they are at cost while sales include the profit margin.

How Useful is ROCE?

Although ROCE is useful for making comparisons over time and between firms in different industries or different economies, it is not without its disadvantages as a measure of managerial efficiency. It is misleading if all capital employed is not included, and if profits are computed at current prices while the capital employed is stated at book value based on historical cost. Even when ROCE is computed a further appraisal must be made to establish the risk taken with the investment to measure whether the ROCE is adequate. The impact of factors outside the control of management must be defined before ROCE can be used to comment on managerial performance. Capital investment is a long-term operation, with projects which may have lives of ten years or more, and perhaps with the return not flowing in evenly over the years of this life. ROCE shows only the result of one year's transactions.

Efficiency is a loose term and means different things to different people, e.g. the engineer, the cost accountant and the economist. To the engineer it might be the input/output ratio of a machine, to the cost accountant the difference between standard and actual cost, and to the economist the achievement of maximum output from a given input (productivity). Profit is the return that a management has made on the capital employed in the business and it is right that their efficiency should be judged on the basis of this return. The risk incurred in the business must be taken into account, by computing a risk factor and applying it to the capital employed, to show how much profit should be made by a particular business. The success of ROCE as a measure of business efficiency also depends upon the objectives of the firm. Not all firms seek to maximize their profits: their objective may be a satisfactory return on capital or the provision of a good service.

Comparison between the operating units within a large organization may help the departmental management by showing how each department compares with others and by pinpointing areas in which improvement can take place. Such comparison may also help the central department in the firm, which is concerned with providing management advisory services to the constituent units. Intra-firm comparison on the basis of ROCE will help central management to judge whether the performance of operating units is satisfactory and will show where improvements can be made and central funds allocated. There are, however, certain points which must be discussed, such as what is meant by efficiency, how it is to be measured, what the causes of differences in efficiency are, and how much similarity is necessary before useful comparisons can be made.

ROCE employed as a measure for comparison compares operating profit to capital employed and acts as a common denominator between firms when comparing the efficiency of managements in using available resources. Other comparison measures which might be used are as follows:

(a) the rate of growth of assets (depends on policy, not efficiency);
(b) profit alone (this has limited benefit unless related to capital employed);
(c) value added per employee;
(d) output per man- or machine-hour;
(e) sales per employee or per £ of payroll.

The last three measures may all show a favourable position while the firm itself is inefficient in other ways. As tests they are not valid, since they do not show an overall view of the business. ROCE is important because it shows whether adequate use is being made of the funds in the business, irrespective of the source of the capital. It must be established whether the funds have earned the return that should have been made from them. Any discussion of business efficiency and ROCE must take into account the fact that good management ensures continuity and expansion, and will not squeeze out extra profits in the short term, which will harm the long-term position of the business. Development periods for large-scale capital projects, when a low return is to be expected, must also be taken into account.

The Limitations of ROCE

1. Definitions of capital employed vary, and confusion may arise when return on capital is discussed unless terms are rationalized.
2. The return on capital is a misleading guide to efficiency unless assets are valued at current prices. Profits are counted in terms of current prices, so it will be misleading if they are compared with capital computed on a historical basis.

3. Comparison of efficiency between firms by means of return on capital employed will be difficult if they are not truly comparable businesses; e.g. one business may lease its plant, another may have new plant, while another may work with old-fashioned plant. Any device to reduce these differences to a common figure will introduce an element of unreality into the comparison.
4. ROCE does not take risk into account. Thus a business may appear to be making a high return, but the fact that a high return is necessary to compensate for risk taken is not taken into account.
5. Capital investment is a long-term phenomenon and often a low return is experienced in the early years of a long-term project. It is therefore necessary that the return on the project over its full life, not just part of its life (say, a year), is used if a true conclusion about its profitability is to be reached. A business is a going concern, while accounting periods tend to be closed systems measuring the return on capital during only part of a full cycle. Difficulty is experienced in deciding what horizon is to be used in measuring efficiency. Some firms will accept low profits at present for larger returns in the future, while others will prefer high profits now and smaller returns later.

Example

The following abbreviated final accounts relate to firms X and Y. Using ratio analysis compare the financial situations of the two companies from the information available.

Profit and Loss Account

	X £	Y £
Sales	2 200 000	2 400 000
Less cost of sales	1 760 000	1 680 000
Gross profit	440 000	720 000
Less expenses	286 000	552 000
Net profit	£154 000	£168 000

Balance Sheet

	£	£	£	£
Share capital and reserves		400 000		1 100 000
Long term liabilities		100 000		100 000
Net capital employed		£500 000		£1 200 000
Fixed assets		200 000		1 000 000
Current assets:				
Stock	400 000		160 000	
Debtors	120 000		400 000	
Cash	40 000		40 000	
	560 000		600 000	
Less current liabilities:				
Trade creditors	260 000		400 000	
Working capital		300 000		200 000
Net assets		£500 000		£1 200 000

Note: 50 per cent of sales are on credit terms. All purchases are on credit terms. Opening stocks are: X, £500 000; Y, £100 000. (Using cost of sales and closing stock you can compute purchases.)

	X	Y
The primary ratio, profitability:		
Net profit to capital employed	154 000 : 500 000	168 000 : 1 200 000
Company X is the more profitable	30.8%	14%
If the gross capital had been		
used in this ratio	154 000 : 760 000	168 000 : 1 600 000
	20.2%	10.5%

This underlines the importance of the definition of the ratio being used. Strictly speaking, the interest on long-term capital should have been added back to net profit.

	X	Y
The secondary ratios:		
Net profit to sales	154 000 : 2 200 000	168 000 : 2 400 000
	7%	7%
Sales to capital employed	2 200 000 : 500 000	2 400 000 : 1 200 000
Turnover ratio	4.4 times	2 times
	4.4 × 7 = 30.8%	2 ×7 = 14%

Both companies earn the same return on their sales, but X makes its capital work harder and is thus more profitable. Further investigation of the asset structure reveals:

	X	Y
Sales to fixed assets	2 200 000 : 200 000	2 400 000 : 1 000 000
	11 times	2.4 times
Sales to working capital	2 200 000 : 300 000	2 400 000 : 200 000
	7.3 times	12 times
Fixed assets to working capital	200 000 : 300 000	1 000 000 : 200 000
	1 :1.5	5 : 1

X is more efficient in the use of fixed assets, while Y makes working capital work harder. The larger proportion of fixed assets to working capital in Y perhaps shows underutilized capacity. Further ratio analysis of the asset structure shows:

	X	Y
Sales to stock	2 200 000 : 400 000	2 400 000 : 160 000
	5.5 times	15 times
Sales to debtors	2 200 000 : 120 000	2 400 000 : 400 000
	18.3 times	6 times

In Y the stocks work three times as hard as in X, whereas the debtors of X support three times as much sales as those of Y. Both companies have the same profit ratio (7 per cent), but what happens with further investigation?

	X	Y
Gross profit to sales	440 000 : 2 200 000	720 000 : 2 400 000
	20%	30%
Expenses to sales	286 000 : 2 200 000	552 000 : 2 400 000
	13%	23%

Company Y has a real advantage over X, either on mark-up or on cost of goods sold, but this is nullified by the impact of higher expenses. Perhaps the higher expenses of Y reflect the impact of extra depreciation and maintenance on the extra fixed assets which it possesses.

THE ALTERNATIVE APPROACH TO RATIO ANALYSIS

This approach investigates one aspect of the firm's affairs at a time. Ratios can be used in groups to comment on solvency, earnings, stocks, capital, sales etc.

Solvency

Two main ratios are used to originate comment on this important aspect of business affairs, and other ratios can be used to substantiate the situation. The first ratio is the working capital ratio, or current ratio, which sets current assets against current liabilities. It expresses the surplus of current assets over current liabilities, or the amount of the firm's own funds used to finance short-term assets. It is also used by short-term creditors to assess the risk of lending to the firm, since a surplus of current assets over current liabilities means that there are sufficient current assets as a fund from which to repay trade creditors and others. When current liabilities exceed current assets (negative working capital) it appears that short-term funds have been recruited to finance long-term assets—a danger sign. Bracketed with the current ratio is the quick asset or 'acid test' ratio, which sets against current liabilities those current assets which can be quickly turned into cash (debtors, investments and cash). This ratio is a useful indicator of whether the firm can meet current liabilities with liquid funds, and a 1 : 1 relationship is considered prudent if a firm is to be able to pay its way. However, it must be made clear that this ratio is somewhat bogus, since the so-called quick assets often cannot be turned into cash in a short time, and in any case many of the current liabilities do not fall due immediately and may be payable in three or four months' time. Many companies are able to operate at a ratio far below the one to one norm. This is because they are in a cash trade so that the inflows of cash are not delayed by waiting for debtors payments, and/or the fact that the company may be in a strong market position. A strong company is able to take extended credit from its suppliers so that operations can be financed using trade credit to a greater extent than is normal.

In the example the current and quick asset ratios are computed as follows. Note the impact of stock on the liquidity of X.

	X	Y
Current ratio	560 : 260	600 : 400
	= 2.2 : 1	= 1.5 : 1
Quick asset ratio	160 : 260	440 : 400
	= 0.6 : 1	= 1.1 : 1

Clearly the solvency position is affected by debtors, creditors and stocks. The ratio of debtors to credit sales comments on the average length of time that debtors take to pay their bills, and the ratio of trade creditors to purchases reveals the average credit period taken by the company. Both these ratios can be computed in terms of time, as follows:

	X	Y
Debtors to credit sales	$\dfrac{120\,000}{1\,100\,000} \times \dfrac{365}{1} = 40$ days	$\dfrac{400\,000}{1\,200\,000} \times \dfrac{365}{1} = 122$ days
Trade creditors to purchase	$\dfrac{260\,000}{1\,660\,000} \times \dfrac{365}{1} = 57$ days	$\dfrac{400\,000}{1\,740\,000} \times \dfrac{365}{1} = 84$ days

Furthermore, the ratio of debtors to creditors highlights the amount of trade credit received and given by the firm.

	X	Y
Debtors to creditors	120 000 : 260 000	400 000 : 400 000
	1 : 2.16	1 : 1

Company Y is in balance, while Company X is seen to use more credit than it gives, which reflects the position as shown by the quick asset ratio.

The ratio of bad debts to credit sales will show up reckless selling, if the volume of bad debts has reached an unacceptable level.

Stocks

The purpose of stock ratios is to comment on the adequacy of stock levels in the light of the reason for holding the stock concerned. These ratios can be computed for different kinds of stock, usually in terms of time and on the basis of the average stock held for the year, i.e. opening plus closing stock divided by two. Alternatively, the ratios can be expressed as a single figure representing the number of times the stock is turned over during the year.

Average material stock to cost of material used

$$= \frac{(\text{Opening stock} + \text{Closing stock} \div 2)}{\text{Material usage}} \times \frac{365}{1} \text{ days} = - \text{ days}$$

If the lead time between ordering raw materials and their delivery is short, then some very convincing reasons will be required to support a high level of investment in stock.

$$\frac{\text{Average work in progress stock}}{\text{Cost of production for a year}} \times \frac{365}{1} \text{ days} = - \text{ days}$$

The above ratio comments on the time spent by semi-finished goods on their way through the factory, and can suggest reasons for production holdups when compared with the estimated time to complete the production cycle. Caution is needed when conclusions are considered, since the stock involved will be incomplete in terms of cost whereas cost of production is at full cost.

$$\frac{\text{Average finished goods stock}}{\text{Cost of sales for a year}} \times \frac{365}{1} \text{ days} = - \text{ days}$$

In circumstances where production and sales are not well co-ordinated, the above ratio helps to reveal the length of time that completed goods wait in the stores before being sold.

Capital

The main ratios used to explore this aspect of a firm's activity are as follows:

1. Capital employed to total indebtedness. This is the ownership ratio, which highlights the proportions of the assets financed by the legal owners and by lenders. Overdependence on finance from outside the firm is a sign of weakness, although in circumstances of inflation it can bring benefits. The ratio can take two forms:

   (a) total assets to long-term liabilities and current liabilities; and
   (b) share capital plus reserves to long-term liabilities and current liabilities.

2. The gearing ratio, which can be computed by a number of alternative formulae, points out the importance of fixed return capital in the capital structure. In a highly geared company the proportion of fixed return capital is high, so when profits exceed the amount required to service the fixed return capital the ordinary shareholders will benefit. An upward fluctuation of profits in these circumstances will lead to a more than proportionate increase in the return to the ordinary shareholders. The usual formulae are:

   (a) ordinary shares to preference shares and long-term liabilities;
   (b) equity interest to equity interest and fixed return capital.

3. Another capital ratio comments on the disposition of the assets financed by the capital employed. The ratio of fixed assets to capital employed, or of fixed assets to current assets, will highlight the proportions in which management have divided their investment of the funds at their disposal in a long- or short-term form.

   Some accountants hold the view that it is prudent to ensure that the fixed assets are covered by the ownership interest in the business, i.e. share capital and reserves, but others, with an eye to the advantage of raising the gearing and post-inflation repayment of long-term loans, are more flexible in their attitude.

Earnings

The managers, shareholders and potential investors all have an interest in these ratios.

1. Net profit after preference dividend and tax to equity interest (ordinary shares plus reserves).

   The return earned on the shareholders' investment in the company must be sufficient to warrant the risk they are taking in entrusting their funds to the management. The funds involved consist in this case of the original investment in shares and profits retained since the company began trading. The return on ownership capital invested shows whether the company is organized in such a way as to maximize the shareholders' proportion of the profit, whether or not it is paid to them as a dividend.

2. The 'pay out' ratio sets profit available for dividend against dividend paid, to explore the dividend policy of the board and at the same time to comment on the ability and/or determination of the company to expand by ploughing back profits. Further analysis using the ratio of profit available for dividend to dividend required or paid shows the dividend cover position. If profits are sufficient to cover the dividend at a certain rate then there is greater security or certainty that the dividend required by a potential investor will be paid. For example, 100 000 ordinary shares of £1 each are in issue. A dividend of 20 pence in the pound is required to meet the investors' calculation of the risk involved, so £20 000 is needed to pay a dividend. If the profit is £40 000 then the required dividend is 'twice covered', and there is an ample margin for profit retention. The amount of profit to be retained in the business is often a very finely balanced decision. If too much profit is retained the dividends will be restricted and demand for the shares will be reduced. If too little is 'ploughed back' then, although dividends are high in the short term, development and replacement of capital equipment is cut back so that obsolence follows and in time earning capacity is reduced.

3. Yield. This ratio sets dividend paid per share against the current market price of the share and shows what return an investor can expect to receive from funds laid out in the purchase of a share. It suffers from the weakness that the dividend paid is only part of the earnings attributable to the shareholder. Another ratio, the P/E (price to earnings) ratio, is often used as an alternative. The earnings per share (EPS) are set against market price to show the shareholder what return is being earned on the current value of his share, both as dividend and profits retained and invested by the directors. The EPS are calculated by dividing the net profit after tax and preference dividend by the average number of ordinary shares in issue during the year.

According to Standard Accounting Practice 3, the EPS should be shown as a note on the face of the published profit and loss account. This standard applies to all quoted companies other than banks and discount companies, and is so arranged that a potential investor can compute a P/E ratio for the company to compare it with those of similar companies, or with its own figure for a previous year. The basis of the calculation of EPS must also be shown as a note to the published accounts. Difficulties arise in the calculation where the number of shares at issue is unclear. If the company has issued convertible loan stock, the owners of such stock could exchange their holdings for ordinary shares, and if these extra potential shares are in the EPS calculation they will dilute the EPS figure. SSAP 3 states that diluted EPS must be shown as well as the basic EPS where equity shares which do not rank for dividend in the period under review are at issue, or where conversion rights exist, or where options have been granted to persons who can exercise them to subscribe for shares.

THE GROSS PROFIT RATIO

This ratio is considered to be so important to accountants that it merits separate discussion. It is computed by setting the gross profit against sales, and is expressed as a percentage. Clearly it can be used as a control device, since it brings together all the elements of the trading account. The gross profit is computed by adding opening stock to purchases and subtracting closing stock to show the cost of goods sold. This figure is then subtracted from sales to give gross profit. The mark-up or profit percentage added to cost when selling price is determined should be reflected by the gross profit percentage, and if there is a difference the accountant knows that some figure in the trading account contains an error.

Many factors can contribute to such a difference. Suppose, for example, that the closing stock figure is wrong. This will have an effect on the cost of goods sold and thus on gross profit. An error in the closing stock can be caused by miscounting the number of items in stock, by extending them at the wrong cost on the stock sheet, or by miscalculating when the amounts are multiplied and added up on the stock sheet. Alternatively, the sales figure may be wrong, perhaps because some sales have not been recorded by mistake, or on purpose if the cash received has been stolen. If stock has been stolen by customers or staff, the cost of the goods sold will increase and the gross profit percentage will not agree with the mark-up. Sometimes the cut-off point is the cause of an error. At the end of an accounting period stock is taken by a physical count, and the books should be closed at this point. If, however, purchases are entered after the cut-off point they will not be in stock, and the cost of goods sold will be distorted.

INTER-FIRM COMPARISON

Managerial ratios can be used to facilitate comparison of one firm with another or of an individual firm with the average for other similar firms in the same industry. An inter-firm comparison (IFC) scheme may be operated by a trade association, or a firm of accountants who audit a number of businesses in the same trade. All participants in the scheme are encouraged to analyse costs according to a set pattern of analytical headings. These costs are then submitted on a pre-designed form to the authority organizing the IFC. Some schemes require participating companies to calculate their own ratios but others ask only for the information. Clearly it is vital to the success of the scheme that the figures of individual businesses remain confidential and are not leaked to other participants in the scheme.

An average is found for the group for each ratio so that the ratios of one company can be compared to the average figures for the group and managers at that company can see if their performance in various aspects of the business is above or below average. It is possible to calculate upper and lower quartiles and even upper and lower deciles to give each firm an idea of how far its performance is below or above the average for each ratio. The key ratios form a scoreboard to indicate the extent of the leeway to be made up, if any, by each firm. This is a management exercise in that managers must examine the position of their company *vis-à-vis* the average, and work out for themselves the reasons why their performance is above or below the norm. It is hoped that ideas to improve efficiency will result from this analysis.

IFC schemes are not without their problems. Difficulties are encountered when making inter-firm comparisons as the outcome is meaningless unless like is compared with like. Terms must be defined and standardized and considerable effort is involved in organizing and initiating a scheme. An exact comparison cannot be made between a firm, say, that owns its premises having bought them 25 years ago, with another firm which owns premises bought last year and yet another firm which does not own premises but pays rent under a lease. It is possible to make adjustments to the figures to bring such disparate firms into line, e.g. by charging a notional rent to those companies who own property, but when this is done the figures depart from reality and the validity of such a comparison is correspondingly reduced. Policy decisions must be made within the scheme as to how to treat investment income which can distort the profit figure. Usually, operating profits are used for IFC, thus neutralizing the effect of non-operating incomes.

An example of the ratios which are likely to be used in an IFC scheme is shown below, with comment as to the likely conclusions which can be drawn from the figures disclosed.

Fragile Structures PLC has joined an inter-firm comparison scheme for civil engineering businesses. The scheme administrators have returned the following ratio analysis for Fragile Structures for the year to 31 December 19-8.

Management Ratio	Q1—1st Quartile M—Median Q3—3rd Quartile	Unit	Industry	Fragile Structures
1. Operating profit / Operating capital	Q1 M Q3	%	6.3 8.7 12.4	5.5%
2. Operating profit / Sales	Q1 M Q3	%	3.7 4.1 4.6	4.2%
3. Sales / Operating capital	Q1 M Q3	Times	1.7 2.1 2.6	1.3
4. Admin. costs / Sales	Q1 M Q3	%	2.1 2.5 3.2	3.3%
5. Marketing costs / Sales	Q1 M Q3	%	0.6 0.8 0.9	0.9%
6. Sales / Fixed assets	Q1 M Q3	Times	2.9 3.6 5.1	5.9
7. Sales / Current assets	Q1 M Q3	Times	2.4 2.9 3.8	2.5
8. Fixed assets / Current assets	Q1 M Q3	Times	0.82 0.80 0.74	0.42
9. Stock of materials / Materials used	Q1 M Q3	Days	51 64 82	60

Management Ratio	Q1—1st Quartile M—Median Q3—3rd Quartile	Unit	Industry	Fragile Structures
10. Work in progress / Cost of production	Q1 M Q3	Days	63 84 91	120
11. Debtors / Sales	Q1 M Q3	Days	30 58 71	90
12. Plant £'s / Production / Employees	Q1 M Q3	£	1000 1250 1620	£950

(a) Draft a report to summarize the performance of Fragile Structures PLC in relation to its competitors.

(b) Recommend aspects of Fragile Structures PLC which merit investigation.

Points which might be included in the report are as follows. Fragile Structures PLC (FS) has a ratio below the first quartile for ROCE. Reasons for this poor performance concern either a lack of activity, or a lack of profitability, or stem from both these factors.

Profitability. Operating profit to sales shows an above average performance but sales earned by capital employed is very weak. This suggests that operating assets may be wastefully employed and that some assets of the business may lie idle, earning nothing. The strong operating profit to sales ratio is satisfactory but this advantage seems to be dissipated by ratios of administrative costs to sales and marketing costs to sales which are well above the average. For ratios such as this a location in the third quartile denotes inefficiency. If operating profit is 4.2 per cent of sales and administration costs and marketing costs are 3.3 per cent and 0.9 per cent of sales, respectively, this implies that when administration and marketing costs are taken away from the operating profit there will be no net profit remaining (3.3 + 0.9 = 4.2).

Activity. The turnover ratio of sales to capital employed suggested a weak performance but ratio 6 shows the fixed assets to be working very hard, since the figure for FS is well above the third quartile. This is an apparent sign of efficiency. Sales to current assets (ratio 7), however, show performance just above the first quartile but below average. The suggestion is that FS has a problem in this area. Ratio 8, however, discloses an extreme imbalance in the asset structure in favour of current assets. The median position for the group is 0.8 to 1 but FS can only show 0.4 to 1 as the relationship of fixed assets to current assets. This must raise the question as to whether the company is using too few fixed assets and whether the suggested efficiency disclosed by ratio 5 is correct. It must be borne in mind that if a company is leasing plant on short-term hire agreements this plant will be working for the business but will not appear on the balance sheet to influence the ratios concerned.

Current Assets. Ratio 9 suggests that the stock-holding period for materials is slightly below average—a sign of efficiency. Work-in-progress stock, however, is well above average as a proportion of annual activity, which may suggest that the production processes used by FS are slow, perhaps because insufficient plant is employed. Ratio 12, which sets plant balance sheet values against production employees, supports this view, because each employee working for FS is supported by only £950 worth of machinery, which is below the first quartile for the industry. The debtor ratio (number 11) suggests that too much credit is given to customers by FS. It appears that three months' credit is given as opposed to two months' as an average for the industry. An analysis of what is meant by administrative costs in this inter-firm comparison may show that the administration costs of FS are artificially high because this figure includes interest on funds borrowed to finance the large stocks of work in progress and the abnormally high debtors.

Aspects of the business of Fragile Structures PLC which might merit further investigation are as follows:

1. Credit control—action must be taken to see if it is feasible to reduce the debtor balances.
2. Work in progress—consideration must be given to completing jobs in less time to bring down the overlong time lag before work in progress is turned into a completed job. Earlier completion will lead to collecting the price for the work at an earlier date, which will economize on capital employed, reduce borrowing and cut the cost of interest.
3. Control should be applied to the administration costs, which seem to be well above the third quartile, let alone the average for the industry.
4. The production process must be investigated with a view to increasing the plant available on site. This may increase the speed with which jobs are completed. The point must be made, however, that extra plant must be financed and since there is no profit this year it may be necessary to borrow, or lease, in order to improve this aspect of the company's performance.

TUTORIAL DISCUSSION TOPICS

24.1 'Solvency is more important than profitability in business.' Discuss.

24.2 'Overdependence on finance from outside the company is a sign of weakness.' Do you agree?

24.3 Discuss the advantages and disadvantages of ratio analysis as a tool of interpretation.

24.4 Explain the interaction of ratios in the diagram approach to ratio analysis.

24.5 Why is the gross profit ratio considered to be so important? What factors can cause this ratio to be different from the mark-up on goods sold by a company?

SEMINAR EXERCISES 15

1. Puzzle Ltd is a small manufacturing company with premises in the East Midlands. The balance sheet of the company is shown below, together with other significant figures extracted from the accounts.

Puzzle Ltd, Balance Sheet as at 31 March

	£	£	£
Capital:			
Ordinary shares of £1 each,			
authorized and issued			240 000
Reserves			480 000
			720 000
Long-term liabilities:			
10 per cent loan stock			800 000
Current liabilities:			
Creditors		200 000	
Tax		60 000	
Overdraft		300 000	560 000
			£2 080 000
Represented by:			
Fixed assets:			
Buildings	400 000		400 000
Plant	800 000	424 000	376 000
Vehicles	30 000	6 000	24 000
	1 230 000	430 000	800 000
Current assets:			
Stock		480 000	
Debtors		720 000	
Investments		80 000	1 280 000
			£2 080 000

Sales: £1 600 000   Gross profit: £320 000   Net profit: £160 000

Using simple ratio analysis, comment on the performance of this company for the year to 31 March.

2. Ours Ltd and Theirs Ltd are two companies of similar size in the same industry. They have drawn up their accounts on a common basis so that they can exchange certain accounting information for their mutual benefit. As accountant to Theirs Ltd you have recently received the following information from Ours Ltd:

Current ratio	2.4 : 1
Stock turnover	5.4 times
Debtors' collection period	32 days
Gross profit	38 per cent
Return on total investment	15.6 per cent

The most recent accounts of Theirs Ltd are as follows:

Income Statement

	£
Opening stock	28 000
Add purchases	384 000
	412 000
Less closing stock	32 000
Cost of sales	380 000
Add overhead expenses	92 000
Add net profit	8 000
Sales	£480 000

Balance Sheet

	£
Share capital	80 000
Add retained profits	40 000
	120 000
10 per cent debentures	20 000
Net capital employed	£140 000

Represented by:

	£	£
Fixed assets		88 000
Current assets:		
Stock	32 000	
Debtors	72 000	
Cash	16 000	
	120 000	
Less creditors	68 000	
Working capital		52 000
Net assets		£140 000

(a) Calculate the relevant ratios for Theirs Ltd.

(b) Suggest reasons for the differences between the two companies revealed by your analysis.

3. The managing director of Roper Ltd, a company in the boot and shoe industry, has just received a statistical bulletin showing the performance of the industry as a whole for the year ended 30 June. He would like to assess the results of the company for the same period, using these statistics for comparison purposes.

The accounts of Roper Ltd for the year ended 30 June this year are given below.

Balance Sheet

Liabilities	£	Assets	£
General reserve	13 000	Trade debtors	75 000
Ordinary share capital	50 000	Equipment at cost	26 000
Trade creditors	47 500	Long-term investment in	
Taxation (payable		associated company	2 500
1 January next year)	7 000	Goodwill	20 000
Long-term loan	30 000	Cash at bank	11 000
Provision for depreciation		Freehold property at cost	21 000
on equipment	13 000	Stock	55 000
Profit and loss account	42 000		
Taxation (payable			
1 January year after next)	8 000		
	£210 500		£210 500

Profit and Loss Account

	£		£
Balance of undistributed			
profit at 30 June this year	42 000	Sales	652 000
Loan interest (10 per cent)	3 000	Balance of undistributed	
General expenses	49 000	profit at 1 July last year	39 400
Depreciation of equipment	2 500	Dividend on shares in	
Cost of goods sold	584 500	associated company	100
Dividend on share capital	2 500		
Corporation tax	8 000		
	£691 500		£691 500

The following ratios were extracted for the industry:

Return on gross capital employed	10 per cent
Stock turnover	15 times
Current ratio	1.8 : 1
Gross profit on sales	20 per cent
Debt ratio	33 per cent

(a) Redraft the accounts in a form suitable for presentation to management.
(b) Calculate the above ratios for Roper Ltd.
(c) Compare the two sets of ratios and advise the managing director.

4. David and Charles each carry on business as wholesalers of the same product. Their respective accounts for the year to 31 January are as follows:

Trading and Profit and Loss Accounts

	David		Charles	
	£	£	£	£
Sales		144 000		140 000
Cost of sales:				
Opening stock	28 000		3 200	
Purchases	124 000		121 600	
	152 000		124 800	
Closing stock	32 000		4 800	
		120 000		120 000
Gross profit		24 000		20 000
Selling expenses	7 200		2 800	
Administration expenses	8 160		9 500	
		15 360		12 300
Net profit		£8 640		£7 700

Balance Sheets at 31 January

	David	Charles
	£	£
Freehold property	20 000	14 000
Fixtures, fittings and equipment	21 750	13 840
Motor vehicles	12 000	6 000
	53 750	33 840
Stock	32 000	4 800
Debtors	28 800	11 200
Bank	8 950	11 360
	£123 500	£61 200
Capital	108 000	30 800
Creditors	15 500	30 400
	£123 500	£61 200

Notes:

  (i) All fixed assets are at written-down value.

 (ii) You may assume that stocks increased over the year at an even rate.

(iii) All sales are on credit.

(iv) The amounts of creditors and debitors have not changed significantly over the year.

Compare the profitability and financial position of the two businesses by:

(a) calculating at least eight suitable ratios for each business;

(b) commenting on the significance of the results of your calculations.

5. Jean Sellar runs a dress shop and her husband acts as a book-keeper. Recently the couple have been worried in case their accounts are not accurate, and they ask you to check the figures. From a preliminary survey of the books you compute a trading account for the last two years ended 31 December.

	Year 1		Year 2	
	£	£	£	£
Sales		571 660		686 480
Opening stock	52 900		62 720	
Add purchases	390 948		502 868	
	443 848		565 588	
Less closing stock	62 720		50 860	
		381 128		514 728
Gross profit		£190 532		£171 752

You meet Jean Sellar and her husband to discuss the figures, and their explanation of the reduction in gross profit is that from January year 2 their suppliers had increased their prices to them by 15 per cent while they have been able to increase their selling price by only 10 per cent.

(a) Verify Jean Sellar's explanation for the fall in gross profit.

(b) Suggest six other reasons which might account for the reduction in gross profit.

(c) Comment briefly to Jean Sellar on her stock level.

REVIEW QUESTIONS 10

1. Your friend Mr Bix is a retailer and has been reading about ratio analysis in a trade journal. He is thinking of using the ratios quoted in the journal in preparing his budget for the year to 31 August 19-4.

    He has listed the ratios as follows and asks for your advice:

(i) Target net profit	£40 000
(ii) Expenses	75 per cent of gross profit
(iii) Mark-up on goods for resale	25 per cent of cost

(iv) Average stock turnover   8× (times)
(v) Opening stock   £75 000
(vi) Return on capital employed   16⅔ per cent
(vii) Return on owner's capital   25 per cent
(viii) Ratio of capital employed
     to working capital   8 : 3
(ix) Current ratio   3.5 : 1
(x) There is a trade investment of £6000. The
     ratio of fixed to current assets is: 8 : 7
     The investment is not part of this ratio.
(xi) Mr Bix expects to draw from the business
     during the year   £30 000

(a) Advise Mr Bix as to whether his method of preparing the 19-4 budget is satisfactory.

(b) Prepare a budgeted trading and profit and loss account and balance sheet for 19-4.

2. Slow PLC and Quick PLC are in the same line of business. Their accounts for the year ending 30 June 19-8 were as follows:

		Quick PLC		Slow PLC
Profit and Loss Account		£000		£000
Sales		7200		8700
Less cost of sales		5400		6960
Gross profit		1800		1740
Less overheads		1200		1260
Net profit before tax		600		480
Corporation tax		240		180
Dividend		90		120
Retained profit for the year		£270		£180
Balance Sheet	£000	£000	£000	£000
Share capital		3000		900
Reserves		1470		630
		4470		1530
Debentures (8 per cent Quick only)		—		600
		£4470		£2130
Represented by:				
Fixed assets: cost		3000		2400
less depreciation		600		480
		2400		1920
Current assets:				
Stock	1650		960	
Debtors	1800		1500	
Cash	150		15	
	3600		2475	
Less current liabilities:				
Taxation	240		180	
Creditors	1290		1920	
Bank overdraft	—		165	
	1530		2265	
Net current assets		2070		210
		£4470		£2130

Compare the profitability and financial position of the two companies using suitable ratios, and comment briefly on your findings.

3. Quorn Brushes are manufacturers in the hardware trade. They operate small factories at Belvoir and Beaufort. The accounting systems of these two subsidiaries are separate, each one maintaining its own set of records. Financial information for the two businesses is set out below:

Balance Sheet as at 30 June 19-2

	Belvoir		Beaufort	
	£000	£000	£000	£000
Share capital		180		540
Retained profit		66		132
Debentures: 9 per cent		30		
15 per cent		30		
14 per cent				150
Net capital employed		£306		£822
Represented by:				
Fixed assets:				
Land and buildings				180
Plant (net of depreciation)		150		315
Vehicles				15
Current assets:				
Stock	60		330	
Debtors	126		135	
Cash	72		15	
	258		480	
Current liabilities:				
Trade creditors	(42)		(72)	
Overdraft			(30)	
Tax payable (1 March 19-3)	(60)		(66)	
		156		312
Net assets		£306		£822

Additional information:	Belvoir	Beaufort
Sales	1320	1860
Cost of sales	1122	1506
Expenses	78	222
Depreciation included in expenses above	15	37.5

When this information is presented to Mr Renard, the group managing director, he comments that Beaufort is a much better firm than Belvoir, because when they are compared, Beaufort has 50 per cent more sales, 100 per cent more retained profit, 240 per cent more in assets and 300 per cent more in capital.

As general manager of the Belvoir subsidiary, you are requested to defend the position of your company to the managing director.

25 | Funds Flow Analysis

The balance sheet shows the sources from which funds have been recruited to finance the business and, on the assets side, the ways in which those funds have been applied. Unfortunately, a balance sheet is produced only at stated intervals to show the position at a specific time. A very useful interpretative tool which the accountant can produce to help the users of accounting information is a statement which analyses the changes that have taken place between two balance sheet dates so far as sources and uses of funds are concerned. Such a statement will show changes in the capital structure and asset structure of a business during the period and will, together with the income statement, explain the events which have led up to the most recent position statement. It is important to note that the position of a business is affected by income (sales less expenses) as well as by the flow of funds both in and out, and it must be recognized that a company can make losses in the short run and survive if it remains solvent, whereas profitable operations can be brought to a halt by a lack of liquid funds to pay wages and creditors in the immediate future. The funds flow statement can be used with accounting ratios, in an interpretation exercise.

WHAT ARE FUNDS?

As one might expect, there is much confusion over the use of the term 'funds'. Some accountants believe that all sources of finance, or means by which a business can gain control over or use of assets, should count as funds employed in the business. Others, however, think that funds should be associated with liquidity, and prefer to define them either as cash resources or as working capital, since the constituent parts will be turned into cash or settled in cash in the near future. Stocks which may be held for longer than the accounting year are sometimes excluded, so the definition of funds is limited to 'monetary items' in the working-capital cycle. This idea restricts the usefulness of the statement to be produced.

Funds introduced into a business, whether or not in the form of cash, enable the firm to use those funds to acquire assets. Share capital raised and long-term loans will flow in as cash, whereas trade credit will be shown by an increase in stocks not yet paid for. Amounts owed to the Inland Revenue for taxation can be used in the business until the due date for payment. A fixed asset sold will provide cash to be used to acquire other assets, fixed or current, or to discharge a liability. In this case a change in the asset structure has liquified funds for use elsewhere in the business. No new funds have been introduced unless the asset was sold at a profit, but the use to which existing funds are put has been changed. When shares are issued in exchange for an asset acquired by the firm no cash has changed hands, but the capital structure and asset structure of the company have both altered. Funds in the form of purchasing power have been created by the company, which has exchanged a liability (its shares) for an asset. The outflow of cash has been avoided by the use of an alternative method of payment or source of finance to support the transaction.

It follows from this discussion that there is a difference between funds and cash and until this difference is fully understood there will be an ever-present confusion between a funds flow statement and a cash flow statement. In summary there are four definitions of funds which could be used in a funds flow statement.

1. Net liquid funds—cash at bank and in hand and cash equivalents such as current asset investments, less overdrafts and other borrowings repayable within one year of the accounting date.
2. Working capital—net liquid funds as above plus stocks and debtors less creditors. This definition, however, excludes some current liabilities from the term creditors, such as taxation owed and dividends payable.
3. Net borrowings—this definition includes net liquid funds as above plus medium- and long-term borrowings.
4. Total external finance—this definition includes net liquid funds plus medium- and long-term borrowings plus share capital.

Clearly there is much confusion as to the meaning of the term funds, and movement of funds statements drafted to disclose changes to one of the definitions may well miss significant changes to other definitions. The absence of an authoritative definition of the term funds from the ASC, and the suggestion of a non-mandatory form for funds flow statements in SSAP 10, has created the situation where there is little comparability between the funds flow statement published by one company and that published by another.

Sources and Uses of Funds

The sources and uses of funds can be set out as follows.

Sources:

(a) funds generated by trading operations; cash received from sales net of cash paid out for expenses (the term cash flow is sometimes given to this amount);
(b) funds injected into the business on a long-term basis; issues of shares plus any premium received on issue; debentures and other long-term loans;
(c) funds released from long-term applications for use elsewhere in the business; sales of fixed assets such as land, buildings, plant and vehicles; loans to subsidiary companies repaid by them;
(d) funds lent to the business on a short-term basis; trade creditors; bank loans and overdrafts; amounts payable to the Inland Revenue; bills of exchange payable.

Uses:

(a) funds lost in trading operations, i.e. when the payment of expenses exceeds receipts from sales;
(b) funds used to acquire permanent assets such as land, buildings, plant, vehicles, fixtures and fittings and long-term investments;
(c) funds paid away outside the business to repay debentures and loan stock, or to redeem share capital;
(d) funds invested outside the business in loans made to subsidiary companies;
(e) funds used to acquire assets of a short-term nature, stocks of material, work in progress and finished goods; trade credit allowed to debtors who have not yet paid for goods sold to them; short-term investments as a temporary repository of idle funds; bills of exchange receivable.

Note that already with this simple analysis shown above items concerning funds moved into and out of the business on a long-term basis are being mixed in with short-term movements, and the source and application of funds from changes in the asset structure.

The funds generated by trading operations can be computed as in sources (a) above, but an alternative method of calculating the same figure is to take the net profit before tax and add back all non-cash costs that have been deducted in the profit calculation. A good example of a cost which has not caused an outflow of cash during the year is depreciation, because it is a means of spreading over a period of years the cash spent when a fixed asset was originally purchased. The term cash flow is often used for net profit plus depreciation and any other non-cash costs identified during the year.

If sources exceed uses there will be a balance of cash representing funds provided but not yet put to use in the business.

The 'capital employed' in figure 12 acts as a reservoir into which funds flow from four major streams. The funds are then tapped off as a result of managerial decisions to irrigate the five fields shown, and any funds remaining in the reservoir will be represented by the bank balance. If, however, uses exceed sources, the reservoir will run dry and, unless extra short-term credit can be arranged at short notice, some of the uses will not receive all the funds they need and the business will suffer as a result. Funds, like water, can run in different directions, so funds from any source can be used to finance any use, although it is imprudent to use short-term funds to acquire fixed assets, unless long-term funds will be raised to cover the position quickly. Circumstances such as these would be highlighted in a funds flow statement.

FUNDS FLOW STATEMENT

This statement has several alternative names. Some accountants refer to it as a movement of funds statement, while to others it is a source and application of funds statement. When projected forward from a recent balance sheet to a budgeted position it is sometimes called a long-term cash budget. There are, of course, alternative forms of statement which express the flow of funds. The statement is computed by finding the differences between the opening and closing balance sheets and arranging them in groups as illustrated in figure 12. For example, if the stock

Sources

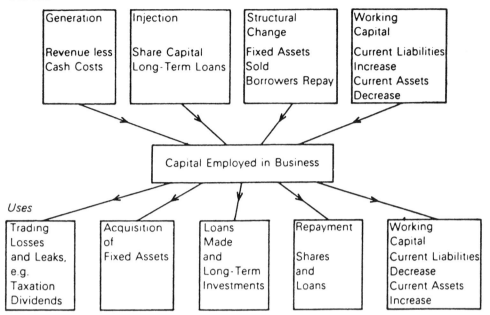

Figure 12. Funds flow diagram.

figure in the earlier balance sheet is deducted from stock in the later balance sheet, the extent of investment or disinvestment in stocks can be ascertained. The basic rule is that if an asset has increased during a period, this is an application of funds, whereas if an asset is reduced, this is counted as a source, since funds have been withdrawn from that asset for use in some other way. If a liability has increased, more funds have been loaned to the business and this is a source, but if a liability is reduced, funds have been applied to repay the liability.

The statement shows more than just the extra funds used during the year: it is extended to show changes in the way in which the funds are used.

Example

The balance sheet of Simpleton Ltd is set out overleaf. Compute a funds flow statement.

Beginning of the Year £	£		£	£	End of the Year £
		Fixed assets			
150 000		Freehold property at cost			190 000
6 000		Leasehold property at cost			—
	176 000	Plant and machinery at cost		217 000	
	74 000	Less depreciation		95 000	
102 000					122 000
258 000					312 000
16 000		Investment in associated company at cost		16 000	
		Add loan to associated company		6 400	
					22 400
274 000					334 000
		Current assets			
	45 000	Stocks		57 000	
	61 000	Debtors		66 000	
	19 800	Cash at bank and in hand		8 400	
	125 800			131 400	
		Less current liabilities			
	83 000	Sundry creditors	85 000		
	10 000	Proposed dividend	12 500		
	15 000	Corporation tax provided	17 900		
	108 000			115 400	
17 800		Working capital			16 000
200		Preliminary expenses			—
292 000					350 400
		Less *deferred liabilities*			
60 000		4 per cent debentures			50 000
£232 000					£300 400
		Represented by:			
		Capital			
190 000		Ordinary shares			240 000
		Capital reserves			
—		Share premium account		10 000	
—		Profit on redemption of debentures		400	10 400
		Revenue reserves			
31 000		General		38 500	
11 000		Unappropriated		11 500	50 000
£232 000					£300 400

Note: The leasehold property was sold during the year at a profit of £2500.

A comparison of the two balance sheets will show how the following figures are derived.

Simpleton Ltd, Funds Flow Statement

Sources	£	£
Cash flow (as calculated below)	57 100	
Sale of leasehold (book value + profit on sale = cash)	8 500	
Shares issued + premium	60 000	
Sundry creditors	2 000	127 600
Uses		
Purchase of freehold property	40 000	
Purchase of plant	41 000	
Loan to associate company	6 400	
Stocks purchased	12 000	
Debtors increased	5 000	
Debentures repaid, cash amount	9 600	
Tax paid	15 000	
Dividend paid	10 000	139 000
Reduction in cash resources £(19 800 − 8400)		£11 400

Uses exceed sources by £11 400. 'Tax paid' and 'Dividend paid' are the amounts owed at the beginning of the year, and shown as current liabilities on the opening balance sheet.

The cash flow figure is found by adding back non-cash costs to net profit. The non-cash costs are depreciation (£21 000) and preliminary expenses written off (£200). Net profit after tax and dividend must equal the amount by which reserves and unappropriated profits have increased, i.e. £5500. The closing balance sheet shows that as current liabilities, £17 900 has been provided out of the profit and loss account to meet corporation tax for the year, and that £12 500 is proposed as dividend payable. These two amounts must be added back to the funds retained in the business this year (£5500) to calculate the net trading profit before tax and dividend for the year. It follows that current liabilities for proposed dividend and corporation tax in the balance sheet at the beginning of the year have been paid during the course of the year, and these amounts are shown as uses of funds.

Calculation of Cash Flow

	£	£
General reserve (38 500 − 31 000) increase		7 500
Unappropriated profit (11 500 − 11 000) increase		500
Unappropriated profit after tax and dividend		8 000
Appropriated to meet taxation	17 900	
Appropriated to pay dividend	12 500	
		30 400
Net profit for the year		38 400
Less profit on sale of leasehold property		(2 500)
Operating profit for the year		35 900
Depreciation for the year		21 000
Other non-cash cost		200
Cash flow		£57 100

The funds flow statement for Simpleton Ltd can be restated in a more informative way as follows:

Sources of funds	£	£
Profit before taxation		35 900
Adjustment for item not involving movement of funds		
+ Depreciation (95 000 − 74 000)	21 000	
+ Other non-cash cost	200	
		21 200
Total generated from operations		57 100
Long-term sources:		
Shares issued	60 000	
Leasehold property sold (6000 + 2500)	8 500	68 500
		125 600
Long-term application:		
Purchase of freehold property	40 000	
Purchase of plant	41 000	
Loan to associate	6 400	
Debenture repaid	9 600	
Tax paid	15 000	
Dividend paid	10 000	122 000
	Surplus	3 600

Working capital:		Source	Application	
Stock			12 000	
Debtors			5 000	
Creditors		2000		
		2000	17 000	Net application 15 000
Reduction in liquid resources (19 800 − 8 400)				11 400

This form of statement tells a story. It shows the funds generated by the business and then the funds injected from outside or made available by the sale of fixed assets. Not only can these sources be compared inter se but also their total can be set against the long-term application of funds. The resulting surplus or deficit shows to what extent long-term applications are funded by long-term sources, and whether working capital has been reduced to finance long-term applications.

The statement provides a useful analysis of how funds have been used during the period, and shows the relative importance of the various sources of funds. A separate section to analyse changes in working capital reveals the funds used or provided by increases and decreases in current assets and current liabilities, and the net effect of the year's transactions on the liquid resources of the business.

Note that in this example the leasehold property was sold during the year at a profit of £2500, which means that the price received for it was £6000 + £2500 = £8500. If the funds flow statement is to show the full amount of funds released by this transaction for use elsewhere in the business, it is necessary to separate the profit on the sale from the operating profit of the business. Accordingly, in the calculation of cash flow the profit on the sale of leasehold property is deducted, so that it can be added to the cost of the leasehold property sold in the long-term sources section of the statement.

Computational Difficulties

Cash flow is the difference between cash flowing in from sales and cash flowing out to pay costs and expenses. It is not the same as net profit, since some costs used in the profit computation do not flow out in cash during the period, e.g. depreciation and preliminary expenses written off. It follows that cash flow can be computed by adding back the non-cash costs to the net profit figure. Any operating costs not paid out in cash by the end of the period yet charged against profit will be picked up in the statement as accruals, which increase the creditors figure. Suppose an electricity bill is unpaid at the year end, yet it has been set against profit, thus reducing cash flow. The bill will also increase the creditors figure, so it will show up on the statement as a short-term source in the working capital section.

The fact that depreciation is added back to compute cash flow may lead to the belief that it is a source of finance. It is true that depreciation is a sum set aside out of profit to replace funds originally invested in the firm which have been used up during the period. Depreciation reduces profit so that less is available for dividend and capital depletion is avoided. Following this line of reasoning, cash flow appears to be an amalgam of funds generated by the business to be reinvested therein and amounts set aside to replace funds used up during the period.

In some problems a balance sheet is available, but there is no income statement from which to take details of profit and depreciation. An accountant can write up the appropriation account, by deduction from the two balance sheets, so the balancing figure in the recreated appropriation account is the trading profit.

In the example above the figures would be:

Dr.		Appropriation Account	Cr.
	£		£
Transfer to general reserve	7 500	Unappropriated profit b/d	11 000
Set aside for taxation	17 900	Profit on sales of fixed	
		assets	2 500
Set aside for dividend	12 500	Trading profit as the	
Loss on sales of fixed		balancing figure	35 900
assets	—		
Unappropriated profit c/f	11 500		
	£49 400		£49 400

It is also possible to work back to the depreciation charge for the year by contrasting the opening and closing positions and taking out the cost and cumulative depreciation of assets sold during the period—see Bradmore Bakeries overleaf.

The sale of fixed assets at more or less than book value presents a computational difficulty. Some accountants prefer to show the profit element in the transaction as part of cash flow and the book value as a long-term source of funds. However, this method has been criticized as showing a confused picture of what has happened, and it is argued that the full cash sum released by the sale should be shown as a long-term source, and the cash flow figure restricted to include only the trading profit.

Overdraft increased or decreased during the year is normally treated in a funds flow statement as part of the computation at the end of the statement to disclose the change in liquid resources during the year, but some authorities argue that the overdraft is a current liability and should therefore be treated as a constituent of working capital like other trade creditors.

Example

The balance sheet of Bradmore Bakeries PLC for the last two years is set out below:

As at 31 December	Last Year £	This Year £
Capital authorized:		
Ordinary shares of £1 each	600 000	700 000
10 per cent redeemable preference shares	40 000	40 000
	£640 000	£740 000
Capital issued:		
Ordinary shares of £1 each, fully paid	410 000	460 000
10 per cent redeemable preference shares	22 000	—
Reserves:		
Share premium account	—	5 000
General reserve	60 000	85 000
Unappropriated profits c/f	5 425	33 196
	£497 425	£583 196

Represented by:

	Last Year Cost £	Last Year Depreciation £	Last Year Net £	This Year Cost £	This Year Depreciation £	This Year Net £
Fixed assets:						
Freehold land and buildings	265 000	—	265 000	215 000	—	215 000
Plant and machinery	250 000	120 000	130 000	320 000	125 000	195 000
Vehicles	50 000	20 000	30 000	40 000	20 000	20 000
	£565 000	£140 000	£425 000	£575 000	£145 000	£430 000
Trade invesments			—			70 000
Current assets:						
Stock	79 896			95 300		
Debtors	60 104			86 210		
Investments	97 100			66 000		
Cash	39 646			—		
		276 746			247 510	
Less current liabilities:						
Trade creditors	74 321			62 503		
Current taxation	12 000			14 000		
Dividend payable	10 000			12 000		
Overdraft	—			2 811		
		96 321			91 314	
Working capital			180 425			156 196
Total assets less current liabilities			605 425			656 196
Long-term liabilities:						
8 per cent debentures		108 000			38 000	
Unsecured loan		—	108 000		35 000	73 000
			£497 425			£583 196

Investigation into the balance sheet figures produces the following significant information:

1. A freehold building was sold during the year for £75 000.

2. Plant which originally cost £30 000 was sold during the year for its written-down value of £5000 and replaced by new machinery which cost £100 000.
3. Some old vehicles which originally cost £10 000 were sold during the year for £750, at a book loss of £1250.
4. Current taxation in the balance sheet represents tax on the profits for that year.
5. The 8 per cent debentures must be completely repaid by the end of next year.

(a) Compute a movement of funds statement for the company, from the data given above.
(b) Prepare a memorandum for submission to the managing director, commenting briefly on the information revealed by the statement.

Some authorities suggest that the latest balance sheet figures should be deducted from those on the earlier balance sheet to reveal the movements which have taken place. It must be stressed, however, that this is only a working document and is not a management statement and, as we shall see, it is inadequate to provide all the details needed. Note that authorized capital is of no significance to a funds flow statement unless it is issued.

The basic rules are:

(a) assets decreased = a source of funds;
(b) assets increased = an application of funds;
(c) liabilities decreased = an application of funds;
(d) liabilities increased = a source of funds.

	Sources £	Applications £
Ordinary shares	50 000	
10 per cent redeemable preference shares		22 000
Share premium	5 000	
General reserve	25 000	
Unappropriated profits	27 771	
8 per cent debentures		70 000
Loan from associate	35 000	
Land and buildings	50 000	
Plant		70 000
Plant depreciation	5 000	
Vehicles	10 000	
Vehicle depreciation	—	—
Trade investments		70 000
Stock		15 404
Debtors		26 106
Investments	31 100	
Cash	39 646	
Creditors		11 818
Tax	2 000	
Dividend	2 000	
Overdraft	2 811	
	£285 328	£285 328

The increase in share premium account suggests that during the year 50 000 £1 ordinary shares have been issued at a premium of 10 pence per share. The fact that redeemable preference shares have been reduced during the year suggests that they have been repaid using funds injected into the business from the issue of fresh ordinary shares.

Next the trading profit must be computed. An income statement is not provided, but one can work back to the appropriation account from the balance sheet. The trading profit is the balancing figure.

Dr.		Profit and Loss Appropriation Account	Cr.
	£		£
Appropriated to general reserve	25 000	Opening balance b/d	5 425
Appropriated to taxation	14 000	Profit on sale of building	25 000
Appropriated to dividend	12 000	Trading profit	55 021
Loss on sale of vehicle	1 250	(balancing figure)	
Closing balance c/f	33 196		
	£85 446		£85 446

The trading profit (or operating profit) should be used to compute the cash flow, but to include the profit on buildings and loss on vehicles in this figure would obscure the amount of funds generated by trading operations. It is preferable to show the full amount of funds released by the sale of the property as a long-term source, rather than to split the amount between book value as a source and the capital profit as funds generated. The choice of this method is reinforced by a consideration of the sale of vehicles at a loss, since it is better to show £750 cash received as a source than to enter the book value of £2000 as a source and then reduce cash flow by the book loss of £1250. Depreciation can be calculated as follows:

Plant £(000s)	Cost	Depreciation	Net
Opening balances	250	120	130
Less sale at written-down value	30	25	5
Remainder	220	95	125
Purchases	100		
Balancing figure = depreciation		30*	70
Closing balances	320	125	195

Vehicles £(000s)	Cost	Depreciation	Net
Opening balances	50	20	30
Sold during year	10	8	2 (written-down value)
	40	12	28
Balancing figure = depreciation	—	8*	8
Closing balances	40	20	20

* Depreciation on plant and vehicles for the year is £38 000

Funds Flow Statement, Year Ending 31 December

Sources of funds	£	£	£
Trading profit			55 021
Items, not involving movement of funds			
Add depreciation			38 000
			93 021
Long-term sources:			
Share capital and premium	55 000		
Loan from associated			
company	35 000		
Sale of fixed assets:			
Freehold	75 000		
Plant	5 000		
Vehicles	750		170 750
			263 771
Long-term applications:			
Preference shares redeemed	22 000		
Debenture repaid	70 000		
Plant purchased	100 000		
Trade investment	70 000		
Tax paid	12 000		
Dividend paid	10 000		284 000
Deficit of long-term application over long-term source			20 229

	£	£	
Working capital changes:	Source	Application	
Creditors		11 818	
Stock		15 404	
Debtors		26 106	
Investment	31 100		
	£31 100	£53 328	
			22 228
Total deficit			£42 457
Financed by a reduction of liquid resources:			
Cash decreased		39 646	
Overdraft increased		2 811	£42 453

Some points which should be included in the explanatory memo to the managing director are as follows:

1. No certain conclusions can be drawn from such sketchy evidence, but the figures in the statement can lead an accountant to form an opinion which can be confirmed by further questioning.
2. The liquidity position of the company has been drastically reduced. Nearly £40 000 of the firm's assets stood idle as a cash balance at the beginning of the year, but these have now been utilized in the business, and overdraft of nearly £3000 has also been drawn on. Short-term investments have been liquified in the sum of £30 000 and these funds have been employed.
3. Funds generated and funds injected are insufficient to finance the long-term application, so £20 000 of cash resources have been used to fill the gap.
4. The purchase of plant and an increase in stocks and debtors suggest an expansion. It is odd that buildings and vehicles have been sold at such a time.

5. The expansion has been financed by several sources: fresh share capital, loan from an associate company, the sale of a freehold and the liquidation of some short-term investments.
6. The expansion has taken place at a time when long-term funds (debentures and preference shares) have been repaid. It is financially imprudent to repay long-term funds when they are needed to finance the expansion scheme. But the debentures are nearing their redemption date. A further £38 000 will flow out in the near future.
7. Why have trade creditors been reduced during the expansion period, when stocks and presumably purchases have increased?
8. The gearing ratio has changed. Fixed return capital has been repaid and fresh ordinary shares have been raised. The loan from an associate is probably at a fixed rate of interest and thus it also will affect the gearing.
9. What has to be paid out in the immediate future? Dividend, taxation and debenture repayment amount to more than £60 000. In the absence of cash resources to meet these payments the remaining short-term investments may have to be sold. Will there be a capital gains tax liability?
10. Further expansion will probably be financed by creditors and the bank. In the absence of an injection of more long-term funds the point at which overtrading commences may have been reached.

Funds Flow Statement: Some Conclusions

The funds flow statement provides a link between the opening balance sheet, the income statement and the closing balance sheet. If this link is to be effective the information must be conveyed in a form that is easily assimilated by the non-technical reader. Statement of Standard Accounting Practice 10 reminds us in its explanatory notes that the funds flow statement is not a substitute for the accounts, but that it contains figures which cover the same transactions except that the information has been selected, reclassified and summarized.

Funds flow analysis reveals the financial changes in a firm during an accounting period. The statement seeks to show the funds generated by the company's own efforts, the funds injected from outside the business, and the changes in asset structure which have made funds available for use elsewhere in the business, e.g. when a fixed asset is sold to help pay for other fixed assets or to ease a liquidity problem, or when current assets are squeezed to provide funds for fixed assets. It also shows how funds have been applied by the management to command more assets, to lend to others, or to repay amounts lent to the business. The analysis is extended to an examination of short- and long-term fluctuations to reveal whether long-term sources are sufficient to cover long-term applications of funds or whether short-term funds are used to finance the purchase of fixed assets—borrowing short to tie up long.

Most funds flow statements show as the bottom line any change in the liquidity position of the company. Therefore they can often be used to explain the situation when, although profits have increased, liquid funds are scarce in a business, by showing how available cash resources have been withdrawn or are tied up in assets. The statement can be projected forward from the present position to a budgeted balance sheet. This long-term cash budget is a useful aid to financial planning in a firm.

SSAP 10 is an advisory standard, rather than a mandatory one. The standard lays down that all financial statements for companies with a turnover in excess of £25 000 per annum must have a movement of funds statement appended thereto and that such a statement must be covered by the normal audit of the accounts. The standard requires that the statement should show comparable figures for a previous year, and stipulates that certain features, e.g. the profit or loss for the period with adjustments for non-cash items, should be revealed. Other amounts which should be shown on a funds flow statement according to SSAP 10 are: dividends paid; acquisitions and disposals of fixed and non-current assets; funds raised by increasing share capital, and long-term loans and funds used to repay capital and loans; any increase or decrease in working capital to show movements of individual current assets or liabilities and changes in liquid funds. The standard also advises that items should not be netted off against other items. The figure for taxation paid is usually shown with other applications of the company's funds.

International Accounting Standard No. 7 uses the term 'statements of changes in financial position' for funds flow statements, and specifies that such statements should be an integral part of the financial statements of a business. It states that funds provided from or used in the operations of an enterprise should be shown separately from unusual items which are not part of the ordinary activities of the enterprise, so that funds generated by the business can be identified. As an alternative to adding back depreciation etc. to net profit, the standard suggests that costs and expenses should be deducted from revenues which provide funds, to compute a figure for funds from operations. Other sources and uses of funds are to be shown separately, but the list includes dividends paid during the period. The term 'funds' for the purpose of this statement refers to cash, cash equivalents and working capital.

A significant criticism of funds flow statements is that the format does not group appropriate items together. It is argued that funds applied to purchase plant should be set in the same part of the statement as funds raised from the sale of plant, or that funds derived from the issue of shares and other long-term sources should be grouped with funds applied to the repayment of long-term loans etc. Research in the USA has suggested that a cash flow statement rather than a funds flow statement should be produced with published accounts. The objectives of such a statement would be to assess:

(a) the ability of the business to generate adequate future cash flow;
(b) the ability of the business to meet its obligations, pay dividends and recruit finance from outside the business;
(c) the reasons for differences between income and associated cash flows;
(d) the cash and non-cash aspects of investing and financial transactions during the period.

In order to achieve these objectives it is suggested that the funds flow statement should be redrafted in a format analysing flows to:

1. *Investing activities* covering the purchase and sale of fixed assets and investments and cash flowing out of the business to make loans to other companies.
2. *Financing activities* such as cash inflows from share issues and long-term debt and outflows generated by the repayment of loans and the payment of dividends.
3. *Operating activities* including all transactions that are not investing and finance activities, i.e. the cash flow generated by business operations.

BALANCE SHEET APPRAISAL

To an experienced accountant each item on the balance sheet of a company has a certain significance which leads to further enquiries. These questions are largely a matter of trying to discover the reality of the situation and to ascertain that all is as it should be. The following are some enquiries an accountant might make to discover the significance of various items in the balance sheet.

1. *Capital.* An accountant would ask whether the issued capital had been called up and, if not, what calls were outstanding. A prospective purchaser of partly called shares should be warned that he will be liable if the remaining calls are made. To a lender the uncalled capital represents a form of security, since if the company is wound up such capital can be called up by the liquidator to meet amounts owed to creditors. The relative voting rights of different classes of share capital are of interest to a prospective purchaser. The existence of convertible loan stock can change the voting pattern of a company in the future. If there are any arrears of preference dividend they may need to be made good before a dividend on ordinary shares is paid.

2. *The reserves.* It is important to discover whether they are available for dividend or are of a capital nature. Reserves created by the issue of shares at a premium reflect the confidence of investors, and reserves built up from the revaluation of fixed assets give an indication of the accuracy of the figure for those assets shown elsewhere in the balance sheet. Capital reserves can be used to pay up shares for a bonus or scrip issue, and their existence makes the tactic a possibility, if not a probability. The size of revenue reserves shows the financial strength of a company, but the rate at which they are increasing reflects the ploughback/pay-out policy of the directors and the ability of the company to grow by retaining its profits. A potential lender to the company may suggest that revenue reserves are capitalized before he lends, since this tactic will prevent the payment of a dividend from such reserves, using the funds that the lender has injected.

3. *Long-term loans* are significant for the gearing of the company. Where debentures are concerned, an accountant automatically asks whether they are secured, whether the security is adequate, when the redemption date is, how they are going to be redeemed (sinking fund?) and how the rate of interest on them compares with the current market rate for such securities. Redemption in the near future can mean an outflow of cash unless a sinking fund has been established or the firm intends to reborrow on the market, where higher interest rates on the replaced funds could mean an increase in costs. A sinking fund implies that funds are set aside annually and invested to produce, with compound interest, a capital sum equal to the amount required on the debenture redemption date.

4. The significance of adequate *working capital* has already been dealt with. The existence of liquid funds in the balance sheet can suggest either an undynamic management which is unable to put all the company's assets to work, or that management are liquifying their assets with some strategic move in view. A company with unutilized cash resources will be a takeover prospect, since profitability can be improved by employing all the assets in the business, and the share price is likely to be depressed by the impact of low profits or dividends.

5. The *trade creditors* deserve analysis to discover, if possible, whether any of them

are secured and so are first to be repaid if the company is liquidated, to the detriment of the claims of other creditors. The existence of a few large creditors who can join together to form a pressure group on the management is important, but if trade creditors are a large disparate group of individuals to whom only small amounts are owed, such co-ordination and pressure are less likely to occur.

6. The size of the *overdraft*, together with amounts owing to other creditors, highlights any overdependence on financial sources other than the owners, and the extent of unused overdraft facilities shows the freedom of action remaining to management.

7. The amount owed to the *Inland Revenue* is always of interest to an accountant. The amount may be an amalgam of corporation tax, VAT, schedule E deductions etc., each with a different payment date. The impact of corporation tax on the cash flow may be reduced if ACT can be set off against it. If a dividend payable is shown among the current liabilities, an accountant will ask how the payment will affect the cash reserves available, and will look for the amount of ACT to be paid consequent upon that dividend.

8. With regard to the *fixed assets*, an accountant will investigate the extent to which the balance sheet figures reflect their market value, and whether the depreciation written off in the past has been sufficient to charge the profit computation with a true amount for the fall in the value of the asset. The impact of inflation on fixed assets, especially property, can be hidden if those assets are shown at historical cost, or were last revalued some years ago. Shareholders could be misled as to the true value of their assets, and may accept a takeover bid for their shares at a low price. If fixed assets are undervalued the depreciation charge will be insufficient and profits will be overstated, and where goodwill has been computed on the basis of these past profits it will also be overstated.

   The precise description of fixed assets will interest the accountant, e.g. to separate such items as freehold and leasehold property. In cases where a company occupies premises held on lease the accountant will consider the terms of the lease, such as when is the next rent review, what will be its impact on the costs of the company, and how long the lease has to run. The adequacy of fixed assets in relation to the business of the company is important. The historical cost of the plant will not be a good guide to its value in a period of inflation, but if the plant is well written down this implies that it is nearing the end of its working life, is likely to be expensive in terms of repair bills, and perhaps will have to be replaced in the near future. If plant resources are small relative to the turnover, it could mean that machinery is leased rather than owned, in which case the terms of the lease should be investigated. If the depreciation rates have not been computed properly the plant may be insufficiently written down, which gives a misleading view of its age and efficiency. An accountant will always ask what method is used to depreciate machinery, and check that the estimated life or rate built into the computation is realistic in current circumstances. Fixed assets may also be set against current assets to ensure the optimum combination to maximize profits. Too much investment in fixed assets can lead to machinery standing idle, while too little in current assets can result in stock shortages and an inadequate credit line to support the efforts of the sales force.

9. *Current assets* raise a separate set of questions in the mind of the accountant. Apart from the adequacy of stock levels and the cost of funds tied up in stock,

the accountant also considers the efficiency with which the stock has been counted at the year end, and the basis used to value stocks once they are entered on the stock sheets. Any mistake in counting, calculation or valuation will not only invalidate the balance sheet figure but will also distort the profit measurement. The computation of the amount for stock of work in progress is also interesting, since some overhead expenses may be wrongly allocated to stocks and carried forward in the stock figures from one accounting period to another, with a consequent effect on profit. The item debtors is significant when compared with credit sales, and the adequacy of the provision for doubtful debts, which also has an impact on profit, must be borne in mind. Further investigation using an 'ageing debtors list' may show up some important discrepancies.

10. *Intangible assets* shown in a balance sheet will always raise questions about their valuation, and whether their existence as assets can be substantiated. Goodwill is an example of an asset which must be treated with caution. It will not be realized until the company is wound up, yet its existence depends on the superprofits made by the company. The accountant considers whether the present and future profitability is sufficient to support the goodwill figure, especially after consideration of the riskiness of the company and the capital employed that is tied up there.

11. It is not unknown for the balance on the *profit and loss account* to be found among the assets on the balance sheet. A debit balance on the profit and loss means that past losses have been made, and this is certainly not an asset of the business. The accountant is alerted by these past losses and asks whether they are likely to continue, what has been done to bring the company into a profit situation, and whether the past losses must be made good before a dividend is paid.

12. The *notes to the accounts* showing an analysis of balance sheet figures and an explanation of accounting policies are very helpful in providing some answers to these questions. It must be realized, however, that the balance sheet shows the position at a specific point in time, and it may be out of date and not at all representative of the current situation. Some significant items appear in the notes rather than on the face of the balance sheet, e.g. information concerning contingent liabilities and future capital commitments.

Example

Dover Electronics PLC plan to build a new warehouse and despatch bay adjacent to the mouth of the Channel Tunnel. Several companies have tendered for this job, and the board have selected Clydeside Contractors Ltd of Glasgow as the contractor to whom they wish to award the contract, which is scheduled to commence in September 19-8. As a final check before committing themselves to a contract, the board have asked you to review the most recent published accounts of Clydeside Contractors to test the financial viability of the company.

Unfortunately, only extracts from the accounts are available, and an opinion is required urgently. In these circumstances despite the inadequacies of the published accounts as a vehicle for business interpretation, comments must be made to assist the board in its decision.

Using the information set out opposite, draft comments concerning Clydeside Contractors Ltd which should in your view be considered by the board of Dover Electronics PLC, and raise matters for further investigation.

Summary Balance Sheet of Clydeside Contractors Ltd as at 31 December 19-7

	Cost	Depreciation	Net
	£	£	£
Fixed assets:			
Plant	2 500 000	1 975 000	525 000
Land/buildings	450 000	108 000	342 000
Vehicles	140 000	90 000	50 000
	3 090 000	2 173 000	917 000
Deferred asset—ACT reclaimable			33 333
Current assets:			
Cash	27 900		
Debtors	97 500		
Stock	365 750		
Work in progress	1 867 143		2 358 293
			£3 308 626
Capital:			
Ordinary shares of £1 (issued and fully paid)			800 000
Reserves			823 619
Loan stock (17 per cent redeemable 19-8–19-9)			1 100 000
			2 723 619
Current liabilities:			
Taxation (ACT £33 333)	152 857		
Dividends	100 000		
Creditors	182 500		
Bank overdraft	149 650		585 007
			£3 308 626

Clydeside Contractors Ltd, Income Statement for the Year Ending 31 December 19-7

	£
Turnover	5 000 000
Net profit after interest	340 000
Taxation for the year	110 000
Net profit after tax	230 000
Dividend	100 000
Retained profit	130 000
Depreciation	275 250
Cash flow	£405 250
Tender price	£1 950 000
Expected completion time	12 months

Solution. A question such as this cannot be answered precisely, but major points which might be included in a solution are as follows:

1. Plant Resources. If Clydeside contractors have adequate plant they may be able to complete the job on time. Plant in the balance sheet shows a cost of £2.5 million written down to £525 000. This suggests that the plant may be old and inefficient and prone to disruption to production from delays caused by breakdowns. The position shown by the balance sheet may not reflect the real circumstances of the company because plant leased by the business may not show up in the balance sheet. The depreciation policy adopted by the business, and the frequency with which plant is revalued for balance sheet purposes, will also influence this comment.

2. The Significance of the Contract for Company Turnover.

$$\frac{\text{Contract price}}{\text{Turnover for the year}} \text{ as a percentage } \quad \frac{£1\ 950\ 000}{£5\ 000\ 000} \times \frac{100}{1} = 39 \text{ per cent}$$

This contract would probably be the most important job in progress with Clydeside Contractors, and might thus receive priority treatment from the management. The calibre of the management team should be investigated. The accounts do not show the value to the business of an efficient management team, nor its reliance on certain key personnel. This is a private limited company which is small in size and is undertaking a job far from its base in Scotland. The existence of a good local management team will be crucial to the progress of the work and the eventual success of the project.

It must be noted that the accounts are six months out of date and the significance of the contract for the turnover of the company may have changed if other contracts have been won which will compete for managerial resources within this business. Conversely some existing jobs may be nearing completion.

3. Financial Viability. Four questions need to be answered.

    (a) Does Clydeside have sufficient capital to undertake this contract?
    (b) Will Clydeside remain solvent until the job is completed?
    (c) To what extent is Clydeside dependent upon outside finance?
    (d) Clydeside appears to have borrowed heavily, and the contractee must attempt to establish the degree of support afforded to that company by the financial institutions which are financing its operations. A private limited company does not have access to the share capital market for an injection of fresh funds.

The working capital ratio looks good at 2358 : 585 = 4 : 1. Consideration of the acid test; however, shows a different picture with the ratio of 125 : 585 = 0.21 : 1. The significance of a comment based on these ratios depends on the situation of the work in progress, and the speed with which it can be converted into architects' certificates and thence into cash. There does, however, appear to be a marked reliance on overdraft and trade credit. It would be interesting to establish whether the company had computed a cash budget for the forthcoming year, and to see what that statement disclosed.

The company proposes to pay a dividend of 12.5 per cent, which will require an outward cash flow of £100 000 + £33 000 for the associated ACT. The cash resources in the balance sheet stand at £28 000. It is difficult to see how the company can meet this dividend requirement as well as its commitment to pay corporation tax, trade creditors, and the bank overdraft if that loan is called in. It should also be noted that the loan stock is redeemable during the contract period for a figure in excess of £1 million.

The corporation tax will probably be payable on 1 October 19-8, immediately after the commencement of this contract. Much depends on whether Clydeside can re-finance the loan stock. The company possesses land and buildings and the accountant should investigate the current value of these assets and their suitability as collateral for a probable re-finance operation. A further question would be to ask whether any of the assets are already charged as security for liabilities in the balance sheet.

Overdependence on outside finance is a sign of weakness. The ratio of total indebtedness to capital employed shows £1 680 000 (loan stock and current liabilities) to £3 308 000, a ratio of 51 per cent. Cash flow for the year is only £405 000 and may prove inadequate to revitalize the finances of this business.

$$\text{ROCE calculated as } \frac{£230\ 000}{£3\ 308\ 000} \times \frac{100}{1} = 6.9 \text{ per cent}$$

The question is raised as to whether this return is sufficient to give confidence to the bank and creditors who can influence the ability of the company to continue as a going concern.

TUTORIAL DISCUSSION TOPIC

A company is currently in negotiation with the branch officials of the trade union to which most of its employees belong. As accountant to the company you have been asked by the managing director to comment on the financial arguments used in a wage claim put forward by local union negotiators. Make a brief comment on each of the following arguments.

1. It is a well-known fact that accountants can manipulate profit and thus it is likely that the figure of £200 000 in the accounts is an understatement of the true position. The accounting policy adopted towards the valuation of stocks of work in progress alone is capable of transferring overhead expenses from one year to another.
2. The profit of £200 000, when set against net capital employed as recorded in the balance sheet, shows a return on investment of 28 per cent. This high profit rate puts the ability of the company to pay higher wages in perspective.
3. Although the accounts for the year show a profit of £200 000 it is noted that during that year £240 000 has been transferred to an associated company and £260 000 has been repaid to debenture holders. This transfer of cash and loan repayment is an attempt to conceal the true profit figure and if it was written back the company's real ability to meet the claim for higher wages would be revealed.
4. In relation to the profit shown in the accounts for the year there are large reserves of undistributed profits built up in past years. It is unfair that past surpluses should be set aside for the shareholders and kept in reserve accounts beyond the reach of employees with wage claims.
5. The dividend rate on the shares of the company has risen over the past ten years from 15 per cent to 25 per cent. The financial press shows the average yield on ordinary shares as about 6 per cent. The distribution to shareholders is therefore excessive and some of this money should be channelled to employees.
6. Profits are retained in the business as a device to avoid the payment of tax on them by shareholders.

The solution to this problem is on p. 508.

SEMINAR EXERCISES 16

1. Gold Bond Ltd is a small firm manufacturing high-quality paper. The bulk of its output has traditionally been purchased by Caxton PLC, a large printing firm.

The management of Gold Bond are becoming increasingly concerned over their almost total reliance on one customer and have obtained summarized financial statements for Caxton PLC in order to monitor financial viability of their major customer. These statements together with information from the inter-firm comparison scheme of the Printing Industry Federation are set out below.

Caxton PLC, Balance Sheets as at 31 December

	19-4	19-5
Assets:	£000s	£000s
Fixed assets at cost	11 516	15 050
Depreciation	4 398	5 031
	7 118	10 019
Goodwill	1 000	500
Current assets:		
Stocks	2 775	2 003
Debtors	8 294	7 098
Cash	353	72
	£19 540	£19 692
Liabilities and shareholders' equity:		
£1 ordinary shares	1 963	1 963
Redeemable preference shares	420	—
Share premium	332	332
Retained earnings	4 780	1 721
Long-term loans	2 931	4 608
Current liabilities:		
Creditors	6 589	6 692
Overdraft	2 174	4 361
Tax	108	7
Dividend	243	8
	£19 540	£19 692

Income Statement for the Year Ended 31 December

	19-4	19-5
Sales	28 846	27 663
Profit before interest and tax	730	(2 311)
Interest	377	712
Tax	103	11
Profit after interest and tax	250	(3 034)
Dividend	130	25

Average Ratios for the Printing Industry

	19-4	19-5
Return on capital employed	13.0%	13.5%
Return on sales	4.8%	5.2%
Asset turnover	2.7	2.6
Current ratio	1.4	1.5
Sales/stocks	7.6	7.7
Average collection period	86 days	79 days

(a) Compute a funds flow statement for Caxton PLC for 19-5.

(b) Prepare a ratio analysis report for the management of Gold Bond Ltd evaluating the financial performance of Caxton PLC. In your report draw particular attention to any areas of weakness you identify and detail any further information you might require in making your analysis.

2. Hypertension PLC is a subcontracting company specializing in the design and construction of bridge decks. Their financial year end is 31 March. The accounts for the year end to 31 March 19-8, and the budget for the year ending 31 March 19-9, are to hand.

   (a) Prepare a budgeted funds flow statement for the company for the year ended 31 March 1990.
   (b) Comment on the manner in which the company plans to finance its operations in the forthcoming year.

Note: £000s

Fixed Assets	Premises	Plant	Vehicles	Fittings	Total
Cost 1 April 19-8	1494	1207	340	109	3150
Acquisitions	800	492	56	27	1375
Disposals	—	(220)	—	—	(220)
Cost 31 March 19-9	2294	1479	396	136	4305
Depreciation:					
1 April 19-8	106	987	153	64	1310
Year	54	123	50	12	239
Disposals	—	(178)	—	—	(178)
31 March 19-9	160	932	203	76	1371
NBV 1 April 19-8	1388	220	187	45	1840
31 March 19-9	2134	547	193	60	2934

Plant was sold during the year for its written-down value.

Budgeted Balance Sheet of Hypertension PLC as at 31 March 19-9

31 March 19-8		£	£	£
1 840 000	Fixed assets (see note)			2 934 000
	Current assets:			
971 000	Stock—materials and work in progress		1 380 000	
1 079 000	Debtors		1 420 000	
460 000	Bank		57 000	
			2 857 000	
	Less current liabilities:			
(610 000)	Trade creditors	814 000		
(170 000)	Tax	240 000		
(250 000)	Dividend	—		
—	Bank overdraft	320 000		
			(1 374 000)	
—	Working capital			1 483 000
3 320 000	Total assets less current liabilities			4 417 000
—	17 per cent debentures			(800 000)
£3 320 000				£3 617 000
	Share capital			
2 500 000	Ordinary shares of £1			2 500 000
500 000	Share premium account			500 000
320 000	Unappropriated profits			617 000
£3 320 000				£3 617 000

3. Soar Valley Services PLC is a company providing a specialized soil mechanics service to the construction industry in the East Midlands.

Balance Sheet as at 30 June 19-8

30.6.19-7				
£		£	£	£
2 650 000	Fixed assets (see note)			3 910 000
	Current assets:			
280 000	Stock—materials and works in progress		570 000	
740 000	Debtors		1 060 000	
71 000	Bank		13 000	
			1 643 000	
	Less current liabilities:			
(410 000)	Trade creditors	565 000		
(80 000)	Taxation	320 000		
(91 000)	Dividends	126 000		
—	Bank overdraft	612 000		
			1 623 000	
	Working capital			20 000
—	Total assets less current liabilities			3 930 000
(400 000)	13 per cent unsecured loan stock			—
—	18 per cent debentures			(400 000)
£2 760 000				£3 530 000
	Share capital:			
2 400 000	Ordinary shares of £1			2 800 000
—	Share premium account			150 000
360 000	Unappropriated profits			580 000
£2 760 000				£3 530 000

Note:

Fixed Assets	Plant	Vehicles	Fittings	Total
Cost 1 July	3 140 000	391 000	229 000	3 760 000
Acquisitions	1 871 000	36 000	—	1 907 000
Disposals	—	—	—	—
Cost 30 June				
	5 011 000	427 000	229 000	5 667 000
Depreciation:				
1 July	881 800	143 400	84 800	1 110 000
Year	520 000	104 100	22 900	647 000
30 June	1 401 800	247 500	107 700	1 757 000
NBV 1 July	2 258 200	247 600	144 200	2 650 000
30 June	3 609 200	179 500	121 300	3 910 000

(a) Prepare a funds flow statement for the company for the year ended 30 June 19-8.

(b) Comment on the financial changes during the year as disclosed by your statement.

4. Holland Swede is a Lincolnshire tenant farmer. One of Mr Swede's main crops is potatoes, and owing to the drought last summer the sale price of potatoes has been very high. Largely because of this Mr Swede made a profit (before taxation) of £75 300 in the year ended 31 March this year, compared to £9500 in the previous year. Because of this abnormal profit Mr Swede decided to give £5000 to his daughter Lindsey and £10 000 to his son Kesteven, who works on the farm. In April last year Mr Swede received a legacy of £10 000 from the estate of his aunt, Mrs Norfolk Dumpling; this he immediately utilized by having a new Dutch barn built at a total cost of £30 000. To finance most of the remainder of the cost he borrowed £15 000 from the Fenland Farmers Friendly Loan Corporation Ltd (repayable over twenty years). Ignore capital transfer tax. The balance sheet of Mr Swede is shown above.

Produce a source and application of funds statement, showing the net increase or decrease of working capital, for Mr Swede covering the year ended 31 March. The statement should include all the information that you consider Mr Swede (a farmer with only an elementary knowledge of book-keeping) would find helpful.

H. Swede Esq., Balance Sheet at 31 March This Year

Last Year £		£	£	£
	Fixed assets (Note 1):			
—	Dutch barn		29 400	
18 200	Farm implements etc.		25 500	54 900
6 000	Trade investment:			10 000
	(Shares in Dumpling and Swede (Grain Dryers) Ltd)			
24 200				64 900
	Current assets:			
21 700	Valuation (Note 2), stocks	32 100		
3 500	Debtors and prepayments	8 500		
—	Bank balance	12 700	53 300	
	Less current liabilities:			
(2 800)	Creditors	4 300		
(6 700)	Bank overdraft	—	4 300	49 000
£39 900				£113 900
	Representing			
—	Loan: Fenland Farmers Friendly Loan Corporation Ltd			15 000
39 900	H. Swede capital account (Note 3)			98 900
£39 900				£113 900

Notes:
1. Fixed assets.

	£ Farm implements etc.	£ Dutch barn
Book value at 31 March last year	18 200	—
Net additions in year	13 700	30 000
	31 900	30 000
Depreciation for year	6 400	600
Book value at 31 March this year	25 500	29 400

2. Valuation. The valuation covers growing crops, live and dead stock, unexhausted manurial values and other 'tenant rights'.
3. Capital account.

Last Year			This Year	
£			£	£
35 600	Balance at 31 March last year		39 900	
9 500	Profit for year (before taxation)		72 300	
—	Legacy: Mrs N. Dumpling		10 000	122 200
—	Gifts to Lindsey and Kesteven		15 000	
	Taxation paid (1 July last year)	2200		
(3 400)	(1 January this year)	2900	5 100	
(1 800)	Other cash drawings		3 200	23 300
£39 900	Balance at 31 March this year			£98 900

5. Forest Ltd is a manufacturer of sportswear with a factory by the River Trent. During the year ended 31 March the company issued £25 000 of shares at par to provide funds to redeem £15 000 of the debenture stock and provide additional working capital. The debentures were redeemed at par and fixed assets (Note 1) were sold at their net book amount. The balance sheet and profit and loss account of Forest Ltd are shown below.

(a) Produce a source and application of funds statement, showing the net increase or decrease in working capital for Forest Ltd for the year ended 31 March.

(b) Discuss five points which you consider to be the main purposes of a source and application of funds statement.

Forest Ltd, Balance Sheet at 31 March This Year

Previous Year				
£		£	£	£
150 000	Ordinary Shares of £1 each			175 000
56 112	Reserves			92 458
206 112				267 458
75 000	10 per cent debenture stock 1991/96			60 000
£281 112				£327 458
	Represented by:			
203 009	Fixed assets (Note 1)			224 117
9 114	Deferred assets, ACT recoverable			9 741
	Current assets:			
110 011	Stock		147 438	
185 783	Debtors		257 610	
			405 048	
	Less current liabilities:			
(122 439)	Creditors	182 873		
(44 720)	Bank overdraft	50 259		
(42 720)	Taxation (Note 2)	59 407		
(16 926)	Dividends	18 909		
			311 448	
	Net current assets			93 600
£281 112				£327 458

Notes:

1. Fixed assets.

	Freehold Land and Buildings £	Plant and Machinery £	Total £
Cost:			
At 1 April last year	120 745	201 514	322 259
Additions	6 660	39 352	46 012
Disposals	—	(7 469)	(7 469)
At 31 March this year	127 405	233 397	360 802
Depreciation:			
At 1 April last year	—	119 250	119 250
Charge for the year	—	21 515	21 515
On disposals	—	(4 080)	(4 080)
At 31 March this year	—	136 685	136 685
Net book amount at 31 March this year	127 405	96 712	224 117

2. Taxation. The taxation creditor at the year end comprises:

	This Year £	Last Year £
Corporation tax on profits for the year at 35 per cent	58 780	41 887
Less ACT on dividends paid in the year	(9 114)	(8 281)
	49 666	33 606
Add ACT on proposed dividends	9 741	9 114
	£59 407	£42 720

3. Forest Ltd, profit and loss account for the year ended 31 March.

Last Year £		£	£
790 754	Turnover		996 455
80 855	Trading profit		114 035
	After charging:		
	Depreciation	21 515	
	Debenture interest	6 750	
	Bank overdraft interest	6 958	
	Corporation tax on profits for the		
41 887	year at 35 per cent		58 780
38 968	Profit after tax		55 255
(16 926)	Dividend, proposed		(18 909)
22 042	Retained profit for the year		36 346
34 070	Reserves at 1 April last year		56 112
£56 112	Reserves at 31 March this year		£92 458

6. The following are the balance sheets and profit and loss account of Landseen Ltd for 19-7 and 19-8.

Balance Sheet for Year Ended 31 May

	19-7		19-8	
	£	£	£	£
Fixed assets:				
Cost		346 500		420 000
Depreciation		82 500		90 000
		264 000		330 000
Current assets:			775 700	
Stocks	722 700		510 000	
Debtors	468 600		15 000	
Bank	13 200			
		1 204 500		1 300 700
		£1 468 500		£1 630 700
Share capital:				
Ordinary shares				
of £1 each		500 000		500 000
10 per cent preference				
shares of £1 each		160 000		160 000
		660 000		660 000
Retained earnings		339 700		362 700
		999 700		
10 per cent debentures 1996/99				100 000
				1 122 700
Current liabilities:				
Trade creditors and				
accruals	303 800		319 000	
Taxation	130 000		151 000	
Dividend	35 000		38 000	
		468 800		508 000
		£1 468 500		£1 630 700

Profit and Loss Accounts

	19-7		19-8	
	£	£	£	£
Net profit before				
taxation		185 000		195 000
Less taxation		86 000		93 000
Profit after taxation		99 000		102 000
Less dividends:				
Preference				
Ordinary	16 000		16 000	
	50 000		63 000	
		66 000		79 000
Profit retained		£33 000		£23 000

The following information is available.

In December 19-7 fixed assets which had cost £35 000 were sold at a profit of £4000. The accumulated depreciation on these assets was £19 000.

(a) Prepare a statement of the source and application of funds for year ended 31 May 19-8.

(b) Discuss the purpose of this statement.

REVIEW QUESTIONS 11

1. Mr Broker has just returned from a course on finance and feels that with his newly acquired knowledge he would like to invest some money on the Stock Exchange. He has been advised by his friend Mr Sharpe to purchase some shares in Sparks & Mincers PLC, a chain of retail stores of high repute.

He has written to the company for their annual accounts and finds that the company's current ratio is less than 1 : 1. He knows very little about accounts but feels that a current ratio of less than 1 : 1 represents a risky company to invest in. He cannot understand why he was advised to purchase shares in such a company.

You are provided with the following extract from the company's accounts.

Sparks & Mincers PLC Profit and Loss Account Extract for Year Ended
31 December 19-2

	19-2	19-1
	£000	£000
Sales	1 275 000	985 000
Profit before tax	94 000	65 000
Tax	15 000	12 000
	79 000	53 000
Dividends	27 000	21 000
Retained profit	£52 000	£32 000

The profit before tax figure has been calculated after deducting depreciation of £14 380 for buildings and £30 090 for equipment (£000).

Using the above and the balance sheet information that follows:

(a) Produce a funds flow statement for the year ending 31 December 19-2.
(b) Explain to Mr Broker whether you consider the company to be in a sound financial position and illustrate your answer with three suitable accounting ratios.

Sparks & Mincers PLC Extract from Balance Sheet as at December 19-2

	£000		£000
Fixed assets:			
Land		150 000	110 000
Buildings (NBV)		210 750	188 630
Equipment (NBV)		84 320	61 910
		445 070	360 540
Current assets:			
Stock	151 450		121 980
Debtors	17 320		11 600
Cash	25 180		17 340
	193 950		150 920
Less current liabilities:			
Creditors	180 370		135 850
Dividend proposed	15 000		12 000
Tax	27 000		21 000
Bank	42 130		31 240
	264 500		200 090

	£000	£000
Working capital	(70 550)	(49 170)
Total net assets	£374 520	£311 370
Financed by:		
Share capital	36 000	31 000
Reserves	323 107	271 170
	359 170	302 170
Long-term loans	15 350	9 200
Total capital employed	£374 520	£311 370

2. Pilbeam PLC is engaged in the distribution of motor cars, the servicing and repair of vehicles and the distribution and retailing of parts and accessories. The company made losses for the three years ended 30 September 19-9. The balance sheets at 30 September 19-8 and 30 September 19-9 and the profit and loss account for the year ended 30 September 19-9 are set out below. Because of the previous losses:

   (i) there is no liability for corporation tax on the 19-8/-9 profit;
   (ii) the directors did not recommend payment of a dividend.

Balance Sheet of Pilbeam PLC

	30 September 19-8		30 September 19-9	
Fixed assets (note 1):	£000	£000	£000	£000
Freehold land and buildings		4653		3509
Leasehold land and buildings		323		305
Plant vehicles and equipment		739		823
		5715		4637
Current assets:				
Stocks and consignment deposits (note 2):	3012		2786	
Debtors and prepayments	2212		1866	
Cash and bank balances	238		160	
	5462		4812	
Less current liabilities:				
Creditors and accrued charges	3447		2876	
Bank loans and overdrafts (secured)	3176		2316	
	6623		5192	
Net current liabilities		(1161)		(380)
		4554		4257
Financed by:				
Share capital		2398		2398
Reserves		918		625
Shareholders' funds		3316		3023
Loans		1238		1234
		4554		4257

Notes:
(a) Fixed assets.

	Freehold land and buildings £000	Leasehold land and buildings £000	Plant, vehicles and equipment £000
Cost or valuation at 1 October 19-8	4653	346	1325
Additions in year	88	5	493
Cost of disposals	(1192)	(15)	(384)
Cost or valuation at 30 September 19-9	3549	336	1434
Depreciation at 1 October 19-8	—	23	586
Charge for year	40	8	229
Disposals	—	—	(204)
Depreciation at 30 September 19-9	40	31	611
Net book value at 30 September 19-9	3509	305	823

(b) Consignment deposits.

Consignment deposits are payments made to manufacturers in respect of vehicles on consignment.

Pilbeam PLC Profit and Loss Account for Year Ended 30 September 19-9

	£000	£000
Turnover		25 607
Profit before taxation and extraordinary items		132
Taxation		Nil
Profit after taxation		132
Extraordinary items:		
Losses against book value on sale of land and buildings	400	
Loss on disposal of plant, etc. ·	25	425
Loss for year		(293)
Reserves brought forward (1 October 19-8)		918
Reserves carried forward (30 September 19-9)		£625

(a) Produce a source and application of funds statement (including showing the net increase/decrease of working capital) for the year ended 30 September 19-9.
(b) Calculate the 'current' ratio at each of two balance sheet dates and comment on the information the ratios have revealed.

3. Quickfoods PLC own a small but expanding chain of well-situated restaurants. The balance sheet at 31 December 19-8 was as follows:

31 December 19-7 £	Funds employed	31 December 19-8 £
300 000	Share capital ordinary shares of £1	400 000
—	Share premium account	150 000
80 000	Unappropriated profits	140 000
380 000		690 000
100 000	8 per cent unsecured loan stock	—
£480 000		£690 000

Employment of Funds

£	£		Gross	Depreciation	Net
350 000		Fixed assets:	£	£	£
		(see Note:)	707 000	37 000	670 000
		Current assets:			
	60 000	Stock		90 000	
	180 000	Debtors		220 000	
	17 000	Cash at bank and			
		cash in hand		1 000	
	257 000			311 000	
		Less current liabilities:			
	30 000	Corporation tax			
		payable 1 Oct -9		70 000	
	27 000	Dividends payable		32 000	
	70 000	Creditors		85 000	
	—	Bank overdraft		104 000	
	127 000			291 000	
130 000		Net current assets			20 000
£480 000					£690 000

Note to Balance Sheet

Fixed assets:

Depreciation on fixed assets (per balance sheet):

19-7		*19-8*
£		£
Nil	Freehold property	1 000
5 000	Fixtures and fittings	13 000
10 000	Motor vehicles	23 000

There were no disposals of fixed assets during the year.

(a) Prepare a statement of source and application of funds for the company for the year ended 31 December 19-8 in a form suitable for publication with the annual accounts.

(b) Interpret the above statement, and supplement your findings with the appropriate ratios.

Solutions

SEMINAR EXERCISES 1

1.

Position Statement Company A as at 31 December

	£
Capital:	
Share capital	50 000
Reserves*	59 072
Ownership interest	109 072
Long-term liabilities, loan	20 000
Capital employed	£129 072

Represented by	£ Cost	£ Depreciation	£ Net
Fixed assets:			
Land and building	95 000	10 000	85 000
Plant	25 000	6 000	19 000
Vehicles	8 000	—	8 000
	£128 000	£16 000	112 000
Investments, shares in Company X			7 000
Current assets:			
Stock		29 941	
Debtors		19 487	
Nottingham bonds		8 000	
Payments in advance		904	
Bank		8 186	
Cash		1 270	
		67 788	
Less current liabilities:			
Creditors	43 614		
Wages payable	1 102		
Taxation owed	13 000	57 716	
Working capital			10 072
Net assets			£129 072

2. (a) Increase capital, liability; increase cash, asset.
   (b) Cash reduced, current liability; 'wages payable' disappears.
   (c) Increase stock, an asset; reduce cash, an asset.
   (d) Increase stock, an asset; increase creditors, a liability.
   (e) Reduce freehold land and buildings, an asset; increase cash, an asset.
   (f) Reduce cash, an asset; reduce creditors, a liability.
   (g) Increase cash, an asset; but the asset 'Nottingham Bonds' disappears.
   (h) Reduce cash, an asset; reduce taxation owed, a liability.

* The balancing figure is that for reserves, since assets less liabilities equals capital, and the share capital is £50 000.

3. (a) Note how the accountant seeks the figures required.

Balance Sheet for Company B as at . . .

	£
Capital:	
Share capital, 100 000 ordinary shares of £1 each	100 000
Reserves*	118 000
Ownership interest	218 000
Long-term liability:	
Mortgage loan (secured on land and buildings)	70 000
Net capital employed	£288 000

Represented by:	£	£	£
Fixed assets:			
Land and building (at valuation)			156 000
Plant and vehicles (at valuation)			64 000
			220 000
Investments			18 000
Current assets:			
Stock		74 000	
Debtors		52 000	
Bank		36 000	
Cash		8 000	
		170 000	
Less current liabilities:			
Creditors	80 000		
Inland Revenue	40 000		
		120 000	
Working capital			50 000
Net assets			£288 000

Notes:
(i) No date for the balance sheet is given in the question.
(ii) The fixed assets are shown as 'at valuation' not 'cost less depreciation'.
(iii) The loan is not set off against land and buildings but a note in brackets shows that it is secured.
(iv) Investments are between fixed and current assets since it is not known whether they are to be held for a long or a short period.
(b) The figure for reserves marked * is a balancing figure. It is needed to ensure that the capital employed equals the net assets. The accounting equation assets − liabilities = capital is needed to find the ownership interest and reserves are that part of ownership interest which is unknown.

4. Note that this balance sheet is drawn up in traditional rather than vertical form.

Balance Sheet of Mr See as at 31 January 19..

	£		£	£
Capital introduced		Fixed assets:		
£(5894 + 2150)	8 044	Premises		13 000
Less withdrawn	285	Fittings		2 714
	7 759	Vehicle		2 150
				17 864
Long-term loan	13 000	Investment		500
Current liabilities		Current assets:		
Creditors £(714 + 1831)	2 545	Stock	2761	
		Bank	2179	4 940
	£23 304			£23 304

Note that capital consists of assets introduced as well as money, and that the purchase of the freezer is outside the scope of the business entity and is treated as a withdrawal of capital.

5. (a) (i) Current asset; (ii) fixed asset, plant; (iii) fixed asset, plant; (iv) not an asset since it is not owned by the business; (v) a cost, not an asset, and should be set against revenue to find the profit figure; wages paid in advance are an asset; (vi) fixed asset; (vii) current asset, stock, but it must be decided whether it is material enough to warrant the expense of counting it for balance sheet purposes; (viii) outside business entity activities, treat as a drawing; (ix) current liability, repayable within twelve months; (x) current asset, debtor; (xi) current asset, payment in advance but only for the proportion not used up at balance sheet date; the amount used up is a cost; (xii) current asset, stock, but it must be decided whether it is material enough to be included; (xiii) current asset; (xiv) long-term liability.
   (b) Air compressor, if bought for resale.
   (c) Capital, reserves and other liabilities.

SEMINAR EXERCISES 2

		£
1. (a)	(i) £2430 in closing balance sheet as stock	35 282
	(ii) £360 is stock and £3840 is a creditor	3 480
	(iii)	800
	(iv)	—
	(v)	230
	(vi) £180 is a payment in advance	180
	(vii)	1 790
	(viii) Depreciation (a non-cash cost)	1 000
	(ix) Accrued expense, creditor in balance sheet	380
		43 142
(b) Net profit		1 858
Sales		£45 000

(c)

Opening Balance Sheet

	£		£
Capital*	6413	Equipment	4000
Creditors	937	Stock	800
		Debtors	2100
		Cash	450
	£7350		£7350

* Balancing figure A − L = C.

(d)

Cash Book

	£		£
Balance at beginning	450	Payments	
Receipts:		Goods. £(37 712 + 937)	38 649
Sales	45 000	Wages	230
Debtors	2 100	Insurance	360
		Expenses	1 790
		Balance at end	6 521
	£47 550		£47 550

(e)

Closing Balance Sheet

	£		£
Opening capital	6 413	Equipment (net of depreciation)	3 000
Add profit	1 858	Stock. £(2430 + 360)	2 790
	8 271	Debtors	Nil
Trade creditors	3 840	Payment in advance	180
Accrued expense	380	Cash	6 521
	£12 491		£12 491

(f)   (i) No capital has been introduced or withdrawn.

    (ii) The opening debtors have all paid.

   (iii) The business is a going concern, so it is correct to depreciate the equipment.

   (iv) Stock will be sold at least for its cost so that no element of loss is ignored in its valuation.

2. The profit made is computed as the difference between the opening and closing capital of John Ash, if this difference is adjusted for capital amounts injected into or drawn from the business. Opening capital, £23 510; closing capital, £24 777; difference, £1267. This represents profit retained, so if 52 × £20 is withdrawn, profit is £2307. It is assumed that the shop premises have not fallen in value during the year.

		£	£
3. (a)	Opening cash (£20 000 + £10 000)		30 000
	Add sales		10 800
	Less payments:		
	Rent	500	
	Expenses	980	
	Insurance	1200	
	Suppliers	7000	
			(9 680)
	Closing cash		£31 120

		£	£
(b)	Sales		53 000
	Cost of sales (£47 000 − £15 000)		32 000
	Gross profit		21 000
	Less expenses:		
	Electricity	50	
	Insurance	100	
	Rent	250	
	Expenses	980	
			1 380
	Net profit		£19 620

Can you now compute a balance sheet as at 31 January? It should balance at net assets of £49 620.

		£		£
4. (a)	Opening capital:		Closing capital:	
	Stock	1200	Stock	1360
	Bank	400	Bank	880
	Debtors	1120	Debtors	3040
	Barrow	800	Barrow	800
		£3520		£6080

Net profit should be £2560

	£	
Cash balance:		
Opening	400	
Cash sales	2520	
Debtors	480	£(1120 + 2400 − 3040)
	3400	
Less paid out	2300	
Closing balance should be	1100	
Closing balance is	880	
Difference	£220	Assume drawings

This means the profit before drawings was £2780. You can check this figure by subtracting cost of sales from sales. In the closing balance sheet capital would be the opening figure plus profit less drawings, and would equal assets of £6080.

(b) Assumptions made, apart from the drawings, include:

(i) no wear and tear to barrow;

(ii) no doubtful debts;

(iii) all stocks are likely to be sold for at least their cost.

5.

Dr.		Rent, Electricity and Insurance Account		Cr.
	£			£
1 July balance, insurance (PIA)	600	1 July balance, electricity (accrued)		200
1 July balance, rent (PIA)	400	30 June profit and loss, insurance		1200
10 July paid, electricity	400	30 June profit and loss, rent		1600
30 September paid, rent	400			
30 September paid, electricity	500			
31 December paid, rent	400			
1 January paid, insurance	1200	30 June profit and loss, electricity		950
31 March paid, rent	400	30 June balance c/f, rent		400
30 June paid, rent	400	30 June balance c/f, insurance		600
30 June balance c/f, electricity accrued	250			
	£4950			£4950
1 July balance, rent	400	1 July balance, electricity		250
1 July balance, insurance	600			

If you cannot make this answer agree, write out separate accounts for the three constituent parts.

SEMINAR EXERCISES 3

2. Grange's capital comprises all the assets he has injected into the business, whether in cash or kind.

Opening Journal Entry

	£ Dr.	£ Cr.
Warehouse	24 000	
Fixtures and fittings	17 000	
Car	2 800	
Van	900	
Bank	8 500	
Capital account		53 200
Being assets injected into the business as capital		
Stock	1 446	
Collie and Co.		471
Lot and Mee		360
Edmunds Ltd		615
Being goods bought for stock on credit terms		

If an account is opened for each of these amounts the nucleus of a set of accounts is formed. The next task is to enter the transactions in the daybook and write up cash and bank accounts. A separate book could be used for returns, but in this case they are merged with purchases in the daybook.

Purchases Daybook

			£
1 September	Apple Ltd	Typewriters	360
5 September	J. Lewin	Goods	171
7 September	J. Lewin	Returns	(20)
9 September	Edmunds Ltd	Goods	280
			£791

Debit purchases	£451
Debit fixtures	£360
Credit returns	£20

Purchases are credited to the suppliers' personal accounts.

Sales Daybook

			£
2 September	T. Veron	Goods	627
2 September	K. Jones	Goods	460
6 September	T. Veron	Returns	(127)
7 September	H. Same Ltd	Goods	430
10 September	H. Same Ltd	Goods	165
			£1555

Credit sales	£1682
Debit returns	£127

Sales are debited to the customers' personal accounts.

Petty Cash

	£		£
1 September, bank	250	4 September, wages	83
		8 September, wages	76
		8 September, office expenses	18
		10 September, drawings	5
		11 September, bank	18
		11 September, balance c/f	50
	£250		£250
12 September, balance b/d	50		

Bank Account

	£		£
1 September, journal	8500	1 September, stationery	174
3 September, sales	165	1 September, petty cash	250
8 September, sales	431	2 September, packing	61
9 September, Veron	475	2 September, cleaning	16
11 September, petty cash	18	5 September, Collie and Co	300
		5 September, Edmunds Ltd	600
		7 September, rent	181
		9 September, insurance	160
		10 September, Lot and Mee	200
		11 September, carriage	29
		11 September, telephone	23
		11 September, balance c/f	7595
	£9589		£9589
12 September, balance b/d	7595		

Discount Allowed

9 September, Veron	25

Discount Received

5 September, Edmunds Ltd	15

Next post the opening journal entries, the total and individual items from the daybooks, and items from bank and petty cash. Remember that bank and petty cash are daybooks as well as ledger accounts. Note that trade discount is deducted from the price but cash discount is the subject of a separate account.

The vehicle transaction on 7 September should go through the journal, but it has been posted direct to the vehicles account.

Warehouse				Vehicles			
	£				£		£
1 September, journal	24 000			1 September, car	2 800	7 September, van to car sales	900
				1 September, van	900	11 September, balance c/f	5 600
Fixtures and Fittings				7 September, van from car sales	2 800		
	£				6 500		6 500
1 September, journal	17 000			12 September, balance b/d	5 600		
11 September, purchases daybook	360						
	17 360						

Capital Account				Collie and Co.			
			£		£		£
		1 September, journal	53 200	5 September, bank	300	1 September, journal	471
				11 September, balance c/f	171		
Stock					471		471
	£		£				
1 September, journal	1446	Balance c/f	1446			12 September, balance b/d	171
	1446		1446				
12 September, balance b/d	1446						

Purchases			
	£		£
11 September, purchases daybook	451	8 September, drawn	53
	451	11 September, balance c/f	398
			451
12 September, balance b/d	398		

Lot and Mee			
	£		£
10 September, bank	200	1 September, journal	360
11 September, balance c/f	160		
	360		360

Returns Outwards			
			£
		11 September, purchases daybook	20
		1 September, balance b/d	160

Sales

	£
3 September, bank	165
8 September, bank	431
11 September, sales daybook	1682
	2278

Edmunds Ltd

	£		£
5 September, bank	600	1 September, journal	615
5 September, discount	15	9 September, purchases daybook	280
11 September, balance c/f	280		
	895		895
		12 September, balance b/d	280

Returns Inwards

	£
11 September, sales daybook	127

Apple Ltd

	£
1 September, purchases daybook	360

Car Sales Ltd

	£		£
7 September, vehicles	900	7 September, vehicles	2800
11 September, balance c/f	1900		
	2800		2800
		12 September, balance b/d	1900

J. Lewin

	£		£
7 September, purchases daybook	20	5 September, purchases daybook	171
11 September, balance c/f	151		
	171		171
		12 September, balance b/d	151

Stationery

	£
1 September, bank	174

T. Veron

	£		£
2 September, sales daybook	627	6 September, sales daybook	127
		9 September, bank	475
		9 September, discount allowed	25
	627		627

Packing

	£
2 September, bank	61

Office Expenses

	£
2 September, bank, cleaning	16
8 September, cash, miscellaneous	18
	34

K. Jones

	£
2 September, sales daybook	460

H. Same

	£
7 September, sales daybook	430
10 September, sales daybook	165
	595

Rent

	£
7 September, bank	181

	Insurance			Wages	
	£			£	
9 September,			4 September,		
bank	160		cash	83	
			8 September,		
			cash	76	
	Carriage			159	
	£				
11 September,				Drawings	
bank	29				
				£	
	Telephone		8 September,		
	£		purchases	53	
11 September,			10 September,		
bank	23		cash	5	
				58	

All daybook items are now posted. If every debit has a credit a trial balance extracted at this stage will balance, but first accounts should be closed off and balances brought down. You should check the entries for all items in the exercise.

Trial Balance of Brian Grange as at 11 September

	£ Debits	£ Credits
Warehouse	24 000	
Fixtures and fittings	17 360	
Vehicles	5 600	
Capital		53 200
Stock at end	1 446	
Purchases	398	
Returns outwards		20
Sales		2 278
Returns inwards	127	
Creditors:		
Car Sales Ltd		1 900
Collie and Co.		171
Lot and Mee		160
Edmunds Ltd		280
Apple Ltd		360
J. Lewin		151
Discount allowed	25	
Debtors:		
K. Jones	460	
H. Same	595	
Discount received		15
Wages	159	
Drawings	58	
Stationery	174	
Packing	61	
Office expenses	34	
Rent	181	
Insurance	160	
Carriage	29	
Telephone	23	
Petty cash	50	
Bank	7 595	
	£58 535	£58 535

SEMINAR EXERCISES 4

1. (b) $\dfrac{\text{Cost} - \text{Scrap}}{\text{Life}}$ $\dfrac{330\ 000 - 10\ 000}{8} = £40\ 000$ $\dfrac{200\ 000}{5} = £40\ 000$

Depreciation year 2 until year 6 = $4 \times 40\ 000 = 160\ 000$

Dr.		Plant Account		Cr.
	£			£
Year 2 purchased	330 000	Year 7 disposal		
		account		330 000
Year 5 purchased	250 000	Year 7 balance c/f		250 000
	£580 000			£580 000
Year 8 balance b/d	£250 000			

Dr.		Disposal Account		Cr.
	£			£
Plant account	330 000	Depreciation account		160 000
		Cash		146 000
		Loss to P/L		24 000
	£330 000			£330 000

Dr.		Depreciation Account		Cr.
	£			£
Year 7 disposal		Year 3 profit and		
account	160 000	loss account		40 000
Year 7 balance c/f	100 000	Year 4 profit and		
		loss account		40 000
		Year 5 profit and		
		loss account		40 000
		Year 6 profit and		
		loss account		90 000
		Year 7 profit and		
		loss account		50 000
				£260 000
	£260 000	Year 8 balance b/d		100 000

Note: A profit on disposal is credited to the profit and loss account. Depreciation has been charged in the year of disposal.

Balance Sheet Entry

	£	£	£
Fixed assets	*Cost*	*Depreciation*	*Net*
Plant	250 000	100 000	150 000

(c) Will this plant be used in years 8, 9 and 10? This is unlikely if the process for which it was purchased is obsolete, so the plant should be written down to an estimate of its current market value. Life and current value are required. If the plant is so specialized that it cannot be used for any other process it should be sold, and any loss or disposal debited to the profit and loss account.

2. Reducing balance methods ensure a high depreciation charge in the early years of machine life and a smaller charge in the later years. This is said to reflect the earning capacity of the asset and to counteract the effect of increasing maintenance costs experienced in later life.

Straight line depreciation: $\dfrac{32\,000 - 1000}{12} = £2583$ per annum.

Assume a 15 per cent reducing balance. Wrong estimation of rate to use may give a false answer as in this case, since the asset is not written off at the end of its life.

Year	Reducing Balance	Maintenance	Total	Total with Straight Line
	31 000			
1	4 650	200	4850	2783
	26 350			
2	3 952	400	4352	2983
	22 398			
3	3 360	600	3960	3183
	19 038			
4	2 856	800	3656	3383
	16 182			
5	2 427	1000	3427	3583
	13 755			
6	2 063	1200	3263	3783
	11 692			
7	1 754	1400	3154	3983
	9 938			
8	1 491	1600	3091	4183
	8 447			
9	1 267	1800	3067	4383
	7 180			
10	1 077	2000	3077	4583
	6 103			
11	915	2200	3115	4783
	5 188			
12	778	2400	3178	4983
WDV	4 410			

Note the difference in the total charge for the two methods in year 1 and year 12 and the different shape of the depreciation 'profile' you would show if the two total columns were graphed.

3. (a) This problem deals with the classic dilemma of depreciation, i.e. should the charge spread the cost evenly over the life of the asset, or should it attempt to charge more in the early years, or should it depreciate according to use?

The straight line, reducing balance and production hour methods should be discussed. A variation of the production hour method based on miles run is recommended, so that use is a prime factor in the depreciation charge. However, this method ignores depreciation in years when little or no use is made of the asset.

$$\frac{\text{Cost} - \text{Scrap}}{\text{Miles in life}} = \frac{£86\ 000 - £1000}{1\ 000\ 000} = 85 \text{ pence per mile}$$

(b) Assume miles run were as follows: last year, 35 000; this year, 21 000; next year, 4000. Depreciation charges: last year, £29 750; this year, £17 850; next year, £3400. This method avoids difficulties which present themselves when an asset is bought part-way through the year. Some businesses depreciate pro rata to time.

Balance Sheet as at 30 September Next Year

Fixed assets	£ Cost	£ Depreciation	£ Net
Vehicles	86 000	51 000	35 000

SEMINAR EXERCISES 5

1. (a)

	£	£
Opening balance of debtors		61 803
Add sales		538 112
		599 915
Less Discount allowed	4 762	
Cash received	519 267	
Returns inwards	26 916	
Bad debts written off	4 328	£555 273
Closing balance of debtors		44 642
Plus cheque written back		1 015
		£45 657

Note: This reconciliation could be expressed in the form of a debtors ledger control account (see Chapter 9).

(b) Dr.   Bad and Doubtful Debts Account   Cr.

	£		£
Bad debts written off	4328	Provision for doubtful debts b/d	4300
Provision c/f	4566	Charge to profit and loss account	4594
	£8894		£8894
		Provision b/d	4566

(c) Current assets:

	£	£
Debtors	45 657	
Less provision	4 566	41 091

Solutions

2. (a)

FIFO

Purchases		Cost of Sales	£	Stock	£
January	1000 × 5				
	600 × 8				
				1000 × 5 }	
				600 × 8 }	
		900 × 5	4 500	100 × 5 }	
				600 × 8 }	
February	600 × 9				
	400 × 10				
				100 × 5 }	
				600 × 8 }	
				600 × 9 }	
				400 × 10 }	
		{ 100 × 5	500		
		1100 { 600 × 8	4 800		
		{ 400 × 9	3 600	200 × 9 }	
				400 × 10 }	
March	1200 × 11			200 × 9 }	
				400 × 10 }	
				1200 × 11 }	
		600 { 200 × 9	1 800		
		{ 400 × 10	4 000	1200 × 11	£13 200
		Cost of sales	19 200		Balance
		Sales	26 300		sheet
		Net profit	£7 100		figure

LIFO

Purchases		Cost of Sales	£	Stock	£
January	1000 × 5				
	600 × 8			1000 × 5 }	
				600 × 8 }	
		900 { 600 × 8	4 800		
		{ 300 × 5	1 500	700 × 5	
February	600 × 9			700 × 5 }	
	400 × 10			600 × 9 }	
				400 × 10 }	
		{ 400 × 10	4 000		
		1100 { 600 × 9	5 400		
		{ 100 × 5	500	600 × 5	
March	1200 × 11			600 × 5 }	
				1200 × 11 }	
		600 × 11	6 600		
				600 × 5 }	
				600 × 11 }	£9 600
		Cost of sales	22 800		Balance
		Sales	26 300		sheet
		Net profit	£3 500		figure

464

Weighted Average

	Purchases			Cost of Sales	£	Stock	£
January	1000 × 5	=	5 000				
	600 × 8	=	4 800				
	1600		9 800				
	$\dfrac{9800}{1600}$	=	6.125			1600 × 6.125 =	9 800
				900 × 6.125	5 512.5	700 × 6.125 =	4 287
February	600 × 9	=	5 400				
	400 × 10	=	4 000				
	700 × 6.125	=	4 287				
	1700		13 687				
	$\dfrac{13\,687}{1\,700}$	=	8.05			1700 × 8.05 =	13 687
				1100 × 8.05	8 855	600 × 8.05 =	4 830
March	1200 × 11	=	13 200				
	600 × 8.05	=	4 830				
	1800		18 030			1800 × 10.01 =	18 030
	$\dfrac{18\,030}{1\,800}$	=	10.01	600 × 10.01	6 006	1200 × 10.01 =	£12 012
				Cost of sales	20 373.5	Balance	
				Sales	26 300	sheet	
				Net profit	£5 926.5	figure	

3. Purchases:

10 Bens @ £30 =	300
20 Bens @ £31 =	620
20 Bens @ £32 =	640
20 Bens @ £33 =	660
20 Bens @ £34 =	680
20 Bens @ £35 =	700
	£3600

	FIFO		*LIFO*
Purchases	3600		3600
Less closing stock			
(20 × 35) + (10 × 34)	1040	(10 × 30) + (20 × 31)	920
Cost of sales	£2560		£2680

The change from FIFO to LIFO increases the cost of sales, thus reducing profit by £120.

SEMINAR EXERCISES 6

1. Workings:

Rent	£	Insurance	£	Heat and Light	£
Trial balance	2600	Trial balance	1460	Trial balance	3574
Paid in advance		Paid in advance		Accrued, balance	
(¼ × 2040), balance		(½ × 642) balance		sheet	140+
sheet	510−	sheet	321−		
					5|3714
	5|2090		5|1139		
Administration ⅕	418−	Administration ⅕	228−	Administration ⅕	743−
Factory ⅘	1662	Factory ⅘	911	Factory ⅘	2971

Repairs		Power		Telephone	
Trial balance	1580	Trial balance	8600	Trial balance	662
Office	83−	Accrued, balance	430+	Accrued, balance	31+
		sheet		sheet	
Works	1497	Works	9030	Administration	693

Depreciation				Doubtful Debts	
Buildings	25 000	Plant	54 000	Debtors	19 600
5 per cent for		10 per cent for		5 per cent for	
year	1 250	year	5 400	year	980
To date	8 000	To date	22 000	Provision now	750
				Increase, profit	
Balance sheet	9 250	Balance sheet	27 400	and loss account	230

John Doe, Manufacturing, Trading and Profit and Loss Account for the Year Ended 31 December

	£	£	£
Sales			140 500
Material, opening stock		7 800	
Add purchases		34 630	
		42 430	
Less closing stock		8 240	
		34 190	
Labour		39 720	
Prime cost		73 910	
Factory overheads:			
Repairs and renewals	1497		
Rent	1672		
Insurance	911		
Heat and light	2971		
Power	9030		
Supervisory wages	8656		
Depreciation			
Buildings	1250		
Plant	5400	31 387	
Factory cost:		105 297	
Finished goods stock adjustment			

	£	£	£
Add opening stock	21 600		
Less closing stock	23 420	(1 820)	
Cost of sales			103 477
Gross profit			37 023
Miscellaneous income, investment and loan interest			2 380
			39 403
Administration expenses:			
Rates	418		
Insurance	228		
Heat and light	743		
Repairs	83		
Telephone	693		
Office expenses	2 140		
Office salaries	5 460	9 765	
Selling and distribution			
Expenses	10 400		
Provision for doubtful debts	230	10 630	20 395
Net profit			19 008
Drawings			7 650
Unappropriated profit c/f			£11 358

John Doe, Balance Sheet as at 31 December

	£	£	£
Capital			68 400
Unappropriated profit c/f			11 358
			£79 758

Represented by:	£	£	£
Fixed assets:	*Cost*	*Depreciation*	*Net*
Land	8 500		8 500
Buildings	25 000	9 250	15 750
Plant	54 000	27 400	26 600
	87 500	36 650	50 850
Investments at cost			8 000
Current assets:			
Stock			
Materials		8 240	
Finished goods		23 420	
Debtors	19 600		
Less provision	980	18 620	
Loans		5 000	
Payments in advance		831	
		56 111	
Current liabilities:			
Creditors	27 970		
Accruals	601		
Overdraft	6 632	35 203	
Working capital			20 908
			£79 758

Solutions

2. (a)   *Paul Over, Manufacturing, Trading and Profit and Loss Account*
                        for the Year Ended 30 April

	£	£
Raw materials:		
Opening stock	24 200	
Plus purchases	125 600	
	149 800	
Less closing stock	28 000	121 800
Factory wages		48 800
Prime cost		170 600
Factory overheads:		
Manager's salary	4 500	
Depreciation:		
Buildings	960	
Plant	1 860	
Power	2 298	
Maintenance	615	
Proportion of expenses	9 640	19 873
Factory cost		190 473
Factory profit loading, 20 per cent		38 094
Transferred to sales department		£228 567

Trading Account	£	£
Sales		255 000
Opening stock of finished goods	7 800	
Transferred from factory	228 567	
	236 367	
Less closing stock	8 400	
Cost of goods sold		227 967
Gross profit		27 033
Selling expenses:		
Manager's salary	4 200	
Wages and salaries	7 100	
Depreciation, cars	2 475	
Proportion of expenses	2 410	
Motor expenses	1 206	
Doubtful debts	453	17 844
Net profit on sales		£9 189

	Factory £	Sales Department £	Total £
Profit	38 094	9 189	47 283
Bonus (1/9)	4 233	1 021	5 254
			42 029
Add discount			600
Less stock provision, £1300 − (1/6 × £8400)			(100)
Net profit			£42 529

468

(b)   *Paul Over, Balance Sheet as at 30 April*

	£	£	£
Capital			95 000
Add profit		42 529	
Less drawings		6 600	35 929
			£130 929

Represented by:

	Cost	Depreciation	Net
Fixed assets:			
Factory	75 000	8 780	66 220
Plant	18 600	8 760	9 840
Vehicles	9 900	8 125	1 775
	103 500	25 665	77 835

	£	£	£
Current assets:			
Stock:			
Material		28 000	
Finished goods	8 400		
Less provision	1 400	7 000	
Debtors, £(14 200 − 298)	13 902		
Less provision	1 275	12 627	
Prepayments		600	
Bank		26 211	
		74 438	
Less current liabilities:			
Creditors	15 600		
Bonus	5 254		
Accruals	490	21 344	
Working capital			53 094
			£130 929

Note that the profit element in stock transferred from the factory but not yet sold cannot be included as a profit since it is not yet realized.

(c) High costs increase the factory profit loading on which the manager's commission is computed. This is not conducive to economy.

3. *Andy Pinder, Manufacturing, Trading and Profit and Loss Account for the Year Ended 31 May*

	£	£	£
Sales, net of returns (£416 per note (e) + £263)			123 109
Opening stock		17 456	
Add purchases (net of returns)		52 362	
		69 818	
Less closing stock		18 760	
		51 058	
Labour		17 020	
Prime cost		68 078	
Factory overheads:			
Power	4511		
Plant:			
Depreciation	1500		
Maintenance	3114		

	£	£	£
Factory:			
Insurance	994		
Light and heat	3 129		
Sundry expenses	600		
Salaries	2 200	16 048	
Factory cost		84 126	
Work in progress stock adjustment:			
Add opening stock	15 900		
Less closing stock	14 900	1 000	
Cost of production		85 126	
Finished goods stock adjustment:			
Add opening stock	18 700		
Less closing stock £(19 100 + 338)	19 438	(738)	
Cost of goods sold			84 388
Gross profit			38 721
Add discounts received			1 830
			40 551
Administration expenses:			
Insurance		331	
Light and heat		1 403	
Sundry expenses		200	
Salaries		13 000	
Depreciation of fixtures		196	
		14 770	
Selling expenses:			
Advertising	1 400		
Transport	1 670		
Vehicle depreciation	276		
Bad debts	181		
Doubtful debts	1 376	4 903	
Financial expenses:			
Loan interest	3 000		
Bank charges	415	3 415	23 088
Net profit			£17 463

Andy Pinder, Balance Sheet as at 31 May

	£	£	£
Capital			57 112
Add profit			17 463
			74 575
Less drawings			4 220
			70 355
Long-term loan			30 000
Net capital employed			£100 355

Represented by:	*Cost*	*Depreciation*	*Net*
Fixed assets:			
Land and buildings	25 000	—	25 000
Plant and machinery	20 000	11 500	8 500
Vehicles	2 604	1 776	828
Fixtures and fittings	3 438	1 666	1 772
	51 042	14 942	36 100

	£	£	£
Current assets:			
Stock:			
Materials		18 760	
Work in progress		14 900	
Finished goods		19 438	
Debtors	17 316		
Less provision	1 732	15 584	
Prepayments		107	
Cash		4 384	
		73 173	
Current liabilities:			
Creditors	5 866		
Accruals	52		
Loan interest	3 000	8 918	
Working capital			64 255
Net assets			£100 355

4. *Sally and Denise, Profit and Loss Account for the Year Ended 30 April 19-8 (£000s)*

	£	£	£
Receipts from customers			4510
Less:			
Materials used up (140 + 400 − 152)		388	
Wages (1080 + 40)		1120	
Depreciation:			
Buildings	10		
Equipment	300		
Furnishings	146	456	
Cleaning expenses		160	
Directors' salaries		40	
Heat, light and power		480	
Rent (490 − 70 − 40)		380	
Salon expense		920	
Doubtful debts		12	
Telephone		210	4166
Net profit before tax			344
Less corporation tax			90
			254
Less proposed dividend			120
Net profit added to reserves in balance sheet			£134

Balance Sheet as at 30 April 19-8 (£000s)

	Cost	Provision for depreciation	WDV
Fixed assets:			
Freehold land and buildings	860	90	770
Equipment and machines	1500	600	900
Salon furnishings	1460	576	884
	3820	1266	2554

Solutions

Current assets:
Stock		152	
Debtors less provision		238	
Prepayments		110	
Cash at bank		435	
Cash in hand		25	
		960	

Less current liabilities:
Creditors	590		
Accruals	40		
Corporation tax payable	90		
Dividend payable	120		
		840	
			120
			2674

Financed by:
Share capital			2000
Reserves (540 + 134)			674
			2674

(b) The important relationship is between dividend and profit for the year available for dividend (i.e. net profit after tax). The ratio is 2.05 : 1, which is more generous than for many PLCs, but still reasonable. Dividends in excess of net profit for the year after tax may be paid out of reserves without breaking the law.

5. *Karl August PLC Manufacturing and Trading and Profit and Loss Account for the Year Ended 31 December 19-8*

Manufacturing account		(£000)
Opening stock of raw materials		1 810
Add raw materials purchases (6035 + 17)		8 052
		7 862
Less closing stock of raw materials (1720 + 17)		1 737
Raw materials consumed		8 125
Add direct labour		1 190
Prime cost		7 315
Add factory expenses:		
Other factory wages	480	
Heat, light and power (555 + 32 elec)	587	
Overhead expenses (892 − 40 rates − 20 ins.)	832	
Repairs and renewals (410 + 8)	418	
Depreciation (buildings) (six-sevenths)	30	
Depreciation (plant)	126	
		2 473
Factory cost of production		9 788
Add opening stock of work in progress		935
		10 723
Less closing stock of work in progress		995
Cost of goods manufactured		9 728

	£	£
Trading account		
Sales less returns		11 275
Less cost of sales		
Opening stock finished goods	1 280	
Add cost of goods manufactured	9 728	
	11 008	
Less closing stock finished goods	1 465	
		9 543
		1 732
Gross profit		
Less expenses:		
Distribution expenses (including proportion of motor depreciation) (635 + 45 dep. + 7 haul. − 5 ins)	682	
Selling expenses (including share of motor depreciation (275 + 6 trav. + 15 dep. + 44 bad debts)	340	
Administration expenses (292 + 25 dir. + 5 dep. bldgs − 8 rates − 5 ins. + 22 commission)	331	
Interest (80 + 80)	160	
		1513
Net profit		219
Less taxation		50
		169
Less proposed dividend 2p per share (× 6 million)		120
Retained profit for the year		49
Add previous year's profits		980
		1029

Note recalculation of commission. In calculating the commission, it is first necessary to work out all other expenses and to deduct these from the gross profit. This would give a provisional net profit of £241 (000). The commission is one-eleventh of this figure (£22 (000)), which is one-tenth of the residual figure.

Balance Sheet as at 31 December 19-8

	£	£	£
Fixed assets:			
Land	600	—	600
Buildings	1750	210	1540
Plant and machinery	1260	526	734
Motor vehicles	420	240	180
	4030	976	3054
Current assets			
Stocks			
Raw materials (1720 + 17)	1737		
Work in progress	995		
Finished goods	1465	4197	
Debtors less provision (2420 − 20 −24)		2376	
Prepayments (48 + 30)		78	
Cash at bank		196	
Cash in hand		15	
		6862	

Solutions

Less current liabilities	
Creditors (+ 17 goods not recorded)	1822
Accruals (32 hlp. + 8 reps + 6 trav. + 7 distrib.	
+ 25 directors + 22 commission + 80 interest)	180
Tax payable	50
Proposed dividend	120
	2172
	4890
	7744
Less long-term liabilities	
8 per cent debenture loan, redeemable 1999–2003	2000
	5744
Financed by:	
Capital and reserves	
Share capital	3000
Share premium account	1715
Profit and loss account	1029
	5744

SEMINAR EXERCISES 7

1.

Mr Feckless, Statement to Compute the Stock as at 30 November

	£	£
Sales, September, October, November		85 627
Less goods despatched in August		7 346
		78 281
Add goods despatched but not yet invoiced		7 912
		86 193
Less mark-up of 25 per cent		21 548
Cost of sales		£64 645
Opening stock per accounts		53 278
Less error of transposition	(1 800)	
Add pricing error	6 120	
Less casting error	(81)	4 239
		57 517
Add purchases during the quarter	64 539	
Less received in August	2 643	
	61 896	
Add received but not yet entered	3 129	
	65 025	
Less returns	958	64 067
		121 584
Less cost of sales net of returns, £[64 645 − (796 × 75%)]		64 048
		57 536
Less scrapped		725
Stock as at 30 November		£56 811

2.   *Reconcile Ltd, Cash Book Adjustment*

	Receipts £	Payments £
Balance c/d	1888	
Standing charges:		
Loan interest		1200
HP		732
Dividend received	1248	
Opening balance c/d in error	9	
Cheque returned written back		167
Cheque drawn entered at a higher figure	27	
Cheque drawn entered as receipt—reversed		341
Cheque drawn entered as it should be		341
Bank charges		213
Receipts side undercast	400	
Balance c/f £578	£3572	£2994

Note. Item (b) is to be ignored.

Reconciliation to Bank Statement

	£
Balance per bank statement	628
Add receipts not yet credited	780
Less cheques not yet presented	(830)
Balance per cash book	£578

Balance per question £516 and bank cheque debited in error £112 = £628.

3. Dr.   *Naunton Knitwear, Suspense Account*   Cr.

	£		£
Opening balance	1227	Debtor balance omitted	57
Sales omitted	83	Cash book undercast	400
		Credit note posted to wrong side	542
		Cash posted to Mr Exe written back	311
	£1310		£1310

(b) A capital revenue adjustment will not affect the trial balance.
(f) This item has not yet been entered in the books and so cannot affect the balance.

Effects of errors:

(a) Debtors increase in balance sheet.
(b) Capitalize £1138, assets increase, expenses decrease, so profits increase. Remember to depreciate the new asset.
(c) Cash increased in balance sheet.
(d) Sales increase, profit increases.
(e) Creditors reduced in balance sheet.
(f) Cost increases, profit decreases.
(g) Cash increases in balance sheet. Provision against this debt can now be removed. Affects profit and balance sheet.

4. *Harold Darby*

	£	£
To plant	2930	
By labour cost		2930
Being capitalization of labour cost of constructing the foundation of a new machine		
To profit and loss	293	
By depreciation		293
Being depreciation on newly capitalized foundation		
Loan interest	1200	
Creditors		1200
Being loan interest for the half year, due but unpaid		
Sales (2 400 + 25 per cent)	3000	
Debtors		3000
Being goods on sale or return written back		
Drawings	179	
Repairs		179
Being repairs to Mr Darby's flat charged to drawings		
Vehicle disposal account	506	
Depreciation on vehicles	1094	
Vehicle account		1600
Being transfer of balances to disposal account		
Cash	506	
Vehicle disposal account		506
Being sale of vehicle at written-down value		
Profit and loss account	400	
Provision for doubtful debts		400
Being provision for a bad debt		

Profit and Loss Reconciliation

		Increase	Decrease
		£	£
(Assume 10 per cent depreciation)	Adjustment 1	2930	293
	2		1 200
	3		3 000
	4	179	
(No effect, sold at written-down value)	5	—	—
	6		400
		3109	4 893
			3 109
	Net decrease		1 784
	Profit per accounts		12 500
	True profit		£10 716

5. *D. Lerr, Trading and Profit and Loss Account for the Year to 31 December*

	£	£
Sales, £(11 600 + 3000 + 1000)		15 600
Purchases	14 800	
Less closing stock	3 500	11 300

	£	£
Gross profit		4 300
Provision for doubtful debts (10 per cent of		
£1000 o/s)	100	
Rent	700	
Petrol and diesel	800	
Expenses	500	
Interest (accrued)	200	
Lorry depreciation (£1680 ÷ 6)	280	2 580
Net profit		£1 720

Balance Sheet as at 31 December

Capital at 1 January			10 000
Add net profit			1 720
Less drawings, £(2080 + 1200)			(3 280)
			8 440
Loan			2 000
Capital employed			£10 440

Represented by:	£	£	£
Fixed assets:			
Lorry at cost			1 680
Less depreciation			280
			1 400
Less loan outstanding			1 280
			120
Current assets:			
Stock, £(3000 + 100 + 400)		3 500	
Debtors less provision		900	
Prepayment		100	
Bank		9 800	
Cash		620	
		14 920	
Less current liabilities:			
Creditors' £(4000 + 400)	4400		
Accruals	200	4 600	
Working capital			10 320
Net assets			£10 440

477

6.

John Grey, Journal

	£	£
Profit and loss account	8 000	
Stock account		8 000
Being stock written down to net realizable value set against profit		
Profit and loss account	12 000	
Sundry debtors, Mr Black		12 000
Being bad debt written off against profit		
Provision for doubtful debts	1 890	
Profit and loss account		1 890
Being adjustment of provision to 10 per cent of debtors		
Machinery account	10 000	
Trade creditors, Mr White		10 000
Being purchase of machinery on credit terms		
Profit and loss account	1 000	
Provision for depreciation		1 000
Being depreciation on new asset, 10 per cent straight line assumed		
Drawings account	1 032	
Profit and loss account		1 032
Being goods withdrawn by proprietor charged to him and cost of sales reduced as appropriate		
Profit and loss account	3 300	
Sundry creditors, Mr Green		3 300
Being loan interest accrued against profit		
Profit and loss account	1 260	
Cash book		1 260
Being interest and bank charges set against profit		
Vehicles account		2 400
Depreciation account	2 000	
Cash book	400	
Being sale of vehicle at book value, cash recorded and vehicle written off		

The balance sheet balances after adjustment at £244 660. Fixed assets £189 018, current assets £97 518, current liabilities £41 876.

7.   Green's Accounts

Dr.	Cash Account			Cr.
	£			£
b/d	100	Bankings		144 700
Sales ledger	16 300	Wages		24 160
Cash sales	*178 480	Repairs		480
		Drawings		8 800
		Printing, etc.		3 760
		Purchase ledger		12 780
		Cash in hand c/f		200
	£194 880			£194 880

*Balancing figure for the account.

Dr.	Debtors Account		Cr.
b/d	3 000	Cash received	16 300
Credit sales	*20 520	Discount allowed	456
		Contra—b/l	680
		c/f	6 084
	£23 520		£23 520

Dr.	Creditors		Cr.
Contra s/l	680	b/d	10 500
Cheques	120 000	Invoices	*135 120
Cash	12 780		
c/f	12 160		
	£145 620		£145 620

Dr.	Rent		Cr.
Paid in advance b/d	2 000	Paid in advance c/f	2 400
Paid by cheque	8 800	Profit and loss a/c	8 400
	£10 800		£10 800

Trading and Profit and Loss Account for the Year Ended 30 June 19-8

	£		£
Stocks at 1 July 19-7	16 000	Sales (20 520 + 178 480)	199 000
Purchases	135 120		
	151 120		
Less stocks 30 June 19-8	19 440		
	131 680		
Gross profit b/d	67 320		
	£199 000		£199 000

	£		£
Wages (1000 + 24 160)	25 160	Gross profit b/d	67 320
Rent	8 400		
Lighting and heating	2 500		
Repairs	480		
Discounts allowed	456		
Printing and sundries	3 760		
Depreciation:			
building	400		
fixtures and			
fittings	1500 → 1 900		
	42 656		
Net profit	24 664		
	£67 320		£67 320

*Balancing figure for the account.

Mr Green Balance Sheet as at 30 June 19-8

	£		£	£
Capital account		Fixed assets		
Opening balance	38 100	Buildings (20 000 − 400)		19 600
Profit for year	24 664	Fixtures (6000 − 1500)		4 500
	62 764			24 100
Less drawings		Current assets		
(8800 plus 10 000)	18 800	Stocks	19 440	
	43 964	Payments in advance	2 400	
		Debtors	6 084	
Creditors	12 160	Cash at bank	3 900	
		Cash in hand	200	
				32 024
	£56 124			£56 124

Workings

Opening capital	£
Shop	20 000
Fixtures	6 000
Stocks	16 000
Rent in advance	2 000
Debtors	3 000
Bank	1 500
Cash	100
	48 600
Less creditors	10 500
	38 100

SEMINAR EXERCISES 8

1. *Check and Mate, Trading, Profit and Loss Appropriation Account for the Year Ended 31 December*

	£	£
Sales		24 800
Opening stock	3 000	
Plus purchases	16 450	
Plus carriage inwards	400	
	19 850	
Less closing stock	3 225	16 625
Gross profit		8 175
Expenses:		
Wages	2150	
Salaries	820	
Rent	325	
Depreciation:		
Plant	300	
Vehicles	800	
Provision for doubtful debts	55	
Interest	300	4 750
		3 425
Net profit for appropriation		
Interest on capital:		
Check	250	
Mate	100	
Salary, Check	575	
Share of profits:		
Check	1250	
Mate	1250	(3 425)

Dr.			Current Account		Cr.
	Check	Mate		Check	Mate
	£	£		£	£
Balance b/d	550	350	Interest on capital	250	100
Contra per guarantee	50		Salary	575	—
Balance c/f	1475	1050	Share of profit	1250	1250
			Contra per guarantee	—	50
	£2075	£1400		£2075	£1400

Check and Mate, Balance Sheet as at 31 December

	£	£	£
Capital:			
Check			5 000
Mate			2 000
			7 000
Current account:			
Check		1475	
Mate		1050	2 525
Owners' equity			9 525
Long-term loan			5 000
Net capital employed			£14 525

Solutions

Represented by:	£	£	£
	Cost	Depreciation	
Fixed assets:			
Buildings	8 000	—	8 000
Plant	6 000	2 300	3 700
Vehicles	3 200	1 600	1 600
	17 200	3 900	13 300
Current assets:			
Stock		3 225	
Debtors	13 100		
Less provision	655	12 445	
Bank		1 200	
		16 870	
Less current liabilities:			
Creditors	15 345		
Interest	300	15 645	
Working capital			1 225
Net assets			£14 525

2. *Utopia Road Nurseries, Trading and Profit and Loss Account for the Year Ended 31 March*

	£	£
Sales, £(101 349 + 25 644 + 18 − 3000 − 773 + 352 + 870)		124 460
Opening stock	7 935	
Plus purchases, £(81 035 + 2900 − 2820 + 3250)	84 365	
	92 300	
Less closing stock	9 080	83 220
Gross profit		41 240
Expenses:		
Wages	16 080	
Repairs	670	
Insurance	835	
Sundries	2 982	
Electricity, £(1300 + 1660 − 180 + 300)	3 080	
Tractor expenses	877	
Tractor depreciation	450	
Van hire	2 400	
Notional rent, Hope	1 500	
Depreciation, greenhouse	1 200	30 074
Net profit for appropriation		11 166
Salary, Crosby	2 500	
Interest on capital:		
Hope	1 000	
Crosby	500	
Share of profits:		
Hope	4 300	
Crosby	2 866	(11 166)

Utopia Road Nurseries, Balance Sheet as at 31 March

	£	£
Capital:		
Hope		10 000
Crosby		5 000
		15 000
Current account:		
Hope, £(1000 + 4300 − 6000 − 350 + 1500)	450	
Crosby, £(2500 + 500 + 2866 − 5500 − 520)	(154)	296
		£15 296

Represented by:	£	£	£
Fixed assets:	Cost	Depreciation	
Greenhouse	12 000	6 400	5 600
Tractor	1 800	1 050	750
	13 800	7 450	6 350
Current assets:			
Stock		9 080	
Debtors		352	
Bank		2 954	
Cash		110	
		12 496	
Less current liabilities, £(3250 + 300)		3 550	
Working capital			8 946
Net assets			£15 296

3. *Leek and Bean, Manufacturing, Trading and Profit and Loss Account for the Year Ended 30 June*

	£	£
Raw materials consumed:		
Stocks at start		4 028
Purchases		28 650
		32 678
Less stocks at end		3 180
		29 498
Productive wages		15 300
		44 798
Add work in progress at start		3 400
		48 198
Less work in progress at end		5 050
Prime cost of goods produced		43 148
Works expenses:		
Factory expenses	14 160	
Depreciation of plant	2 575	16 735
Works cost of goods produced		59 883
Factory profit		8 517
Value of goods transferred to warehouse		68 400
Stock of finished goods at start		48 000
		116 400
Stock of finished goods at end		40 500
Cost of goods sold		75 900
Sales		111 020
Gross profit		35 120

	£	£
General expenses:		
Warehouse wages	6 030	
Warehouse expenses	11 100	
Depreciation of vans	1 610	
Depreciation of car	800	
Provision for doubtful debts	200	19.740
Net profit on trading		15 380
Add profit earned by factory		8 517
Net profit for the year		£23 897

			£
Appropriation	*Leek*	*Bean*	
	£	£	
Factory profit	6 388	2 129	
Selling profit	3 845	11 535	
	10 233	13 664	
Adjustment (see below)	(75)	75	
	10 158	13 739	23 897
Interest on drawings	(600)	(500)	
Interest on capital	2 400	2 450	
	1 800	1 950	Difference £150

The partnership agreement is silent as to how this amount is to be charged to the partners. Therefore the Act applies and they share equally, so Leek must transfer £75 to Bean.

Leek and Bean, Balance Sheet as at 30 June

	£	£	£
	Cost	*Depreciation*	
Fixed assets:			
Freehold factory	42 150	—	42 150
Plant	25 750	8 625	17 125
Vans	8 050	5 060	2 990
Car	4 000	800	3 200
	79 950	14 485	65 465
Current assets:			
Stocks and work in progress		48 730	
Debtors	18 000		
Less provision for doubtful debts	1 800	16 200	
		64 930	
Less current liabilities:			
Sundry creditors	9 450		
Bank overdraft	7 048	16 498	48 432
			£113 897

	£	£	£
Represented by:			
Current accounts:			
	Leek	*Bean*	
Balance 1 July	48 000	49 000	
Add profit for the year	10 158	13 739	
Capital introduced	4 000	—	
	62 158	62 739	
Less drawings	6 000	5 000	
	56 158	57 739	£113 897

Leek and Bean, Workings

	£
Lawnmowers	
Stock of completed items at start	1 200
Produced (to warehouse 1520 × £45 = £68 400)	1 520
	2 720
Less sold	1 820
Stock at end	900
Stock to be valued at £45	£40 500

Overheads

	Trial Balance	Creditors	Total Profit and Loss Account	Manufacturing Account
	£	£	£	£
Factory overheads	12 070	2090		14 160
Warehouse overheads	10 020	1080	11 100	
Factory wages	15 020	280		15 300
		3450		
Creditors from trial balance		6000		
Creditors for balance sheet		£9450		

Depreciation

	Cost		Depreciation for Year	Depreciation at Start	Balance Sheet
	£		£	£	£
Plant	25 750	10%	2575	6050	8625
Vans	8 050	20%	1610	3450	5060
Car	4 000	20%	800	—	800

Provision for Doubtful Debts

Debtors	£18 000	10% required	1800
b/f			1600
Charge to profit and loss account			£200

4.

Dr.   Capital Accounts   Cr.

	Henrietta £	Maud £	Nellie £	Emma £		Henrietta £	Maud £	Nellie £	Emma £
Cash	18 000				Balances b/d	10 000	8 000	2000	
Balances c/f		13 300	5700		Salary	—	1 000	—	
					Interest	1 000	800	200	
					Share of profit	3 500	1 750	1750	
					Revaluation	500	250	250	
					Goodwill	3 000	1 500	1500	
	£18 000	13 300	5700			£18 000	13 300	5700	
Goodwill		2 000	2000	2000	Balances b/d		13 300	5700	
Balances c/f		11 300	3700	5000	Cash				5000
					Car				2000
	£	13 300	5700	7000		£	13 300	5700	7000

Balance Sheet as at 1 January

		£			£	£
Capital accounts:			Fixed assets:			
Maud		11 300	Freehold property			25 000
Nellie		3 700	Vehicle			2 000
Emma		5 000	Fixtures and fittings			2 000
		20 000				29 000
Creditors		2 500	Current assets:			
			Stock		3000	
Bank overdrawn		10 500	Debtors		1000	4 000
		£33 000				£33 000

5. (a)

Dr.   Red, Green and Blue, Capital Accounts   Cr.

	Red £	Green £	Blue £		Red £	Green £	Blue £
Goodwill written back	6 000	—	3 000	Balances b/d	13 000	5000	7 000
Loss on revaluation	600	600	600	Goodwill	3 000	3000	3 000
Cash	—	4000	—				
Loan	—	3400	—				
Balances c/f	9 400	—	6 400				
	£16 000	8000	10 000		£16 000	8000	10 000

Balance Sheet after Retirement of Green

	£		£	£
Capitals:		Fixed assets:		
Red	10 900	Freehold		2 500
Blue	4 900	Plant		3 000
	15 800			5 500
Loan account, Green	3 400	Current assets:		
Current liabilities, creditors	5 000	Stock	7300	
		Debtors	6900	
		Cash	4500	18 700
	£24 200			£24 200

SEMINAR EXERCISES 10

1. (a) *Assembly PLC Manufacturing, Trading and Profit and Loss Account for Year Ended 31 December 19-6*

	£	£	£
Opening stock of raw material			164 290
Plus purchases			1 396 730
carriage inwards			34 670
			1 595 690
Less closing stock			130 470
Material cost			1 465 220
Factory wages			367 200
Prime cost			1 832 420
Production overheads:			
Depreciation machinery		144 930	
Plant repairs		15 150	
Power		27 080	
Rent		10 400	197 560
			2 029 980
Factory costs			
Work in progress:			
Plus opening stock		23 460	
Less closing stock		25 490	2 030
			2 027 950
Cost of production			
Finished goods stock:			
Add opening stock		83 460	
Less closing stock		75 430	8 030
Cost of goods sold			2 035 980
Sales			2 996 800
Gross profit			960 820
Selling and distribution expenses:			
Advertising	13 560		
Delivery	14 950		
Salaries	49 500		
Doubtful debts	4 620	82 630	

	£	£	£
Administration expenses:			
Depreciation: fixtures + fittings	11 250		
Directors' fees	45 000		
Insurance	2 420		
Salaries	204 000		
Light and heat	1 400		
Post, stationery, telephone	4 190		
Rent	5 200		
Audit fee	6 000	279 460	
Financial expenses:			
Bank charges	1 430		
Interest	30 000	31 430	
			393 520
Net profit			£567 300

(b)   *Assembly Limited Profit and Loss Account for Publication*

	£	£
Turnover		2 996 800
Cost of sales		2 035 980
Gross profit		960 820
Selling and distribution costs	82 630	
Administration expenses	280 890	
Interest paid	30 000	393 520
Net profit before tax and extraordinary items		567 300
UK corporation tax based on profits		
for the year at 35 per cent		250 000
Net profit after tax		317 300
Appropriations:		
Transfer to plant replacement reserve	200 000	
Dividend proposed:		
Preference (6 per cent)	60 000	
Ordinary (12½ per cent)	125 000	
		385 000
		(67 700)
Unappropriated profit b/d		86 520
Unappropriated profit c/f		£18 820

Notes
1. Depreciation £156 180
2. Audit fee £6000
3. Directors' emoluments £88 100 (fees £45 000, salaries £43 100)
   Chairman £25 000
   Highest-paid director received £43 100
   Number in salary band £5001–£10 000 = two
4. Number of employees in salary band £30 001–£35 000 = one
Tutorial note:
Bank charges are included in administration expenses.

2.   *Sandal Ltd Workings*

Cost analysis	Selling and distribution £	Administration £
Motor expenses	78 482	
Overhead expenses		38 240
General expenses		6 564
Directors' salaries	16 000	26 500
Directors' fees (accrued)	5 500	11 000 (b/s creditors)
Other salaries	28 679	20 000
Audit fee		1 050
Depreciation: Buildings		2 000
Vehicles	6 509	
Fittings		540
Directors' pension		950
Superannuation scheme		8 250
	£135 170	£115 094

More detail in the question would enable a more accurate apportionment to be made.

	£
Unappropriated profit 31 December per balance sheet	84 691
Less: unappropriated profit c/f in error from profit and loss account	52 356
Equals b/d from last year	32 335

	£	
Investment income (net)	1970	(Cash)
Grossed up 3/7 × 1970 = tax suffered	844	(p/l tax)
Investment income (gross)	2814	(p/l income)

	£	
Dividend paid preference	7 500	
Dividend proposed ordinary	10 000	
	£17 500	× 3/7 = ACT payable
£17 500 × 3/7 = £7500		= ACT recoverable

Fraction is 25/75 or 1/3 when tax rate is at 25 per cent.

	£	
Corporation tax owed December balance sheet	29 244	
Corporation tax provided December profit and loss	13 104	(payable in January next year)
∴ Corporation tax owed at beginning of year	£16 140	(payable in January this year)

Sandal Ltd Profit and Loss Account for the Year Ended 31 December

	£	£
Turnover		1 638 740
Cost of sales		1 333 871
Gross profit		304 869
Distribution costs	135 170	
Administration expenses	115 094	
Interest	800	251 064

	£	£
Net trading profit		53 805
Income from investments (gross)	2 814	
Miscellaneous income	685	3 499
Net profit before tax		57 304
UK corporation tax	13 104	
Based on profit for the year		
Tax deducted from investment income	844	13 948
Net profit after tax		43 356
Dividends:		
Preference shares paid (7½ per cent)	7 500	
Ordinary shares proposed (10 per cent)	10 000	
		17 500
Unappropriated profit for the year		25 856
Unappropriated profit b/d		32 335
Unappropriated profit c/f		£58 191

Sandal Ltd Balance Sheet as at 31 December

	£ Cost	£ Depreciation	£
Fixed assets (tangible):			
Land and buildings	90 000	5 000	85 000
Vehicles	25 600	12 800	12 800
Fixtures	10 400	4 840	5 560
	126 000	22 640	103 360
Investments: listed		10 000	
unlisted		5 000	15 000
			118 360
Deferred asset—ACT recoverable			7 500
Current assets:			
Stock (at cost)		105 246	
Debtors (net of provision)		162 522	
Bank + cash		60 912	
		328 680	
Creditors payable within one year:			
Trade creditors	89 605		
Current taxation owed	16 140		
Proposed dividend	10 000		
ACT payable	7 500	123 245	
Net current assets:			205 435
Total assets less current liabilities			331 295
Creditors due after more than one year:			
8 per cent debentures (1990–2001)		10 000	
Corporation tax		13 104	23 104
			£308 191

	£	£	£
		Authorized	*Issued*
Capital:			
Ordinary shares of 50 pence each		150 000	100 000
7½ per cent preference of £1 each		150 000	100 000
		300 000	200 000
Reserves: share premium		20 000	
general reserve		30 000	
unappropriated profit		58 191	108 191
			£308 191

Notes

1. Directors' emoluments—£62 808 (salaries £42 500, fees £16 500, pension contributions £3808)
   Chairman—£5500
   Highest-paid director—£32 000
   Number of directors in salary band £20 001–£25 000 is one.
2. Capital expenditure during year—£20 000 on freehold land and buildings.
3. Total depreciation—£9049 for the year.
4. Listed investments have a market value of £17 582.
5. Average number of employees is six.
   Total wages and salaries net of directors—£48 679
   Total superannuation net of directors—£5392

3.   *Candlestickmakers PLC—Workings*

	Cost of sales	*Administration expenses*	*Distribution cost*	
	£	£	£	
	1 886 666	330 623	213 211	
Directors	36 000	67 241	40 000	→ 143 241
Depreciation	95 800	8 185	9 000	
Bad debts		8 445		
Pension contributions		60 000		
Audit		1 000		
Accounting		500		
	2 018 466	475 994	262 211	

Debtors	70 450
Bad debt written off	4 000 (p/l)
	66 450
Provision 10 per cent	6 645 (p/l 6645 − 2200 = 4445)
Balance sheet	59 805
Debenture interest	500 000 ×10% = 50 000 (p/l)
	Paid 25 000
	Accrued 25 000 (b/s)
Creditors 66 409 + 25 000 + 1500	92 909

Solutions

Candlestickmakers PLC Profit and Loss Account for the Year Ended 31 December 19-2

	£	£
Turnover (sales net of VAT)		2 884 782
Cost of sales		2 018 466
Gross profit		866 316
Distribution cost	262 211	
Administration expenses	475 994	
Finance charges		
Interest on loan repayable more than five years hence	50 000	
		788 205
Net trading profit before tax		78 111
Corporation tax based on profit for the year		40 000
Net profit after tax		38 111
Appropriations:		
Transfer to general reserve	8 000	
Proposed dividend on ordinary shares	30 000	
		38 000
Unappropriated profit for the year		111
Unappropriated profit b/d		25 955
Unappropriated profit c/f		£26 066

Candlestickmakers PLC Balance Sheet as at 31 December 19-2

Fixed assets		1 177 365
Deferred assets—ACT recoverable		12 857
Current assets:		
Stock	292 452	
Debtors	59 805	
Cash	675	
	352 932	
Creditors payable within one year:		
Trade creditors	92 909	
Bank overdraft	8 322	
Corporation tax	40 000	
Dividend payable	30 000	
ACT payable	12 857	
	184 088	
Net current assets		168 844
Total assets less current liabilities		1 359 066
Creditors payable more than one year hence		
Debentures 10 per cent		500 000
		£859 066

	Authorized	*Issued*
Capital		
£1 ordinary shares	1 000 000	750 000
General reserve		83 000
Unappropriated profit		26 066
		£859 066

Notes:

1. Fixed Assets	Land	Building	Plant	Vehicles	Fittings	Total
	£	£	£	£	£	£
Cost at 1 January	700 000	120 000	446 000	62 462	43 850	1 372 372
Additions	—	—	61 000	—	14 000	75 000
Disposals	—	—	(28 000)	—	—	(28 000)
Closing cost	700 000	120 000	479 000	62 462	57 850	1 419 312
Depreciation:						
Opening balance	—	20 000	83 000	26 462	19 500	148 962
Disposals	—	—	(20 000)	—	—	(20 000)
Provision	—	2 400	95 800	9 000	5 785	112 985
Closing balance	—	22 400	158 800	35 462	25 285	241 947
WDV	700 000	97 600	320 200	27 000	32 565	1 177 365

Depreciation rates   buildings   2 per cent on cost
                             plant   20 per cent on cost
                             vehicles   25 per cent on WDV
                             fittings   10 per cent on cost

2. Directors' emoluments—£143 241 (salaries £123 241, pension contributions £20 000)
Chairman—£14 000
Highest-paid director—£40 000
Number of directors in salary band £35 001–£40 000 is one
Number of directors in salary band £30 000–£35 000 is one
3. 10 per cent debentures are secured on the freehold property
They are repayable in ten years' time
4. Auditor's remuneration is £1000

SEMINAR EXERCISES 11

Value PLC Value Added Statement

		£000	%
Turnover		24 926	
Bought-in materials and services (including subcontract)			
[£6431 + £1211 + £3461 + £312 + £479 + £57]		11 951	
Value added		£12 975	100%
Applied as follows:			
Employees		10 748	83
[£7903 + £1064 + £1085 +£100 +£106 + £309 + £181]			
Providers of finance:			
Lenders	400		
Shareholders	220		
		620	5
Government		358	3
To provide for maintenance and the expansion of assets:			
Depreciation [£874 + £83 + £98]	1055		
Retained profit	194		
		1249	9
		£12 975	100%

SEMINAR EXERCISES 13

1. Ginger Ltd.

		1 January		31 December	Change
Current assets:	£	£	£	£	£
Stock		17 000		70 000	+ 53 000
Debtors		7 000		10 000	+ 3 000
Cash		18 000		20 000	+ 2 000
		42 000		100 000	
	£	£	£	£	£
Current liabilities:					
Trade creditors	12 000		14 000		+ 2 000
Tax	11 000		12 000		+ 1 000
Dividends proposed	6 000		8 000		+ 2 000
		29 000		34 000	
Working capital		£13 000		£66 000	

The major factor in the change in working capital is the increase in stocks. Small increases in debtors and cash are balanced by increases in current liabilities. The stock increase appears to have been financed in part by a long-term loan.

2.

Mr Smith, Cash Budget

	Jan.	Feb.	March	Apr.	May	June
	£	£	£	£	£	£
Receipts	Nil	6 000	8000	10 000	12 000	12 000
Payments:						
Purchases	—	10 500	7500	9 000	9000	9000
Wages	350	450	500	500	500	500
Expenses	350	350	350	350	350	350
Rent	500	—	—	500	—	—
Insurance	—	—	—	160	—	—
Assets	3000	1 500	—	—	—	—
Total	4200	12 800	8350	10 510	9850	9850
Surplus/deficit	(4200)	(6 800)	(350)	(510)	2150	2150
Opening balance	5000	800	(6000)	(6 350)	(6860)	(4710)
Closing balance	800	(6 000)	(6350)	(6 860)	(4710)	(2560)

3.

Alpha PLC, Cash Budget for the First Six Months

	July	Aug.	Sept.	Oct.	Nov.	Dec.
	£	£	£	£	£	£
Receipts:						
Opening balance	50 000	39 000	(3 800)	(58 000)	(88 600)	(115 000)
Sales	—	—	36 000	60 000	80 000	120 000
	50 000	39 000	32 200	2 000	(8 600)	5 000
Payments:						
Purchases		34 000	41 000	53 000	89 000	65 000
Commission		800	1 200	1 600	2 400	2 000
Rent	3 000			3 000		
Wages and salaries	5 000	5 000	5 000	5 000	5 000	5 000
Other overheads	3 000	3 000	3 000	4 000	4 000	4 000
Motor car				24 000		
Plant						
Advertisement			40 000		6 000	
Closing balance	39 000	(3 800)	(58 000)	(88 600)	(115 000)	(71 000)
	50 000	39 000	32 200	2 000	(8 600)	5 000

Anticipated Profit and Loss Account for the First Six Months

	July	Aug.	Sept.	Oct.	Nov.	Dec.	Total
Sales	40 000	60 000	80 000	120 000	100 000	100 000	500 000
Cost of sales	24 000	36 000	48 000	84 000	60 000	60 000	312 000
Gross profit	16 000	24 000	32 000	36 000	40 000	40 000	188 000
Expenses:							
Advertisement						40 000	
Commission at							
2 per cent						10 000	
Rent						6 000	
Wages and salaries						30 000	
Other overheads						21 000	
Depreciation:							
Plant					200		
Motor vehicle					1 500	1 700	108 700
Net profit							£79 300

4.   Ranch William, Cash Budget January to April

	Jan.	Feb.	March	Apr.
	£	£	£	£
Budgeted opening balance b/f	2000	(2930)	(6730)	(5 130)
Add budgeted receipts:				
Sales of cattle (no. × £115/£100)	4600	4600	4600	4 600
Auctions:				
Steers (no. × £50)	600	1000	1000	1 300
Beef cattle (no. × £125)	1000	2000	2000	2 500
Supplementary payments:				
Interim		700		
Final				2 100
Development Board subsidy			1000	
Total receipts	6200	8300	8600	10 500
Sub-total	8200	5370	1870	5 370
Less budgeted payments:				
Salaries:				
Basic	800	800	800	800
Bonus (5 per cent of auction sales)	80	150	150	190
Wages, hired hands:				
Regular	1 350	1 350	1350	1350
Casual	1 500	1 200	1200	900
Fodder	900	900	900	500
Grazing rights		300		
Rights of way	100			
Other costs	400	400	400	400
Capital expenditure:				
Buildings		6 000		
Truck:				
Deposit			1200	
Instalment				150
Personal drawings	1 000	1 000	1000	1000
Tax	5 000			
Total payments	11 130	12 100	7000	5290
Budgeted closing balance c/f	(2 930)	(6 730)	(5130)	80

Solutions

SEMINAR EXERCISES 14

1. (a) Limitations of published accounts—points should cover:
   1. Weakness of historical cost accounts in a period of inflation.
   2. Timeliness—produced after event, situation could have changed.
   3. Limited to disclosures required by Act—explained in complicated notes, segmental analysis.
   4. Accounting policies—read note with care to discover affect of methods on income and position. Business income still depends on estimates—doubtful debts/asset lives/accruals.
   5. Historical—no clue as to future operations, nor information about potential or planned results in the year under review.
   6. Asset values in balance sheet do not give information as to true value of items as individuals, or on the value of the business as a whole. The investor is left to judge the risk.

   (b) Items requiring deeper investigation—discussion of *three* from:
   1. Budget—to test future plans, strength of order book.
   2. Adequacy of plant—age/ownership/suitability.
   3. Calibre of management—training/lab. turnover.
   4. Financial support by creditors—and need for more working capital.
   5. Value of fixed assets—premises/stock/debtors.
   6. Relationship with clients—volume of work in progress—speed of payment on certificate—jobs under negotiation—order book.

2. (a) *Assets Basis*

	£
Net book value	60 000
Write up land and buildings	30 000
Provide for doubtful debts	(1 000)
Value of business	£89 000

   Assumptions:

   (i) The assets will realize their book values. Property has been revalued and doubtful debts provided for, but will fixtures and stock sell for the book amounts?
   (ii) The business is worth only the market value of its constituent assets. There is no goodwill.

   Yield Basis

Average profits for last three years, £115 000 ÷ 3	£38 333
Net tangible assets of £89 000 should earn 25 per cent	£22 250
Superprofits	£16 083
Net tangible assets	89 000
Three years' purchase of superprofits = goodwill	48 249
Value of business	£137 249

Assumptions:

  (i) Past average profits represent future. Should they have been weighted to be more representative of recent years?
 (ii) Is a three-year purchase of superprofits suitable in the circumstances? This means that intangible assets are given a capitalization rate of 33 per cent.
(iii) Is it fair to apply the 25 per cent rate for all companies to this particular company?

Capitalization Basis. Average annual profit × capitalization rate =

$$£38\ 333 \times \frac{100}{25} = £153\ 332$$

= value of business. Assumptions (i) and (iii) above apply to this method.

3. (a) The major assumption which must be made to compute superprofit is the capitalization rate or rate of return which can be earned in a similar business. The return on an annuity is not helpful, since it includes an element of capital repayment and depends on life expectancy rather than business risk. The building society return of 9 per cent is post-tax and when grossed up might give a pre-tax return of 14 per cent, but this too is a relatively risk-free investment. The income from quoted and unquoted companies is not a satisfactory guide, since it is post-tax and is computed on profits distributed as dividend, not on all of the profit made. The investor may accept a small return in order to achieve capital growth. The return is also typical of small holdings of shares and thus cannot be used to value a company as a whole. A required return of 20 per cent should be assumed in a small private company, since this reflects the interest rate paid by the company on its loan.

   Other considerations are whether Mr Parsnip can be replaced at the same salary (£12 000 per annum), whether the loss on the car is an extraordinary item, whether the bad debts are normal, and whether the profit figures are normal and reflect future performance.

	£
Net profit	30 000
Add back:	
Mrs Carrott's fees	7 500
Loss on car	2 500
Expected future profit	£40 000

Capital employed, net tangible assets, £110 000

Expected return, £110 000 × 20 per cent	£22 000	Expected return
	£40 000	Adjusted future profit
	£18 000	Superprofit

(b) Depreciation has increased by £20 000 this year. This must be the charge for the year, and would put back £5000 into profit if the rate is reduced from 20 per cent to 15 per cent (¼). Superprofit would then be £23 000 and at three years' purchase, goodwill would be worth £46 000. Net tangible assets and goodwill combined make the company worth £156 000.

4. (a) The net tangible assets of this company are nil after revaluation of property and stock. Any value of the business depends on the fact that the shareholders own the assets and combine them in such a way as to show a profit. In this case all profits are superprofits so far as the shareholders are concerned, since their investment has been lost by past trading losses and the revaluation.

Since the losses are not likely to be repeated, it seems fair to take a weighted average profit of the last three years as a goodwill foundation.

Year 13	5 000 × 1	=	5 000			
Year 14	10 000 × 2	=	20 000			
Year 15	15 000 × 3	=	45 000			
	6		70 000	$\dfrac{70\ 000}{6}$	=	£11 666

Average profit times the capitalization rate is $£11\ 666 \times \dfrac{100}{20} = £58\ 330$

This is what an investor expecting a 20 per cent return would pay for the right to receive these profits. Each ordinary share is worth £1.94.

5. (a)

				£
Net tangible assets				70 000

Profits	Year Before Last	Last Year	This Year	
	£	£	£	
Profits	60 000	90 000	100 000	
Adjust, Mr Almond	(20 000)	(20 000)	(20 000)	
Adjust, depreciation	(10 000)	(15 000)	(20 000)	
	30 000	55 000	60 000	145 000
			Offer price	£215 000
Weight	1	2	3	
Profit	30 000	110 000	180 000	

$$\frac{320\ 000}{6} = £53\ 333 \text{ as PAWA}$$

(b) (i) $\dfrac{53\ 333}{215\ 000}$ = 25 per cent. Almond is valuing his business at a high-risk capitalization rate.

(ii) Superprofits, not profits, should be used to value the firm.

(iii) Tangible assets comprise only one-third of the price.

(iv) The advantage of material from associate company will be lost.

(v) Enquire about past losses: How? When? Will they be repeated?

SEMINAR EXERCISES 15

1. Net profit to capital employed = 160 : 2080 = 7.7 per cent. Disappointing return. Investigate whether the profitability of operations or the underuse of capacity is the cause.

Net profit to sales = 160 : 1600 = 10 per cent. Sales to capital employed = 1600 : 2080 = 0.77 times. The profit margin on sales is fairly good, but could be improved. Resources do not appear to be working hard enough, since every £1 of assets earns only 77 pence of sales in the year. 0.77 × 10 per cent = 7.7 per cent.

Sales to fixed assets = 1600 : 800 = 2 times. Sales to current assets = 1600 : 1280 = 1.25 times. Fixed assets to current assets = 800 : 1280 = 1 : 1.6. Current assets earn less per £1 than fixed assets, yet current assets have more weight in the asset structure. This may reflect the nature of the business, or could be evidence of over-investment in current assets.

$$\text{Debtor period} = \frac{720}{1600} \times \frac{365}{1} = 164 \text{ days} = \text{five months} +.$$

$$\text{Stock turnover} = \frac{480}{1280} \times \frac{365}{1} = 137 \text{ days} = \text{four months} +.$$

Five months' credit to customers seems excessive. Credit control could reduce the investment here, so long as it did not harm sales effort. Perhaps stock control could reduce the four-month period which, on average, stocks wait in stores before being used.

Gross profit to sales = 320 : 1600 = 20 per cent. Expenses to sales = 160 : 1600 = 10 per cent. Half of the gross profit margin is used up by the expenses.

2. It must be stressed that apparent reasons for differences are derived from speculation, and therefore should not be treated as definite conclusions, but should be investigated further.

Current ratio = 120 : 68 = 1.77 : 1 (Ours 2.4 : 1). Theirs has less current asset cover for its current liabilities. Therefore it may be more dependent on short-term credit than Ours.

$$\text{Stock turnover} = \frac{\text{Average stock}}{\text{Cost of sale}} = \frac{30}{380} = 12.7 \text{ times (Ours 5.4 times). Stocks are}$$

turned over faster at Theirs, so the capital employed in stocks works harder. This may mean that they have good stock control or that they prefer to take the risks inherent in low stocks. If they are dependent on creditors for finance they would tend to reduce stocks to minimize borrowings.

$$\text{Debtor collection} = \frac{72}{380} \times \frac{365}{1} = 69 \text{ days (Ours 32 days). Theirs give more}$$

trade credit to their customers, perhaps to support sales effort, perhaps through inefficient credit control.

$$\text{Gross profit} = \frac{100}{480} \times \frac{100}{1} = 21 \text{ per cent (Ours 38 per cent). Ours is more}$$

profitable than Theirs, perhaps because of a different pricing policy or a lower cost of sales resulting from better buying (see stock turnover above).

$$\text{Return on total investment} = \frac{8}{208} \times \frac{100}{1} = 3.8 \text{ per cent or} \frac{8}{140} \times \frac{100}{1} = 5.7$$

per cent (Ours 15.6 per cent). Theirs is less profitable than Ours. This reflects the difference in gross profit rate, or more interest to pay (current ratio).

Solutions

3. (a)

Roper Ltd, Trading and Profit and Loss Account to 30 June

	£	£
Sales		652 000
Less cost.of sales		584 500
Gross profit		67 500
Add investment income		100
		67 600
Less expenses:		
Loan interest	3 000	
General	49 000	
Depreciation	2 500	54 500
Net profit		13 100
Less appropriations:		
Taxation	8 000	
Dividend	2 500	10 500
Unappropriated profit for the year		2 600
Unappropriated profit b/d		39 400
Unappropriated profit c/f		£42 000

Balance Sheet as at 30 June

	£	£	£
Share capital			50 000
General reserve			13 000
Unappropriated profit			42 000
Equity interest			105 000
Long-term loan			30 000
Net capital employed			£135 000
Represented by:			
Intangible asset, goodwill			20 000

	Cost	Depreciation	
Fixed assets:			
Freehold property	21 000	—	21 000
Equipment	26 000	13 000	13 000
Investment			2 500
			56 500
Current assets:			
Stock		55 000	
Debtors		75 000	
Cash		11 000	
		141 000	
Current liabilities:			
Creditors	47 500		
Taxation	15 000		
		62 500	
Working capital			78 500
Net assets			£135 000

(b), (c) $\text{ROCE} = \dfrac{13\ 100}{197\ 500} \times \dfrac{100}{1} = 6.6$ per cent (industry 10 per cent). Less profitable than average for industry. Investigate profitability and underuse of capacity.

$\text{Stock turnover} = \dfrac{584.5}{55} = 10.6$ times (industry 15 times). This suggests that stocks are not working hard enough. Other companies manage with less stock per £1 of sales. Stock control.

Current ratio = 141 : 62.5 = 2.3 : 1 (industry 1.8 : 1). Less dependent on outside finance to fund current assets. Perhaps does not take as much trade credit as it could.

$\text{Gross profit} = \dfrac{67.5}{652} \times \dfrac{100}{1} = 10.4$ per cent (industry 20 per cent). Less profitable per £1 of sales made than average for industry. Investigate pricing policy or buying department to isolate mark-up or cost of sales as the reason.

$\text{Debt ratio} = \dfrac{75}{652} \times \dfrac{100}{1} = 11.5$ per cent or 1.38 months (industry 33 per cent or 4 months). The company is giving less credit than average to customers. This reflects efficient collection policy, but is the sales effort being supported by a good credit line? More credit may mean more sales and a faster stock turnover at higher prices.

4. (a)

	David	Charles
ROCE	7 per cent	12.6 per cent
Net profit to sales	6 per cent	5.5 per cent
Sales to capital employed	1.16 times	2.29 times
Gross profit	16.7 per cent	14.3 per cent
Expenses to sales	10.7 per cent	8.8 per cent
Fixed assets to sales	2.68 times	4.14 times
Current assets to sales	2.06 times	5.12 times
Fixed assets to current assets	1 : 1.3	1 : 0.8
Stock turnover	4 times	30 times
Debtors	10 weeks	4 weeks
Current ratio	4.5 : 1	0.9 : 1

(b) Charles has a better return on capital than David, not because his business is more profitable, but because he works his capital harder. He has a lower gross profit margin, but his expenses ratio is lower too, so this compensates for much of the difference. Charles earns more sales per pound on both fixed and current assets, but this difference is most marked for current assets. The two firms have different asset structures. Charles uses less current assets and this is reflected in his much better stock turnover and debtor performance and in the current ratio. The profitable operations of Charles may be halted, since he has negative working capital.

5. (a)

	Year 1	Year 2
Gross profit rate	$\dfrac{190\ 532}{571\ 660} \times \dfrac{100}{1} = 33.3$ per cent	$\dfrac{171\ 752}{686\ 480} \times \dfrac{100}{1} = 25$ per cent

Solutions

Gross profit has fallen from one-third to one-quarter. A gross profit of 33 per cent last year means a mark-up on cost of 50 per cent. Thus goods costing £100 would be sold for £150. If Jean's explanation is correct, this year the same goods would cost £115 (£100 + 15 per cent) and sell for £165 (£150 + 10 per cent) to show a profit of £50. Gross profit rate would be $\frac{50}{165} \times \frac{100}{1} = 30$ per cent. Thus Jean's explanation accounts for only part (⅜) of the fall in gross profit.

(b) Other reasons:
   (i)   Stock errors in opening or closing stocks, e.g. items omitted or costs or extensions wrong.
  (ii) Cash from sales stolen, not banked. False sales figure.
 (iii) Goods stolen by customers or staff.
 (iv) Cash or goods withdrawn by Jean Sellar: not in books.
  (v) Wrong 'cut-off point'. Goods in purchases but not in stock.
 (vi) Gross profit is an average. Change mixture of sales to less profitable lines.

(c) *Stock Turnover*

	Year 1	Year 2
$\frac{\text{Average stock}}{\text{Cost of sales}} \times \frac{52}{1}$	$\frac{57\,810}{381\,128} \times \frac{52}{1} = 7.9$ weeks	$\frac{56\,790}{514\,727} \times \frac{52}{1} = 5.7$ weeks

SEMINAR EXERCISES 16

1. (a)   *Caxton PLC, Funds Flow Statement 19-5*

	£	£
Net loss (after interest but before tax)		(3023)
Deduct non-cash costs:		
Depreciation	633	
Goodwill W/O	500	1133
Negative cash flow generated by operations		(1890)
Sources of funds—long-term loans		1677
		(213)
Application of funds:		
Fixed assets purchased	3534	
Preference shares redeemed	420	
Tax paid (108 + 11−7)	112	
Dividend paid (243 + 25 − 8)	260	(4326)
Long-term deficit		(4539)
Working capital:		
Stock (decrease)	772	
Debtors (decrease)	1196	
Creditors (increase)	103	
Funds saved by working capital measures		2071
Remaining deficit		(2468)
Change in liquidity	281	
Overdraft increased	2187	
		2468

502

Notes:

1. Considerable fixed asset purchases are made at a time when stocks and debtors are reduced and turnover is stable. Is this a reorganization? Perhaps trading losses stem from this.
2. Preference shares redeemed during a period of fixed asset purchase and loss. This is strategically wrong. The company is in contravention of the Companies Act 1985—shares redeemed without a fresh issue yet no capital redemption reserve is created from distributable profit.
3. Losses and fixed asset purchases (1890 + 3534) financed by loans/overdraft/ working capital economies (1677/2187/2071).

(b)   *Caxton PLC, Ratio Analysis*

	19-4		19-5	
	Caxton	Industry	Caxton	Industry
ROCE (Owners/Overall)	3.3%/3.7%	13%	(75%)/(11.7%)	13.5%
Net profit: sales	1.2%	4.8%	(10.9%)	5.2%
Turnover ratio	1.47	2.7	1.40	2.6
Current ratio	1.25	1.4	0.83	1.5
Sales/stocks	10.4	7.6	13.8	7.7
Average collection	105 days	86 days	94 days	79 days

Report

Points to be considered:

1. Losses experienced in 19-5 lead to a reduction of reserves and capital depletion.
2. A five-year trend will show if the loss in 19-5 is a sudden isolated incident.
3. Sales to stocks is not a meaningful ratio—stock at cost should be set against cost of sales. The purchases figure is needed in order to calculate this ratio.
4. Current ratio is falling against the industry trend. 19-5 gives cause for concern which is accentuated if the acid test is applied (0.65 in 19-5). Creditors show no change but overdraft has doubled. Action by the bank manager could seriously embarrass the company.
5. *Stocks*—rapidly increasing stock-turn requires analysis, does this change stem from materials or finished goods or both? Is the company holding insufficient stocks to service its activities?
6. *Debtors*—the credit period has been reduced but it is still longer than the average for the industry.
7. *Retained profit*—was inadequate in 19-4 (250 − 130) and negative in 19-5. Payment of a dividend in this situation constitutes a significant disinvestment.
8. *Gearing*

$$19\text{-}4: \frac{2931}{10\,426} \times \frac{100}{1} = 28 \text{ per cent} \qquad 19\text{-}5: \frac{4608}{8624} \times \frac{100}{1} = 53 \text{ per cent}$$

Gearing has increased to reflect increased long-term loans and a reduction of shareholders' funds through losses. The debt/equity ratio has increased from 1.6 : 1 to 3.9 : 1 and is a danger signal reflecting the increase in overdraft.

2. (a) *Hypertension PLC, Budgeted Funds Flow Statement Year Ending 31 March 19-9 (£000s)*

	£	£
Funds generated from operations:		
Net proft before tax and dividend [297 + 240]		537
Items not involving the movement of funds		
Depreciation		239
		776
Funds from other sources:		
17 per cent debentures	800	
Sale of assets	42	
		842
		1618
Application of funds:		
Tax paid	170	
Dividend paid	250	
Plant purchased	492	
Premises purchased	800	
Vehicles purchased	56	
Fixtures purchased	27	
		1795
Deficit of long-term application over source		177
Working capital:		
Stock—increased	409	
Debtors—increased	341	
Creditors—increased	(204)	
		546
Total deficit		723
Financed by: Overdraft	320	
Cash used up	403	
		723

(b) *Comments*

(i) Funds generated (776 − tax and dividend) of 356 are less than half of funds injected.

(ii) Assets sold are relatively unimportant.

(iii) Debentures issued = premises purchased—is this a coincidence?

(iv) Idle cash resources are put to work.

(v) Short-term sources—CRS 204 and O/D 320 are used to bridge the gap.

(vi) Gearing is increased—LTL increase faster than shareholders' funds.

3. (a) *Soar Valley Services PLC Funds Flow Statement for the Year Ending 30 June 19-8*

	£	£
Funds generated from operations:		
Net profit before tax (220 000 + 320 000 + 126 000)		666 000
Items not involving the movement of funds		
Depreciation		647 000
		1 313 000
Funds from other sources:		
Share capital issued at a premium	550 000	
18 per cent debentures issued	400 000	
		950 000
		2 263 000
Application of funds:		
Tax paid	80 000	
Dividend paid	91 000	
Plant purchased	1 907 000	
12 per cent unsecured loan stock repaid	400 000	
		2 478 000
Deficit of long-term application over source		(215 000)
Working capital:		
Stock—increased	(290 000)	
Debtors—increased	(320 000)	
Creditors—increased	(155 000)	
		(455 000)
		(670 000)
Overdraft increase	612 000	
Bank decrease	58 000	
		£670 000

(b) (i) Implied expansion—plant, stock, debtors increase £2 597 000. Major item is purchase of plant for £1 871 000.

   (ii) Financed by fresh share capital, generated funds ploughed back, a sizeable overdraft, an increase in creditors, and spare cash used up—deficit of LTA over source.

   (iii) Gearing reduced—but debt : equity situation gives cause for concern— moved from 2.8 times last year to 1.7 times. Reflects greater use of short-term finance, which can of course be withdrawn at short notice.

   (iv) Unsecured loan 12 per cent repaid—replaced by debenture at 18 per cent; cost £20 000 p.a. in increased interest. What is the security for the debenture?

   (v) Liquidity reduced—cash replaced by large overdraft, plus extra creditors. Working capital ratio 1.01 : 1 reduced from 1.87 : 1. Is it now safe? Acid test at 0.66 : 1 is a danger signal.

   (vi) Fresh shares issued at large premium—company has confidence of investors.

4.   *H. Swede Esq., Funds Flow Statement for the Year to 31 March*

	£	£	£
Cash flow:			
Net profit		72 300	
Depreciation		7 000	
		79 300	
Less:			
Cash withdrawn	3 200		
Gifts made	15 000		
Tax paid	5 100	23 300	56 000
Long-term sources:			
Capital introduced (legacy)		10 000	
Loan from Fenland Farmers		15 000	25 000
			81 000
Long-term applications:			
Dutch barn		30 000	
New implements		13 700	
Investments		4 000	47 700
Surplus			£33 300

Working capital movements:	Source	Application	
Stock		10 400	
Debtors		5 000	
Creditors	1 500		
Cash, £(6700 + 12 700)		19 400	
	1 500	34 800	
Net application to working capital			£33 300
These figures can be reconciled:			
Opening working capital			15 700
Closing working capital			49 000
Increase			£33 300

Mr Swede should be told of the improvement in his liquid position resulting from a profitable year with a large proportion of the profits retained in the business. He must be warned, however, that his profits will attract tax, resulting in a cash outflow next year.

(a)   *Forest Ltd, Funds Flow Statement for the Year Ended 31 March*

	£	£
Sources of funds:		
Profit before tax and dividend		114 035
Depreciation		21 515
Total generated from operations		135 550
Funds from other sources:		
Issue of shares	25 000	
Disposal of fixed assets	3 389	28 389
		163 939
Application of funds:		
Dividends paid	16 926	
Tax paid	42 720	
Additions to buildings	6 660	
Additions to plant	39 352	
Debentures redeemed	15 000	120 658
		£43 281

	£	£
Increase/decrease in working capital:		
Increase in stocks	37 427	
Increase in debtors	71 827	
Increase in creditors	(60 434)	
	48 820	
Movement of liquid funds:		
Increase in bank overdraft	(5 539)	£43 281

Note: This form of statement is more in line with the example in SSAP 10 than previous examples given. Although it shows the amounts paid out in tax and dividend, it does not show the funds generated to be retained in the business or the extra credit from tax and dividend owed at the year end. ACT owed and recoverable cancel each other out.

6. (a)   *Landseen Ltd, Funds Flow Statement*

	£000s	£000s
Cash flow—net profit before tax (195−4)		191
Add items not involving the movement of funds		
Depreciation		26.5
Funds generated by operation		217.5
Other sources:		
Sale of fixed assets [WDV + profit = cash]	20	
[35 − 19 + 4 = 20]		
Debentures issued	100	
		120
		337.5
Long-term applications:		
Fixed assets purchased	108.5	
Tax paid [130 + 93 − 151]	72	
Dividend paid [35 + 79 − 38]	76	
		256.5
		81

Surplus	Source	Application	
Worktime capital			
Stock (increase)		53	
Debtors (increase)		41.4	
Creditors (increase)	15.2		
	15.2	94.4	
		79.2	Application
Reduction in liquid resources (bank)		1.8	

Workings:

Calculation of depreciation and asset purchases for the year

	Cost	Depreciation	Net
Opening balance sheet	346 500	82 500	264 000
Assets sold	(35 000)	(19 000)	(16 000)
	311 500	63 500	248 000
Closing balance sheet	420 000	90 000	330 000
Assets purchased	£108 500		
Depreciation charged		£26 500	

SOLUTION TO TUTORIAL DISCUSSION TOPIC, CHAPTER 25

1. The profit figure for a period can show different results if computed using different accounting policies. Such policies, however, must be used consistently and if a new policy is adopted the impact of the change on the profit figure should be shown by way of a note to the accounts. It is true that a proportion of overhead expenses charged against the work in progress can be carried forward to another year and set off against revenue in that year when the goods are finished and sold. This practice seems fair, especially when it is applied consistently year after year.

2. The return on capital employed may be artificially high. Net capital employed ignores current liabilities, which contain such sources of capital as bank overdraft, taxation and trade credit. Fixed assets, especially property, shown in the balance sheet at historical cost may be undervalued in a period of inflation. Depreciation based on historical cost may be insufficient for the same reason, so profits may be overstated.

3. The transfer of cash and loan repayment have no effect on the current profit position. Even if the transactions could be reversed (and the loan repayment cannot) this would affect liquidity, not profitability. If cash is available this does not necessarily mean that it is part of a profit surplus. It may represent part of the capital of the business held in liquid form, and to pay increased wages from such funds would deplete the capital of the business and reduce its ability to employ its labour force. The repayment of debentures will reduce future interest charges, and thus increase the profitability of the company.

4. Undistributed profits represent profits made in the past which could have been distributed in full to shareholders when they were made. It was decided instead to plough these profits back into the company, to enable it to expand and thus maintain the employment it provides in the area. These reserves are part of the shareholders' investment in the business and, although it is not illegal to use them to meet wage claims if the shareholders agree, it is imprudent, since increased costs are borne by running down the capital employed. Reserves may not be in the form of cash.

5. The dividend rate is quoted on the face or nominal value of the shares. Yield is the dividend per share expressed as a percentage of the current price and represents the true return on the investors' income. Shareholders bear the risk of the business, allow their capital to be tied up, and also pay income tax on dividends received, thus their return at 6 per cent is not excessive.

6. Profits retained are reinvested in the business to expand or maintain its productive capacity and to avoid recourse to the capital market. Thus these retained profits help the company to improve employment opportunities for its labour force. Tax must be paid on such profits when and if they are eventually distributed, and they have already suffered corporation tax.

Index

Accountants
  financial accountants *see* Financial accountant
  large practices   4–5
  management accountants   5
  professional bodies   6–7
  work of   3–5
Accounting
  historical development of   5–6
  purpose of   7–8
  theoretical framework *see* Theoretical
    framework of accounting
Accounting bases   24
Accounting equation   32–4
Accounting information, users of   9–11
Accounting period, choice of   40–1
Accounting Standards Board (ASB)   293
Accounting Standards Committee (ASC)   274,
  290, 386
  compliance enforcement   292, 294
  criticisms of   291–3
  funding   292, 294
  see also Standards
Accounting statements *see* Financial statements
Accretion   269–70
Accruals principle   21, 41–2, 280
  costs and   41–2
  criticism of   274
  income and   38
  prepayments and   42–5
  stocks and   89
Acid test ratio   281
Activity   412
Adjustments to accounts   147–9
  appropriation of profit   147
  capital/revenue allocation   147
  cash book errors   148
  casting errors   149
  cost or appropriation omitted   148
  credit sales understated   147
  debtor balance gone bad   148
  depreciation at wrong rate   148
  goods on sale or return   148
  loan interest outstanding   148
  omissions when statements made up   147
  stock write-down   148
  vehicle sale without entry   148
  wrong posting of debits and credits   148
Advance corporation tax   223–5
Allocation principle   68
Apportionment   109
Appropriation account   38–40
  partnerships   172–3
  taxation and   112
Appropriation of profit by proprietor   147
Assets
  current *see* Current assets
  fixed *see* Depreciation; Fixed assets
  fixed to current ratio   402
  gross   277
  historic cost   27
  holding gains   27
  intangible   27, 28, 436
    disclosure of   240, 242, 251

  market value of   27
  premature retirement   76–9
  tangible, disclosure of   241, 251
Association of Accounting Technicians   7
Association of Public Accountants (USA)   5
Auditors   195–216, 277
  appointment   198–200
  confidence level   198
  definition   195–6
  disagreements with accountants   289
  external   197
  fee   199
  financial accountant as   195–216
  going concern concept and   15–16
  ICQs   198
  internal   197
  lack of flexibility of   289
  liability of   202–4
  qualification of report   201–2
  Recognized Qualifying Bodies   199
  Recognized Supervisory Body   199, 200
  registered   199
  removal from office   201
  remuneration of   238
  rights and duties of   200–1
Audits
  divisible profits   204–6
  errors
    of commission   206
    compensating   206–7
    of location   207
    of omission   206
    of principle   206
  final   197
  in-depth checking   198
  interim audits   197
  internal audits   196–7
  internal check   207–8
  internal control   207
    cash sales   210–11
    computer systems   212–15
    credit sales   212
    payment of wages   208–9
    raw materials   209–10
  methods   197–8
  population   198
  qualification of report   201–2
  sampling   198
  statutory   196
AVCO   93–4, 95, 96

Bad debts *see* Debtors
Balance sheet   8–9, 26–37, 427
  accounting equation   32–4
  assets   26–9
    unquantifiable   276
    see also Assets
  criticism of   276–8
  disclosure required in   238–47
  form of   30–2
  formats   231–4
  information from   434–9

liabilities   29–30
  unquantifiable   276–7
  see also Liabilities
static funds statement   280
window dressing   276
see also Position statement
Balances *see* Trial balances
Bank reconciliations   153–6
Bank statements
  cash books and   153–4
  incomplete accounts and   135–6
Bias, lack of   11
Bonus shares   332–3
Book value   300, 375
Budget   9
Building societies   327–8
Buildings
  depreciation of   81–2
  Investment Property Revaluation Reserve   82
  SSAPs   81–2
Business cycle   28
  revenue recognition in   267
Business entity concept   17–18, 28
Business finance *see* Finance for business
Business valuation *see* Valuation of business
Businesses *see individual enterprises e.g.*
    Companies

Capital   434
  capital employed   277
  circulating capital   28
  economic ideas   296–7
  expenditure   45–6
  gearing   315, 336–9, 343, 434
  inflation and   307
  maintenance of   69, 318, 349
  ratio analysis   408
  reserves   29, 32
  share capital   29, 239
  venture capital   29
  see also Capital structure; Finance for business;
      Working capital
Capital structure
  bonus shares   332–3
  debentures   332, 334–6, 343
  loan stock issue   343
  ordinary shares   330–2
    call option   331–2
    floating   331
    marketability   331
  preference shares   333–4
  share issue *see* Finance for business
Capital/revenue allocation   147
Cash balances   361
Cash book   138
  adjustment for errors in   148
  bank statements and   153–4
Cash budgets   363–5
Cash discounts   356
Cash flow   427, 430
Cash sales   210–11
Casting errors   149
Certainty theory   268
Chairman's statement   275
Charitable gifts   221
Chartered Association of Certified
    Accountants   6

Chartered Institute of Management
    Accountants   6
Chartered Institute of Public Finance
    Accountants   6
Cheques dishonoured   154
Clubs *see* Non-trading organizations
Companies   324–6
  gearing   315, 336–9, 343, 434
  guarantee companies   325
  limited by shares   325–6
  partnerships and   180–2, 183–5, 326
  unlimited companies   325
  see also Capital structure; Finance for business;
      Valuation of business
Comparability   12
Completed contract method   268
Completeness   11
Computers
  double-entry book-keeping and   54, 58–60
  internal control systems   212–15
Conceptual framework   14
Conservatism concept *see* Prudence concept
Consistency   19, 275
Consultative Committee for Accountancy Bodies
    (CCAB)   6, 290
Contingencies, disclosure of   250
Contingent liability   30, 240
Control accounts   149–53
Controlling interest valuation   374–8
Co-operative societies   327
Corporate objectives statement   285
Corporate Report, The   282–6
  corporate objectives statement   285
  employment report   285
  foreign currency transactions   285
  future prospects   285
  money exchanges with Government   285
  value added statement   283–4
Corporation tax *see* Advance corporation tax;
    Taxation
Cost-effectiveness   12
Costs   9, 22
  accrual principle   41–2
  accrued expenses   42, 44
  cost of capital   349
  cost of sales   305–6, 313–14
  debt cost   350
  deferred revenue expenditure   44–5
  development expenditure   45
  flow of costs   92
  historic cost   27, 71
  overheads   89–90, 92, 111
  stocks and   89–90
Cover   374, 399
Credit balances   108
Credit rating agencies   11
Credit sales   212
Creditors
  disclosure of   239–40
  trade   434–5
  working capital and   360, 361
Crystallization   335
Current assets   27, 28, 412, 435–6
  debtors   99–101
  flow of costs   92
  IAS   13, 88
  investments   101–2

long-term work in progress   98–9
stocks *see* Stocks
Current cost accounting (CCA)   309–10, 317
  examples of   313–15
  SSAP 16   310, 311–12
Current liabilities   30
  disclosure of   240
Current purchasing power method (CPP)   309,
  310, 316, 317
Customers, as users of information   11

Debentures   332, 334–6, 434
  crystallization of   335
  issue   343
Debt cost   350
Debtors   28, 99–101
  adjustment to accounts   148
  bad debts
    later collected   100–1
    written off to profit and loss account   99–100
  disclosure of   243–4
  doubtful debts
    overestimate of provision for   101
    which go bad later   100
  in trial balances   111
  taxation and   222
  working capital and   360, 361
Decision-making   296
Deferred revenue expenditure   44–5
Deferred taxation   250
Depreciation   16, 44, 46, 67–87, 298
  accounting entries   76–80
  adjustments to accounts   148
  allocation principle   68
  buildings   81–2
  calculation of   244–5
  capital maintenance concept   69
  as concept   68–70
  definition   67
  disclosure of   238, 250
  in funds flow statement   427
  historical costs   71
  incomplete accounts and   138
  inflation and   303–5, 314
  judgemental approach   70–2
  objective of   80
  premature retirement   76–9
  production hour method   75
  production unit method   75
  reasons for value loss   67–8
  reducing balance method   73–4
  replacement and   69
  residual value   71–2
  revaluation method   74–5
  SSAPs   80–2
  straight line method   72–3
  taxation and   221
  in trial balances   110, 112
  useful economic life   71, 79–80
Deprival value   300–1
Development expenditure   45
Directors
  directors' report   247–8, 275
  emoluments   237
  loans to   241

Disclosure   21
  accounting policies   23
  alternative accounting rules   251–2
  balance sheet
    disclosure required in   238–47
    formats   231–4
  Companies Act requirements   230–63
  directors' report   247–8
  medium-sized company exemptions   250–1
  profit and loss account
    formats   234–7
    information specified   237–8
  segmental reporting   253
  small company exemptions   250–1
  in SSAPs   249–50
  statistical supplements   253–4
  summarized accounts   252
  true and fair view override   230, 231
Discounted present value   296
Discounts, trade and cash   356
Dishonoured cheques   154
Dividends, disclosure of   238
Double entry   22–3, 51–66
  accounting system   55
  computer transaction lists   54
  computers and book-keeping   58–60
  daybooks   54, 59
  journal   54–5
  ledgerless book-keeping   54
  petty cash book   56–8
    imprest system   57–8
  prime documents   53–4
  principles of   51–3
  quadrant and sextant   60–4
  recording transactions   53–4
  trial balance   55–6

Earnings, ratio analysis   408–9
Earnings per share   377, 387
  calculation   245
  disclosure of   249
Economic ideas   295–302
  capital   296–7
  income   297–9
  perfection assumption   296
  value   299–300
EEC Fourth Directive   386
Employees
  as users   10
  disclosure of   237
Employment report   285
Entertaining, taxation and   221
Equity cost   350
Estate Duties Investment Trust (Edith)   346
Expenditure, capital and revenue   45–6
Extended trial balance   113
Extraordinary items
  disclosure of   238, 249
  revenue recognition   271

Factoring   353
Factory overheads   92, 111
Fairness concept   18–19
FIFO   92, 93, 94, 95, 96

Finance for business   341–54
  capital maintenance   349
  cost of capital   349
  debenture issue   343
  debt cost   350
  equity cost   350
  factoring   353
  fixed capital   342
  gearing and   343
  grants and incentives   352
  hire purchase   351
  institutional investors   346–7
  invoice discounting   353
  leasing   351
  loan stock issue   343
  long-term capital market   343–6
  management buy-outs (MBOs)   348–9
  mortgage   351
  overdrafts   352, 427
  price of money   341
  profit retention as source   343
  risk   342
  sale and lease-back   351
  share issue   343
    by prospectus   344
    introduction   345
    market making   345
    offer by tender   345
    offer for sale   344
    placing   344–5
  short-term financial requirements   352–3
  small business   341–2
  start-up funds   348
  third market   347
  trade credits   352–3
  Unlisted Securities Market (USM)   345, 347–8
  venture capital   348
  working capital   342
Finance for Industry   346
Financial accountant   4–5
  as auditor *see* Auditors
  work of *see individual aspects*
Financial Reporting Council (FRC)   293
Financial statements   8–9
  characteristics of   11–12
  monetary measurement   14–15
  see also individual statements e.g. Balance sheet
Financial strength   398
Fixed assets   27–8, 44, 435
  disclosure of   241, 242, 251, 252
  fixed to current ratio   402
  inflation and   303–5
  revaluation and deferred tax   227
  sale not at book value   427
  tangible, disclosure of   241, 251
  see also Depreciation
Flow of costs   92
Foreign currency transactions   285
Funds flow analysis   420–50
  funds explained   420–1
    net borrowings   421
    net liquid funds   421
    total external finance   421
    working capital   421
  sources and use of funds   421–2
  see also Funds flow statement
Funds flow statement   9, 422–33

  cash flow in   427, 430
  computational difficulties   427–32
  depreciation in   427
  financial changes revealed   432
  format   433
  liquidity changes   432
  overdrafts in   427
  SSAP 10   433
Future prospects statement   285

Gearing   336–9, 434
  finance for business and   343
  inflation adjustment   315
Gifts to charity   221
Going concern principle   15–16, 28, 274
Going concern value   300
Goodwill   28
  accounting treatment of   384–7
  amortization   386–7
  definition   378
  factors contributing to existence of   379
  negative   385
  partnerships   171, 174, 175–7
  purchased and inherent   384–5
  valuation of   374, 375, 378–87
  write-off to reserves   387
Government
  as users of information   11
  grants and incentives   352
  money exchanges with   285
Gross assets   277
Gross profit margins   136–7
Gross profit ratio   409–10
Groups, segmental reporting   253
Guarantee companies   325

Hire of plant or machinery   238
Hire purchase
  finance by   351
  revenue recognition   270
Historical cost   27
  adjusted for inflation   307–9
  criticism of   273
Holding gains   27, 315–17

IAS *see* International Accounting Standards
Imputation system   223–5
Income
  economic ideas   297–9
  from investments   238
Income statement
  accruals principle   38, 41–2
  appropriation account   38–9
  capital and revenue expenditure   45–6
  criticism of   278–9
  deferred revenue expenditure   44–5
  manufacturing account   38
  position statement and   279–82
  prepayments and accruals   42–5
  reserves and provisions   46–7
  trading account   38
  see also Profit and loss account
Income tax *see* Taxation

Incomplete records   135–40
Industrial and Commercial Finance
   Corporation   346
Inflation   303–20
   capital and   307
   cost of sales and   305–6, 313–14
   cost principle undermined   273
   current cost accounting (CCA)   309–10, 317
      examples of   313–15
      SSAP 16   310, 311–12
   current purchasing power (CPP)   309, 310,
      316, 317
   depreciation and   303–5, 314
   economic and accountancy attitudes   296
   fixed assets and   303–5
   gearing adjustment   315
   historical cost accounting adjusted   307–9
   holding gains   315–17
   monetary items   306, 310–11
   monetary working capital adjustment   314–15
   operating capital maintenance   318
   purchasing power   307
   realization and   273–4
Information *see* Accounting information
Institute of Chartered Accountants in England
   and Wales   5, 6, 290
Institute of Chartered Accountants in Ireland   6,
   290
Institute of Chartered Accountants in
   Scotland   5, 6, 290
Intangible assets   27, 28, 436
   disclosure of   240, 251
   fixed   151
Inter-firm comparison   410–13
Interest
   disclosure of analysis of   238
   loan interest outstanding   148
Internal Control Questionnaires (ICQs)   198
International Accounting Standards   88, 94, 98,
   433
International Accounting Standards
   Committee   386
Interpretation of accounts *see individual aspects*
   e.g. Ratio analysis
Introduction   345
Inventory *see* Stocks
Investment Property Revaluation Reserve   82
Investment trust   346–7
Investments   101–2, 242
   income from   238
Invoice discounting   353

Joint ventures   185–7
Journal   54–5
   entries   136, 149
   incomplete accounts and   136
'Just in time' stock control   359

Leasing   351
Lenders, as users   10–11
Liabilities
   capital reserves   29
   contingent   30, 240
   current   30, 240
   long-term   29

present obligations   30
   trial balances and   109
   venture capital   29
Life, useful economic life   71, 79–80
LIFO   92, 93, 94, 95, 96
Limited companies   325–6
   conversion of partnership to   183–5
   sale of partnership to   180–2
Liquidity   398, 432
Loan stock, annual interest on   111
Loans
   disclosure of   239–40, 243–4
   interest outstanding   148
   revenue recognition and interest   270
   to directors and officers   241
Long-term contracts   269

MacMillan gap   346
Mainstream corporation tax   225–6
Management, as user   10
Management accountants   5
Management buy-outs (MBOs)   9, 348–9
Managerial ratios   410–13
Manufacturing account   38
Mark-up   118
   incomplete accounts and   136–7
Market making   345
Market value   300
Matching principle *see* Accruals principle
Materiality concept   20, 275
Medium-sized companies exemptions   250–1
Merchant banks   346, 347
Monetary items, inflation and   306, 310–11
Monetary measurement   14–15
Mortgage   351

Nationalized industries   328–9
Net realizable value   89, 90, 300
Net worth   276, 378
Next in first out (NIFO)   305
Non-monetary terms   275
Non-trading organizations
   accounts of   141–6
   accumulated fund   142, 144
   bank accounts   145
   bar trading account   145
   building fund   142, 145
   general expenses   145
   information relevant to accounts   143–4
   life fund   142, 145
   subscriptions   142, 144–5

Objectivity concept   18
Operating capital maintenance concept   318
Opportunity cost   300
Overdrafts   352
   in funds flow statement   427
Overheads   89–90
   factory overheads   92, 111
Over-trading   357
Owner's equity   276
Ownership of business   398

Partnerships   169–94, 323–4
   agreement   170–1
   appropriation account   172–3

change of partners   174–8
  retirement   171, 174, 178
companies and   326
conversion to limited company   183–5
debts of partnership   178
dissolution   178–9
goodwill   171, 174, 175–7
joint ventures   185–7
Partnership Act   171–2
realization account   180–2
remuneration   170–1
sale to limited company   180–2
utmost good faith   169
Past adjusted weighted average profit   374–5, 376
Patents   27, 28
Payments
  in advance   109–10
  incomplete accounts and   136
  for raw materials   209–10
  of wages   208–9
Pension commitments disclosure   241
Percentage of completion method   268
Petty cash   56–8, 138
  imprest system   57–8
Pie charts   254
Placing   344
Position statement   295
  income statement and   279–82
  see also Balance sheet
Post-balance sheet events   250, 276
Preference shares   333–4
Present obligations   30
Price/earnings ratio   377, 378, 409
Primary ratio *see* Return on capital employed
Prior-year adjustments
  disclosure of   249
  revenue recognition   271
Production cycle   407
Production hour method   75
Production unit method   75
Profit and loss account   8–9
  cash budgets and   365
  disclosure required in   237–8
  formats   234–7
  see also Income statement
Profit margin on sales   118
Profitability   397–8, 402, 412
Profits
  forecasts   9
  measurement not determination   278
  past adjusted weighted average   374–5, 376
  ploughed back   46–7
  retention   343
  superprofits   376–7, 384
Property revaluation   274
Prospectus   344
Provisions   46–7, 239
Prudence concept   20, 28, 273, 278
  stocks and   89
Purchasing power   307

Ratio analysis   281, 399–410
  capital   408
  as comparators   399–400
  earnings   408–9
  fixed to current assets   402

gross profit ratio   409–10
  inter-firm comparison   410–13
  pay-out ratio   409
  price to earnings ratio   409
  profit margin on sales   118
  ROCE *see* Return on capital employed
  solvency   406–7
  stocks   402, 407–8
  turnover ratio   402, 412
  yield   409
Raw materials   209–10
Realization account   180–2
Realization concept   16–17, 20, 273–4
Receipts, incomplete accounts and   136
Recognition of revenue *see* Revenue recognition
Reconciliations, bank   153–6
Reducing balance method   73–4
Relevance   11
Reliability   11
Rents, revenue from   238
Replacement
  depreciation and   69
  value   300
Research and development   250
Reserves   434
  capital reserves   29, 32
  disclosure of   238, 239
  goodwill write-off to   387
  provisions and   46–7
Residual value   71–2
Return on capital employed   357–8, 397–8, 400–6
  analysis using ratios   401–2
  business efficiency and   402–3
  definition of capital employed   401
  limitations of   403–6
  usefulness of   402–3
Revaluation   74–5, 276
Revenue expenditure   45–6
Revenue profit account *see* Income statement; Profit and loss account
Revenue recognition   267–72
  accretion   269–70
  certainty theory   268
  completed contract method   268
  critical points   268–9
  delivery critical   270
  extraordinary items   271
  hire purchase terms   270
  inflation and   305
  instalment terms   270
  loan interest   270
  long-term contracts   269
  percentage of completion method   268
  prior year adjustments   271
  unascertained goods   268
  work in progress   269
Review Panel   294
Risk   404
  cover   374, 399
  finance for business and   342
  valuation of business and   373–4
ROCE *see* Return on capital employed

Sale and lease-back   351
Sales
  accruals principle and revenue from   45

cash 210–11
cost of *see* Costs: cost of sales
credit sales 147, 212
goods on sale or return 148
gross profit margins 136–7
profit margin on 118
revenue recognition 270
stock to sales ratio 402
Satisficer 296
Scrap value 299
Segmental reporting 253
Share capital 29, 239
Share issue *see* Finance for business
Shareholders, as users 10
Shares *see* Capital structure
Short-term financial requirements 352–2
Sinking fund 69
Small businesses, finance for 341–2
Small company disclosure exemptions 250–1
Sole traders 323
Solvency 398
ratio analysis 406–7
Spreadsheets 60
SSAPs 80–2, 89–90, 94, 98, 223, 227, 228–9, 288
disclosure in 249–50
list of 291
see also Standards
Standards
achievement of objectives 289
compliance enforcement 292, 294
harmonization 293
need to standardize 288
procedures for setting 290–1
see also Accounting Standards Committee; SSAPs
Start-up funds 348
Statement of Standard Accounting Practice *see* SSAPs
Statistical supplements 253–4
Stock Exchange 345, 346
Stocks 28
accounting treatment 89–92
annual interest on loan stock 111
closing stock figures 110–11
conservation of funds in 358–60
correct level decisions 359–60
costs and 89–90
disclosure of 242–3, 250
economic order quantity 96
in income statement 43
'just in time' stock control 359
net realizable value 89, 90, 300
ratio analysis 407–8
records 96–8
re-order point 96
safety margin 96
SSAP 9 89–90, 94, 98
stock to sales ratio 402
stock turnover period 90
taxation and 222
unused items 89
valuation methods 92–5, 275
AVCO 93–4, 95, 96
FIFO 92, 93, 94, 95, 96
LIFO 92, 93, 94, 95, 96
standard cost methods 93, 94
weeks' usage held in 359
work in progress 89, 98–9
write-down 148
see also Current assets
Straight line method 72–3
Substance over form 23
Summarized accounts 252
Superprofits 376–7, 384
Suspense account 149

Takeover bids 9
Tangible assets 241
fixed 251
Task Force 294
Taxation 217–29
advance corporation tax 223–5
appropriation of profit for 112
capital allowances 226
capital grants 217
corporation tax 220, 224
deferred 226–9
disclosure of 250
revaluation of fixed assets 227
timing difference 226–7
disclosure of 238, 250
expenditure
for business 221
domestic 221
gifts 221
forms of 218–20
imputation system 223–5
income tax 217
negative 218
schedules 220
mainstream corporation tax 225–6
progressive and regressive 218
road fund licence 218
taxable profit 220–3
debtors 222
depreciation and 221
entertaining 221
stocks 222
see also Expenditure
value added tax 217, 218
wealth tax 219
Technical Development Capital Ltd 346
Tender offer 345
Terminology misuse 273
Theoretical framework of accounting 13–25
concepts
business entity 17–18
conservatism *see* Prudence
consistency 19, 275
disclosure 21
fairness 18–19
materiality 20, 275
objectivity 18
prudence 20, 28, 89, 273, 278
concepts, standards and the law 23–4
conceptual framework 14
postulates
going concern concept 15–16, 28, 274
monetary measurement 14–15
realization 16–17, 20, 273–4
principles
accruals *see* Accruals principle

cost   22
dual aspect   22–3
matching *see* Accruals principle
substance over form   23
'Third market'   347
Timeliness   11–12
Trade credit   352–3, 361, 434–5
Trade discounts   356
Trade unions as users of information   10
Trademarks   27, 28
Trading account   38
Trading profit   430
Trial balances   55–6
accounts from   106–32
adjustment by amounts in notes   109–12
annual interest   111
apportionment   109
appropriation of profit for tax   112
bad and doubtful debts   111
closing stock figures   110–11
credit balances   108
depreciation   110, 112
extended   113
figures from   116–18
list of balances converted to   108
payments in advance   109–10
procedure   108–18
suspense account   149
'True and fair' view   3–5, 24–5
override   230, 231
Turnover
disclosure of   237
ratio   402, 412

Understandability   11
Unit trusts   328, 347
Unlimited companies   325
Useful economic life   71, 79–80
Users   9–11

Valuation of business   372, 372–93
book value   300, 375
controlling interest   374–8
earnings per share   377, 387
goodwill *see* Goodwill
past adjusted weighted average profit   374–5, 376
price/earnings ratio   377, 378
risk and   373–4
superprofits   376–7, 384

Value   9, 22
book value   300, 375
deprival value   300–1
discounted present value   296
economic ideas   299–300
going concern value   300
market value   300
net realizable value   89, 90, 300
opportunity cost   300
property revaluation   274
replacement value   300
residual value   71–2
scrap value   299
stock *see* Stocks: valuation methods
Value added statements   254, 283–4
Value added tax (VAT)   217, 218
Venture capital   29, 348

Wages payment   208–9
Weighted average method *see* AVCO
Window dressing   276
Work in progress   28, 89
accretion   269–70
complete contract method   98–9
costs   89
disclosure of   250
long-term   98–9
percentage of completion method   98
revenue recognition   269
see also Stocks
Workforce, employment report   285
Working capital   355–71
adequate   355–6
cash budgets   363–5
conserving funds in current assets   358–60; *see also* Stocks
conserving resources of   357–8
cycle   360
debtors and creditors   360, 361
finance for *see* Finance for business
inflation adjustment   314–15
insufficient   356–7
ratio   281
return on capital employed   357–8
trade-off strategies   362–3

Yield   409